The South Since Reconstruction

THE AMERICAN HERITAGE SERIES

Under the General Editorship of
LEONARD W. LEVY AND ALFRED F. YOUNG

The South

Since Reconstruction

Edited by

THOMAS D. CLARK

THE BOBBS-MERRILL COMPANY, INC.
Publishers · Indianapolis · New York

For

Edwin Hemphill Clark

12-13-23

Foreword

THOMAS D. CLARK, THE FORMER EDITOR OF THE *Southern Historical Review* and a past president of the Southern Historical Association, is one of the nation's most distinguished scholars of the South. Among his many books are *Three Paths to the Modern South, The Emerging South,* and *The South Since Appomattox.* His expertise has made this the best documentary on the South since Reconstruction. The book is dominated by the two problems, race relations and the economy, that have fixed the character of the South for so long. The theme of the book, in Clark's words, is that from Reconstruction to the present "the South has been essentially a young region seeking new directions in its economic and political life. Socially, however, it has been an old region bound emotionally to a tradition and a myth." Clark's selection of primary sources, together with his perceptive introduction and headnotes, substantiate his theme and his determination of the dominant problems of the South.

As Clark says, the South has departed from the ways of its past with an astonishing rapidity in the past few decades. The South still retains its special character but is no longer, as Franklin D. Roosevelt once called it, the nation's number one problem. The rate of change has in fact progressed geometrically, and traumatically, in the very recent past. The South of Aunt Jemima and Uncle Tom, of a one-party system, of virulent racism, lynchers, massive resistance, of fundamentalism, of pellagra and hookworm, of unbelievable squalor, poverty, child labor, and of agricultural dependency is dead and unlamented. An egocentric particularism that once amounted to a virtual southern nationalism or separate civilization has yielded to a rampant homogenization that has remade the South in the nation's image. Regionalism has succeeded sectionalism. The South has become little different from Pasadena, Pontiac, and Forest Hills. Within a few years of the time that three young civil rights workers were brutally murdered, the local police of the same Mississippi community shot night-riders who tried to fire-bomb the home of a desegregationist, and the state prosecuted the Grand Dragon of the Ku Klux Klan. The number of black children in integrated schools is proportionally greater today in the states of the old Confederacy than in those that composed the Union. Republicans and blacks are political forces whose power is burgeoning, while industry and the growth of a huge middle class, as well as cities and suburbs, have made the South little different from any other region of the country.

This book is one of a series created to provide the essential primary sources of the American experience, especially of American thought. The series constitutes a documentary library of American history, filling a need long felt among scholars, students, libraries, and general readers for authoritative collections of original materials. Some volumes illuminate the thought of significant individuals, such as James Madison or John Marshall; some deal with movements, such as the Antifederalist or the Populist; others are organized around special themes, such as Puritan political thought or American Catholic thought on social questions. Many volumes take up the large number of subjects traditionally studied in American history for which surprisingly there are no documentary anthologies; others pioneer in introducing new subjects of increasing importance to scholars and to the contemporary world. The series aspires to maintain the high standards demanded of contemporary editing, providing authentic texts, intelligently and unobtrusively edited. It also has the distinction of presenting pieces of substantial length which give the full character and flavor of the original. The series is, we believe, the most comprehensive and authoritative of its kind.

Leonard W. Levy
Alfred F. Young

Contents

Contents

A Heritage of Change

THE CENTURY OF SOUTHERN HISTORY SINCE 1865 HAS SEEN EVEN more revolutionary change than that of the East or the old Northwest. Every phase of change has been accompanied by a new crop of analyses of some sort. Out of this staggering collection of writings some landmark articles can be culled to identify central forces that stirred the South at a particular moment. Such writings express a regional point of view—so much so that every writer who seeks to trace the intertwinings of the strands of modern southern history becomes conscious that he examines his material against, but somehow apart from, a background of shifting national standards. It was beyond the borders of the South that most American standards were set, and from which the region's failures to approximate the new standards drew public criticism. Yet the South had its own standards and its own self image.[1]

The postwar South's self image was partly selected from a glittering dream of the past, partly dictated by pressing regional problems that demanded rapid solutions.[2] Like any old and

[1] Dewey E. Grantham, ed., *The South and the Sectional Image: the Sectional Theme Since Reconstruction* (New York: Harper & Row, 1967), 23–26; W. Clement Eaton, *The Waning of the Old South Civilization, 1860–1880's* (Athens: University of Georgia Press, 1968), 139–171.

[2] C. Vann Woodward, *Origins of the New South, 1877–1913* (Baton Rouge: Louisiana State University Press, 1951); Benjamin B. Kendrick

established institution, the South confronted the inevitability of changes. In the postwar years the region was called upon to undergo the traumatic process of internal reexamination and self-appraisal. Inevitably the resulting changes greatly disrupted southern desires for a gradual recovery.[3] Two distinct lines of progress were involved: the free Negro in southern society, and the burden of a peculiar regional economics for the masses. Underlying both was the greatly enlarged challenge of universal education.[4] In many respects these problems were purely regional in nature.

Discussion of such regional issues during the past century in the South and elsewhere has gone far toward giving the area a sectional, even a nationalistic image. Most Southerners' image of the post-Civil War South was cast largely within the matrix of a myth formed from the glories of an old South, exaggerated partly by the extreme hardships inflicted on the region during Reconstruction. Yet out of post-war and post-Reconstruction gloom there came into focus a brighter image of the future. This new image embraced all the advantages of the burgeoning nation, but retained many of the softening and humanizing influences of the southern past. There was every evidence that realists in the South understood that certain changes and modifications would be pressed upon them, if only by the presence of so large an asset in unexploited natural resources.[5] Believing,

---

and Alex M. Arnett, *The South Looks at Its Past* (Chapel Hill: The University of North Carolina Press, 1935); Stuart Noblin, *Leonidas Polk, Agrarian Crusader* (Chapel Hill, The University of North Carolina Press, 1849); A. D. Kirwan, *The Revolt of the Rednecks: Mississippi Politics, 1876–1925* (Lexington: The University of Kentucky Press, 1951).

[3] Thomas D. Clark, *Pills, Petticoats and Plows: The Southern Country Store* (Indianapolis: The Bobbs-Merrill Company, 1944); Vernon O. Key, *Southern Politics* (New York: Alfred A. Knopf, 1949); C. Vann Woodward, *Origins of the New South.*

[4] The best general coverage of this subject is Charles W. Dabney, *Universal Education in the South,* 2 vols. (Chapel Hill: The University of North Carolina Press, 1936); See also, Oliver H. Orr, *Charles Brantley Aycock* (Chapel Hill: The University of North Carolina Press, 1961).

[5] Walter Cooper, ed., *The Piedmont Region, Embracing Georgia, Alabama, Florida, and the Carolinas* (Atlanta: Charles P. Boyd, Publisher and Printer, 1895); W. D. Kelly, *The Old South and the New, a Series of*

however, in his particular regionalism, the southern writer viewed his section with a high degree of consideration for human values, measured against the progress made by the new industries and businesses. At the same time, it was virtually impossible to separate the political, social, and economic forces at work in the South. Because of this, authors have often tended either to treat their subjects within an integrated regional theme dealing with central issues, or to resort to some degree of general defensive oratory. Thus, the various forces that worked so powerfully within the section in the latter part of the nineteenth century were merged into an integrated image.[6]

Certainly there was no shortage of outsiders eager to analyze and guide the South in its perplexities. In the years after the Civil War only the far West approached the South in receiving so many inquiring visitors and critical journalistic observers. Mountains of contemporary accounts were created by these people, who were so anxious not only to rush home and write about what they had seen but also to give their opinions of the direction in which the section should move.[7] Most of the travelers who viewed the South prior to 1885 looked upon it as a pallid and spent giant that stumbled aimlessly in a stupefied daze, waiting for some leader or some centralizing force to shove it forward. Edward King, in the Great South: A Record of Journeys, drew such a picture.[8] So did the more superficial,

---

Letters by Honorable William D. Kelly (London: G. P. Putnam's Sons, 1888); Edward King, The Great South; a Record of Journeys in Louisiana, Texas, the Indian Territory, Missouri, Arkansas, Mississippi, Alabama, Georgia, Florida, South Carolina, North Carolina, Kentucky, Tennessee, Virginia, West Virginia, and Maryland (Hartford, Conn.: American Pub. Company, 1875).

[6] Jay B. Hubbell, The South in American Literature, 1606–1900 (Durham, The Duke University Press, 1954); John Ezell, The South Since 1865 (New York: The Macmillan Company, 1963); Thomas D. Clark and Albert D. Kirwan, The South Since Appomattox, A Century of Regional Change (New York: The Oxford University Press, 1967), 202–228.

[7] Thomas D. Clark, ed., Travels in the New South: A Bibliography. The Postwar South, 1865–1903 (Norman: University of Oklahoma Press, 1962).

[8] King, Great South.

but no less self-assured, Henry Ward Beecher in *A Circuit of the Continent: Account of a Tour Through the West and the South.* Carl Shurz's *The New South* gauged a South for social and political purposes, and with far less focus on the currents of regional change. This book was respected because of the author's journalistic and political standing.

Many within the South also wished to discuss the region. Once freed of the clogs of Reconstruction, the region became host to hordes of spokesmen. Among them were editors, politicians, businessmen and industrial promoters, emotionally-maimed native sons, casual travelers, and even ministers of the gospel.[9] Until 1910 it seemed that one of the leading products of the South was its annual crop of booster publications. Moreover, editors of the new national magazines opened their columns to stories about the recovering South and the place of the Negro in the new regional social structure. A rising new generation of southern authors found a ready market for its writings in the national journals, and even some of the old diehard authors were given opportunities to sing the literary requiem of a dying order. The image younger authors created of their section depended upon the mood in which they cast their materials, and upon the impulses that stirred them to write. Some were nostalgic and romantic, others were defensive and critical.

Wherever they came from, the truly observant saw that, despite its surface failures, the South possessed vast resources, both human and natural. Like a comely maid, the land with its timber and minerals awaited the spoilers. These came quickly. Yet one of the most interesting facts about the era, 1865–1880, was the positive changes underway; these were changes of sufficient

---

[9] Examples of this literature are: *South Carolina: A Home for the Industrious Immigrant* (Charleston: Joseph Walker's Power Press Book and Job Printing Office and Bindery, 1867); George M. Barbour, *Florida for Tourists, Invalids, and Settlers, Containing Practical Information Regarding Climate, Soil, and Production; Cities, Towns, and People; the Culture of the Orange and other Tropical Fruits; Farming and Gardening; Scenery and Resorts; Sports, Routes of Travel, etc., etc.* (New York: D. Appleton and Co., 1882); *Garden Spots of the South* (Louisville, Passenger Department of Louisville and Nashville Railroad Company, 1891).

depth to initiate in time a revolution of major breadth. The old South, if it was an invention of postwar Southerners, was already fading rapidly in the birth throes of sectional redirection.

Because of this, authors often tended either to treat their subjects within an integrated theme dealing with central issues, or to resort to some degree of general oratory. Thus, the internal forces that worked so powerfully within the section in the latter part of the nineteenth century were in fact highly stratified, even though an integrated southern image emerged.

The major gains that have been made in every phase of southern life since 1880 have come about either as the result of long and arduous campaigning, a regional or national crisis, or radical changes in the world situation.[10] Under these conditions, it mattered little to the reformers and activists after 1880 whether or not they spoke for a "New South" or simply described a region struggling to produce change. This despite the fact that Henry W. Grady had popularized the term "New South" in 1886.[11] True, the South was a land of lingering nostalgia, but it was likewise a land of vigorous anticipation. Contemporary authors hoped, without saying so specifically, that progress could be attained by maintaining a considerable amount of continuity between the future and the past, and thus without explosive and revolutionary redirection of the currents of southern life.

In fact, after 1875 many southern problems actually had little relationship with the past, though they promised to have enormous bearings on the future. Because of recurring epidemics, public health problems became acute. It was true, of course, that endemic fevers had always taken a heavy toll of life, but with the rise of towns and cities, and the improvement of transportation facilities, communicable diseases became even more threat-

---

[10] Arnett and Kendrick, *The South Looks at Its Past*; Virginius Dabney, *Liberalism in the South* (Chapel Hill: The University of North Carolina Press, 1932).

[11] Anniversary Celebration of the New England Society in the City of New York (New York: Annual of the Society, December 22, 1886); Joel Chandler Harris, *Joel Chandler Harris' Life of Henry W. Grady; Including His Writings and Speeches* (New York: Cassell Publishing Company, 1890), 83–93.

ening.[12] Along with this, as the cotton system failed to maintain a level of reasonable human welfare, the ravages of poverty played havoc with human life.[13]

Advances in medical knowledge during the latter part of the nineteenth century placed southern social conditions in entirely new perspectives, and made new demands on society to support an extended program of preventive measures.[14] Discoveries of the sources of parasitic infestations, and of the nature of respiratory diseases and their treatment, became parts of social change. These discoveries and other advances in the life sciences brought home to Southerners a new sense of the value of human life, a fuller understanding of the economic waste of diseases, and a realization that these were color-blind in their attacks upon human beings.

The South was already establishing some clear lines of procedure for the future by 1885, and many of these approaches have kept the same basic objectives. Uppermost in this area was

[12] The subject of health and disease is discussed in numerous sources. Among these are: Gerald M. Capers, Jr., *The Biography of a River Town: Memphis Its Heroic Age* (Chapel Hill: The University of North Carolina Press, 1939); William H. Glasson, "The Rockefeller Commission's Campaign Against the Hookworm," *South Atlantic Quarterly* 10 (April 1911), 142–148; "The Report of the Rockefeller Sanitary Commission," *South Atlantic Quarterly* 10 (April 1911), 180–183; Charles W. Stiles, "The Industrial Condition of the Tenant Class (White and Black) as Influenced by the Medical Conditions," in *Economic History, 1865–1910*, ed. James Curtis Ballagh, *The South in the Building of the Nation*, vol. VI (Richmond: Southern Publication Society, 1909), 594–600; D. G. Gill, *Health in Alabama, Then and Now* (Montgomery, Alabama: Department of Health, 1956); *History of Public Health in Georgia, 1733–1950* (Atlanta, Georgia: Department of Public Health, 1950); Thomas D. Clark, *The Emerging South* (New York: Oxford University Press, 1961), 24–39.

[13] Henry W. Grady, "Cotton and Its Kingdom," *Harper's Magazine* 63 (October 1881), 719–734; Charles S. Johnson, Edwin R. Embree, W. W. Alexander, *The Collapse of Cotton Tenancy: Summary of Field Studies & Statistical Surveys, 1933–35* (Chapel Hill: The University of North Carolina Press, 1935); Harold D. Woodman, *King Cotton & His Retainers: Financing & Marketing the Cotton Crop of the South, 1800–1925* (Lexington: University of Kentucky Press, 1968), 395–433.

[14] Rupert B. Vance, *Human Geography of the South, A Study in Regional Resources and Human Adequacy* (Chapel Hill: The University of North Carolina Press, 1932), 382–385; D. G. Gill, *Health in Alabama*.

the South's virginal field of economic opportunity in many areas, which helped to bring regional thinking more nearly into the scope of national expansion to the benefit of the nation. Vast stands of virgin timber, rich mineral beds, and untapped sources of industrial energy were readily available to supplement the similar resources being exhausted in other parts of the Union.[15]

Also, much of the human resource came to be regarded in a new light. Many looked upon the Negro as a source of human energy in fields other than agriculture. Yet training the ex-slave and his children for productive lives involved enormous expenditures, and the utilization of his services involved emotional problems and prejudices. The Southerner readily acknowledged that the presence of large numbers of Negroes created much of southern society's peculiar mores.[16] Even deeper emotions were involved in the re-establishment of the white Southerner himself within his region as an American involved in a diversity of national issues. In what ways, if any, did he differ from other Americans? Was there such a thing as a distinct southern type, and if so what was its nature? All of these questions intrigued Americans. Albert Bushnell Hart, a visiting young scholar made a particularly astute investigation of the southern temperament.[17] His analysis on the whole was without bias, and without the kind of supercilious criticism found in most traveler observations.

In his book, Professor Hart indicated a belief that there were problems in the South which only Southerners could solve. One such problem was the region's desperate need to organize an effective system of universal education. Despite a beginning,

[15] Especially good is the timber report in the United States Census, 1890. See also James Curtis Ballagh, ed. *Economic History, 1865–1910, The South in the Building of the Nation*, vol. VI (Richmond: Southern Publication Society, 1909); Nollie Hickman, *Mississippi Harvest: Lumbering in the Longleaf Pine Belt, 1840–1915* (University, Mississippi: University of Mississippi Press, 1962).

[16] Dabney, *Universal Education in the South*, vol. I., 433–526; Carter G. Woodson, *Mis-education of the Negro* (Washington, D.C.: The Associated Publishers, Inc., 1933).

[17] Albert Bushnell Hart, *The Southern South* (New York: D. Appleton and Company, 1910), 66–79.

accomplishments in this area amounted to little more than token gestures. If the South expected to advance with the rest of the nation, its educational burden would indeed become heavy.[18]

None of the commentators on conditions of southern life in the latter half of the nineteenth century failed to appreciate that the Negro laid both a heavy educational and social burden on the region. No matter how ardently the educational crusaders in the South argued for the building of school systems, or how much they stressed that both races should be educated, they reserved for the white man a dominant position in this field.[19]

After 1880 the masses of Southerners were unwilling to accept as permanent most of the economic and political concessions which had been made in the earlier years in Reconstruction. The Negro had, they felt to win these rights by long and arduous serving on the farms and in the industries, by rigid educational preparation, and by a change in social behavior. Time and again the moral issue of social and intellectual inferiority was injected into discussions of the Negro's place in southern society.[20] Great masses of Southerners believed he would have to accomplish improvements in these areas largely on his own.

Economically the Negro found himself in the latter part of the nineteenth century suspended between slavery and tenant farmer peonage. The mass of the black population had neither educational nor economic maturity—nor economic means—to thrust itself forward. Perhaps more significantly it lacked racial leadership to accomplish improvements. They were dependent upon former masters, if not for direct support, then as credit guarantors. This economic need was two-sided, and in large segments of society and economy both races were wholly dependent on cotton or one of the other staple crops to provide an economic base.[21] Thus, under prevailing conditions it was im-

---

[18] *Ibid.*

[19] Clark, *Travels in the New South;* Claude Nolan, *The Negro's Image in the South: The Anatomy of White Supremacy* (Lexington: University of Kentucky Press, 1967).

[20] Josephus Daniels, "The Progress of Southern Education," *Annals of the Academy of Political Science* 18 (July 1901), 310–320.

[21] Woodman, *King Cotton & His Retainers;* Grady, "Cotton and Its Kingdom"; and Johnson, Embree, and Alexander, *The Collapse of Cotton Tenancy.*

possible for the Negro to achieve the ideals that even the most charitable whites had for him. The latter envisioned race progress largely in the idealistic terms of the older South. They believed that the Negro should initiate and sustain schools, churches, businesses, and otherwise demonstrate his capability to lift himself into the status of an honest and independent yeoman farmer who would strive for the same vague goals as the white man. At some unspecified date it was hoped he would have matured culturally to the point that he would find himself in harmony with white culture and traditions.[22] At that point he would have attained the necessary maturity to become a responsible voter. In many ways the white Southerner's aspiration for the Negro was the goal he set for himself by improving his own educational and economic status.[23] Differing in only the slightest degree was the problem of lifting the social standards and vocational capabilities of the poor white man. He was no less a theme of the betterment crusades. But the problem of improving the Negro's condition and at the same time establishing a racially controllable situation was a continually vexing issue in southern society—so vexing that it distracted many Southerners from educational and economic improvements that would have benefited the whole region.

As a result of set social patterns many articulate Southerners prior to 1920 viewed the Negro as still a primitive man who physically, intellectually, and socially, had made little if any real progress toward earning equality in the South. No part of Negro civilization, or lack of it, disturbed the southern mind more than did intimate personal and social relationships of the two races engaged in a series of common enterprises in which each was so thoroughly dependent upon the other.[24]

[22] Horace M. Bond, *Negro Education in Alabama: A Study in Cotton and Steel* (Washington: The Associated Publishers, Inc., 1939); C. W. Dabney, *Universal Education in the South*, vol. I, 492–526.

[23] *Ibid.*, vol. I.

[24] Harris Dickson, "The Vardaman Idea," *Saturday Evening Post* 179 (April 27, 1907), 3–5; M. D. S. Noble, *A History of the Public Schools of North Carolina* (Chapel Hill: The University of North Carolina Press, 1930); Henry W. Grady, "In Plain Black and White," *Century Magazine* 29 [Old Series] (April 1885), 909–917.

Clearly in the broad strand of southern literature relating to this subject, there is reflected a generous amount of fear and guilt. So eloquent a spokesman as Henry W. Grady revealed on several occasions this uneasy mixture of southern emotions. Speaking in Dallas, Texas, in October 1887, he addressed himself largely to the youth in his audience in terms of a lingering tradition of southern nationalism. He said, "But the future holds a problem, in solving which the South must stand alone, in dealing with which, she must come closer together than ambition or despair have driven her, and on the outcome of which her very existence depends. This problem is to carry within her body two separate races, and near equal in numbers. She must carry these races in peace—for discord means ruin. She must carry them separately—for assimilation means debasement. She must carry them in equal justice—for this she pledged in honor and in gratitude. She must carry them even unto the end, for in human probability she will never be quit of either."[25] This statement of a moderate view of the South's situation was made at a time when active steps were already underway to disfranchise the Negro by writing restrictive franchise clauses in the new state constitutions.[26] Other authors reflected a like sense of fear and guilt.

Grady assured the Texans that white voters should not be put in a position of opposing the great mass of Negroes reaching for political control. To him, "The clear and unmistakable domination of the white race, dominating not through violence, not through past alliance, but through the integrity of its own vote and the eagerness of its sympathy and justice through which it shall compel the support of the better classes of the colored races—that is the hope of the South."[27]

The Dallas speech, not the one before the New England So-

---

[25] Joel Chandler Harris, *Life of Henry W. Grady*, 96.

[26] Mississippi Constitution (Jackson, 1890), Sections 241–243; Louisiana Constitution (Baton Rouge, 1898), Sections 3–5, 78–81. Characteristic views of Southerners were expressed by the editor of the *Butler* (Alabama) *Weekly Enterprise,* April 10, 1901, and the *Demopolis* (Alabama) *Marengo Democrat,* October 18, 1901. Both editors proclaimed the South "white man's country."

[27] Harris, *Life of Henry W. Grady*, 99.

ciety that popularized the term "New South", was Henry W.
Grady's true voice of the New South. Here he defined in regional
temper for a regional audience future southern challenges in
terms of political and economic decisions. This speech had much
more solid substance than the "New South" one, which depended more upon eloquent oratory touched with piquant
humor. Grady's speech in Dallas was also predicated upon current issues which were disturbing Southerners to the point of
action in this highly significant transitional period.

The Grady and southern points of view on racial associations
in the South during the opening years of constitutional revision
and redemption were sharply challenged by George W. Cable
of New Orleans. This gentle local colorist author had pleased a
wide audience with his Cajun stories and accounts of the gentler
phases of life in the romantic Old South. However, he lost favor
suddenly with people of the region upon publication of his
highly accusative article which appeared in *Century Magazine*
under the title "The Freedman's Case in Equity," and subsequently he developed the theme in the essays in his book the
Silent South.[28]

Cable looked upon the presence of the Negro in American
society as the nation's greatest social problem, and saw that it
had been so for the past century. With the astuteness of a com
petent novelist he wrote, "One of the marvels of future history
will be that it was counted a small matter, by a majority of the
nation, for six million people within, made its own decree a component part of it, to be subjected to a system of oppression so
rank that nothing could make it seem small except the fact that
they had already been ground under it for a century and a
half."[29] He foresaw that an ultimate and responsible full freedom—would be forthcoming, and that it would not be framed
within the traditional patterns of southern life.

The venerable historian and spokesman for the French Loui-

[28] George W. Cable, "The Freedman's Case in Equity," *Century Magazine* 29 [Old Series] (February 1884), 409–418; idem, *The Silent South,
Together with The Freedman's Case in Equity and The Convict Lease
System* (New York: Charles Scribner's Sons, 1885).
[29] Cable, "The Freedman's Case in Equity," 413.

sianans, Charles Gayarré, responded immediately to the contentions in Cable's article. Gayarré's strictures, however, got no
more than local circulation since they appeared in two installments in the *New Orleans Times-Democrat*.[30] A thundering reply before a national audience came from Henry W. Grady, who
published his rebuttal in *Century Magazine* under the title, "In
Plain Black and White."[31] The style of his article was oratorical,
and he appealed to the dead past, waved to the future, and
trumpeted for the present South.

In his answer to Cable, Henry Grady said he spoke for another "silent South." He claimed the right of the South to solve
the race problem in its way. "The race problem is hers," he
wrote, "whether or not of her seeking, and her very existence
depends on its proper solution. Her responsibility is greater, her
knowledge of the case is more thorough than that of others can
be. . . . As a matter of course, this implies the clear and unmistakable domination of the white race in the South."[32]

His conclusions were clear: the South was white man's country, and the white man had to retain dominance, George Cable
to the contrary. In fact, writers within the region, such as
Gayarré and Robert Y. Hayne were critical even of Grady. They
felt he should have laid the licks on heavier.[33] Grady's reply to
George W. Cable was but a forerunner of numerous articles in
which authors voiced this central theme, none more clearly than
the politicians, Benjamin Tillman and James K. Vardaman.

For almost eighty years following the Civil War, farming was
a central economic fact in the South. Whether or not this meant
grubbing a bare existence from sandy hillside soil on a rented
farm, laboring from "sun-to-sun" with utmost diligence to retain possession of a yeoman farm, or managing a new type
southern plantation by use of sharecroppers, the story varied
little. By 1930, though, farming as an economic way of life for

---

[30] Charles Gayarré, *New Orleans Times-Democrat*, January 8, 11, 1885.
[31] Grady, "In Plain Black and White," 909–917.
[32] *Ibid.*, 917.
[33] Clement Eaton, *Waning of Old South Civilization*, 143–148.

large numbers of Southerners was a lost battle. In fact many observers of southern life even at the turn of this century saw the fate which lay ahead, while they did not fully comprehend its broad social and economic implications. They were aware enough to know that in the end the South would face a reckoning which would be even more frustrating and disappointing than those faced by individuals at "settling up" time each year in the country or furnishing stores. From the vigorously critical Alliance-Populist reformer Charles Otken to the calmer, more scholarly Matthew Brown Hammond, Southerners still pictured cotton as the economic mainstay for the masses; even so, southern farming practices gathered a host of caustic critics.[34] A broad spectrum of southern economic and social history is based in this area of regional life.[35]

At no point in their daily lives did Negro and white fortunes run so completely in the same grooves, or did the two races have such common causes for grievance in their struggle to survive during the decades 1870–1920, as in the failures of cotton farming. Though there may have been much racial discrimination in the furnishing trade, and in the mode of granting and administering credit advances, the truth was that the two races were yoked together inseparably in an agricultural economy which promised no final rewards for either.[36]

Even open critics of the Negro such as Otken, Grady, and the southern country journalists saw this. They found fault with the individual white or black husbandry for tolerating his plight,

---

[34] M. B. Hammond, *The Cotton Industry—An Essay in American Economic History* (New York: Published for the American Economic Association by The Macmillan Company, 1897); Charles Otken, *Ills of the South: or, Related Causes Hostile to the General Prosperity of the Southern People* (New York: G. P. Putnam's Sons, 1894).

[35] Arthur F. Raper and Ira De A. Reid, *Share Croppers All* (Chapel Hill: The University of North Carolina Press, 1941); Arthur F. Raper, *Tenants of the Almighty* (New York: The Macmillan Company, 1943); John Leonard Fulmer, *Agricultural Progress in the Cotton Belt Since 1920* (Chapel Hill: The University of North Carolina Press, 1950); Carl Kelsey, *The Negro Tenant Farmer* (Chicago: Jennings & Pye, 1903).

[36] Thomas D. Clark, "The Furnishing and Supply System in America Since 1865," *Journal of Southern History* 12 (February 1846), 24–44.

but they offered him no concrete suggestions by which he could overcome his problems.[37] Clearly the whole system of southern agricultural economy was at fault; the system from the end of the cotton row to the banker's desk as far away as New York was riddled with failure. Hundreds of books, pamphlets, critical articles, and an endless stream of editorials were written to point out the evils of the system. Later historians have been no more imaginative than were hillside farmers in treating the woes of this period. They have tended to follow along in the deeply eroded furrows plowed by Otken, Hammond, Holmes, Banks, and others. They themselves have built up an enduring myth that only major research and statistical comparison can destroy.[38] Over the years since 1910 they have varied their story little; they have not validated it with fresh findings. In this respect there is no doubt but what the southern agrarian mercantile system was inefficient and even exploitative; so, however, were the practices of commercial fertilizer manufacturers, cotton buyers, wholesalers, and even southern legislators.

For the southern masses, farming prior to the great Depression and the New Deal denied them the great American ideal of well being. A disproportionate part of the population was concentrated upon land which was incapable of sustaining even smaller numbers of people under prevailing modes of cultivation. Under careless and ignorant management the land was reduced well below the subsistence level for even the most straitened farm family. H. H. Bennett of the Soils Division of the United States Department of Agriculture in an article in the *American Geographic Review* in 1933 estimated that there were 75,000,000 acres of severely impaired soil in the South. For literally millions of persons this worn-out farmland became a desolate island of economic and human defeat on which people

[37] Thomas D. Clark, *The Southern Country Editor* (Indianapolis: The Bobbs-Merrill Company, Inc., 1948), 264–282.

[38] A good example of this is Fred A. Shannon, *The Farmer's Last Frontier: Agriculture, 1860–1897* (New York: Farrar & Rinehart, 1945), 76–100.

who were unskilled and untrained for other forms of employment were marooned. Here both races were caught in the dusty web of illiteracy, and showed a high rate of parasitic infestation, a disproportionate rate of local violence, a narrow fundamentalism, racial discrimination, and broken spirits.[39]

Back of this, however, were more causes than those that were assigned by contemporary critics. Often critics attacked only the highly visible offenders. They charged stubbornness and ignorance as reasons for failure to diversify crops, lack of scientific land use and conservation, failure to exploit intelligently local resources, lack of market facilities, and use of poor grades of field crops and of inadequate fertilization. These were sound enough reasons, of course, to explain agricultural economic failures, but the critics failed to suggest a social blueprint to correct the variety of conditions that led to failure. Poor grade schools (perpetuated by low per capita expenditures for education and a staggering failure to enforce attendance), a lack of venture capital to develop markets, too little scientific knowledge as to the control of parasites and diseases among farm animals, a lack of governmental concern with human affairs in these areas, and a constant harking back to ill-defined southern traditions—all were to blame.[40] As Howard W. Odum said later, focussing on one fundamental problem, "Many failed to see that backwardness in the development of an adequate system of universal education with the strict enforcement of compulsory attendance laws was a greater cause of southern waste of resources than were farming methods."[41]

It was not until the South had suffered the ruinous impact of a depression and its lingering effects for more than a decade that Southerners and other Americans were able to gauge the full

[39] H. H. Bennett, "The Quantitative Study of Erosion Technique and Some Preliminary Results," *The Geographic Review* 23 (July 1933), 423–434.
[40] Howard W. Odum, *Southern Regions of the United States* (Chapel Hill: The University of North Carolina Press, 1936), section IV, 15.
[41] *Ibid.*

depth of agricultural backwardness, and only then when it stood uncovered in stark-naked defeat.[42] In the 1930s New Deal measures and agencies brought into clear focus basic conditions of adversity prevailing in the South. Agencies like the Agricultural Adjustment and the Farm Security Administrations revealed many old wounds and failures unsuspected by earlier critics.[43]

A new crop of southern authors after 1920 wrote of the failures of the agricultural South with boldness and with much fuller understanding of their region. They backed up their materials with endless tables of social and economic statistics.[44] One of the clearest voices among this new breed of social scientists was that of Howard W. Odum. He had no timidity about discussing the region's problems and he offered no self-effacing apologies. "The picture of the cotton-tobacco agrarian South," he wrote, "may also be described as a landscape of dilemmas. The tenant type bordering on poverty and hopelessness is only one. The human factors of waste, product of the single crop systems, have already been enumerated, as have the waste of land and forests. The instability that comes from great mobility and lack of purpose on the part of millions of citizens is another problem. Disgracefully low standards of housing follow a logical shiftlessness and irresponsibility. Instability of prices and income, speculation, and lost fortunes, lack of capital for efficient farm management and machinery, the low standards of wages due partly to the Negro, the debtor character of southern economy—these and others cry out for a more adequate analysis and long time planning."[45]

[42] Rupert B. Vance, *Human Factors in Cotton Culture: A Study in the Social Geography of the American South* (Chapel Hill: The University of North Carolina Press, 1929); Arthur F. Raper, *Preface to Peasantry: A Tale of Two Black Belt Counties* (Chapel Hill: The University of North Carolina Press, 1936).

[43] T. J. Woofter, Jr., *Landlord and Tenant on the Cotton Plantation* (Washington: Works Progress Administration, Division of Social Research, 1936); William C. Halley, Ellen Winston, and T. J. Woofter, Jr., *The Plantation South, 1934–37* (Washington: Government Printing Office, 1940).

[44] *Ibid.*

[45] Howard W. Odum, *Southern Regions*, 62–63.

A significant deterrent to southern progress in the post World War I years was the failure of both the Federal Government and private industry to act with greater integrity and decision in the development of the Tennessee Valley. The promise of this great public works facility was no less in the 1920s than in the 1930s. The area had a longstanding need for such development; a major reason for the creation of this project in the first place was the manufacture of cheaper and more reliable grades of ingredients for chemical fertilizers. When planners and experts of The Tennessee Valley Authority, along with the southern experiment station scientists, began sincerely to tackle the problems of the Valley many of the ills discussed so thoroughly by economists and sociologists in the 1930s either began to disappear or to come under control.[46] There were, however, other fundamental problems to be solved beyond those of the Tennessee Valley.

In the tender moment of frustration and demoralization in the troubled decade, 1930–1940, no study produced greater regional trauma than did the 1938 report of the National Emergency Council on Economic Conditions in the South. The crisis revealed in this report went too deep and was too grave to be glossed over. So far as landless farmers and tenants were concerned their way of life had perished suddenly after a lingering illness dating back through three generations. The United States Government now recorded its passing in a highly upsetting report[47]—upsetting both to Southerners and federal officials because its truths were manifestly obvious. This slender publication was in the truest sense a requiem for the old staple-crop South, burdened with its below-subsistence level farms, its oppressed hordes of sharecroppers, and its ever-expanding ranks of tenants.

[46] David Lilienthal, *T.V.A.—Democracy on the March* (New York: Harper & Brothers, 1944); Gordon R. Clapp, *The T.V.A.: An Approach to the Development of a Region* (Chicago: University of Chicago Press, 1955).

[47] U.S. National Emergency Council, *Report on Economic Conditions of the South, Prepared for the President* (Washington: U.S. Government Printing Office, 1938).

In its passing the old cotton staple crop system left a hard legacy of wasted men and land throughout the whole history of the modern South. This story involved every strand of the region's development. Behind it was a record of racial discriminations, economic displacements and failures, a tremendous cultural lag, and a far too pronounced sense of regional frustration and defeat. This is not to say that a chapter of southern history closed cleanly and sharply in 1938 or on any other specific date. The great Depression succeeded by World War II, and a postwar period of farm mechanism, use of non-row crops, and the re-conversion of millions of acres of farm land delayed the ending, though they made it no less certain. Some of the last of the human victims of the old economy are still marooned on a desolate shoal of defeat between the old and deficient agricultural system and the rising new southern industrial suburbia.[48]

In 1950 the big social and economic task immediately confronting the South was the reintegration of its whole organization of society, politics, and economy into a rapidly shifting national system. This meant, of course, the destruction of many ancient myths, the restructuring of many regional postures, and the development of new folk mores. Only in the innermost folds of southern sentiment and history itself could the nostalgic Southerner retreat into the past, and then he found himself on unfamiliar and uncertain ground because of fresh historical interpretation. This was hard to accept. Still, as early as 1900, a realist could see that the path to the future was already being hacked boldly and widely by the coming of industry, changing world conditions, federal court decisions, and Congressional acts.

The conflict of rigid tradition and onrushing change has been especially real in the field of racial relations. One of the tragedies of southern history has been the fact that the South, which has

[48] Rupert B. Vance and Nicholas J. Demarath, eds., *The Urban South* (Chapel Hill: The University of North Carolina Press, 1954); Clark and Kirwan, *The South Since Appomattox,* 330–346.

had such a heavy concentration of Negro population, proclaimed so stoutly during the past century that the region was white man's country. Trying to sustain this thesis has indeed led the region along a politically devious and self-frustrating path. It has deluded people into accepting a deficient system of government, and expending an enormous amount of precious time and talent in constitutional maneuvering, in the framing and adoption of worthless legislation, and in endless court litigation. It would be difficult to estimate the social and economic cost to the South of constitutional weaknesses created by this attitude. In perspective, the example of subterfuge set by the franchise clause in the Mississippi Constitution of 1890 headed the South toward ultimate, humiliating defeat at the hands of the Congress and the United States Supreme Court.[49] Moreover the principle embodied in the "Mississippi Plan" was the culmination of a struggle not only to cut the Negro off from the main stream of public life, but to reduce materially the influence of a significant segment of the white vote.[50] The adoption of this clause and the extension of its essential principle in other southern constitutions not only concluded the last dramatic act of undoing Reconstruction, it opened a new era of political discrimination and abuse of power. In 1898 when the United States Supreme Court upheld the Mississippi clause in *Williams* v. *Mississippi* it assured white Southerners that their region was now under the dominance of favored white men, and that the source of political power and decision was to stay in the hands of a restricted white electorate.[51]

Two years before, in *Plessy* v. *Ferguson,* the South had been given a virtually impenetrable barrier of racial discrimination, behind which it quickly took refuge.[52] Although not dealing *per se* with the issue of segregation by establishing the principle of "separate but equal," *Plessy* v. *Ferguson* was interpreted

[49] *Smith* v. *Allwright*, 321 (U.S. Reports, 1944), 757–768; *Grovey* v. *Townsend; Classic* v. *United States*, 313 (U.S. Reports), 1031–1043.
[50] Woodward, *Origins of the New South*, 321–349.
[51] *Williams* v. *Mississippi*, 170 (U.S. Reports, 1898), 215–225.
[52] *Plessy* v. *Ferguson*, 45 (U.S. Reports, 1895), 540–552.

broadly by Southerners as a judicial approval of the custom. In 1904 the Kentucky General Assembly dealt directly with the question of segregation by enacting the Day Law, which was intended to destroy the co-racial program of Berea College. This law was upheld by the United States Supreme Court, but again the Court dealt with an abstract issue of constitutional law rather than with the social intent of the state statute.[53] Even as late as 1927 the Supreme Court again upheld the principle of separate but equal educational facilities in the Meridian, Mississippi, case of *Gong Lum* v. *Rice*.[54] This latter decision, however, was the final act in this era of southern history.

Three important changes took place in the South after 1930. One was the revolution that came to southern agriculture and that resulted in the separation of hundreds of thousands of people from their traditional mode of life. Second, was the impact of the New Deal and its social policies and legislation which brought a social and economic revolution.[55] Third was the occurrence of World War II followed by the rise of the new industry. All these things had an effect upon the southern Negro who prior to 1945 found himself well-nigh helpless to strike back, because he lacked political voice or legal support from either the state or federal governments. He was unprepared by either education or skill to take his place competitively in industry. Fortunately for him the shifting membership of the United States Supreme Court was to begin a long process of assuring him legal access to the polls and the schoolroom. Beginning with the Lloyd Gaines Case in Missouri in 1938[56] down through a series of decisions the barriers to Negro participation in education and politics were removed; so were economic barriers. For the first time, in the Depression years, a large number of Negroes began to define positive goals in American society.

Brown v. *Board of Education,* 1954, was a watershed case

---

[53] *Berea College Case,* 45 (U.S. Reports, 1908), 100–102, 122.

[54] *Gong Lum* v. *Rice,* 275 (U.S. Reports, 1927), 101–102.

[55] George B. Tindall, *The Emergence of the New South, 1913–1945* (Baton Rouge: Louisiana State University Press, 1967), 443–472.

[56] *Missouri ex rel. Gaines* v. *Canada,* 305 (U.S. Reports, 1938), 334–337.

principally because it destroyed the last vestiges of legal sanction for the doctrine of "separate but equal" facilities. This decision no doubt struck the severest blow to southern racial policies to date. However, fourteen years later the issue of desegregating in public schools still appeared in one form or another before the federal courts.[57] *Brown* v. *Board of Education* was actually only a single milestone on the road to court decreed social and political actions, and to the adoption of two major civil rights acts by Congress. Large numbers of Southerners were unwilling to acknowledge that social and economic conditions had undergone such revolutionary changes. They were still entranced by the conciliatory words that Booker T. Washington had uttered at the Southern Cotton Exposition in Atlanta, and by the philosophy enunciated by the United States Supreme Court in *Plessy* v. *Ferguson,* and *Gong Lum* v. *Rice.* It appears clear that much of the southern leadership placed its faith in the belief that these attitudes would prove as lasting as the Fourteenth Amendment itself.

Time and social change caught up with Southerners unexpectedly after 1930. They perhaps were too vexed by seemingly insoluble economic problems which arose after 1920 to be able to focus clearly on the serious erosion which was occurring in regional economic and social relationships with the rest of the nation. In the great crusade to balance, and even to supplant agriculture with industry there was little indication that southern political leadership was aware of the approaching revolution.[58]

When future historians are finally able to bring the era, 1920–1970, into full perspective they no doubt will be in a position to analyze more fully the dynamics by which southern nationalism and southern images were changed. Already it is clear that within three decades the South has departed further from the ways of the past than in any other like period in its entire his-

---

[57] *Brown* v. *Board of Education,* 349 (U.S. Reports, 1955), 28, 55, 150–151.
[58] Clark, *The Emerging South.*

tory. No prophet, even the most foolhardy, could have predicted in 1945 and the end of World War II that this would happen in so brief a span of time. Angry voices have cried out on all sides of issues raised by the departures from earlier southern practices. Conservative Southerners have protested vociferously in public speeches, editorials, handbills, pamphlets, and letters to editors. Extremists have been even more angry in their protestations. They have run mimeograph machines and printing presses full blast to create a voluminous record of their displeasures.[59] Editors of highly respected newspapers have at times joined the rabble in their criticisms of the courts, of Congress, and the central administrations. At the same time the Negro and his friends have spoken with new found boldness and angry defiance against the traditions which have discriminated against him. The southern mind generally has been thrown into confusion by all this storm of protest. In this crisis Southerners advanced few if any new arguments in defense of the old system that once promised to stay the approach of a new industrial age for the South. Following the debacle of the Central High School confrontation in Little Rock, Arkansas was to see its industrial expansion come to a standstill.

Current Negro views have been expressed in much more clearly defined terms than were those during the first two decades of this century, such as "The Freedman's Case in Equity," and W. E. B. Du Bois's critical article on the South's failure to educate its Negro citizens. Still, fundamental issues remained the same. The Negro in the early modern South sought prompt emancipation from restrictive laws and customs which had held him in thraldom in political, economic, and social areas. In the new age the Negro found that he was able to shift his dependence from the local white establishment to the federal courts, while the locus of his leadership moved to areas outside the

[59] Some examples: Judge Tom P. Brady, *Segregation and the South*, 1957; James O. Eastland, "The Supreme Court's Modern Scientific Authorities in the Segregation Cases," 1955, Marvin Mobley, *The Red Hens are Coming Home to Roost*, n.d.

South. This latter shift was predicted by Negroes who drafted the Durham Manifesto in 1944. In that document they undertook to persuade reasonable white leaders to liberalize policies in several areas before time ran out on them.[60] Such a mild argument, however, was ineffective.

Once the southern Negro actively joined his cause to that of the Negro in the Nation, with the discontented of other minority groups, he became a major part of a national movement which the old line southern leadership was powerless either to control or to influence. Too, any racially restrictive move made in the South after 1945 almost immediately had to stand review in the courts, with reasonable expectations that the act would be declared in conflict with the United States Constitution.

In the carrying out of the mandate advanced in *Baker* v. *Carr* to relocate congressional and legislative district lines, Southerners had to face the extent to which the region had shifted away from its old rural base of political controls to one suspended between town and country, or even held by the urban centers.[61] A shifting population rather than an impressive growth had wrought tremendous changes. With this shift a second revolt was in the making—this time in the distribution of power wielded by rural and urban voters. And thus the South's problems have become the concern of the nation as a whole, while the South has become involved in problems not confined to its own territory.

No clearer outline of the recent South's advance into this nationalistic age has been presented than in the papers and messages of two recent North Carolina governors. In 1955 Governor Luther Hodges faced the immediate challenge of leading his people out of the emotional storm which had struck following the rendering of *Brown* v. *Board of Education*. Both in a television address to North Carolinians in general and in a speech to the faculty and students of the Technological College

[60] *New South* 7, pp. 6–8.
[61] *Baker* v. *Carr*, 369 (U.S. Reports, 1962).

in Greensboro he revealed his own bondage to southern traditions, but at the same time he indicated that he saw the South facing an entirely new set of realities.

In his two addresses, Governor Hodges expressed a hope that within the year of grace allowed by the Supreme Court for facilitating the Brown decision some legal means could be found to soften its impact. At Greensboro he reviewed in considerable detail the advances which Negroes had made under the "separate but equal" doctrine. His Negro audience was ill-tempered and impatient if not downright rude. He learned that the white man could no longer appeal to the southern Negro in the old patronizing vein.[62] Elsewhere in the South white leaders met hostility and resistance when they attempted to persuade Negro educators to accept increased financial support in lieu of racial equality and mixing in the classroom.[63]

Governor Terry Sanford, Hodges' successor, had the advantage of the passage of time. He could view the problems of his state and of the South in much clearer perspective. In an address to the South Carolina Work Conference for Teachers in Columbia he spoke in positive terms of the educational needs of the modern South. Using for his subject the popular slang expression, "The South will Rise Again!" he spoke as a contemporary Walter Hines Page, thinking in up-to-date terms of the "Forgotten Man." He said this time the battle of the South would be fought in the classrooms with textbooks as weapons. In an eloquent perioration he told South Carolinians, "We will not be firing on Fort Sumter, we will be firing on the dungeons of ignorance."[64] Governor Sanford did fire on the dungeons of ignorance from his office in Raleigh, opening more dark corners than those of Southern schoolrooms. In several sharply worded messages, for example, he told members of the Ku Klux Klan

[62] James W. Patton, ed., *Messages, Addresses, and Papers of Luther Hartwell Hodges, Governor of North Carolina, 1954–1961* (Raleigh: Council of State, State of North Carolina, 1963), 249–257.

[63] Clark, *The Emerging South*, 193–200.

[64] Memory F. Mitchell, ed., *Messages, Addresses, and Public Papers of Governor Terry Sanford, Governor of North Carolina, 1961–1965* (Raleigh: Council of State, State of North Carolina, 1966), 150–158.

that their shabby and brutal acts would not be tolerated in the South.

Elsewhere, in Alabama, Mississippi, Arkansas, and Louisiana, governors gave early indication that they believed they could withstand the passage of time and preserve untarnished the myth of white supremacy. They discovered, however, how costly their errors could be not only in terms of outbreaks of violence, but also in terms of frightening away new industries which were so desperately needed to sustain the region in an era of funda- mental social and economic transition. Southern governors learned quickly that neither they nor their legislatures could control this change.

Thus for a century, southern voices have been eloquent in paying tribute to the past, in expressing an uneasiness about the present, and confidently beckoning to the future. Quieter voices have spoken in the more realistic terms of historical fact and statistical information. They have cautioned the region about cultural lags and institutional deficiencies. Nothing has documented so clearly the South's approach to this point in the twentieth century as this cacophony of voices. These in large measure have been the creators of the South's image. Yet what- ever the viewpoints of the spokesmen, one thing they held in common was a hope that the image of the South could be shaped in keeping with their emotions and wishes, rather than by the pressures of a region being lifted drastically nearer the shoals of loss of identity by national and world changes. Be- sides, underneath all the diversity of viewpoints there is an underlying belief that the region would in time come to realize its great potential. From 1880 to date the South has been essentially a young region seeking new directions in its eco- nomic and political life. Socially, however, it has been an old region bound emotionally to a tradition and a myth. Often the past has been the Southerner's escape from present reality; yet immediately painful problems have pulled him back to the present and have forced him to balance dream and reality as he shaped his future. Thus few if any American people are so well conditioned to face the realities of changing patterns of society, economy, and even thought. The reflections contained in the selections in this book reveal, if nothing more, that modern southern history has felt the unceasing impact of change. Still, from the comments of the new editor of the *Century Magazine* in 1885 to those of Secretary of Commerce, Luther Hodges in 1965, the South has kept its youthful confidence that in some way it is a land of promise. The problem has been to find the formula by which the promise could be realized.

Selected Bibliography

Alexander, Charles C. *The Ku Klux Klan in the Southwest.* Lexington: University of Kentucky Press, 1965.

Ashmore, Harry S. *An Epitaph for Dixie.* New York: Norton, 1958.

―――. *The Negro and the Schools.* Chapel Hill: The University of North Carolina Press, 1954.

Baker, Ray Stannard. *Following the Color Line; An Account of Negro Citizenship in the American Democracy.* New York: Doubleday, Page, and Company, 1908.

Banks, Enoch. *The Economics of Land Tenure in Georgia.* New York: The Columbia University Press, The Macmillan Co., agents, 1905.

Blaustein, Albert B. and Ferguson, Clarence Clyde Jr. *Desegregation and the Law: The Meaning and Effect of the School Segregation Cases.* New Brunswick: Rutgers University Press, 1957.

Cash, Wilbur J. *The Mind of the South.* New York: Alfred A. Knopf, 1941.

Clark, Thomas D. *The Southern Country Editor.* Indianapolis: The Bobbs-Merrill Co., 1948.

―――. *Three Paths to the Modern South.* Athens: University of Georgia Press, 1965.

―――, ed. *Travels in the New South: A Bibliography.* Vol. I, *The Postwar South, 1865–1900: An Era of Reconstruction and Readjustment,* Norman: University of Oklahoma Press, 1962.

Dabbs, James McBride. *The Southern Heritage.* New York: Alfred A. Knopf, 1958.

Dabney, Charles W. *Universal Education in the South.* 2 vols. Chapel Hill: The University of North Carolina Press, 1936.

Dabney, Virginius. *Liberalism in the South.* Chapel Hill: The University of North Carolina Press, 1932.

Daniels, Josephus. *Tar Heel Editor.* Chapel Hill: The University of North Carolina Press, 1939.

Davidson, Elizabeth H. *Child Labor Legislation in the Southern Textile States.* Chapel Hill: The University of North Carolina Press, 1939.

Eaton, Clement. *The Waning of the Old South Civilization, 1860–1880's.* Athens: University of Georgia Press, 1968.

Fulmer, John Leonard. *Agricultural Progress in the Cotton Belt Since 1920.* Chapel Hill: The University of North Carolina Press, 1950.

Grantham, Dewey W. *The Democratic South.* Athens: University of Georgia Press, 1963.

Harlan, Louis R. *Separate and Unequal: Public School Campaigns and Racism in the Southern Seaboard States, 1901–1915.* Chapel Hill: The University of North Carolina Press, 1958.

Highsaw, Robert B., ed. *The Deep South in Transformation, A Symposium.* Tuscaloosa: University of Alabama Press, 1964.

Hillyard, M. B. *The New South. A Description of the Southern States. Noting Each State Separately, and Giving Their Distinctive Features and Most Salient Characteristics.* Baltimore: Manufacturer's Record Co., 1887.

Hubbard, Preston J. *Origins of the T. V. A.: The Muscle Shoals Controversy, 1920–1932.* Nashville: Vanderbilt University Press, 1961.

Kelley, William Darrah. *The Old South and the New: A Series of Letters by Honorable William D. Kelley.* New York: G. P. Putnam's Sons, 1888.

Kendrick, Benjamin B., and Arnett, Alex M. *The South Looks at Its Past.* Chapel Hill: The University of North Carolina Press, 1935.

Key, Valdimer O., Jr. *Southern Politics in State and Nation.* New York: Alfred A. Knopf, 1949.

King, Edward, *The Great South: a Record of Journeys in Louisiana, Texas, the Indian Territory, Missouri, Arkansas, Mississippi, Alabama, Georgia, Florida, South Carolina, North Carolina, Kentucky, Tennessee, Virginia, West Virginia, and Maryland.* Hartford: American Publishing Co., 1875.

Kirwan, A. D. *Revolt of the Rednecks: Mississippi Politics, 1876–1925.* Lexington: University of Kentucky Press, 1957. Gloucester, Mass.: P. Smith, 1964.

Lilienthal, David. *T.V.A.—Democracy on the March.* New York: Harper & Brothers, 1944.

Link, Arthur S. and Patrick, Rembert W. *Writing Southern History: Essays in Historiography in Honor of Fletcher M. Green.* Baton Rouge: Louisiana State University Press, 1965.

Logan, Rayford W., ed. *What the Negro Wants.* Chapel Hill: The University of North Carolina Press, 1944.

Malone, Dumas. *Edwin H. Alderman: A Biography.* New York: Doubleday, Doran & Company, Inc., 1940.

McKinney, John C., and Thompson, Edgar T. *The South in Continuity and Change.* Durham: Duke University Press, 1965.

Mitchell, Broadus. *The Rise of the Cotton Mills in the South.* Baltimore: The Johns Hopkins Press, 1921.

Mitchell, Memory F., ed. *Messages, Addresses, and Public Papers of Terry Sanford, Governor of North Carolina 1961–1965.* Raleigh: North Carolina History Commission, 1966.

Mitchell, Samuel Chiles, ed. *History of the Social Life of the Southern States,* Vol. X. *The South in the Building of the Nation.* Richmond: The Southern Historical Publication Society, 1909.

Murphy, Edgar Gardner. *Problems of the Present South: A Discussion of Certain of the Educational, Industrial and Political Issues in the Southern States.* New York: The Macmillan Company, 1904.

Myrdal, Gunnar. *An American Dilemma: The Negro Problem and Modern Democracy.* New York: Harper & Brothers, 1944.

Nolen, Claude H. *The Negro's Image in the South: The Anatomy of White Supremacy.* Lexington: University of Kentucky Press, 1967.

Ogden, Frederick D. *The Poll Tax in the South.* University, Ala.: University of Alabama Press, 1958.

Orr, Oliver H., Jr. *Charles Brantly Aycock.* Chapel Hill: The University of North Carolina Press, 1961.

Parkin, Almon D. *The South: Its Economic-Geographic Development.* New York: J. Wiley and Sons, Inc., 1928; London: Chapman and Hall, Limited, 1938.

Patton, James W., ed. *Messages, Addresses, and Public Papers of Luther Hartwell Hodges, Governor of North Carolina 1954–*

1961. 2 vols. Raleigh: Council of State, State of North Carolina, 1962.

Peck, Elisabeth. *Berea's First Century, 1855–1955.* Lexington: University of Kentucky Press, 1955.

Pierce, Truman M., *et al. White and Negro Schools in the South: An Analysis of Biracial Education.* Englewood Cliffs, New Jersey: Prentice-Hall, 1955.

[Ransom, John Crowe, ed.] *I'll Take My Stand: The South and the Agrarian Tradition.* New York: Harper & Brothers, 1930; new edition reprinted, Peter Smith, 1951.

Rice, Arnold S. *The Ku Klux Klan in American Politics.* Washington: Public Affairs Press, 1962.

Robertson, Ben. *Red Hills and Cotton: An Upcountry Memory.* New York: Alfred A. Knopf, 1942.

Saloutos, Theodore. *Farmer Movements in the South, 1865–1933.* Berkeley: University of California Press, 1960.

Savage, Henry, Jr. *Seeds of Time: The Background of Southern Thinking.* New York: Holt, 1959.

Shoemaker, Don, ed. *With All Deliberate Speed: Segregation—Desegregation in Southern Schools.* New York: Harper & Brothers, 1957.

Simkins, Francis Butler. *A History of the South.* 3rd rev. ed. New York: Alfred A. Knopft, 1963.

Sindler, Allan P., ed. *Change in the Contemporary South.* Durham, N.C.: Duke University Press, 1963.

Skaggs, William H. *The Southern Oligarchy, An Appeal in Behalf of the Silent Masses of Our Country Against the Despotic Rule of the Few.* New York: The Devin-Adair Company, 1924.

Tannenbaum, Frank. *Darker Phases of the South.* New York: G. P. Putnam's Sons, 1924.

Tindall, George B. *The Emergence of the New South, 1913–1945.* Baton Rouge: Louisiana State University Press, 1967.

Turner, Arlin, and Cable, George W. *A Biography.* Durham, N.C.: Duke University Press, 1956.

Vance, Rupert B. *Human Factors in Cotton Culture: A Study in the Social Geography of the American South.* Chapel Hill: The University of North Carolina Press, 1929.

————. *Human Geography of the South: A Study in Regional Resources and Human Adequacy.* Chapel Hill: The University of North Carolina Press, 1932.

Washington, Booker T. *The Future of the American Negro.* Boston: Small, Maynard & Company, 1899.

Washington, E. D., ed. *Selected Speeches of Booker T. Washington.* Garden City: Doubleday and Page, 1932.

Wharton, Vernon L. *The Negro in Mississippi, 1865–1890.* Chapel Hill: The University of North Carolina Press, 1947.

Woodman, Harold D. *King Cotton & His Retainers: Financing & Marketing the Cotton Crop of the South, 1800–1925.* Lexington: University of Kentucky Press, 1968.

Editor's Note

TO MAKE SPECIFIC SELECTIONS FROM THE GREAT MASS OF WRITINGS about the South since 1880 presents many challenges. Perhaps no two scholars would agree on a fully representative selection. They would agree, however, that certain persons in the passing decades have been able to speak for the region in varying degrees of clarity and precision. In turn their statements have become important regional documents. There can be no doubt that Henry W. Grady, Walter Hines Page, Edwin A. Alderman, James K. Vardaman, Theodore G. Bilbo, Edgar G. Murphy, and Booker T. Washington acted as regional spokesmen. In their speeches and writings they revealed some of the main currents of southern thought. Thus they have found a place in this collection.

Other men spoke at variance with the tenor of southern thinking. They perhaps had a better sense of southern history than did many who assumed the central roles of speaking directly for the South. Among these were George Washington Cable, W. E. B. Du Bois, William H. Skaggs, and Thomas Stribling. Modern Negro authors have introduced a new dimension to southern comment.

An attempt also has been made in this volume to bring into a single grouping most of the constitutional and judicial decisions which have guided the South in its uncertain course of political and social development. If the principles enunciated in the "Mississippi Plan," *Williams* v. *Mississippi,* and *Plessy* v. *Ferguson* gave the South a false sense of security in maintaining the region as "white man's country," then *Missouri ex rel. Gaines* v. *Canada, Smith* v. *Allwright, Grovey* v. *Townsend, Brown* v. *Board of Education,* and *Baker* v. *Carr* shattered this concept and in fact dislodged the anchor of southern nationalism itself.

The latter three decades of this century have produced such sudden and unsettling changes that literally thousands of people have presented themselves voluntarily as spokesmen for the South. Shrill voices have cried out for and against those implacable forces which have sought to remake the region. Daily newspaper editors have fed the great stream of current comment, much of it revealing a constant soul-searching. Also ministers, businessmen, educators, and even the extremist rabble have been vociferous in their offerings. There is no lack of materials from which to make selections. Thus it would indeed be little short of ridiculous to select certain individuals and say that they alone have spoken for the modern South. Trying to identify definitely the spokesmen of the region and to assess the quality of their utterances is largely an exercise in frustration. Who can say with certainty that one spokesman uttered more clearly the central views? Edwin A. Alderman, Booker T. Washington, Rayford Logan, Judge Tom Brady, and members of the Ku Klux Klan of America all have spoken with regional voices, and what they said has in some way borne upon the shaping of the regional image.

An attempt has been made in this volume to present as wide a range of material as is physically possible. Some of the selections may appear to be ephemeral, and no doubt they are. Much of what has been said about the South is ephemeral. It has been impossible to compress in a single volume more than a sampling of materials, but this sampling may be broad enough to give more than a glimpse of the South through a century of its most important growth.

Some articles in this collection have been cut internally, and it has been necessary to cut severely some of the Supreme Court decisions. Cuts within the text are marked by ellipses, except for the omission of citations in legal documents; footnotes, section headings, etc., have been deleted except when especially relevant. Otherwise, the documents are reprinted as first published.

The South Since Reconstruction

PART 1 The New South

BY 1880 THE SOUTH CLEARLY WAS INVOLVED IN FUNDAMENTAL social and political change. Indications of this fact included political elevation of the Negro, disruption of the plantation system, attempts to readjust regional economy, and the grip which extra-regional capitalism had secured on the South.[1] Long before Henry W. Grady delivered his famous New England Society oration in New York on December 22, 1886, there was public consciousness of a new South.[2] The larger question, however, was the nature and degree of the newness in the post-Reconstruction region. Hundreds of visitors, American and foreign, came to view the former Confederacy and to determine how southern energies were being redirected.[3]

First, there was the matter of the Southerner himself. In what ways did he differ from other Americans? What were his temperament, his political views, his economic conditions, and his

[1] Edward King, *The Great South;* James Bryce, *The American Commonwealth* (New York: The Macmillan Co., 1889), vol. II, 491–511; Sir George Campbell, *White and Black: The Outcome of a Visit to the United States* (London: Chatto & Windus, 1879).

[2] William Darrah Kelley, *The Old South and the New;* M. B. Hillyard, *The New South,* 5–57; *U.S. Eleventh Census* (1890), vol. 16, 516–546, 595, 606.

[3] Thomas D. Clark, ed., *Travels in the New South, 1865–1900.*

1

prospects for the future?[4] Some observers appeared to feel the Southerner was almost an American set apart because of the region's war experience and the presence of the free Negro. More perceptive visitors looked upon southern youth as an enormously important reservoir of potential manpower and intellectual talent if it were educated and fitted to take its place in a rising industrial nation.[5] It was true the Civil War had taken a ruinous toll of the human resource, but a new generation of Southerners was rapidly making up for this deficit. In 1882 the editor of the new *Century Magazine* was much nearer understanding what was occurring in the post-war South than were many of his contemporaries; he foresaw a real "competition for leadership" between northern and southern young men.[6]

Nothing indicated the social and intellectual youthfulness of the South after 1880 so much as did the crusade to establish a system of universal education.[7] This movement embraced many challenges to southern life well beyond the establishing of schools. For example, health problems ranged from annually recurring fevers to heavy parasitic infestations. Before masses of young Southerners in many parts of the South could become functionally effective in the new economic system they had to be free of debilitating diseases and parasites.[8] It was often meaningless to crusade for schools in areas where the wits of school-age children were dulled by systemic disorders. Thus Southerners were forced to undertake social and economic reforms on a much broader scale than most other Americans.[9]

In addition to the abundance of youth, southern natural re-

---

[4] Albert Bushnell Hart, *The Southern South*, 30–47, 66–79; Edgar Gardner Murphy, *Problems of the Present South* (1909), 3–27.

[5] Murphy, *Problems of the Present South* (1909), 97–125; Elizabeth H. Davidson, *Child Labor Legislation in the Southern Textile States*.

[6] "The Young South," *Century Magazine*, 24 [Old Series] (October 1882), 939–940; Joel Chandler Harris, *Joel Chandler Harris' Life of Henry W. Grady; Including His Writings and Speeches*, 94–120.

[7] Charles William Dabney, *Universal Education in the South*, 2 vols., (Chapel Hill: The University of North Carolina Press, 1936).

[8] Rupert B. Vance, *Human Geography of the South*, 380–390.

[9] Dabney, *Universal Education in the South*, II, pp. 246–264.

sources remained either untouched or poorly exploited.[10] The railway system was for the first time being connected in most parts of the region, and new manufacturing industries were being located in strategic places.[11] However, the rise of industry sometimes created about as many problems as it solved. This was especially true in the field of community organization and child labor. Moreover, yeoman farmers merely were converted from subsistence farmers into meager wage-earners who depended upon the mill as they once had depended upon the land. In their conversion, however, they were still pioneers seeking their difficult way to economic independence.[12]

[10] *U.S. Eleventh Census* (1890), 516–546.

[11] James Curtis Ballagh, ed., *Economic History, 1865–1910*, vol. VI, *The South in the Building of the Nation;* esp. Victor S. Clark, "Manufactures," 253–304; Ulrich B. Phillips, "Railway Transportation in the South," 305–316; Logan W. Page, "Steel Railways in the South Since the War," 316–325.

[12] Broadus and George S. Mitchell, *The Industrial Revolution in the South* (Baltimore: The Johns Hopkins Press, 1930); Nannie May Tilley, *The Bright-Tobacco Industry, 1860–1929* (Chapel Hill: The University of North Carolina Press, 1948).

1 The Young South

By 1880 the South was again inching its way slowly into the mainstream of American economic and social growth. Reconstruction was behind, and leaders of the region looked to the future. Observers like Albert Bushnell Hart, the historian, sought to define the southern character and temperament, and to place the economy of the region in the context of national growth. Henry W. Grady was certain as to where the region should place its political and economic emphases. The white man was supreme and must remain so, and cotton made the southern farmer a king in his own right. As time unfolded there were other voices that spoke no less positively, but not of cotton kings and superior statesmen. A shocking revelation was that of Walter Hines Page who portrayed a large segment of southern society lost in the fog of ignorance and neglect. He spoke of the South's most precious resource. William M. Glasson in a twentieth-century report on the Rockefeller Commission's campaign against the devitalizing parasite hookworm gave a good insight into the reason why so large a mass of Southerners were forgotten men.

The great depression of the late 1920s and the 1930s brought other forgotten men in the South into social focus. In an eloquent statement of his life experiences, Smith Coon of Cameron, North Carolina, spoke for the forgotten men of his generation, and revealed an intimately personal aspect of the economic expansion in the South, and of human frustrations.

In 1882, before Henry W. Grady had made his famous "New South" speech, the editor of the newly formed *Century Magazine* took occasion to editorialize on the South. He viewed the region,

which had just come through Reconstruction, with hope and ex-
pectancy. Well might northern politicians and businessmen turn
their attention southward. The editor even suggested they could
make a wise investment by contributing to the establishment of
schools and colleges to train people who would bring southern
resources under exploitation.

It is a commonplace of Northern politicians that the
South has always wielded an influence in our national affairs altogether disproportionate to its population, its wealth, and its
general intelligence. How this came about, under the old régime, it is easy to see: the men who owned the property and
possessed the culture were forced to the front to look after their
interests; there was, therefore, always in Congress, from the
South, a trained band of expert parliamentarians and adroit
managers, who easily took the lead in legislation.

These conditions have passed away, and we still see Southern
men maintaining much of the old ascendency in our national
discussions. We may explain this partly as a political survival.
The habit of sending their best men to Congress still holds in
the Southern communities. It is a good habit and ought never
to be abandoned. There is no call for sectional competition, but
a State is fairly entitled to whatever advantage it may gain by
keeping in Congress a strong delegation.

From that large class who were able to devote an ample
leisure to the pursuits of statesmanship came the Southern
leaders of the last generation. Most of the families belonging to
this class have lost their property, and have been obliged to turn
their energies to bread-winning; the new organization of labor
promises far larger rewards, but it demands also much more
careful attention; the time and thought of the ruling class of
the South must henceforth be largely given to business. Shall
we, then, find in the South, in the next generation, the
stuff out of which leaders can be made? The prospect might

"The Young South," *Century Magazine*, 24 [Old Series] (October
1882), 939–940.

seem dubious to a superficial observer, yet there are signs that the Southern people will be as well led in the future as they have been in the past.

The Southern States are now rearing a large number of young men before whom the outlook is bright. Some of them are sons of the old ruling families, but many of them have sprung from the lower and middle classes. They enjoy the advantages of poverty; they have no money to spend in luxuries or diversions; they have fortunes to retrieve or to gain; they have grown up since the war, and have inherited less than could be expected of its resentments. "Well," said a bright fellow at the close of a college commencement in Virginia last summer, "Lee and Jackson have been turned over in their graves but once to-day." The sigh of relief with which he said it indicates the feeling of many of these young men. They keep no grudges and have no wish to fight the war over again. The sentiment of patriotism is getting a deep root in their natures.

Yet they are full of faith in the future of their own section. Well they may be. During their lifetime the industry of the South has been revolutionized, and the results already achieved are marvelous. An era of prosperity has begun; and there are few intelligent men at the South to-day who will not at once confess that it is destined to be a far brighter era than they have ever seen. Free labor is unlocking the wealth of farms and mines and falling waters in a way that slave-labor never could have done. New machinery, new methods are bringing in a new day. In the midst of the stir and movement of this industrial revolution these young men are growing up. Hope and expectation are in the air: the stern discipline of poverty goads them on, and the promise of great success allures them. All the conditions are favorable for the development of strong character; and any one who will visit the Southern colleges and schools will find in them a generation of students, alert, vigorous, manly, and tremendously in earnest. Probably they do not spend, on an average, one-third as much money *per capita* as is spent by the students of the New England colleges; and in the refinements of scholarship the average Southern student would be found inferior to the average Northern student; but they are making the most of their opportunities. They ought to have better opportunities. Most of the Southern colleges and schools are crippled for lack of funds, and much more of the flood of Northern bounty might well be turned southward, to the endowment of schools and colleges for whites as well as blacks. The generous sentiment of the young South would thus be strengthened, and the bonds of union more firmly joined. But whatever may be done in this direction, it is evident that a race of exceptional moral earnestness and mental vigor is now growing up in the South, and that it is sure to be heard from. If the young fellows in the Northern colleges expect to hold their own in the competition for leadership, they must devote less of their resources to base-ball and rowing and champagne suppers, and "come down to business."

2 Southern Temperament

In 1910 the young Harvard University historian Albert Bushnell Hart tried his hand at assessing the southern temperament and personality. Perhaps there could have been no more detached viewer of the southern scene than this ambitious, young, and objective scholar. He could scarcely be said to be prejudiced in favor of the Southerner, or to have been won over by long or frequent associations with the natives. The following essay, published as a chapter in *The Southern South* (1910), did not present as many basic differences between Northerners and Southerners as he might have supposed existed. Many of the South's problems were also those of an expanding America. But though Hart discussed both abolition and the modern race problem, he wrote in a remarkably conciliatory vein. Actually Professor Hart seemed to portray himself in the role of healer of national wounds, and to see the South's being as fundamental to national progress as the other sections.

THE SOUTH HAS NOT ONLY ITS OWN DIVISION OF SPECIAL CLASSES, its own methods of influence, it has also its own way of looking at the problems of the universe, and especially that department of the universe south of Mason and Dixon's line. To discover the temperament of the South is difficult, for upon the face of things

Albert Bushnell Hart, *The Southern South* (New York: D. Appleton and Company, 1910), 66–79.

the differences of the two sections are slight. Aside from little peculiarities of dialect, probably no more startling than Bostonese English is to the Southerner when he first hears it, the people whom one meets in Southern trains and hotels appear very like their Northern kinsfolk. The Memphis drummer in the smoker tells the same stories that you heard yesterday from his Chicago brother; the members of the Charleston Club talk about their ancestors just like the habitués of the Rittenhouse Club in Philadelphia; the President of the University of Virginia asks for money for the same reasons as the President of Western Reserve University; Northern and Southern men, meeting on mutual ground and avoiding the question of the Negro, which sometimes does not get into their conversation for half an hour together, find their habits of thought much the same: the usual legal reasoning, economic discussion, and religious controversy all appeal to the same kind of minds. Northerners read Lanier with the same understanding with which Southerners read Longfellow.

Nevertheless there is a subtle difference of temperament hard to catch and harder to characterize, which may perhaps be illustrated by the difference between the Northern "Hurrah" and the "Rebel yell"; between "Yankee Doodle" and "Dixie," each stirring, each lively, yet each upon its separate key. Upon many questions, and particularly upon all issues involving the relations of the white and negro races, the Southerner takes things differently from the Northerner. He looks upon himself from an emotional standpoint. Thomas Dixon, Jr., characterizes his own section as "The South, old-fashioned, medieval, provincial, worshipping the dead, and raising men rather than making money, family-loving, home-building, tradition-ridden. The South, cruel and cunning when fighting a treacherous foe, with brief, volcanic bursts of wrath and vengeance. The South, eloquent, bombastic, romantic, chivalrous, lustful, proud, kind and hospitable. The South, with her beautiful women and brave men."

This self-consciousness is doubtless in part a result of external conditions, such as the isolation of many parts of the South; but

still more is due to an automatic sensitiveness to all phases of
the race question. People in the South often speak of their "two
peoples" and "two civilizations"; and at every turn, in every
relation, a part of every discussion, is the fact that the population
of the South is rigidly divided into two races marked off from
each other by an impassable line of color. The North has race
questions, but no race question: the foreign elements taken together are numerous enough, and their future is uncertain
enough to cause anxiety; but they are as likely to act against
each other as against the group of people of English stock; as
likely to harmonize with native Anglo-Saxon people as to oppose
them—they are not a combined race standing in a cohort, watchful, suspicious, and resentful. The North has twenty race problems; the South has but one, which for that very reason is
twenty times as serious. In every field of Southern life, social,
political, economic, intellectual, the presence of two races
divides and weakens. The blacks and the Whites in the South
are the two members of a pair of shears, so clumsily put together that they gnash against each other continually. Though
one side be silver, and the other only bronze, neither can perform its function without the other, but there is a terrible strain
upon the rivet which holds them together.

This state of tension is not due wholly to the Negroes, nor re-
movable by improving them, as though the straightening only
the bronze half of the shears you could make them cut truly. If
no Negroes had ever come over from Africa, or if they were all
to be expatriated to-morrow, there would still remain a Southern
question of great import. One of the mistakes of the Abolition
controversy was to suppose that the South was different from
the North simply because it had slaves; and that the two sections
would be wholly alike if only the white people felt differently
toward the Negro. The Negro does not make all the trouble,
cause all the concern, or attract all the attention of thoughtful
men in the South. In every part of that section, from the most
remote cove in the Tennessee mountains to the stateliest quarter
of New Orleans, there is a Caucasian question, or rather a series

of Caucasian questions, arising out of the peculiar make-up of the white community, though alongside it is always the shadow of the African.

Nobody can work out any of the Caucasian problems as though they stood by themselves; what now draws together most closely the elements of the white race is a sense of a race issue. The white man cannot build new schoolhouses or improve his cotton seed or open a coal mine without remembering that there is a negro race and a negro problem. This consciousness of a double existence strikes every visitor and confronts every investigator. As Du Bois says, the stranger "realizes at last that silently, resistlessly, the world about flows by him in two great streams: they ripple on in the same sunshine, they approach and mingle their waters in seeming carelessness,—then they divide and flow wide apart." Henry W. Grady asserted that "The race problem casts the only shadow that rests on the South." Murphy says, "The problems of racial cleavage, like problems of labor and capital, or the problems of science and religion, yield to no precise formulæ; they are problems of life, persistent and irreducible."

Various as are the opinions in the South with regard to the race problem and the modes of its solution, society is infused with a feeling of uneasiness and responsibility. Sometimes the visitor seems to catch a feeling of pervading gloom; sometimes he hears the furious and cruel words of those who would end the problem by putting the Negro out of the question; sometimes he listens to the hopeful voice of those who expect a peaceful and a just solution; but all thinking men in the South agree that their section has a special, a peculiar, a difficult and almost insoluble problem in which the North has little or no share.

Here comes in the first of many difficulties in dealing with the Southern question, a diversity of voices such that it is hard to know which speaks for the South, or where the average sentiment is to be found. Public opinion on some moral and social questions is less easily concentrated than in the North; though the prohibitionists have recently made a very successful campaign through a general league, all efforts to focus public opinion on the negro question through general societies and public meetings have so far failed.

Agitation or even discussion of the race problem is not much aided by the press, though in some ways journalism is on a higher plane than in the North. Most cities, even small ones, have a newspaper which is edited with real literary skill, and which does not seem to be the servant of any commercial interest. There is a type of Southern paper of which the *Charleston News and Courier* is the best example, which has for its stock-in-trade, ultra and Bourbon sentiments. No paper in the South is more interesting than the *News and Courier,* but it represents an age that is past. The conservative, readable, and on the whole, high-toned Southern newspapers, do not in general seem to lead public sentiment, and the yellow journal has begun to compete with them. Still the paper which by its lurid statement of facts, large admixture of lies, and use of ferocious headlines, was one of the chief agents in bringing about the Atlanta riots of 1907 afterwards went into the hands of a receiver; and journals of that type have less influence than in the North.

A temperamental Southern characteristic is an impatience of dissent, a characteristic which has recently been summed up as follows by a foreigner who has lived twelve years in the South and is identified with it. "There are three phases of public sentiment that I must regard as weaknesses, . . . The public attitude of Southern temper is over-sensitive and too easily resents criticism . . . Then, I think the Southern people are too easily swayed by an apparent public sentiment, the broader and higher conscience of the people gives way too readily to a tin-pan clamor, the depth and real force of which they are not disposed to question. . . . Again, . . . the South as a section, does not seem fully to appreciate the importance of the inevitables in civilization—the fixed and unalterable laws of progress." Illustrations of this sensitiveness to criticism are abundant. For instance, the affectionate girl in the Southern school when a Yankee teacher gives her a low mark, bursts into tears, and wants to know why the teacher does not love her.

From slavery days down, there has been a disposition to look upon Northern writers and visitors with suspicion. Still inquirers are in all parts of the South received with courtesy by those whose character and interest in the things that make for the uplift of both the white and black race furnish the most convincing argument that there is an enlightened public sentiment which will work out the Southern problem. In any case there is no public objection to criticism of Southerners by other Southerners; nothing, for instance, could be more explicit and mutually unfavorable than the opinions exchanged between Hoke Smith and Clark Howells in 1907, when rival candidates for the governorship of Georgia. In politics one may say what he likes, subject to an occasional rebuke from the revolver's mouth.

It is not the same in the discussion of the race question. In half a dozen instances in the last few years, attempts have been made to drive out professors from Southern colleges and universities, on the ground that they were not sufficiently Southern. In one such case, that of Professor Bassett, at Trinity College, North Carolina, who said in print that Booker Washington was the greatest man except Lee, born in the South in a hundred years, it stood by him manfully, and his retention was felt to be a triumph for free speech. Other boards of trustees have rallied in like manner, and there is a fine spirit of fearless truth among professors of colleges, ministers, lawyers, and public men. It is no small triumph for the cause of fair play that John Sharp Williams, of Mississippi, in 1907 came out in opposition to Governor Vardaman's violent abuse of the Negro, on that issue triumphed over him in the canvass for the United States Senate; and then in a public address committed himself to a friendly and hopeful policy toward the Negro.

In part, this frame of mind is due to a feeling neatly stated by a Southern banker: "The Southern people are not a bad kind, and a kind word goes a long way with them; they have odd peculiarities; they cannot argue, and as soon as you differ with them, you arouse temper, not on the Negro question especially, but on any." This diagnosis is confirmed by "Nicholas Worth": "Few men cared what opinion you held about any subject. . . .

I could talk in private as I pleased with Colonel Stover himself about Jefferson Davis or about educating the negro. He was tolerant of all private opinions, privately expressed among men only. But the moment that an objectionable opinion was publicly expressed, or expressed to women or to negroes, that was another matter. Then it touched our sacred dead, our hearthstones, etc." This state of feeling has much affected politics in the South and is in part responsible for the phenomenon called the Solid South, under which, whatever be its causes, the South is deprived of influence either in nominating or supplying candidates for national office, because its vote may be relied upon in any case for one party and one only.

The dislike of the critic is specially strong when criticism comes from foreigners, and aggravated when it comes from Northerners. A recent Southern speaker says: "Now, as since the day the first flagship was legalized in its trade in Massachusetts, . . . the trouble in the race question is due to the persistent assertion on the part of northern friends and philanthropists that they understand the problem and can devise the means for its solution." That Northerners do not all lay claim to such understanding, or hold themselves responsible for race troubles, is admitted by a Southerner of much greater weight, Edgar Gardner Murphy, who has recently said: "Beneath the North's serious and rightful sense of obligation the South saw only an intolerant 'interference.' Beneath the South's natural suspicion and solicitude the North saw only an indiscriminating enmity to herself and to the negro."

To these characteristics another is added by "Nicholas Worth," in his discussion of the "oratorical habit of mind" of a generation ago—"Rousing speech was more to be desired than accuracy of statement. An exaggerated manner and a tendency to sweeping generalizations were the results. You can now trace this quality in the mind and in the speech of the great majority of Southern men, especially men in public life. We call it the undue development of their emotional nature. It is also the result of a lack of any exact training,—of a system that was mediæval." Another form of this habit of mind is the love of round numbers, a fondness for stating a thing in the largest terms; thus the clever but no-wise distinguished professor of Latin is "Probably the greatest classical scholar in the United States," the siege of Vicksburg was "the most terrific contest in the annals of warfare"; the material progress of the South is "the most marvelous thing in human history."

This difference of temperament between North and South is not confined to members of the white race. The mental processes of the Southern Negro differ not only from those of the Southern White, but to a considerable degree from those of the Northern Negro; and the African temperament has, in the course of centuries, in some ways reacted upon the minds of the associated white race. The real standards and aspirations of the Negroes are crudely defined and little known outside themselves, and if they were better understood they would still have scant influence upon the white point of view. The "Southern temperament," therefore means the temperament of the Southern Whites, of the people who control society, forum, and legislature. It is always more important to know what people think than what they do, and every phase of the race question in the South is affected by the habits of thought of thinking white people.

Both sections need to understand each other; and that good result is impeded by the belief of a large number of people in the South that the North as a section feels a personal hostility to the South; that in Reconstruction it sought to humiliate the Southern Whites, and to despoil them of their property; that it planted schools in the South with the express purpose of bringing about a social equality hateful to the Whites; that it arouses in the Negro a frame of mind which leads to the most hideous of crimes; and that Northern observers and critics of the South are little better than spies.

The North is doubtless blamable for some past ill feeling and some ill judgment, but it cannot be charged now with prejudice against the South. It is not too much to say that the North as a section is weary of the negro question; that it is disappointed in the progress of the race both in the South and

in the North; that it is overwhelmed with a variety of other
questions, and less inclined than at any time during forty
years to any active interference in Southern relations. An
annual floodtide carries many Northern people into Florida
and other pleasure resorts, where they see the surface of the
negro question and accept without verification the conventional
statements that they hear; the same tide on its ebb brings them
North with a tone of discouragement and irritation toward
the Negro, which much affects Northern public sentiment.

This apathy or disappointment is unfortunate, for from many
points of view, the North has both an interest and a responsibility for what goes on in the South. First of all, from its considerable part in bringing about present conditions. Besides
an original share in drawing slavery upon the colonies, the
North by the emancipation of the slaves disturbed the pre-
ëxisting balance of race relations, such as it was. Then in Reconstruction the North attempted to bring about a new political
system with the honest expectation that it would solve the race
question. Surely it has a right to examine the results of its
action, with a view either to justify its attitude, or to accept
censure for it.

If either through want of patience or skill or by sheer force
of adverse circumstance a dangerous condition has come about
in the South for which the dominant white Southerners are not
responsible, they are entitled to an understanding of their case
and to sympathy, encouragement and aid in overcoming their
troubles. No thinking person in the North desires anything but
the peaceful removal of the evils which undeniably weigh upon
the South. To that end the North might offer something out
of its own experience, for it has expert knowledge of race
troubles and of ways to solve them. The Indian question ever
since the Civil War has been chiefly in the hands of Northern
men; and if it has been a botchy piece of work, at least a way
out has been found in the present land-in-severalty plan; and
from the North in considerable part has proceeded the government of the Filipinos. The North carries almost alone a mass
of foreigners who contribute difficulties which in diversity much

exceed the negro problem, and which so far have been so handled that in few places is there a crisis, acute or threatening. The North has further its own experiences with Negroes, beginning in Colonial times; it now harbors a million of them; and it has in most places found a peaceful living basis for the two races, side by side.

Perhaps Southern people do not make sufficient allowance for the scientific love of inquiry of the North. It is a region where Vassar students of sociology visit the probation courts; where Yale men descend upon New York and investigate Tammany Hall; where race relations are thought a fit subject for intercollegiate debate and scientific monographs, on the same footing with the distribution of immigrants, or the career of discharged convicts. In Massachusetts, people are ready to attack any insoluble problem, from the proper authority of the Russian Douma to the reason why cooks give notice without previous notice. As a study of human nature, as an exercise in practical sociology, the Southern race problem has for the North much the same fascination as the preceding slavery question.

Doubtless the zeal for investigation, and the disposition to give unasked advice, would both be lessened if the Southern problem were already solved or on the road to solution by the people nearest to it. The Southern Whites have had control of every Southern state government since 1876 and some of them longer; they are dominant in legislature, court and plantation; yet they have not yet succeeded in putting an end to their own perplexities. Some of them still defiantly assert themselves against mankind; thus Professor Smith, of New Orleans, says apropos of the controversy over race relations: "The attitude of the South presents an element of the pathetic. The great world is apparently hopelessly against her. Three-fourths of the virtue, culture, and intelligence of the United States seems to view her with pitying scorn; the old mother, England, has no word of sympathy, but applauds the conduct that her daughter reprehends; the continent of Europe looks on with amused perplexity, as unable even to comprehend her position, so childish and absurd." Professor Smith's answer to his own question is: "The South cares nothing, in themselves, for the personal friendships or appreciations of high-placed dignitaries and men of light and leading." He does not speak for his section; for most intelligent Southern people, however extreme their views, desire to be understood; they want their position to seem humane and logical to their neighbors; they are sure that they are the only people who can be on the right road; but they do not feel that they are approaching a permanent adjustment of race relations.

How could such an adjustment be expected now? The negro question has existed ever since the first landing of negro slaves in 1619, became serious in some colonies before 1700, gave rise to many difficulties and complications during the Revolution, was reflected in the Constitutional Convention of 1787, later proved to be the rock of offense upon which the Union split, and has during the forty years since the Civil War been the most absorbing subject of discussion in the South. It hardly seems likely that it will be put to rest in our day and generation.

Yet some settlement is necessary for the peace and the prosperity of both races; and one of the means to that end is a frank, free and open discussion in all parts of the Union. Nothing was so prejudicial to slavery as the attempt to silence the Northern abolitionists; for a social system that was too fragile to be discussed was doomed to be broken. One of the most encouraging things at present is the willingness of the South to discuss its problems on its own ground, and to admit that there can be a variety of opinions; and to meet rather than to defy the criticisms of observers.

If the thinking people of the South were less willing to share the discussion with the North, it would still be a Northern concern; for the Southern race problem, like the labor unions of the manufacturing North, the distribution of lands in the far West, and the treatment of Mongolians on the Pacific Coast, is nobody's exclusive property. There must be freedom for the men of every section to discuss every such question; it is the opportunity for mutual helpfulness. For instance, how much might be contributed to an understanding of the decay of the New England hill towns by a Southern visitor who should visit them and then report upon them from his point of view. Violent, ignorant, and prejudiced discussion of any section of the Union by any other section is, of course, destructive of national harmony; but the days have gone by when it could be thought unfriendly, hostile, or condemnatory for Northern men to strive to make themselves familiar with the race questions of the South. "We are everyone members of another," and the whole body politic suffers from the disease of any member. The immigrant in the North is the concern of the Southerner for he is to become part of America. The status of the plantation hand in Alabama is likewise a Northern problem; as Murphy has recently said: "The Nation, including the South as well as the North, and the West as well as the South and the North, has to do with every issue in the South that touches any national right of the humblest of its citizens. Too long it has been assumed, both at the North and at the South, that the North is the Nation. The North is not the Nation. The Nation is the life, the thought, the conscience, the authority, of all the land."

3 The South and Her Problems

Speaking in Dallas, Texas, on October 26, 1887, before a state fair audience, Henry W. Grady expressed freely his views on the southern race problem and the problems of southern industry. Nowhere else is the prevailing southern attitude just prior to the rewriting of the southern state constitutions stated so forcibly. Professing a strong nationalism, Grady nevertheless spoke in sectional terms. He was clearly a white supremacist. To him the Anglo-Saxon was predestined by God to rule the South, and he proposed to his Texas audience that Southerners yield not an inch on this proposition. Never in his papers and speeches did Grady specifically define what the Negro's place should be as an active participant in government and regional economy.

Grady also believed that southern economy rested upon a foundation of cotton culture. His speech in 1887 might well have been made to one of the antebellum trade conventions. Though critical at times of the monopoly which cotton held on much of the South, he saw the staple as the region's chief stock in trade. Cotton was king and it would remain king. His comparative figures showed the South claiming a safe margin of production over its competitors from abroad. Though proclaiming cotton king, however, Grady suggested, in what almost amounted to an oratorical aside, that the region develop its iron ores and timber resources, and grow at home the food that it consumed.

I SHALL BE PARDONED FOR RESISTING THE INSPIRATION OF this presence and adhering to-day to blunt and rigorous speech —for there are times when fine words are paltry, and this seems to me to be such a time. So I shall turn away from the thunders of the political battle upon which every American hangs intent, and repress the ardor that at this time rises in every American heart—for there are issues that strike deeper than any political theory has reached, and conditions of which partisanry has taken, and can take, but little account. Let me, therefore, with studied plainness, and with such precision as is possible—in a spirit of fraternity that is broader than party limitations, and deeper than political motive—discuss with you certain problems upon the wise and prompt solution of which depends the glory and prosperity of the South.

But why—for let us make our way slowly—why "the South." In an indivisible union—in a republic against the integrity of which sword shall never be drawn or mortal hand uplifted, and in which the rich blood gathering at the common heart is sent throbbing into every part of the body politic—why is one section held separated from the rest in alien consideration? We can understand why this should be so in a city that has a community of local interests; or in a State still clothed in that sovereignty of which the debates of peace and the storm of war has not stripped her. But why should a number of States, stretching from Richmond to Galveston, bound together by no local interests, held in no autonomy, be thus combined and drawn to a common center? That man would be absurd who declaimed in Buffalo against the wrongs of the Middle States, or who demanded in Chicago a convention for the West to consider the needs of that section. If then it be provincialism that holds the South together, let us outgrow it; if it be sectionalism, let us root it out of our hearts; but if it be something deeper than these and essential to our system, let us declare

Joel Chandler Harris, *Joel Chandler Harris' Life of Henry W. Grady: Including His Writings and Speeches* (New York: Cassell Publishing Company, 1890), 94–115.

it with frankness, consider it with respect, defend it with firmness, and in dignity abide its consequence. What is it that holds the southern States—though true in thought and deed to the Union—so closely bound in sympathy to-day? For a century these States championed a governmental theory—but that, having triumphed in every forum, fell at last by the sword. They maintained an institution—but that, having been administered in the fullest wisdom of man, fell at last in the higher wisdom of God. They fought a war—but the prejudices of that war have died, its sympathies have broadened, and its memories are already the priceless treasure of the republic that is cemented forever with its blood. They looked out together upon the ashes of their homes and the desolation of their fields—but out of pitiful resource they have fashioned their homes anew, and plenty rides on the springing harvests. In all the past there is nothing to draw them into essential or lasting alliance—nothing in all that heroic record that cannot be rendered unfearing from provincial hands into the keeping of American history.

But the future holds a problem, in solving which the South must stand alone; in dealing with which, she must come closer together than ambition or despair have driven her, and on the outcome of which her very existence depends. This problem is to carry within her body politic two separate races, and nearly equal in numbers. She must carry these races in peace—for discord means ruin. She must carry them separately—for assimilation means debasement. She must carry them in equal justice—for to this she is pledged in honor and in gratitude. She must carry them even unto the end, for in human probability she will never be quit of either.

This burden no other people bears to-day—on none hath it ever rested. Without precedent or companionship, the South must bear this problem, the awful responsibility of which should win the sympathy of all human kind, and the protecting watchfulness of God—alone, even unto the end. Set by this problem apart from all other peoples of the earth, and her unique position emphasized rather than relieved, as I shall show hereafter, by her material conditions, it is not only fit but it is essential that she should hold her brotherhood unimpaired, quicken her sympathies, and in the light or in the shadows of this surpassing problem work out her own salvation in the fear of God—but of God alone.

What shall the South do to be saved? Through what paths shall she reach the end? Through what travail, or what splendors, shall she give to the Union this section, its wealth garnered, its resources utilized, and its rehabilitation complete—and restore to the world this problem solved in such justice as the finite mind can measure, or finite hands administer?

In dealing with this I shall dwell on two points.

First, the duty of the South in its relation to the race problem.

Second, the duty of the South in relation to its no less unique and important industrial problem.

. . . What of the negro? This of him. I want no better friend than the black boy who was raised by my side, and who is now trudging patiently with downcast eyes and shambling figure through his lowly way of life. I want no sweeter music than the crooning of my old "mammy," now dead and gone to rest, as I heard it when she held me in her loving arms, and bending her old black face above me stole the cares from my brain, and led me smiling into sleep. I want no truer soul than that which moved the trusty slave, who for four years while my father fought with the armies that barred his freedom, slept every night at my mother's chamber door, holding her and her children as safe as if her husband stood guard, and ready to lay down his humble life on her threshold. History has no parallel to the faith kept by the negro in the South during the war. Often five hundred negroes to a single white man, and yet through these dusky throngs the women and children walked in safety, and the unprotected homes rested in peace. Unmarshaled, the black battalions moved patiently to the fields in the morning to feed the armies their idleness would have starved, and at night gathered anxiously at the big house to "hear the news from marster," though conscious that his victory made their chains enduring. Everywhere humble and kindly; the bodyguard of the helpless;

the rough companion of the little ones; the observant friend; the silent sentry in his lowly cabin; the shrewd counselor. And when the dead came home, a mourner at the open grave. A thousand torches would have disbanded every Southern army, but not one was lighted. When the master going to a war in which slavery was involved said to his slave, "I leave my home and loved ones in your charge," the tenderness between man and master stood disclosed. And when the slave held that charge sacred through storm and temptation, he gave new meaning to faith and loyalty. I rejoice that when freedom came to him after years of waiting, it was all the sweeter because the black hands from which the shackles fell were stainless of a single crime against the helpless ones confided to his care.

From this root, imbedded in a century of kind and constant companionship, has sprung some foliage. As no race had ever lived in such unresisting bondage, none was ever hurried with such swiftness through freedom into power. Into hands still trembling from the blow that broke the shackles, was thrust the ballot. In less than twelve months from the day he walked down the furrow a slave, the negro dictated in legislative halls from which Davis and Calhoun had gone forth, the policy of twelve commonwealths. When his late master protested against his misrule, the federal drum beat rolled around his strongholds, and from a hedge of federal bayonets he grinned in good-natured insolence. From the proven incapacity of that day has he far advanced? Simple, credulous, impulsive—easily led and too often easily bought, is he a safer, more intelligent citizen now than then? Is this mass of votes, loosed from old restraints, inviting alliance or awaiting opportunity, less menacing than when its purpose was plain and its way direct?

My countrymen, right here the South must make a decision on which very much depends. Many wise men hold that the white vote of the South should divide, the color line be beaten down, and the southern States ranged on economic or moral questions as interest or belief demands. I am compelled to dissent from this view. The worst thing in my opinion that could happen is that the white people of the South should stand in opposing factions, with the vast mass of ignorant or purchasable negro votes between. Consider such a status. If the negroes were skillfully led,—and leaders would not be lacking, —it would give them the balance of power—a thing not to be considered. If their vote was not compacted, it would invite the debauching bid of factions, and drift surely to that which was the most corrupt and cunning. With the shiftless habit and irresolution of slavery days still possessing him, the negro voter will not in this generation, adrift from war issues, become a steadfast partisan through conscience or conviction. In every community there are colored men who redeem their race from this approach, and who vote under reason. Perhaps in time the bulk of this race may thus adjust itself. But, through what long and monstrous periods of political debauchery this status would be reached, no tongue can tell.

The clear and unmistakable domination of the white race, dominating not through violence, not through party alliance, but through the integrity of its own vote and the largeness of its sympathy and justice through which it shall compel the support of the better classes of the colored race,—that is the hope and assurance of the South. Otherwise, the negro would be bandied from one faction to another. His credulity would be played upon, his cupidity tempted, his impulses misdirected, his passions inflamed. He would be forever in alliance with that faction which was most desperate and unscrupulous. Such a state would be worse than reconstruction, for then intelligence was banded, and its speedy triumph assured. But with intelligence and property divided—bidding and overbidding for place and patronage—irritation increasing with each conflict—the bitterness and desperation seizing every heart—political debauchery deepening, as each faction staked its all in the miserable game— there would be no end to this, until our suffrage was hopelessly sullied, our people forever divided, and our most sacred rights surrendered.

One thing further should be said in perfect frankness. Up to this point we have dealt with ignorance and corruption—but beyond this point a deeper issue confronts us. Ignorance may struggle to enlightenment, out of corruption may come the incorruptible. God speed the day when,—every true man will work and pray for its coming,—the negro must be led to know and through sympathy to confess that his interests and the interests of the people of the South are identical. The men who, from afar off, view this subject through the cold eye of speculation or see it distorted through partisan glasses, insist that, directly or indirectly, the negro race shall be in control of the affairs of the South. We have no fears of this; already we are attaching to us the best elements of that race, and as we proceed our alliance will broaden; external pressure but irritates and impedes. Those who would put the negro race in supremacy would work against infallible decree, for the white race can never submit to its domination, because the white race is the superior race. But the supremacy of the white race of the South must be maintained forever, and the domination of the negro race resisted at all points and at all hazards—because the white race is the superior race. This is the declaration of no new truth. It has abided forever in the marrow of our bones, and shall run forever with the blood that feeds Anglo-Saxon hearts.

In political compliance the South has evaded the truth, and men have drifted from their convictions. But we cannot escape this issue. It faces us wherever we turn. It is an issue that has been, and will be. The races and tribes of earth are of Divine origin. Behind the laws of man and the decrees of war, stands the law of God. What God hath separated let no man join together. The Indian, the Malay, the Negro, the Caucasian, these types stand as markers of God's will. Let not man tinker with the work of the Almighty. Unity of civilization, no more than unity of faith, will never be witnessed on earth. No race has risen, or will rise, above its ordained place. Here is the pivotal fact of this great matter—two races are made equal in law, and in political rights, between whom the caste of race has set an impassable gulf. This gulf is bridged by a statute, and the races are urged to cross thereon. This cannot be. The fiat of the Almighty has gone forth, and in eighteen centuries of history it is written. We would escape this issue if we could. From the depths of its soul the South invokes from heaven "peace on earth, and good will to man." She would not, if she could, cast this race back into the condition from which it was righteously raised. She would not deny its smallest or abridge its fullest privilege. Not to lift this burden forever from her people, would she do the least of these things. She must walk through the valley of the shadow, for God has so ordained. But he has ordained that she shall walk in that integrity of race, that created in His wisdom has been perpetuated in His strength. Standing in the presence of this multitude, sobered with the responsibility of the message I deliver to the young men of the South, I declare that the truth above all others to be worn unsullied and sacred in your hearts, to be surrendered to no force, sold for no price, compromised in no necessity, but cherished and defended as the covenant of your prosperity, and the pledge of peace to your children, is that the white race must dominate forever in the South, because it is the white race, and superior to that race by which its supremacy is threatened.

It is a race issue. Let us come to this point, and stand here. Here the air is pure and the light is clear, and here honor and peace abide. Juggling and evasion deceives not a man. Compromise and subservience has carried not a point. There is not a white man North or South who does not feel it stir in the gray matter of his brain and throb in his heart. Not a negro who does not feel its power. It is not a sectional issue. It speaks in Ohio, and in Georgia. It speaks wherever the Anglo-Saxon touches an alien race. It has just spoken in universally approved legislation in excluding the Chinaman from our gates, not for his ignorance, vice or corruption, but because he sought to establish an inferior race in a republic fashioned in the wisdom and defended by the blood of a homogeneous people.

. . . And yet that is just what is proposed. Not in twenty years have we seen a day so pregnant with fate to this section as the sixth of next November. If President Cleveland is then defeated, which God forbid, I believe these States will be led through sorrows compared to which the woes of reconstruction will be as the fading dews of morning to the roaring flood. To dominate these States through the colored vote, with such aid as federal patronage may debauch or federal power deter, and thus through its chosen instruments perpetuate its rule, is in my opinion the settled purpose of the Republican party. I am appalled when I measure the passion in which this negro problem is judged by the leaders of the party. Fifteen years ago Vice-President Wilson said—and I honor his memory as that of a courageous man: "We shall not have finished with the South until we force its people to change their thought, and think as we think." I repeat these words, for I heard them when a boy, and they fell on my ears as the knell of my people's rights—"to change their thought, and make them think as we think." Not enough to have conquered our armies—to have decimated our ranks, to have desolated our fields and reduced us to poverty, to have struck the ballot from our hands and enfranchised our slaves—to have held us prostrate under bayonets while the insolent mocked and thieves plundered—but their very souls must be rifled of their faiths, their sacred traditions cudgeled from memory, and their immortal minds beaten into subjection until thought had lost its integrity, and we were forced "to think as they think." And just now General Sherman has said, and I honor him as a soldier:

> The negro must be allowed to vote, and his vote must be counted; otherwise, so sure as there is a God in heaven, you will have another war, more cruel than the last, when the torch and dagger will take the place of the muskets of well-ordered battalions. Should the negro strike that blow, in seeming justice, there will be millions to assist them.

And this General took Johnston's sword in surrender! He looked upon the thin and ragged battalions in gray, that for four years had held his teeming and heroic legions at bay. Facing them, he read their courage in their depleted ranks, and gave them a soldier's parole. When he found it in his heart to taunt these heroes with this threat, why—careless as he was twenty years ago with fire, he is even more careless now with his words. If we could hope that this problem would be settled within our

lives I would appeal from neither madness nor unmanliness.
But when I know that, strive as I may, I must at last render this
awful heritage into the untried hands of my son, already dearer
to me than my life, and that he must in turn bequeath it unsolved to his children, I cry out against the inhumanity that
deepens its difficulties with this incendiary threat, and beclouds
its real issue with inflaming passion.

This problem is not only enduring, but it is widening. The
exclusion of the Chinese is the first step in the revolution that
shall save liberty and law and religion to this land, and in peace
and order, not enforced on the gallows or at the bayonet's end,
but proceeding from the heart of an harmonious people, shall
secure in the enjoyment of these rights, and the control of this
republic, the homogeneous people that established and has
maintained it. The next step will be taken when some brave
statesman, looking Demagogy in the face, shall move to call to
the stranger at our gates, "Who comes here?" admitting every
man who seeks a home, or honors our institutions, and whose
habit and blood will run with the native current; but excluding
all who seek to plant anarchy or to establish alien men or measures on our soil; and will then demand that the standard of
our citizenship be lifted and the right of acquiring our suffrage
be abridged. When that day comes, and God speed its coming,
the position of the South will be fully understood, and everywhere approved. Until then, let us—giving the negro every
right, civil and political, measured in that fullness the strong
should always accord the weak—holding him in closer friendship and sympathy than he is held by those who would crucify
us for his sake—realizing that on his prosperity ours depends—
let us resolve that never by external pressure, or internal division, shall he establish domination, directly or indirectly, over
that race that everywhere has maintained its supremacy. Let this
resolution be cast on the lines of equity and justice. Let it be the
pledge of honest, safe and impartial administration, and we
shall command the support of the colored race itself, more dependent than any other on the bounty and protection of government. Let us be wise and patient, and we shall secure through

its acquiescence what otherwise we should win through conflict, and hold in insecurity.

All this is no unkindness to the negro—but rather that he
may be led in equal rights and in peace to his uttermost good.
Not in sectionalism—for my heart beats true to the Union, to
the glory of which your life and heart is pledged. Not in disregard of the world's opinion—for to render back this problem
in the world's approval is the sum of my ambition, and the height
of human achievement. Not in reactionary spirit—but rather to
make clear that new and grander way up which the South is
marching to higher destiny, and on which I would not halt her
for all the spoils that have been gathered unto parties since
Catiline conspired, and Cæsar fought. Not in passion, my
countrymen, but in reason—not in narrowness, but in breadth—
that we may solve this problem in calmness and in truth, and
lifting its shadows let perpetual sunshine pour down on two
races, walking together in peace and contentment. Then shall
this problem have proved our blessing, and the race that
threatened our ruin work our salvation as it fills our fields with
the best peasantry the world has ever seen. Then the South—
putting behind her all the achievements of her past—and in war
and in peace they beggar eulogy—may stand upright among the
nations and challenge the judgment of man and the approval
of God, in having worked out in their sympathy, and in His
guidance, this last and surpassing miracle of human government.

What of the South's industrial problem? When we remember
that amazement followed the payment by thirty-seven million
Frenchmen of a billion dollars indemnity to Germany, that the
five million whites of the South rendered to the torch and sword
three billions of property—that thirty million dollars a year, or
six hundred million dollars in twenty years, has been given willingly of our poverty as pensions for Northern soldiers, the wonder is that we are here at all. There is a figure with which history has dealt lightly, but that, standing pathetic and heroic in
the genesis of our new growth, has interested me greatly—our
soldier-farmer of '65. What chance had he for the future as he

wandered amid his empty barns, his stock, labor, and implements gone—gathered up the fragments of his wreck—urging kindly his borrowed mule—paying sixty per cent. for all that he bought, and buying all on credit—his crop mortgaged before it was planted—his children in want, his neighborhood in chaos—working under new conditions and retrieving every error by a costly year—plodding all day down the furrow, hopeless and adrift, save when at night he went back to his broken home, where his wife, cheerful even then, renewed his courage, while she ministered to him in loving tenderness. Who would have thought as during those lonely and terrible days he walked behind the plow, locking the sunshine in the glory of his harvest, and spreading the showers and the verdure of his field—no friend near save nature that smiled at his earnest touch, and God that sent him the message of good cheer through the passing breeze and the whispering leaves—that he would in twenty years, having carried these burdens uncomplaining, make a crop of $800,000,000. Yet this he has done, and from his bounty the South has rebuilded her cities, and recouped her losses. While we exult in his splendid achievement, let us take account of his standing.

. . . Amid this universal conflict, where stands the South? While the producer of everything we eat or wear, in every land, is fighting through glutted markets for bare existence, what of the southern farmer? In his industrial as in his political problem he is set apart—not in doubt, but in assured independence. Cotton makes him king. Not the fleeces that Jason sought can rival the richness of this plant, as it unfurls its banners in our fields. It is gold from the instant it puts forth its tiny shoot. The shower that whispers to it is heard around the world. The trespass of a worm on its green leaf means more to England than the advance of the Russians on her Asiatic outposts. When its fibre, current in every bank, is marketed, it renders back to the South $350,000,000 every year. Its seed will yield $60,000,000 worth of oil to the press and $40,000,000 in food for soil and beast, making the stupendous total of $450,000,000 annual income from this crop. And now, under the Tompkins patent, from its stalk—news paper is to be made at two cents per pound. Edward Atkinson once said: "If New England could grow the cotton plant, without lint, it would make her richest crop; if she held monopoly of cotton lint and seed she would control the commerce of the world."

But is our monopoly, threatened from Egypt, India and Brazil, sure and permanent? Let the record answer. In '72 the American supply of cotton was 3,241,000 bales,—foreign supply 3,036,000. We led our rivals by less than 200,000 bales. This year the American supply is 8,000,000 bales—from foreign sources, 2,100,000, expressed in bales of four hundred pounds each. In spite of new areas elsewhere, of fuller experience, of better transportation, and unlimited money spent in experiment, the supply of foreign cotton has decreased since '72 nearly 1,000,000 bales, while that of the South has increased nearly 5,000,000. Further than this: Since 1872, population in Europe has increased 13 per cent., and cotton consumption in Europe has increased 50 per cent. Still further: Since 1880 cotton consumption in Europe has increased 28 per cent., wool only 4 per cent., and flax has decreased 11 per cent. As for new areas, the uttermost missionary woos the heathen with a cotton shirt in one hand and the Bible in the other, and no savage I believe has ever been converted to one, without adopting the other. To summarize: Our American fibre has increased its product nearly three-fold, while it has seen the product of its rival decrease one-third. It has enlarged its dominion in the old centers of population, supplanting flax and wool, and it peeps from the satchel of every business and religious evangelist that trots the globe. In three years the American crop has increased 1,400,000 bales, and yet there is less cotton in the world to-day than at any time for twenty years. The dominion of our king is established; this princely revenue assured, not for a year, but for all time. It is the heritage that God gave us when he arched our skies, established our mountains, girt us about with the ocean, tempered the sunshine, and measured the rain—ours and our children's forever.

Not alone in cotton, but in iron, does the South excel. The

Hon. Mr. Norton, who honors this platform with his presence,
once said to me: "An Englishman of the highest character predicted that the Atlantic will be whitened within our lives with
sails carrying American iron and coal to England." When he
made that prediction the English miners were exhausting the
coal in long tunnels above which the ocean thundered. Having
ores and coal stored in exhaustless quantity, in such richness,
and in such adjustment, that iron can be made and manufacturing done cheaper than elsewhere on this continent, is to now
command, and at last control, the world's market for iron. The
South now sells iron, through Pittsburgh, in New York. She has
driven Scotch iron first from the interior, and finally from American ports. Within our lives she will cross the Atlantic, and fulfill
the Englishman's prophecy. In 1880 the South made 212,000
tons of iron. In 1887, 845,000 tons. She is now actually building,
or has finished this year, furnaces that will produce more than
her entire product of last year. Birmingham alone will produce
more iron in 1889 than the entire South produced in 1887. Our
coal supply is exhaustless, Texas alone having 6000 square miles.
In marble and granite we have no rivals, as to quantity or quality. In lumber our riches are even vaster. More than fifty per
cent. of our entire area is in forests, making the South the best
timbered region of the world. We have enough merchantable
yellow pine to bring, in money, $2,500,000,000—a sum the vast-
ness of which can only be understood when I say it nearly
equaled the assessed value of the entire South, including cities,
forests, farms, mines, factories and personal property of every
description whatsoever. Back of this our forests of hard woods,
and measureless swamps of cypress and gum. Think of it. In
cotton a monopoly. In iron and coal establishing swift mastery.
In granite and marble developing equal advantage and resource.
In yellow pine and hard woods the world's treasury. Surely the
basis of the South's wealth and power is laid by the hand of the
Almighty God, and its prosperity has been established by divine
law which work in eternal justice and not by taxes levied on its
neighbors through human statutes. Paying tribute for fifty years
that under artificial conditions other sections might reach a

prosperity impossible under natural laws, it has grown apace—
and its growth shall endure if its people are ruled by two max-
ims, that reach deeper than legislative enactment, and the
operation of which cannot be limited by artificial restraint, and
but little hastened by artificial stimulus.

First. No one crop will make a people prosperous. If cotton
held its monopoly under conditions that made other crops impossible—or under allurements that made other crops exceptional—its dominion would be despotism.

Whenever the greed for a money crop unbalances the wisdom
of husbandry, the money crop is a curse. When it stimulates
the general economy of the farm, it is the profiting of farming.
In an unprosperous strip of Carolina, when asked the cause
of their poverty, the people say, "Tobacco—for it is our only
crop." In Lancaster, Pa., the richest American county by the
census, when asked the cause of their prosperity, they say, "Tobacco—for it is the golden crown of a diversified agriculture."
The soil that produces cotton invites the grains and grasses,
the orchard and the vine. Clover, corn, cotton, wheat, and barley
thrive in the same inclosure; the peach, the apple, the apricot,
and the Siberian crab in the same orchard. Herds and flocks
graze ten months every year in the meadows over which winter
is but a passing breath, and in which spring and autumn meet
in summer's heart. Sugar-cane and oats, rice and potatoes, are
extremes that come together under our skies. To raise cotton
and send its princely revenues to the west for supplies, and to
the east for usury, would be misfortune if soil and climate
forced such a curse. When both invite independence, to remain
in slavery is a crime. To mortgage our farms in Boston for
money with which to buy meat and bread from western cribs
and smokehouses, is folly unspeakable. I rejoice that Texas is
less open to this charge than others of the cotton States. With
her eighty million bushels of grain, and her sixteen million head
of stock, she is rapidly learning that diversified agriculture
means prosperity. Indeed, the South is rapidly learning the same
lesson; and learned through years of debt and dependence it will
never be forgotten. The best thing Georgia has done in twenty

years was to raise her oat crop in one season from two million to nine million bushels, without losing a bale of her cotton. It is more for the South that she has increased her crop of corn—that best of grains, of which Samuel J. Tilden said, "It will be the staple food of the future, and men will be stronger and better when that day comes"—by forty-three million bushels this year, than to have won a pivotal battle in the late war. In this one item she keeps at home this year a sum equal to the entire cotton crop of my State that last year went to the west.

This is the road to prosperity. It is the way to manliness and sturdiness of character. When every farmer in the South shall eat bread from his own fields and meat from his own pastures, and disturbed by no creditor, and enslaved by no debt, shall sit amid his teeming gardens, and orchards, and vineyards, and dairies, and barnyards, pitching his crops in his own wisdom, and growing them in independence, making cotton his clean surplus, and selling it in his own time, and in his chosen market, and not at a master's bidding—getting his pay in cash and not in a receipted mortgage that discharges his debt, but does not restore his freedom—then shall be breaking the fullness of our day. Great is King Cotton! But to lie at his feet while the usurer and the grain raiser bind us in subjection, is to invite the contempt of man and the reproach of God. But to stand up before him and amid the crops and smokehouses wrest from him the magna charta of our independence, and to establish in his name an ample and diversified agriculture, that shall honor him while it enriches us—this is to carry us as far in the way of happiness and independence as the farmer, working in the fullest wisdom, and in the richest field, can carry any people.

But agriculture alone—no matter how rich or varied its resources—cannot establish or maintain a people's prosperity. There is a lesson in this that Texas may learn with profit. No commonwealth ever came to greatness by producing raw material. Less can this be possible in the future than in the past. The Comstock lode is the richest spot on earth. And yet the miners, gasping for breath fifteen hundred feet below the earth's surface, get bare existence out of the splendor they dig from the earth. It goes to carry the commerce and uphold the industry of distant lands, of which the men who produce it get but dim report. Hardly more is the South profited when, stripping the harvest of her cotton fields, or striking her teeming hills, or leveling her superb forests, she sends the raw material to augment the wealth and power of distant communities.

Texas produces a million and a half bales of cotton, which yield her $60,000,000. That cotton, woven into common goods, would add $75,000,000 to Texas's income from this crop, and employ 220,000 operatives, who would spend within her borders more than $30,000,000 in wages. Massachusetts manufactures 575,-000 bales of cotton, for which she pays $31,000,000, and sells for $72,000,000, adding a value nearly equal to Texas's gross revenue from cotton, and yet Texas has a clean advantage for manufacturing this cotton of one per cent. a pound over Massachusetts. The little village of Grand Rapids began manufacturing furniture simply because it was set in a timber district. It is now a great city and sells $10,000,000 worth of furniture every year, in making which 125,000 men are employed, and a population of 40,000 people supported. The best pine districts of the world are in eastern Texas. With less competition and wider markets than Grand Rapids has, will she ship her forests at prices that barely support the wood-chopper and sawyer, to be returned in the making of which great cities are built or maintained? When her farmers and herdsmen draw from her cities $126,000,000 as the price of their annual produce, shall this enormous wealth be scattered through distant shops and factories, leaving in the hands of Texas no more than the sustenance, support, and the narrow brokerage between buyer and seller? As one-crop farming cannot support the country, neither can a resource of commercial exchange support a city. Texas wants immigrants—she needs them—for if every human being in Texas were placed at equi-distant points through the State no Texan could hear the sound of a human voice in your broad areas.

So how can you best attract immigration? By furnishing work for the artisan and mechanic if you meet the demand of your population for cheaper and essential manufactured articles. One half million workers would be needed for this, and with their families would double the population of your State. In these mechanics and their dependents farmers would find a market for not only their staple crops but for the truck that they now despise to raise or sell, but is at least the cream of the farm. Worcester county, Mass., takes $720,000,000 [$62,000,000?] of our material and turns out $87,000,000 of products every year, paying $20,000,000 in wages. The most prosperous section of this world is that known as the Middle States of this republic. With agriculture and manufacturers in the balance, and their shops and factories set amid rich and ample acres, the result is such deep and diffuse prosperity as no other section can show. Suppose those States had a monopoly of cotton and coal so disposed as to command the world's markets and the treasury of the world's timber, I suppose the mind is staggered in contemplating the majesty of the wealth and power they would attain. What have they that the South lacks?—and to her these things were added, and climate, ampler acres and rich soil. It is a curious fact that three-fourths of the population and manufacturing wealth of this country is comprised in a narrow strip between Iowa and Massachusetts, comprising less than one-sixth of our territory, and that this strip is distant from the source of raw materials on which its growth is based, of hard climate and in a large part of sterile soil. Much of this forced and unnatural development is due to slavery, which for a century fenced enterprise and capital out of the South. Mr. Thomas, who in the Lehigh Valley owned a furnace in 1845 that set that pattern for iron-making in America, had at that time bought mines and forest where Birmingham now stands. Slavery forced him away. He settled in Pennsylvania. I have wondered what would have happened if that one man had opened his iron mines in Alabama and set his furnaces there at that time. I know what is going to happen since he has been forced to come to Birmingham and put up two furnaces nearly forty years after his survey.

Another cause that has prospered New England and the Middle States while the South languished, is the system of tariff taxes levied on the unmixed agriculture of these States for the protection of industries to our neighbors to the North, a system on which the Hon. Roger Q. Mills—that lion of the tribe of Judah —has at last laid his mighty paw and under the indignant touch of which it trembles to its center. That system is to be revised and its duties reduced, as we all agree it should be, though I should say in perfect frankness I do not agree with Mr. Mills in it. Let us hope this will be done with care and industrious patience. Whether it stands or falls, the South has entered the industrial list to partake of his bounty if it stands, and if it falls to rely on the favor with which nature has endowed her, and from this immutable advantage to fill her own markets and then have a talk with the world at large.

With amazing rapidity she has moved away from the one-crop idea that was once her curse. In 1880 she was esteemed prosperous. Since that time she has added 393,000,000 bushels to her grain crops, and 182,000,000 head to her live stock. This has not lost one bale of her cotton crop, which, on the contrary, has increased nearly 200,000 bales. With equal swiftness has she moved away from the folly of shipping out her ore at $2 a ton and buying it back in implements from $20 to $100 per ton; her cotton at 10 cents a pound and buying it back in cloth at 20 to 80 cents per pound; her timber at $8 per thousand and buying it back in furniture at ten to twenty times as much. In the past eight years $250,000,000 have been invested in new shops and factories in her States; 225,000 artisans are now working that eight years ago were idle or worked elsewhere, and these added $227,000,000 to the value of her raw material—more than half the value of her cotton. Add to this the value of her increased grain crops and stock, and in the past eight years she has grown in her fields or created in her shops manufactures more than the value of her cotton crop. The incoming tide has begun to rise. Every train brings manufacturers from the East and West seeking to establish themselves or their sons near the raw material and in this growing market. Let the fullness of the tide roll in.

It will not exhaust our materials, nor shall we glut our markets.

When the growing demand of our southern market, feeding on its own growth, is met, we shall find new markets for the South. Under our new condition many indirect laws of commerce shall be straightened. We buy from Brazil $50,000,000 worth of goods, and sell her $8,500,000. England buys only $29,000,000, and sells her $35,000,000. Of $65,000,000 in cotton goods bought by Central and South America, over $50,000,000 went to England. Of $331,000,000 sent abroad by the southern half of our hemisphere, England secures over half, although we buy from that section nearly twice as much as England. Our neighbors to the South need nearly every article we make; we need nearly everything they produce. Less than 2,500 miles of road must be built to bind by rail the two American continents. When this is done, and even before, we shall find exhaustless markets to the South. Texas shall command, as she stands in the van of this new movement, its richest rewards.

The South, under the rapid diversification of crops and diversification of industries, is thrilling with new life. As this new prosperity comes to us, it will bring no sweeter thought to me, and to you, my countrymen, I am sure, than that it adds not only to the comfort and happiness of our neighbors, but that it makes broader the glory and deeper the majesty, and more enduring the strength, of the Union which reigns supreme in our hearts. In this republic of ours is lodged the hope of free government on earth. Here God has rested the ark of his covenant with the sons of men. Let us—once estranged and thereby closer bound, —let us soar above all provincial pride and find our deeper inspirations in gathering the fullest sheaves into the harvest and standing the staunchest and most devoted of its sons as it lights the path and makes clear the way through which all the people of this earth shall come in God's appointed time. . . .

4 Child Labor in Alabama

At the turn of the twentieth century Southerners began to realize that the textile industry was growing rapidly, and that with it the evils of child labor were multiplied. As some mills were owned by New England millmasters, there developed considerable discussion between the southern crusaders and the New Englanders. Even though the New England-owned mills actually were in the minority their managers represented a highly articulate opposition to southern reformers seeking legislation similar to that which had already been enacted in the New England states to curb the abuse of children.[1] Especially active in this struggle was the Executive Committee on Child Labor in Alabama, headed by the Reverend Edgar Gardner Murphy of Montgomery. Murphy was well able to take to task the New England millmasters who undertook either to justify or excuse their child labor policies,[2] as in the following exchange of letters with officials of two Massachusetts textile companies.[3]

In 1907 at a textile conference held in Nashville, Tennessee, and at another the next year in New Orleans, manufacturers were presented with resolutions that not only proposed to establish fourteen

---

[1] *Boston Evening Transcript*, October 30, 1901.

[2] Edgar Gardner Murphy replied to the Nichols letter on November 2, 1901. This letter also appeared in the *Boston Evening Transcript*.

[3] The Sears letter appeared first in the *Boston Evening Transcript* and then in the *Monthly Leader*, organ of the Christian Social Union, December 1901. Both this and the letter above appeared in Murphy, *Problems of the Present South*, 309–329.

years as the minimum age for child labor but also proposed to limit hours from sixty to fifty-four per week. Beyond this, proposals were made to reduce working hours for women, and to prohibit night work for either children or women under twenty-one years of age. In time all the southern states enacted child labor legislation, though laws and their enforcement left much to be accomplished.[4]

To the Editor of the Transcript:

My attention has been called to an article in your paper of the 23d inst., signed by gentlemen from Alabama, in reference to child labor.

As treasurer of a mill in that State, erected by Northern capital, I am interested in the subject. From the starting of our mill, I have never been South without protesting to the agent, and overseer of spinning (the only department in which small help can be employed), against allowing children under twelve years of age to come into the mill, as I did not consider them intelligent enough to do good work. On a visit last June, annoyed that my instructions were not more carefully observed, before leaving I wrote the agent a letter of which the following is a copy:—

"Every time I visit this mill, I am impressed with the fact that it is a great mistake to employ small help in the spinning room. Not only is it wrong from a humanitarian standpoint but it entails an absolute loss to the mill. We prepare the stock and make it into roving, and, because of the small spinners, send back to the pickers an excessive amount of roving waste, and meantime lose the work of the spindles. I again express the wish that you prevent the overseer, as far as possible, from employing children under twelve years of age. I know it is sometimes difficult to get at the real age—and in some cases the parents may threaten to leave our employ unless we give work to their small children, but we must take this stand—and

[4] Walter B. Palmer, "Economic and Legal Aspects of the Labor of Women and Children in the South," in *Economic History, 1865–1910*, ed. James Curtis Ballagh, *The South in the Building of the Nation*, vol. VI, 53–58.

I trust an honest effort will be made to carry out my wishes."

In defence of our officials, it is doubtless true that the trouble comes largely from the parents, who make every effort to get their children into the mill, and often because of refusal, take their families containing needed workers, to other mills, where no objection is made to the employment of children. The statement that twice as many children under twelve years of age are employed in mills under Northern control as in Southern mills, if it means, as it should, in proportion to spindles on same number of yarns, is absolutely false so far as relates to our company, and I have reason to believe the same can be said of other mills under Northern ownership.

Now in regard to the attempted legislation of last winter: The labor organization at the North imported from England a very bright and skillful female labor agitator and sent her to Alabama. She held meetings at central points, and when the Legislature convened, appeared at Montgomery with her following, and a bill against employing children was promptly introduced. The manufacturers and other business men of Alabama resented this outside interference, well knowing the source from which it came, and they were also aware that manufacturers at the North were being solicited for funds with which to incite labor troubles in the South.

As they recognized that this bill was only the entering wedge, they determined that action must come from within the State, and not outside. They also felt that the adjoining State of Georgia, having double the number of spindles, should act first. With these considerations in mind, the manufacturers selected among others our agent, a native Alabamian, to appear before the legislative committee, with the result that the bill was defeated. I think it may be said with truth, that the interference of Northern labor agitators is retarding much needed legislation in all the manufacturing States of the South.

As to our mill and the little town of 2300 people which has grown up around it, there is nothing within the mill or without, of which any citizen of Massachusetts need be ashamed. On the contrary, I challenge either of the gentlemen from Alabama whose names are attached to the letter referred to, to mention among the forty mills in the State, of which only four are directly operated from the North, any one which will compare with ours, in the expenditure which has been made for the comfortable housing of the operatives, and the appliances introduced for their comfort and uplift. From the inception of this enterprise, the purpose has been to build up a model town that should be an object lesson to the South, and we are assured that its influences have been helpful. In addition to a school supported by public tax, the company has always carried on a school of its own, with an experienced and devoted teacher, who has been instructed to make special effort to get in the young children, and thus allure them from the mill. We have built and have in operation a beautiful library—the first erected for this special purpose in the State of Alabama, and we have a church building which would be an ornament in any village of New England, and is in itself an education to our people. We are now building a modern schoolhouse from plans by Boston architects which will accommodate all the children of our community. These are a few of the things we have done and are doing, in our effort to meet the responsibility we have assumed, in dealing with a class of people who have some most excellent traits, and who appeal to us strongly, because many of them have hitherto been deprived of needed comforts and largely of elementary advantages.

What we are attempting to do for our operatives may seem to the gentlemen who signed the appeal in your columns as "spectacular philanthropy" and a "heartless policy"; but this is not the opinion of our employees, nor of visitors who have acquainted themselves with the facts, nor of the communities adjacent to us.

J. HOWARD NICHOLS,
Treasurer Alabama City Mill, Alabama.

TO THE EDITOR OF THE TRANSCRIPT:

I note in your issue of October 30th a reply to a statement to the press and the people of New England, on the subject of child labor in Alabama. Our statement bore the signatures of six

representative citizens of Alabama, among them the Superin-
tendent of Public Schools of Birmingham and ex-Governor
Thomas G. Jones, of Montgomery. The reply to the address of
the committee is signed, not by a disinterested citizen of the
State, but by Mr. J. Howard Nichols, Treasurer of the Alabama
City Mill, at Alabama City.

I thank you for publishing Mr. Nichols's letter. The well-
known citizens of Alabama with whom I have the honor to be
associated, have welcomed the discussion of this subject, and
they desire the frankest and fullest showing of the facts.

I note, however, with some amazement, that the Treasurer of
the Alabama City Mill begins his argument by conceding the
two fundamental principles for which we are contending—the
social wrong and the economic error of child labor under twelve.
He declares that from the starting of that mill he has repeatedly
protested against the use of children under this age and that
last June he wrote to his local agent that the employment of such
help "is not only wrong from a humanitarian standpoint, but it
entails an absolute loss to the mill." Now this is substantially,
and in admirable form, the whole case of our committee.

Yet what must be our added amazement when, in the next
paragraph but one, we read the further admission that, in order
to continue this economic and social wrong and in order to defeat a simple and effective remedy for this wrong, the salaried
representative of his own mill, during the preceding February,
had appeared in this city before our Legislature, in aggressive
and persistent antagonism to the protection of little children
under twelve! This, in the teeth of protests which Mr. Nichols
declares he has made since "the starting" of his mill. Who, then,
is the responsible representative of the actual policy of the
Alabama City Mill—its Treasurer or its representative before
the Legislature? Or is the policy of the mill a policy which con-
cedes the principle, only to deny the principle its fruit? If this
be the true interpretation of the conditions, what are we to say
to the explanations which are suggested; explanations offered
"in defence of our [Mr. Nichols's] officials."

Mr. Nichols assures us that the officials have been put under grave pressure from the parents. Let us concede that this is true. Yet Mr. Nichols himself is not satisfied with this "defence," and he declares wisely and bravely that his officials must take their stand against the pressure of unscrupulous and idle parents. His agents must resist the threat of such parents to leave the Alabama City Mill for mills having a lower standard of employment. Does not Mr. Nichols see that our legislation was precisely directed toward ending this pressure, toward breaking up this ignoble competition, and toward the preservation of the standard of employment which he professes? There could be no pressure to withdraw the children and to enter them in other mills, if such labor were everywhere prohibited by statute. But we are grateful to Mr. Nichols for his declaration. And yet, is he ignorant of the need of legislation in the State at large? His very argument is a confession of knowledge. If the Alabama City Mill is fairly represented by the profession of Mr. Nichols, why should the paid and delegated agent of that mill labor here for weeks to thwart a simple legislative remedy for the abuses he deplores?

Is it sufficient for your correspondent to declare that this legislation met with local opposition simply because such reforms should come "from within the State and not from outside"? This is a strange objection upon the part of one who represents investments from outside. The evils may be supported from the East, but the remedies (sic) must be indigenous! Nor is there the slightest ground for the suggestion that the initiative for our movement of reform came from "a skillful female labor agitator imported from England." We yield sincere gratitude to the American Federation of Labor for their earnest, creditable, and effective coöperation. Their interest in the situation is entirely intelligible. When the younger children are thrust into the labor market in competition with the adult, they contend that the adult wage is everywhere affected. But the agent of the Federation of Labor—earnest and devoted woman that she is—did her work, not in the spirit of interference, but in the spirit of helpfulness. She was not responsible for the beginning of the agitation. The demand for this legislative protection of our children was made by the Ministers' Union of Montgomery and by the Woman's Christian Temperance Union of Alabama, before she was ever heard of in the South.

Nothing could be more baseless than the assumption that our local effort for reforms is due to outside forces. But if it were —what of it? There is at stake here to-day the welfare of our little children, the happiness and efficiency of our future operatives, the moral standard of our economic life; and this committee frankly proposes, in every honorable way, to secure all the aid, from every quarter of our common country, which we can possibly command. The criticism of such a policy is a little out of place from the representative of a mill here operated upon investments from Massachusetts.

Mr. Nichols then informs us that the reform legislation was defeated because "the adjoining State of Georgia, having double the number of spindles, should act first." This, we have contended, is to miss the very essence of the statesmanship of the situation. The very fact that Georgia has twice as many spindles as Alabama, makes it twice as hard for Georgia to precede us. The cost of such an economic readjustment must be obviously twice as great in Georgia as in Alabama. That Alabama is not so deeply involved in the system of child labor as some other Southern States is clearly the reason why Alabama should take the lead.

It has been conservatively estimated that in some of the Southern States more than twenty per cent of the mill operatives are under fourteen years of age. Does Mr. Nichols wish Alabama to delay until that becomes the condition of the industry in this State? According to the logical demand of his argument, the State having the most spindles, the State most deeply and inextricably involved, must be the first to face the delicate and difficult problem of readjustment!

Mr. Nichols also declares that our reform measure was defeated because it was believed to be "the entering wedge" of other troublesome labor legislation. We must not protect our little children under twelve, we must not do a compassionate and reasonable thing, because, forsooth, somebody might then demand an inconsiderate and unreasonable thing! Do the corporate interests in Alabama wish to predicate their liberties upon such an argument?

Yet, says Mr. Nichols, "with these considerations in mind, the manufacturers selected, among others, our agent, a native Alabamian, to appear before the Legislative Committee, with the result that the bill was defeated." Mr. Nichols neglects to state that on the second hearing of the bill, his agent appeared alone as the chosen spokesman of all the opponents of reform. He, too, made much of this hoary scare about "the entering wedge."

What iniquities of reaction, what bitter stultification of human progress has that argument not supported! In such a case as this, it is not an argument, it is a provocation. It is a challenge to the common sense and the common humanity of our people. If the corporate interests of this State, whether operated by Northerners or Southerners, are to rest the great cause of their unrestricted development upon the cruel refusal of protection to our younger children, then let them beware lest, having rejected "the entering wedge," they invite the cyclone. What greater folly, viewed from the strictly selfish standpoint of certain corporate interests, than to involve their fate in the issues of so odious an argument?

I concur in the claim that the Alabama City Mill is in some respects wholly exceptional. Says Mr. Nichols: "I challenge either of the gentlemen from Alabama to mention among the mills of the State . . . any one which compares with ours in the expenditure which has been made for the comfortable housing of the operatives and the appliances introduced for their comfort and uplift." In one breath the friends of this mill ask us to believe it exceptional, and yet in the next breath they ask that the need for reform legislation in relation to all the mills of the State, shall be determined from the conditions it presents! If the Alabama City Mill is so unique, then it is not representative or typical. If it is not representative of the average conditions of child labor in Alabama, it has nothing to do with this argument.

As to the proportionate number of little children in our Southern and Northern mills, the facts have been accurately stated by the committee. The statement of Mr. Nichols that there are only four mills in the State "directly operated from the North" is unintelligible to me. Upon my desk, as I write, there are the figures from eleven Alabama mills which, upon the word of their own managers, are controlled by Northern capital.

It seems to have grieved Mr. Nichols that we should have characterized certain unique philanthropies in connection with one or two of our Eastern mills as "spectacular." The gentlemen of this committee have no desire to express themselves in the language of impulsive epithet. We are sincerely grateful for every motive and for every work which touches and blesses the lot of the unprivileged. But when large photographs of the exceptional philanthropies of a single bill are seriously brought before the committee of our Legislature as an argument for the perpetuation of the general conditions of child labor in this State, when the advertisements of a unique establishment are used to cloak the wretched lot of the average factory; when, upon the basis of the representations of Alabama City, men are taught to ignore the essential cruelty of the whole miserable system, and are made blind to the misery of hundreds whom that factory can never touch, then I frankly declare that such philanthropies are indeed "spectacular," for they have actually cursed more than they have ever blessed. They have become a mockery of love. They may have benefited the employees of one mill; but they have served to rivet the chains of a heart-breaking and wretched slavery upon hundreds of our little children in the State at large. And no philanthropy, however exceptional, and no institutional compassion, however effective, ever justify the refusal, at the door of the factory, of legislative protection to the little child under twelve years of age. That is the sole contention of this committee.

Is that asking too much? If Massachusetts protects at fourteen years, may not Alabama protect at twelve? Is this too drastic a demand upon the exceptional philanthropy of the mill at Alabama City? I hope not. I do not mean to write with the slightest personal unkindness, but I do write with an intense earnestness of concern in behalf of the sad and unnatural fate of the little people of our factories. We, for their sakes, do not want enemies anywhere. We want friends everywhere. It is with pleasure therefore that I recur to the instructions forwarded by Mr. Nichols to his agent. Speaking of the employment of little children, he said, "Not only is it wrong from a humanitarian standpoint, but it entails an absolute loss to the mill." There speaks the man of wisdom and the man of heart. Does Mr. Nichols mean it? Does the mill at Alabama City mean it? Will Massachusetts join hands with Alabama?

That mill, with its great influences, has led the fight in this State against the protection of our factory children. Will it continue to represent a policy of opposition and reaction? Or, will it represent a policy of coöperation and of progress? Will it send its representative, with this committee, before our next Legislature and there declare that the cotton industry of the South, as here undertaken by Massachusetts, is too important in its dignity and its value to be longer involved in the odium and the horror of an industrial system which all the world has cast off? If so, that representative may indeed find himself in the company of some of the nobler forces from "outside." The whole world has a way of taking the little child to its heart. But he will also find himself in the company—the increasingly resolute company—of thousands of the people of Alabama.

EDGAR GARDNER MURPHY.
MONTGOMERY, ALA., November 2, 1901.

EDITOR THE *Leader*:

It would be difficult to think that such misleading statements as those which appeared under the communication entitled, "Child Labor in Alabama," were intended seriously, were it not for the importance of the subject and the evident stress of feeling under which its authors labored. Such appeals do far more to hinder than to help the welfare of the children, which many manufacturers have more truly at heart than have the professional labor agitator and the well-meaning but ill-advised humanitarian.

But I have read with interest, and wish to indorse throughout, the thoughtful and dispassionate reply to this appeal in your issue of October 30 by Mr. J. Howard Nichols, treasurer of the Alabama City Mill. In the light of his statement, a statement with which I, in common with most manufacturers, agree, that the employment of child labor is not only "wrong from a humanitarian standpoint, but entails absolute loss to the mill," the fervid rhetoric of the executive committee "of the exploitation of childhood for the creation of dividends" seems just a little strained.

If, instead of giving utterance to sentimental heroics and berating those who are in no wise responsible for, but are trying to better, these conditions (which conditions are not nearly as deplorable as this over-wrought appeal would indicate), the executive committee would join the manufacturers in trying to obtain remedial legislation that would strike at the root of the trouble, and to awaken a deeper sense of parental responsibility, much would be gained towards improving the industrial system as far as it affects the employment of children in the cotton mills of the South.

At the hearing before the legislative committee at Montgomery last winter (which I am constrained to believe none of this executive committee attended or they would have a more intelligent conception of the situation to-day), the president of our mill joined with other manufacturers in urging that the Legislature pass a compulsory education law. If such a law were passed and then adequately enforced after enactment, it would be impossible for the children to work in the mills for a large part of the year, a condition which most manufacturers would welcome as gladly as the executive committee. As it is, no mill can afford, as Mr. Nichols states, to lose some of its most desirable and skilful operatives, through the parents' insisting that their children be given employment to swell the family revenues, and removing to a mill that will grant such employment, if the mill where they are located refuses to do so. At our mill the superintendent has sometimes taken this risk, and refused to allow children to work unless the parents would first agree to have them attend school for a part of the term at least. All possible pressure is brought to bear to get the children into school, but many will not go at all of their own volition, neither will their parents always require it. And without a compulsory education law we know they are better off in the mill than running wild in the streets and fields, exposed to the danger of growing up into an ignorant, idle, and vicious citizenship.

Any compulsory education law which is passed, however, should be made operative only upon the passage of similar laws by the States of Georgia, South Carolina, and North Carolina. Otherwise it would be prejudicial to the interests of Alabama as a cotton manufacturing State and make it very difficult for the mills to retain some of their best and most skilful hands. While I doubt not that the people of New England would be glad, as always, to do anything in their power for the elevation of the toiling masses, especially of the children, and for the amelioration of any adverse conditions that surround them, yet there is little in this instance that they can do, except to advise our friends in Alabama, who have interested themselves in the matter, to cultivate a calm and judicial mind, study the situation with intelligence and wise discrimination, and then act under the responsibility which they state that they feel rests upon them. Nor can they do better than to follow the lead of Massachusetts, which long ago successfully grappled with the problem, by

1st—Awakening a sense of parental responsibility, so that parents will deny themselves and make any reasonable sacrifice to win an education for their children.

2d—The enactment of a compulsory education law.

3d—Its energetic enforcement.

The statement that the actual number of children employed in mills representing Northern investments is twice as great as in the mills controlled by Southern capital is unworthy of attention. I challenge its accuracy, and deplore the partisan spirit which leads to such an unfounded accusation.

The executive committee appears to include representatives of the Church, the school, and the State. Let me call their attention to the fact that many of the families who are now happy in their work and growing into finer manhood and womanhood at the mills, came from isolated and distant homes where the Church and the school never reached them, and where the State was felt only through its unsympathetic and restraining, although necessary, laws. Through the opportunity which the mills have offered, and under their watchful and sympathetic care, many a community has been built up and surrounded with Christianizing, educational, and civilizing influences, that the Church, the school, and the State would never have been able to throw around them.

Although our mill village is provided with a church which was built at the expense of the mill in its very inception, with schools supported in part by the State, in part by the parents, and in part by the mill, whose superintendent is instructed to see that the tuition of every child desiring to attend school is paid by the mill if not otherwise provided for, with an assembly hall, a library, and a reading room, it did not occur to us that this was "spectacular philanthropy," for we neither knew nor cared whether it came to the notice of the outside world, save as it would influence other corporations to do likewise. Indeed, we do not consider it philanthropy at all, but simply rendering willing service in our turn to those who are faithfully serving us.

The neighboring factory village at Lanett, Ala., is similarly provided for at the expense and under the fostering care of the Lanett Cotton Mill, and my personal observation and knowledge lead me to believe that instead of one or two mills of a "spectacular philanthropy," the majority of the mills throughout the South, and especially those under Northern management, have, without any appeal to the galleries, quietly and gladly given their operatives and their families all desired privileges of church and school and social and literary life, that were not already offered by the town in which they were located.

Turning from the appeal of the executive committee, a picture arises before me of the peaceful, happy mill settlement at Langdale, with its pretty church filled to the doors on Sundays with an attentive, God-fearing congregation, with its large and en-

thusiastic Sunday-school, with its fine school and kindergarten
department, with its well-selected library of over 1000 volumes,
with its pleasant reading room open every week-day evening,
with its assembly hall often filled with an audience attracted by
a programme of the debating club, or the literary society, or the
entertainment committee, with its streets lighted by electricity,
and with the mill agent and his beloved wife going in and out
among the homes of the people, participating in all their joys
and sorrows; and knowing that this is typical of many another
manufacturing village in the South, especially of those under
Northern management or controlled by Northern capital, I rub
my eyes and wonder whether the animus of this appeal of the
executive committee is that of ignorance, or of mischievous
labor agitation, or of sectional hatred, which we had hoped
was long since deservedly laid away in its grave-clothes.

HORACE S. SEARS,
Treasurer of the West Point Manufacturing
Company, Langdale, Ala.

TO THE EDITOR OF THE *Monthly Leader:*

A number of the considerations presented by Mr. Horace S.
Sears I have dealt with in my reply to Mr. J. Howard Nichols.
This reply was published in the *Evening Transcript* of Boston,
and I will gladly forward a copy of it to any of your readers upon
receipt of a postal card request.

There are, however, a few additional suggestions in the letter
of Mr. Sears.

He contends that, while "the employment of little children is
not only wrong from a humanitarian standpoint, but entails
absolute loss to the mill," yet Alabama should not provide any
legislative protection for her children under twelve, until the
State can be won to the acceptance of a compulsory education
law. In other words, we are not to attempt a possible reform
until we have first secured another reform which every practical
man in Alabama knows is just now impossible.

But granting that Mr. Sears is right, and admitting that Massachusetts may fairly labor to defeat one method of reform be-

cause Alabama will not adopt another, is Mr. Sears really ready
for his remedy? Not by any means. If our Executive Committee
should adopt his advice, should abandon its own conception of
the statesmanship of the situation, and should "join the manufacturers" in first assisting upon a comprehensive scheme of
compulsory education, would the forces represented by Mr.
Sears stand by the compact? Not for a moment! He is quite
frank in his disavowal of any such intention. Says Mr. Sears, "any
compulsory education law which is passed, however, should be
operative only upon the passage of similar laws by the States of
Georgia, South Carolina, and North Carolina."

This enthusiasm for reform, only on condition that all the
rest of the world will reform too, is very familiar to the students
of economic progress. Over in Georgia and the Carolinas, some
of the mill men are claiming that they "are only waiting upon
Alabama." And there you are!

The suggestion from Mr. Sears that the members of our Committee were not present at the legislature hearings last winter is,
I think, unworthy of this discussion. If Mr. Sears was there
himself, he knows that one of the members of our Committee
was Chairman of the Legislative Committee of the lower House
which had the Child-labor Bill under consideration, that he pre-
sided at the public hearing on this bill given by the joint Committee of both Houses, and that he was personally in charge of
the compulsory education bill (which Mr. Sears claims to have
favored); that the writer of these lines appeared in behalf of
the Child-labor Bill at both hearings; that those who fought
our Child-labor law selected, as the most prominent man in
Alabama whom they could get to oppose us, the State's most
conspicuous opponent of compulsory education; and that the
representative of Massachusetts investments who so vigorously
fought the proposed legislative protection of our children, took
no part whatever in the public discussion of the bill for compulsory education.

Moreover, Mr. Sears neglects to state that the compulsory
education law, which he declares the president of his mill supported, owed its origin not to Massachusetts, nor to the mills,

but to the same devoted woman whom Mr. Nichols condemns as "a skilful female labor agitator imported from England," which description Mr. Sears approves! In other words, the very remedy which Mr. Sears suggests with such commendable unction was offered to Alabama, not by the forces of Massachusetts, nor by the mills, but by the forces which Mr. Sears has so persistently opposed and which he ventures to charge with "sentimental heroics."

At the hearings upon the compulsory education bill I was not personally present, for, realizing the utter futility of then placing our dependence upon the practical coöperation of the mill men, I knew the bill was doomed. But other members of our Committee were untiring in its support, and had the mill forces expended one-fifth of the energy in favor of this bill that they expended in opposition to our Child-labor Bill, the compulsory education measure might at least have been put upon its passage.

In the face of such facts and in the face of all the convenient conditions suggested, under which "any compulsory education law should be made operative only upon the passage of similar laws by the States of Georgia, South Carolina, and North Carolina," it is not strange that suspicion should be abroad, and that some of our reform forces should have adopted the opinion that all this strenuous talk about compulsory education is but part of an attempt to block a reform which is possible, by the safe proposal of a reform which is impossible—that the effort is simply a neat and effective element in the diplomacy of estoppel.

Is the suspicion totally unfounded? I do not doubt that, in the hearts of some, the proposal is sincere. Those who are not face to face with our local conditions, may think compulsory education a practical alternative. But that the representative of the cotton mill, the representative of the system of child labor in this State, should sincerely advocate a policy of compulsory education, is something which many of our hard-headed, sensible people cannot understand. These people are confronted, not merely by a few exceptional mills, but by the average conditions of the child-labor system. They see little children under twelve, sometimes as young as six, working eight and twelve and thirteen hours a day—sometimes sent into the mills at night; they see the burden and the wretchedness of this system; and they cannot see how a man who is identified with such conditions can be sincerely an advocate of the system of compulsory education—and for the very obvious reason that he himself, in supporting the child-labor system of Alabama, is manifestly supporting a system of compulsory ignorance.

"But," Mr. Sears may say, "it is not true that I am identified with such conditions. Our mill is a good mill." The claim cannot stand. I am not prepared to charge the darkest conditions upon the mills controlled by Massachusetts, but I do contend that when the representatives of the Massachusetts mills, upon their own published confession, unite in public opposition to legislative reform for our abuses, when they themselves continue to oppose the legislative protection of children under twelve, and when they are actually employing hundreds of such children, then they are morally responsible for the general evils which they have labored to continue. We must have the aid of the law, not primarily for the good mill, but for the bad mill, just as every community needs a law against theft, not to protect it from the honest, but from the dishonest. In urging this suggestion upon our many friends in New England, I ask them to realize that any factory here, whatever its advantages, stands intimately related to the whole industrial system of the State. There are true men and true women associated with some of these factories. But the effort of the good mill to prevent the legislative protection of children under twelve, means, in its effect, the continuation of the present conditions in the worst mills of the State. Kindness may modify the evils of child labor in one mill without legislation, yet nothing but legislation will enable us to protect the child which has fallen into the hands of the unkind.

I am personally of the opinion that there is no mill on earth good enough to be permitted to work a little child under twelve years of age, but, if there be such a mill and if that mill be controlled by brave and good men, it will make its sacrifices and will put forth its labors, not only to continue the supposed good fortune of the few, but to avert the pitiable misfortunes of the many.

New England might find analogies in our situation. Was New England solicitous for the policy of "non-interference" from outside the State, in relation to the evils of slavery? Yet Mr. Nichols and Mr. Sears do not wish anybody outside of Alabama to take an interest in the local question of child labor! More than a generation ago it was argued, for the system of slavery, that there were good plantations upon which the slaves were well treated. The statement was true, but the argument was weak. The presence of the good plantation could not offset the perils and evils of the system in itself, any more than the "good factory" can justify the system of child labor. The need for any social or economic reform may never be determined from the conditions presented by the best phases of a system, but from the essential genius of the system, and from the average conditions which it presents. The very idea of enforced labor for the child under twelve is monstrous, both from a moral and an economic standpoint. The very essence of the system, as with the system of slavery, is an error. There can be no "good" child labor. And this system is monstrous, not only in principle, but in results.

Mr. Sears is sure that we have exaggerated the evil of these results. I would respectfully ask, who are the more likely to make accurate report of the results—Mr. Sears and Mr. Nichols, living in Boston and directly interested in the system they defend, or a representative committee of seven men who are passing their lives in Alabama and who have no financial connection whatever, direct or indirect, with the system they attack? Among these men are Dr. Phillips, the Superintendent of Public Schools at Birmingham, and ex-Governor Thos. G. Jones, lately selected by President Roosevelt for the Federal bench (although a Democrat) upon the ground of his breadth of learning, his sterling integrity, and his judicial capacity and temper. It is hardly necessary for Mr. Sears to accuse such men of "sentimental heroics" or to exhort such men "to cultivate a calm and judicial mind and to study the situation with intelligence and wise discrimination."

Let us take another of the issues of fact. Mr. Sears, in urging a compulsory education law and in opposition to a child-labor law, declares in support of his mill, that "all possible pressure is brought to bear to get the children into school, but many will not go at all of their own volition, neither will their parents always require it." The impression is created even upon the mind of the editor of the *Leader* (in whose large-heartedness I have every confidence) that present conditions are possibly better than they would be under the law proposed by the Committee. This rather ignores the fact that the law proposed by the Committee had an admirable educational provision—as good a provision as we thought it possible to pass. But, is it true that these children are stubbornly opposed to education? Conditions vary. No man can speak for the children of every mill in Alabama. Yet, as Mr. Sears has told about the children in one factory, I will tell of those in another. The mill is less than twenty miles from my study. There are about seventy-five children in it. They are worked twelve hours out of twenty-four, from 6 A.M. to 6:30 P.M., allowing a half-hour for dinner. Last year they were refused a holiday, even on Thanksgiving. A night school, taught by volunteers, has been opened near them, through those whom Mr. Sears has called "well-meaning but ill-advised humanitarians." I have watched the experiment with some hesitation, because the teaching is real teaching and I am not sure that any child, after twelve hours of work, should be wearied with much of an effort at education. But fifty children out of the seventy-five are flocking into this school voluntarily, eager to learn, and disappointed when the crowded session is brought to its early end. Now, which law is the more needed by these children—a provision for compulsory education, or a provision which will strike at the system of compulsory ignorance surrounding them; which will close for them the door of the mill, and open to them the opportunities of knowledge by daylight?

Says Mr. Sears, "We know that they are better off in the mill than running wild in the streets and fields, exposed to the dangers of growing up into an ignorant, idle, and vicious citizenship." Mr. Sears seems to miss the point. He seems to forget that our legislation is directed simply toward the protection of the freedom of children under twelve. In view of this cardinal fact, I may suggest, in the words of Mr. Sears himself, that his language "seems just a little strained." What are the perils of vice "in the fields," or even in the streets of our rural South (or even in the streets of the model villages of Mr. Nichols and Mr. Sears), for the little child under twelve?

In attempting to arrive at the "animus" of the appeal of our Committee, Mr. Sears seems inclined to attribute our statement to "ignorance," or to "mischievous labor agitation," or to "sectional hatred." Sectional hatred! And which is the more likely to induce that malignant and excuseless passion—the spectacle of the attitude of the South toward the capital of Massachusetts, or the attitude of the capital of Massachusetts toward the little children of the South? The fact that these are white children, and that Massachusetts—always solicitous for the negro—should be largely indifferent to the fate of our white children, does not relieve the situation. Suppose the conditions were reversed, and that the mills of Southern men were full of negro children under twelve—how quickly and how justly New England would ring with denunciation!

The fundamental principle of our appeal is not that Alabama is guiltless, or that gentlemen like Mr. Nichols and Mr. Sears are intentionally brutal. That would be unjust to them and unjust to our own sense of right and truth. Our elementary contention is, simply, that the common conscience will hold, and should hold, the capital of Massachusetts to the moral and economic standards of Massachusetts. Both Mr. Nichols and Mr. Sears have admitted that the employment of little children is "wrong" from an economic and a humanitarian standpoint. Neither gentleman has told us, and no single representative of New England investments in Alabama has yet told us, that he is ready to join with us to right this wrong by direct and effective legislation.

But the appeal of our Committee has not been without response. We care to indulge in no recriminations for the past. We have prayed that, in our approaching struggle, New England will stand with us and not against us, for we have no intention whatever of seeing her investments here embarrassed by complex and oppressive labor legislation. Our motives cannot long be misunderstood. For such response as has come to us from the New England press, and from many of the people of New England, we are sincerely grateful. I close this letter with an expression which has just reached me. It is a telegram from Seth Low, the Mayor-elect of Greater New York, in reference to our bill now pending before the Legislature of the State of Georgia. It reflects what we believe will be the real, the ultimate, response of the North to the situation at the South. It is as follows:—

> I am heartily glad to throw whatever influence I can exert, in favor of protective legislation for the children of Georgia, strictly defining the permitted age and hours of labor in factories, on lines of similar legislation in Massachusetts and New York. Georgia ought to profit by the experience of other States. She ought not to pay for her own experience with the lives of her children. I say this as one having indirectly an interest in the Massachusetts mills in Georgia.
>
> SETH LOW.

That is statesmanship, that is religion, that is intersectional fraternity, and that is "Education."

EDGAR GARDNER MURPHY.
MONTGOMERY, ALA., December 15, A.D. 1901.

PART 2 The Cotton South in Transition

THE DREAM OF RESTORING COTTON TO ITS PRIME ECONOMIC position in the post-Civil War South faded rapidly after 1880. It did not begin to tarnish, however, until a large segment of the region's population had become ensnared in all the evils and failures of the one-crop system. And although contemporary Southerners like Henry W. Grady, Charles Otken, George K. Holmes, and Matthew Brown Hammond were explicit in their comments upon the impact of cotton on the lives of the people, the most they could do was to criticize the system of staple agriculture without saying specifically what other economic course the South could pursue.[1]

Later authors commenting on the course of southern economy revealed the intimate relationship between southern resources and the development of new industries. Contrary views were presented by promoters who had produced bales of seductive advertising materials to attract immigrants to the South. They often hinted at industry as a solution, but they were too close to

[1] C. Vann Woodward, *Origins of the New South 1887–1913*, 175–204; 235–263; Thomas D. Clark and Albert D. Kirwan, *The South Since Appomattox*, 51–107; Almon E. Parkins, *The South: Its Economic-Geographic Development*, 239–299; John Leonard Fulmer, *Agricultural Progress in the Cotton Belt Since 1920* (Chapel Hill: The University of North Carolina Press, 1950) review generally the changes which came in southern agriculture between 1880 and 1940.

the staple agricultural system to speak in more than general
terms on the subject.[2] Finally, though, the coming of the boll
weevil and the post-World War I recession magnified the economic plight of the South.[3] Later in the span of the New Deal
hundreds of reports of surveys, commentaries, and sociological
analyses were published almost as a benediction to much of
cotton culture. No publication, however, had a greater impact
on the southern mind than the report of the President's Emergency Council.[4]

Although many forces after 1910 helped turn the South away
from cotton and tobacco culture as major sources of income, no
single act hastened the economic revolution more than passage
by Congress of the Tennessee Valley Authority Act. The influence of this New Deal act was to be felt well beyond the
confines of the Tennessee Valley. Throughout the South it
hastened the adoption of new approaches to industrialization,
conservation, public education, and the general improvement
of the southern way of life.[5]

[2] This material is voluminous, but some good specific sources are M. B.
Hillyard, *The New South;* Robert Newman *et al., Southern Lands: Induce-
ments to Emigrants;* Julian Alvin Chandler, ed., *Economic History, 1865–
1910,* in *The South in the Building of the Nation,* vol. VI.

[3] Rupert B. Vance, *The Human Factors in Cotton Culture;* Thomas D.
Clark, *Pills, Petticoats, and Plows: The Southern Country Store* (India-
napolis: The Bobbs-Merrill Company, 1944); Almon E. Parkins, *The South
Its Economic-Geographic Development.*

[4] Arthur Raper, *Tenants of the Almighty;* Arthur Raper and Ira De A.
Ried, *Share Croppers All;* Howard W. Odum, *Southern Regions of the
United States;* and Rupert B. Vance, *Human Geography of the South: A
Study in Regional Resources and Human Adequacy.*

[5] David Lilienthal, *TVA-Democracy on the March;* and Joseph S.
Ransmeier, *The Tennessee Valley Authority: A Case Study in the Eco-
nomics of Multiple Purpose Stream Planning* (Nashville: The Vanderbilt
University Press, 1942).

5 The Main Crop

Though antebellum Southerners had proclaimed cotton economic king of the South and post-war Southerners hoped to sustain this boast, the depression years of the 1880s and 1890s shook their confidence. In these years Matthew Brown Hammond, a member of the distinguished South Carolina family, questioned the royalty of cotton. In a well documented study he analyzed precisely the place the crop occupied not only in the whole structure of southern agriculture, but in agrarian society and industrial economy. Fifteen years before, Henry W. Grady had published a more superficial observation that was no less biting and incisive in its general conclusions. In full context Hammond did not condemn the planting of cotton as such. He was convinced that the production of the staple was a necessity in the American economy. He did, however, ask pointedly whether or not the system of credit, labor, and an impoverished society could lead the region anywhere but to further social and economic failure. Under the prevailing practices of cotton production, the South could only expect one depression after another.

BY 1876 THE CULTURE OF COTTON HAD APPARENTLY RECOVERED from the industrial paralysis caused by the Civil War and the

Matthew Brown Hammond, *The Cotton Industry—An Essay in American History* (New York: Published for the American Economic Association by The Macmillan Company, 1897).

subsequent era of reconstruction. The crop harvested that year corresponded in amount closely to that gathered in 1860, the largest of the antebellum crops. The price of the staple had steadily declined since 1864, but at thirteen cents a pound (average New York prices), was still far from discouraging, while the causes which had operated to bring about this decline, such as the greater reliability and efficiency of labor, and the adoption of better methods of tillage, were generally favorable to the producer.

There is very little in the history of cotton growing to excite attention during the fifteen years following 1876, except the rapid growth in production. Many writers in both England and America had predicted that emancipation would result in an increase in the production of cotton in the southern states, but no one could have foreseen the extent of this increase, nor the rapidity with which it came about when order and quiet had been restored, and the South was left free to guide her own course of development.

The cotton crop harvested in 1876 is stated to have been slightly in excess of two billion pounds, grown on a little less than twelve million acres. By 1880 the amount produced was in excess of two billion, six hundred million pounds; by 1890, nearly three and one-half billion pounds were raised, and by 1895 production had swelled to four billion, seven hundred and ninety-two million pounds, and the cotton area was estimated at twenty-three million acres. Despite this rapid increase in both acreage and yield, trade conditions continued to favor the producer until 1890. There was, it is true, a continuation of the fall in prices, but the rate of decline was small when compared to the increase in production, as may be seen in the following table:

Years	Average Annual Production Million Pounds	Increase Per Cent	Average New York Prices	Decrease Per Cent
1876–80	2.612		11.77 cents	
1881–85	2.805	7.38	11.06 cents	6.51
1886–90	3.217	14.71	10.44 cents	5.93

Only once during all these years did the average price of cotton on the New York market fall below ten cents per pound for the commercial year, while in the South the improvements effected in agriculture, cheaper transportation, and the greater yield per acre served to compensate for the decline in the price of the staple, which was slowly taking place. For in spite of the enormous increase in production, the comsumption of cotton by the European and American mills was increasing at a still more rapid pace. Had it not been for the relatively important part which Indian cotton still played in European consumption, there probably would have been no decline whatever in the price of the American staple.

It is only since 1890 that the condition of the cotton grower has been rendered serious by the depreciation in the price of his product. The agricultural depression which has befallen the South as a result of these low prices has excited the attention of the whole country, and the keenest controversy has been waged over the question as to what has caused the fall in prices and the accompanying financial distress among the agricultural classes. The extent of this fall of prices and what it has cost the southern farmer, can only be appreciated when the total selling value of the cotton crop during recent years is compared with the years preceding and it is seen what a falling off there must have been in the farmer's income. In 1875–76 the cotton crop of the United States amounted to a sum total of 4,632,313 bales, and its value computed on the basis of average New York prices for middling uplands was $267,540,000. In spite of an almost steady fall in prices between 1875 and 1890, the total selling value of the crop generally showed an increase, so that the large crop of 1890–91 whose average price showed a decrease of two and one-half cents per pound under that of the preceding year, had a total selling value of $429,792,716. The decline in values since that year is shown in the table on the following page.

According to this exhibit, the planter who in 1894 raised twice as much cotton as in 1875, received a total income from his crop no larger than that received in the earlier year, and he received nearly one-third less than that received from a much smaller crop in 1890.

Year	Total Crop Bales	Average New York Prices	Total Selling Value
1890–91	8,652,597	9.03 cents	$429,792,047
1891–92	9,035,379	7.64 cents	391,424,716
1892–93	6,700,365	8.24 cents	284,279,066
1893–94	7,549,817	7.67 cents	294,593,859
1894–95	9,901,251	6.50 cents	289,809,616
1895–96	7,157,346	8.16 cents	294,095,347
1896–97	8,757,964	7.72 cents	338,057,410

In 1893 the Senate Committee on Agriculture and Forestry made a lengthy report to Congress on the condition of cotton growers in the United States. In this report it is stated that "there is a general consensus of opinion that cotton cannot, except under the most favorable circumstances, be raised profitably at less than eight cents per pound, nor without loss under seven cents." Now when we remember that from the prices quoted in the above table, which for the seven years average only 7.85 cts. per pound, must be deducted charges for transportation and commissions for selling the crop, we find that the plantation price of cotton since 1890 has seldom been high enough to allow the producer a profit and not infrequently it has caused him an actual loss. With an ever increasing acreage and with every increasing effort on the part of the farmer to extricate himself from his perilous situation, there has followed a further fall in the price of his produce and a steady decline in his annual income. No wonder, then, that the result of these discouragements has been "to produce wide-spread discontent among cotton producers and a disposition to discredit their old time conservative methods and to induce a too ready acceptance of plausible theories for relief."

Among the causes which have combined to bring about this fall of prices there are doubtless some that have been a direct benefit to the producer. Such are the improved methods of cultivation which have enabled the planter to secure a greater yield from a given acreage than heretofore. According to the statistics of acreage which we possess, and which can be considered as

only approximately accurate, the average yield per acre throughout the cotton belt for the decade 1881–90 was 168 pounds, while
in the five years 1891–95 the average was 197 pounds. It would,
of course, be incorrect to represent this as a clear gain to the
farmer. The increase has been caused by the expenditure of additional labor and capital on the land, and this expenditure,
especially for fertilizers, has been considerable. In 1879 the
average yield of cotton per acre in Alabama was 136.02 pounds
and in 1889, 158.11 pounds. The amount of fertilizers purchased
in the state during the latter year was more than double that
purchased in 1879. In Georgia where there was a similar increase in the yield per acre, the amount of commercial fertilizers
inspected for sale increased from 48,648 tons in 1874–5 to 315,-
612 tons in 1893–4. Similar though less noticeable results were
produced in South Carolina and Louisiana. But while the increased yield per acre has, therefore, not been a net gain to the
farmer, it is safe to say that it has yielded him a profit; otherwise
the purchase of fertilizers would not have continued. The price
of these fertilizers has also declined more than *pari passu* to the
decline in the price of cotton.

The producer has also gained by the decline in the cost of
other elements necessary to production. The increase in white
labor has rendered labor more efficient and therefore cheaper.
Plows, mules and horses, cotton bagging and iron ties, trace
chains, hoes, gins and presses, food and clothing have all shown
a decline in price, which has been advantageous to the cotton
raiser. "It also costs much less to handle cotton after it gets to
market; commissions for selling, storage, insurance, drayage,
etc., are all cheaper than formerly.".

Probably the greatest factor in cheapening the cost of production has been the lowering of transportation rates. The cost of
sending one hundred pounds of cotton by steamer from New
Orleans to New York was in 1873 sixty cents, in 1880 forty-five
cents, and in 1892 thirty-two cents. In 1886 it cost eighty-five
cents to send one hundred pounds of cotton by rail from Atlanta
to New York. In 1893 the price had fallen to sixty-seven cents.
While the advantage gained by the farmers through the cheaper

and improved means of production can only be estimated, it is probably fair to say that eight cent cotton is as remunerative to-day as ten cent cotton was in 1860.

There is another way in which the loss to the farmer through lower prices of cotton has been partly offset, and that is through the sale of the cotton seed, a product whose uses were scarcely known previous to the war, and which was not highly valued for many years afterward. In 1885 there were only forty cotton seed oil mills in the country. There are now three hundred of them, and still further expansion of this industry may be expected. In 1889 the cotton growers of the South disposed of 1,793,369 tons of cotton seed at an average price of $8.84 per ton, giving a total value of $15,852,525. Not all of the farmers have sold their cotton seed. Those of the Atlantic states have usually preferred to retain it for the purpose of fertilizing their land. While the power of the cotton seed oil trust to depress prices has not always allowed the producers to obtain the full value of their seed, yet the returns from its sale have contributed not a little to increase the income of those who have thus disposed of this product.

But after making all due allowance for the above circumstances that have served to reduce the loss which the cotton growers have suffered from falling prices, it must be admitted that they fail to explain away this loss or to account for the rapid decline in the price of cotton since 1890. And it is easy to exaggerate the importance of these factors and their influence on the cost of production, as seems to be the tendency of some writers.

Cotton seed may undoubtedly be made an important source of income. Yet the total price of that sold in 1889 was but little more than four per cent. of the total value of the cotton crop for that year, and this would compensate for less than one-half per cent. decline in the price of the lint. There has no doubt been a decline in freight rates, but the reduction has been less in the South than in the northern and western states, and unjust discriminations in favor of certain southern cities have worked to the disadvantage of cotton growers situated near the less important shipping points. It is impossible to measure the gain to the cotton growers secured through the lowering of the cost of production on the plantation, but it may be said that while it is true that food is cheaper, the increased acreage in cotton has caused the planter to raise less of his own supplies and to buy more from the North and West, and this has more than offset the advantage gained from a lowering of the price of provisions.

And even the most liberal allowance for a reduction in the cost of producing and marketing cotton, while it might be accepted as an explanation of the gradual decline in the price of cotton between 1876 and 1890, utterly fails to account for the sudden fall from an average of 10.44 cents between 1880 and 1890 to an average of 7.81 cents for the years 1891–95. It cannot be said that causes tending to lower the cost of producing cotton since 1890 were not operative in the decade preceding.

It has been usual to attribute the cause of low prices and the agricultural depression in the South to over-production of cotton, although there are some writers who are inclined to deny that there has been any over-production. . . . I have sought to show by a study of the conditions prevailing on the world's market for cotton that over-production has actually taken place, and that the southern farmers are themselves directly responsible for the low price of their chief product. To merely assert, however, that low prices have been caused by over-production is about as satisfactory as to assert that fluctuations in prices are caused by changes in supply and demand, without pointing out what these changes have been. Admitting that there has been over-production in recent years, we are justified in asking what has caused it and what are the conditions surrounding the southern farmer which has caused him to continue to produce for a steadily declining market.

Prominent among the causes which have led to over-production in recent years is the increase in the cotton acreage west of the Mississippi river, especially in the great state of Texas. The opening up of new lands in this region has affected the cultivators of cotton in other sections in the same way as the settlement of the Mississippi bottom lands and the extension of cotton culture in the 'thirties and 'forties affected the planters in the Atlantic states, causing them to suffer from the phenomenally low prices which reigned between 1840 and 1850.

In 1859 and again in 1869, Texas stood sixth in rank among the cotton growing states, producing in the former year about one-twelfth and in the latter year about one-ninth of the total crop for the year. In 1879 Texas had moved up to third place among the cotton states, but even then produced but little more than one-seventh of the cotton grown in the country. A decade later she had passed her former rivals, Georgia and Mississippi, in both acreage and production, and in 1894–5 had over one-quarter the total cotton acreage and produced nearly one-third the cotton grown in the country. Looked at merely from the standpoint of the western increase, it might with truth be said that the planters in the older states could not be charged with over-production of cotton, but that the responsibility for this must be shouldered by the Texas cotton growers. From the following table it appears that there has been but little increase in the quantity of cotton produced outside of Texas since 1890, certainly not more than would have been demanded by the increasing consumption of the American and European mills.

Year	Total U.S. Crop Thousands of Bales	Texas Crop Thousands of Bales	Annual Rate of Increase or Decrease Per cent	U.S. Crop outside of Texas Thousands of Bales	Annual Rate of Increase or Decrease Per cent	Annual Rate of Increase in World's Consumption	Average New York Prices. Cents	Annual Rate of Increase or Decrease Per cent
1889–90	7,297	1,770		5,527			11.53	
1890–91	8,674	2,000	13.0	6,674	20.7	6.06	9.03	−21.6
1891–92	9,018	2,400	20.0	6,618	− 0.8	−0.04	7.64	−15.3
1892–93	6,664	2,235	− 6.9	4,429	−35.0	−3.27	9.24	7.8
1893–94	7,552	1,925	−13.8	5,607	28.8	3.03	7.67	− 6.9
1894–95	9,837	3,219	72.4	6,618	18.0	7.58	6.50	−15.2
1895–96	7,157	1,990	−38.1	5,167	−21.9	−0.24	8.16	24.1
Average	8,028	2,220	7.	5,806	1.6	2.18	8.39	− 4.5

The rapid increase of cotton growing in Texas is largely due to the natural advantages which this state possesses. The new and fertile lands enable the producer to raise as much or more cotton per acre without the use of fertilizers, and with less labor than can his competitor in the eastern states, who in order to produce a good crop is compelled to adopt intensive methods of farming. "Fertilizers are not used in Texas, except barn-yard, and not much of that," writes a correspondent to the Senate Committee on Agriculture; and he goes on to say that, "four-fifths of the black land of Texas is capable of producing one bale per acre with favorable seasons, which come once in about every three years. The timbered sandy land about averages, one year with another, a bale to three acres." Outside of the river bottom lands very little of the cultivated area east of the Mississippi will produce one-third of a bale to the acre, without the use of fertilizers.

But Texas' superiority in cotton raising is not due entirely to her soil and climate. Her people are, without question, more thrifty, more hopeful and more progressive than the residents of the older states. In 1860 Texas was still a new state, just beginning to feel the touch of slavery. The war bore on her people less heavily than on those east of the Mississippi, and she had less to lose by emancipation. The negroes were always in a minority in this state, and their proportion has been steadily decreasing since the war. The number of blacks engaged in the cultivation of cotton is comparatively small, and it seems probable that this number is decreasing, although no definite statement can be made to that effect. Texas has been to some extent an exception to the rule that the cotton states have failed to attract any considerable number of the foreign born population of the country. Although the increase in foreign born has not quite kept pace with the increase of native born, Texas has received a considerable addition to her population from this source in the last thirty years. She has also gained large numbers of immigrants from the northern states. The quality of her labor has as a consequence steadily improved in most parts of the state, and probably this, as much as cheaper and more fertile lands, has given Texas her present advantage over other cotton states. Her more intelligent and efficient labor has enabled the cotton growers to take advantage of any improvements in implements or methods that have been made.

From the estimates furnished the Senate Committee on Agriculture, it would seem that cotton can be produced in Texas at from 1½ to 2 cents a pound cheaper than it can be raised in the eastern states. The cotton growers of Texas have not become victims of the crop lien system to the extent that their competitors in other states have, and it is worthy of note that whatever reduction in the acreage and production of cotton has taken place in recent years as a result of low prices, has for the most part been effected in Texas. The reports of correspondents of the Senate Committee on Agriculture show that with few exceptions the cotton growers of Texas are in much more favorable circumstances than are those elsewhere, and in the case of these exceptions, the bad conditions are usually attributed to the failure of the farmers to raise their own supplies and to diversify their farming. A correspondent from Van Zandt county writes as follows: "Twenty years ago cotton raising in this county was an exception to the rule, and then our people were universally prosperous; ten years ago cotton raising became general, and the system of crop mortgages among farmers came with it, and now the mortgage system is nearly as general among farmers as cotton raising. Now cotton raising and crop mortgaging are practically synonymous terms."

But if it can be shown that the increase in the cotton area and production in recent years has come almost entirely from the region beyond the Mississippi, it does not follow that the cotton growers of the older states are not responsible for overproduction and low prices. Prudence and their own experience should have taught them that they could not compete with the western farmers in the production of this staple. The farmers of the New England and Middle states have felt the effects of a similar competition on the part of the wheat growers of the Northwest, but they have adjusted themselves to the changed conditions. "The farmers of New York have greatly decreased the relative production of wheat and other staples adversely affected by changing railway rates, and have increased that of hay and potatoes, but little modified in that way. It is otherwise in most of the Gulf states of the South. They still rely upon the old staples which like wheat have been lowered in value at the seaboard by changed cost of transportation, and such staples as cotton, that by greatly increased production have over-stocked the market and thus fallen in price. The farmers in such states suffer the full effect of the losses by modern economic changes affecting the price of agricultural staples." Instead of maintaining and seeking to increase his cotton acreage, the farmer east of the Mississippi should have reduced his acreage in cotton as rapidly as possible, increasing that of other crops, and raising cotton, if at all, as a surplus crop. The farmer can scarcely plead ignorance as an excuse for not having done so. For sixty years or more, southern agricultural writers and speakers have besought him to raise his own food supplies, and the practice of his more prosperous neighbors has furnished him with an example of the practicability and wisdom of so doing. As early as 1875 the commissioner of agriculture of Georgia showed that allowing for only a very moderate yield of corn and cow peas, the raising of these two staples would have yielded the farmer a net profit of $8.32 per acre, while cotton, then selling at 15 cts. per pound on the New York market, gave a net profit of only $4.52 an acre. In reading over the reports of the correspondents of the Senate Committee on Agriculture, one cannot but be struck with the practical unanimity with which these practical men whatever be their own theories as to the cause of low prices have asserted that those farmers who raise their own supplies have prospered, while their neighbors who raised cotton exclusively are in desperate circumstances. An Alabama planter sums up the general verdict when he says: "As a rule cotton raisers are prosperous in proportion as they grow their supplies on the farm."

In justice to the cotton growers it should be said, however, that the majority of them have in recent years, been unable to exercise their own discretion as to what staples they should cultivate. The crop lien system has taken away their industrial freedom and made them dependent on the merchants for the food and provisions which they might otherwise have raised at home. "Cotton raising has grown to be a necessity more than a choice. As a general rule, supplies cannot be obtained from the merchants on any other crop than cotton; consequently they are forced to raise it to get credit." It is the system of agricultural credit, therefore, to which in the last analysis must be referred the cause of over-production of cotton and under-production of food crops.

Uneconomical methods of production and bad farm management are not the least among the causes which have contributed to the financial depression among cotton growers, and they have been an indirect cause if not a direct one of the excessive planting of this staple. Cotton is the "lazy man's crop" in the South, although it is an expensive one to produce. In no one way has lack of economy contributed more to its over-production than in the purchase of commercial fertilizers. There can be no question of the benefits which the South has derived from the finding of rich deposits of phosphates and marl in various portions of her territory, which have been utilized only since the Civil War. In many localities the use of fertilizers is indispensable to the profitable production of cotton. A South Carolina farmer writes: "Most of our land without the aid of fertilizer would produce about one-fourth of a bale the first year, and in the course of a few years would not produce over one-eighth or one-tenth of a bale per acre. Without fertilizer we would have to quit planting cotton." But the expense incurred for commercial fertilizers is a heavy one, usually ranging from 12 to 33 per cent. of the total value of the crop, depending on the amount applied as well as on the price of cotton, and this expense could usually be partly if not entirely saved by preserving and using barn-yard manures or home made composts. The commercial fertilizers are almost without exception bought on credit and seldom used on any other than the cotton lands. They are usually placed in the center of the ridge where they feed the cotton, but do little to bring up the fertility of the soil.

There is a noticeable lack of economy in many other respects on the majority of southern plantations, although southern planters are not the only ones who are guilty of this charge. Many of the cotton growers have no gardens and still many more keep no live stock except their work animals. Better implements have come into almost general use within the last twenty years, but these are often left unhoused when not in use and in a few years are "worn out." "There is a neglect and want of thrift which are a burden in themselves. The farmer is not willing to lend a hand to delay the dilapidation of his buildings. The plow is left at the end of the last furrow until the next year; a few nails or screws would save dollars of loss or of eventual credit with the merchants in scores of places." There is far more truth than is generally appreciated at the South in the sentiment of an Alabama planter who writes: "I am unable to say that this depression or distress is produced by causes coming from the action or non-action of Congress or of our state legislatures. The trouble arises from bad management and want of proper economy at home."

In discussing the causes which have produced the agricultural depression in the cotton states, too much emphasis cannot be laid upon the inefficiency and unreliability of agricultural labor. A Texas correspondent of the Senate Committee writes that, "of all causes mentioned as contributing to the financial depression of the cotton raiser, the want of reliable labor is perhaps the most important and the most difficult to remedy." The difficulties which arise from this source are more noticeable in those parts of the South where cotton cultivation is in a large measure dependent on negro labor. It is commonly supposed that the cultivation of this staple is mainly carried on by colored labor, as was the case in slavery days. . . . we have shown that the tendency during reconstruction days was toward an increase of white labor in the cultivation of this plant. By 1876 thirty-nine per cent. of the laborers in the cotton fields were whites. While statistics are not available for showing the rate of increase there is no doubt but that the proportion of whites engaged in the cultivation of this staple has steadily increased since 1876. Mr. Tillett estimates that white labor produced in 1883 forty-four per cent. of the cotton crop; in 1884, forty-eight per cent., and in 1885, over fifty per cent. Reckoning on a gain of two and one-half per cent. annually, Otken came to the conclusion that "the cotton produced by white labor in 1893 is about seventy per cent. of the entire crop." But, without relying too much on these individual estimates, the fact that in Texas the cotton crop has more than doubled in the last two decades, while the increase in white population for the same period has been more than twice that of the blacks, is an indication if not a certain proof of the increase of white labor in cotton cultivation.

It is perhaps hardly correct to say, as have some writers, that the decline in the proportion of the cotton crop raised by the negroes is partly to be explained by a desertion of cotton culture by this race in order to engage in other pursuits. It is true that in certain sections of the South, as in the sea island cotton country of lower Georgia, the thrifty white labor has pushed the blacks off the plantations into the turpentine forests, or to engage in railroad building; and it is also true that in the outskirts of most of the southern cities and towns there has been a congregation of negroes who by means of "odd jobs" in the towns have been able to maintain a hand to mouth existence. But it cannot be said that as a class the negroes are leaving the farms in large numbers to engage in other industrial pursuits, or that they have shown that marked preference for urban life that has characterized both the foreign born and native white population of the United States during recent years.

Mr. Van de Graaff's excellent detailed study of the geographical distribution of the black race in 1890 has failed to show any radical change from the conditions prevailing in 1860, when, with few exceptions, the large negro populations were to be found in the chief cotton producing counties of the South. The negroes still remain agricultural laborers in the cotton belt and the tendency for the country people to drift into the cities has probably affected the blacks less than any other class of the population.

But it is equally true that the negro has not deserted cotton culture in order to grow other crops. His preference for cotton is as great as it was in slavery days or during the early years of freedom. In fact, the tendency which existed previous to the war for the blacks to congregate on the rich cotton lands of the river bottoms and to leave the hill country to the whites, has continued since the negro has been free to control his own movements. In the so-called "delta region," bordering on the Mississippi, Yazoo and Red rivers, the blacks comprised in 1890, 68.71 per cent. of the entire population; their rate of increase during the preceding decade being 20.59 percent., as compared to a white increase of 14.58 per cent. The comparatively small white population in this region is largely due to the malarious character of these alluvial lands. The negroes stand the climate better, and as a result the large planters in this region give them the preference as agricultural laborers.

We may look at the question as to the efficiency of the negro labor for cotton culture from two standpoints. Is his labor as valuable as that of the white man under the same circumstances? Is his labor improving? The facts already mentioned seem to furnish a negative answer to both questions. Not only has there been an increase in the proportion of whites engaged in the cultivation of cotton, but a corresponding increase in the production of this staple has taken place in precisely those regions where the increase of white labor is most noticeable. Mr. Hoffman has pointed out the fact that in Mississippi, where the proportion of blacks to the white population has almost steadily increased since 1860, the production of cotton has actually shown a falling off, while in Texas, where the proportion of colored to the white population has decreased fifteen per cent. since 1860, the production of cotton is seven times as great as in the earlier year. The white farmers who cultivate the sea-island cotton in Georgia raise three or four times as much per acre as do the blacks who raise the same variety a little farther to the south in Florida. These indications of the inferiority of the negro labor in cotton culture are confirmed by the statements of southern planters from almost every portion of the cotton belt. The fact is further proven by the wages paid to colored labor, when these are compared with the wages received by white men employed in the same pursuits.

The only exception to this general preference for white labor comes from the "delta region." Here the negro is generally preferred to the white man for cotton cultivation. The preference, however, is not due to the greater efficiency of the black man, for here as elsewhere wages of white labor are higher. But the malaria in this region affects the negroes less than it does the whites, and negro labor is accordingly more steady and reliable. Negro labor is also much cheaper, for the negro's lower standard of living allows him to dispense with many things which seem indispensable to the white man. The latter demands a good house, stoves, and a diversified diet, while the negro seems content with a log cabin and a fire place, and with corn, bacon and molasses as articles of food. The superiority which this region possesses for cotton raising and the advantages which it has for negro labor, make it certain that a considerable portion of the cotton crop will for years to come be cultivated by negro labor.

It is generally conceded at the South that not only are the negroes less efficient laborers than they were under slavery, but that the best workers among the blacks are ex-slaves, men and women now perhaps sixty or seventy years of age, who under slavery had been trained in the methods of cultivating cotton and have not under freedom entirely lost their skill in this direction nor become victims of idleness. "It takes on an average to-day two negroes of the old class to do as much as one did formerly, three of the class of young men to do the work that one did in a former period, and five women of this latter class to do the work of one in past time. There are worthy exceptions in these groups, but they are few. The equation resulting from the character of this labor may be thus expressed: the work of three negroes in 1860 equals the work of ten negroes in 1890."

The freedmen and their descendants are generally lacking in energy and ambition. They possess none of the qualities which are found in all progressive workers. Their labor succeeds only when it is subject to constant supervision. On the big Mississippi plantations an authority little short of compulsion is often exercised by the managers, and in such cases the negroes are fairly successful laborers. But poorer farming can scarcely be found than on those numerous plantations in the South where the absentee proprietor has rented out his land to the negro "cropper" and has left the latter free to conduct the farming in his own way. There are to be found in every southern community negro farmers who are prosperous, respected citizens, and whose agriculture is fully on a par with that of their white neighbors. They prove the possibility of the negro attaining economic independence and prosperity where he is industrious and saving. But these men are only the notable exceptions to the general rule of negro idleness and shiftlessness. The majority of the freedmen will not work unless compelled to by dire necessity; they spend all their surplus earnings for useless luxuries as soon as they are paid, and they are hopelessly content with a bare subsistence.

The negro's preference for cotton, and his apparent inability to raise other crops, have contributed not a little to over-production of the white staple. "It is, indeed, a commonplace in the South that the negro can only grow cotton—that he cannot grow corn. Corn will not bear neglect; to fail to plough at the proper time means loss of the crop. Though cotton must be worked much more, it bears the delays incident to negro methods much better." In spite of falling prices, therefore, the negro continues the cultivation of this staple. The "cropping system" facilitates this and the "credit system" often compels it, but neither the "cropping system" nor the "credit system" would have proved such serious obstacles to the reduction of the cotton acreage had it not been for the natural preference for cotton felt by so large a proportion of those engaged in its cultivation.

In the cultivation of cotton the negro women seem to participate in a much less degree than they did in slavery days. They still form an important addition to the labor force in picking time. But their evident desire to live as do the white women has generally caused them to shun out-door employments, and

the quality of their work has deteriorated even more than that
of the men.

Closely connected with this question of negro labor is the
problem of land tenure in the cotton states. During the period
of industrial reconstruction we saw that the failure of the planters to secure steady labor from the freedmen, under the wage
system, led to the abandonment of this method of farming, and
to the adoption throughout the greater part of the cotton belt
of the "share" or "cropping" system—a plan aptly described by
Mr. J. R. Dodge as "a partnership in which labor wrought without hire and capital was advanced without security." This mode
of tilling the cotton lands still continues at the South, and while
the following table compiled from the returns of the Tenth and
Eleventh Censuses shows a slight decrease in the percentage of
farms cultivated on the share system in some of the states, in
the leading cotton states, especially those where negro labor
is largely employed, it is seen that the "cropping" system has
more than held its own.

TENURE OF FARMS IN THE COTTON STATES

States	Percentage Cultivated by Owner		Percentage Rented for Fixed Money Rental		Percentage Rented for Share of Products	
	1880	1890	1880	1890	1880	1890
North Carolina	66.55	65.86	5.48	5.93	27.97	28.21
South Carolina	49.69	44.72	23.41	27.75	26.90	27.53
Georgia	55.15	46.46	13.39	17.19	31.46	36.35
Florida	69.11	76.37	15.14	11.50	15.75	12.13
Alabama	53.15	51.43	16.85	24.68	30.00	23.89
Mississippi	56.22	47.16	17.14	21.04	26.64	31.80
Louisiana	64.78	55.62	13.81	16.95	21.41	27.43
Arkansas	69.09	67.89	10.50	13.21	20.41	18.90
Texas	62.41	58.13	6.94	8.80	30.65	33.07
Tennessee	65.47	69.16	11.63	11.33	22.90	19.51

More noticeable than the increase in the number of farms
cultivated on shares, is the decrease in the percentage of those

cultivated by owners, which appears in all the leading cotton states. This decrease is not an absolute one, however, for in all the cotton states the decrease which has taken place in the average size of landed properties has been accompanied by an increase in the number of those cultivated by owners, as well as in the number of those farmed by tenants. It is not easy to explain the greater increase in the number of rented farms, especially when one considers the low selling value of southern farming lands and their relatively high rental value. The negroes do not seem to have acquired land in recent years to any appreciable extent, while the facilities for renting land have increased the number of negro "croppers." Perhaps it is not to be regretted that the majority of the negroes, in their present state of efficiency, have not acquired ownership of land; for, as Mr. Hoffman says, "As a rule their 'farms' are such in name only, and the cultivation of the soil and the condition of the grounds, are of the lowest order. The value of the negro as an agricultural laborer becomes impaired. The small produce of his farm, together with the earnings of his wife and children in peanut or strawberry season, enable him to live in comparative comfort, adding little or nothing to the aggregate wealth of the community." But if the choice lays between negro ownership and negro tenancy, the advantages of the former to society far outweigh those of the latter. The negro's cultivation of the land as a tenant is even worse than as an owner. His dependence on the merchant is much greater, and there is the additional dependence on the land owner. Land owning has stimulated the ambition of some negroes and has caused them to carry out agricultural improvements. And while the majority of negro cultivators are not yet in a condition to make the best use of the land if ownership in farming property were suddenly conferred upon them, it may be said that the fact that a freedman has accumulated enough capital to buy a farm, is evidence that he will be able to manage it with considerable prudence and economy.

As regards the "share system" or "tenant system" (for some writers draw a distinction between the two), there is a unanimity of opinion among writers on the subject as to its present unfitness and its deleterious effects upon both the worker and the soil. The tenant is interested only in the crop that he is raising, and makes no effort to keep up the fertility of the land, by means of careful cultivation, judicious fertilizing and the rotation of crops. Cotton is always the preferred crop to the land owner, because he is able to secure larger rents than he could in cash, and because there is less danger of a complete failure of the cotton crop than would be the case if other crops were planted; while the cotton has the additional advantage of always finding an open market and a ready sale. The tenant also prefers cotton, partly because it bears neglect better and gives him more time for fishing and camp-meetings, and partly because he is able to live on the crop in advance of its harvesting, owing to the credit which it gives him at the store.

The whole tendency of the share system, therefore, is to encourage wasteful methods of cultivation, diminish the fertility of the soil, increase the number of crop liens, cause over-production of cotton, foster the natural inclination of the negroes to remain idle, and it is, doubtless, largely responsible for that curious phenomenom of southern agriculture—the fact that the rental value of the land is often equal to from one-half to the total selling value. "The tenant system of farming has proven more wasteful and destructive than slavery ever was anywhere. The productiveness of the lands has been lowered, buildings have undergone great deterioration, live stock has decreased in quantity and is of inferior quality; orchards and gardens have disappeared. Poverty and even destitution may be found where of old there was good living for all. The negroes accumulated nothing; they are still living on the credit of the crop yet to be grown. In good times they have gotten but a subsistence; under the stress of hard times very many have been brought literally to the ragged edge of starvation."

There is no question as to the desirability of a change. The present system is entirely too bad to continue for any length of time. The only question is as to the direction of the change and the means of bringing it about.

6 The Peons of the South

George K. Holmes's essay, written in 1893, has been accepted as a standard summary of the failures of the southern staple crop agricultural system. Although the author had no opportunity to examine the account books of farmers and merchants to document the charges he made against them, he nevertheless was able to get a good overall view of the system from his position in the Department of Agriculture in Washington. Not all of Holmes's charges against the staple crop system were aimed at the evils of the crops themselves, nor at the Negroes who helped produce them. White farmers showed a lack of pride in their farm premises, and a lack of thrift in the management of their lands. There was little use to waste time talking to farmers about living off the land when such a large percentage of them did not have even a garden to grow vegetables for the family table.

The greatest tragedy in Holmes's eyes was the fact that southern farmers had followed their wasteful and primitive practices of cultivation so long that they appeared to be past the point of rehabilitation. Moreover, those then on the land could not be expected to adopt new and scientific methods of farming on soil which was exhausted, or when they were in a condition of bankruptcy at the store. The crop lien was as devastating in its effects as the crude modes of cultivation.

THAT COTTON RAISING ON SMALL HOLDINGS, AS NOW CARRIED ON IN the South, has economic disadvantage against which the farmer finds it difficult to struggle, may be true; but the situation of the farmer can not be understood nor the direction of its improvement indicated until the non-essential conditions under which he lives are taken into account, especially the sort of peonage under which he is held by the merchant.

Before the Civil War the agricultural land of the South was owned and cultivated in large areas by white planters who were wealthy and independent. Their purchases and sales were made through agents and brokers whose accounts showed balances in favor of the planters sufficient to meet all purchases made in their behalf and all drafts made by them for cash. When a planter wanted sugar, coffee, clothing for slaves and other supplies that could not be produced on the plantation, they were bought by the agent and their cost charged against the balance in his hands remaining from sales of cotton or other products. It rested with the planter to decide how much cotton he would raise, and, if he had preferred to abandon cotton for other products, no one was in a situation to prevent him from doing so. He made bacon and raised corn, but not so much as he should have done, and, as far as he could economically and conveniently do so, he produced other supplies. His plantation was an independent little principality, on which the small economies were attended to, and these were of considerable importance. The slaves kept the various implements in repair, did the work of blacksmiths and carpenters, pruned and grafted in the orchards, and guarded the poultry from hawks and foxes; their labor, in numerous directions, was superintended intelligently and effectively and with a view to prevent waste, losses and idleness.

A devastating and exhausting war, in which nearly all of the able-minded white men of the South were engaged on one side, made an immediate and radical change in the agricultural

George K. Holmes, "The Peons of the South," *Annals of the American Academy of Political and Social Science*, 4 (September 1893), 265–274.

system of that region. The planters, their sons, the "poor whites," and their comrades of other descriptions, returned from the camp, in poverty, worn out, dispirited, hopeless of the future and dazed with the collapse of their dream. Their old home surroundings were gone and they must create such new ones as were permitted by expediency and the limited means at command. Their first concern was food and the strict necessaries of life, which they must produce or borrow from those who had not lost all of their wealth and credit. Large plantations could not be cultivated as of yore for want of equipment, and a subdivision into tenancies was the only course. The ex-slaves were still there, unprovided, as many of their former masters were, with food sufficient to last until the harvesting of the next year's crops. Freed from their bondage to the soil, many of the freedmen drifted to the towns, which they had not been allowed to frequent before.

So it happened that tenant farming largely replaced the old system. Farmers who owned the farms that they cultivated and landlords alike had to obtain from merchants the supplies of food, clothing and farm equipment that were needed, and these on credit, giving in return pledges of the crop to come, out of which the debts must be paid. The tenants, even less prepared to choose, adopted the same system and lived on their interest in the future crop.

The merchants then took the helm. Such crops as they could most readily market must be produced under their orders, regardless of the fact that they might not be the ones most advantageous to their debtors. The kind of crop that best accorded with this requirement in the cotton regions was cotton, and it was demanded in quantities proportionate to the indebtedness that was allowed to accumulate. The sale of the cotton, too, was taken charge of by the merchants, and as the system in this respect was much like that which prevailed before the war, its necessity was readily accepted by the farm owners; but now the balance of the account was with the merchant and agent. His cry for cotton and more cotton, to keep pace with the indebtedness, has led to so enormous an increase in the production of this fibre since the war that the North,

ignorant of the real situation, has pointed to it as an evidence of
the superiority of the free, over the slave, labor of the blacks.
But the situation is not misunderstood in the South. The merchants, who advance plantation supplies, have replaced the
former masters and have made peons of them and of their
former slaves.

Every crop of cotton is mostly consumed before it is harvested, and after the harvest the farm owner or tenant has to
place a lien on the next year's crop, often before the seed goes
into the ground. These liens bear high rates of interest, regardless of usury laws, because the supplies are advanced at excessive prices. The road to wealth in the South, outside of the cities
and apart from manufactures, is "merchandising." It is the general opinion in many counties where inquiries have been made,
that the interest and profit on crop liens amount to not less than
25 per cent yearly of the capital advanced, that the common
proportion is from 40 to 80 per cent and that even 200 per cent
is exacted in some places. Doubtless an unusual degree of risk
may warrant a charge therefor in the rate of interest; but the
rates much more than cover this and effectually transfer the
farmers' profit to the pocket of the merchant. Hence the farmer
finds himself in that oft-mentioned situation between the upper
and the nether millstone. He has lost his independence, and the
cotton raising that is forced upon him by his creditor, supple-
mented by his own unwillingness to raise anything in addition
to cotton, makes it impossible for him to regain his independence.

This being the state of affairs the agricultural land of the cotton States has little sale. Merchants will not accept it as security
for debt unless they are compelled to do so when crop, mules,
cattle and other personal property are insufficient. This is one
reason why mortgages on Southern farm land are so few. Only
3.38 per cent of the farms of Georgia, cultivated by owners,
were mortgaged in 1890, and only 8 per cent in South Carolina,
while in Iowa the proportion was 53.29 per cent; in Maine, 22.09
per cent; in Maryland, 30.01 per cent; in Massachusetts, 30.46
per cent; in Montana, 15.58 per cent; in Wisconsin, 42.85 per
cent; and in New Jersey, 48.91 per cent. Georgia's and South

Carolina's small percentages tell a story of unfortunate conditions to those who are familiar with the reasons for their smallness.

The farm tenant does not rise to ownership in the South, because, as his affairs are managed, he can not acquire ownership. Generally speaking, it is probable that he owes more than he owns, and what he owns is of little value—hardly worth taxing. In this region, where he can build his own dwelling of logs and where land can be bought for a very few dollars an acre, about half of the farms are hired and the proportion is increasing. Such an effect indicates the badness of the case more than pages of description could do. In Georgia 58.10 per cent of the farms were hired in 1890, an increase of 13.25 in the percentage since 1880; in South Carolina the percentage has increased from 50.31 to 61.49. The system of peonage, at least to a great extent, is immediately responsible for this, but it may be that there is escape from it for tenants who are exceptionally industrious and saving. It is more easy for the cultivating farm owners and for the landlords.

The white farmers of the cotton States are "in a rut," in which they are kept by the persistence of the habits and customs which developed out of the necessities that followed the war. They have no good excuse for buying their bacon and some of their corn year after year, as they are doing. They can produce and make much that they now purchase and can exercise a better supervision over their tenants. They can restore many of the small economies that were practiced before the war. Indeed, it is to the system that then prevailed that they must and can return in a large degree, as far as consistent with the thirteenth amendment to the Constitution. Some of them have done so and their old-time independence has been restored.

One of the best known cotton planters of Georgia returned from the war a young man with no possessions but the clothing on his body. He bought land entirely on credit, received advancements of supplies from a merchant, also entirely on credit, and prepared to raise a crop of cotton. In the meantime, being a man of exceptional force of character, he was faithful as far as possible, to the system that prevailed on his father's plantation before the war, and he at once began to produce on his own plantation the supplies needed thereon. His supervision was excellent and it prevented waste, enforced economy and secured repairs. It may everywhere be observed that the more thriving farmers are those who are constantly guarding against outgoes that are charges against their crops. They live mostly on the direct and indirect products of their farm, they produce fertilizers instead of buying them, they do rough carpenter's work, repair their implements and other articles of equipment, and so maintain a high degree of independence except in relation to the purchasers of their crops. This was the policy pursued by the Georgia planter referred to above, with the result that in two or three years he was able to begin to reduce the mortgage on his farm and eventually to pay it in full.

The prices of cotton in later years have made such an achievement of slower accomplishment, but not impossible. It is only by following such a course that the cotton planter and landlord can emancipate themselves from their peonage to the merchant. Once let him reach a position where they can defy him and resist his demand for cotton, they can check its over-production, diversify their agriculture, pay more attention to the rearing of domestic animals and to the raising of fruits and vegetables, at the same time aiming to master a specialty. It is most unwise for a farmer to put all his eggs into one basket. With one product he may thrive for a time, but, in the long run, under present competition, he should have many reliances, one of which may be a specialty, if it is wisely selected.

Doubtless the Southern planters can not escape from their enthrallment to cotton without much effort, but there are assurances that, where this effort has been made, it promises success, if it has not already won success. It would seem as if no great effort were required from a cotton farmer to make it unnecessary for him to buy cabbages at fifteen cents apiece, Irish potatoes at $1.50 a bushel, and hay at $20 a ton, which he was not long ago seen to do in Arkansas, although he had land that would produce cabbages and two crops of clover and potatoes in a year. Nor need he pay $10 for a barrel of flour that cost the merchant $3, and $1 a bushel for corn that cost forty cents, as he was doing in a certain Georgia town last summer, although he could raise both wheat and corn.

On the Southern farm there is a neglect and a want of thrift which are a burden in themselves. The farmer is not ready to lift a hand to delay the dilapidation of his buildings. The plow is left at the end of the last furrow until the next year; a few nails or screws would save dollars of loss or of eventual credit with the merchant, in scores of places. What shall be said of farmers who have no gardens? And yet gardens are rarely seen on Southern farms, although the South is peculiarly the clime for them. Such has been the subjection of the cotton planter to his unthrifty habits and to the system, of which the merchant is king, that not until very recent years did the product of corn in the cotton States exceed that of 1850.

But the black tenant has more to overcome. He too is living on the next crop, but he operates on so small a scale on his one-mule or two-mule holding that his net product of wealth gives him no more than a poor subsistence. The tenant system, as now managed, is economically inferior to the previous slave system, and, while he did not get a due share of the products of his labor as a slave, he gets even less now, because he receives a share of the incidence of the comparative economic loss. As a slave he was better fed and better housed than he now is, he had the best medical attendance in the county, and, if he was disposed to neglect his master's interests, which would have been his own as well, had he been free, he was restrained. Now he is almost as helpless as a child, and is still as thoughtless of the morrow. The merchant who has a lien on his share of the crop pays his taxes, buries his wife or child, buys him a mule if he needs one, and feeds and clothes him and his family to the extent that his improvidence and laziness are allowed credit. The high prices that the tenant pays for supplies are partly due to his untrustworthiness; not infrequently he is missing, after his living has been advanced to him until it is time to pick cotton, or he carries off cotton in the night without accounting for it to the merchant.

The first step in the tenants' elevation now consists in their producing their own food and, as far as possible, other supplies, which are now mostly a charge against their share of the crop. They may then have a margin for saving, if they are economical, and it is only with this that they can elevate themselves to farm ownership and give themselves the independence that was their vision at their emancipation. That any considerable number of them will ever do this is not believed in the South.

The blacks prefer a tenancy to selling their labor for wages, and in some regions, at least, the white owners who cultivate their farms find that only the inferior laborers can be hired, because the superior ones prefer tenancies. As the planters become independent of merchants, they are unfriendly to these tenancies, but, in some instances, have to grant very small ones, in order to hold the services of the blacks, who, under such circumstances work for wages during a part of the year on the plantation cultivated by their landlord. If white landlords arrive at independence from debt before the black tenants do, as it may be assumed that they will, if either class is to improve, it seems likely that the blacks will see a service for wages encroaching upon the tenant system.

Some of the more hopeful and thriving of the cotton planters believe that progress will be made by the plantation owners out of the present bad state of affairs in the direction which, in a general way, has been indicated; but a contrary opinion is held by some observers who are familiar with the data of the problem. The plantation owners, most of whom are landlords, often live in towns, having abandoned their plantations to irresponsible tenants who care to work only indifferently and for a bare subsistence of the poorest sort. A tenant whose crop by chance more than suffices to meet his obligations, will pick enough cotton to discharge his debts to the landlord and the merchant and abandon the remainder, knowing that he can live on the next crop until it is harvested. There is complaint that the blacks and the poor whites can not be controlled to secure efficient service and economical production. At any rate, the owners make little effort to control them and leave the merchants to drive them away from their stores and the towns, where they are loafing, when they should be working, by threats of cutting off their supplies.

When plantation owners are asked why they do not make bacon, the frequent answer is that it is discouraging to struggle against hog cholera and that it is cheaper to buy bacon. Energetic efforts to suppress the disease are wanting and there seems to be a nursing of the spirit of helplessness. The objection is also advanced that hogs will stray away because fences are wanting, and that under the tenant system fences can not be built. Although this is true the obstacle is not too great to be overcome by an industrious farm landlord, who will make a beginning by cultivating a portion of his farm, instead of leaving it all to tenants. That a movement in this direction has been made is indicated by the increased production of corn in very recent years.

Customs that have prevailed in the South since early times still prevent an adaptation of the owners of plantations to the radically changed conditions consequent upon the war. Their traditions forbid them to work. Had they been reared among the surroundings and customs of the Northern farmers, they would long ago have recovered from the disasters of the war by making their plantations provide most of their subsistence; by their own labor and thrifty supervision they would have diversified agriculture, gone into fruit culture and stock raising and emancipated themselves from peonage to merchants and slavery to cotton. It would have required a sacrifice of sentiment and the traditional standing of a "gentleman" for some time to have achieved these results, but it must now be realized that the loss would have been insubstantial and temporary, while the gain would have been fundamental and permanent.

It is deeply to be regretted that custom and sentiment, at this late day, should be preventing a regeneration of Southern agriculture, and the regret would be still greater if there were to be a considerable immigration of foreign agriculturists. The South, with its weak economic instincts, is peculiarly a prosperous region for those in whom these instincts are active, especially if their style of living is simple and cheap. If German, Polish, Bohemian, and Swedish agriculturists were to invade the South in large numbers, they would dispossess the plantation owners by their industry and economy. They were born to work and to slave. Already the process has begun in Texas, where large plantations are passing piecemeal into the hands of these people, and where in a few years the purchasers are entirely out of debt.

There is no doubt that the plantation owners can work out their own salvation, if they will, in spite of the low quality of labor that they must hire. The question is whether they have the will to do so, whether long custom and tradition have not so incrusted them that they have lost their adaptability. From the tenants little can be expected. Most of them are so wanting in the instincts on which their rise from the kind of peonage under which they live depends, that they will not do better than they are doing.

It rests with the plantation owners to determine whether the South shall escape from the thralldom of the crop lien. Southern farming, both large and small, needs to shun the storekeeper as much as it can. When the supplies for farm and family are derived mostly from the farm itself, it is apparent that the charges against the cotton crop will be reduced, a margin for saving established and that peonage will be abolished. After this has been done cotton production can not be forced upon the farmer and he can begin the diversification of agricultural products and branch out into stock raising, truck farming, fruit culture and other occupations according to his opportunities and his markets. The ills of the farmers are not going to be cured by legislation; "our remedies oft in ourselves do lie, which we ascribe to heaven."

7 Peonage and Serfdom in the Southern States

Looking back on southern history in the early 1920s many Southerners were disillusioned by their region's failure to correct so many of the evils with which it had been charged in the era of Reconstruction. One major evil was the agricultural system. Inevitably the postwar Southerner turned back to an agrarianism that lacked the necessary capital to place it one year ahead and out of debt. White Southerners in great numbers were inextricably caught right at the start in the vise of debt. The Negro was even more entrapped. Once the tenant farmer, black or white, signed a lien note to be redeemed by a future cotton or tobacco crop, he virtually sold himself and members of his family into peonage. Thus between 1865 and 1930 while the lien system prevailed under the sanction of state law, a system of peonage prevailed with it.

Critics of the South's economic failures in the depression decades after 1920 were biting in their comments. They had little difficulty in uncovering materials to sustain their contentions, especially concerning the failure of the old tenant and credit systems with its heavy social and economic deficits. It took little exploring to see that resulting peonage was more widely spread than in Ireland, India, or other places where human beings found themselves under heavy economic bondage. Nothing did more to document this fact in human terms than did the heavy migration of Negroes from the South after 1910.

THE HISTORY OF PEONAGE IN THE SOUTHERN STATES IS ANOTHER story of sordid injustice and appalling horrors, the execrable details of which are beyond the limits of this volume. In detestable and flagrant violation of Federal laws, open and defiant has been the practice of peonage under the protection of the Oligarchy in the South.

A peon is defined in the *Century Dictionary* as "a species of serf compelled to work for his creditor until his debts are paid." The most common form of peonage in the Southern States is found among the tenant croppers, under farming contracts whereby the unscrupulous landlord or merchant, by dishonest practices, manages to keep the tenant continuously in debt for supplies. This form of peonage is sanctioned in some cases by the State laws, in other cases it continues through the maladministration of the law by venal officers of the law, and almost universally, in the cotton and rice-producing States, and in the turpentine and lumber camps of the South. Justice Brewer of the United States Supreme Court, gave the following definition of peonage:

> It may be defined as a status or condition of compulsory service based upon the indebtedness of the peon to the master. The basal fact is indebtedness. One fact exists universally; all were indebted to their masters. This was the cord by which they seemed to be bound to their master's service.

It was during the early years of the Roosevelt Administration that the prevalence of peonage in the South was brought to public attention. Through the prosecutions that were started in the Federal courts under that Administration, every effort possible, within the limits of the Federal courts, was made to remove the evil. Among the early prosecutions for peonage under the Roosevelt Administration was the rather notorious case in South Alabama where a white man and his entire family were held in peonage by another white man. There had been a "fake trial" before a Justice of the Peace "specially elected for the business." A fine was imposed which the unfortunate

C/R 1924 by The Devin-Adair Company. Reprinted from *The Southern Oligarchy* by William Skaggs by permission of the publisher.

man was not able to pay and he was "turned over to work out his fine." As reported by "Raymond," staff correspondent of *The Chicago Tribune*,—

> newly arrived immigrants are in chain gangs in Alabama charged with no crime whatsoever except their unwillingness or inability to pay their debts which may or may not have been just ones. . . . Several instances were cited to show that newly arrived immigrants were made victims of the old-fashioned laws of the Southern States, by means of which a person who makes a contract to labor and fails to fulfill it, or who runs in debt for advances made to him as a laborer or tenant, can be compelled to work by force, or actually be sent to the chain gang.

It was reported that more than 3,000 men were held in a state of peonage in Florida. These men, it was stated, had been induced to accept employment in the South. Further regarding the peonage investigations in Florida, "Raymond" of *The Chicago Tribune* said:

> Men have been tried and punished for peonage in Florida, and in other cases, in which the Florida East Coast Railway was concerned, the juries have returned a verdict of acquittal in spite of convincing evidence to the contrary.

Peonage, like the appalling record of the convict system, is an old story of sordid brutalities in Florida. It has been in common practice in this State for forty years or more, with little interference or abatement except, as we have seen, when, during the Roosevelt Administration, the Department of Justice was active in prosecuting cases of peonage in the South.

The appalling record of peonage in Georgia is only a little less shocking than the gruesome story of the convict system. When the Department of Justice was actively engaged in an investigation of the charges of peonage in the South, Judge Emory Speer of the United States District Court in Georgia, on one occasion,—

> devoted his entire charge to the grand jury to the matter of peonage. . . . He said there was no doubt that men held in involuntary

servitude were really in worse condition than those held in slavery, for the latter had the countenance of law to give it a certain standing, while peonage, under whatever guise it is hidden, is totally outside the pale.

The investigation of secret service agents in Georgia, in 1903, developed "some horrible cases" of peonage. Among other notorious and shocking cases was that of "three prominent politicians and wealthy citizens of South Georgia." They operated a manufacturing plant and for some years they worked State and county convicts under the lease system; later, they made arrangements with the officers in some of the surrounding counties whereby they paid the fines of convicted mis- demeanor prisoners, and the prisoners were turned over to them to work out the fine. But these rapacious landlords did not limit their traffic in human beings to the resources of State and county officials who apprehended unfortunate citizens for minor and frequently for no offense. They resorted to kid- napping, a practice not uncommon in Georgia for many years.

One of the most diabolical and shocking cases against these exploiters was that of a Negro girl, fifteen years old, who, while on her way to visit a sister in Florida, was so unfortunate as to enter the territory preëmpted by these robbers. She was kid- napped while she was at a boarding-house and accused of a crime of which she was wholly innocent, and was threatened with prosecution unless she could pay the sum of $25. She was unable to pay the ransom demanded by her kidnappers where- upon she was told that she would be accused and prosecuted in court for the crime with which she was charged unless she agreed to go to the camp of the exploiters and work until she had paid the sum of $25. She finally accepted the proposition and went to the camp, where she remained at work for three months, until her mother, after employing a lawyer, was re- quired to pay $15 for the release of her daughter, although no criminal charge had been made against her in any court. Ac- cording to the statement of a United States Revenue Agent, "there were scores of similar cases."

Two special representatives of the Italian Government were

sent to Mississippi to investigate the unfortunate condition of twenty-two Italians held in peonage in that State. The efforts of the Italian Government to protect the treaty rights of its nationals in Mississippi were met with the usual refusal on the part of that State to protect the Italians and the assertion that the charges were "an unwarranted attack on the South." With respect to the investigations of the United States Government in Mississippi, among other statements, it was reported as follows:

> From evidence obtained by Miss Mary Grace Quackenbos, a woman lawyer, and other federal investigators, Sunnyside plantation is worked by "slaves," who are induced by false promises to go upon the soil there. Once they set foot within its boundaries they are, to all practical purposes, prisoners. If they attempt to leave, debt charges are trumped up against them, and they are arrested. They are brought before a county justice of the peace, who probably has "peons" on his own plantation, and tried.
>
> None ever is acquitted, and outrageous fines are entered against them. Of course, they cannot pay them, and these immigrants, who believed America was a free country are sent to the chain gang, back into prison to work out as a felon the fines assessed against them.
>
> So flagrant and numerous have these crimes against written and human laws become that foreign nations have protested time and again to the State Department in Washington for relief. Secretary Root appealed to Governor Vardaman of Mississippi, asking that he take steps to protect aliens in that State, but to no purpose.

The investigations and prosecutions of peonage during the Roosevelt Administration did not eradicate the inhuman practice in the Southern States, but the activities of the Department of Justice brought relief to many unfortunate victims, and it rivetted public attention on the pernicious evil. It created alarm among the guilty who were not detected and apprehended and there was a marked decrease in the number of violations of the Federal laws against this common and shameful practice. Investigations and prosecutions by the Department of Justice attracted public attention and aroused indignation which

resulted in an investigation of the situation by a committee of
Congress in 1908. Had the vigorous policy of the Federal
Government continued, after the Roosevelt Administration, in
a thorough investigation of all charges relating to reported cases
of peonage, and an energetic prosecution of all cases where the
evidence appeared sufficient to convict the accused parties, the
evil of peonage would have been greatly reduced and eventually
eradicated. But the leaders of the Southern Oligarchy are
well-trained and crafty politicians and expert traders. They
have always fought investigations of corrupt practices and lawlessness, and all proposed Federal legislation to punish crimes
in the South; and they have usually succeeded in evading all
laws which conflicted with their policies and the practices
of their agents and confederates. But they were never able to
bluff or bamboozle President Roosevelt; their later efforts along
this line were more successful.

After the Roosevelt Administration, and prior to the beginning of the Harding Administration, the public heard very
little about prosecution of peonage cases. During the Taft Administration the activities of the Federal agents in apprehending and bringing to trial persons charged with peonage declined
and the evil increased. Practically nothing was done during
the Wilson Administration in the matter of prosecuting peonage cases.

Immediately after the election of Mr. Harding, and the return to power of the Republican party, with some promise of
virile Americanism and a suggestion of law enforcement, the
newspapers began to publish news items from the Southern
States, Georgia in particular, relating to peonage. The situation may be illustrated by comparison. For instance, the annual
report of the United States Attorney General (1920, p. 128)
contains the following reference to peonage:

> A number of complaints have reached the Department during
> the past fiscal year, charging that the crime of peonage is being
> practiced, which complaints, for the most part, have been investi-
> gated and found to allege circumstances of a character insufficient
> upon which to institute prosecutions under the Act. There are

several of these complaints, however, in which the investigations have not been completed. No new cases have been instituted and none have been disposed of during the year.

While the Attorney-General was writing this report respecting the matter of peonage in violation of the Federal laws, it is a fact that peonage was more prevalent, widespread and more diabolical than it had been at any time in the history of this country. Within less than sixty days after the publication of the report of the Attorney-General, from which I have quoted, a press telegram from Atlanta, Georgia (January 13, 1921), contains the following statement:

> Coincident with the announcement that peonage indictments had been served against a farmer and two of his tenants, one of whom is a Negro in connection with the death of another Negro, United States District Attorney, Hooper Alexander, in a statement today said that wrongs were being perpetrated against Negroes in this State that "run all the gamut from the meanest of petty cheating to deliberate and plotted murder." . . . Comparatively little effort is being made by the proper officers to end these conditions. In a large proportion of the cases judicial processes are issued by magistrates that are used in the most shameless manner in the aid of crimes, and the attendant circumstances are such as should call for indictment for malpractice. Cases have occurred in which there is the gravest reason to fear that other officers of the law have been active participants in the gravest kind of wrongs. If the people of the State permit the continuance of conditions that now prevail, sooner or later and in some way we will suffer a dreadful retribution.

It was stated during the month of April, 1921 that there had been numerous investigations in the South in the past ten years in which peonage conditions had been exposed and "countless indictments" had been returned against farmers and planters who were alleged to be holding Negroes in bondage. In only a few cases, however, have verdicts of guilty been returned, and in these few cases light sentences have been imposed. A large number of planters and officials, it was stated, were under indictment and had been under indictment for years, the cases never being called for trial. It was further alleged that Federal agents "who have taken a hand in the case," now charge that the murders on the John S. Williams "murder farm" began as far back as 1910, and cite the killing of three Negroes to support their claims. They produced witnesses to prove that two of the Negroes—one a woman—were killed because they were too old to work and a useless expense to the farmer. Aleck Dyer, a Negro laborer, was knocked on the head with an ax and instantly killed while he worked in the field on the Williams plantation, and Nick and Mamie Walker, aged Negroes, were shot to death after they had lived on the "death farm" for twenty years. These killings "were said by the one-time farm hands" to have occurred in 1910 and 1911.

It was late in February, 1921, that Federal officials first appeared at the Williams plantation to investigate alleged peonage conditions. Immediately after the beginning of that investigation, the "bonded" Negroes began to disappear. It was stated by Federal agents engaged in an investigation of conditions in Jasper County, Georgia, in the matter of alleged peonage in that county, that the Negroes on the Williams farm were taken from the city stockades. For many years it has been a common practice to take Negroes from the city prisons and hold them in peonage as security for the payment of actual or alleged fines and costs imposed by the city courts.

During the month of April, 1921, a few weeks before the expiration of his term of office, Governor Hugh M. Dorsey, of Georgia, published a pamphlet on *The Negro in Georgia* which—

> deals with lynching, cruelty, and holding in peonage of blacks. . . . The Governor divided his discussion into four parts—the Negro lynched, the Negro held in peonage, the Negro driven out by organized lawlessness, and the Negro subject to individual acts of cruelty. One hundred and thirty-five examples of alleged mistreatment of Negroes in Georgia were mentioned.

Concerning actual conditions in Georgia and the treatment of Negroes, Governor Dorsey said:

If conditions indicated by these charges should continue, both God and man would justly condemn Georgia more severely than man and God have condemned Belgium and Leopold for Congo atrocities. In some counties the Negro is being driven out as though he were a wild beast. In others he is being held as a slave. In others no Negroes remain. In only a few cases was there any prosecution of white men guilty of attacking Negroes. Acquittal or light fines was the usual result of the trials.

The Atlanta Constitution quoted a "high official" of the State of Georgia as follows:

Since the State of Georgia has failed absolutely in handling peonage, lynching and cruelty to Negroes, I believe the Federal Government should be asked to take complete charge of the situation and remain in control until these violations of the law are checked.

In upholding Governor Dorsey in his attitude respecting the charges of peonage and other criminal offenses of which the Negroes were the victims, *The Constitution* said:

Another fact Georgia must face is that recently the most revolting instance of peonage ever known was brought to light in this State, and with other disclosures that followed, emphasized the seriousness of the situation.

Further respecting the charges contained in the pamphlet by Governor Dorsey, *The Constitution* said:

Strongly defending Governor Hugh M. Dorsey's position in the peonage situation in Georgia, the United States District Attorney, Hooper Alexander, issued a statement Thursday declaring that conditions described in the Governor's pamphlet really do exist in Georgia and offering to furnish names of witnesses who will testify in a number of cases not even listed by the Governor. "The laws of the State of Georgia are violated and defied in cruel treatment of Negroes with a frequency that warrants inquiry and demands correction. . . . Negroes have been killed on the public highways and their bodies left exposed to the public gaze, and though their slayers are known, no action has been taken to hale them before the jury," the District Attorney stated.

In a preceding paragraph of this chapter, I quoted from the report (1920) of the United States Attorney-General, while America was under rule of the Southern Oligarchy, in which the Department of Justice, in an official report to Congress, asserted that complaints charging peonage had been investigated and "for the most part . . . found to allege circumstances of a character insufficient upon which to institute prosecutions . . . no new cases have been instituted and none have been disposed of during the year." I also quoted from the United States District Attorney of Atlanta, a statement in which he said that peonage existed in the most exaggerated form and that "comparatively little effort was being made to end these conditions," and that "officers of the law have been active participants in the gravest kind of wrongs."

In order to show the shameless neglect of official duty, and also the utter unreliability of certain public officials, State and Federal, under rule of the Southern Oligarchy, in all matters relating to corrupt practices and law defiance in the Southern States, it may be well to call attention to certain statements in the first annual report of the Attorney General under the Harding Administration. This report (December, 1921) contains some comments on the violation of Federal laws relating to peonage from which I quote as follows:

> Peonage, or the holding of persons in involuntary servitude, still continues in many of the Southern States. The victims are almost always extremely poor, ignorant and friendless. Many times it appears that county officers conspired with employers to force these unfortunates into bondage, which is worse than outright slavery. Bureau agents have been instructed to make vigorous efforts to put a stop to this vicious practice, and a number of cases have been successfully prosecuted and substantial sentences imposed. Some of the cases reported in the hundreds of reports received have been extremely aggravated and in several instances the poor victims have been murdered when it was discovered by the employer that this bureau was conducting an investigation.
>
> Complaints arising under this act increased during the year, and peonage was found to exist to a shocking extent in Georgia, Alabama, and some parts of Texas.

It will be observed that the Attorney-General under the Harding Administration corroborates and amplifies the charges made by the District Attorney of Atlanta. In most cases where the organization of labor is attempted in the South it is met with bitter opposition and frequently with persecution and violence. By a system of legal chicanery the poor and ignorant whites and Negroes, but more especially the Negroes, are cheated of their earnings, especially on farms, and held in a state of economic dependence, frequently in a state of peonage and a life of serfdom. The report of the Attorney-General (1921) from which I have quoted states the actual situation when he refers to cases of "bondage" in the South as "worse than outright slavery."

In the preceding chapter on the evils of the fee system I referred to the common practice in the South of apprehending poor Negroes (and sometimes poor whites), taking them before petty courts where for misdemeanors, or other minor offences, or no offence, fines and heavy costs are imposed which the poor defendants cannot pay and they are sold to contractors, manufacturers, farmers, or anybody who needs unskilled labor and is willing to pay the fines and fees. This is one method used for making peons; the other and more common practice is to keep farm tenants in debt until they are reduced to a state of peonage.

A system of rapacious landlordism in the South by which tenants are swindled, frequently with the help of public officials, has developed a condition of tenancy more distressing and inhuman than can be found in any civilized country. The condition of the tenant in Italy under the Cæsars was better than the present condition of the tenant in the Southern States. Prior to, and during the early years of the Christian era, the Roman tenant had certain rights which were respected and could be enforced; so long as he paid his rent he could remain a free man and a Roman citizen. In the Southern States the tenant has few civil or political rights that are enforceable. The civil and political rights of which the average American is so boastful exist only in theory, so far as the tenant and the average laborer in

the South are concerned. The corrupt and dishonorable practices of the landlord in numerous cases make it impossible for
the tenant to pay his rent or other contractual obligations. The
tenant is in fact neither a citizen nor a freeman; he is a serf,
bound to the soil at the will of the landlord.

8 The South's Manufacturing Possibilities

By 1911 the boll weevil had made its first major impact on the western half of the cotton belt. Southern farming felt the pinch of competition from many sources in this period, and southern industry was still in a highly formative stage. More than this, the region lacked diversity of industrial enterprises. Delegates to the Southern Commercial Congress in Atlanta discussed the place of the South in light of the impending opening of the Panama Canal, then three years in the future. In the following speech Harry Wise, editor of the *Tradesman,* reviewed the South's promise in slightly old-fashioned southern rhetorical terms; beneath the froth, however, was a serious vein suggesting major future revisions of southern economic approaches. Some of the things which Wise said had been said many times before, but this was the first time that a southern audience could really be wooed away from the "moonlight and roses" view of the future to see that the industrialization of the region was not only necessary but inevitable.

THE SOUTH IN REFERENCE TO ITS MANUFACTURING POSSIBILITIES can send forth to the world the message, that within its boundaries lies the territory that in the not far distant future will embrace the center of industrial America.

Harry Wise, "The South's Manufacturing Possibilities," *Proceedings of the Third Annual Convention, Southern Commercial Congress* (Washington: Southern Commercial Congress, 1911), 564–571.

Not an idle boast this, not a statement at random, but a conclusion based on the fact, that this day and age, industries of all kinds are gravitating toward logical centers. The laws governing this are based on the location of raw material, economies in manufacturing and facilities for distribution.

When we speak of the South we naturally think of that historically poetic country, whose history is fraught with romance and tragedy, that lives in fiction as in fact and has at one time or another and in one way or another been the happiest and saddest of earth's habitations.

It is another South that we are here to consider, the geographical South, the industrial South, and more particularly the manufacturing South. Take the territory south of a line following the course of the Potomac and Ohio rivers, where the latter flows into the Mississippi, then west including the States of Arkansas, Oklahoma and Texas, and we have fourteen States, covering an area of 888,122 square miles and in which are living 27,559,-113 of our people, nearly 30 per cent of all of continental United States. This is the geographical South that is now being developed along lines that are destined to make it the most productive of any section of our productive country.

In considering the adaptability of any section for manufacturing purposes, the questions to be considered, as referred to before, are the securing of raw material, the economical and economic possibilities in the conversion to the finished product and the necessary facilities for distribution.

It is unnecessary to dwell at any length on the first condition, the raw material. The South produces in cotton, almost the world's supply. Of iron, bituminous coal and lumber there are within its bounds a supply that will make it more than possible to build within its borders plants that would enable the doubling of our present products in which these enter, without going outside of its confines for any of the necessary materials.

As to the economical and economic possibilities, the climatic conditions in the major portion of the territory make it possible to maintain a plant at less expense. The fact that land is cheaper and greater areas can thus be used, provides more adequate facilities for handling and storing.

The laborer also lives cheaper and better, congested conditions and the evils incidental thereto, are removed and increased efficiency naturally follows.

But most important of all is the question of distribution. We do not pretend that our future industrial expansion lies wholly within the borders of our own country, it is the trade from without that makes us great and will make us still greater. I purposely omit making any extended reference to the possibilities that the completion of the Panama Canal opens up, but shortsighted indeed must be the man who can look forward to this, one of the wonders of the age, and not recognize the part the South is destined to play in connection with what will be the main artery of the Nation's future industrial expansion.

It is not my purpose or intention to'review what the South has done in the development along any lines. We know that it has fully demonstrated that its possibilities are only limited by its resources and resourcefulness and both of these have developed into rather good sized propositions.

A comparatively few years ago, it was contended that cotton mills could not be successfully operated in the South, for the same reason no doubt, that it was traditional in years gone by that Georgia could not raise anything but cotton and razorback hogs. At any rate, it was maintained that the textile industry had been perfected in the New England field and could not successfully be competed with elsewhere. After textile mills were operated in the South the prophecy was somewhat modified to mean, that the finer grades of textiles were what was meant, and when this was accomplished, there must have followed a spell of wet weather and "all signs failed."

It is not so very long ago that it was said that the South offered a market for second-hand machinery only, and that high-grade tools and equipments could not be sold in that section. Those who said it and never learned otherwise are out of business today.

What we are most interested in just now is not what we've got but what we haven't and ought to have and that brings me to the very center of the subject that calls for our best thoughts and efforts, the enlarging of the manufacturing possibilities and the husbanding of our resources.

In 1905, the Southern States, including Missouri, contained 15.3 per cent of the manufacturing plants, representing 11 per cent of the total capital invested and produced 10.5 per cent of the finished products. The middle and central States contained about two-thirds of all the plants in the country, about equally divided among them. These ratios have not materially changed in the past five years.

In 1910, the South is credited with a fraction less than 10 per cent of the total pig iron production, and about 22 per cent of the bituminous coal. In lumber, over 20 million feet were cut. Cotton of course is our monopoly. Here we have the necessary raw materials entering into a large percentage of the finished products that go to make up what the manufacturing world today produces.

. . . No one for a moment can question the fact that the South's manufacturing development will increase in direct proportion to the intelligent exploiting of its resources and possibilities.

No section of the Southland can meet all requirements, no restricted territory exists where all classes of industries will thrive alike, and just as the manufacturer and merchant, to sell his goods in any given section of the country, has to meet the requirements of that territory, just so every section of the South must first study its possibilities and then concentrate on such lines as are absolutely logical. West Virginia will hardly make any effort to secure cotton mills, and Texas no very strenuous effort, comparatively, toward extensive coal mine development, and yet, West Virginia coal supplies the needs of innumerable manufacturing plants outside of its own boundaries, and Texas furnishes practically one-third of the entire cotton supply of the country and has not enough spindles in operation to make it worth mentioning in polite society.

On the other hand, in the State of Texas there are under

cultivation something less than 4,000,000 acres of land, or to be exact, 3,797, 967, about 11 per cent of what can be classed as tillable. This State in 1909 produced 122,250,000 bushels of corn and 2,653,000 bales of cotton; if, therefore, instead of 11 per cent of the possible land cultivated, 33 per cent were tilled, and the same proportionate yield were had, this one State would be able to produce nearly half of the entire corn yield of the United States, and nearly three times as much cotton as the entire South marketed in the seasons of 1909 and 1910.

You have, no doubt, all of you read the Bob Ballads and recall the story of the two men who were cast on a desert land. One side produced only oysters and the other, if I remember right, terrapin. The man on the oyster side could not endure the sight of oysters but was very fond of terrapin, the other fairly hated terrapin but doted on oysters.

In view of the fact, however, that they had never been properly introduced they could not according to the rules of etiquette discuss the matter, and would, we are led to believe, have starved to death if they had not been brought together by a fortunate occurrence, which however, has no bearing on the analogy I wish to make.

While as cities, communities and States, we have made progress in cooperative work, we have not as yet been all together properly introduced, and have therefore fallen into the common error of wishing to increase our manufacturing possibilities simply to get it away from the other fellow and without first determining whether our special location be a logical one.

Climate is a great thing, geographical location and natural environments are valuable assets, but these and others too often used as arguments should be made minor considerations, for to increase our manufacturing possibilities ill advisedly, will be a mistake. We must encourage and establish what bids fair to be successful enterprises, let every city study its own possibilities, take into consideration the class of industries best adapted for that special location, and then concentrate its efforts in that particular line.

In a very few years it will be necessary for all manufacturers who do, or contemplate doing, business with the South American and Oriental countries, to have at least an auxiliary plant somewhere in the South. This can be confidentially looked forward to and it behooves us therefore, to know ourselves not as individuals, but as an entire section, and work not singly, but united, not as the South, but for the South.

. . . The industrial South is no less the garden spot because it has awakened the spirit of progressiveness. On the contrary, its beauty is enhanced, its desirability as a habitation has increased and its sphere of usefulness enlarged by this very thing, and as it grows and expands, its very environments will serve to add new dignity to labor and to rest.

The sun will never shine less brightly, the rivers flow less placidly, but in common with nature, will beckon all mankind to the coming manufacturing section of the country—the South.

9 The Decline of Cotton

By 1921 few Southerners doubted that the reign of King Cotton was ended for the great masses of cotton growers. Cotton was still being grown by little farmers, but wreckage of the old staple crop system was becoming more and more visible. The depression of 1929 brought the ruin into full focus. Between the onset of the panic and the first year of the New Deal an understanding of how seriously the system of cotton culture had failed became clearly mandatory. All sorts of surveys and reports were made on the evils of cotton tenancy. Charles S. Johnson, Edwin R. Embree, and Dr. Will W. Alexander, three humane Southerners who had concerned themselves with human needs in their region, made their own report in a slender volume which did more to narrate the problems of cotton tenancy than did many of the more voluminous reports. Not only did they report an end of much of the traditional plantation system in the South, but their findings revealed a shifting of the economic bases for large segments of the southern population by a turning away from the land.

THE COTTON TENANTS LIVE AT THE LEVEL OF MERE SUBSISTENCE. But they are not the only sufferers under the evil despotism of King Cotton. The devotion to a single crop has left the whole

Charles S. Johnson, Edwin R. Embree, and W. W. Alexander, *The Collapse of Cotton Tenancy: Summary of Field Studies & Statistical Surveys, 1933–35* (Chapel Hill: The University of North Carolina Press, 1935), 1–24.

region of the Old South dependent upon the fluctuations of one commodity, at the mercy of the success of a single plant. Continuous tilling of one crop has worn out soil over wide areas which previously were rich and fertile. Devotion to a commercial harvest has left an abundant farm region destitute of food crops, and its people living on a shockingly meager and ill-balanced diet.

The past five years of economic depression have accentuated the problems and aggravated the evils of American cotton culture. Changes in world markets and the development of substitute materials now threaten the life of the industry. The growth of cotton in the Southwest, and the prospect of increasing use of machinery in tilling and picking, make it certain that the ancient order of cotton culture in the Old South is doomed. Sweeping changes in southern farming must come swiftly if millions of former plantation workers are not to be completely wrecked —if the region itself is not to suffer violent ruin.

THE COTTON BELT

The cotton belt as determined by soil, climate, and rainfall, lies between 25° and 37° north latitude. Cotton culture now occupies a belt 300 miles north and south, stretching 1,600 miles from the Carolinas to western Texas. In this area 125 million acres are devoted to this single crop—nearly as great an amount of land as is given to all other crops together in this huge region.

. . . The belt is marked by dense farm populations. While the South, as a whole, is the most thickly populated rural area in America, the cotton belt is the most densely peopled region in the South. Negroes, remaining from slavery times, contribute large numbers to the older sections, forming over forty per cent of the total inhabitants of South Carolina, Georgia, and Alabama, and slightly more than half the population of Mississippi. But Negroes no longer make up the bulk of cotton tenants. White workers, in an increasing flood, have been drawn into the cotton fields, until today they outnumber the blacks more than five to three.

TENANCY

In the ten chief cotton states over sixty per cent of those engaged in the production of this crop are tenants. The computations of Rupert B. Vance place the number of tenant families in the cotton belt at 1,790,783. Of these, 1,091,944 are white, and 698,839 are colored. The family units of white tenants are larger than the colored, due in part to the earlier break-up of Negro families and the high infant death rate. The total number of individuals in these tenant families runs to approximately five and a half million whites and slightly over three million Negroes.

Tenancy for decades has been steadily increasing. The number of farms operated by tenants in the South was high enough in 1880, when 36.2 per cent were run by tenants. By 1920 the percentage of tenancy had reached 49.6, and in 1930 it was 55.5. These figures are for the South as a whole. In the cotton belt the percentage of tenancy is still higher. Out of every hundred cotton farms, over sixty are operated by tenants.

Up to the Civil War cotton laborers universally were Negro slaves. It is one of the strange facts of the history of the slave period that white non-slaveholding families, in spite of their numbers and their destitution, were given no place in the expanding cotton culture, save where they were able to hang on to the fringes of the industry as overseers or as small independent farmers. After Emancipation, however, white families began to compete with Negroes for the new kind of slavery involved in tenancy. The white tenants have increased steadily, filling the new openings in the expanding industry, and taking places left vacant by Negroes who migrated from the plantations to northern and southern cities. In the decade from 1920 to 1930, white tenants in the cotton states increased by 200,000 families—approximately a million persons. During the same decade Negro tenants decreased by 2,000 families as a result of mass movements to cities. Since 1914, this Negro migration to the North alone has exceeded a million and a half persons. Increasingly, therefore, the problems of the rural South in general, and of cotton tenancy in particular, are those of native white families much more than of Negroes.

WHAT IS A TENANT?

A farm tenant, in the widest meaning of the term, is any person who hires the farm which he operates, paying for the use of the land either by a share of the crop which he raises or by cash rental or both. Now the renting of land is not in itself a bad thing; it is customary in other parts of America and to a limited extent in Europe. It is a simple means of getting access to land by persons who have not capital enough to purchase farms. Normally it is regarded as a step on the road to independent ownership. The evil is not in renting land but in the traditions and practices which have grown up about it in the South.

Tenants may be divided into three main classes: (a) renters who hire land for a fixed rental to be paid either in cash or its equivalent in crop values; (b) share tenants, who furnish their own farm equipment and work animals and obtain use of land by agreeing to pay a fixed per cent of the cash crop which they raise; (c) share-croppers who have to have furnished to them not only the land but also farm tools and animals, fertilizer, and often even the food they consume, and who in return pay a larger per cent of the crop.

In considering cotton tenancy, the first group may be almost ignored. Those who have definite agreements with landlords as to exact rental prices are few in number and their status is so independent as to remove them from the system of subservient tenancy. The share tenants and share-croppers are the two great subdivisions of the dependent workers in the cotton belt. The difference between these two classes is simply one of degree. The share tenants, since they supply much of their own equipment, are able to rent the land on fairly good terms, usually on the basis of paying to the owner not more than one-fourth or one-third of the crop raised. The share-croppers, on the other hand, having almost nothing to offer but their labor, must pay as rent a higher share of the product, usually one-half of the crop. In addition, of course, both tenants and croppers must pay out of their share of the crop for all that is supplied to them in the way of seed, fertilizer, and food supplies. "Tenancy," as used in the present report and as commonly applied in the South, is a general term covering both the share tenants and the share-croppers, but not the renters. As a matter of fact, over one-third of all tenants in the South, and over half of the Negro tenants are croppers, that is, in the lowest category of poverty and dependence.

The risk of the tenant increases, of course, in proportion to what he is able to contribute to the contract. There is almost no financial risk assumed by the share cropper who furnishes only his labor (and that of his family), who receives his equipment and supplies and even his food, from the owner. The share tenant, who supplies his own tools and work animals, assumes more risk, and in return expects a larger share of the earnings. The renter of course assumes much greater risk. In turn the landlord's potential profits increase as he assumes more and more of the risk. Therein lies a danger to the tenant. It is to the advantage of the owner to encourage the most dependent form of share cropping as a source of largest profits. And he wishes to hold in greatest dependence just those workers who are most efficient. A shiftless and inefficient cropper is of little value to the owner and is expelled, unless, in a serious labor shortage, absence of any worker is even more costly than the presence of an incompetent one. The industrious and thrifty tenant is sought by the landlord. The very qualities which might normally lead a tenant to attain the position of renter, and eventually of owner, are just the ones which make him a permanent asset as a cropper. Landlords, thus, are most concerned with maintaining the system that furnishes them labor and that keeps this labor under their control, that is, in the tenancy class. The means by which landowners do this are: first, the credit system; and second, the established social customs of the plantation order.

As a part of the age-old custom in the South, the landlord keeps the books and handles the sale of all the crops. The owner returns to the cropper only what is left over of his share of the profits after deductions for all items which the landlord has advanced to him during the year: seed, fertilizer, working equipment, and food supplies, plus interest on all this indebtedness, plus a theoretical "cost of supervision." The landlord often supplies the food—"pantry supplies" or "furnish"—and other current necessities through his own store or commissary. Fancy prices at the commissary, exorbitant interest, and careless or manipulated accounts, make it easy for the owner to keep his tenants constantly in debt.

The plight of the tenant at annual settlement time is so common that a whole folklore about it has grown up in the South.

> A tenant offering five bales of cotton was told, after some owl-eyed figuring, that this cotton exactly balanced his debt. Delighted at the prospect of a profit this year, the tenant reported that he had one more bale which he hadn't yet brought in. "Shucks," shouted the boss, "why didn't you tell me before? Now I'll have to figure the account all over again to make it come out even."

Of course every story of this kind, and such stories are innumerable, can be matched by tales of unreliability and shiftlessness on the part of the tenant. The case against the system cannot be rested on any personal indictment of landlords any more than it can be vindicated by stories of the improvidence of tenants. The fact is that landlords generally act as they find it necessary to act under the system; tenants do likewise. The development of bad economic and social habits of whatever kind on the part of both landlords and tenants is direct evidence of a faulty system.

Even more than the credit system, the traditions of the region hold the tenant in thrall. The plantation system developed during slavery. It continues on the old master and slave pattern. For many years, even after Emancipation, black tenants were the rule in the cotton fields and the determination to "keep the Negro in his place" was, if anything, stronger after the Civil War than before. Although white families now form the great majority of the cotton tenants, the old "boss and black" attitude still pervades the whole system. Because of his economic condition, and because of his race, color, and previous condition of servitude, the rural Negro is helpless before the white master. Every kind of exploitation and abuse is permitted because of the old caste prejudice. The poor white connives in this abuse of the Negro; in fact, he is the most violent protagonist of it. This fixed custom of exploitation of the Negro has carried over to the white tenant and cropper. Yet it has been impossible to bring about any change, even to get the poor white workers to take a stand, since any movement for reform is immediately confused with the race issue. Because of their insistence upon the degrading of three million Negro tenants, five and a half million white workers continue to keep themselves in virtual peonage.

WHAT THE TENANT EARNS

The average American farm family in 1929 earned $1,240, and this was about a third of the average for non-farm families. The lowest general earnings were in the southern states. The Carolinas, Mississippi, Arkansas, Alabama, Georgia, and Tennessee, the states of the old cotton belt, stood at the bottom of the list. Here, even at the period of national prosperity, a vast farm population barely earned subsistence.

Every study of wages and income in the South makes perfectly clear the low economic position of the rural South. Clarence Heer's exhaustive study of wages and income, covering a period of thirty years, showed that southern agriculture had provided its farmers just about half the per capita income of farmers in other sections. This includes all the "independent farmers, plantation owners, tenants, and the share croppers." When tenants alone are considered, the family earnings slump distressingly below the level of decent subsistence.

The debts are a part of the system and are of two kinds: those accumulating from year to year; and current debts arising from the "furnishing" system. More than a third of the tenants have debts of more than a year's standing. In six widely differing counties included in the field studies of our Committee, 43.4 per cent of the tenants were in debt before they planted their 1934 crop. The average indebtedness, according to the Alabama tenants who were able to keep any record of their accounts, was $80.00.

As to current earnings or deficits, a study of Negro tenant farmers in Macon County, Alabama, in 1932, published in *Shadow of the Plantation,* showed that 61.7 per cent "broke even," 26.0 per cent "went in the hole," and 9.4 per cent made some profit. Of this latter group the total income ranged from about $70 to $90 per year. The special inquiry into tenant farmer earnings by this Committee, which covered some 2,000 families in 1934 and 1935 in Mississippi, Texas, Alabama, and South Carolina, found variations in earnings according to soil fertility and types of management, but universally a substandard. Inseparable from the small gross earnings of these farmers was the stern factor of landlord policy, prerogative, alleged supervision charges, and interest rates. It must be remembered that the tenant's actual income is very different from the earnings of his farm as listed in agricultural reports. The landlord's share is taken from the earnings together with the operator's gross expenses.

For the small number of all these 2,000 tenant families who received a cash income in 1933, the average was $105.43. The actual earnings per family, when distributed among five persons, would give a monthly income per person of $1.75. And these incomes, theoretically at least, were benefiting from the federal program of aid to farmers as administered in 1933.

Tenants in general have to consider themselves fortunate if they can farm for subsistence only. One cropper complained dismally: "For 18 years we ain't cleared a thing or made any real money." Another had received his cash in a manner which made it difficult to remember the amounts: "I couldn't possibly go to task and tell you. I got it in dribbles and couldn't keep a record of it, but it wasn't over $75.00." Still another farmer "cleared $45.00 last year; nothing the year before and no settlement; cleared $117.00 the year before that. The most I ever cleared was $260.00—just before the war." Few of the tenants interviewed had cleared cash incomes since 1921, and many had made nothing since the World War.

There could, perhaps, be some compensation for low incomes if the farms were supplying food for the families. But the production of a cash crop rules out the raising of general produce. This much is obvious: if there is any advantage in cotton farming as a profitable business, the tenant does not share it.

HOW THE TENANT LIVES

Cotton has always been a cheap-labor crop; its development has rested on keeping this labor cost low. In fact many declare that profit is impossible "if all the labor it requires were paid for." The results appear in the living standards of the millions of families whose men, women, and children produce the crop.

The cultural landscape of the cotton belt has been described as a "miserable panorama of unpainted shacks, rain-gullied fields, straggling fences, rattle-trap Fords, dirt, poverty, disease, drudgery, and monotony that stretches for a thousand miles across the cotton belt." It used to be said that "cotton is and must remain a black man's crop, not a white man's, because the former's standard of living has always been low, and his natural inferiority makes it unnecessary to change it." Now that white families make up nearly two-thirds of the workers, it is clear that meager and pinched living is not a racial trait but a result of the system of cotton tenancy. Submerged beneath the system which he supports, the cotton tenant's standard of living approaches the level of bare animal existence. The traditional status of the slave required only subsistence. The cotton slave —white or colored—has inherited a rôle in which comfort, education, and self-development have no place. For the type of labor he performs, all that is actually required is a stomach indifferently filled, a shack to sleep in, some old jeans to cover his nakedness.

This age-old condition of the cotton worker and the necessity to keep it unchanged, lead to some interesting rationalizing by supporters of the existing order. Serious statements about the happiness of the tenant in his dependent rôle are taking the place of the earlier stories of the contentment of the slaves. Anecdotes of ludicrous spending whenever he gets his hands on money are used to justify the regular condition of poverty. Shiftlessness and laziness are reported as reasons for the dependent state, whereas, in fact, in so far as they exist, they are not necessarily inherent, but are caused by the very conditions of the share-cropping system.

The studies made of tenant families confirm the indignant assertion of a writer in the Dallas, Texas, *News* that "the squalid condition of the cotton raisers of the South is a disgrace to the southern people. They stay in shacks, thousands of which are unfit to house animals, much less human beings. Their children are born under such conditions of medical treatment, food and clothing, as would make an Eskimo rejoice that he did not live in a cotton growing country."

The drab ugliness of tenant houses might be condoned if they were comfortable. Many of them are old, some have actually come down from the period of slavery, and all of them, unpainted and weather-beaten, appear ageless. They are crudely constructed, windows and doors are out of alignment, they leak even while still new. Family size and size of house have no relationship. Whatever the number in the family it must occupy the customary three rooms. In fact a family of any size may live in a two-room house; as many as thirteen have been found living in a single bedroom and kitchen.

A Children's Bureau study of the welfare of children in cotton-growing areas of Texas, showed 64 per cent of the white and 77 per cent of the Negro families living under conditions of housing congestion, and this in spite of the common belief that over-crowding is a phenomenon of the city. Another study of white tenant families in Tennessee estimated an average value of all personal belongings of tenants at less than a hundred dollars. In one cotton-growing county of Alabama, reported in *Shadow of the Plantation,* over half of the families lived in one- and two-room cabins, and the comment on the character and inadequacy of these by one of the tenants does not exaggerate the lot of this majority: "My house is so rotten you can jest take up the boards in your hands and cromple 'em up. Everything done swunk about it."

Although living on abundant land in the south temperate zone, tenant families have probably the most meager and ill-balanced diet of any large group in America. Devotion to the single cash-crop, and the fact that food crops mature during the same season as cotton, make it virtually impossible under the system to raise subsistence crops. Because the growing of household produce does not fit into the economy of a cash-crop, it is not encouraged by landlords, whose prerogative it is to determine the crops grown. As a result the diet is limited largely to imported foods, made available through the commissaries and local stores. This diet can be, and commonly is, strained down to the notorious three M's,—meat (fat salt pork), meal, and molasses. Evidence of the slow ravages of this diet are to be found in the widespread incidence of pellagra, which Dr. Joseph Goldberger of the United Public Health Service bluntly attributes to lack of proper food. This diet is a part of the very culture of tenancy, supported by habit, convenience, and cheapness. A dietary survey reported by Rupert B. Vance revealed significantly that the maize kernel constituted 23 per cent of the total food intake of white Tennessee and Georgia mountaineers, 32.5 per cent of that of southern Negroes, chiefly tenant farmers, but only 1.6 per cent of that of northern families in comfortable circumstances. Pork—chiefly fat salt pork—makes up 40 per cent of the food of southern tenant farmers.

Food is the largest item in the tenant's budget, and since almost no food is produced, it must be purchased. In six counties, the average monthly expenditure for food in 1934 was $12.34, or about $3.08 per week for the average family of five. As small as these amounts seem, they consume the major portion of the tenant's income. . . .

WHAT THE STATUS OF TENANCY MEANS

It is a notorious and shameful fact that the stock arguments employed against any serious efforts to improve the lot of the cotton tenant are based upon the very social and cultural conditions which tenancy itself creates. The mobility of the tenant, his dependence, his lack of ambition, shiftlessness, his ignorance and poverty, the lethargy of his pellagra-ridden body, provide a ready excuse for keeping him under a stern paternalistic control. There is not a single trait alleged which, where true, does not owe its source and continuance to the imposed status itself.

The status of tenancy demands complete dependence; it requires no education and demands no initiative, since the landlord assumes the prerogative of direction in the choice of crop, the method by which it shall be cultivated, and how and when and where it shall be sold. He keeps the records and determines the earnings. Through the commissary or credit merchant, even the choice of diet is determined. The landlord can determine the kind and amount of schooling for the children, the extent to which they may share benefits intended for all the people. He may even determine the relief they receive in the extremity of their distress. He controls the courts, the agencies of law enforcement and, as in the case of share-croppers in eastern Arkansas, can effectively thwart any efforts at organization to protect their meager rights.

The present system is so constructed that the landless remain landless and the propertyless remain propertyless. To accumulate property, to increase independence, is to oppose the system itself. In a plantation area it is easier to be a cropper and conform to the system than to be a small owner or renter. For a share tenant to rise above his status he must overcome insuperable obstacles: (1) the agriculture that he knows fits only the old system, (2) the banks canot finance him because they are geared to finance the plantations, (3) the cost of merchant credit dissipates his accumulated working capital, and (4) the crop lien credit system has destroyed his independence in the marketing of his crop.

Neither ambition, nor thrift, nor self-respect can thrive in such a climate. Not only is it impossible to develop a hardy stock of ambitious farm owners—the persistent American ideal—but it is impossible to avoid physical and moral decadence.

If the tenant is lazy, this is a result of his mode of life. As a Mississippian, H. Snyder, writing candidly in the *North American Review*, observes: "Certainly the common run of people in the South are poor, and we are told this poverty is born of their laziness. But this is upside down, as their laziness is born of their poverty."

Attempts to justify the existing system of tenure on the score that is an adaptation to the latent and innate characteristics and capacities of the southern farm population are as baseless as they are vicious. All such observable characteristics can be traced directly to the system of tenure and the mode of livelihood that it promotes. The system, says Arthur N. Moore of the Georgia Experiment Station, does not provide ". . . a friendly atmosphere for the development of latent capacities."

Such in brief detail is the life of the tenant—drear, meager, and changeless. Upon this is reared an agricultural system which custom and a temporary federal subsidy are holding together against the insistent need of complete reorganization. . . .

10 The Nation's Number One Economic Problem

In 1939, after all sorts of sociological and economic studies had been made in the South, the National Emergency Council made its famous report to President Franklin D. Roosevelt. This pride-shattering report discussed five categories of southern life, and in the process labeled the South the Nation's number one problem. In the section on economic resources it revealed that the South had enormous natural resources but its people had not exploited them to their advantage. Southern people were the poorest in the nation and were growing progressively poorer. They were last in almost every standard of measurement, as Howard Odum was to point out so eloquently in his *Southern Regions*.

The National Emergency Council reported that one of the South's most serious ills stemmed from lack of credit facilities which could deal leniently with low income farm people. The South shared meagerly indeed in the capital income of the country. Before economic improvement could be accomplished, a reservoir of credit had to be built up to be supplied on terms that poverty-stricken small farmers could hope to pay back without forcing themselves into starvation.

THERE HAS NEVER BEEN ENOUGH CAPITAL AND CREDIT IN THE South to meet the needs of its farmers and its industry. Its people

U.S. National Emergency Council, *Report on Economic Conditions of the South, Prepared for the President* (Washington, D.C.: Government Printing Office, 1938), 5–8, 49–52.

have been living so close to poverty that the South has found it almost impossible to scrape together enough capital to develop its natural resources for the benefit of its own citizens.

Lacking capital of its own the South has been forced to borrow from outside financiers, who have reaped a rich harvest in the form of interest and dividends. At the same time it has had to hand over the control of much of its business and industry to investors from wealthier sections.

A glance at the bank reports show how difficult it has been for the southern people, whose average income is the lowest in the Nation, to build up savings of their own. Although the region contains 28 percent of the country's population, in July 1937, its banks held less than 11 percent of the Nation's bank deposits, or only $150 per capita, as compared with $471 per capita for the rest of the United States. Savings deposits were less than 6 percent of the national total. Of the 66 banks having deposits of $100,000,000 or more only two are in the South, and they barely qualify.

Even these figures do not fully disclose how small a share the South plays in the country's financial life. Southern investment banking firms managed only 0.07 percent of the security issues larger than $1,000,000 which were offered for sale between July 1, 1936, and June 1, 1938—and it is the investment bankers who find the money for virtually all important industries.

Insurance company funds reflect the same story. Southern companies hold only $756,000,000 or about 2.6 percent, of the $28,418,000,000 of assets held by the Nation's life-insurance companies.

The scarcity of local credit sources results in high interest rates and lays a heavy burden both on individuals and local governments. The average interest paid on southern State, county, and municipal bonds is 4.4 percent, while the rest of the country pays only 3.98. The weighted average interest rates charged by banks in 27 large southern and western cities in June 1938 was 4.14 percent, while for New York City it was only 2.36 percent, and for 8 other northern and eastern cities only 3.38 percent.

State banks outside the Federal Reserve System, but insured by the Federal Deposit Insurance Corporation, charge average interest rates in the South ranging from 6.5 percent in Virginia to 10.43 percent in Texas and 11.5 percent in Oklahoma. In the New England and the Middle Atlantic States, on the other hand, it is 5.75 percent. In the Mountain States the highest average is 8.5 percent, which is lower than in 5 of the Southern States.

Banking laws and regulations have contributed still further to the scarcity of southern credit. Ordinarily, banks can make credit available for capital purposes only by the purchase of readily marketable securities. This makes it almost necessary for a security to be listed on an exchange or to have an active over-the-counter market. Locally owned southern industries are usually too small to meet these requirements. Recently these requirements have been liberalized, but it is too early to tell whether the change will be helpful.

Faced with these handicaps, the South has had to look beyond its boundaries for the financing of virtually all of its large industries and many of its small ones. This has turned policy-making powers over to outside managements whose other interests often lead them to exercise their authority against the South's best advantage. For example, many such companies buy most of their goods outside of the South, and often their sales policies are dictated in the interest of allied corporations in other sections of the country.

If the high cost of credit has hampered southern industry, its effect on farming might be illustrated by the remark of Louis XIV: "Credit supports agriculture, as the rope supports the hanged." Almost the only sources of credit for small farmers— aside from Federal agencies—are (1) local banks, (2) landlords, and (3) merchants and dealers.

The banks cannot meet all credit demands, because whatever scant deposits they may have are largest in the fall and winter, after harvest, and smallest in the spring and summer, when the need for farm financing is greatest.

As a result, the majority of southern tenant farmers must de-

pend for credit on their landlords or the "furnish merchant"
who supplies seed, food, and fertilizer. Their advances, in fact,
have largely replaced currency for a considerable part of the
rural population. For security the landlord or merchant takes
a lien on the entire crop, which is to be turned over to him immediately after harvest in settlement of the debt. Usually he
keeps the books and fixes the interest rate. Even if he is fair
and does not charge excessive interest, the tenants often find
themselves in debt at the end of the year. This is not necessarily
a reflection on the planter-merchant, very often he would like
to improve the lot of his tenants but must exploit them in order
that he himself may survive.

The credit difficulties of the landlord are only a little less
oppressive than those of his tenants. Because he ordinarily
stakes everything on a single cash crop—cotton or tobacco—
which is subject to wildly fluctuating markets, the landowner is
a poor credit risk. Consequently he often must pay interest rates
as high as 20 percent, making the rates for tenants range considerably higher.

Attempts to find a remedy through credit unions have met
with slight success, although such organizations are spreading.
On January 1, 1938, there were 564 Federal credit unions in the
South, with 80,530 members and assets totaling $2,851,500. The
unions are not evenly distributed throughout the region, however, since Texas alone had 167 while Kentucky had only 4.

Some of the South's credit difficulties have been slightly
relieved in recent years by the extension of credit from Federal
agencies—to the business man by the Reconstruction Finance
Corporation, to the farmer by the Farm Security and Farm
Credit Administrations, to municipalities by the Public Works
Administration. Many other agencies, ranging from the Works
Progress Administration to the Soil Conversation Service, have
brought desperately needed funds into the South.

The fact remains, however, that the South has not yet been
able to build up an adequate supply of credit—the basis of the
present-day economic system.

In the South, as elsewhere, the two most important economic

endowments are its people and its physical resources. The 1937 census estimates showed that the 13 Southern States had more than 36 million persons. While this population is descended from the peoples of virtually every country of the world, a larger percentage derives from early American stock than that of any other region in the United States; 97.8 percent, according to the last census, was native born; 71 percent white, and 29 percent colored.

The birth rate in the South exceeds that of any other region, and the excess of births over deaths makes the South the most fertile source for replenishing the population of the United States. At a time when the population of the country as a whole is becoming stationary, there is a continuous stream of people leaving the South to work in other parts of the Nation—greatly in excess of the corresponding migration to the South.

The South is a huge crescent embracing 552 million acres in 13 States from Virginia on the east to Texas on the west. It has widely varying topographic conditions—vast prairies, wooded plains, fertile valleys, and the highest mountains in the eastern United States.

The transportation facilities of the South are, for the most part, excellent. It is covered by rail lines which connect the interior with ports and give easy access to other regions. Both the Mississippi and the Ohio Rivers' navigation facilities serve the South. The Warrior-Tombigbee system taps the important industrial region around Birmingham, while the Tennessee River system, now being developed by the Tennessee Valley Authority, will bring water transportation to the very heart of the Southeast. The highways of the South are well advanced. Roads are built cheaply and are usable in all seasons. The region is well served by air lines. Bordered by both the Atlantic and the Gulf, the South has ideal harbors and many fine ports. Trade with Europe has been important for three centuries. Across the Gulf and Caribbean the South can expect further trade development.

The South has been richly endowed with physical resources. No other region offers such diversity of climate and soil. With a climate ranging from temperate to subtropical, nearly half of that part of the country where there is a frostless growing season for more than 6 months of the year is in the South. Throughout almost the entire South is ample annual rainfall and little artificial irrigation is required.

The soils of the South are the most widely varied of the Nation. Alabama, a typical southern State, has 7 major types and almost 300 soil subtypes. These soils permit the growing of a wide variety of products: cotton, tobacco, grains, fruits, melons, vegetables, potatoes, hay nuts, sugar cane, and hemp. The South leads the world in production of cotton and tobacco.

Soil and climate combine to give it forests of many kinds. With 40 percent of the Nation's forests, the South has found its woodlands second only to cotton as a source of wealth. Approximately 30 percent of the land is still in forests. Despite exploitation and abuse, forests still cover almost 200,000,000 acres, and more than half of the country's second-growth saw timber is in the South.

The region leads the world in naval stores production. Because southern pine reseeds itself and grows rapidly, the South has great potentialities for the production of paper.

The South lags, however, in the production of livestock, despite its wealth of grasslands. Its 20,000,000 cattle amount to less than a third of the total found on American farms; and because of the poor quality of many of them, the value of the annual production of cattle is only one-sixth of the Nation's total.

Fish and game are as plentiful as in any part of the country. Louisiana is our largest raw fur producer.

The South has more than 300 different minerals: Asbestos, asphalt, barite, bauxite, clays, coal, diamonds, feldspar, fluorspar, gypsum, lead, limestone, marble, mercury, phosphate rock, pyrites, salt, sand and gravel, silica, sulphur, zinc, and so on by the scores.

With less than 2 percent of its seams so far tapped, the Southeast contains a fifth of the Nation's soft coal. It mines a full tenth of our iron ore annually, but it produces only slightly more than 7 percent of our pig iron.

The South possesses approximately 27 percent of the Nation's installed hydroelectric generating capacity, although it produces only 21 percent of the electric power actually generated. The region contains 13 percent of the country's undeveloped hydroelectric power.

Nearly two-thirds of the Nation's crude oil is produced in the South, and over two-thirds of our supply of natural gas comes from southern fields. In 1935 the South furnished about half of the country's marble output. Florida and Tennessee produce 97 percent of all our phosphates, and Texas and Louisiana supply over 99 percent of our sulphur.

Commercial fisheries flourish on both the Atlantic and Gulf coasts. Shore fisheries engaged in taking oysters, clams, menhaden, mackerel, sponges, and shrimp are especially important.

In spite of this wealth of population and natural resource, the South is poor in the machinery for converting this wealth to the uses of its people. With 28 percent of the Nation's population, it has only 16 percent of the tangible assets, including factories, machines, and the tools with which people make their living. With more than half the country's farmers, the South has less than a fifth of the farm implements. Despite its coal, oil, gas, and water power, the region uses only 15 percent of the Nation's factory horsepower. Its potentialities have been neglected and its opportunities unrealized.

The paradox of the South is that while it is blessed by Nature with immense wealth, its people as a whole are the poorest in the country. Lacking industries of its own, the South has been forced to trade the richness of its soil, its minerals and forests, and the labor of its people for goods manufactured elsewhere. If the South received such goods in sufficient quantity to meet its needs, it might consider itself adequately paid.

11 The Tennessee Valley Authority

After almost fifteen years of discussion and a considerable amount of maneuvering by politicians and American businessmen, the Tennessee Valley issue came to a head in the passage of the Tennessee Valley Authority Act on May 18, 1933. This was an early New Deal law, and for the South it was the beginning of an industrial and social revolution. In many respects the Tennessee Valley Authority Act was one of the most unusual pieces of broad public legislation ever enacted by Congress. It may well be true that the social and economic history of the South can be divided at the point of passage of this act.

The Act itself is long and detailed, and administrative details have been deleted from the version which appears here. Congress was feeling its way into the field of public management of a facility which had a wide diversity of purposes, and which offered active competition with private enterprise. Never had a public enterprise proposed to deal so thoroughly with the internal affairs of so large a region. But drastic action was necessary. The South was in the throes of a depression which perhaps bit deeper into the lives of people than it did in most other parts of the Nation. Moreover the land suffered from misuse and abuse. Resources were dangerously near exhaustion, and floods annually took their tolls of life and property. If the region was to progress, it had to have plentiful electric power, to develop a dependable source of chemical fertilizer, and to bring about a massive program of reforestation and forest management.

Too, cheap transportation was a necessity if industry was to thrive in the Tennessee Valley.

. . . THAT FOR THE PURPOSE OF MAINTAINING AND OPERATING THE properties now owned by the United States in the vicinity of Muscle Shoals, Alabama, in the interest of the national defense and for agricultural and industrial development, and to improve navigation in the Tennessee River and to control the destructive flood waters in the Tennessee River and Mississippi River Basins, there is hereby created a body corporate by the name of the "Tennessee Valley Authority" (hereinafter referred to as the "Corporation"). The board of directors first appointed shall be deemed the incorporators, and the incorporation shall be held to have been effected from the date of the first meeting of the board.

. . . SEC. 2. (a) The board of directors of the Corporation (hereinafter referred to as the "board") shall be composed of three members, to be appointed by the President, by and with the advice and consent of the Senate. In appointing the members of the board, the President shall designate the chairman. All other officials, agents, and employees shall be designated and selected by the board.

(b) The terms of office of the members first taking office after the approval of this Act shall expire as designated by the President at the time of nomination, one at the end of the third year, one at the end of the sixth year, and one at the end of the ninth year, after the date of approval of this Act. A successor to a member of the board shall be appointed in the same manner as the original members and shall have a term of office expiring nine years from the date of the expiration of the term for which his predecessor was appointed.

(c) Any member appointed to fill a vacancy in the board occurring prior to the expiration of the term for which his pred-

U.S., *Statutes at Large*, 73rd Cong., 1st Sess., May 18, 1933, Chap. 32, pp. 58–72.

ecessor was appointed shall be appointed for the remainder of such term.

(d) Vacancies in the board so long as there shall be two members in office shall not impair the powers of the board to execute the functions of the Corporation, and two of the members in office shall constitute a quorum for the transaction of the business of the board.

(e) Each of the members of the board shall be a citizen of the United States, and shall receive a salary at the rate of $10,000 a year, to be paid by the Corporation as current expenses. Each member of the board, in addition to his salary, shall be permitted to occupy as his residence one of the dwelling houses owned by the Government in the vicinity of Muscle Shoals, Alabama, the same to be designated by the President of the United States. Members of the board shall be reimbursed by the Corporation for actual expenses (including traveling and subsistence expenses) incurred by them in the performance of the duties vested in the board by this Act. No member of said board shall, during his continuance in office, be engaged in any other business, but each member shall devote himself to the work of the Corporation.

(f) No director shall have financial interest in any public-utility corporation engaged in the business of distributing and selling power to the public nor in any corporation engaged in the manufacture, selling, or distribution of fixed nitrogen or fertilizer, or any ingredients thereof, nor shall any member have any interest in any business that may be adversely affected by the success of the Corporation as a producer of concentrated fertilizers or as a producer of electric power.

(g) The board shall direct the exercise of all the powers of the Corporation.

(h) All members of the board shall be persons who profess a belief in the feasibility and wisdom of this Act.

Sec. 3. The board shall without regard to the provisions of Civil Service laws applicable to officers and employees of the United States, appoint such managers, assistant managers, officers, employees, attorneys, and agents, as are necessary for the transaction of its business, fix their compensation, define their duties, require bonds of such of them as the board may designate, and provide a system of organization to fix responsibility and promote efficiency. Any appointee of the board may be removed in the discretion of the board. No regular officer or employee of the Corporation shall receive a salary in excess of that received by the members of the board.

All contracts to which the Corporation is a party and which require the employment of laborers and mechanics in the construction, alteration, maintenance, or repair of buildings, dams, locks, or other projects shall contain a provision that not less than the prevailing rate of wages for work of a similar nature prevailing in the vicinity shall be paid to such laborers or mechanics.

In the event any dispute arises as to what are the prevailing rates of wages, the question shall be referred to the Secretary of Labor for determination, and his decision shall be final. In the determination of such prevailing rate or rates, due regard shall be given to those rates which have been secured through collective agreement by representatives of employers and employees.

Where such work as is described in the two preceding paragraphs is done directly by the Corporation the prevailing rate of wages shall be paid in the same manner as though such work had been let by contract.

... (i) [The Agency] Shall have power to acquire real estate for the construction of dams, reservoirs, transmission lines, power houses, and other structures, and navigation projects at any point along the Tennessee River, or any of its tributaries, and in the event that the owner or owners of such property shall fail and refuse to sell to the Corporation at a price deemed fair and reasonable by the board, then the Corporation may proceed to exercise the right of eminent domain, and to condemn all property that it deems necessary for carrying out the purposes of this Act, and all such condemnation proceedings shall be had pursuant to the provisions and requirements hereinafter specified, with reference to any and all condemnation proceedings.

(j) Shall have power to construct dams, reservoirs, power houses, power structures, transmission lines, navigation projects, and incidental works in the Tennessee River and its tributaries, and to unite the various power installations into one or more systems by transmission lines.

SEC. 5. The board is hereby authorized—

(a) To contract with commercial producers for the production of such fertilizers or fertilizer materials as may be needed in the Government's program of development and introduction in excess of that produced by Government plants. Such contracts may provide either for outright purchase of materials by the board or only for the payment of carrying charges on special materials manufactured at the board's request for its program.

(b) To arrange with farmers and farm organizations for large-scale practical use of the new forms of fertilizers under conditions permitting an accurate measure of the economic return they produce.

(c) To cooperate with National, State, district, or county experimental stations or demonstration farms, for the use of new forms of fertilizer or fertilizer practices during the initial or experimental period of their introduction.

(d) The board in order to improve and cheapen the production of fertilizer is authorized to manufacture and sell fixed nitrogen, fertilizer, and fertilizer ingredients at Muscle Shoals by the employment of existing facilities, by modernizing existing plants, or by any other process or processes that in its judgment shall appear wise and profitable for the fixation of atmospheric nitrogen or the cheapening of the production of fertilizer.

(e) Under the authority of this Act the board may make donations or sales of the product of the plant or plants operated by it to be fairly and equitably distributed through the agency of county demonstration agents, agricultural colleges, or otherwise as the board may direct, for experimentation, education, and introduction of the use of such products in cooperation with practical farmers so as to obtain information as to the value, effect, and best methods of their use.

(f) The board is authorized to make alterations, modifications, or improvements in existing plants and facilities, and to construct new plants.

(g) In the event it is not used for the fixation of nitrogen for agricultural purposes or leased, then the board shall maintain in stand-by condition nitrate plant numbered 2, or its equivalent, for the fixation of atmospheric nitrogen, for the production of explosives in the event of war or a national emergency, until the Congress shall by joint resolution release the board from this obligation, and if any part thereof be used by the board for the manufacture of phosphoric acid or potash, the balance of nitrate plant numbered 2 shall be kept in stand-by condition.

(h) To establish, maintain, and operate laboratories and experimental plants, and to undertake experiments for the purpose of enabling the Corporation to furnish nitrogen products for military purposes, and nitrogen and other fertilizer products for agricultural purposes in the most economical manner and at the highest standard of efficiency.

. . . (a) The exclusive use, possession, and control of the United States plants numbered 1 and 2, including steam plants, located, respectively, at Sheffield, Alabama, and Muscle Shoals, Alabama, together with all real estate and buildings connected therewith, all tools and machinery, equipment, accessories, and materials belonging thereto, and all laboratories and plants used as auxiliaries, thereto; the fixed-nitrogen research laboratory, the Waco limestone quarry, in Alabama, and Dam Numbered 2, located at Muscle Shoals, its power house, and all hydroelectric and operating appurtenances (except the locks), and all machinery, lands, and buildings in connection therewith, and all appurtenances thereof, all other property to be acquired by the Corporation in its own name or in the name of the United States of America, are hereby intrusted to the Corporation for the purposes of this Act.

(b) The President of the United States is authorized to provide for the transfer to the Corporation of the use, possession, and control of such other real or personal property of the United States as he may from time to time deem necessary and proper for the purposes of the Corporation as herein stated.

Sec. 8. (a) The Corporation shall maintain its principal office in the immediate vicinity of Muscle Shoals, Alabama. The Corporation shall be held to be an inhabitant and resident of the northern judicial district of Alabama within the meaning of the laws of the United States relating to the venue of civil suits.

(b) The Corporation shall at all times maintain complete and accurate books of accounts.

(c) Each member of the board, before entering upon the duties of his office, shall subscribe to an oath (or affirmation) to support the Constitution of the United States and to faithfully and impartially perform the duties imposed upon him by this Act.

Sec. 9. (a) The board shall file with the President and with the Congress, in December of each year, a financial statement and a complete report as to the business of the Corporation covering the preceding governmental fiscal year. This report shall include an itemized statement of the cost of power at each power station, the total number of employees and the names, salaries, and duties of those receiving compensation at the rate of more than $1,500 a year.

(b) The Comptroller General of the United States shall audit the transactions of the Corporation at such times as he shall determine, but not less frequently than once each governmental fiscal year, with personnel of his selection. In such connection he and his representatives shall have free and open access to all papers, books, records, files accounts, plants, warehouses, offices, and all other things, property and places belonging to or under the control of or used or employed by the Corporation, and shall be afforded full facilities for counting all cash and verifying transactions with and balances in depositaries. He shall make report of each such audit in quadruplicate, one copy for the President of the United States, one for the chairman of the board, one for public inspection at the principal office of the corporation, and the other to be retained by him for the uses of the Congress. The expenses for each such audit may be paid from moneys advanced therefor by the Corporation, or from any appropriation or appropriations for the General Accounting Office, and appropriations so used shall be reimbursed promptly by the Corporation as billed by the Comptroller General. All such audit expenses shall be charged to operating expenses of the Corporation. The Comptroller General shall make special report to the President of the United States and to the Congress of any transaction or condition found by him to be in conflict with the powers or duties intrusted to the Corporation by law.

SEC. 10. The board is hereby empowered and authorized to sell the surplus power not used in its operations, and for operation of locks and other works generated by it, to States, counties, municipalities, corporations, partnerships, or individuals, according to the policies hereinafter set forth; and to carry out said authority, the board is authorized to enter into contracts for such sale for a term not exceeding twenty years, and in the sale of such current by the board it shall give preference to States, counties, municipalities, and cooperative organizations of citizens or farmers, not organized or doing business for profit, but primarily for the purpose of supplying electricity to its own citizens or members: *Provided,* That all contracts made with private companies or individuals for the sale of power, which power is to be resold for a profit, shall contain a provision authorizing the board to cancel said contract upon five years' notice in writing, if the board needs said power to supply the demands of States, counties, or municipalities. In order to promote and encourage the fullest possible use of electric light and power on farms within reasonable distance of any of its transmission lines the board in its discretion shall have power to construct transmission lines to farms and small villages that are not otherwise supplied with electricity at reasonable rates, and to make such rules and regulations governing such sale and distribution of such electric power as in its judgment may be just and equitable: *Provided further,* That the board is hereby authorized and directed to make studies, experiments, and

determinations to promote the wider and better use of electric
power for agricultural and domestic use, or for small or local
industries, and it may cooperate with State governments, or
their subdivisions or agencies, with educational or research
institutions, and with cooperatives or other organizations, in
the application of electric power to the fuller and better balanced development of the resources of the region.

SEC. 11. It is hereby declared to be the policy of the Government so far as practical to distribute and sell the surplus power
generated at Muscle Shoals equitably among the States,
counties, and municipalities within transmission distance. This
policy is further declared to be that the projects herein provided
for shall be considered primarily as for the benefit of the people
of the section as a whole and particularly the domestic and rural
consumers to whom the power can economically be made available, and accordingly that sale to and use by industry shall be a
secondary purpose, to be utilized principally to secure a sufficiently high load factor and revenue returns which will permit
domestic and rural use at the lowest possible rates and in such
manner as to encourage increased domestic and rural use of
electricity. It is further hereby declared to be the policy of the
Government to utilize the Muscle Shoals properties so far as
may be necessary to improve, increase, and cheapen the production of fertilizer and fertilizer ingredients by carrying out
the provisions of this Act.

SEC. 12. In order to place the board upon a fair basis for making such contracts and for receiving bids for the sale of such
power, it is hereby expressly authorized, either from appropriations made by Congress or from funds secured from the sale of
such power, or from funds secured by the sale of bonds hereafter
provided for, to construct, lease, purchase, or authorize the construction of transmission lines within transmission distance from
the place where generated, and to interconnect with other
systems. The board is also authorized to lease to any person,
persons, or corporation the use of any transmission line owned
by the Government and operated by the board, but no such lease
shall be made that in any way interferes with the use of such

transmission line by the board: *Provided,* That if any State, county, municipality, or other public or cooperative organization of citizens or farmers, not organized or doing business for profit, but primarily for the purpose of supplying electricity to its own citizens or members, or any two or more of such municipalities or organizations, shall construct or agree to construct and maintain a properly designed and built transmission line to the Government reservation upon which is located a Government generating plant, or to a main transmission line owned by the Government or leased by the board and under the control of the board, the board is hereby authorized and directed to contract with such State, county, municipality, or other organization, or two or more of them, for the sale of electricity for a term not exceeding thirty years; and in any such case the board shall give to such State, county, municipality, or other organization ample time to fully comply with any local law now in existence or hereafter enacted providing for the necessary legal authority for such State, county, municipality, or other organization to contract with the board for such power: *Provided further,* That all contracts entered into between the Corporation and any municipality or other political subdivision or cooperative organization shall provide that the electric power shall be sold and distributed to the ultimate consumer without discrimination as between consumers of the same class, and such contract shall be voidable at the election of the board if a discriminatory rate, rebate, or other special concession is made or given to any consumer or user by the municipality or other political subdivision or cooperative organization: *And provided further,* That as to any surplus power not so sold as above provided to States, counties, municipalities, or other said organizations, before the board shall sell the same to any person or corporation engaged in the distribution and resale of electricity for profit, it shall require said person or corporation to agree that any resale of such electric power by said person or corporation shall be made to the ultimate consumer of such electric power at prices that shall not exceed a schedule fixed by the board from time to time as reasonable, just, and fair; and in case of any such sale, if an amount is charged the ultimate consumer which is in excess of the price so deemed to be just, reasonable, and fair by the board, the contract for such sale between the board and such distributor of electricity shall be voidable at the election of the board: *And provided further,* That the board is hereby authorized to enter into contracts with other power systems for the mutual exchange of unused excess power upon suitable terms, for the conservation of stored water, and as an emergency or break-down relief.

SEC. 13. Five per centum of the gross proceeds received by the board for the sale of power generated at Dam Numbered 2, or from any other hydropower plant hereafter constructed in the State of Alabama, shall be paid to the State of Alabama; and 5 per centum of the gross proceeds from the sale of power generated at Cove Creek Dam, hereinafter provided for, or any other dam located in the State of Tennessee, shall be paid to the State of Tennessee. Upon the completion of said Cove Creek Dam the board shall ascertain how much additional power is thereby generated at Dam Numbered 2 and at any other dam hereafter constructed by the Government of the United States on the Tennessee River, in the State of Alabama, or in the State of Tennessee, and from the gross proceeds of the sale of such additional power 2½ per centum shall be paid to the State of Alabama and 2½ per centum to the State of Tennessee. These percentages shall apply to any other dam that may hereafter be constructed and controlled and operated by the board on the Tennessee River or any of its tributaries, the main purpose of which is to control flood waters and where the development of electric power is incidental to the operation of such flood-control dam. In ascertaining the gross proceeds from the sale of such power upon which a percentage is paid to the States of Alabama and Tennessee, the board shall not take into consideration the proceeds of any power sold or delivered to the Government of the United States, or any department or agency of the Government of the United States, used in the operation of any locks on the Tennessee River or for any experimental purpose, or for the manufacture of fertilizer or any of the ingredients thereof, or for any other governmental purpose: *Provided*, That the percentages to be paid to the States of Alabama and Tennessee, as provided in this section, shall be subject to revision and change by the board, and any new percentages established by the board, when approved by the President, shall remain in effect until and unless again changed by the board with the approval of the President. No change of said percentages shall be made more often than once in five years, and no change shall be made without giving to the States of Alabama and Tennessee an opportunity to be heard.

SEC. 14. The board shall make a thorough investigation as to the present value of Dam Numbered 2, and the steam plants at nitrate plant numbered 1, and nitrate plant numbered 2, and as to the cost of Cove Creek Dam, for the purpose of ascertaining how much of the value or the cost of said properties shall be allocated and charged up to (1) flood control, (2) navigation, (3) fertilizer, (4) national defense, and (5) the development of power. The findings thus made by the board, when approved by the President of the United States, shall be final, and such findings shall thereafter be used in all allocation of value for the purpose of keeping the book value of said properties. In like manner, the cost and book value of any dams, steam plants, or other similar improvements hereafter constructed and turned over to said board for the purpose of control and management shall be ascertained and allocated.

. . . SEC. 16. The board, whenever the President deems it advisable, is hereby empowered and directed to complete Dam Numbered 2 at Muscle Shoals, Alabama, and the steam plant at nitrate plant numbered 2, in the vicinity of Muscle Shoals, by installing in Dam Numbered 2 the additional power units according to the plans and specifications of said dam, and the additional power unit in the steam plant at nitrate plant numbered 2.

SEC. 17. The Secretary of War, or the Secretary of the Interior, is hereby authorized to construct, either directly or by contract to the lowest responsible bidder, after due advertisement, a dam in and across Clinch River in the State of Tennessee, which has by long custom been known and designated as the Cove Creek Dam, together with a transmission line from Muscle Shoals, according to the latest and most approved designs, including power house and hydroelectric installations and equipment for the generation of power, in order that the waters of the said Clinch River may be impounded and stored above said dam for the purpose of increasing and regulating the flow of the Clinch River and the Tennessee River below, so that the maximum amount of primary power may be developed at Dam Numbered 2 and at any and all other dams below the said Cove Creek Dam: *Provided, however,* That the President is hereby authorized by appropriate order to direct the employment by the Secretary of War, or by the Secretary of the Interior, of such engineer or engineers as he may designate, to perform such duties and obligations as he may deem proper, either in the drawing of plans and specifications for said dam, or to perform any other work in the building or construction of the same. The President may, by such order, place the control of the construction of said dam in the hands of such engineer or engineers taken from private life as he may desire: *And provided further,* That the President is hereby expressly authorized without regard to the restriction or limitation of any other statute, to select attorneys and assistants for the purpose of making any investigation he may deem proper to ascertain whether, in the control and management of Dam Numbered 2, or any other dam or property owned by the Government in the Tennessee River Basin, or in the authorization of any improvement therein, there has been any undue or unfair advantage given to private persons, partnerships, or corporations, by any officials or employees of the Government, or whether in any such matters the Government has been injured or unjustly deprived of any of its rights.

SEC. 18. In order to enable and empower the Secretary of War, the Secretary of the Interior, or the board to carry out the authority hereby conferred, in the most economical and efficient manner, he or it is hereby authorized and empowered in the exercise of the powers of national defense in aid of navigation, and in the control of the flood waters of the Tennessee and Mississippi Rivers, constituting channels of interstate commerce, to exercise the right of eminent domain for all purposes of this Act, and to condemn all lands, easements, rights of way, and other area necessary in order to obtain a site for said Cove Creek Dam, and the flowage rights for the reservoir of water above said dam, and to negotiate and conclude contracts with States, counties, municipalities, and all State agencies and with railroads, railroad corporations, common carriers, and all public utility commissions and any other person, firm, or corporation, for the relocation of railroad tracks, highways, highway bridges, mills, ferries, electric-light plants, and any and all other properties, enterprises, and projects whose removal may be necessary in order to carry out the provisions of this Act. When said Cove Creek Dam, transmission line, and power house shall have been completed, the possession, use, and control thereof shall be intrusted to the Corporation for use and operation in connection with the general Tennessee Valley project, and to promote flood control and navigation in the Tennessee River.

. . . SEC. 22. To aid further the proper use, conservation, and development of the natural resources of the Tennessee River drainage basin and of such adjoining territory as may be related to or materially affected by the development consequent to this Act, and to provide for the general welfare of the citizens of said areas, the President is hereby authorized, by such means or methods as he may deem proper within the limits of appropriations made therefor by Congress, to make such surveys of and general plans for said Tennessee basin and adjoining territory as may be useful to the Congress and to the several States in guiding and controlling the extent, sequence, and nature of development that may be equitably and economically advanced through the expenditure of public funds, or through the guidance or control of public authority, all for the general purpose of fostering an orderly and proper physical, economic, and social development of said areas; and the President is further authorized in making said surveys and plans to cooperate with the States affected thereby, or subdivisions or agencies of such States, or with cooperative or other organizations, and to make such studies, experiments, or demonstrations as may be necessary and suitable to that end.

SEC. 23. The President shall, from time to time, as the work provided for in the preceding section progresses, recommend to Congress such legislation as he deems proper to carry out the general purposes stated in said section, and for the especial purpose of bringing about in said Tennessee drainage basin and adjoining territory in conformity with said general purposes (1) the maximum amount of flood control; (2) the maximum development of said Tennessee River for navigation purposes; (3) the maximum generation of electric power consistent with flood control and navigation; (4) the proper use of marginal lands; (5) the proper method of reforestation of all lands in said drainage basin suitable for reforestation; and (6) the economic and social well-being of the people living in said river basin. . . .

PART 3 The Ordeal of White Supremacy

SOME SOUTHERNERS IN THE 1880s AND 1890s ARGUED THAT THE Negro should atone for the excesses of Reconstruction by surrendering the political gains granted him in the Fourteenth and Fifteenth Amendments, and in the Civil Rights Act of 1870. He should, it was said, take time to condition himself intellectually to exercise the ballot; at some unspecified future date he would have the right to vote restored to him.[1] In any event delegates to the Mississippi Constitutional Convention in 1890 took active steps to disfranchise the state's Negro voters. The "Mississippi Plan" devised in this convention was to be copied by other ex-Confederate states. Louisiana added the novelty of the "Grandfather Clause." In time the United States Supreme Court upheld the constitutionality of the Mississippi Plan but nullified Louisiana's Grandfather Clause.[2]

Racial segregation was taken a step further in Louisiana in a law which forbade Negroes and whites to ride together in a railway coach. Homer Plessy, a seven-eighths mulatto, brought suit in both the state and federal courts to have criminal proceedings against himself reversed. In *Plessy* v. *Ferguson* the United States Supreme Court gave further encouragement to

[1] Albert D. Kirwan, *Revolt of the Rednecks*, 53–84.
[2] *Williams* v. *Mississippi,* 170 U.S. 213 (1898); *Louisiana Constitution* (1898), Secs. 3, 4, and 5, pp. 78–81.

147

segregation or "Jim Crowism" by promulgating the doctrine of "separate but equal" accommodations. This doctrine prevailed until it was specifically overturned in *Brown* v. *Board of Education.*[3]

The southern Negro has had to fight his way back to political and social freedom through a tremendously complicated legal campaign of court trials and decisions. In a series of educational cases which reached the Supreme Court, beginning in 1938, barriers were breached in the segregated professional schools in southern universities.[4] The Negro was equally successful in destroying the exclusiveness of the white Democratic primary.[5] Before he did this, however, he caused the Court to make a penetrating reexamination and a major rationalization of the principles which had guided it in the past through a series of decisions. In the action *Smith* v. *Allwright* the Negro gained a major political victory for every individual who suffered discrimination under the restrictive principles of the "Mississippi Plan." The Court did not arrive at this decision until it had made an intricate restudy of the place of the white Democratic primary as a central fact in the election process, reversing its earlier decision in *Grovey* v. *Townsend.*[6]

In 1962 the Supreme Court decision, *Baker* v. *Carr*, completed the destruction of the traditional southern political structure's discriminatory rationale. Devoid of mention of race, the Court's mandate remanded the re-districting cases to the lower courts, and opened the way for rising urban majorities across the South to snatch control of state and courthouse from entrenched rural voters and their representatives.[7]

Thus the South's years have been troubled since 1938 by the fear that on almost any Monday when the Supreme Court was in chambers another landmark decision could further lower the barriers of white supremacy and rural political domination.

[3] *Plessy* v. *Ferguson,* 163 U.S. 540–552 (1895).
[4] C. Vann Woodward, *The Strange Career of Jim Crow,* 70–80.
[5] V. O. Key, Jr., *Southern Politics in State and Nation* (New York, 1949), 619–643.
[6] *Smith* v. *Allwright,* 321 U.S. 757–768 (April 3, 1944).
[7] Thomas D. Clark, *The Emerging South* (New York, 1968), 287–288.

12 The Mississippi Plan

By 1890 the white redeemers set out to gain control of political affairs in Mississippi. The safest way to accomplish this was by revising the Reconstruction constitution. In that year a new constitution was drafted, which contained a new and effective franchise provision that disfranchised nearly all of the Negro voters and a considerable number of white voters. The so-called "Mississippi Plan" was embodied in Sections 241, 242, 243, and 244, containing the literacy provision, the poll tax, the mode of registration, and a list of the indiscretions against the law that would disfranchise a voter. These sections became the models by which other ex-Confederate states revised their constitutions to disfranchise both Negro and borderline white voters.[1]

In 1898 the Mississippi Plan was tested in the courts in *Williams* v. *Mississippi*,[2] and was upheld by the United States Supreme Court. It was not until the passage of the two twentieth-century civil rights acts, in 1962 and 1965, that the last vestiges of these restrictions on voters were swept away.[3] The poll tax and literacy sections were to cause a tremendous amount of legislative debating and public reaction before they were nullified.

---

[1] Mississippi, *Constitution* (1890), Sections 241, 242, 243, and 244; Kirwan, *Revolt of the Red Necks;* C. Vann Woodward, *Origins of the New South* (Baton Rouge, 1951), 321–344.

[2] *Williams* v. *Mississippi*, 170 U.S. 213 (1898).

[3] U.S., *Civil Rights Acts*, 1957, 1964, and 1966.

Section 241. Every inhabitant of this state, except idiots, insane persons and Indians not taxed, who is a citizen of the United States of America, twenty-one years old and upwards, who has resided in this state for two years, and one year in the election district, or in the incorporated city or town in which he offers to vote, and who is duly registered as provided in this article, and who has never been convicted of bribery, theft, arson, obtaining money or goods under false pretense, perjury, forgery, embezzlement or bigamy, and who has paid on or before the first day of February of the year in which he shall offer to vote, all poll taxes which may have been legally required of him, and which he has had an opportunity of paying according to law, for the two preceding years, and who shall produce to the officers holding the election satisfactory evidence that he has paid such taxes, is declared to be a qualified elector; but any minister of the gospel in charge of an organized church, or his wife legally residing with him, shall be entitled to vote after six months' residence in the election district, incorporated city or town, if otherwise qualified.

Section 242. The legislature shall provide by law for the registration of all persons entitled to vote at any election, and all persons offering to register shall take the following oath or affirmation: "I, ———, do solemnly swear (or affirm), that I am twenty-one years old (or will be before the next election in this county), and that I will have resided in this state two years and ——— election district of ——— county one year next preceding the ensuing election (or if it be stated in the oath that the person proposing to register is a minister of the gospel in charge of an organized church, then it will be sufficient to aver therein two years' residence in the state and six months in said election district), and am now in good faith a resident of the same, and that I am not disqualified from voting by reason of having been convicted of any crime named in the constitution of this state as a disqualification to be an elector; that I will truly answer all questions propounded to me concerning my antecedents so far as they relate to my right to vote, and also as to my residence before my citizenship in this district; that I will faithfully support the Constitution of the United States and of the state of Mississippi, and will bear true faith and allegiance to the same. So help me God." In registering voters in cities and towns not wholly in one election district, the name of such city or town may be substituted in the oath for the election district. Any wilful and corrupt false statement in said affidavit, or in answer to any material questions propounded as herein authorized, shall be perjury.

Section 243. A uniform poll tax of two dollars, to be used in aid of common schools, and for no other purpose, is hereby imposed on every inhabitant of this state, male or female, between the ages of twenty-one and sixty years, except persons who are deaf and dumb, or blind, or who are maimed by loss of hand or foot; said tax to be a lien only upon taxable property. The board of supervisors of any county may, for the purpose of aiding the common schools in that county, increase the poll tax in said county but in no case shall the entire poll tax exceed in any one year three dollars on each poll. No criminal proceedings shall be allowed to enforce the collection of the poll tax.

Section 244. Every elector shall, in addition to the foregoing qualifications be able to read and write any section of the Constitution of this State and give a reasonable interpretation thereof to the county registrar. He shall demonstrate to the county registrar a reasonable understanding of the duties and obligations of citizenship under a constitutional form of government.

The person applying to register shall make a sworn, written application for registration on a form to be prescribed by the state board of election commissioners, exhibiting therein the essential facts and qualifications necessary to show that he is entitled to register and vote, said application to be entirely written, dated and signed by the applicant in the presence of the county registrar, without assistance or suggestion from any person or memorandum whatever; provided, however, that if the applicant is unable to write his application by reason of physical disability, the same, upon his oath of such disability, shall be written at his unassisted dictation by the county registrar.

13 The Grandfather Clause

The revised Louisiana Constitution of 1898 contained essentially the same restrictive provisions as the 1890 Mississippi Constitution, but there was added a novel restriction—or rather a novel loophole by which the restrictive parts of the new constitution would not disfranchise the bi-lingual and illiterate white citizens of that state, but at the same time would enable registrars to prevent Negroes from registering to vote. An immediate, and maybe unexpected, result of the new franchise sections was a reduction of illiterate white registration as well as the almost complete disappearance of Negro voters.[1] In 1915 the United States Supreme Court ruled the Louisiana "grandfather clause" unconstitutional.[2]

A second part of the Louisiana Constitution which raised the barrier of discrimination was the property qualification. Under the assessment practices of 1898 it took a fairly well-to-do farmer to own property assessed on the public tax rolls at $300.

Sec. 3. He [the registrant] shall be able to read and write, and shall demonstrate his ability to do so when he applies for registration, by making, under oath administered by the registration officer or his deputy, written application therefor, in the English language, or his mother tongue, which application shall

[1] *Louisiana Constitution* (1898), Sec. 3, 4, and 5, pp. 78–81.
[2] Woodward, *Origins of the New South*, 330–337.

contain the essential facts necessary to show that he is entitled
to register and vote, and shall be entirely written, dated and
signed by him, in the presence of the registration officer or his
deputy, without assistance or suggestion from any person or any
memorandum whatever, except the form of application hereinafter set forth; provided, however, that if the applicant be unable to write his application in the English language, he shall
have the right, if he so demands, to write the same in his mother
tongue from the dictation of an interpreter; and if the applicant
is unable to write his application by reason of physical disability, the same shall be written at his dictation by the registration
officer or his deputy, upon his oath of such disability. The application for registration, above provided for, shall be a copy of the
following form, with the proper names, dates and numbers substituted for the blanks appearing therein, to wit:

I am a citizen of the State of Louisiana. My name is . . . . I was
born in the State (or country) of . . . ., Parish (or county) of
. . . ., on the . . day of . . . ., in the year . . I am now . . years, . .
months and . . days of age. I have resided in this State since . . . .,
in this parish . . ., and in Precinct No. . ., of Ward No. . ., of this
parish, since . ., and I am not disfranchised by any provision of
the Constitution of this State.

Sec. 4. If he be not able to read and write, as provided by
Section three of this article, then he shall be entitled to register
and vote if he shall, at the time he offers to register, be the bona
fide owner of property assessed to him in this State at a valuation
of not less than three hundred dollars on the assessment roll of
the current year in which he offers to register, or on the roll of
the preceding year, if the roll of the current year shall not then
have been completed and filed, and on which, if such property
be personal only, all taxes due shall have been paid. The applicant for registration under this section shall make oath before
the registration officer or his deputy, that he is a citizen of the
United States and of this State, over the age of twenty-one years;
that he possesses the qualifications prescribed in section one of
this article, and that he is the owner of property assessed in this
State to him at a valuation of not less than three hundred dollars,

and if such property be personal only, that all taxes due thereon have been paid.

Sec. 5. No male person who was on January 1st, 1867, or at any date prior thereto, entitled to vote under the Constitution or statutes of any State of the United States, wherein he then resided, and no son or grandson of any such person not less than twenty-one years of age at the date of the adoption of this Constitution, and no male person of foreign birth, who was naturalized prior to the first day of January, 1898, shall be denied the right to register and vote in this State by reason of his failure to possess the educational or property qualifications prescribed by this Constitution; provided, he shall have resided in this State for five years next preceding the date at which he shall apply for registration, and shall have registered in accordance with the terms of this article prior to September 1, 1898, and no person shall be entitled to register under this section after said date.

Every person claiming the benefit of this section shall make application to the proper registration officer, or his deputy, for registration, and he shall make oath before such registration officer or his deputy, in the form following, viz.: I am a citizen of the United States and of this State, over the age of twenty-one years; I have resided in this State for five years next preceding this date. I was on the . . day of . . entitled to vote under the Constitution or statutes of the State of . . . , herein I then resided (or, I am the son, or grandson) of . . . ., who was on the . . . . day of . . . . entitled to vote under the Constitution or statutes of the State of . . ., wherein he then resided, and I desire to avail myself of the privileges conferred by section 5 of Article 197 of the Constitution of this State.

14 Plessy v. Ferguson

Homer Plessy was of one-eighth Negro blood. In the October 1895 term of the United States Supreme Court, he challenged a ruling of the Louisiana Supreme Court upholding the principle of separate but equal facilities on the state's railroads.[1] In 1894 Plessy purchased a ticket for a short journey on an intrastate railroad and boarded the white coach; when he was unchallenged by the conductor, he reported himself.[2] He was so light of skin that he had some difficulty proving himself by Louisiana definition a Negro. In the ensuing trial in *Ex parte Plessy* the state court found him guilty of violating the Louisiana segregation law of 1890,[3] and at the same time ruled Plessy a Negro. Plessy then sued the state's Judge Ferguson, who had tried the plaintiff on criminal charges.[4]

The Supreme Court of the United States was confronted with three issues in this case: first, who was a Negro; second, could a state legislate equality in racial matters; and, third, in light of the Fourteenth Amendment, did the state have a right to make laws concerning race, and did the Louisiana law violate the Thirteenth and Fourteenth Amendments? In the preceding *Civil Rights* and *Slaughter-house* cases, the Court had ignored the amendments.[5] The

[1] *Plessy v. Ferguson*, 163 U.S. 540–552 (1896).
[2] Louisiana, *Acts* (1890), No. 111, p. 152.
[3] *Ex parte Plessy*, 45 *Louisiana Annual* 50.
[4] Albert P. Blaustein and Clarence C. Ferguson, Jr., *Desegregation and the Law: The Meaning and Effect of the School Segregation Cases* (New Brunswick, N.J.: Rutgers University Press, 1957), 95–103.
[5] *Ibid.*, 95–96.

Court's decision rested almost altogether on whether Louisiana had the right to adopt reasonable regulations of public facilities. The issue of segregation of the races per se was not actually examined. So long as some court held the Louisiana law reasonable, the United States Supreme Court refused to reverse it. In his dissent Justice John Marshall Harlan pointed out the fact that the United States Constitution of necessity was color-blind. Nevertheless the Court had established the principle of "separate but equal," and Southerners took refuge behind it until 1954 and *Brown* v. *Board of Education. Plessy* v. *Ferguson* was the basic case behind decisions reached in the *Berea College Case* and *Gong Lum* v. *Rice*.[6]

THIS CASE TURNS UPON THE CONSTITUTIONALITY OF AN ACT OF the General Assembly of the State of Louisiana, passed in 1890, providing for separate railway carriages for the white and colored races.

The first section of the statute enacts "that all railway companies carrying passengers in their coaches in this State, shall provide equal but separate accommodations for the white, and colored races, by providing two or more passenger coaches for each passenger train, or by dividing the passenger coaches by a partition so as to secure separate accommodations: *Provided*, That this section shall not be construed to apply to street railroads. No person or persons, shall be admitted to occupy seats in coaches, other than, the ones, assigned, to them on account of the race they belong to."

By the second section it was enacted

> that the officers of such passenger trains shall have power and are hereby required to assign each passenger to the coach or compartment used for the race to which such passenger belongs; any passenger insisting on going into a coach or compartment to which by race he does not belong, shall be liable to a fine of twenty-five dollars, or in lieu thereof to imprisonment for a period of not more than twenty days in the parish prison, and any officer of any

[6] *Berea College Case*, 45 U.S. 100–102 and 222 (1908); *Gong Lum* v. *Rice*, 275 U.S. 78, 101–102 (1927).

railroad insisting on assigning a passenger to a coach or compartment other than the one set aside for the race to which said passenger belongs, shall be liable to a fine of twenty-five dollars, or in lieu thereof to imprisonment for a period of not more than twenty days in the parish prison; and should any passenger refuse to occupy the coach or compartment to which he or she is assigned by the officer of such railway, said officer shall have power to refuse to carry such passenger on his train, and for such refusal neither he nor the railway company which he represents shall be liable for damages in any of the courts of this State.

The third section provides penalties for the refusal or neglect of the officers, directors, conductors and employes of railway companies to comply with the act, with a proviso that "nothing in this act shall be construed as applying to nurses attending children of the other race." The fourth section is immaterial.

The information filed in the criminal District Court charged in substance that Plessy, being a passenger between two stations within the State of Louisiana, was assigned by officers of the company to the coach used for the race to which he belonged, but he insisted upon going into a coach used by the race to which he did not belong. Neither in the information nor plea was his particular race or color averred.

The petition for the writ of prohibition averred that petitioner was seven eighths Caucasian and one eighth African blood; that the mixture of colored blood was not discernible in him, and that he was entitled to every right, privilege and immunity secured to citizens of the United States of the white race; and that, upon such theory, he took possession of a vacant seat in a coach where passengers of the white race were accommodated, and was ordered by the conductor to vacate said coach and take a seat in another assigned to persons of the colored race, and having refused to comply with such demand he was forcibly ejected with the aid of a police officer, and imprisoned in the parish jail to answer a charge of having violated the above act.

The constitutionality of this act is attacked upon the ground that it conflicts both with the Thirteenth Amendment of the

Constitution, abolishing slavery, and the Fourteenth Amendment, which prohibits certain restrictive legislation on the part
of the States.

1. That it does not conflict with the Thirteenth Amendment,
which abolished slavery and involuntary servitude, except as a
punishment for crime, is too clear for argument. Slavery implies
involuntary servitude—a state of bondage; the ownership of
mankind as a chattel, or at least the control of the labor and
services of one man for the benefit of another, and the absence
of a legal right to the disposal of his own person, property and
services. This amendment was said in the *Slaughter-house cases*,
16 Wall. 36, to have been intended primarily to abolish slavery,
as it had been previously known in this country, and that it
equally forbade Mexican peonage or the Chinese coolie trade,
when they amounted to slavery or involuntary servitude, and
that the use of the word "servitude" was intended to prohibit
the use of all forms of involuntary slavery, of whatever class or
name. It was intimated, however, in that case that this amendment was regarded by the statesmen of that day as insufficient
to protect the colored race from certain laws which had been
enacted in the Southern States, imposing upon the colored race
onerous disabilities and burdens, and curtailing their rights in
the pursuit of life, liberty and property to such an extent that
their freedom was of little value; and that the Fourteenth
Amendment was devised to meet this exigency.

So, too, in the *Civil Rights cases*, 109 U.S. 3, 24, it was said
that the act of a mere individual, the owner of an inn, a public
conveyance or place of amusement, refusing accommodations
to colored people, cannot be justly regarded as imposing any
badge of slavery or servitude upon the applicant, but only as
involving an ordinary civil injury, properly cognizable by the
laws of the State, and presumably subject to redress by those
laws until the contrary appears. "It would be running the slavery
argument into the ground," said Mr. Justice Bradley, "to make
it apply to every act of discrimination which a person may see
fit to make as to the guests he will entertain, or as to the people
he will take into his coach or cab or car, or admit to his concert

or theatre, or deal with in other matters of intercourse or business."

A statute which implies merely a legal distinction between the white and colored races—a distinction which is founded in the color of the two races, and which must always exist so long as white men are distinguished from the other race by color— has no tendency to destroy the legal equality of the two races, or reestablish a state of involuntary servitude. Indeed, we do not understand that the Thirteenth Amendment is strenuously relied upon by the plaintiff in error in this connection.

2. By the Fourteenth Amendment, all persons born or naturalized in the United States, and subject to the jurisdiction thereof, are made citizens of the United States and of the State wherein they reside; and the States are forbidden from making or enforcing any law which shall abridge the privileges or immunities of citizens of the United States, or shall deprive any person of life, liberty or property without due process of law, or deny to any person within their jurisdiction the equal protection of the laws.

The proper construction of this amendment was first called to the attention of this court in the *Slaughter-house cases*, which involved, however, not a question of race, but one of exclusive privileges. The case did not call for any expression of opinion as to the exact rights it was intended to secure to the colored race, but it was said generally that its main purpose was to establish the citizenship of the negro; to give definitions of citizenship of the United States and of the States, and to protect from the hostile legislation of the States the privileges and immunities of citizens of the United States, as distinguished from those of citizens of the States.

The object of the amendment was undoubtedly to enforce the absolute equality of the two races before the law, but in the nature of things it could not have been intended to abolish distinctions based upon color, or to enforce social, as distinguished from political equality, or a commingling of the two races upon terms unsatisfactory to either. Laws permitting, and even requiring, their separation in places where they are liable to be brought into contact do not necessarily imply the inferiority of either race to the other, and have been generally, if not universally, recognized as within the competency of the state legislatures in the exercise of their police power. The most common instance of this is connected with the establishment of separate schools for white and colored children, which has been held to be a valid exercise of the legislative power even by courts of States where the political rights of the colored race have been longest and most earnestly enforced.

One of the earliest of these cases is that of *Roberts* v. *City of Boston*, 5 Cush. 198, in which the Supreme Judicial Court of Massachusetts held that the general school committee of Boston had power to make provision for the instruction of colored children in separate schools established exclusively for them, and to prohibit their attendance upon the other schools. "The great principle," said Chief Justice Shaw, "advanced by the learned and eloquent advocate for the plaintiff," (Mr. Charles Sumner,) "is, that by the constitution and laws of Massachusetts, all persons without distinction of age or sex, birth or color, origin or condition, are equal before the law. . . . But, when this great principle comes to be applied to the actual and various conditions of persons in society, it will not warrant the assertion, that men and women are legally clothed with the same civil and political powers, and that children and adults are legally to have the same functions and be subject to the same treatment; but only that the rights of all, as they are settled and regulated by law, are equally entitled to the paternal consideration and protection of the law for their maintenance and security." It was held that the powers of the committee extended to the establishment of separate schools for children of different ages, sexes and colors, and that they might also establish special schools for poor and neglected children, who have become too old to attend the primary school, and yet have not acquired the rudiments of learning, to enable them to enter the ordinary schools. Similar laws have been enacted by Congress under its general power of legislation over the District of Columbia, as well as by the legislatures of many of the States, and have been generally, if not uniformly, sustained by the courts.

Laws forbidding the intermarriage of the two races may be said in a technical sense to interfere with the freedom of contract, and yet have been universally recognized as within the police power of the State.

The distinction between laws interfering with the political equality of the negro and those requiring the separation of the two races in schools, theatres and railway carriages has been frequently drawn by this court. Thus in *Strauder* v. *West Virginia*, 100 U.S. 308, it was held that a law of West Virginia limiting to white male persons, 21 years of age and citizens of the State, the right to sit upon juries, was a discrimination which implied a legal inferiority in civil society, which lessened the security of the right of the colored race, and was a step toward reducing them to a condition of servility. Indeed, the right of a colored man that, in the selection of jurors to pass upon his life, liberty and property, there shall be no exclusion of his race, and no discrimination against them because of color, has been asserted in a number of cases.

So, where the laws of a particular locality or the charter of a particular railway corporation has provided that no person shall be excluded from the cars on account of color, we have held that this meant that persons of color should travel in the same car as white ones, and that the enactment was not satisfied by the company's providing cars assigned exclusively to people of color, though they were as good as those which they assigned exclusively to white persons.

Upon the other hand, where a statute of Louisiana required those engaged in the transportation of passengers among the States to give to all persons travelling within that State, upon vessels employed in that business, equal rights and privileges in all parts of the vessel, without distinction on account of race or color, and subjected to an action for damages the owner of such a vessel, who excluded colored passengers on account of their color from the cabin set aside by him for the use of whites, it was held to be so far as it applied to interstate commerce, unconstitutional and void. The court in this case, however, expressly disclaimed that it had anything whatever to do with the statute as a regulation of internal commerce, or affecting anything else than commerce among the States.

In the *Civil Rights case*, 109 U.S. 3, it was held that an act of Congress, entitling all persons within the jurisdiction of the United States to the full and equal enjoyment of the accommodations, advantages, facilities and privileges of inns, public conveyances, on land or water, theatres and other places of public amusement, and made applicable to citizens of every race and color, regardless of any previous condition of servitude, was unconstitutional and void, upon the ground that the Fourteenth Amendment was prohibitory upon the States only, and the legislation authorized to be adopted by Congress for enforcing it was not direct legislation on matters respecting which the States were prohibited from making or enforcing certain laws, or doing certain acts, but was corrective legislation, such as might be necessary or proper for counteracting and redressing the effect of such laws or acts. In delivering the opinion of the court Mr. Justice Bradley observed that the Fourteenth Amendment

> does not invest Congress with power to legislate upon subjects that are within the domain of state legislation; but to provide modes of relief against state legislation, or state action, of the kind referred to. It does not authorize Congress to create a code of municipal law for the regulation of private rights; but to provide modes of redress against the operation of state laws, and the action of state officers, executive or judicial, when these are subversive of the fundamental rights specified in the amendment. Positive rights and privileges are undoubtedly secured by the Fourteenth Amendment; but they are secured by way of prohibition against state laws and state proceedings affecting those rights and privileges, and by power given to Congress to legislate for the purpose of carrying such prohibition into effect; and such legislation must necessarily be predicated upon such supposed state laws or state proceedings, and be directed to the correction of their operation and effect.

Much nearer, and, indeed, almost directly in point, is the case of the *Louisville, New Orleans &c. Railway* v. *Mississippi*, 133 U. S. 587, wherein the railway company was indicted for a violation of a statute of Mississippi, enacting that all railroads carrying passengers should provide equal, but separate, accommodations for the white and colored races, by providing two or more passenger cars for each passenger train, or by dividing the passenger cars by a partition, so as to secure separate accommodations. The case was presented in a different aspect from the one under consideration, inasmuch as it was an indictment against the railway company for failing to provide the separate accommodations, but the question considered was the constitutionality of the law. In that case, the Supreme Court of Mississippi, 66 Mississippi, 662, had held that the statute applied solely to commerce within the State, and, that being the construction of the state statute by its highest court, was accepted as conclusive. "If it be a matter," said the court, p. 591, "respecting commerce wholly within a State, and not interfering with commerce between the States, then, obviously, there is no violation of the commerce clause of the Federal Constitution. . . . No question arises under this section, as to the power of the State to separate in different compartments interstate passengers, or affect, in any manner, the privileges and rights of such passengers. All that we can consider is, whether the State has the power to require that railroad trains within her limits shall have separate accommodations for the two races; that affecting only commerce within the State is no invasion of the power given to Congress by the commerce clause."

A like course of reasoning applies to the case under consideration, since the Supreme Court of Louisiana in the case of the *State ex rel. Abbott* v. *Hicks, Judge, et al.*, 41 La. Ann. 770, held that the statute in question did not apply to interstate passengers, but was confined in its application to passengers travelling exclusively within the borders of the State. The case was decided largely upon the authority of *Railway Co.* v. *State*, 66 Mississippi, 662, and affirmed by this court in 188 U. S. 587.

In the present case no question of interference with interstate commerce can possibly arise, since the East Louisiana Railway appears to have been purely a local line, with both its termini within the State of Louisiana.

While we think the enforced separation of the races, as applied to the internal commerce of the State, neither abridges the privileges or immunities of the colored man, deprives him of his property without due process of law, nor denies him the equal protection of the laws, within the meaning of the Fourteenth Amendment we are not prepared to say that the conductor, in assigning passengers to the coaches according to their race, does not act at his peril, or that the provision of the second section of the act, that denies to the passenger compensation in damages for a refusal to receive him into the coach in which he properly belongs, is a valid exercise of the legislative power. Indeed, we understand it to be conceded by the State's attorney, that such part of the act as exempts from liability the railway company and its officers is unconstitutional. The power to assign to a particular coach obviously implies the power to determine to which race the passenger belongs, as well as the power to determine who, under the laws of the particular State, is to be deemed a white, and who a colored person. This question, though indicated in the brief of the plaintiff in error, does not properly arise upon the record in this case, since the only issue made is as to the unconstitutionality of the act, so far as it requires the railway to provide separate accommodations, and the conductor to assign passengers according to their race.

It is claimed by the plaintiff in error that, in any mixed community, the reputation of belonging to the dominant race, in this instance the white race, is *property*, in the same sense that a right of action, or of inheritance, is property. Conceding this to be so, for the purposes of this case, we are unable to see how this statute deprives him of, or in any way affects his right to, such property. If he be a white man and assigned to a colored coach, he may have his action for damages against the company for being deprived of his so called property. Upon the other hand, if he be a colored man and be so assigned, he has been deprived of no property, since he is not lawfully entitled to the reputation of being a white man.

In this connection, it is also suggested by the learned counsel for the plaintiff in error that the same argument that will justify the state legislature in requiring railways to provide separate accommodations for the two races will also authorize them to require separate cars to be provided for people whose hair is of a certain color, or who are aliens, or who belong to certain nationalities, or to enact laws requiring colored people to walk upon one side of the street, and white people upon the other, or requiring white men's houses to be painted white, and colored men's black, or their vehicles or business signs to be of different colors, upon the theory that one side of the street is as good as the other, or that a house or vehicle of one color is as good as one of another color. The reply to all this is that every exercise of the police power must be reasonable, and extend only to such laws as are enacted in good faith for the promotion for the public good, and not for the annoyance or oppression of a particular class. Thus in *Yick Wo* v. *Hopkins,* 118 U.S. 356, it was held by this court that a municipal ordinance of the city of San Francisco, to regulate the carrying on of public laundries within the limits of the municipality, violated the provisions of the Constitution of the United States, if it conferred upon the municipal authorities arbitrary power, at their own will, and without regard to discretion, in the legal sense of the term, to give or withhold consent as to persons or places, without regard to the competency of the persons applying, or the propriety of the places selected for the carrying on of the business. It was held to be a covert attempt on the part of the municipality to make an arbitrary and unjust discrimination against the Chinese race. While this was the case of a municipal ordinance, a like principle has been held to apply to acts of a state legislature passed in the exercise of the police power.

So far, then, as a conflict with the Fourteenth Amendment is concerned, the case reduces itself to the question whether the statute of Louisiana is a reasonable regulation, and with respect to this there must necessarily be a large discretion on the part of the legislature. In determining the question of reasonableness it is at liberty to act with reference to the established usages, customs and traditions of the people, and with a view to the promotion of their comfort, and the preservation of the public peace and good order. Gauged by this standard, we cannot say that a law which authorizes or even requires the separation of the two races in public conveyances is unreasonable, or more obnoxious to the Fourteenth Amendment than the acts of Congress requiring separate schools for colored children in the District of Columbia, the constitutionality of which does not seem to have been questioned, or the corresponding acts of state legislatures.

We consider the underlying fallacy of the plaintiff's argument to consist in the assumption that the enforced separation of the two races stamps the colored race with a badge of inferiority. If this be so, it is not by reason of anything found in the act, but solely because the colored race chooses to put that construction upon it. The argument necessarily assumes that if, as has been more than once the case, and is not unlikely to be so again, the colored race should become the dominant power in the state legislature, and should enact a law in precisely similar terms, it would thereby relegate the white race to an inferior position. We imagine that the white race, at least, would not acquiesce in this assumption. The argument also assumes that social prejudices may be overcome by legislation, and that equal rights cannot be secured to the negro except by an enforced commingling of the two races. We cannot accept this proposition. If the two races are to meet upon terms of social equality, it must be the result of natural affinities, a mutual appreciation of each other's merits and a voluntary consent of individuals. As was said by the Court of Appeals of New York in *People* v. *Gallagher*, 93 N. Y. 438, 448, "this end can neither be accomplished nor promoted by laws which conflict with the general sentiment of the community upon whom they are designed to operate. When the government, therefore, has secured to each of its citizens equal rights before the law and equal opportunities for improvement and progress, it has accomplished the end for which it was organized and performed all of the functions respecting social advantages with which it is endowed." Legislation is powerless to eradicate racial instincts or to abolish distinctions based upon physical differences, and the attempt to do so can only result in accentuating the difficulties of the present situation. If the civil and political rights of both races be equal one cannot be inferior to the other civilly or politically. If one race be inferior to the other socially, the Constitution of the United States cannot put them upon the same plane.

It is true that the question of the proportion of colored blood necessary to constitute a colored person, as distinguished from a white person, is one upon which there is a difference of opinion in the different States, some holding that any visible admixture of black blood stamps the person as belonging to the colored race, others that it depends upon the preponderance of blood, and still others that the predominance of white blood must only be in the proportion of three fourths. But these are questions to be determined under the laws of each State and are not properly put in issue in this case. Under the allegations of his petition it may undoubtedly become a question of importance whether, under the laws of Louisiana, the petitioner belongs to the white or colored race.

The judgment of the court below is, therefore,

Affirmed.

15 Williams v. Mississippi

The "Mississippi Plan" was tested before the United States Supreme Court in *Williams* v. *Mississippi*, March 25, 1898. It was brought into court on the grounds that Henry Williams, a Negro of Washington County, Mississippi, had been denied his constitutional rights because he had been convicted of murder by an all-white jury. The Mississippi Supreme Court had denied Williams's contentions that under Sections 241–244 of the 1890 Mississippi Constitution he as a Negro was discriminated against. The Supreme Court justices reached an interesting conclusion based largely upon the grounds that white supremacists had cited in writing the discriminatory sections in the first place. The state constitution was not racially discriminatory in wording; rather, officials were given power to disqualify voters possessing *traits* associated with the Negro race. The Court based its affirmation of the Mississippi court decision on the additional grounds that, regardless of the broad powers the state constitution gave the registrar, the registrar was not involved in the Williams complaint anyway.*

AT JUNE TERM 1896 OF THE CIRCUIT COURT OF WASHINGTON County, Mississippi, the plaintiff in error was indicted by a grand jury composed entirely of white men for the crime of murder. On the 15th day of June he made a motion to quash the

* *Williams* v. *Mississippi*, 170 (U.S.), 215–225 (1898).

168

indictment, which was in substance as follows, omitting repetitions and retaining the language of the motion as nearly as possible:

Now comes the defendant in this cause, Henry Williams by name, and moves the Circuit Court of Washington County, Mississippi, to quash the indictment herein filed and upon which it is proposed to try him for the alleged offence of murder: (1) Because the laws by which the grand jury was selected, organized, summoned and charged, which presented the said indictment, are unconstitutional and repugnant to the spirit and letter of the Constitution of the United States of America, Fourteenth Amendment thereof, in this, that the Constitution prescribes the qualifications of electors, and that to be a juror one must be an elector; that the Constitution also requires that those offering to vote shall produce to the election officers satisfactory evidence that they have paid their taxes; that the legislature is to provide means for enforcing the Constitution, and in the exercise of this authority enacted section 3643, also section 3644 of 1892, which respectively provide that the election commissioners shall appoint three election managers, and that the latter shall be judges of the qualifications of electors, and are required "to examine on oath any person duly registered and offering to vote touching his qualifications as an elector." And then the motion states that "the registration roll is not *prima facie* evidence of an elector's right to vote, but the list of those persons having been passed upon by the various district election managers of the county to compose the registration book of voters as named in section 2358 of said code of 1892, and that there was no registration books of voters prepared for the guidance of said officers of said county at the time said grand jury was drawn." It is further alleged that there is no statute of the State providing for the procurement of any registration books of voters of said county, and (it is alleged in detail) the terms of the constitution and the section of the code mentioned, and the discretion given to the officers, "is but a scheme on the part of the framers of that constitution to abridge the suffrage of the colored electors in the State of Mississippi on account of the previous condition of servitude by granting a discretion to the said officers as mentioned in the several sections of the constitution of the State and the statute of the State adopted under the said constitution, the use of said discretion can be and has been used in the said Washington County to the end complained of." After some detail to the same effect, it is further alleged that the constitutional convention was composed of 134 members, only one of whom was a negro; that under prior laws there were 190,000 colored voters and 69,000 white voters; the makers of the new constitution arbitrarily refused to submit it to the voters of the State for approval, but ordered it adopted, and an election to be held immediately under it, which election was held under the election ordinances of the said constitution in November, 1891, and the legislature assembled in 1892 and enacted the statutes complained of, for the purpose to discriminate aforesaid, and but for that the "defendant's race would have been represented impartially on the grand jury which presented this indictment," and hence he is deprived of the equal protection of the laws of the State. It is further alleged that the State has not reduced its representation in Congress, and generally for the reasons aforesaid, and because the indictment should have been returned under the constitution of 1869 and statute of 1889 it is null and void. The motion concludes as follows: "Further, the defendant is a citizen of the United States, and for the many reasons herein named asks that the indictment be quashed, and he be recognized to appear at the next term of the court."

This motion was accompanied by four affidavits, subscribed and sworn to before the clerk of the court, on June 15, 1896, to wit:

1st. An affidavit of the defendant, "who, being duly sworn, deposes and says that the facts set forth in the foregoing motion are true to the best of his knowledge, of the language of the constitution and the statute of the State mentioned in said motion, and upon information and belief as to the other facts, and that the affiant verily believes the information to be reliable and true."

2d. Another affidavit of the defendant, "who, being first duly sworn, deposes and says: That he has heard the motion to quash the indictment herein read, and that he thoroughly understands the same, and that the facts therein stated are true, to the best of his knowledge and belief. As to the existence of the several sections of the state constitution, and the several sections of the state statute, mentioned in said motion to quash, further affiant states: That the facts stated in said motion, touching the manner and method peculiar to the said election, by which the delegates to said constitutional convention were elected, and the purpose for which said objectionable provisions were enacted, and the fact that the said discretion complained of as aforesaid has abridged the suffrage of the number mentioned therein, for the purpose named therein; all such material allegations are true, to the best of the affiant's knowledge and belief, and the fact of the race and color of the prisoner in this cause, and the race and color of the voters of the State whose elective franchise is abridged as alleged therein, and the fact that they who are discriminated against, as aforesaid, are citizens of the United States, and that prior to the adoption of the said constitution and said statute the said State was represented in Congress by seven Representatives in the lower House, and two Senators, and that since the adoption of the said objectionable laws there has been no reduction of said representation in Congress. All allegations herein, as stated in said motion aforesaid, are true to the best of affiant's knowledge and belief."

3d. An affidavit of John H. Dixon, "who, being duly sworn, deposes and says that he had heard the motion to quash the indictment filed in the *Henry Williams case,* and thoroughly understands the same, and that he has also heard the affidavit sworn to by said Henry Williams, carefully read to him, and thoroughly understands the same. And in the same manner the facts are sworn to in the said affidavit, and the same facts alleged therein upon information and belief, are hereby adopted as in all things the sworn allegations of affiant, and the facts alleged therein, as upon knowledge and belief, are made hereby the allegations of affiant upon his knowledge and belief."

4th. An affidavit of C. J. Jones, "who, being duly sworn, deposes and says that he has read carefully the affidavit filed in the *John Dixon case* sworn to by him (said C. J. Jones), and that he, said affiant, thoroughly understands the same, and adopts the said allegations therein as his deposition in this case upon hearing this motion to quash the indictment herein, and that said allegations are in all things correct and true as therein alleged."

The motion was denied and the defendant excepted. A motion was then made to remove the cause to the United States Circuit Court, based substantially on the same grounds as the motion to quash the indictment. This was also denied and an exception reserved.

The accused was tried by a jury composed entirely of white men and convicted. A motion for a new trial was denied, and the accused sentenced to be hanged. An appeal to the Supreme Court was taken and the judgment of the court below was affirmed.

The following are the assignments of error:

1. The trial court erred in denying motion to quash the indictment, and petition for removal.

2. The trial court erred in denying motion for new trial, and pronouncing death penalty under the verdict.

3. The Supreme Court erred in affirming the judgment of the trial court.

Mr. Justice McKunna, after stating the case, delivered the opinion of the court.

The question presented is, are the provisions of the constitution of the State of Mississippi and the laws enacted to enforce the same repugnant to the Fourteenth Amendment of the Constitution of the United States? That amendment and its effect upon the rights of the colored race have been considered by this court in a number of cases, and it has been uniformly held that the Constitution of the United States, as amended, forbids, so far as civil and political rights are concerned, discriminations by the General Government, or by the States, against any citizen because of his race; but it has also been held, in a very recent case, to justify a removal from a state court to a Federal court of a cause in which such rights are alleged to be denied, that such denial must be the result of the constitution or laws of the State, not of the administration of them. Nor can the conduct of a criminal trial in a state court be reviewed by this court unless the trial is had under some statute repugnant to the Constitution of the United States, or was so conducted as to deprive the accused of some right or immunity secured to him by that instrument. Upon this general subject this court in *Gibson* v. *Mississippi*, 162 U. S. 566, 581, after referring to previous cases, said: "But those cases were held to have also decided that the Fourteenth Amendment was broader than the provisions of section 641 of the Revised Statutes; that since that section authorized the removal of a criminal prosecution before trial, it did not embrace a case in which a right is denied by judicial action during a trial, or in the sentence, or in the mode of executing the sentence; that for such denials arising from judicial action after a trial commenced, the remedy lay in the revisory power of the higher courts of the State, and ultimately in the power of review which this court may exercise over their judgments whenever rights, privileges or immunities claimed under the Constitution or laws of the United States are withheld or violated; and that the denial or inability to enforce in the judicial tribunals of the States rights secured by any law providing for the equal civil rights of citizens of the United States to which section 641 refers and on account of which a criminal prosecution may be removed from a state court, is primarily, if not exclusively, a denial of such rights or an inability to enforce them resulting from the constitution or laws of the State rather than a denial first made manifest at or during the trial of the case."

It is not asserted by plaintiff in error that either the constitution of the State or its laws discriminate in terms against the negro race, either as to the elective franchise or the privilege or duty of sitting on juries. These results, if we understand plaintiff in error, are alleged to be effected by the powers vested in certain administrative officers.

Plaintiff in error says:

Section 241 of the constitution of 1890 prescribes the qualifications for electors; that residence in the State for two years, one year in the precinct of the applicant, must be effected; that he is twenty-one years or over of age, having paid all taxes legally due of him for two years prior to 1st day of February of the year he offers to vote. Not having been convicted of theft, arson, rape, receiving money or goods under false pretences, bigamy, embezzlement.

Section 242 of the constitution provides the mode of registration. That the legislature shall provide by law for registration of all persons entitled to vote at any election, and that all persons offering to register shall take the oath; that they are not disqualified for voting by reason of any of the crimes named in the constitution of this State; that they will truly answer all questions propounded to them concerning their antecedents so far as they relate to the applicant's right to vote, and also as to their residence before their citizenship in the district in which such application for registration is made. The court readily sees the scheme. If the applicant swears, as he must do, that he is not disqualified by reason of the crimes specified, and that he has effected the required residence, what right has he to answer all questions as to his former residence? Section 244 of the constitution requires that the applicant for registration after January, 1892, shall be able to read any section of the constitution, or he shall be able to understand the same (being any section of the organic law), or give a reasonable interpretation thereof. Now we submit that these provisions vest in the administrative officers the full power, under section 242, to ask all sorts of vain, impertinent questions, and it is with that officer to say whether the questions relate to the applicant's right to vote; this officer can reject whomsoever he chooses, and register whomsoever he chooses, for he is vested by the constitution with that power. Under section 244 it is left with the administrative officer to determine whether the applicant reads, understands or interprets the section of the constitution designated. The officer is the sole judge of the examination of the applicant, and even though the applicant be qualified, it is left with the officer to so determine; and the said officer can refuse him registration.

To make the possible dereliction of the officers the dereliction of the constitution and laws, the remarks of the Supreme Court of the State are quoted by plaintiff in error as to their intent. The constitution provides for the payment of a poll tax, and by a section of the code its payment cannot be compelled by a seizure and sale of property. We gather from the brief of counsel that its payment is a condition of the right to vote, and in a case to test whether its payment was or was not optional, *Ratcliff* v. *Beale*, 20 So. Rep. 865, the Supreme Court of the State said: "Within the field of permissible action under the limitations imposed by the Federal Constitution, the convention swept the field of expedients, to obstruct the exercise of suffrage by the negro race." And further the court said, speaking of the negro race: "By reason of its previous condition of servitude and dependencies, this race had acquired or accentuated certain peculiarities of habit, of temperament, and of character, which clearly distinguished it as a race from the whites. A patient, docile people; but careless, landless, migratory within narrow limits, without forethought; and its criminal members given to furtive offences, rather than the robust crimes of the whites. Restrained by the Federal Constitution from discriminating against the negro race, the convention discriminates against its characteristics, and the offences to which its criminal members are prone." But nothing tangible can be deduced from this. If weakness were to be taken advantage of, it was to be done "within the field of permissible action under the limitations imposed by the Federal Constitution," and the means of it were alleged characteristics of the negro race, not the administration of the law by officers of the State. Besides, the operation of the constitution and laws is not limited by their language or effects to one race. They reach weak and vicious white men as well as weak and vicious black men, and whatever is sinister in their intention, if anything, can be prevented by both races by the exertion of that duty which voluntarily pays taxes and refrains from crime.

It cannot be said, therefore, that the denial of the equal protection of the laws arises primarily from the constitution and laws of Mississippi, nor is there any sufficient allegation of an evil and discriminating administration of them. The only allegation is ". . . by granting a discretion to the said officers, as mentioned in the several sections of the constitution of the State, and the statute of the State adopted under the said constitution, the use of which discretion can be and has been used by said officers in the said Washington County to the end here complained of, to wit, the abridgment of the elective franchise of the colored voters of Washington County, that such citizens are denied the right to be selected as jurors to serve in the Circuit Court of the county, and that this denial to them of the right to equal protection and benefits of the laws of the State of Mississippi on account of their color and race, resulting from the exercise of the discretion partial to the white citizens, is in accordance with and the purpose and intent of the framers of the present constitution of said State. . . ."

It will be observed that there is nothing direct and definite in this allegation either as to means or time as affecting the proceedings against the accused. There is no charge against the officers to whom is submitted the selection of grand or petit jurors, or those who procure the lists of the jurors. There is an allegation of the purpose of the convention to disfranchise citizens of the colored race, but with this we have no concern, unless the purpose is executed by the constitution or laws or by those who administer them. If it is done in the latter way, how or by what means should be shown. We gather from the statements of the motion that certain officers are invested with discretion in making up lists of electors, and that this discretion can be and has been exercised against the colored race, and from these lists jurors are selected. The Supreme Court of Mississippi, however, decided, in a case presenting the same questions as the one at bar, "that jurors are not selected from or with reference to any lists furnished by such election officers."

16 Berea College v. Kentucky

The Kentucky General Assembly enacted a law in 1904 known as the "Day Law" which forbade co-racial education.[1] Berea College had from its founding in 1854 accepted Negroes,[2] and in 1904 it was the only co-racial school in Kentucky. The college appealed the law to the Kentucky Court of Appeals and then to the United States Supreme Court. The Supreme Court, following the precedent of *Plessy* v. *Ferguson*, refused to decide the Berea issue on the basis of co-racial education, but chose to evade this issue and to confine its consideration to the very narrow question of whether or not the state had the right to prescribe conditions for the operation of institutions to which it granted charters. Thus in 1908 the Supreme Court might well have taken the step which it took in 1954 by deciding against the racially discriminatory nature of the law. With *Plessy* v. *Ferguson* and *Berea College* v. *Kentucky*, the South now had two powerful precedents for ordering the maintenance of separate schools for Negroes and whites. This particular case was in many ways an even more important precedent than the Ferguson case because the Court did discuss briefly desegregating the races, an issue which had not risen specifically in the former case.[3]

[1] *Acts*, Kentucky General Assembly (Frankfort, 1904), Chap. 85, pp. 181–182.
[2] Elisabeth S. Peck, *Berea's First Century, 1855–1955* (Lexington: University of Kentucky Press, 1955), 49–53.
[3] *Berea College* v. *Kentucky*, 211 (U.S.), 45–58 (1908).

THAT THE LEGISLATURE OF KENTUCKY DESIRED TO SEPARATE THE teaching of white and colored children may be conceded, but it by no means follows that it would not have enforced the separation so far as it could do so, even though it could not make it effective under all circumstances. In other words, it is not at all unreasonable to believe that the legislature, although advised beforehand of the constitutional question, might have prohibited all organizations and corporations under its control from teaching white and colored children together, and thus made at least uniform official action. The rule of construction in questions of this nature is stated by Chief Justice Shaw in *Warren* v. *Mayor of Charlestown*, 2 Gray, 84, quoted approvingly by this court in *Allen* v. *Louisiana*, 103, U.S. 80–84.

> But if they are so mutually connected with and dependent on each other, as conditions, considerations or compensations for each other as to warrant a belief that the legislature intended them as a whole, and that if all could not be carried into effect, the legislature would not pass the residue independently, and some parts are unconstitutional, all the provisions which are thus dependent, conditional or connected, must fall with them.
>
> . . . As one section of a statute may be repugnant to the Constitution without rendering the whole act void, so, one provision of a section may be invalid by reason of its not conforming to the Constitution, while all the other provisions may be subject to no constitutional infirmity. One part may stand, while another will fall, unless the two are so connected or dependent on each other in subject-matter, meaning or purpose, that the good cannot remain without the bad. The point is, not whether the parts are contained in the same section for, the distribution into sections is purely artificial; but whether they are essentially and inseparably connected in substance—whether the provisions are so interdependent that one cannot operate without the other.

Further, inasmuch as the Court of Appeals considered the act separable, and while sustaining it as an entirety gave an independent reason which applies only to corporations, it is obvious that it recognized the force of the suggestions we have made. And when a state statute is so interpreted this court should hesitate before it holds that the Supreme Court of the

State did not know what was the thought of the legislature in its enactment.

. . . While the terms of the present charter are not given in the record, yet it was admitted on the trial that the defendant was a corporation organized and incorporated under the general statutes of the State of Kentucky, and of course the state courts, as well as this court on appeal, take judicial notice of those statutes. Further, in the brief of counsel for the defendant is given a history of the incorporation proceedings, together with the charters. From that it appears that Berea College was organized under the authority of an act for the incorporation of voluntary associations, approved March 9, 1854, . . . which act was amended by an act of March 10, 1856, . . . and which in terms reserved to the General Assembly "the right to alter or repeal the charter of any associations formed under the provisions of this act, and the act to which this act is an amendment, at any time hereafter." After the constitution of 1891 was adopted by the State of Kentucky, and on June 10, 1899, the college was reincorporated under the provisions of chap. 32, art. 8, Ky.Stat., . . . the charter defining its business in these words: "Its object is the education of all persons who may attend its institution of learning at Berea, and, in the language of the original articles, 'to promote the cause of Christ.'" The constitution of 1891 provided in §3 of the bill of rights that "Every grant of a franchise, privilege or exemption shall remain, subject to revocation, alteration or amendment." So that the full power of amendment was reserved to the legislature.

It is undoubtedly true that the reserved power to alter or amend is subject to some limitations, and that under the guise of an amendment a new contract may not aways be enforceable upon the corporation or the stockholders; but it is settled "that a power reserved to the legislature to alter, amend or repeal a charter authorizes it to make any alteration or amendment of a charter granted subject to it, which will not defeat or substantially impair the object of the grant, or any rights vested under it, and which the legislature may deem necessary to secure either that object or any public right.

Construing the statute, the Court of Appeals held that "if the same school taught the different races at different times, though at the same place or at different places at the same time it would not be unlawful." Now, an amendment to the original charter, which does not destroy the power of the college to furnish education to all persons, but which simply separates them by time or place of instruction, cannot be said to "defeat or substantially impair the object of the grant." The language of the statute is not in terms an amendment, yet its effect is an amendment, and it would be resting too much on mere form to hold that a statute which in effect works a change in the terms of the charter is not to be considered as an amendment, because not so designated. The act itself, being separable, is to be read as though it in one section prohibited any person, in another section any corporation, and in a third any association of persons to do the acts named. . . .

There is no dispute as to the facts. That the act does not violate the constitution of Kentucky is settled by the decision of its highest court, and the single question for our consideration is whether it conflicts with the Federal Constitution. The Court of Appeals discussed at some length the general power of the State in respect to the separation of the two races. It also ruled that "the right to teach white and negro children in a private school at the same time and place is not a property right. Besides, appellant as a corporation created by this State has no natural right to teach at all. Its right to teach is such as the State sees fit to give to it. The State may withhold it altogether, or qualify it."

Upon this we remark that when a state court decides a case upon two grounds, one Federal and the other non-Federal, this court will not disturb the judgment if the non-Federal ground, fairly construed, sustains the decision.

Again, the decision by a state court of the extent and limitation of the powers conferred by the State upon one of its own corporations is of a purely local nature. In creating a corporation a State may withhold powers which may be exercised by and cannot be denied to an individual. It is under no obligation to treat both alike. In granting corporate powers the legislature may deem that the best interests of the State would be subserved by some restriction, and the corporation may not plead that in spite of the restriction it has more or greater powers because the citizen has. "The granting of such right or privilege [the right or privilege to be a corporation] rests entirely in the discretion of the State, and, of course, when granted, may be accompanied with such conditions as its legislature may judge most befitting to its interests and policy."

The act of 1904 forbids "any person, corporation or association of persons to maintain or operate any college," etc. Such a statute may conflict with the Federal Constitution in denying to individuals powers which they may rightfully exercise, and yet, at the same time, be valid as to a corporation created by the State.

It may be said that the Court of Appeals sustained the validity of this section of the statute, both against individuals and corporations. It ruled that the legislation was within the power of the State, and that the State might rightfully thus restrain all individuals, corporations and associations. But it is unnecessary for us to consider anything more than the question of its validity as applied to corporations.

The statute is clearly separable and may be valid as to one class while invalid as to another. Even if it were conceded that its assertion of power over individuals cannot be sustained, still it must be upheld so far as it restrains corporations.

There is no force in the suggestion that the statute, although it substantially declares that any authority given by previous charters to instruct the two races at the same time and in the same place is forbidden, and that prohibition being a departure from the terms of the original charter in this case may properly be adjudged an amendment.

Again, it is insisted that the Court of Appeals did not regard the legislation as making an amendment, because another prosecution instituted against the same corporation under the fourth section of the act, which makes it a misdemeanor to teach pupils of the two races in the same institution, even although one race is taught in one branch and another in another branch, provided the two branches are within twenty-five miles of each other, was held could not be sustained, the court saying: "This last section, we think, violates the limitations upon the police power: it is unreasonable and oppressive." But while so ruling it also held that this section could be ignored and that the remainder of the act was complete notwithstanding. Whether the reasoning of the court concerning the fourth section be satisfactory or not is immaterial, for no question of its validity is presented, and the Court of Appeals, while striking it down, sustained the balance of the act. We need concern ourselves only with the inquiry whether the first section can be upheld as coming within the power of a State over its own corporate creatures.

We are of opinion, for reasons stated, that it does come within that power, and on this ground the judgment of the Court of Appeals of Kentucky is

Affirmed.

17 Missouri ex rel. Gaines v. Canada

In preparing the majority opinion in the landmark Gaines case, Mr. Chief Justice Charles Evans Hughes wrote one of the clearest statements of the position of the Negro in higher education in the South prior to 1938. He outlined in considerable detail the essential issue: the processes by which Negroes were denied access to professional education in their own states. At the same time the Court alluded to the inadequacy of funds with which to send Negroes into other state professional schools where there would be no discrimination.

Some of the states undertook to avoid co-racial educational classes by establishing "paper" schools in which they promised at some future date to provide training, in law especially. In Missouri, Justice Hughes and an overwhelming majority of the Court said there was limited demand for law among Negro students, and because of this it would be impossible to establish and maintain a Negro law school of comparable quality and prestige with that of the University of Missouri. At this point, efforts to discriminate against Negroes involved segregationists in their most difficult bind. By their own admissions, makeshift efforts to provide professional training could never be more than a gesture, and in a final analysis could not meet *Plessy* v. *Ferguson*'s demands of "separate but equal" opportunities. Thus the 1938 decision in the Gaines case began the toppling of the segregationists' house of cards, and portended the *Brown* v. *Board of Education* decision in 1954. Now the issue of racial discrimination was firmly conjoined in the Missouri case. The first dissent below was written by several members of the Court. In a separate opinion

Mr. Justice John Clark McReynolds dissented on the grounds that segregation of the races in classrooms in Missouri had long been a fixed policy. He contended that education was a matter for the state and that the Supreme Court was not within its rights to upset such a policy. He also contended that the Supreme Court of Missouri well understood the implications of upsetting the legislative policy of that state and had refused to find for the plaintiff.°

STATEMENT OF FACTS

1. The State of Missouri provides separate schools and universities for whites and negroes. At the state university, attended by whites, there is a course in law; at the Lincoln University, attended by negroes, there is as yet none, but it is the duty of the curators of that institution to establish one there whenever in their opinion this shall be necessary and practicable, and pending such development, they are authorized to arrange for legal education of Missouri negroes, and to pay the tuition charges therefor, at law schools in adjacent States where negroes are accepted and where the training is equal to that obtainable at the Missouri State University. Pursuant to the State's policy of separating the races in its educational institutions, the curators of the state university refused to admit a negro as a student in the law school there because of his race; whereupon he sought a mandamus, in the state courts, which was denied. *Held:*

(1) That inasmuch as the curators of the state university represented the State, in carrying out its policy, their action in denying the negro admission to the law school was state action, within the meaning of the Fourteenth Amendment.

(2) The action of the State in furnishing legal education within the State to whites while not furnishing legal education within the State to negroes, was a discrimination repugnant to the Fourteenth Amendment.

If a State furnishes higher education to white residents, it is bound to furnish substantially equal advantages to negro residents, though not necessarily in the same schools.

° *Missouri ex rel. Gaines* v. *Canada,* 305 U.S. 334–337 (1938).

(3) The unconstitutional discrimination is not avoided by the purpose of the State to establish a law school for negroes whenever necessary and practicable in the opinion of the curators of the University provided for negroes.

(4) Nor are the requirements of the equal protection clause satisfied by the opportunities afforded by Missouri to its negro citizens for legal education in other States.

The basic consideration here is not as to what sort of opportunities other States provide, or whether they are as good as those in Missouri, but as to what opportunities Missouri itself furnishes to white students and denies to negroes solely upon the ground of color. The admissibility of laws separating the races in the enjoyment of privileges afforded by the State rests wholly upon the equality of the privileges which the laws give to the separated groups within the State. By the operation of the laws of Missouri a privilege has been created for white law students which is denied to negroes by reason of their race. The white resident is afforded legal education within the State; the negro resident having the same qualifications is refused it there and must go outside the State to obtain it. That is a denial of the equality of legal right to the enjoyment of the privilege which the State has set up, and the provision for the payment of tuition fees in another State does not remove the discrimination.

(5) The obligation of the State to give the protection of equal laws can be performed only where its laws operate, that is, within its own jurisdiction. It is there that the equality of legal right must be maintained. That obligation is imposed by the Constitution upon the States severally as governmental entities —each responsible for its own laws establishing the rights and duties of persons within its borders.

(6) The fact that there is but a limited demand in Missouri for the legal education of negroes does not excuse the discrimination in favor of whites.

(7) Inasmuch as the discrimination may last indefinitely— so long as the curators find it unnecessary and impracticable to provide facilities for the legal education of negroes within the State, the alternative of attendance at law schools in other States

being provided meanwhile—it can not be excused as a temporary discrimination.

The state court decided this case upon the merits of the federal question, and not upon the propriety of remedy by mandamus.

THE DISSENT

The Supreme Court of Missouri has held that the laws of Missouri do not entitle the petitioner to be admitted as a student in the University of Missouri, and that those laws provide for the separation of the white and negro races for the purpose of higher education. The second part of the decision, fully recognizing petitioner's constitutional right to equal facilities for legal education, finds as a fact that the State has accorded him equal facilities—which finding of fact, supported as it is by strong and uncontradicted evidence, is binding upon this Court. The absence of a substantial federal question is manifest.

Petitioner refused to avail himself of the facilities for a legal education provided by the State. If he had applied to the Lincoln University curators for a legal education, it is to be presumed that they would have given it to him in accordance with their mandatory duty under the Act. His refusal to avail himself of his legal rights is fatal to his case.

The State of Missouri has not denied petitioner the equal protection of the laws by excluding him from the School of Law of the University of Missouri.

Separation of the white and negro races for purposes of education does not infringe the rights of either race guaranteed by the Fourteenth Amendment.

Social equality is not a legal question and can not be settled by law or by the judgments of courts.

The facilities for legal education available to petitioner under the Lincoln University Act are substantially equal to the facilities afforded white students in the School of Law of the University of Missouri.

In separating the races, and in determining the particular

facilities to be used by the two races, the State is allowed a large measure of discretion; and the courts will not interfere with the exercise of that discretion as unconstitutional, except in case of a very clear and unmistakable disregard of rights secured by the Constitution of the United States.

The Lincoln University board of curators are not merely authorized, but are required, to reorganize the institution so that it shall afford opportunity to negroes equal to that accorded to white students; and, pending the full development of Lincoln University, are required, to arrange for the attendance of negro residents of the State at the university of any adjacent State, to take any course of study provided at the University of Missouri but not at Lincoln University; and they are not merely authorized, but are required, to pay the reasonable tuition fees for such attendance. The duty to do these things is mandatory and peremptory.

The responsibility and duty to carry out this plan has been placed by law—not upon these respondents, the curators of the University of Missouri—but upon the curators of Lincoln University.

If petitioner pursues his legal rights and makes application to the Lincoln University curators for an education in the law, it will then become their mandatory duty (a) to establish a school of law in Lincoln University and to admit petitioner as a student therein; and (b) pending that, and as a temporary matter, to arrange for the attendance of petitioner in one or another of the schools of law already established in the Universities of Kansas, Nebraska, Iowa or Illinois (all of which admit negroes), and to pay his tuition fees while he is attending such school.

Substantial equality and not identity of school facilities is what is guaranteed by the Fourteenth Amendment.

The fact that in order to avail himself of legal education in any one of the four law schools in adjacent states, the petitioner (a grown man) would be put to the necessity of traveling farther from his home in St. Louis than the distance from St. Louis to Columbia (where the University of Missouri is located), is a mere matter of inconvenience, which must necessarily arise as an incident to any classification or any school system; and the court below held that this furnishes no substantial ground of complaint by petitioner. Petitioner's expense of travel to any of these adjacent state universities would be no greater than the traveling expense of students living in various parts of Missouri, who attend the University of Missouri at Columbia.

The question of the constitutionality of the provision for out-of-state instruction is, strictly speaking, not presented for review, since petitioner never made any application to Lincoln University curators for the establishment of a law course in that institution; and, therefore, it is impossible to know whether the curators of Lincoln University, had he knocked at the door, would have immediately established a law course there, rendering it unnecessary for him to go out-of-state for a legal education.

Mandamus against respondents was not a proper remedy, because petitioner must exhaust his administrative remedies before seeking extraordinary relief; and this he failed to do. Petitioner is in no position to appeal to the courts for any remedy, and certainly not for mandamus, to compel the board of curators of Lincoln University to provide him with the opportunity for legal education which he says he desires, but which he has never requested from the authorities charged with the duty to provide it for him. A fortiori, he could not appeal to the courts for mandamus to compel the board of curators of the University of Missouri to provide him with a legal education which he has not requested from the authorities charged with the duty to provide it for him.

THE DECISION

Mr. Chief Justice Hughes delivered the opinion of the Court.

Petitioner Lloyd Gaines, a negro was refused admission to the School of Law at the State University of Missouri. Asserting that this refusal constituted a denial by the State of the equal protection of the laws in violation of the Fourteenth Amendment of the Federal Constitution, petitioner brought this action for mandamus to compel the curators of the University to admit him. On final hearing, an alternative writ was quashed and a peremptory writ was denied by the Circuit Court. The Supreme Court of the State affirmed the judgment. We granted certiorari, October 10, 1938.

Petitioner is a citizen of Missouri. In August, 1935, he was graduated with the degree of Bachelor of Arts at the Lincoln University, an institution maintained by the State of Missouri for the higher education of negroes. That University has no law school. Upon the filing of his application for admission to the law school of the University of Missouri, the registrar advised him to communicate with the president of Lincoln University and the latter directed petitioner's attention to § 9622 of the Revised Statutes of Missouri (1929), providing as follows:

> Sec. 9622. *May arrange for attendance at university of any adjacent state—Tuition fees.*—Pending the full development of the Lincoln university, the board of curators shall have the authority to arrange for the attendance of negro residents of the state of Missouri at the university of any adjacent state to take any course or to study any subjects provided for at the state university of Missouri, and which are not taught at the Lincoln university and to pay the reasonable tuition fees for such attendance; *provided* that whenever the board of curators deem it advisable they shall have the power to open any necessary school or department.

Petitioner was advised to apply to the State Superintendent of Schools for aid under that statute. It was admitted on the trial that petitioner's "work and credits at the Lincoln University would qualify him for admission to the School of Law of the University of Missouri if he were found otherwise eligible." He was refused admission upon the ground that it was "contrary to the constitution, laws and public policy of the State to admit a negro as a student in the University of Missouri." It appears that there are schools of law in connection with the state universities of four adjacent States, Kansas, Nebraska, Iowa and Illinois, where nonresident negroes are admitted.

The clear and definite conclusions of the state court in construing the pertinent state legislation narrow the issue. The action of the curators, who are representatives of the State in the management of the state university, must be regarded as state action. The state constituion provides that separate free public schools shall be established for the education of children of African descent, and by statute separate high school facilities are supplied for colored students equal to those provided for white students. While there is no express constitutional provision requiring that the white and negro races be separated for the purpose of higher education, the state court on a comprehensive review of the state statutes held that it was intended to separate the white and negro races for that purpose also. Referring in particular to Lincoln University, the court deemed it to be clear "that the Legislature intended to bring the Lincoln University up to the standard of the University of Missouri, and give to the whites and negroes an equal opportunity for higher education—the whites at the University of Missouri, and the negroes at Lincoln University." Further, the court concluded that the provisions of § 9622 (above quoted) to the effect that negro residents "may attend the university of any adjacent State with their tuition paid, pending the full development of Lincoln University," made it evident "that the Legislature did not intend that negroes and whites should attend the same university in this State." In that view it necessarily followed that the curators of the University of Missouri acted in accordance with the policy of the State in denying petitioner admission to its School of Law upon the sole ground of his race.

In answering petitioner's contention that this discrimination constituted a denial of his constitutional right, the state court has fully recognized the obligation of the State to provide negroes with advantages for higher education substantially equal to the advantages afforded to white students. The State has sought to fulfill that obligation by furnishing equal facilities in separate schools, a method the validity of which has been sustained by our decisions. *Plessy* v. *Ferguson,* 163 U.S. 537, 544; *McCabe* v. *Atchison, T. & S. F. Ry. Co.*, 235 U.S. 151, 160; *Gong Lum* v. *Rice*, 275 U.S. 78, 85, 86. Compare *Cumming* v. *Board of Education,* 175 U.S. 528, 544, 545. Respondents' counsel have appropriately emphasized the special solicitude of the State for the higher education of negroes as shown in the establishment of Lincoln University, a state institution well conducted on a plane with the University of Missouri so far as the offered courses are concerned. It is said that Missouri is a pioneer in that field and is the only State in the Union which has established a separate university for negroes on the same basis as the state university for white students. But, commendable as is that action, the fact remains that instruction in law for negroes is not now afforded by the State, either at Lincoln University or elsewhere within the State, and that the State excludes negroes from the advantages of the law school it has established at the University of Missouri.

It is manifest that this discrimination, if not relieved by the provisions we shall presently discuss, would constitute a denial of equal protection. That was the conclusion of the Court of Appeals of Maryland in circumstances substantially similar in that aspect. *University of Maryland* v. *Murray,* 169 Md. 478, 182 A. 590. It there appeared that the State of Maryland had "undertaken the function of education in the law" but had "omitted students of one race from the only adequate provision made for it, and omitted them solely because of their color"; that if those students were to be offered "equal treatment in the performance of the function, they must, at present, be admitted to the one school provided." A provision for scholarships to enable negroes to attend colleges outside the State, mainly for the purpose of professional studies, was found to be inadequate and the question, "whether with aid in any amount it is sufficient to send the negroes outside the State for legal education," the Court of Appeals found it unnecessary to discuss. Accordingly, a writ of mandamus to admit the applicant was issued to the officers and regents of the University of Maryland as the agents of the State entrusted with the conduct of that institution.

The Supreme Court of Missouri in the instant case has distinguished the decision in Maryland upon the grounds—(1) that in Missouri, but not in Maryland, there is "a legislative declaration of a purpose to establish a law school for negroes at Lincoln University whenever necessary or practical"; and (2) that, "pending the establishment of such a school, adequate provision has been made for the legal education of negro students in recognized schools outside of this State."

As to the first ground, it appears that the policy of establishing a law school at Lincoln University has not yet ripened into an actual establishment, and it cannot be said that a mere declaration of purpose, still unfulfilled, is enough. The provision for legal education at Lincoln is at present entirely lacking. Respondents' counsel urge that if, on the date when petitioner applied for admission to the University of Missouri, he had instead applied to the curators of Lincoln University it would have been their duty to establish a law school; that this "agency of the State," to which he should have applied, was "specifically charged with the mandatory duty to furnish him what he seeks." We do not read the opinion of the Supreme Court as construing the state statute to impose such a "mandatory duty" as the argument seems to assert. The state court quoted the language of § 9618, R.S. Mo. 1929, set forth in the margin, making it the mandatory duty of the board of curators to establish a law school in Lincoln University "whenever necessary and practicable in their opinion." This qualification of their duty, explicitly stated in the statute, manifestly leaves it to the judgment of the curators to decide when it will be necessary and practicable to establish a law school, and the state court so construed the statute. Emphasizing the discretion of the curators, the court said:

> The statute was enacted in 1921. Since its enactment no negro, not even appellant, has applied to Lincoln University for a law education. This fact demonstrates the wisdom of the legislature in leaving it to the judgment of the board of curators to determine when it would be necessary or practicable to establish a law school for negroes at Lincoln University. Pending that time adequate provision is made for the legal education of negroes in the university of some adjacent State, as heretofore pointed out.

The state court has not held that it would have been the duty of the curators to establish a law school at Lincoln University for the petitioner on his application. Their duty, as the court defined it, would have been either to supply a law school at Lincoln University as provided in § 9618 or to furnish him the opportunity to obtain his legal training in another State as provided in § 9622. Thus the law left the curators free to adopt the latter course. The state court has not ruled or intimated that their failure or refusal to establish a law school for a very few students, still less for one student, would have been an abuse of the discretion with which the curators were entrusted. And, apparently, it was because of that discretion, and of the postponement which its exercise in accordance with the terms of the statute would entail until necessity and practicability appeared, that the state court considered and upheld as adequate the provision for the legal education of negroes, who were citizens of Missouri, in the universities of adjacent States. We may put on one side respondent's contention that there were funds available at Lincoln University for the creation of a law department and the suggestions with respect to the number of instructors who would be needed for that purpose and the cost of supplying them. The president of Lincoln University did not advert to the existence or prospective use of funds for that purpose when he advised petitioner to apply to the State Superintendent of Schools for aid under § 9622. At best, the evidence to which argument as to available funds is addressed admits of conflicting inferences, and the decision of the state court did not hinge on any such matter. In the light of its ruling we must regard the question whether the provision for the legal education in other States of negroes resident in Missouri is sufficient to satisfy the constitutional requirement of equal protection, as the pivot upon which this case turns.

The state court stresses the advantages that are afforded by the law schools of the adjacent States,—Kansas, Nebraska, Iowa and Illinois,—which admit non-resident negroes. The court considered that these were schools of high standing where one desiring to practice law in Missouri can get "as sound, comprehensive, valuable legal education" as in the University of Missouri; that the system of education in the former is the same as that in the latter and is designed to give the students a basis for the practice of law in any State where the Anglo-American system of law obtains; that the law school of the University of Missouri does not specialize in Missouri law and that the course of study and the case books used in the five schools are substantially identical. Petitioner insists that for one intending to practice in Missouri there are special advantages in attending a law school there, both in relation to the opportunities for the particular study of Missouri law and for the observation of the local courts, and also in view of the prestige of the Missouri law school among the citizens of the State, his prospective clients. Proceeding with its examination of relative advantages, the state court found that the difference in distances to be traveled afforded no substantial ground of complaint and that there was an adequate appropriation to meet the full tuition fees which petitioner would have to pay.

We think that these matters are beside the point. The basic consideration is not as to what sort of opportunities other States provide, or whether they are as good as those in Missouri, but as to what opportunities Missouri itself furnishes to white students and denies to negroes solely upon the ground of color. The admissibility of laws separating the races in the enjoyment of privileges afforded by the State rests wholly upon the equality of the privileges which the laws give to the separated groups within the State. The question here is not of a duty of the State to supply legal training, or of the quality of the training which it does supply, but of its duty when it provides such training to furnish it to the residents of the State upon the basis of an equality of right. By the operation of the laws of Missouri a privilege has been created for white law students which is denied to negroes by reason of their race. The white resident is afforded legal education within the State; the negro resident having the same qualifications is refused it there and must go outside the State to obtain it. That is a denial of the equality of legal right to the enjoyment of the privilege which the State has set up, and the provision for the payment of tuition fees in another State does not remove the discrimination.

The equal protection of the laws is "a pledge of the protection of equal laws." *Yick Wo* v. *Hopkins*, 118 U.S. 356, 369. Manifestly, the obligation of the State to give the protection of equal laws can be performed only where its laws operate, that is, within its own jurisdiction. It is there that the equality of legal right must be maintained. That obligation is imposed by the Constitution upon the States severally as governmental entities, —each responsible for its own laws establishing the rights and duties of persons within its borders. It is an obligation the burden of which cannot be cast by one State upon another, and no State can be excused from performance by what another State may do or fail to do. That separate responsibility of each State within its own sphere is of the essence of statehood maintained under our dual system. It seems to be implicit in respondents' argument that if other States did not provide courses for legal education, it would nevertheless be the constitutional duty of Missouri when it supplied such courses for white students to make equivalent provision for negroes. But that plain duty would exist because it rested upon the State independently of the action of other States. We find it impossible to conclude that what otherwise would be an unconstitutional discrimination, with respect to the legal right to the enjoyment of opportunities within the State, can be justified by requiring resort to opportunities elsewhere. That resort may mitigate the inconvenience of the discrimination but cannot serve to validate it.

Nor can we regard the fact that there is but a limited demand in Missouri for the legal education of negroes as excusing the discrimination in favor of whites. We had occasion to consider a cognate question in the case of *McCabe* v. *Atchison, T. & S. F. Ry. Co., supra*. There the argument was advanced, in relation to the provision by a carrier of sleeping cars, dining and chair cars, that the limited demand by negroes justified the State in permitting the furnishing of such accommodations exclusively for white persons. We found that argument to be without merit. It made, we said, the constitutional right "depend upon the number of persons who may be discriminated against, whereas the essence of the constitutional right is that it is a personal one.

Whether or not particular facilities shall be provided may doubtless be conditioned upon there being a reasonable demand therefor, but, if facilities are provided, substantial equality of treatment of persons traveling under like conditions cannot be refused. It is the individual who is entitled to the equal protection of the laws, and if he is denied by a common carrier, acting in the matter under the authority of a state law, a facility or convenience in the course of his journey which under substantially the same circumstances is furnished to another traveler, he may properly complain that his constitutional privilege has been invaded."

Here, petitioner's right was a personal one. It was as an individual that he was entitled to the equal protection of the laws, and the State was bound to furnish him within its borders facilities for legal education substantially equal to those which the State there afforded for persons of the white race, whether or not other negroes sought the same opportunity.

It is urged, however, that the provision for tuition outside the State is a temporary one,—that it is intended to operate merely pending the establishment of a law department for negroes at Lincoln University. While in that sense the discrimination may be termed temporary, it may nevertheless continue for an indefinite period by reason of the discretion given to the curators of Lincoln University and the alternative of arranging for tuition in other States, as permitted by the state law as construed by the state court, so long as the curators find it unnecessary and impracticable to provide facilities for the legal instruction of negroes within the State. In that view, we cannot regard the discrimination as excused by what is called its temporary character.

We do not find that the decision of the state court turns on any procedural question. The action was for mandamus, but it does not appear that the remedy would have been deemed inappropriate if the asserted federal right had been sustained. In that situation the remedy by mandamus was found to be a proper one in *University of Maryland* v. *Murray, supra.* In the instant case, the state court did note that petitioner had not ap-

plied to the management of Lincoln University for legal training. But, as we have said, the state court did not rule that it
would have been the duty of the curators to grant such an application, but on the contrary took the view, as we understand it,
that the curators were entitled under the state law to refuse
such an application and in its stead to provide for petitioner's
tuition in an adjacent State. That conclusion presented the federal question as to the constitutional adequacy of such a provision while equal opportunity for legal training within the State
was not furnished, and this federal question the state court en-
tertained and passed upon. We must conclude that in so doing
the court denied the federal right which petitioner set up and
the question as to the correctness of that decision is before us.
We are of the opinion that the ruling was error, and that petitioner was entitled to be admitted to the law school of the State
University in the absence of other and proper provision for his
legal training within the State.

The judgment of the Supreme Court of Missouri is reversed
and the cause is remanded for further proceedings not inconsistent with this opinion.

SEPARATE OPINION OF MR. JUSTICE McREYNOLDS

Considering the disclosures of the record, the Supreme Court
of Missouri arrived at a tenable conclusion and its judgment
should be affirmed. That court well understood the grave difficulties of the situation and rightly refused to upset the settled
legislative policy of the State by directing a mandamus.

In *Cumming* v. *Richmond County Board of Education*, this
Court through Mr. Justice Harlan declared—"The education of
the people in schools maintained by state taxation is a matter
belonging to the respective States, and any interference on the
part of Federal authority with the management of such schools
cannot be justified except in the case of a clear and unmistakable disregard of rights secured by the supreme law of the
land." *Gong Lum* v. *Rice*, opinion by Mr. Chief Justice Taft—
asserts: "The right and power of the state to regulate the method

of providing for the education of its youth at public expense is clear."

For a long time Missouri has acted upon the view that the best interest of her people demands separation of whites and negroes in schools. Under the opinion just announced, I presume she may abandon her law school and thereby disadvantage her white citizens without improving petitioner's opportunities for legal instruction; or she may break down the settled practice concerning separate schools and thereby, as indicated by experience, damnify both races. Whether by some other course it may be possible for her to avoid condemnation is matter for conjecture.

The State has offered to provide the negro petitioner opportunity for study of the law—if perchance that is the thing really desired—by paying his tuition at some nearby school of good standing. This is far from unmistakable disregard of his rights and in the circumstance is enough to satisfy any reasonable demand for specialized training.

18 Heman Marion Sweatt, Petitioner *v.* Theophilus Shickel Painter, et al.

In the Negro's long and litigacious route to full access to public institutions, no case was of greater importance than *Sweatt* v. *Painter*, in which the Court ruled that the University of Texas must admit Heman Marion Sweatt to its Law School. This decision was rendered on June 5, 1950, and though the McLaurin and Sipuel cases had already been decided, the Sweatt decision had more meaning in finally breaking down segregated resistance in southern universities. It answered the question of whether a special school designed to forestall desegregation could be substituted for the one in which the petitioner sought to enter, and especially whether the prestige and tradition of an older institution could be ignored in satisfying the petitioner. Subsequently other states tried to circumvent the desegregation of their professional schools in this manner, but *Sweatt* v. *Painter* laid to rest such attempts.[°]

THIS CASE AND *McLaurin* v. *Oklahoma State Regents, post,* . . . present different aspects of this general question: To what extent does the Equal Protection Clause of the Fourteenth Amendment limit the power of a state to distinguish between students of different races in professional and graduate education in a state university? Broader issues have been urged for our consideration, but we adhere to the principle of deciding constitu-

[°] *Sweatt* v. *Painter*, 339 (U.S.), 629 (1950).

tional questions only in the context of the particular case before the Court. We have frequently reiterated that this Court will decide constitutional questions only when necessary to the disposition of the case at hand, and that such decisions will be drawn as narrowly as possible. Because of this traditional reluctance to extend constitutional interpretations to situations or facts which are not before the Court, much of the excellent research and detailed argument presented in these cases is unnesessary to their disposition.

In the instant case, petitioner filed an application for admission to the University of Texas Law School for the February, 1946 term. His application was rejected solely because he is a Negro. Petitioner thereupon brought this suit for mandamus against the appropriate school officials, respondents here, to compel his admission. At that time, there was no law school in Texas which admitted Negroes.

The State trial court recognized that the action of the State in denying petitioner the opportunity to gain a legal education while granting it to others deprived him of the equal protection of the laws guaranteed by the Fourteenth Amendment. The court did not grant the relief requested, however, but continued the case for six months to allow the State to supply substantially equal facilities. At the expiration of the six months, in December, 1946, the court denied the writ on the showing that the authorized university officials had adopted an order calling for the opening of a law school for Negroes the following February. While petitioner's appeal was pending, such a school was made available, but petitioner refused to register therein. The Texas Court of Civil Appeals set aside the trial court's judgment and ordered the cause "remanded generally to the trial court for further proceedings without prejudice to the right of any party to this suit."

On remand, a hearing was held on the issue of the equality of the educational facilities at the newly established school as compared with the University of Texas Law School. Finding that the new school offered petitioner "privileges, advantages,

and opportunities for the study of law substantially equivalent
to those offered by the State to white students at the University
of Texas," the trial court denied mandamus. The Court of Civil
Appeals affirmed. . . . Petitioner's application for a writ of error
was denied by the Texas Supreme Court. We granted certiorari,
because of the manifest importance of the constitutional issues
involved.

The University of Texas Law School, from which petitioner
was excluded, was staffed by a faculty of sixteen full-time and
three part-time professors, some of whom are nationally recognized authorities in their field. Its student body numbered 850.
The library contained over 65,000 volumes. Among the other
facilities available to the students were a law review, moot
court facilities, scholarship funds, and Order of the Coif affilia-
tion. The school's alumni occupy the most distinguished positions in the private practice of the law and in the public life of
the State. It may properly be considered one of the nation's
ranking law schools.

The law school for Negroes which was to have opened in February, 1947, would have had no independent faculty or library.
The teaching was to be carried on by four members of the University of Texas Law School faculty, who were to maintain their
offices at the University of Texas while teaching at both institutions. Few of the 10,000 volumes ordered for the library had
arrived; nor was there any full-time librarian. The school
lacked accreditation.

Since the trial of this case, respondents report the opening
of a law school at the Texas State University for Negroes. It is
apparently on the road to full accreditation. It has a faculty of
five full-time professors; a student body of 23; a library of some
16,500 volumes serviced by a full-time staff; a practice court and
legal aid association; and one alumnus who has become a
member of the Texas Bar.

Whether the University of Texas Law School is compared
with the original or the new law school for Negroes, we cannot
find substantial equality in the educational opportunities offered white and Negro law students by the State. In terms of

number of the faculty, variety of courses and opportunity for specialization, size of the student body, scope of the library, availiability of law review and similar activities, the University of Texas Law School is superior. What is more important, the University of Texas Law School possesses to a far greater degree those qualities which are incapable of objective measurement but which make for greatness in a law school. Such qualities, to name but a few, include reputation of the faculty, experience of the administration, position and influence of the alumni, standing in the community, traditions and prestige. It is difficult to believe that one who had a free choice between these law schools would consider the question close.

Moreover, although the law is a highly learned profession, we are well aware that it is an intensely practical one. The law school, the proving ground for legal learning and practice, cannot be effective in isolation from the individuals and institutions with which the law interacts. Few students and no one who has practiced law would choose to study in an academic vacuum, removed from the interplay of ideas and the exchange of views with which the law is concerned. The law school to which Texas is willing to admit petitioner excludes from its student body members of the racial groups which number 85% of the population of the State and include most of the lawyers, witnesses, jurors, judges, and other officials with whom petitioner will inevitably be dealing when he becomes a member of the Texas Bar. With such a substantial and significant segment of society excluded, we cannot conclude that the education offered petitioner is substantially equal to that which he would receive if admitted to the University of Texas Law School.

It may be argued that excluding petitioner from that school is no different from excluding white students from the new law school. This contention overlooks realities. It is unlikely that a member of a group so decisively in the majority, attending a school with rich traditions and prestige which only a history of consistently maintained excellence could command, would claim that the opportunities afforded him for legal education were unequal to those held open to petitioner. That such a claim, if made, would be dishonored by the State, is no answer. "Equal protection of the laws is not achieved through indiscriminate imposition of inequalities."

It is fundamental that these cases concern rights which are personal and present. This Court has stated unanimously that "The State must provide [legal education] for [petitioner] in conformity with the equal protection clause of the Fourteenth Amendment and provide it as soon as it does for applicants of any other group." *Sipuel* v. *Board of Regents,* 332 U. S. 631, 633 (1948). That case "did not present the issue whether a state might not satisfy the equal protection clause of the Fourteenth Amendment by establishing a separate law school for Negroes." *Fisher* v. *Hurst,* 333 U. S. 147, 150 (1948). In *Missouri ex rel. Gaines* v. *Canada,* 305 U. S. 337, 351 (1938), the Court, speaking through Chief Justice Hughes, declared that ". . . petitioner's right was a personal one. It was as an individual that he was entitled to the equal protection of the laws, and the State was bound to furnish him within its borders facilities for legal education substantially equal to those the State there afforded for persons of the white race, whether or not other Negroes sought the same opportunity." These are the only cases in this Court which present the issue of the constitutional validity of race distinctions in state-supported graduate and professional education.

In accordance with these cases, petitioner may claim his full constitutional right: legal education equivalent to that offered by the State to students of other races. Such education is not available to him in a separate law school as offered by the State. We cannot, therefore, agree with respondents that the doctrine of *Plessy* v. *Ferguson,* 163 U. S. 537 (1896), requires affirmance of the judgment below. Nor need we reach petitioner's contention that *Plessy* v. *Ferguson* should be reexamined in the light of contemporary knowledge respecting the purposes of the Fourteenth Amendment and the effects of racial segregation.

We hold that the Equal Protection Clause of the Fourteenth Amendment requires that petitioner be admitted to the University of Texas Law School. The judgment is reversed and the cause is remanded for proceedings not inconsistent with this opinion.

Reversed.

19 Heman Sweatt, an Editorial View

The editor of the *Mexia* (Texas) *News* voiced an opinion which was diametrically contrary to those held by Southerners resting comfortably behind the wall of *Plessy* v. *Ferguson* until 1954. Tragically, not more Southerners shared the editor's understanding of the real needs of all Southerners for adequate educational training.

DURING THE PAST WEEK A TEXAS COURT MADE A RULING WHICH might well become one of the most momentous decisions ever handed down from a Southern court. Heman Sweatt, Houston Negro, was granted permission to enter the law school of the University of Texas, the action being suspended in order to allow time for the establishment of a Negro professional school. The far-reaching effects of this decision may be judged by the manner in which citizens of Texas regarded the litigation. Every respectable Southerner immediately came forth with statements in the Rebel tradition such as, "No child of mine will ever go to school with a Negro." Even candidates in the gubernatorial race have chosen to make this a major campaign issue.

A TEST OF WHITE CITIZENS

It would be wise to remember, however, when considering

"The Texas Negro Education Suit as Seen by a Texas Newspaper," *New South* 2 (July 1946), 6.

Sweatt's application for university admission, that the Negro in all probability does not desire to attend school with white students. He is simply faced with the proposition of asking for that type of education or none at all. Conservatives were correct when they labeled Sweatt's application a "test case"—but it provided to be a test of white citizens, not the Negroes. Would Texans keep their promises by establishing a university of the first class for Negroes? Earlier attempts to do this resulted in the opening of Prairie View University and later the appropriation of funds to make it "first class." Notwithstanding, Negro education in Texas is poor, even for a Southern State.

The question is not one of upholding or condemning a Negro in his effort to get an education. Nor is it one of wanting Negroes in white institutions. Should the governor's committee recommend the establishment of professional schools for Negroes, there would no longer be occasion for action such as Sweatt took. Should the state, on the other hand, fail once again in this respect, it is possible that similar applications will flood all state-supported institutions.

A HELPFUL ADVANCE

For this reason, if none other, Texans may have witnessed an advance that will help bridge the wide gap between institutional and technological progress.

Our success or failure will be measured by the quality of education that is offered for Negroes in Negro schools, not by our ability to bar the doors of white institutions to them. And unless we are successful this time, Texans may very possibly find themselves forced to uphold that portion of the Constitution of the United States which guarantees that citizens shall not be discriminated against because of "race, color, or previous conditions of servitude."

20 Grovey v. Townsend

The United States Supreme Court brought *Grovey* v. *Townsend*[1] up from the Supreme Court of Texas on writ of *Certiorari*. This case involved a key point in racial discrimination in voting. Townsend, a County Clerk in Harris County, Texas, refused to issue to the plaintiff Grovey an absentee ballot so he could vote in the upcoming Democratic primary in July 1934. The Clerk's refusal was predicated on a resolution adopted by the Democratic convention May 24, 1932. The Supreme Court affirmed the state court decision, giving the color of legality to the Democratic Party's discriminatory practices in denying Negroes the right to express themselves in a primary election which essentially resulted in the selection of officials. Subsequently this decision was to be overturned in the *Classic* decision in 1944,[2] and *Smith* v. *Allwright*[3] stated even more clearly that Democratic party rule in Texas, which excluded Negro voters, was unconstitutional.

THE PETITIONER, BY COMPLAINT FILED IN THE JUSTICE COURT OF Harris County, Texas, alleged that although he is a citizen of the United States and of the State and County, and a member of and believer in the tenets of the Democratic party, the respondent, the county clerk, a state officer, having as such only

[1] 295 *United States*, 46–55 (1936).
[2] *United States* v. *Classic*, 313 U.S. 299–341 (May 26, 1941).
[3] *Smith* v. *Allwright*, 321 U.S. 757–768 (April 3, 1944).

public functions to perform, refused him a ballot for a Democratic party primary election because he is of the negro race.
He demanded ten dollars damages. The pleading quotes articles
of the Revised Civil Statutes of Texas which require the nomination of candidates at primary elections by any organized
political party whose nominees received one hundred thousand
votes or more at the preceding general election, and recites that
agreeably to these enactments a Democratic primary election
was held on July 28, 1934, at which petitioner had the right to
vote. Referring to statutes which regulate absentee voting at
primary elections, the complaint states the petitioner expected
to be absent from the county on the date of the primary election,
and demanded of the respondent an absentee ballot, which was
refused him in virtue of a resolution of the state Democratic
convention of Texas, adopted May 24, 1932, which is:

> Be it resolved that all white citizens of the State of Texas who are
> qualified to vote under the Constitution and laws of the state
> shall be eligible to membership in the Democratic party and as
> such entitled to participate in its deliberations.

The complaint charges that the respondent acted without
legal excuse and his wrongful and unlawful acts constituted a
violation of the Fourteenth and Fifteenth Amendments of the
Federal Constitution.

A demurrer, assigning as reasons that the complaint was
insufficient in law and stated no cause of action, was sustained;
and a motion for a new trial, reasserting violation of the federal
rights mentioned in the complaint, was overruled. We granted
certiorari, because of the importance of the federal question
presented, which has not been determined by this court. Our
jurisdiction is clear, as the Justice Court is the highest state
court in which a decision may be had, and the validity of the
constitution and statutes of the state was drawn in question
on the ground of their being repugnant to the Constitution of
the United States.

The charge is that respondent, a state officer, in refusing
to furnish petitioner a ballot, obeyed the law of Texas, and

the consequent denial of petitioner's right to vote in the primary election because of his race and color was state action forbidden by the Federal Constitution; and it is claimed that former decisions require us so to hold. The cited cases are, however, not in point. In *Nixon* v. *Herndon,* 273 U.S. 536, a statute which enacted that "in no event shall a negro be eligible to participate in a Democratic party primary election held in the State of Texas," was pronounced offensive to the Fourteenth Amendment. In *Nixon* v. *Condon,* 286 U.S. 73, a statute was drawn in question which provided that "every political party in this State through its State Executive Committee shall have the power to prescribe the qualifications of its own members and shall in its own way determine who shall be qualified to vote or otherwise participate in such political party." We held this was a delegation of state power to the state executive committee and made its determination conclusive irrespective of any expression of the party's will by its convention, and therefore the committee's action barring negroes from the party primaries was state action prohibited by the Fourteenth Amendment. Here the qualifications of citizens to participate in party counsels and to vote at party primaries have been declared by the representatives of the party in convention assembled, and this action upon its face is not state action. The question whether under the constitution and laws of Texas such a declaration as to party membership amounts to state action was expressly reserved in *Nixon* v. *Condon, supra,* pp. 84–85. Petitioner insists that for various reasons the resolution of the state convention limiting membership in the Democratic party in Texas to white voters does not relieve the exclusion of negroes from participation in Democratic primary elections of its true nature as the act of the state.

First. An argument pressed upon us in *Nixon* v. *Condon, supra,* which we found it unnecessary to consider, is again presented. It is that the primary election was held under statutory compulsion; is wholly statutory in origin and incidents; those charged with its management have been deprived by statute and judicial decision of all power to establish qualifications for participation therein inconsistent with those laid down by the laws of the state, save only that the managers of such elections have been given the power to deny negroes the vote. It is further urged that while the election is designated that of the Democratic party, the statutes not only require this method of selecting party nominees, but define the powers and duties of the party's representatives, and of those who are to conduct the election, so completely, and make them so thoroughly officers of the state, that any action taken by them in connection with the qualifications of members of the party is in fact state action and not party action.

In support of this view petitioner refers to Title 50 of the Revised Civil Statutes of Texas of 1925, which by Article 3101 requires that any party whose members cast more than one hundred thousand ballots at the previous election, shall nominate candidates through primaries, and fixes the date at which they are to be held; by Article 2939 requires primary election officials to be qualified voters; by Article 2955 declares the same qualifications for voting in such an election as in the general elections; by Article 2956 permits absentee voting as in a general election; by Article 2978 requires that only an official ballot shall be used, as in a general election; by Articles 2980–2981 specifies the form of ballot and how it shall be marked, as other sections do for general elections; by Article 2984 fixes the number of ballots to be provided, as another article does for general elections; by Articles 2986, 2987 and 2990 permits the use of voting booths, guard rails, and ballot boxes which by other statutes are provided for general elections; by Articles 2998 and 3104 requires the officials of primary elections to take the same oath as officials at the general elections; by Article 3002 defines the powers of judges at primary elections; by Articles 3003–3025 provides elaborately for the purity of the ballot box; by Article 3028 commands that the sealed ballot boxes be delivered to the county clerk after the election, as is provided by another article for the general election; and by Article 3041 confers jurisdiction of election contests upon district courts, as is done by another article with respect to general elections. A perusal of these provisions, so it is said, will convince that the state has prescribed and regulated party primaries as fully as general elections, and has made those who manage the primaries state officers subject to state direction and control.

While it is true that Texas has by its laws elaborately provided for the expression of party preference as to nominees, has required that preference to be expressed in a certain form of voting, and has attempted in minute detail to protect the suffrage of the members of the organization against fraud, it is equally true that the primary is a party primary; the expenses of it are not borne by the state, but by members of the party seeking nomination; the ballots are furnished not by the state, but by the agencies of the party; the votes are counted and the returns made by instrumentalities created by the party; and the state recognizes the state convention as the organ of the party for the declaration of principles and the formulation of policies.

We are told that in *Love* v. *Wilcox*, 119 Tex. 256; 28 S. W. (2d) 515, the Supreme Court of Texas held the state was within its province in prohibiting a party from establishing past party affiliations or membership in nonpolitical organizations as qualifications or tests for participation in primary elections, and in consequence issued its writ of mandamus against the members of the state executive committee of the Democratic party on the ground that they were public functionaries fulfilling duties imposed on them by law. But in that case it was said (p. 272):

> We are not called upon to determine whether a political party has power, beyond statutory control, to prescribe what persons shall participate as voters or candidates in its conventions or primaries. We have no such state of facts before us.

After referring to Article 3107, which limits the power of the state executive committee of a party to determine who shall be qualified to vote at primary elections, the court said:

> The Committee's discretionary power is further restricted by the statute directing that a single, uniform pledge be required of the primary participants. The effect of the statutes is to decline to

give recognition to the lodgment of power in a State Executive Committee, to be exercised at its discretion.

Although it did not pass upon the constitutionality of § 3107, as we did in *Nixon* v. *Condon, supra,* the Court thus recognized the fact upon which our decision turned, that the effort was to vest in the state executive committee the power to bind the party by its decision as to who might be admitted to membership.

In *Bell* v. *Hill,* 74 S. W. (2d) 113, the same court, in a mandamus proceeding instituted after the adoption by the state convention of the resolution of May 24, 1932, restricting eligibility for membership in the Democratic party to white persons, held the resolution valid and effective. After a full consideration of the nature of political parties in the United States, the court concluded that such parties in the state of Texas arise from the exercise of the free will and liberty of the citizens composing them; that they are voluntary associations for political action, and are not the creatures of the state; and further decided that §§ 2 and 27 of Article 1 of the State Constitution guaranteed to citizens the liberty of forming political associations, and the only limitation upon this right to be found in that instrument is the clause which requires the maintenance of a republican form of government. The statutes regulating the nomination of candidates by primaries were related by the court to the police power, but were held not to extend to the denial of the right of citizens to form a political party and to determine who might associate with them as members thereof. The court declared that a proper view of the election laws of Texas, and their history, required the conclusion that the Democratic party in that state is a voluntary political association and, by its representatives assembled in convention, has the power to determine who shall be eligible for membership and, as such, eligible to participate in the party's primaries.

We cannot, as petitioner urges, give weight to earlier expressions of the state courts said to be inconsistent with this declaration of the law. The Supreme Court of the state has decided, in a case definitely involving the point, that the legislature of Texas has not essayed to interfere, and indeed may not interfere, with the constitutional liberty of citizens to organize a party and to determine the qualifications of its members. If in the past the legislature has attempted to infringe that right and such infringement has not been gainsaid by the courts, the fact constitutes no reason for our disregarding the considered decision of the state's highest court. The legislative assembly of the state, so far as we are advised, has never attempted to prescribe or to limit the membership of a political party, and it is now settled that it has no power so to do. The state, as its highest tribunal holds, though it has guaranteed the liberty to organize political parties, may legislate for their governance when formed and for the method whereby they may nominate candidates, but must do so with full recognition of the right of the party to exist, to define its membership, and to adopt such policies as to it shall seem wise. In the light of the principles so announced, we are unable to characterize the managers of the primary election as state officers in such sense that any action taken by them in obedience to the mandate of the state convention respecting eligibility to participate in the organization's deliberations, is state action.

Second. We are told that §§ 2 and 27 of the Bill of Rights of the Constitution of Texas as construed in *Bell* v. *Hill, supra,* violate the Federal Constitution, for the reason that so construed they fail to forbid a classification based upon race and color, whereas in *Love* v. *Wilcox, supra,* they were not held to forbid classifications based upon party affiliations and membership or non-membership in organizations other than political parties, which classifications were by Article 3107 of Revised Civil Statutes, 1925, prohibited. But, as above said, in *Love* v. *Wilcox* the court did not construe or apply any constitutional provision and expressly reserved the question as to the power of a party in convention assembled to specify the qualifications for membership therein.

Third. An alternative contention of petitioner is that the state Democratic convention which adopted the resolution here involved was a mere creature of the state and could not lawfully do what the Federal Constitution prohibits to its creator. The argument is based upon the fact that Article 3167 of the Revised Civil Statutes of Texas, 1925, requires a political party desiring to elect delegates to a national convention, to hold a state convention on the fourth Tuesday of May, 1928, and every four years thereafter; and provides for the election of delegates to that convention at primary conventions, the procedure of which is regulated by law. In *Bell* v. *Hill, supra,* the Supreme Court of Texas held that Article 3167 does not prohibit declarations of policy by a state Democratic convention called for the purpose of electing delegates to a national convention. While it may be, as petitioner contends, that we are not bound by the state court's decision on the point, it is entitled to the highest respect, and petitioner points to nothing which in any wise impugns its accuracy. If, as seems to be conceded, the Democratic party in Texas held conventions many years before the adoption of Article 3167, nothing is shown to indicate that the regulation of the method of choosing delegates or fixing the times of their meetings, was intended to take away the plenary power of conventions in respect of matters as to which they would normally announce the party's will. Compare *Nixon* v. *Condon, supra,* 84. We are not prepared to hold that in Texas the state convention of a party has become a mere instrumentality or agency for expressing the voice or will of the state.

Fourth. The complaint states that candidates for the offices of Senator and Representative in Congress were to be nominated at the primary election of July 9, 1934, and that in Texas nomination by the Democratic party is equivalent to election. These facts (the truth of which the demurrer assumes) the petitioner insists, without more, make out a forbidden discrimination. A similar situation may exist in other states where one or another party includes a great majority of the qualified electors. The argument is that as a negro may not be denied a ballot at a general election on account of his race or color, if exclusion from the primary renders his vote at the general election insignificant and useless, the result is to deny him the suffrage altogether. So to say is to confuse the privilege of membership in a party with the right to vote for one who is to hold a public office. With the former the state need have no concern, with the latter it is bound to concern itself, for the general election is a function of the state government and discrimination by the state as respects participation by negroes on account of their race or color is prohibited by the Federal Constitution.

Fifth. The complaint charges that the Democratic party has never declared a purpose to exclude negroes. The premise upon which this conclusion rests is that the party is not a state body but a national organization, whose representative is the national Democratic convention. No such convention, so it is said, has resolved to exclude negroes from membership. We have no occa sion to determine the correctness of the position, since even if true it does not tend to prove that the petitioner was discriminated against or denied any right to vote by the State of Texas. Indeed, the contention contradicts any such conclusion, for it assumes merely that a state convention, the representative and agent of a state association, has usurped the rightful authority of a national convention which represents a larger and superior country-wide association.

We find no ground for holding that the respondent has in obedience to the mandate of the law of Texas discriminated against the petitioner or denied him any right guaranteed by the Fourteenth and Fifteenth Amendments.

Judgment affirmed.

21 United States v. Classic

In the following decision the Supreme Court reversed the Fifth District Court ruling negating a Louisiana primary election in which congressmen were chosen. The plaintiffs charged that a conspiracy had prevailed in the Second Precinct of the Tenth Ward in New Orleans, in which eighty-three ballots had been falsely certified. In a lengthy discussion of Paragraphs 19 and 20 of the United States Criminal Code, and a considerable amount of discussion of the role of the Democratic primary in the election of officials, the Supreme Court reversed the lower court. It did, however, establish that the primary election process was legally a part of the official means of selecting officers of state and federal governments. It upheld the major arguments in *Grovey* v. *Townsend,* but subsequently reversed itself in *Smith* v. *Allwright.* The significance of the Classic case was the fact that it brought the Supreme Court a step nearer to declaring unconstitutional much of the election process in which the Democratic primary discriminated against Negroes and other persons.[*]

Two counts of an indictment found in a federal district court charged that appellees, Commissioners of Elections, conducting a primary election under Louisiana law, to nominate a candidate of the Democratic Party for representative in Congress, willfully altered and falsely counted and certified the bal-

[*] *United States* v. *Classic,* 313 U.S. 299–341 (May 26, 1941).

lots of voters cast in the primary election. The questions for decision are whether the right of qualified voters to vote in the Louisiana primary and to have their ballots counted is a right "secured * * * by the Constitution" within the meaning of §§ 19 and 20 of the Criminal Code, and whether the acts of appellees charged in the indictment violate those sections.

On September 25, 1940, appellees were indicted in the District Court for Eastern Louisiana for violations of §§ 19 and 20 of the Criminal Code. The first count of the indictment alleged that a primary election was held on September 10, 1940, for the purpose of nominating a candidate of the Democratic Party for the office of Representative in Congress for the Second Congressional District of Louisiana, to be chosen at an election to be held on November 10th; that in that district nomination as a candidate of the Democratic Party is and always has been equivalent to an election; that appellees were Commissioners of Election, selected in accordance with the Louisiana law to conduct the primary in the Second Precinct of the Tenth Ward of New Orleans, in which there were five hundred and thirty-seven citizens and qualified voters.

The charge based on these allegations, was that the appellees conspired with each other and with others unknown, to injure and oppress citizens in the free exercise and enjoyment of rights and privileges secured to them by the Constitution and Laws of the United States, namely, (1) the right of qualified voters who cast their ballots in the primary election to have their ballots counted as cast for the candidate of their choice, and (2) the right of the candidates to run for the office of Congressman and to have the votes in favor of their nomination counted as cast. The overt acts alleged were that the appellees altered eighty-three ballots cast for one candidate and fourteen cast for another, marking and counting them as votes for a third candidate, and that they falsely certified the number of votes cast for the respective candidates to the chairman of the Second Congressional District Committee.

The second count, repeating the allegations of fact already detailed, charged that the appellees, as Commissioners of Election willfully and under color of law subjected registered voters at the primary who were inhabitants of Louisiana to the deprivation of rights, privileges and immunities secured and protected by the Constitution and Laws of the United States, namely their right to cast their votes for the candidates of their choice and to have their votes counted as cast. It further charged that this deprivation was effected by the willful failure and refusal of defendants to count the votes as cast, by their alteration of the ballots, and by their false certification of the number of votes cast for the respective candidates in the manner already indicated.

The District Court sustained a demurrer to counts 1 and 2 on the ground that §§ 19 and 20 of the Criminal Code under which the indictment was drawn do not apply to the state of facts disclosed by the indictment and that, if applied to those facts, §§ 19 and 20 are without constitutional sanction. The case comes here on direct appeal from the District Court under the provisions of the Criminal Appeals Act, Judicial Code, which authorize an appeal by the United States from a decision or judgment sustaining a demurrer to an indictment where the decision or judgment is "based upon the invalidity, or construction of the statute upon which the indictment is founded."

Upon such an appeal our review is confined to the questions of statutory construction and validity decided by the District Court. Hence, we do not pass upon various arguments advanced by appellees as to the sufficiency and construction of the indictment.

Section 19 of the Criminal Code condemns as a criminal offense any conspiracy to injure a citizen in the exercise "of any right or privilege secured to him by the Constitution or laws of the United States". Section 20 makes it a penal offense for anyone who, "acting under color of any law" "willfully subjects, or causes to be subjected, any inhabitant of any State * * * to the deprivation of any rights, privileges, or immunities secured or protected by the Constitution and laws of the United States." The Government argues that the right of a qualified voter in a Louisiana congressional primary election to have his vote counted as cast is a right secured by Article I, §§ 2 and 4 of the Constitution, and that a conspiracy to deprive the citizen of that right is a violation of § 19, and also that the willful action of appellees as state officials, in falsely counting the ballots at the primary election and in falsely certifying the count, deprived qualified voters of that right and of the equal protection of the laws guaranteed by the Fourteenth Amendment, all in violation of § 20 of the Criminal Code.

Article I, § 2 of the Constitution, commands that "The House of Representatives shall be composed of Members chosen every second Year by the People of the several States, and the Electors in each State shall have the qualifications requisite for Electors of the most numerous Branch of the State Legislature." By § 4 of the same article "The Times, Places and Manner of holding Elections for Senators and Representatives, shall be prescribed in each State by the Legislature thereof; but the Congress may at any time by Law make or alter such Regulations, except as to the Places of chusing Senators." Such right as is secured by the Constitution to qualified voters to choose members of the House of Representatives is thus to be exercised in conformity to the requirements of state law subject to the restrictions prescribed by § 2 and to the authority conferred on Congress by § 4, to regulate the times, places and manner of holding elections for representatives.

We look then to the statutes of Louisiana here involved to ascertain the nature of the right which under the constitutional mandate they define and confer on the voter and the effect upon its exercise of the acts with which appellees are charged, all with the view to determining, first, whether the right or privilege is one secured by the Constitution of the United States, second, whether the effect under the state statute of appellee's alleged acts is such that they operate to injure or oppress citizens in the exercise of that right within the meaning of § 19 and to deprive inhabitants of the state of that right within the meaning of § 20, and finally, whether §§ 19 and 20 respectively are in other respects applicable to the alleged acts of appellees.

Pursuant to the authority given by § 2 of Article I of the Constitution, and subject to the legislative power of Congress under § 4 of Article I, and other pertinent provisions of the Constitution, the states are given, and in fact exercise a wide discretion in the formulation of a system for the choice by the people of representatives in Congress. In common with many other states Louisiana has exercised that discretion by setting up machinery for the effective choice of party candidates for representative in Congress by primary elections and by its laws it eliminates or seriously restricts the candidacy at the general election of all those who are defeated at the primary. All political parties, which are defined as those that have cast at least 5 per cent of the total vote at specified preceding elections, are required to nominate their candidates for representative by direct primary elections.

The primary is conducted by the state at public expense. The primary, as is the general election, is subject to numerous statutory regulations as to the time, place and manner of conducting the election, including provisions to insure that the ballots cast at the primary are correctly counted, and the results of the count correctly recorded and certified to the Secretary of State, whose duty it is to place the names of the successful candidates of each party on the official ballot. The Secretary of State is prohibited from placing on the official ballot the name of any person as a candidate for any political party not nominated in accordance with the provisions of the Act.

One whose name does not appear on the primary ballot, if otherwise eligible to become a candidate at the general election, may do so in either of two ways, by filing nomination papers with the requisite number of signatures or by having his name "written in" on the ballot on the final election. No. 46 provides "No one who participates in the primary election of any political party shall have the right to participate in any primary election of any other political party, with a view of nominating opposing candidates, nor shall he be permitted to sign any nomination papers for any opposing candidate or candidates; nor shall he be permitted to be himself a candidate in opposition to any one nominated at or through a primary election in which he took part."

Section 15 of Article VIII of the Constitution of Louisiana as amended by Act 80 of 1934, provides that "no person whose name is not authorized to be printed on the official ballot, as the nominee of a political party or as an independent candidate, shall be considered a candidate," unless he shall file in the appropriate office at least ten days before the general election a statement containing the correct name under which he is to be voted for and containing the further statement that he is willing and consents to be voted for for that office. The article also provides that "no commissioners of election shall count a ballot as cast for any person whose name is not printed on the ballot or who does not become a candidate in the foregoing manner." Applying these provisions the Louisiana Court of Appeals for the Parish of Orleans has held that an unsuccessful candidate at the primary may not offer himself as a candidate at a general election, and that votes for him may not lawfully be written into the ballot or counted at such an election.

The right to vote for a representative in Congress at the general election is, as a matter of law, thus restricted to the successful party candidate at the primary, to those not candidates at the primary who file nomination papers, and those whose names may be lawfully written into the ballot by the electors. Even if, as appellees argue, contrary to the decision in *Serpas* v. *Trebucq*, *supra*, voters may lawfully write into their ballots, cast at the general election, the name of a candidate rejected at the primary and have their ballots counted, the practical operation of the primary law in otherwise excluding from the ballot on the general election the names of candidates rejected at the primary is such as to impose serious restrictions upon the choice of candidates by the voters save by voting at the primary election. In fact, as alleged in the indictment, the practical operation of the primary in Louisiana, is and has been since the primary election was established in 1900 to secure the election of the Democratic primary nominee for the Second Congressional District of Louisiana.

Interference with the right to vote in the Congressional primary in the Second Congressional District for the choice of Democratic candidate for Congress is thus as a matter of law and in fact an interference with the effective choice of the voters at the only stage of the election procedure when their choice is of significance, since it is at the only stage when such interference could have any practical effect on the ultimate result, the choice of the Congressman to represent the district. The primary in Louisiana is an integral part of the procedure for the popular choice of Congressman. The right of qualified voters to vote at the Congressional primary in Louisiana and to have their ballots counted is thus the right to participate in that choice.

Obviously included within the right to choose, secured by the Constitution, is the right of qualified voters within a state to cast their ballots and have them counted at Congressional elections. This Court has consistently held that this is a right secured by the Constitution.

. . . But we are now concerned with the question whether the right to choose at a primary election, a candidate for election as representative, is embraced in the right to choose representatives secured by Article I, § 2. We may assume that the framers of the Constitution in adopting that section, did not have specifically in mind the selection and elimination of candidates for Congress by the direct primary any more than they contemplated the application of the commerce clause to interstate telephone, telegraph and wireless communication which are concededly within it. But in determining whether a provision of the Constitution applies to a new subject matter, it is of little significance that it is one with which the framers were not familiar. For in setting up an enduring framework of government they undertook to carry out for the indefinite future and in all the vicissitudes of the changing affairs of men, those fundamental purposes which the instrument itself discloses. Hence we read its words, not as we read legislative codes which are subject to continuous revision with the changing course of events, but as the revelation of the great purposes which were intended to be achieved by the Constitution as a continuing instrument of government. If we remember that "it is a Constitution we are expounding", we cannot rightly prefer, of the possible meanings of its words, that which will defeat rather than effectuate the Constitutional purpose.

That the free choice by the people of representatives in Congress, subject only to the restrictions to be found in §§ 2 and 4 of Article I and elsewhere in the Constitution, was one of the great purposes of our Constitutional scheme of government cannot be doubted. We cannot regard it as any the less the constitutional purpose or its words as any the less guarantying the integrity of that choice when a state, exercising its privilege in the absence of Congressional action, changes the mode of choice from a single step, a general election, to two, of which the first is the choice at a primary of those candidates from whom, as a second step, the representative in Congress is to be chosen at the election.

. . . Long before the adoption of the Constitution the form and mode of that expression had changed from time to time. There is no historical warrant for supposing that the framers were under the illusion that the method of effecting the choice of the electors would never change or that if it did, the change was for that reason to be permitted to defeat the right of the people to choose representatives for Congress which the Constitution had guaranteed. The right to participate in the choice of representatives for Congress includes, as we have said, the right to cast a ballot and to have it counted at the general election whether for the successful candidate or not. Where the state law has made the primary an integral part of the procedure of choice, or where in fact the primary effectively controls the choice, the right of the elector to have his ballot counted at the primary, is likewise included in the right protected by Article I, § 2. And this right of participation is protected just as is the right to vote at the election, where the primary is by law made an integral part of the election machinery, whether the voter exercises his right in a party primary which invariably, sometimes or never determines the ultimate choice of the representative. Here, even apart from the circumstance that the Louisiana primary is made by law an integral part of the procedure of choice, the right to choose a representative is in fact controlled by the primary because, as is alleged in the indictment, the choice of candidates at the Democratic primary determines the choice of the elected representative. Moreover, we cannot close our eyes to the fact already mentioned that the practical influence of the choice of candidates at the primary may be so great as to affect profoundly the choice at the general election even though there is no effective legal prohibition upon the rejection at the election of the choice made at the primary and may thus operate to deprive the voter of his constitutional right of choice. This was noted and extensively commented upon by the concurring Justices in *Newberry* v. *United States*. Unless the constitutional protection of the integrity of "elections" extends to primary elections, Congress is left powerless to effect the constitutional purpose, and the popular choice of representatives is stripped of its constitutional protection save only as Congress, by taking over the control of state elections, may exclude from them the influence of the state primaries. Such an expedient would end that state autonomy with respect to the elections which the Constitution contemplated that Congress should be free to leave undisturbed, subject only to such minimum regulation as it should find necessary to insure the freedom and integrity of the choice. Words, especially those of a constitution are not to be read with such stultifying narrowness

There remains the question whether §§ 19 and 20 are an exercise of the congressional authority applicable to the acts with which appellees are charged in the indictment. Section 19 makes it a crime to conspire to "injure" or "oppress" any citizen "in the free exercise * * * of any right or privilege secured to him by the Constitution." In *Ex parte Yarbrough, supra*, and in *United States* v. *Mosley, supra*, as we have seen, it was held that the right to vote in a congressional election is a right secured by the Constitution, and that a conspiracy to prevent the citizen from voting or to prevent the official count of his ballot when cast, is a conspiracy to injure and oppress the citizen in the free exercise of a right secured by the Constitution within the meaning of § 19. In reaching this conclusion the Court found no uncertainty or ambiguity in the statutory language, obviously devised to protect the citizen "in the free exercise * * of any right or privilege secured to him by the Constitution," and concerned itself with the question whether the right to participate in choosing a representative is so secured. Such is our function here. Conspiracy to prevent the official count of a citizen's ballot, held in *United States* v. *Mosley, supra,* to be a violation of § 19 in the case of a congressional election, is equally a conspiracy to injure and oppress the citizen when the ballots are cast in a primary election prerequisite to the choice of party candidates for a congressional election. In both cases the right infringed is one secured by the Constitution. The injury suffered by the citizen in the exercise of the right is an injury which the statute describes and to which it applies in the one case as in the other.

The suggestion that § 19, concededly applicable to the conspiracies to deprive electors of their votes at congressional elections, is not sufficiently specific to be deemed applicable to primary elections, will hardly bear examination. Section 19 speaks neither of elections nor of primaries. In unambiguous language it protects "any right or privilege secured * * * by the Constitution," a phrase which as we have seen extends to the right of the voter to have his vote counted in both the general election and in the primary election, where the latter is a part of the election machinery, as well as to numerous other constitutional rights which are wholly unrelated to the choice of a representative in Congress.

But we are troubled by no such doubt here. Hence, the right to participate through the primary in the choice of representatives in Congress—a right clearly secured by the Constitution—is within the words and purpose of § 19 in the same manner and to the same extent as the right to vote at the general election. It is no extension of the criminal statute, as it was not of the civil statute in *Nixon* v. *Herndon, supra,* to find a violation of it in a new method of interference with the right which its words protect. For it is the constitutional right, regardless of the method of interference, which is the subject of the statute and which in precise terms it protects from injury and oppression.

It is hardly the performance of the judicial function to construe a statute, which in terms protects a right secured by the

Constitution, here the right to choose a representative in Congress, as applying to an election whose only function is to ratify a choice already made at the primary but as having no application to the primary which is the only effective means of choice. To withdraw from the scope of the statute, an effective interference with the constitutional right of choice, because other wholly different situations not now before us may not be found to involve such an interference, is to say that acts plainly within the statute should be deemed to be without it because other hypothetical cases may later be found not to infringe the constitutional right with which alone the statute is concerned.

The alleged acts of appellees were committed in the course of their performance of duties under the Louisiana statute requiring them to count the ballots, to record the result of the count, and to certify the result of the election. Misuse of power, possessed by virtue of state law and made possible only because the wrongdoer is clothed with the authority of state law, is action taken "under color of" state law. Here the acts of appellees infringed the constitutional right and deprived the voters of the benefit of it within the meaning of § 20, unless by its terms its application is restricted to deprivations "on account of [an] inhabitant being an alien, or by reason of his color, or race."

The last clause of § 20 protects inhabitants of a state from being subjected to different punishments, pains or penalties by reason of alienage, color or race, than are prescribed for the punishment of citizens. That the qualification with respect to alienage, color and race, refers only to differences in punishment and not to deprivations of any rights or privileges secured by the Constitution, is evidenced by the structure of the section and the necessities of the practical application of its provisions. The qualification as to alienage, color and race, is a parenthetical phrase in the clause penalizing different punishments "than are prescribed for * * * citizens" and in the common use of language could refer only to the subject matter of the clause and not to that of the earlier one relating to the deprivation of rights to which it makes no reference in terms.

Moreover the prohibited differences of punishment on account of alienage, color or race, are those referable to prescribed punishments which are to be compared with those prescribed for citizens. A standard is thus set up applicable to differences in prescribed punishments on account of alienage, color or race, which it would be difficult if not impossible to apply to the willful deprivations of constitutional rights or privileges, in order to determine whether they are on account of alienage, color or race. We think that § 20 authorizes the punishment of two different offenses. The one is willfully subjecting any inhabitant to the deprivation of rights secured by the Constitution; the other is willfully subjecting any inhabitant to different punishments on account of his color or race, than are prescribed for the punishment of citizens. The meager legislative history of the section supports this conclusion. So interpreted § 20 applies to deprivation of the constitutional rights of qualified voters to choose representatives in Congress. The generality of the section made applicable as it is to deprivations of any constitutional right, does not obscure its meaning or impair its force within the scope of its application, which is restricted by its terms to deprivations which are willfully inflicted by those acting under color of any law, statute and the like.

We do not discuss the application of § 20 to deprivations of the right to equal protection of the laws guaranteed by the Fourteenth Amendment, a point apparently raised and discussed for the first time in the Government's brief in this Court. The point was not specially considered or decided by the court below, and has not been assigned as error by the Government. Since the indictment on its face does not purport to charge a deprivation of equal protection to voters or candidates, we are not called upon to construe the indictment in order to raise a question of statutory validity or construction which we are alone authorized to review upon this appeal.

Reversed.

22 Smith v. Allwright

Lonnie E. Smith sought of Democratic election officials in the Forty-Eighth Precinct of Harris County, Texas, a ballot to enable him to vote in a Democratic primary for United States Senator, a congressman, and state officials. After being refused the ballot, he brought suit against S. E. Allwright and James Liuzza, judge and associate judge of the precinct. Before the Court was the whole question of the nature of the Democratic primary and its meaning in the electoral process, especially as it might deny a Negro the right to vote under terms of the Fourteenth and Fifteenth Amendments. Since 1923 the primary and its meaning had been an issue before the Court in one form or another. Both *Grovey* v. *Townsend* and *Classic* v. *United States* bore directly on this issue. In *Smith* v. *Allwright* the Court was specifically concerned with *Grovey* v. *Townsend*. The majority decision in this case is a masterful rationalization of why the Court reversed itself so quickly. Actually the decision is about as much a defense of the Court's change of view as constitutional reinterpretation. Mr. Justice Roberts in his penetrating dissent took his colleagues to task on this point of reversal. Whatever the rationale of the majority of the justices, or the objection of Mr. Justice Roberts, *Smith* v. *Allwright* was indeed of major importance in destroying the racial exclusiveness of the Democratic primary.°

THIS WRIT OF CERTIORARI BRINGS HERE FOR REVIEW A CLAIM FOR damages in the sum of $5,000 on the part of petitioner, a Negro

° *Smith* v. *Allwright*, 321 U.S. 757–768 (April 3, 1944).

citizen of the 48th precinct of Harris County, Texas, for the refusal of respondents, election and associate election judges respectively of that precinct, to give petitioner a ballot or to permit him to cast a ballot in the primary election of July 27, 1940,
for the nomination of Democratic candidates for the United
States Senate and House of Representatives, and Governor and
other state officers. The refusal is alleged to have been solely
because of the race and color of the proposed voter.

. . . The State of Texas by its Constitution and statutes provides that every person, if certain other requirements are met
which are not here an issue, qualified by residence in the district or county "shall be deemed a qualified elector." Constitution of Texas.

Primary elections for United States Senators, Congressmen
and state officers are provided for by Chapters Twelve and Thirteen of the statutes. Under these chapters, the Democratic Party
was required to hold the primary which was the occasion of the
alleged wrong to petitioner.

[The Texas Supreme Court held that]

> Since the right to organize and maintain a political party is one
> guaranteed by the Bill of Rights of this state, it necessarily fol-
> lows that every privilege essential or reasonably appropriate to
> the exercise of that right is likewise guaranteed, including, of
> course, the privilege of determining the policies of the party and
> its membership. Without the privilege of determining the policy
> of a political association and its membership, the right to organize
> such an association would be a mere mockery. We think these
> rights, that is, the right to determine the membership of a po-
> litical party and to determine its policies, of necessity are to be
> exercised by the State Convention of such party, and cannot,
> under any circumstances, be conferred upon a state or govern-
> mental agency.

The Democratic party on May 24, 1932, in a State Convention
adopted the following resolution, which has not since been
"amended, abrogated, annulled or avoided":

> Be it resolved that all white citizens of the State of Texas who
> are qualified to vote under the Constitution and laws of the State

shall be eligible to membership in the Democratic party, and, as such, entitled to participate in its deliberations.

It was by virtue of this resolution that the respondents refused to permit the petitioner to vote.

[1] Texas is free to conduct her elections and limit her electorate as she may deem wise, save only as her action may be affected by the prohibitions of the United States Constitution or in conflict with powers delegated to and exercised by the National Government. The Fourteenth Amendment forbids a state from making or enforcing any law which abridges the privileges or immunities of citizens of the United States and the Fifteenth Amendment specifically interdicts any denial or abridgement by a state of the right of citizens to vote on account of color. Respondents appeared in the District Court and the Circuit Court of Appeals and defended on the ground that the Democratic party of Texas is a voluntary organization with members banded together for the purpose of selecting individuals of the group representing the common political beliefs as candidates in the general election. As such a voluntary organization, it was claimed, the Democratic party is free to select its own membership and limit to whites participation in the party primary. Such action, the answer asserted, does not violate the Fourteenth, Fifteenth or Seventeenth Amendments as officers of government cannot be chosen at primaries and the Amendments are applicable only to general elections where governmental officers are actually elected. Primaries, it is said, are political party affairs, handled by party not governmental officers. No appearance for respondents is made in this Court. Arguments presented here by the Attorney General of Texas and the Chairman of the State Democratic Executive Committee of Texas, as amici curiae, urged substantially the same grounds as those advanced by the respondents.

. . . The question of a political party in Texas "without restraint by any law to determine its own membership" was left open.

In *Grovey* v. *Townsend*, this Court had before it another suit for damages for the refusal in a primary of a county clerk, a Texas officer with only public functions to perform, to furnish petitioner, a Negro, an absentee ballot. The refusal was solely on the ground of race. This case differed from *Nixon* v. *Condon, supra,* in that a state convention of the Democratic party had passed the resolution of May 24, 1932, hereinbefore quoted. It was decided that the determination by the state convention of the membership of the Democratic party made a significant change from a determination by the Executive Committee. The former was party action, voluntary in character. The latter, as had been held in the Condon case, was action by authority of the State. The managers of the primary election were therefore declared not to be state officials in such sense that their action was state action. A state convention of a party was said not to be an organ of the state. This Court went on to announce that to deny a vote in a primary was a mere refusal of party membership with which "the state need have no concern," while for a state to deny a vote in a general election on the ground of race or color violated the Constitution. Consequently, there was found no ground for holding that the county clerk's refusal of a ballot because of racial ineligibility for party membership denied the petitioner any right under the Fourteenth or Fifteenth Amendments.

Since *Grovey* v. *Townsend* and prior to the present suit, no case from Texas involving primary elections has been before this Court. We did decide, however, *United States* v. *Classic,* 313 U.S. 299, 61 S.Ct. 1031, 85 L.Ed. 1368. We there held that Section 4 of Article I of the Constitution authorized Congress to regulate primary as well as general elections, "where the primary is by law made an integral part of the election machinery." Consequently, in the Classic case, we upheld the applicability to frauds in a Louisiana primary of §§ 19 and 20 of the Criminal Code, 18 U.S.C.A. §§ 51, 52. Thereby corrupt acts of election officers were subjected to Congressional sanctions because that body had power to protect rights of Federal suffrage secured by the Constitution in primary as in general elections. This decision depended, too, on the determination that under the Loui-

siana statutes the primary was a part of the procedure for choice
of Federal officials. By this decision the doubt as to whether or
not such primaries were a part of "elections" subject to Federal
control, which had remained unanswered since Newberry v.
United States, was erased. The Nixon cases were decided under
the equal protection clause of the Fourteenth Amendment without a determination of the status of the primary as a part of the
electoral process. The exclusion of Negroes from the primaries
by action of the State was held invalid under that Amendment.
The fusing by the Classic case of the primary and general elections into a single instrumentality for choice of officers has a
definite bearing on the permissibility under the Constitution of
excluding Negroes from primaries. This is not to say that the
Classic case cuts directly into the rationale of *Grovey* v. *Townsend*. This latter case was not mentioned in the opinion. Classic
bears upon *Grovey* v. *Townsend* not because exclusion of Negroes from primaries is any more or less state action by reason
of the unitary character of the electoral process but because the
recognition of the place of the primary in the electoral scheme
makes clear that state delegation to a party of the power to fix
the qualifications of primary elections is delegation of a state
function that may make the party's action the action of the
state. When *Grovey* v. *Townsend* was written, the Court looked
upon the denial of a vote in a primary as a mere refusal by a
party of party membership.

As the Louisiana statutes for holding primaries are similar to
those of Texas, our ruling in Classic as to the unitary character
of the electoral process calls for a reexamination as to whether
or not the exclusion of Negroes from a Texas party primary was
state action.

The statutes of Texas relating to primaries and the resolution
of the Democratic party of Texas extending the privileges of
membership to white citizens only are the same in substance
and effect today as they were when *Grovey* v. *Townsend* was
decided by a unanimous Court. The question as to whether the
exclusionary action of the party was the action of the State persists as the determinative factor. In again entering upon consid-

eration of the inference to be drawn as to state action from a substantially similar factual situation, it should be noted that *Grovey* v. *Townsend* upheld exclusion of Negroes from primaries through the denial of party membership by a party convention. A few years before this Court refused approval of exclusion by the State Executive Committee of the party. A different result was reached on the theory that the Committee action was state authorized and the Convention action was unfettered by statutory control. Such a variation in the result from so slight a change in form influences us to consider anew the legal validity of the distinction which has resulted in barring Negroes from participating in the nominations of candidates of the Democratic party in Texas. Other precedents of this Court forbid the abridgement of the right to vote.

[2] It may now be taken as a postulate that the right to vote in such a primary for the nomination of candidates without discrimination by the State, like the right to vote in a general election, is a right secured by the Constitution. By the terms of the Fifteenth Amendment that right may not be abridged by any state on account of race. Under our Constitution the great privilege of the ballot may not be denied a man by the State because of his color.

[3] We are thus brought to an examination of the qualifications for Democratic primary electors in Texas, to determine whether state action or private action has excluded Negroes from participation. Despite Texas' decision that the exclusion is produced by private or party action, *Bell* v. *Hill, supra,* Federal courts must for themselves appraise the facts leading to that conclusion. It is only by the performance of this obligation that a final and uniform interpretation can be given to the Constitution, the "supreme Law of the Land." Texas requires electors in a primary to pay a poll tax. Every person who does so pay and who has the qualifications of age and residence is an acceptable voter for the primary.

. . . Texas requires by the law the election of the county officers of a party. These compose the county executive committee. The county chairmen so selected are members of the district executive committee and choose the chairman for the district. Precinct primary election officers are named by the county executive committee. Statutes provide for the election by the voters of precinct delegates to the county convention of a party and the selection of delegates to the district and state conventions by the county convention. The state convention selects the state executive committee. No convention may place in platform or resolution any demand for specific legislation without endorsement of such legislation by the voters in a primary. Texas thus directs the selection of all party officers.

Primary elections are conducted by the party under state statutory authority. The county executive committee selects precinct election officials and the county, district or state executive committees, respectively, canvass the returns. These party committees or the state convention certify the party's candidates to the appropriate officers for inclusion on the official ballot for the general election. No name which has not been so certified may appear upon the ballot for the general election as a candidate of a political party. No other name may be printed on the ballot which has not been placed in nomination by qualified voters who must take oath that they did not participate in a primary for the selection of a candidate for the office for which the nomination is made.

The state courts are given exclusive original jurisdiction of contested elections and of mandamus proceedings to compel party officers to perform their statutory duties.

[4, 5] We think that this statutory system for the selection of party nominees for inclusion on the general election ballot makes the party which is required to follow these legislative directions an agency of the state in so far as it determines the participants in a primary election. The party takes its character as a state agency from the duties imposed upon it by state statutes; the duties do not become matters of private law because they are performed by a political party. The plan of the Texas primary follows substantially that of Louisiana, with the exception that in Louisiana the state pays the cost of the primary while Texas assesses the cost against candidates. In

numerous instances, the Texas statutes fix or limit the fees to be charged. Whether paid directly by the state or through state requirements, it is state action which compels. When primaries become a part of the machinery for choosing officials, state and national, as they have here, the same tests to determine the character of discrimination or abridgement should be applied to the primary as are applied to the general election. If the state requires a certain electoral procedure, prescribes a general election ballot made up of party nominees so chosen and limits the choice of the electorate in general elections for state offices, practically speaking, to those whose names appear on such a ballot, it endorses, adopts and enforces the discrimination against Negroes, practiced by a party entrusted by Texas law with the determination of the qualifications of participants in the primary. This is state action within the meaning of the Fifteenth Amendment.

[6] The United States is a constitutional democracy. Its organic law grants to all citizens a right to participate in the choice of elected officials without restriction by any state because of race. This grant to the people of the opportunity for choice is not to be nullified by a state through casting its electoral process in a form which permits a private organization to practice racial discrimination in the election. Constitutional rights would be of little value if they could be thus indirectly denied.

[7, 8] The privilege of membership in a party may be, as this Court said in *Grovey* v. *Townsend*, no concern of a state. But when, as here, that privilege is also the essential qualification for voting in a primary to select nominees for a general election, the state makes the action of the party the action of the state. In reaching this conclusion we are not unmindful of the desirability of continuity of decision in constitutional questions. However, when convinced of former error, this Court has never felt constrained to follow precedent. In constitutional questions, where correction depends upon amendment and not upon legislative action this Court throughout its history has freely exercised its power to reexamine the basis of its constitutional decisions. This has long been accepted practice, and this practice has continued

to this day. This is particularly true when the decision believed erroneous is the application of a constitutional principle rather than an interpretation of the Constitution to extract the principle itself. Here we are applying, contrary to the recent decision in *Grovey* v. *Townsend*, the well established principle of the Fifteenth Amendment, forbidding the abridgement by a state of a citizen's right to vote. *Grovey* v. *Townsend* is overruled.

Judgment reversed.

23 Brown v. Board of Education

In the years after 1938 it became increasingly clear that the United States Supreme Court would have to deal directly with the question of racial segregation in the public educational system, both at the elementary level and at the graduate or professional school level. On May 17, 1954, it rendered the great landmark decision in *Brown v. Board of Education*. The court faced issues raised in four separate cases which ultimately combined with the Brown case.° These were grouped under a single decision. In rendering its decision the Court departed somewhat from its usual style and procedures and took into consideration the greater social implications of public education. Beyond this it considered the inequalities in the nature of education being offered not only to Negroes but to children in different sections of the United States. Prime consideration was given to the findings of educational historians and sociologists. The appearance of these sources in the footnotes in the case caused considerable disturbance among lawyers and southern legislators who believed the judicial body should have relied solely upon traditional legal sources. This was especially true in regard to footnote 11. In particular, the extreme segregationists singled out Gunar Myrdal, the Swedish sociologist and general author of *An American Dilemma*, as one of the authors of their undoing.

° *Davis v. County School Board, Gebhart v. Belton, Brown v. Board of Education, Bolling v. Sharpe.* (*Brown v. Board of Education*, 347, U.S. 483 [1954]).

In the body of the *Brown* v. *Board of Education* decision the Court suggested that since the rendering of *Sweatt* v. *Painter* it had given clear indication that it would be only a matter of time until *Plessy* v. *Ferguson* would be reversed. Nevertheless few decisions rendered by the United States Supreme Court have stirred emotions as did this one. Social and political involvements with the issues it raised will long remain an active fact in American life.

MR. CHIEF JUSTICE WARREN DELIVERED THE OPINION OF THE Court.

These cases come to us from the States of Kansas, South Carolina, Virginia, and Delaware. They are premised on different facts and different local conditions, but a common legal question justifies their consideration together in this consolidated opinion.

In each of the cases, minors of the Negro race, through their legal representatives, seek the aid of the courts in obtaining admission to the public schools of their community on a non-segregated basis. In each instance, they had been denied admission to schools attended by white children under laws requiring or permitting segregation according to race. This segregation was alleged to deprive the plaintiffs of the equal protection of the laws under the Fourteenth Amendment. In each of the cases other than the Delaware case, a three-judge federal district court denied relief to the plaintiffs on the so-called "separate but equal" doctrine announced by this Court in *Plessy* v. *Ferguson*, 163 U.S. 537. Under that doctrine, equality of treatment is accorded when the races are provided substantially equal facilities, even though these facilities be separate. In the Delaware case, the Supreme Court of Delaware adhered to the doctrine, but ordered that the plaintiffs be admitted to the white schools because of their superiority to the Negro schools.

The plaintiffs contend that segregated public schools are not "equal" and cannot be made "equal," and that hence they are deprived of the equal protection of the laws. Because of the obvious importance of the question presented, the Court took jurisdiction. Argument was heard in the 1952 Term, and reargu-

ment was heard this Term on certain questions propounded by
the Court.

Reargument was largely devoted to the circumstances surrounding the adoption of the Fourteenth Amendment in 1868.
It covered exhaustively consideration of the Amendment in
Congress, ratification by the states, then existing practices in
racial segregation, and the views of proponents and opponents
of the Amendment. This discussion and our own investigation
convince us that, although these sources cast some light, it is
not enough to resolve the problem with which we are faced. At
best, they are inconclusive. The most avid proponents of the
post-War Amendments undoubtedly intended them to remove
all legal distinctions among "all persons born or naturalized in
the United States." Their opponents, just as certainly, were antagonistic to both the letter and the spirit of the Amendments
and wished them to have the most limited effect. What others
in Congress and the state legislatures had in mind cannot be
determined with any degree of certainty.

An additional reason for the inconclusive nature of the
Amendment's history, with respect to segregated schools, is the
status of public education at that time. In the South, the movement toward free common schools, supported by general taxation, had not yet taken hold. Education of white children was
largely in the hands of private groups. Education of Negroes
was almost nonexistent, and practically all of the race were illiterate. In fact, any education of Negroes was forbidden by law
in some states. Today, in contrast, many Negroes have achieved
outstanding success in the arts and sciences as well as in the
business and professional world. It is true that public education
had already advanced further in the North, but the effect of the
Amendment on Northern States was generally ignored in the
congressional debates. Even in the North, the conditions of public education did not approximate those existing today. The
curriculum was usually rudimentary; ungraded schools were
common in rural areas; the school term was but three months a
year in many states; and compulsory school attendance was
virtually unknown. As a consequence, it is not surprising that

there should be so little in the history of the Fourteenth Amendment relating to its intended effect on public education.

In the first cases in this Court construing the Fourteenth Amendment, decided shortly after its adoption, the Court interpreted it as proscribing all state-imposed discriminations against the Negro race. The doctrine of "separate but equal" did not make its appearance in this Court until 1896 in the case of *Plessy* v. *Ferguson, supra,* involving not education but transportation. American courts have since labored with the doctrine for over half a century. In this Court, there have been six cases involving the "separate but equal" doctrine in the field of public education. In *Cumming* v. *County Board of Education,* 175 U.S. 528, and *Gong Lum* v. *Rice,* 275 U.S. 78, the validity of the doctrine itself was not challenged. In more recent cases, all on the graduate school level, inequality was found in that specific benefits enjoyed by white students were denied to Negro students of the same educational qualifications. *Missouri ex rel. Gaines* v. *Canada,* 305 U.S. 337; *Sipuel* v. *Oklahoma State Regents,* 339 U.S. 637. In none of these cases was it necessary to re-examine the doctrine to grant relief to the Negro plaintiff. And in *Sweatt* v. *Painter, supra,* the Court expressly reserved decision on the question whether *Plessy* v. *Ferguson* should be held inapplicable to public education.

In the instant cases, that question is directly presented. Here, unlike *Sweatt* v. *Painter,* there are findings below that the Negro and white schools involved have been equalized, or are being equalized, with respect to buildings, curricula, qualifications and salaries of teachers, and other "tangible" factors. Our decision, therefore, cannot turn on merely a comparison of these tangible factors in the Negro and white schools involved in each of the cases. We must look instead to the effect of segregation itself on public education.

In approaching this problem, we cannot turn the clock back to 1868 when the Amendment was adopted, or even to 1896 when *Plessy* v. *Ferguson* was written. We must consider public education in the light of its full development and its present place in American life throughout the Nation. Only in this way can it be determined if segregation in public schools deprives these plaintiffs of the equal protection of the laws.

Today, education is perhaps the most important function of state and local governments. Compulsory school attendance laws and the great expenditures for education both demonstrate our recognition of the importance of education to our democratic society. It is required in the performance of our most basic public responsibilities, even service in the armed forces. It is the very foundation of good citizenship. Today it is a principal instrument in awakening the child to cultural values, in preparing him for later professional training, and in helping him to adjust normally to his environment. In these days, it is doubtful that any child may reasonably be expected to succeed in life if he is denied the opportunity of an education. Such an opportunity, where the state has undertaken to provide it, is a right which must be made available to all on equal terms.

We come then to the question presented: Does segregation of children in public schools solely on the basis of race, even though the physical facilities and other "tangible" factors may be equal, deprive the children of the minority group of equal educational opportunities? We believe that it does.

In *Sweatt* v. *Painter, supra*, in finding that a segregated law school for Negroes could not provide them equal educational opportunities, this Court relied in large part on "those qualities which are incapable of objective measurement but which make for greatness in a law school." In *McLaurin* v. *Oklahoma State Regents, supra*, the Court, in requiring that a Negro admitted to a white graduate school be treated like all other students, again, restored to intangible considerations: ". . . his ability to study, to engage in discussions and exchange views with other students, and, in general, to learn his profession." Such considerations apply with added force to children in grade and high schools. To separate them from others of similar age and qualifications solely because of their race generates a feeling of inferiority as to their status in the community that may affect their hearts and minds in a way unlikely ever to be undone. The effect of this separation on their educational opportunities was well stated by a finding in the Kansas case by a court which nevertheless felt compelled to rule against the Negro plaintiffs:

> Segregation of white and colored children in public schools has a detrimental effect upon the colored children. The impact is greater when it has the sanction of the law; for the policy of separating the races is usually interpreted as denoting the inferiority of the Negro group. A sense of inferiority affects the motivation of a child to learn. Segregation with the sanction of law, therefore, has a tendency to retard the educational and mental development of Negro children and to deprive them of some of the benefits they would receive in a racially integrated school system.

Whatever may have been the extent of psychological knowledge at the time of *Plessy* v. *Ferguson,* this finding is amply supported by modern authority. Any language in *Plessy* v. *Ferguson* contrary to this finding is rejected.

We conclude that in the field of public education the doctrine of "separate but equal" has no place. Separate educational facilities are inherently unequal. Therefore, we hold that the plaintiffs and others similarly situated for whom the actions have been brought are, by reason of the segregation complained of, deprived of the equal protection of the laws guaranteed by the Fourteenth Amendment. This disposition makes unnecessary any discussion whether such segregation also violates the Due Process Clause of the Fourteenth Amendment.

Because these are class actions, because of the wide applicability of this decision, and because of the great variety of local conditions, the formulation of decrees in these cases presents problems of considerable complexity. On reargument, the consideration of appropriate relief was necessarily subordinated to the primary question—the constitutionality of segregation in public education. We have now announced that such segregation is a denial of the equal protection of the laws. In order that we may have the full assistance of the parties in formulating decrees, the cases will be restored to the docket, and the parties are requested to present further argument on Questions 4 and 5 previously propounded by the Court for the reargument this Term. The Attorney General of the United States is again invited to participate. The Attorneys General of the states requiring or permitting segregation in public education will also be permitted to appear as *amici curiae* upon request to do so by September 15, 1954, and submission of briefs by October 1, 1954. It is so ordered.

24 Testing Brown v. Board of Education

In September 1957, the first major test of desegregating a large high school system came in Little Rock, Arkansas. Every conceivable legal device was used to stay the inevitable moment of obeying the mandate of the Court. A great deal of legal confusion was created in the minds of southern people by the passage of numerous state laws, and by state and federal court decisions. Actually the federal courts had dealt gently with the Little Rock School Board, ordering it to begin gradual integration only. Just prior to school opening the issue of state law versus federal court decision was brought before Federal Judge Ronald N. Davies, and the first of the editorials from the *Arkansas Gazette* reprinted below describes the results. A subsequent editorial attacks Governor Orval Faubus for making a mess of school opening. The paper even accuses him of creating the Central High School crisis.

THE TESTING

In his clear and forthright ruling in the Little Rock school case Federal Judge Ronald N. Davies has swept away the legal confusion generated by the apparent conflict between state and federal laws.

The judge ordered the Little Rock School Board to proceed

The Arkansas Gazette, September 1 and 4, 1957.

on schedule with its plan for limited, gradual integration at the High School level—and he enjoined "all persons, in any manner, directly or indirectly, from interfering with the plan of integration as approved by the United States District Court."

This means that on Tuesday some 15 Negro children will be enrolled at Little Rock Central High School along with more than 2,000 whites. There are those who have suggested that this cannot be done without inciting the populace of this city to violence. They have, we believe, too little faith in the respect of our people for law and order.

We do not believe any organized group of citizens would under any circumstances undertake to do violence to school children of any race. And if there are any individuals who might embark upon such a reckless and indefensible course we have no doubt that our law enforcement officers can and will preserve order.

This is a time of testing for all of us. Few of us are entirely happy over the necessary developments in the wake of changes in the law. But certainly we must recognize that the School Board is simply carrying out its clear duty—and is doing so in the ultimate best interests of all the school children of Little Rock, white and colored alike.

We are confident that the citizens of Little Rock will demonstrate on Tuesday for the world to see that we are a law-abiding people.

THE CRISIS

Little Rock arose yesterday to gaze upon the incredible spectacle of an empty high school surrounded by National Guard troops called out by Governor Faubus to protect life and property against a mob that never materialized.

Mr. Faubus says he based this extraordinary action on reports of impending violence. Dozens of local reporters and national correspondents worked through the day yesterday without verifying the few facts the governor offered to explain why his appraisal was so different from that of local officials—who have asked for no such action.

Mr. Faubus contends that he has done nothing that can be construed as defiance of the federal government.

Federal Judge Ronald N. Davies last night accepted the governor's statement at its face value, and ordered the School Board to proceed on the assumption that the National Guard would protect the right of the nine enrolled Negro children to enter high school without interference.

Now it remains for Mr. Faubus to decide whether he intends to pose what could be the most serious constitutional question to face the national government since the Civil War. The effect of his action so far is to interpose his state office between the local School District and the United States Court. The government, as Judge Davies implied last night, now has no choice but to proceed against such interference or abandon its right to enforce its rulings and decisions.

Thus the issue is no longer segregation vs. integration. The question has now become the supremacy of the government of the United States in all matters of law. And clearly the federal government cannot let this issue remain unsolved, no matter what the cost to this community.

Until last Thursday the matter of gradual, limited integration in the Little Rock schools was a local problem which had been well and wisely handled by responsible local officials who have had—and we believe still have—the support of a majority of the people of this city. On that day Mr. Faubus appeared in Chancery Court on behalf of a small but militant minority and chose to make it a state problem. On Monday night he called out the National Guard and made it a national problem.

It is one he must now live with, and the rest of us must suffer under. If Mr. Faubus in fact has no intention of defying federal authority now is the time for him to call a halt to the resistance which is preventing the carrying out of a duly entered court order. And certainly he should do so before his own actions become the cause of the violence he professes to fear.

52 Baker v. Carr

Few cases decided by the United States Supreme Court have promised to go so deeply into the foundations of the state political system as does *Baker* v. *Carr*.* This case was brought from the Middle District Court of Tennessee to insure better representation for Nashville and Davidson County. This issue, however, was of broad national interest, and in time the Nashville mayor was to be joined in the case by mayors from many American cities. In remanding the case to the district courts for adjudication, the Supreme Court declared the issue constitutionally justiciable. Beyond this it struck a fatal blow at a great American political tradition by seriously weakening the position of the rural politician, and by giving more power to the urban representative.

The decision, the dissents, and the historical matter connected with *Baker* v. *Carr* constitute an interesting discourse on representative government. Research was thorough, and in places the dissertation is masterful. The Court felt it was venturing on to some uncertain ground, and it was indeed cautious in reaching its decision. In the long run this case may have more fundamental political meaning in the South than *Brown* v. *Board of Education*. It may in fact sound the death knell for the tight control of state government by rural voters and representatives. The material which appears here is but a small portion of the Court's discourse.

* *Baker* v. *Carr*, 369 U.S. (March 26, 1962).

ACTION UNDER THE CIVIL RIGHTS STATUTE, BY QUALIFIED VOTERS
of certain counties of Tennessee for a declaration that a state
apportionment statute was an unconstitutional deprivation of
equal protection of the laws, for an injunction, and other relief.
A three-judge District Court, for the Middle District of Tennessee, 179 F.Supp. 824, entered an order dismissing the complaint, and plaintiffs appealed. The Supreme Court, Mr. Justice
Brennan, held that complaint containing allegations that a state
statute effected an apportionment that deprived plaintiffs of
equal protection of the laws in violation of the Fourteenth
Amendment presented a justiciable constitutional cause of action, and the right asserted was within reach of judicial protection under the Fourteenth Amendment, and did not present a
nonjusticiable political question.

Reversed and remanded.

This civil action was brought under 42 U.S.C. §§ 1983 and
1988, 42 U.S.C.A. §§ 1893, 1988 to redress the alleged deprivation
of federal constitutional rights. The complaint, alleging that by
means of a 1901 statute of Tennessee apportioning the members
of the General Assembly among the State's 95 counties, "these
plaintiffs and others similarly situated, are denied the equal
protection of the laws accorded them by the Fourteenth Amendment to the Constitution of the United States by virtue of the
debasement of their votes," was dismissed by a three-judge court
convened under 28 U.S.C. § 2281, 28 U.S.C.A. § 2281 in the
Middle District of Tennessee. The court held that it lacked
jurisdiction of the subject matter and also that no claim was
stated upon which relief could be granted. We noted probable
jurisdiction of the appeal. We hold that the dismissal was error,
and remand the cause to the District Court for trial and further
proceedings consistent with this opinion.

The General Assembly of Tennessee consists of the Senate
with 33 members and the House of Representatives with 99
members. The Tennessee Constitution provides in Art. II as
follows:

Sec. 3. Legislative authority—Term of office.—The Legislative authority of this State shall be vested in a General Assembly, which shall consist of a Senate and House of Representatives, both dependent on the people; who shall hold their offices for two years from the day of the general election.

Sec. 4. Census.—An enumeration of the qualified voters, and an apportionment of the Representatives in the General Assembly, shall be made in the year one thousand eight hundred and seventy-one, and within every subsequent term of ten years.

Sec. 5. Apportionment of representatives.—The number of Representatives shall, at the several periods of making the enumeration, be apportioned among the several counties or districts, according to the number of qualified voters in each; and shall not exceed seventy-five, until the population of the State shall be one million and a half, and shall never exceed ninety-nine; Provided, that any county having two-thirds of the ratio shall be entitled to one member.

Sec. 6. Apportionment of senators.—The number of Senators shall, at the several periods of making the enumeration, be apportioned among the several counties or districts according to the number of qualified electors in each, and shall not exceed one-third the number of representatives. In apportioning the Senators among the different counties, the fraction that may be lost by any county or counties, in the apportionment of members to the House of Representatives, shall be made up to such county or counties in the Senate, as near as may be practicable. When a district is composed of two or more counties, they shall be adjoining; and no county shall be divided in forming a district.

Thus, Tennessee's standard for allocating legislative representation among her counties is the total number of qualified voters resident in the respective counties, subject only to minor qualifications. Decennial reapportionment in compliance with the constitutional scheme was effected by the General Assembly each decade from 1871 to 1901. The 1871 apportionment was preceded by an 1870 statute requiring an enumeration. The 1881 apportionment involved three statutes, the first authorizing an enumeration, the second enlarging the Senate from 25 to 33 members and the House from 75 to 99 members, and the third apportioning the membership of both Houses. In 1891 there were both an enumeration and an apportionment. In 1901 the General Assembly abandoned separate enumeration in favor of reliance upon the Federal Census and passed the Apportionment Act here in controversy. In the more than 60 years since that action, all proposals in both Houses of the General Assembly for reapportionment have failed to pass.

Between 1901 and 1961, Tennessee has experienced substantial growth and redistribution of her population. In 1901 the population was 2,020,616, of whom 487,380 were eligible to vote. The 1960 Federal Census reports the State's population at 3,567,089, of whom 2,092,891 are eligible to vote. The relative standings of the counties in terms of qualified voters have changed significantly. It is primarily the continued application of the 1901 Apportionment Act to this shifted and enlarged voting population which gives rise to the present controversy.

Indeed, the complaint alleges that the 1901 statute, even as of the time of its passage, "made no apportionment of Representatives and Senators in accordance with the constitutional formula * * *, but instead arbitrarily and capriciously apportioned representatives in the Senate and House without reference * * * to any logical or reasonable formula whatever." It is further alleged that "because of the population changes since 1900, and the failure of the Legislature to reapportion itself since 1901," the 1901 statute became "unconstitutional and obsolete." Appellants also argue that, because of the composition of the legislature effected by the 1901 Apportionment Act, redress in the form of a state constitutional amendment to change the entire mechanism for reapportioning, or any other change short of that, is difficult or impossible. The complaint concludes that "these plaintiffs and others similarly situated, are denied the equal protection of the laws accorded them by the Fourteenth Amendment to the Constitution of the United States by virtue of the debasement of their votes." They seek a declaration that the 1901 statute is unconstitutional and an injunction restraining the appellees from acting to conduct any further elections under it.

They also pray that unless and until the General Assembly enacts a valid reapportionment, the District Court should either decree a repportionment by mathematical application of the Tennessee constitutional formulae to the most recent Federal Census figures, or direct the appellees to conduct legislative elections, primary and general, at large. They also pray for such other and further relief as may be appropriate.

. . . A federal court enforcing the Federal Constitution is not, to be sure, bound by the remedial doctrines of the state courts. But it must consider as pertinent to the propriety or impropriety of exercising its jurisdiction those state-law effects of its decree which it cannot itself control. A federal court cannot provide the authority requisite to make a legislature the proper governing body of the State of Tennessee. And it cannot be doubted that the striking down of the statute here challenged on equal protection grounds, no less than on grounds of failure to reapportion decennially, would deprive the State of all valid apportionment legislation and—under the ruling in McCanless—deprive the State of an effective law-based legislative branch. Just such considerations, among others here present, were determinative in *Luther* v. *Borden* and the Oregon initiative cases.

Although the District Court had jurisdiction in the very restricted sense of power to determine whether it could adjudicate the claim, the case is of that class of political controversy which, by the nature of its subject, is unfit for federal judicial action. The judgment of the District Court, in dismissing the complaint for failure to state a claim on which relief can be granted, should therefore be affirmed.

26 Voter Registration, Citizenship Tests, and Poll Taxes

The shabby system of voter discrimination displayed itself no more openly than in Mississippi. In 1965 the United States Civil Rights Commission held hearings on voter registration and the various modes of intimidation and discrimination practiced in the state. Three black belt delta counties were brought under close scrutiny. The results were almost unbelievable. Perhaps in all the literature pertaining to the thwarting of free exercise of the ballot there is no more eloquent testimony than that given by G. H. Hood, Registrar of Humphreys County. He was choked in the noose that he himself had used so many times when Negroes sought to register. Nothing could have revealed more clearly the sham and hypocrisy of white supremacy as practiced in voter registration than this testimony by one of the system's flunkies.

THE COMMISSION'S INVESTIGATION OF REGISTRARS FOCUSED ON three Delta counties. In all three there had been a Negro voter registration drive within the past year.

Issaquena County was chosen for the most extensive investigation. It is a sparsely populated agricultural county bordering on the Mississippi River at the southern edge of the Delta. Most

U.S. Commission on Civil Rights, *Voting in Mississippi* (Washington, D.C.: Government Printing Office, 1965), 13–19.

of its farms are large plantations, and its largest town, Mayersville, has a population of less than 500. Negroes constitute 68 percent of a population of 2,700. When the Commission began its investigation in October 1964, 100 percent of the white voting age population was registered to vote, while none of the Negro population was registered. In prior years only a few Negroes had attempted to register and they were not successful.

In June 1964 civil rights workers began an organized registration effort in the county. During the next seven months about 90 Negroes, approximately 10 percent of the voting age Negro population, attempted to register. When the registration drive began the county sheriff visited several Negro residents, cautioned them against involvement with civil rights workers, and advised that they could safely visit the courthouse and attempt to register.

When Negroes began attempting to register, the principal barrier they encountered was the conduct of the registrar. From July 1961 to February 10, 1965, approximately 150 forms were completed by white applicants and 128 by Negroes. The 128 represented multiple attempts by 90 Negroes. All 150 white applicants passed on their first attempt. Only nine Negroes passed, most after repeated attempts, and only after the initiation of Commission and Department of Justice investigations.

The relative lack of success of Negro applicants resulted from three practices of the registrar: (1) discrimination in the choice of the constitutional sections; (2) discrimination in judging the interpretations and in application of the "letter-perfect" rule; and (3) discrimination in rendering assistance to whites but not to Negroes. Although the registrar chose not to appear at the hearing, the application forms from the files, analyzed by Commission staff attorneys, evidenced her practices.

During the two years preceding the first Negro effort, the period covered by the applications in her files, the registrar relied primarily on three of the shorter and less difficult sections of the Mississippi constitution in administering the interpretation test. Of the 133 white applicants who took the test during this period, 107 were given one of these three sections:

Section 35. The senate shall consist of members chosen every four years by the qualified electors of the several districts.

Section 8. All persons, resident in this state, citizens of the United States, are hereby declared citizens of the state of Mississippi.

Section 240. All elections by the people shall be by ballot.

The remaining sections used prior to July 3, 1964, were also, for the most part, short and easy to understand.

After the first Negro attempted to register, the pattern changed. The registrar began choosing more varied and slightly more difficult sections for testing whites. While some Negroes received sections comparable to these, nearly one-half of them received very difficult sections. Witnesses who appeared before the Commission had received sections on tax exemptions for corporations (§ 182), judicial sale of land (§ 111), eminent domain (§ 190), concurrent jurisdiction of chancery and circuit courts (§ 161), and habeas corpus (§ 21). Not a single white applicant received any of these sections. The complexity of these provisions is illustrated by section 182, which provides as follows:

> The power to tax corporations and their property shall never be surrendered or abridged by any contract or grant to which the state or any political subdivision thereof may be a party, except that the legislature may grant exemption from taxation in the encouragement of manufactures and other new enterprises of public utility extending for a period of not exceeding five years, the time of such exemptions to commence from date of charter, if to a corporation; and if to an individual enterprise, then from the commencement of work; but when the legislature grants such exemptions for a period of five years or less, it shall be done by general laws, which shall distinctly enumerate the classes of manufactures and other new enterprises of public utility entitled to such exemptions, and shall prescribe the mode and manner in which the right to such exemptions shall be determined.

The other sections mentioned are of comparable difficulty.

The records also show discrimination in the acceptance of answers. One white applicant, asked to interpret section 35

("The senate shall consist of members chosen every four years by the qualified electors of the several districts"), wrote only "equible wrights" and was passed. Another successful white applicant's interpretation of this section read, "The government is for the people and by the people." Six white applicants left question 20 on the duties of citizenship blank and were passed. Six other white applicants failed to sign their applications, and 13 others mistakenly signed the special oath for ministers. All were passed.

The registrar refused to accept Negro forms with similar deficiencies. Three Negro applicants were denied registration for failure to sign on the appropriate line. Negroes also gave inadequate interpretations of constitutional sections, but unlike white applicants, they did not succeed in passing the test.

Beginning in November 1964, after Commission investigators and Justice Department attorneys had interviewed the registrar, a few Negroes were passed. It appears that after October the registrar relaxed her standards for some Negro applicants. Mrs. Unita Zelma Blackwell, a leader of the registration drive, who had taken and failed the registration test on two prior occasions, testified about her third attempt in January 1965:

> Mrs. Blackwell: I filled it out and I had section 97 and I wrote it down and looked it over and I picked some of the words out of, you know, what I had wrote down; put that in there and turned it over. And I misspelled "length" and I said "Oh, my Lord." And so then I filled out the rest of it and when I got through I handed it to her, and I said "Well, I misspelled this, and well, I didn't date the top," and she said "Oh, that's all right, it's all right, it's all right." And then she ran and got the book and [registered me].

The forms provide evidence that the registrar had previously given assistance to white applicants. Many of the whites' forms bore similar or identical answers. Fifteen of the 48 whites who interpreted section 35 gave, verbatim, the following answer: "To elect the Senate members every four years in order to get people who keep abreast of the times." One person gave the same answer, but omitted the word "abreast." Fourteen of these same 15 persons described the duties of citizenship with the following: "To obey the laws of the state and serve in a useful capacity whenever possible." The other person gave substantially the same response. Nine of the 21 applicants interpreting section 240 ("All elections by the people shall be by ballot") wrote: "Election of the people shall be held by secret ballot." The word "secret" is not suggested by the wording of section 240. All nine also used identical words to answer question 20 on the duties of citizenship: "Obey the duties of the government and carry out the rules and laws to the best of your ability."

The practices of the Issaquena County registrar are by no means atypical. At the time of the hearing the Department of Justice had brought 23 lawsuits against Mississippi registrars to eliminate the effects of discrimination in the registration process. In addition, an analysis of records from 31 counties shows that registrars in at least two-thirds of these counties have required Negroes to interpret more difficult sections of the constitution than whites. In virtually all of these counties the records show discrimination against Negroes in the grading of applications and in the furnishing of assistance. The United States Court of Appeals for the Fifth Circuit described some of these practices in deciding the first Mississippi voting case to end in a final decree:

> The Negro citizens were not treated in the same manner as the white citizen. The application was treated largely as an information form when submitted by a white person. It was a test of skill for the Negro. It was not even a test of literacy for the white, whereas any Negro applicant demonstrated his literacy in filling out the form. Much more difficult sections of the Constitution were given to the Negroes to write and construe than those given to the white applicants. Delay and refusal of deputies to serve the Negroes were uniform, whereas speed and dispatch, to the extent of permitting the applicant to sign immediately, were the lot of the white.

The Commission also heard testimony on the administration of the constitutional interpretation test by the registrar of Humphreys County.

Humphreys County lies in the heart of the Delta. Negroes constitute 66 percent of its population of 19,000. At the time of the Commission's hearing in February 1965, approximately 68 percent of the voting age white population, but none of the Negro population, was registered to vote. No Negroes had even attempted to register between 1955, when one Negro registration leader was killed by a shotgun blast and another severely wounded, and August 1964, when a new registration drive began. Between August and the time of the Commission's hearing, 16 Negroes had attempted to register, but none had succeeded in passing the test.

The Humphreys County registrar, G. H. Hood, testified that in administering the test he followed the practice of choosing constitutional sections consecutively. When he reached the end of the 286-section constitution, he would begin again. Mr. Hood stated that he did not draw any distinction between hard or easy sections. Each section was given in turn. This testimony was supported by records he submitted in response to the Commission's subpoena.

While Mr. Hood did not appear to discriminate in choosing sections, he did not eliminate very difficult sections, such as section 182, concerning the power to tax corporations, which the registrar of Issaquena County had reserved for Negro applicants. By using these sections he imposed a test which neither he nor the majority of white Mississippians had been required to take when they registered. When asked at the hearing whether he could interpret this section, the following colloquy ensued:

> Commissioner Griswold: I hand you a copy of section 182 of the Mississippi constitution. Would you please make a reasonable interpretation of section 182 for the Commission?
> (Pause.)
> Mr. Hood: You say 182?
> Commissioner Griswold: Yes.
> Mr. Hood: I'm sorry, sir. I've been reading 183.
> (Pause.)
> Mr. Hood: Well, it means that the power to tax corporations,

their property, shall never be surrendered or abridged by any contract. And—

Commissioner Griswold: I didn't ask you to read it, Mr. Hood. I asked you to interpret it.

Mr. Bridges (Aside to Mr. Hood).

Commissioner Griswold: Mr. Chairman, I think it should be the witness' interpretation; not his counsel's.

Mr. Bridges: If you please, gentlemen, the conference between the witness and his attorney had nothing to do with the question. It was a question whether he was to answer it or not.

Mr. Hood: Which I will not.

Mr. Bridges: Which he will not.

Commissioner Griswold: You decline to interpret section 182?

Mr. Hood: On pressure being put on me before a Committee like this.

Commissioner Griswold: On the ground that it may incriminate you?

Mr. Hood: That's right.

                                        ❂   ❂   ❂

Commissioner Griswold: I find it a little hard to see how citizens of Mississippi are expected to interpret the section if the registrar is unable to do so and he is the person who grades the interpretation which is made by a citizen of Mississippi.

The administration of the registration test by the registrar of Washington County contrasts with the practices of officials in Issaquena and Humphreys Counties. Washington borders the Mississippi River north of Issaquena and has a population of 77,000, of which 56 percent is Negro. Greenville, the county seat, has been an industrial and cultural center of the Delta since the Civil War. It has a population of 41,000.

Negro witnesses from Greenville testified that the county registrar applies the constitutional interpretation test without using the harder constitutional sections. An applicant draws a slip bearing one of a number of relatively easy sections from a box. In the opinion of the witnesses, the registrar has been fair in his grading of the tests.

The fairer administration of registration tests in Washington County accounts, in part, for the fact that it is one of a handful of Mississippi counties where Negro registration exceeds 10 percent. As of February 1965, Negro registration for Washington County was estimated at 2,500. Based on this estimate, Negro registration is approximately 12 percent of the 1960 voting age Negro population, which is significantly higher than in adjacent Delta counties. A local voter registration organization has been active since 1943, and was assisted by a number of civil rights organizations during 1964.

While Negroes in Washington County fare better at the hands of the registrar than in most other Mississippi counties, the percentage of Negroes registered still falls far below average Negro registration in other Southern States. In part this results from inferior educational opportunities afforded Negro citizens. Public schools are segregated in Washington County and the median education level is 5th grade for Negroes and 12th grade for whites.

COLLECTION OF THE POLL TAX

As described in Chapter I, payment of a poll tax was made a prerequisite for voting in Mississippi in 1890 to restrict or eliminate exercise of the franchise by Negro citizens. Since that time Negroes have experienced difficulty in certain counties in paying the tax. Under Mississippi law the sheriff is the tax collector. In 1955, when Negroes in Humphreys County started a voter registration drive, the sheriff refused to accept their poll tax payments until compelled to do so by court order. Negroes seeking to qualify to vote for the first time experienced difficulty in paying poll taxes in Issaquena County in 1959. Between 1956 and 1964, when the Department of Justice brought suit, the sheriff of Holmes County refused to accept poll taxes from Negroes. Between 1948 and 1963, when the Department of Justice filed suit to enjoin the practice, officials in Chickasaw County allegedly refused to accept poll tax payments from Negroes. In recent years, the Commission has also received complaints that Negroes had not been permitted to pay poll taxes in Amite, Bolivar, Jefferson Davis, and Tallahatchie Counties.

There is evidence that officials have used more subtle methods than outright refusal to prevent Negroes from paying the tax. The sheriff of Tallahatchie County, where most whites but few Negroes had registered to vote, admitted that he instructed his deputies to require all persons paying poll taxes for the first time to apply to him personally. This requirement was voided by Federal court order in 1961. A Carroll County witness described a different official technique:

> Commissioner Freeman: Do the officers try to get the people to pay the poll tax?
>
> Mr. Eskridge: Well, they will ask every white person that come in there, and every Negro they won't say a word. I was in there paying taxes here in February, and every white person come in there, white women especially they ask them about paying tax. When I paid my tax, they hand me just my tax receipt and didn't ask for a poll tax. ° ° °

The Commission's investigation of registration practices indicated that the constitutional interpretation test, devised as an instrument of disfranchisement, is used in many counties to maximum advantage by the registrar to prevent any registration by Negroes or to limit such registration to token numbers. Even where the test is fairly administered it remains a significant impediment to Negro registration. In addition to overcoming the hurdle of registration, a Negro who wishes to vote must succeed in having his poll tax payment accepted by the sheriff for two successive years. Together, these requirements present a formidable obstacle to Negro registration and voting in Mississippi.

PART 4 The Negro as Southerner

THE NEGRO HAS AT LAST BEEN GIVEN A CENTRAL CHAPTER OF southern history. Every phase of southern life is deeply involved with the Negro. Even as he has suffered from the abuses of segregation in so many social, economic, and political areas, he has taken his place in southern patterns of thought and in the ever-evolving mores of the South. Little more than a sampling of materials on the Negro can be included in so brief a space.[1] Since 1954 alone approximately 4000 books and pamphlets have been published on the Negro in America.[2] Even though the

[1] Gunar Myrdal, *An American Dilemma;* W. E. B. Du Bois, *Black Reconstruction: An Essay Toward a History of the Part which Black Folk Played in the Attempt to Reconstruct Democracy in America, 1860–1880* (New York: Harcourt, Brace and Company, 1935), and *The Souls of Black Folk: Essays and Sketches* (Chicago: A. C. McClurg & Co., 1903); John Dollard, *Caste and Class in a Southern Town* (New Haven: Yale University Press, 1937); E. Franklin Frazier, *The Negro in the United States* (New York: Macmillan Co., 1949; Horace M. Bond, *The Education of the Negro in the American Social Order* (New York: Prentice-Hall, Inc., 1934); and Claude H. Nolen, *The Negro's Image in the South.*

[2] Elizabeth W. Miller, compiler, *The Negro in America, A Bibliography* (Cambridge: Harvard University Press, 1966). Specific titles for this era are Harry S. Ashmore, *The Negro and the Schools* (Chapel Hill: The University of North Carolina Press, 1954); James McBride Dabbs, *The Southern Heritage* (New York: Alfred A. Knopf, 1958), and *Who Speaks for the South?* (New York: Funk & Wagnalls, 1964); Albert P. Blaustein and Clarence Clyde Ferguson Jr., *Desegregation and the Law.* The periodical,

selection of materials included here is brief, a consistent thread runs through the writings of both white and Negro describing discriminations, conditions and quality of life, and the struggle to achieve political and economic equality. The rationale of segregation seems to be a consistent one, and the Negro protest against discrimination is equally consistent.[3]

The history of racial relations in the South since 1865 appears as little more than prologue to the revolution which has occurred since 1945. But despite phenomenal changes that have taken place in many areas of racial associations, it is to be doubted that the attitude of the mass of southern whites has undergone radical changes. The Negro, however, has found his own voice and possesses enough courage to make known in a flood of published materials his aspirations, angers, and determinations. Where once only a few men like Du Bois or Washington spoke for the Negro, there are now spokesmen on every hand. They now speak out as Southerners and Americans, and not as submissive freedmen or victims of Jim Crowism.[4]

New South, published by the Southern Regional Council since 1945, is one of the most consistent sources for tracing the course of southern racial attitudes and reactions.

[3] Howard W. Odum, *Race and Rumor of Race* gives a calm and thoughtful analysis of this subject. Lerone Bennett, Jr., *The Negro Mood and Other Essays* (Chicago: Johnson Pub. Co., 1964), and Martin Luther King, Jr., *Why We Can't Wait* are samples of the Negro mood at this point in the twentieth century.

[4] Rayford Logan, ed., *What the Negro Wants*. Added to this are hundreds of voices listed in Elizabeth Miller, compiler, *The Negro in America, A Bibliography*.

27 The Freedman's Case in Equity

No more courageous voice was heard in the South in 1885 than that of the novelist and public reader George Washington Cable. He delivered the main part of "The Freedman's Case in Equity" in a two hour speech before the National Conference of Charities and Correction in 1882 in Louisville. Between that date and 1884 when the essay was published in the *Century Magazine* there was some editorial comment on the speech. After its publication in the popular national magazine there occurred a veritable tornado of criticism.

Cable had used great care in his search for documentary proof for his assertions. In this article he reviewed the abuses of convicts in several of the southern states, and tied his observations in with the race problem. Although published eleven years before the famous racial decision, *Plessy* v. *Ferguson*, which sustained "Jim Crow" practices in southern life, the essay raised the biting question of defining the freedman's place in an open and free society. Beyond this he called the white Southerner's attention to the fact he could not force two-fifths of the South's population into a debased social role in the region without condemning southern society as a whole to shabby mediocrity.

An interesting test of the validity of Cable's views is how well they described the situation in the South down to 1960. He might well have offered this article, except for the convict section, for publication in 1960 with slight changes of phraseology.[*]

[*] Louis D. Rubin, *George W. Cable: The Life and Times of a Southern Heretic* (New York: Pegasus, 1969), 110–115.

THE GREATEST SOCIAL PROBLEM BEFORE THE AMERICAN PEOPLE
to-day is, as it has been for a hundred years, the presence among
us of the negro.

No comparable entanglement was ever drawn round itself by
any other modern nation with so serene a disregard of its ultimate issue, or with a more distinct national responsibility. The
African slave was brought here by cruel force, and with everybody's consent except his own. Everywhere the practice was
favored as a measure of common aggrandizement. When a few
men and women protested, they were mobbed in the public interest, with the public consent. There rests, therefore, a moral
responsibility on the whole nation never to lose sight of the results of African-American slavery until they cease to work mis-
chief and injustice.

It is true these responsibilities may not fall everywhere with
the same weight; but they are nowhere entirely removed. The
original seed of trouble was sown with the full knowledge and
consent of the nation. The nation was to blame; and so long as
evils spring from it, their correction must be the nation's duty.

The late Southern slave has within two decades risen from
slavery to freedom, from freedom to citizenship, passed on into
political ascendency, and fallen again from that eminence. The
amended Constitution holds him up in his new political rights
as well as a mere constitution can. On the other hand, certain
enactments of Congress, trying to reach further, have lately
been made void by the highest court of the nation. And another
thing has happened. The popular mind in the old free States,
weary of strife at arm's length, bewildered by its complications,
vexed by many a blunder, eager to turn to the cure of other
evils, and even tinctured by that race feeling whose grosser excesses it would so gladly see suppressed, has retreated from its
uncomfortable dictational attitude and thrown the whole matter
over to the States of the South. Here it rests, no longer a main

George W. Cable, "The Freedman's Case in Equity," *Century Magazine*, 24 [Old Series] (February 1884), 409–418.

party issue, but a group of questions which are to be settled by each of these States separately in the light of simple equity and morals, and which the genius of American government does not admit of being forced upon them from beyond their borders. Thus the whole question, become secondary in party contest, has yet reached a period of supreme importance.

Before slavery ever became a grave question in the nation's politics,—when it seemed each State's private affair, developing unmolested,—it had two different fates in two different parts of the country. In one, treated as a question of public equity, it withered away. In the other, overlooked in that aspect, it petrified and became the corner-stone of the whole social structure; and when men sought its overthrow as a national evil, it first brought war upon the land, and then grafted into the citizenship of one of the most intelligent nations in the world six millions of people from one of the most debased races on the globe.

And now this painful and wearisome question, sown in the African slave trade, reaped in our civil war, and garnered in the national adoption of millions of an inferior race, is drawing near a second seed-time. For this is what the impatient proposal to make it a dead and buried issue really means. It means to recommit it to the silence and concealment of the covered furrow. Beyond that incubative retirement no suppressed moral question can be pushed; but all such questions, ignored in the domain of private morals, spring up and expand once more into questions of public equity; neglected as matters of public equity, they blossom into questions of national interest; and, despised in that guise, presently yield the red fruits of revolution.

This question must never again bear that fruit. There must arise, nay, there has arisen, in the South itself, a desire to see established the equities of the issue; to make it no longer a question of endurance between one group of States and another, but between the moral débris of an exploded evil and the duty, necessity, and value of planting society firmly upon universal justice and equity. This, and this only, can give the matter final burial. True, it is still a question between States; but only sec-

ondarily, as something formerly participated in, or as it concerns
every householder to know that what is being built against his
house is built by level and plummet. It is the interest of the
Southern States first, and *consequently* of the whole land, to
discover clearly these equities and the errors that are being committed against them.

If we take up this task, the difficulties of the situation are
plain. We have, first, a revision of Southern State laws which has
forced into them the recognition of certain human rights dis-
cordant with the sentiments of those who have always called
themselves the community; second, the removal of the entire
political machinery by which this forcing process was effected;
and third, these revisions left to be interpreted and applied
under the domination of these antagonistic sentiments. These
being the three terms of the problem, one of three things must
result. There will arise a system of vicious evasions eventually
ruinous to public and private morals and liberty, or there will
be a candid reconsideration of the sentiments hostile to these
enactments, or else there will be a division, some taking one
course and some the other.

This is what we should look for from our knowledge of men
and history; and this is what we find. The revised laws, only
where they could not be evaded, have met that reluctant or
simulated acceptance of their narrowest letter which might have
been expected—a virtual suffocation of those principles of human equity which the unwelcome decrees do little more than
shadow forth. But in different regions this attitude has been
made in very different degrees of emphasis. In some the new
principles have grown, or are growing, into the popular conviction, and the opposing sentiments are correspondingly dying
out. There are even some limited districts where they have received much practical acceptance. While, again, other sections
lean almost wholly toward the old sentiments; an easy choice,
since it is the conservative, the unyielding attitude, whose
strength is in the absence of intellectual and moral debate.

Now, what are the gains, what the losses of these diverse attitudes? Surely these are urgent questions to any one in our coun-

try who believes it is always a losing business to be in the wrong.
Particularly in the South, where each step in this affair is an
unprecedented experience, it will be folly if each region, small
or large, does not study the experiences of all the rest. And yet
this, alone, would be superficial; we would still need to do more.
We need to go back to the roots of things and study closely,
analytically, the origin, the present foundation, the rationality,
the rightness, of those sentiments surviving in us which prompt
an attitude qualifying in any way peculiarly the black man's
liberty among us. Such a treatment will be less abundant in incident, less picturesque; but it will be more thorough.

First, then, what are these sentiments? Foremost among them
stands the idea that he is of necessity an alien. He was brought
to our shores a naked, brutish, unclean, captive, pagan savage,
to be and remain a kind of connecting link between man and the
beasts of burden. The great changes to result from his contact
with a superb race of masters were not taken into account. As a
social factor he was intended to be as purely zero as the brute
at the other end of his plow-line. The occasional mingling of his
blood with that of the white man worked no change in the sentiment; one, two, four, eight, multiplied upon or divided into
zero, still gave zero for the result. Generations of American
nativity made no difference; his children and children's children
were born in sight of our door, yet the old notion held fast. He
increased to vast numbers, but it never wavered. He accepted
our dress, language, religion, all the fundamentals of our civilization, and became forever expatriated from his own land; still
he remained, to us, an alien. Our sentiment went blind. It did
not see that gradually, here by force and there by choice, he was
fulfilling a host of conditions that earned at least a solemn moral
right to that naturalization which no one at first had dreamed
of giving him. Frequently he even bought back the freedom of
which he had been robbed, became a tax-payer, and at times
an educator of his children at his own expense; but the old idea
of alienism passed laws to banish him, his wife, and children by
thousands from the state, and threw him into loathsome jails
as a common felon for returning to his native land.

It will be wise to remember that these were the acts of an enlightened, God-fearing people, the great mass of whom have passed beyond all earthly accountability. They were our fathers. I am the son and grandson of slave-holders. These were their faults; posterity will discover ours; but these things must be frankly, fearlessly taken into account if we are ever to understand the true interests of our peculiar state of society.

Why, then, did this notion that the man of color must always remain an alien stand so unshaken? We may readily recall how, under ancient systems, he rose not only to high privileges, but often to public station and power. Singularly, with us the trouble lay in a modern principle of liberty. The whole idea of American government rested on all men's equal, inalienable right to secure their life, liberty, and the pursuit of happiness by governments founded in their own consent. Hence, our Southern forefathers, shedding their blood, or ready to shed it, for this principle, yet proposing in equal good conscience to continue holding the American black man and mulatto and quadroon in slavery, had to anchor that conscience, their conduct, and their laws in the conviction that the man of African tincture was, not by his master's arbitrary assertion merely, but by nature and unalterably, an alien. If that hold should break, one single wave of irresistible inference would lift our whole Southern social fabric and dash it upon the rocks of negro emancipation and enfranchisement. How was it made secure? Not by books, though they were written among us from every possible point of view, but, with the mass of our slave-owners, by the calm hypothesis of a positive, intuitive knowledge. To them the statement was an axiom. They abandoned the methods of moral and intellectual reasoning, and fell back upon this assumption of a God-given instinct, nobler than reason, and which it was an insult to a freeman to ask him to prove on logical grounds.

Yet it was found not enough. The slave multiplied. Slavery was a dangerous institution. Few in the South to-day have any just idea how often the slave plotted for his freedom. Our Southern ancestors were a noble, manly people, springing from some

of the most highly intelligent, aspiring, upright, and refined nations of the modern world; from the Huguenot, the French
Chevalier, the Old Englander, the New Englander. Their acts
were not always right; whose are? But for their peace of mind
they had to believe them so. They therefore spoke much of the
negro's contentment with that servile condition for which nature
had designed him. Yet there was no escaping the knowledge
that we dared not trust the slave caste with any power that could
be withheld from them. So the perpetual alien was made also a
perpetual menial, and the belief became fixed that this, too, was
nature's decree, not ours.

Thus we stood at the close of the civil war. There were always
a few Southerners who did not justify slavery, and many who
cared nothing whether it was just or not. But what we have described was the general sentiment of good Southern people.
There was one modifying sentiment. It related to the slave's
spiritual interests. Thousands of pious masters and mistresses
flatly broke the shameful laws that stood between their slaves
and the Bible. Slavery was right; but religion, they held, was for
the alien and menial as well as for the citizen and master. They
could be alien and citizen, menial and master, in church as well
as out; and they were.

Yet over against this lay another root of to-day's difficulties.
This perpetuation of the alien, menial relation tended to perpetuate the vices that naturally cling to servility, dense ignorance and a hopeless separation from true liberty; and as we
could not find it in our minds to blame slavery with this perpetuation, we could only assume as a further axiom that there was,
by nature, a disqualifying moral taint in every drop of negro
blood. The testimony of an Irish, German, Italian, French, or
Spanish beggar in a court of justice was taken on its merits; but
the colored man's was excluded by law wherever it weighed
against a white man. The colored man was a prejudged culprit.
The discipline of the plantation required that the difference
between master and slave be never lost sight of by either. It
made our master caste a solid mass, and fixed a common master-

hood and subserviency between the ruling and the serving race.* Everyone of us grew up in the idea that he had, by birth and race, certain broad powers of police over any and every person of color.

All at once the tempest of war snapped off at the ground every one of these arbitrary relations, without removing a single one of the sentiments in which they stood rooted. Then, to fortify the freedman in the tenure of his new rights, he was given the ballot. Before this grim fact the notion of alienism, had it been standing alone, might have given way. The idea that slavery was right did begin to crumble almost at once. "As for slavery," said an old Creole sugar-planter and former slave-owner to me, "it was damnable." The revelation came like a sudden burst of light. It is one of the South's noblest poets who has but just said:

> I am a Southerner;
> I love the South; I dared for her
> To fight from Lookout to the sea,
> With her proud banner over me:
> But from my lips thanksgiving broke,
> As God in battle-thunder spoke,
> And that Black Idol, breeding drouth
> And dearth of human sympathy
> Throughout the sweet and sensuous South,
>   Was, with its chains and human yoke,
> Blown hellward from the cannon's mouth,
>   While Freedom cheered behind the smoke!

With like readiness might the old alien relation have given way if we could only, while letting that pass, have held fast by the other old ideas. But they were all bound together. See our embarrassment. For more than a hundred years we had made these sentiments the absolute essentials to our self-respect. And

---

* The old Louisiana Black Code says, "That free people of color ought never to . . . presume to conceive themselves equal to the white; but, on the contrary, that they ought to yield to them in every occasion, and never speak or answer to them but with respect, under the penalty of imprisonment according to the nature of the offense." (Section 21, p. 164.)

yet if we clung to them, how could we meet the freedman on equal terms in the political field? Even to lead would not compensate us; for the fundamental profession of American politics is that the leader is servant to his followers. It was too much. The ex-master and ex-slave—the quarter-deck and the forecastle, as it were—could not come together. But neither could the American mind tolerate a continuance of martial law. The agonies of reconstruction followed.

The vote, after all, was a secondary point, and the robbery and bribery on one side, and whipping and killing on the other, were but huge accidents of the situation. The two main questions were really these: on the freedman's side, how to establish republican State government under the same recognition of his rights that the rest of Christendom accorded him; and on the former master's side, how to get back to the old semblance of republican State government, and—allowing that the freedman was *de facto* a voter—still to maintain a purely arbitrary superiority of all whites over all blacks, and a purely arbitrary equality of all blacks among themselves as an alien, menial, and dangerous class.

Exceptionally here and there some one in the master caste did throw off the old and accept the new ideas, and, if he would allow it, was instantly claimed as a leader by the newly liberated thousands around him. But just as promptly the old master race branded him also an alien reprobate, and in ninety-nine cases out of a hundred, if he had not already done so, he soon began to confirm by his actions the brand on his cheek. However, we need give no history here of the dreadful episode of reconstruction. Under an experimentative truce its issues rest to-day upon the pledge of the wiser leaders of the master class: Let us but remove the hireling demagogue, and we will see to it that the freedman is accorded a practical, complete, and cordial recognition of his equality with the white man before the law. As far as there has been any understanding at all, it is not that the originally desired ends of reconstruction have been abandoned, but that the men of North and South have agreed upon a new, gentle, and peaceable method for reaching them; that, without change as to the ends in view, compulsory reconstruction has been set aside and a voluntary reconstruction is on trial.

It is the fashion to say we paused to let the "feelings engendered by the war" pass away, and that they are passing. But let not these truths lead us into error. The sentiments we have been analyzing, and upon which we saw the old compulsory reconstruction go hard aground—these are not the "feelings engendered by the war." We must disentangle them from the "feelings engendered by the war," and by reconstruction. They are older than either. But for them slavery would have perished of itself, and emancipation and reconstruction been peaceful revolutions.

Indeed, as between master and slave, the "feelings engendered by the war" are too trivial, or at least were too short-lived, to demand our present notice. One relation and feeling the war destroyed: the patriarchal tie and its often really tender and benevolent sentiment of dependence and protection. When the slave became a freedman the sentiment of alienism became for the first time complete. The abandonment of this relation was not one-sided; the slave, even before the master, renounced it. Countless times, since reconstruction began, the master has tried, in what he believed to be everybody's interest, to play on that old sentiment. But he found it a harp without strings. The freedman could not formulate, but he could see, all our old ideas of autocracy and subserviency, of master and menial, of an arbitrarily fixed class to guide and rule, and another to be guided and ruled. He rejected the overture. The old master, his well-meant condescensions slighted, turned away estranged, and justified himself in passively withholding that simpler protection without patronage which any one American citizen, however exalted, owes to any other, however humble. Could the freedman in the bitterest of those days have consented to throw himself upon just that one old relation, he could have found a physical security for himself and his house such as could not, after years of effort, be given him by constitutional amendments, Congress, United States marshals, regiments of regulars, and ships of war. But he could not; the very nobility of the civilization that had held him in slavery had made him too much a man to go back to that shelter; and by his manly neglect to do so he has proved to us who once ruled over him that, be his relative standing among the races of men what it may, he is worthy to be free.

To be a free man is his still distant goal. Twice he has been a freedman. In the days of compulsory reconstruction he was freed in the presence of his master by that master's victorious foe. In these days of voluntary reconstruction he is virtually freed by the consent of his master, but the master retaining the exclusive right to define the bounds of his freedom. Many everywhere have taken up the idea that this state of affairs is the end to be desired and the end actually sought in reconstruction as handed over to the States. I do not charge such folly to the best intelligence of any American community; but I cannot ignore my own knowledge that the average thought of some regions rises to no better idea of the issue. The belief is all too common that the nation, having aimed at a wrong result and missed, has left us of the Southern States to get now such other result as we think best. I say this belief is not universal. There are those among us who see that America has no room for a state of society which makes its lower classes harmless by abridging their liberties, or, as one of the favored class lately said to me, has "got 'em so they don't give no trouble." There is a growing number who see that the one thing we cannot afford to tolerate at large is a class of people less than citizens; and that every interest in the land demands that the freedman be free to become in all things, as far as his own personal gifts will lift and sustain him, the same sort of American citizen he would be if, with the same intellectual and moral caliber, he were white.

Thus we reach the ultimate question of fact. Are the freedman's liberties suffering any real abridgment? The answer is easy. The letter of the laws, with but few exceptions, recognizes him as entitled to every right of an American citizen; and to some it may seem unimportant that there is scarcely one public relation of life in the South where he is not arbitrarily and unlawfully compelled to hold toward the white man the attitude of an alien, a menial, and a probable reprobate, by reason of his race and color. One of the marvels of future history will be that it was counted a small matter, by a majority of our nation, for six millions of people within it, made by its own decree a component part of it, to be subjected to a system of oppression so rank that nothing could make it seem small except the fact that they had already been ground under it for a century and a half.

Examine it. It proffers to the freedman a certain security of life and property, and then holds the respect of the community, that dearest of earthly boons, beyond his attainment. It gives him certain guarantees against thieves and robbers, and then holds him under the unearned contumely of the mass of good men and women. It acknowledges in constitutions and statutes his title to an American's freedom and aspirations, and then in daily practice heaps upon him in every public place the most odious distinctions, without giving ear to the humblest plea concerning mental or moral character. It spurns his ambition, tramples upon his languishing self-respect, and indignantly refuses to let him either buy with money, or earn by an excellence of inner life or outward behavior, the most momentary immunity from these public indignities even for his wife and daughters. Need we cram these pages with facts in evidence, as if these were charges denied and requiring to be proven? They are simply the present avowed and defended state of affairs peeled of its exteriors.

Nothing but the habit, generations old, of enduring it could make it endurable by men not in actual slavery. Were we whites of the South to remain every way as we are, and our six million blacks to give place to any sort of whites exactly their equals, man for man, in mind, morals, and wealth, provided only that they had tasted two years of American freedom, and were this same system of tyrannies attempted upon them, there would be as bloody an uprising as this continent has ever seen. We can say this quietly. There is not a scruple's weight of present danger. These six million freedmen are dominated by nine million whites immeasurably stronger than they, backed by the virtual consent of thirty-odd millions more. Indeed, nothing but the habit of oppression could make such oppression possible to a people of the intelligence and virtue of our Southern whites, and the invitation to practice it on millions of any other than the children of their former slaves would be spurned with a noble indignation.

Suppose, for a moment, the tables turned. Suppose the courts of our Southern States, while changing no laws requiring the impaneling of jurymen without distinction as to race, etc., should suddenly begin to draw their thousands of jurymen all black, and well-nigh every one of them counting not only himself, but all his race, better than any white man. Assuming that their average of intelligence and morals should be not below that of jurymen as now drawn, would a white man, for all that, choose to be tried in one of those courts? Would he suspect nothing? Could one persuade him that his chances of even justice were all they should be, or all they would be were the court not evading the law in order to sustain an outrageous distinction against him because of the accidents of his birth? Yet only read white man for black man, and black man for white man, and that—I speak as an eye-witness—has been the practice for years, and is still so to-day; an actual emasculation, in the case of six million people both as plaintiff and defendant, of the right of trial by jury.

In this and other practices the outrage falls upon the freedman. Does it stop there? Far from it. It is the first premise of American principles that whatever elevates the lower stratum of the people lifts all the rest, and whatever holds it down holds all down. For twenty years, therefore, the nation has been working to elevate the freedman. It counts this one of the great necessities of the hour. It has poured out its wealth publicly and privately for this purpose. It is confidently expected that it will soon bestow a royal gift of millions for the reduction of the illiteracy so largely shared by the blacks. Our Southern States are, and for twenty years have been, taxing themselves for the same end. The private charities alone of the other States have given twenty millions in the same good cause. Their colored

seminaries, colleges, and normal schools dot our whole Southern country, and furnish our public colored schools with a large
part of their teachers. All this and much more has been or is
being done in order that, for the good of himself and everybody
else in the land, the colored man may be elevated as quickly
as possible from all the debasements of slavery and semi-slavery
to the full stature and integrity of citizenship. And it is in the
face of all this that the adherent of the old régime stands in the
way to every public privilege and place—steamer landing,
railway platform, theater, concert-hall, art display, public library, public school, court-house, church, everything—flourish-
ing the hot branding-iron of ignominious distinctions. He forbids the freedman to go into the water until *he* is satisfied that
he knows how to swim, and for fear he should learn hangs mill-
stones about his neck. This is what we are told is a small matter
that will settle itself. Yes, like a roosting curse, until the outraged intelligence of the South lifts its indignant protest against
this stupid firing into our own ranks.

I say the outraged intelligence of the South; for there are
thousands of Southern-born white men and women in the minority in all these places—in churches, courts, schools, libraries,
theaters, concert-halls, and on steamers and railway carriages—
who see the wrong and folly of these things, silently blush for
them, and withhold their open protests only because their belief is unfortunately stronger in the futility of their counsel than
in the power of a just cause. I do not justify their silence; but
I affirm their sincerity and their goodly numbers. Of late years,
when condemning these evils from the platform in Southern
towns, I have repeatedly found that those who I had earlier
been told were the men and women in whom the community
placed most confidence and pride—they were the ones who,
when I had spoken, came forward with warmest hand-grasps
and expressions of thanks, and pointedly and cordially justified
my every utterance. And were they the young South? Not by
half! The gray-beards of the old times have always been among
them, saying in effect, not by any means as converts, but as
fellow-discoverers, "Whereas we were blind, now we see."

Another sort among our good Southern people make a similar but feebler admission, but with the time-worn proviso that expediency makes a more imperative demand than law, justice, or logic, and demands the preservation of the old order. Somebody must be outraged, it seems; and if not the freedman, then it must be a highly refined and enlightened race of people constantly offended and grossly discommoded, if not imposed upon, by a horde of tatterdemalions, male and female, crowding into a participation in their reserved privileges. Now, look at this plea. It is simply saying in another way that though the Southern whites far outnumber the blacks, and though we hold every element of power in greater degree than the blacks, and though the larger part of us claim to be sealed by nature as an exclusive upper class, and though we have the courts completely in our own hands, with the police on our right and the prisons on our left, and though we justly claim to be an intrepid people, and though we have a superb military experience, with ninety-nine hundredths of all the military equipment and no scarcity of all the accessories, yet with all the facts behind us we cannot make and enforce that intelligent and approximately just assortment of persons in public places and conveyances on the merits of exterior decency that is made in all other enlightened lands. On such a plea are made a distinction and separation that not only are crude, invidious, humiliating, and tyrannous, but which do not reach their ostensible end or come near it; and all that saves such a plea from being a confession of driveling imbecility is its utter speciousness. It is advanced sincerely; and yet nothing is easier to show than that these distinctions on the line of color are really made not from any necessity, but simply for their own sake—to preserve the old arbitrary supremacy of the master class over the menial without regard to the decency or indecency of appearance or manners in either the white individual or the colored.

See its every-day working. Any colored man gains unquestioned admission into innumerable places the moment he appears as the menial attendant of some white person, where he could not cross the threshold in his own right as a well-dressed and well-behaved master of himself. The contrast is even greater in the case of colored women. There could not be a system which when put into practice would more offensively condemn itself. It does more: it actually creates the confusion it pretends to prevent. It blunts the sensibilities of the ruling class themselves. It waives all strict demand for painstaking in either manners or dress of either master or menial, and, for one result, makes the average Southern railway coach more uncomfortable than the average of railway coaches elsewhere. It prompts the average Southern white passenger to find less offense in the presence of a profane, boisterous, or unclean white person than in that of a quiet, well-behaved colored man or woman attempting to travel on an equal footing with him without a white master or mistress. The holders of the old sentiments hold the opposite choice in scorn. It is only when we go on to say that there are regions where the riotous expulsion of a decent and peaceable colored person is preferred to his inoffensive company, that it may seem necessary to bring in evidence. And yet here again it is *primâ facie* evidence; for the following extract was printed in the Selma (Alabama) "Times" not six months ago, and not as a complaint, but as a boast:

A few days since, a negro minister, of this city, boarded the east-bound passenger train on the E. T., V. & G. Railway and took a seat in the coach occupied by white passengers. Some of the passengers complained to the conductor and brakemen, and expressed considerable dissatisfaction that they were forced to ride alongside of a negro. The railroad officials informed the complainants that they were not authorized to force the colored passenger into the coach set apart for the negroes, and they would lay themselves liable should they do so. The white passengers then took the matter in their own hands and ordered the ebony-hued minister to take a seat in the next coach. He positively refused to obey orders, whereupon the white men gave him a sound flogging and forced him to a seat among his own color and equals. We learned yesterday that the vanquished preacher was unable to fill his pulpit on account of the severe chastisement inflicted upon him. Now [says the delighted editor] the query that puzzles is, "Who did the flogging?"

And as good an answer as we can give is that likely enough they were some of the men for whom the whole South has come to a halt to let them get over the "feelings engendered by the war." Must such men, such acts, such sentiments, stand alone to represent us of the South before an enlightened world? No. I say, as a citizen of an extreme Southern State, a native of Louisiana, an ex-Confederate soldier, and a lover of my home, my city, and my State, as well as of my country, that this is not the best sentiment in the South, nor the sentiment of her best intelligence; and that it would not ride up and down that beautiful land dominating and domineering were it not for its tremendous power as the *traditional* sentiment of a conservative people. But is not silent endurance criminal? I cannot but repeat my own words, spoken near the scene and about the time of this event. Speech may be silvern and silence golden; but if a lump of gold is only big enough, it can drag us to the bottom of the sea and hold us there while all the world sails over us.

The laws passed in the days of compulsory reconstruction requiring "equal accommodations," etc., for colored and white persons were freedmen's follies. On their face they defeated their ends; for even in theory they at once reduced to half all opportunity for those more reasonable and mutually agreeable self-assortments which public assemblages and groups of passengers find it best to make in all other enlightened countries, making them on the score of conduct, dress, and price. They also led the whites to overlook what they would have seen instantly had these invidious distinctions been made against themselves: that their offense does not vanish at the guarantee against the loss of physical comforts. But we made, and are still making, a mistake beyond even this. For years many of us have carelessly taken for granted that these laws were being carried out in some shape that removed all just ground of complaint. It is common to say, "We allow the man of color to go and come at will, only let him sit apart in a place marked off for him." But marked off how? So as to mark him instantly as a menial. Not by railings and partitions merely, which, raised against any other class in the United States with the same invidious intent, would be kicked down as fast as put up, but by giving him besides, in every instance and without recourse, the most uncomfortable, uncleanest, and unsafest place; and the unsafety, uncleanness, and discomfort of most of these places are a shame to any community pretending to practice public justice. If any one can think the freedman does not feel the indignities thus heaped upon him, let him take up any paper printed for colored men's patronage, or ask any colored man of known courageous utterance. Hear them:

> We ask not Congress, nor the Legislature, nor any other power, to remedy these evils, but we ask the people among whom we live. Those who *can* remedy them if they *will*. Those who have a high sense of honor and a deep moral feeling. Those who have one vestige of human sympathy left. . . . Those are the ones we ask to protect us in our weakness and ill-treatments. . . . As soon as the colored man is treated by the white man as a *man*, that harmony and pleasant feeling which should characterize all races which dwell together, shall be the bond of peace between them.

Surely their evidence is good enough to prove their own feelings. We need not lean upon it here for anything else. I shall not bring forward a single statement of fact from them or any of their white friends who, as teachers and missionaries, share many of their humiliations, though my desk is covered with them. But I beg to make the same citation from my own experience that I made last June in the far South. It was this: One hot night in September of last year I was traveling by rail in the State of Alabama. At rather late bed-time there came aboard the train a young mother and her little daughter of three or four years. They were neatly and tastefully dressed in cool, fresh muslins, and as the train went on its way they sat together very still and quiet. At the next station there came aboard a most melancholy and revolting company. In filthy rags, with vile odors and the clanking of shackles and chains, nine penitentiary convicts chained to one chain, and ten more chained to another, dragged laboriously into the compartment of the car where in one corner sat this mother and child, and packed it full, and the train moved on. The keeper of the convicts told me he should take them in that car two hundred miles that night. They were going to the mines. My seat was not in that car, and I staid in it but a moment. It stank insufferably. I returned to my own place in the coach behind, where there was, and had all the time been, plenty of room. But the mother and child sat on in silence in that foul hole, the conductor having distinctly refused them admission elsewhere because they were of African blood, and not because the mother was, but because she was *not*, engaged at the moment in menial service. Had the child been white, and the mother not its natural but its hired guardian, she could have sat anywhere in the train, and no one would have ventured to object, even had she been as black as the mouth of the coal-pit to which her loathsome fellow-passengers were being carried in chains.

Such is the incident as I saw it. But the illustration would be incomplete here were I not allowed to add the comments I made upon it when in June last I recounted it, and to state the two opposite tempers in which my words were received. I said: "These are the facts. And yet you know and I know we belong to communities that, after years of hoping for, are at last taking comfort in the assurance of the nation's highest courts that no law can reach and stop this shameful foul play until we choose to enact a law to that end ourselves. And now the east and north and west of our great and prosperous and happy country, and the rest of the civilized world, as far as it knows our case, are standing and waiting to see what we will write upon the white page of to-day's and to-morrow's history, now that we are simply on our honor and on the mettle of our far and peculiarly famed Southern instinct. How long, then, shall we stand off from such ringing moral questions as these on the flimsy plea that they have a political value, and, scrutinizing the Constitution, keep saying, 'Is it so nominated in the bond? I cannot find it; 'tis not in the bond.'"

With the temper that promptly resented these words through many newspapers of the neighboring regions there can be no propriety in wrangling. When regions so estranged from the world's thought carry their resentment no further than a little harmless invective, it is but fair to welcome it as a sign of progress. If communities nearer the great centers of thought grow impatient with them, how shall we resent the impatience of these remoter ones when their oldest traditions are, as it seems to them, ruthlessly assailed? There is but one right thing to do: it is to pour in upon them our reiterations of the truth without malice and without stint.

But I have a much better word to say. It is for those who, not voiced by the newspapers around them, showed, both then and constantly afterward in public and private during my two days' subsequent travel and sojourn in the region, by their cordial, frequent, specific approval of my words, that a better intelligence is longing to see the evils of the old régime supplanted by a wiser and more humane public sentiment and practice. And I must repeat my conviction that if the unconscious habit of oppression were not already there, a scheme so gross, irrational, unjust, and inefficient as our present caste distinctions could not find place among a people so generally intelligent and high-minded. I ask attention to their bad influence in a direction not often noticed.

In studying, about a year ago, the practice of letting out public convicts to private lessees to serve out their sentences under private management, I found that it does not belong to all our once slave States nor to all our once seceded States. Only it is no longer in practice outside of them. Under our present condition in the South, it is beyond possibility that the individual black should behave mischievously without offensively rearousing the old sentiments of the still dominant white man. As we have seen, too, the white man virtually monopolizes the jury-box. Add another fact: the Southern States have entered upon a new era of material development. Now, if with these conditions in force the public mind has been captivated by glowing pictures of the remunerative economy of the convict-lease system, and by the seductive spectacle of mines and railways, turn-pikes and levees, that everybody wants and nobody wants to pay for, growing apace by convict labor that seems to cost nothing, we may almost assert beforehand that the popular mind will—not so maliciously as unreflectingly—yield to the tremendous temptation to hustle the misbehaving black man into the State prison under extravagant sentence, and sell his labor to the highest bidder who will use him in the construction of public works. For ignorance of the awful condition of these penitentiaries is extreme and general, and the hasty, half-conscious assumption naturally is, that the culprit will survive this term of sentence, and its fierce discipline "teach him to behave himself."

But we need not argue from cause to effect only. Nor need I repeat one of the many painful rumors that poured in upon me the moment I began to investigate this point. The official testimony of the prisons themselves is before the world to establish the conjectures that spring from our reasoning. After the erroneous takings of the census of 1880 in South Carolina had been corrected, the population was shown to consist of about twenty blacks to every thirteen whites. One would therefore look for a preponderance of blacks on the prison lists; and inasmuch as they are a people only twenty years ago released from servile captivity, one would not be surprised to see that preponderance large. Yet, when the actual numbers confront us, our speculations are stopped with a rude shock; for what is to account for the fact that in 1881 there were committed to the State prison at Columbia, South Carolina, 406 colored persons and but 25 whites? The proportion of blacks sentenced to the whole black population was one to every 1488; that of the whites to the white population was but one to every 15,644. In Georgia the white inhabitants decidedly out-number the blacks; yet in the State penitentiary, October 20, 1880, there were 115 whites and 1071 colored; or if we reject the summary of its tables and refer to the tables themselves (for the one does not agree with the other), there were but 102 whites and 1083 colored. Yet of 52 pardons granted in the two years then closing, 22 were to whites and only 30 to blacks. If this be a dark record, what shall we say of the records of lynch law? But for them there is not room here.

A far pleasanter aspect of our subject shows itself when we

turn from courts and prisons to the school-house. And the explanation is simple. Were our educational affairs in the hands of that not high average of the community commonly seen in jury-boxes, with their transient sense of accountability and their crude notions of public interests, there would most likely be no such pleasant contrast. But with us of the South, as elsewhere, there is a fairly honest effort to keep the public-school interests in the hands of the State's most highly trained intelligence. Hence our public educational work is a compromise between the unprogressive prejudices of the general mass of the whites and the progressive intelligence of their best minds. Practically, through the great majority of our higher educational officers, we are fairly converted to the imperative necessity of elevating the colored man intellectually, and are beginning to see very plainly that the whole community is sinned against in every act or attitude of oppression, however gross or however refined.

Yet one thing must be said. I believe it is wise that all have agreed not to handicap education with the race question, but to make a complete surrender of that issue, and let it find adjustment elsewhere first and in the schools last. And yet, in simple truth and justice and in the kindest spirit, we ought to file one exception for that inevitable hour when the whole question must be met. There can be no more real justice in pursuing the freedman's children with humiliating arbitrary distinctions and separations in the school-houses than in putting them upon him in other places. If, growing out of their peculiar mental structure, there are good and just reasons for their isolation, by all means let them be proved and known; but it is simply tyrannous to assume them without proof. I know that just here looms up the huge bugbear of Social Equality. Our eyes are filled with absurd visions of all Shantytown pouring its hordes of unwashed imps into the company and companionship of our own sunny-headed darlings. What utter nonsense! As if our public schools had no gauge of cleanliness, decorum, or moral character! Social Equality? What a godsend it would be if the advocates of the old Southern régime could only see that the color line points straight in the direction of social equality by tending toward the equalization of all whites on one side of the line and of all blacks on the other. We may reach the moon some day, not social equality; but the only class that really effects anything toward it are the makers and holders of arbitrary and artificial social distinctions interfering with society's natural self-distribution. Even the little children everywhere are taught, and begin to learn almost with their A B C, that they will find, and must be guided by the same variations of the social scale in the public school as out of it; and it is no small mistake to put them or their parents off their guard by this cheap separation on the line of color.

But some will say this is not a purely artificial distinction. We hear much about race instinct. The most of it, I fear, is pure twaddle. It may be there is such a thing. We do not know. It is not proved. And even if it were established, it would not necessarily be a proper moral guide. We subordinate instinct to society's best interests as apprehended in the light of reason. If there is such a thing, it behaves with strange malignity toward the remnants of African blood in individuals principally of our own race, and with singular indulgence to the descendants of— for example—Pocahontas. Of mere race *feeling* we all know there is no scarcity. Who is stranger to it? And as another man's motive of private preference no one has a right to forbid it or require it. But as to its being an instinct, one thing is plain: if there is such an instinct, so far from excusing the malignant indignities practiced in its name, it furnishes their final condemnation; for it stands to reason that just in degree as it is a real thing it will take care of itself.

It has often been seen to do so, whether it is real or imaginary. I have seen in New Orleans a Sunday-school of white children every Sunday afternoon take possession of its two rooms immediately upon their being vacated by a black school of equal or somewhat larger numbers. The teachers of the colored school are both white and black, and among the white teachers are young ladies and gentlemen of the highest social standing. The pupils of the two schools are alike neatly attired, orderly, and in every respect inoffensive to each other. I have seen the two races sitting in the same public high-school and grammar-school rooms, reciting in the same classes and taking recess on the same ground at the same time, without one particle of detriment that any one ever pretended to discover, although the fiercest enemies of the system swarmed about it on every side. And when in the light of these observations I reflect upon the enormous educational task our Southern States have before them, the inadequacy of their own means for performing it, the hoped-for beneficence of the general Government, the sparseness with which so much of our Southern population is distributed over the land, the thousands of school districts where, consequently, the multiplication of schools must involve both increase of expense and reduction of efficiency, I must enter some demurrer to the enforcement of the tyrannous sentiments of the old régime until wise experiments have established better reasons than I have yet heard given.

What need to say more? The question is answered. Is the freedman a free man? No. We have considered his position in a land whence nothing can, and no man has a shadow of right to, drive him, and where he is multiplying as only oppression can multiply a people. We have carefully analyzed his relations to the finer and prouder race, with which he shares the ownership and citizenship of a region large enough for ten times the number of both. Without accepting one word of his testimony, we have shown that the laws made for his protection against the habits of suspicion and oppression in his late master are being constantly set aside, not for their defects, but for such merit as they possess. We have shown that the very natural source of these oppressions is the surviving sentiments of an extinct and now universally execrated institution; sentiments which no intelligent or moral people should harbor a moment after the admission that slavery was a moral mistake. We have shown the outrageousness of these tyrannies in some of their workings, and how distinctly they antagonize every State and national interest involved in the elevation of the colored race. Is it not well to have done so? For, I say again, the question has reached a moment of special importance. The South stands on her honor before the clean equities of the issue. It is no longer whether constitutional amendments, but whether the eternal principles of justice, are violated. And the answer must—it shall—come from the South. And it shall be practical. It will not cost much. We have had a strange experience: the withholding of simple rights has cost us much blood; such concessions of them as we have made have never yet cost a drop. The answer is coming. Is politics in the way? Then let it clear the track or get run over, just as it prefers. But, as I have said over and over to my brethren in the South, I take upon me to say again here, that there is a moral and intellectual intelligence there which is not going to be much longer beguiled out of its moral right of way by questions of political punctilio, but will seek that plane of universal justice and equity which it is every people's duty before God to seek, not along the line of politics,—God forbid!—but across it and across it and across it as many times as it may lie across the path, until the whole people of every once slave-holding State can stand up as one man, saying, "Is the freedman a free man?" and the whole world shall answer, "Yes."

28 In Plain Black and White

The most striking effect of the publication of Cable's views (document 27) was to elicit from Henry W. Grady of the *Atlanta Constitution* the following revealing stricture. The editors of *Century* received so many letters from the South critical of Cable's essay[1] that Richard Watson Gilder undertook to have Joel Chandler Harris answer it. After he refused, the editor appealed to Grady. His reply, though somewhat more moderate than the angry letters to Gilder had been, was an exceedingly clear statement of the white supremacist's position on Negro political rights. Extremists of later decades were unable to improve greatly on the Atlanta editor's statement; they even repeated his views many times.

It is doubtful that Grady or any of his fellow Southerners, who shared a like view, clearly understood, or were charitable enough to try to understand, many of the things which Cable foresaw. Gilder proposed to publish Cable's rebuttal in the same issue of the *Century Magazine*, but the author was too busy on the lecture circuit to prepare his reply. It was not until later that he responded to his southern critics in an essay, and later, in a book entitled *The Silent South*.[2]

IT IS STRANGE THAT DURING THE DISCUSSION OF THE NEGRO QUES-tion, which has been wide and pertinent, no one has stood up to

[1] Louis D. Rubin, *George W. Cable: The Life and Times of a Southern Heretic* (New York: Pegasus, 1969), 109–112.
[2] Rubin, 179–184.

speak the mind of the South. In this discussion there has been much of truth and more of error—something of perverseness, but more of misapprehension—not a little of injustice, but perhaps less of mean intention.

Amid it all, the South has been silent.

There has been, perhaps, good reason for this silence. The problem under debate is a tremendous one. Its right solution means peace, prosperity, and happiness to the South. A mistake, even in the temper in which it is approached or the theory upon which its solution is attempted, would mean detriment, that at best would be serious, and might easily be worse. Hence the South has pondered over this problem, earnestly seeking with all her might the honest and the safe way out of its entanglements, and saying little because there was but little to which she felt safe in committing herself. Indeed, there was another reason why she did not feel called upon to obtrude her opinions. The people of the North, proceeding by the right of victorious arms, had themselves undertaken to settle the negro question. From the Emancipation Proclamation to the Civil Rights Bill they hurried with little let or hindrance, holding the negro in the meanwhile under a sort of tutelage, from part in which his former masters were practically excluded. Under this state of things the South had little to do but watch and learn.

We have now passed fifteen years of experiment. Certain broad principles have been established as wise and just. The South has something to say which she can say with confidence. There is no longer impropriety in her speaking or lack of weight in her words. The people of the United States have, by their suffrages, remitted to the Southern people, temporarily at least, control of the race question. The decision of the Supreme Court on the Civil Rights Bill leaves practically to their adjustment important issues that were, until that decision was rendered, covered by straight and severe enactment. These things deepen the responsibility of the South, increase its concern, and con-

Henry W. Grady, "In Plain Black and White," *Century Magazine* 24 [Old Series] (April 1884), 909–917.

front it with a problem to which it must address itself promptly and frankly. Where it has been silent, it now should speak. The interest of every American in the honorable and equitable settlement of this question is second only to the interest of those specially—and fortunately, we believe—charged with its adjustment. "What will you do with it?" is a question any man may now ask the South, and to which the South should make frank and full reply.

It is important that this reply shall be plain and straightforward. Above all things it must carry the genuine convictions of the people it represents. On this subject and at this time the South cannot afford to be misunderstood. Upon the clear and general apprehension of her position and of her motives and purpose everything depends. She cannot let pass unchallenged a single utterance that, spoken in her name, misstates her case or her intention. It is to protest against just such injustice that this article is written.

In a lately printed article, Mr. George W. Cable, writing in the name of the Southern people, confesses judgment on points that they still defend, and commits them to a line of thought from which they must forever dissent. In this article, as in his works, the singular tenderness and beauty of which have justly made him famous, Mr. Cable is sentimental rather than practical. But the reader, enchained by the picturesque style and misled by the engaging candor with which the author admits the shortcomings of "We of the South," and the kindling enthusiasm with which he tells how "We of the South" must make reparation, is apt to assume that it is really the soul of the South that breathes through Mr. Cable's repentant sentences. It is not my purpose to discuss Mr. Cable's relations to the people for whom he claims to speak. Born in the South, of Northern parents, he appears to have had little sympathy with his Southern environment, as in 1882 he wrote, "To be in New England would be enough for me. I was there once,—a year ago—and it seemed as if I had never been home till then." It will be suggested that a man so out of harmony with his neighbors as to say, even after he had fought side by side with them on the battle-field, that he

never felt at home until he had left them, cannot speak under-
standingly of their views on so vital a subject as that under
discussion. But it is with his statement rather than his personality that we have to deal. Does he truly represent the South?
We reply that he does not! There may be here and there in the
South a dreaming theorist who subscribes to Mr. Cable's teachings. We have seen no signs of one. Among the thoughtful
men of the South,—the men who felt that all brave men might
quit fighting when General Lee surrendered,—who, enshrining
in their hearts the heroic memories of the cause they had lost,
in good faith accepted the arbitrament of the sword to which
they had appealed, who bestirred themselves cheerfully amid
the ruins of their homes, and set about the work of rehabilitation,
—who have patched and mended and builded anew, and fashioned out of pitiful resource a larger prosperity than they
ever knew before,—who have set their homes on the old red
hills, and staked their honor and prosperity and the peace and
well-being of the children who shall come after them on the
clear and equitable solution of every social, industrial, or political problem that concerns the South,—among these men, who
control and will continue to control, I do know, there is general
protest against Mr. Cable's statement of the case, and universal
protest against his suggestions for the future. The mind of
these men I shall attempt to speak, maintaining my right to
speak for them with the pledge that, having exceptional means
for knowing their views on this subject, and having spared no
pains to keep fully informed thereof, I shall write down nothing
in their name on which I have found even a fractional difference
of opinion.

A careful reading of Mr. Cable's article discloses the following argument: The Southern people have deliberately and persistently evaded the laws forced on them for the protection of
the freedman; this evasion has been the result of prejudices
born of and surviving the institution of slavery, the only way to
remove which is to break down every distinction between the
races; and now the best thought of the South, alarmed at the
withdrawal of the political machinery that forced the passage

of the protective laws, which withdrawal tempts further and more intolerable evasions, is moving to forbid all further assortment of the races and insist on their intermingling in all places and in all relations. The first part of this argument is a matter of record, and, from the Southern stand-point, mainly a matter of reputation. It can bide its time. The suggestion held in its conclusion is so impossible, so mischievous, and, in certain aspects, so monstrous, that it must be met at once.

It is hard to think about the negro with exactness. His helplessness, his generations of enslavement, his unique position among the peoples of the earth, his distinctive color, his simple, lovable traits,—all these combine to hasten opinion into conviction where he is the subject of discussion. Three times has this tendency brought about epochal results in his history. First, it abolished slavery. For this all men are thankful, even those who, because of the personal injustice and violence of the means by which it was brought about, opposed its accomplishment. Second, it made him a voter. This, done more in a sense of reparation than in judgment, is as final as the other. The North demanded it; the South expected it; all acquiesced in it, and, wise or unwise, it will stand. Third, it fixed by enactment his social and civil rights. And here for the first time the revolution faltered. Up to this point the way had been plain, the light clear, and the march at quick-step. Here the line halted. The way was lost; there was hesitation, division, and uncertainty. Knowing not which way to turn, and enveloped in doubt, the revolutionists heard the retreat sounded by the Supreme Court with small reluctance, and, to use Mr. Cable's words, "bewildered by complication, vexed by many a blunder," retired from the field. See, then, the progress of this work. The first step, right by universal agreement, would stand if the law that made it were withdrawn. The second step, though irrevocable, raises doubts as to its wisdom. The third, wrong in purpose, has failed in execution. It stands denounced as null by the highest court, as inoperative by general confession, and as unwise by popular verdict. Let us take advantage of this halt in the too rapid revolution, and see exactly where we stand and what is best for us to do. The situation is critical. The next moment may formulate the work of the next twenty years. The tremendous forces of the revolution, unspent and still terrible, are but held in arrest. Launch them mistakenly, chaos may come. Wrong-headedness may be as fatal now as wrong-heartedness. Clear views, clear statement, and clear understanding are the demands of the hour. Given these, the common sense and courage of the American people will make the rest easy.

Let it be understood in the beginning, then, that the South will never adopt Mr. Cable's suggestion of the social intermingling of the races. It can never be driven into accepting it. So far from there being a growing sentiment in the South in favor of the indiscriminate mixing of the races, the intelligence of both races is moving farther from that proposition day by day. It is more impossible (if I may shade a superlative) now than it was ten years ago; it will be less possible ten years hence. Neither race wants it. The interest, as the inclination, of both races is against it. Here the issue with Mr. Cable is made up. He denounces any assortment of the races as unjust, and demands that white and black shall intermingle everywhere. The South replies that the assortment of the races is wise and proper, and stands on the platform of equal accommodation for each race, but separate.

The difference is an essential one. Deplore or defend it as we may, an antagonism is bred between the races when they are forced into mixed assemblages. This sinks out of sight, if not out of existence, when each race moves in its own sphere. Mr. Cable admits this feeling, but doubts that it is instinctive. In my opinion it is instinctive—deeper than prejudice or pride, and bred in the bone and blood. It would make itself felt even in sections where popular prejudice runs counter to its manifestation. If in any town in Wisconsin or Vermont there was equal population of whites and blacks, and schools, churches, hotels, and theaters were in common, this instinct would assuredly develop; the races would separate, and each race would hasten the separation. Let me give an example that touches this supposition closely. Bishop Gilbert Haven, of the Methodist

Episcopal Church, many years ago came to the South earnestly,
and honestly, we may believe, devoted to breaking up the assortment of the races. He was backed by powerful influences
in the North. He was welcomed by resident Northerners in the
South (then in control of Southern affairs) as an able and
eloquent exponent of their views. His first experiment toward
mixing the races was made in the church—surely the most
propitious field. Here the fraternal influence of religion emphasized his appeals for the brotherhood of the races. What was
the result? After the first month his church was decimated. The
Northern whites and the Southern blacks left it in squads. The
dividing influences were mutual. The stout bishop contended
with prayer and argument and threat against the inevitable, but
finally succumbed. Two separate churches were established,
and each race worshiped to itself. There had been no collision,
no harsh words, no discussion even. Each race simply obeyed
its instinct, that spoke above the appeal of the bishop and
dominated the divine influences that pulsed from pew to pew.
Time and again did the bishop force the experiment. Time and
again he failed. At last he was driven to the confession that
but one thing could effect what he had tried so hard to bring
about, and that was miscegenation. A few years of experiment
would force Mr. Cable to the same conclusion.

The same experiment was tried on a larger scale by the Methodist Episcopal Church (North) when it established its
churches in the South after the war. It essayed to bring the races
together, and in its conferences and its churches there was no
color line. Prejudice certainly did not operate to make a division
here. On the contrary, the whites and blacks of this church were
knit together by prejudice, pride, sentiment, political and even
social policy. Underneath all this was a race instinct, obeying
which, silently, they drifted swiftly apart. While white Methodists of the church North and of the church South, distant from
each other in all but the kinship of race and worship, were struggling to effect once more a union of the churches that had been
torn apart by a quarrel over slavery, so that in every white conference and every white church on all this continent white Meth-

odists could stand in restored brotherhood, the Methodist Church (North) agreed, without serious protest, to a separation of its Southern branch into two conferences of whites and of blacks, and into separate congregations where the proportion of either race was considerable. Was it without reason—it certainly was not through prejudice—that this church, while seeking anew fusion with its late enemies, consented to separate from its new friends?

It was the race instinct that spoke there. It spoke not with prejudice, but against it. It spoke there as it speaks always and everywhere—as it has spoken for two thousand years. And it spoke to the reason of each race. Millaud, in voting in the French Convention for the beheading of Louis XVI, said: "If death did not exist, it would be necessary to-day to invent it." So of this instinct. It is the pledge of the integrity of each race, and of peace between the races. Without it, there might be a breaking down of all lines of division and a thorough intermingling of whites and blacks. This once accomplished, the lower and the weaker elements of the races would begin to fuse and the process of amalgamation would have begun. This would mean the disorganization of society. An internecine war would be precipitated. The whites, at any cost and at any hazard, would maintain the clear integrity and dominance of the Anglo-Saxon blood. They understand perfectly that the debasement of their own race would not profit the humble and sincere race with which their lot is cast, and that the hybrid would not gain what either race lost. Even if the vigor and the volume of the Anglo-Saxon blood would enable it to absorb the African current, and after many generations recover its own strength and purity, not all the powers of earth could control the unspeakable horrors that would wait upon the slow process of clarification. Easier far it would be to take the population of central New York, intermingle with it an equal percentage of Indians, and force amalgamation between the two. Let us review the argument. If Mr. Cable is correct in assuming that there is no instinct that keeps the two races separate in the South, then there is no reason for doubting that if intermingled they would fuse. Mere prejudice would not long survive perfect equality and social intermingling; and the prejudice once gone, intermarrying would begin. Then, if there is a race instinct in either race that resents intimate association with the other, it would be unwise to force such association when there are easy and just alternatives. If there is no such instinct, the mixing of the races would mean amalgamation, to which the whites will never submit, and to which neither race should submit. So that in either case, whether the race feeling is instinct or prejudice, we come to but one conclusion: The white and black races in the South must walk apart. Concurrent their courses may go—ought to go—will go—but separate. If instinct did not make this plain in a flash, reason would spell it out letter by letter.

Now, let us see. We hold that there is an instinct, ineradicable and positive, that will keep the races apart, that would keep the races apart if the problem were transferred to Illinois or to Maine, and that will resist every effort of appeal, argument, or force to bring them together. We add in perfect frankness, however, that if no such instinct existed, or if the South had reasonable doubt of its existence, it would, by every means in its power, so strengthen the race prejudice that it would do the work and hold the stubbornness and strength of instinct. The question that confronts us at this point is: Admitted this instinct, that gathers each race to itself. Then, do you believe it possible to carry forward on the same soil and under the same laws two races equally free, practically equal in numbers, and yet entirely distinct and separate? This is a momentous question. It involves a problem that, all things considered, is without a precedent or parallel. Can the South carry this problem in honor and in peace to an equitable solution? We reply that for ten years the South has been doing this very thing, and with at least apparent success. No impartial and observant man can say that in the present aspect of things there is cause for alarm, or even for doubt. In the experience of the past few years there is assuredly reason for encouragement. There may be those who discern danger in the distant future. We do not. Beyond the apprehensions which must for a long time attend a matter so serious, we see nothing but cause for congratulation. In the common sense and the sincerity of the negro, no less than in the intelligence and earnestness of the whites, we find the problem simplifying. So far from the future bringing trouble, we feel confident that another decade or so, confirming the experience of the past ten years, will furnish the solution to be accepted of all men.

Let us examine briefly what the South has been doing, and study the attitude of the races towards each other. Let us do this, not so much to vindicate the past as to clear the way for the future. Let us see what the situation teaches. There must be in the experience of fifteen years something definite and suggestive. We begin with the schools and school management, as the basis of the rest.

Every Southern State has a common-school system, and in every State separate schools are provided for the races. Almost every city of more than five thousand inhabitants has a public-school system, and in every city the schools for whites and blacks are separate. There is no exception to this rule that I can find. In many cases the law creating this system requires that separate schools shall be provided for the races. This plan works admirably. There is no friction in the administration of the schools, and no suspicion as to the ultimate tendency of the system. The road to school is clear, and both races walk therein with confidence. The whites, assured that the school will not be made the hot-bed of false and pernicious ideas, or the scene of unwise associations, support the system cordially, and insist on perfect equality in grade and efficiency. The blacks, asking no more than this, fill the schools with alert and eager children. So far from feeling debased by the separate-school system, they insist that the separation shall be carried further, and the few white teachers yet presiding over negro schools supplanted by negro teachers. The appropriations for public schools are increased year after year, and free education grows constantly in strength and popularity. Cities that were afraid to commit themselves to free schools while mixed schools were a possibility commenced building school-houses as soon as separate schools were assured.

In 1870 the late Benjamin H. Hill found his matchless eloquence
unable to carry the suggestion of negro education into popular
tolerance. Ten years later nearly one million black children attended free schools, supported by general taxation. Though the
whites pay nineteen-twentieths of the tax, they insist that the
blacks shall share its advantages equally. The schools for each
race are opened on the same day and closed on the same day.
Neither is run a single day at the expense of the other. The negroes are satisfied with the situation. I am aware that some of
the Northern teachers of negro high-schools and universities
will controvert this. Touching their opinion, I have only to say
that it can hardly be considered fair or conservative. Under the
forcing influence of social ostracism, they have reasoned im-
patiently and have been helped to conclusions by quick sympathies or resentments. Driven back upon themselves and
hedged in by suspicion or hostility, their service has become a
sort of martyrdom, which has swiftly stimulated opinion into
conviction and conviction into fanaticism. I read in a late issue
of "Zion's Herald" a letter from one of these teachers, who declined, on the conductor's request, to leave the car in which she
was riding, and which was set apart exclusively for negroes. The
conductor, therefore, presumed she was a quadroon, and stated
his presumption in answer to inquiry of a young negro man
who was with her. She says of this:

> Truly, a glad thrill went through my heart—a thrill of pride.
> This great autocrat had pronounced me as not only in sympathy,
> but also one in blood, with the truest, tenderest, and noblest race
> that dwells on earth.

If this quotation, which is now before me over the writer's
name, suggests that she and those of her colleagues who agree
with her have narrowed within their narrowing environment,
and acquired artificial enthusiasm under their unnatural conditions, so that they must be unsafe as advisers and unfair as witnesses, the sole purpose for which it is introduced will have been
served. This suggestion does not reach all Northern teachers of
negro schools. Some have taken broader counsels, awakened

wider sympathies, and, as a natural result, hold more moderate views. The influence of the extremer faction is steadily diminishing. Set apart, as small and curious communities are set here and there in populous States, stubborn and stiff for a while, but overwhelmed at last and lost in the mingling currents, these dissenting spots will be ere long blotted out and forgotten. The educational problem, which is their special care, has already been settled, and the settlement accepted with a heartiness that precludes the possibility of its disturbance. From the stand-point of either race the experiment of distinct but equal schools for the white and black children of the South has demonstrated its wisdom, its policy, and its justice, if any experiment ever made plain its wisdom in the hands of finite man.

I quote on this subject Gustavus J. Orr, one of the wisest and best of men, and lately elected, by spontaneous movement, president of the National Educational Association. He says: "The race question in the schools is already settled. We give the negroes equal advantages, but separate schools. This plan meets the reason and satisfies the instinct of both races. Under it we have spent over five million dollars in Georgia, and the system grows in strength constantly." I asked if the negroes wanted mixed schools. His reply was prompt: "They do not. I have questioned them carefully on this point, and they make but one reply: They want their children in their own schools and under their own teachers." I asked what would be the effect of mixed schools. "I could not maintain the Georgia system one year. Both races would protest against it. My record as a public-school man is known. I have devoted my life to the work of education. But I am so sure of the evils that would come from mixed schools that, even if they were possible, I would see the whole educational system swept away before I would see them established. There is an instinct that gathers each race about itself. It is as strong in the blacks as in the whites, though it has not asserted itself so strongly. It is making itself manifest, since the blacks are organizing a social system of their own. It has long controlled them in their churches, and it is now doing so in their schools."

In churches, as in schools, the separation is perfect. The negroes, in all denominations in which their membership is an
appreciable percentage of the whole, have their own churches,
congregations, pastors, conferences, and bishops, their own missionaries. There is not the slightest antagonism between them
and the white churches of the same denomination. On the contrary, there is sympathetic interest and the utmost friendliness.
The separation is recognized as not only instinctive but wise.
There is no disposition to disturb it, and least of all on the part
of the negro. The church is with him the center of social life, and
there he wants to find his own people and no others.

... In their social institutions, as in their churches and schools,
the negroes have obeyed their instinct and kept apart from the
whites. They have their own social and benevolent societies,
their own military companies, their own orders of Masons and
Odd Fellows. They rally about these organizations with the
greatest enthusiasm and support them with the greatest liberal-
ity. If it were proposed to merge them with white organizations
of the same character, with equal rights guaranteed in all, the
negroes would interpose the stoutest objection. Their tastes, associations, and inclinations—their instincts—lead them to
gather their race about social centers of its own. I am tempted
into trying to explain here what I have never yet seen a stranger
to the South able to understand. The feeling that, by mutual
action, separates whites and blacks when they are thrown together in social intercourse is not a repellent influence in the
harsh sense of that word. It is centripetal rather than centrifu-
gal. It is attractive about separate centers rather than expulsive
from a common center. There is no antagonism, for example,
between white and black military companies. On occasions they
parade in the same street, and have none of the feeling that
exists between Orangemen and Catholics. Of course the good
sense of each race and the mutual recognition of the possible
dangers of the situation have much to do with maintaining the
good-will between the distinct races. The fact that in his own
church or society the negro has more freedom, more chance for
leadership and for individual development, than he could have

in association with the whites, has more to do with it. But beyond all this is the fact that, in the segregation of the races, blacks as well as whites obey a natural instinct, which, always granting that they get equal justice and equal advantages, they obey without the slightest ill-nature or without any sense of disgrace. They meet the white people in all the avenues of business. They work side by side with the white bricklayer or carpenter in perfect accord and friendliness. When the trowel or the hammer is laid aside, the laborers part, each going his own way. Any attempt to carry the comradeship of the day into private life would be sternly resisted by both parties in interest.

We have seen that in churches, schools, and social organizations the whites and blacks are moving along separately but harmoniously, and that the "assortment of the races," which has been described as shameful and unjust, is in most part made by the instinct of each race, and commands the hearty assent of both. Let us now consider the question of public carriers. On this point the South has been sharply criticised, and not always without reason. It is manifestly wrong to make a negro pay as much for a railroad ticket as a white man pays, and then force him to accept inferior accommodations. It is equally wrong to force a decent negro into an indecent car, when there is room for him or for her elsewhere. Public sentiment in the South has long recognized this, and has persistently demanded that the railroad managers should provide cars for the negroes equal in every respect to those set apart for the whites, and that these cars should be kept clean and orderly. In Georgia a State law requires all public roads or carriers to provide equal accommodation for each race, and failure to do so is made a penal offense. In Tennessee a negro woman lately gained damages by proving that she had been forced to take inferior accommodation on a train. The railroads have, with few exceptions, come up to the requirements of the law. Where they fail, they quickly feel the weight of public opinion, and shock the sense of public justice. This very discussion, I am bound to say, will lessen such failures in the future. On four roads, in my knowledge, even better has been done than the law requires. The car set apart

for the negroes is made exclusive. No whites are permitted to
occupy it. A white man who strays into this car is politely told
that it is reserved for the negroes. He has the information repeated two or three times, smiles, and retreats. This rule works
admirably and will win general favor. There are a few roads
that make no separate provision for the races, but announce that
any passenger can ride on any car. Here the "assortment" of
the races is done away with, and here it is that most of the outrages of which we hear occur. On these roads the negro has no
place set apart for him. As a rule, he is shy about asserting himself, and he usually finds himself in the meanest corners of the
train. If he forces himself into the ladies' car, he is apt to provoke
a collision. It is on just one of these trains where the assortment
of the passengers is left to chance that a respectable negro
woman is apt to be forced to ride in a car crowded with negro
convicts. Such a thing would be impossible where the issue is
fairly met, and a car, clean, orderly, and exclusive, is provided
for each race. The case could not be met by grading the tickets
and the accommodations. Such a plan would bring together in
the second or third class car just the element of both races between whom prejudice runs highest, and from whom the least
of tact or restraint might be expected. On the railroads, as elsewhere, the solution of the race problem is, equal advantages for
the same money,—equal in comfort, safety, and exclusiveness,—
but separate.

There remains but one thing further to consider—the negro
in the jury-box. It is assumed generally that the negro has no
representation in the courts. This is a false assumption. In the
United States courts he usually makes more than half the jury.
As to the State courts, I can speak particularly as to Georgia. I
assume that she does not materially differ from the other States.
In Georgia the law requires that commissioners shall prepare
the jury-list for each county by selection from the upright, intelligent, and experienced citizens of the county. This provision
was put into the Constitution by the negro convention of reconstruction days. Under its terms no reasonable man would have
expected to see the list made up of equal percentage of the

races. Indeed, the fewest number of negroes were qualified under the law. Consequently, but few appeared on the lists. The number, as was to be expected, is steadily increasing. In Fulton County there are seventy-four negroes whose names are on the lists, and the commissioners, I am informed, have about doubled this number for the present year. These negroes make good jurymen, and are rarely struck by attorneys, no matter what the client or cause may be. About the worst that can be charged against the jury system in Georgia is that the commissioners have made jurors of negroes only when they had qualified themselves to intelligently discharge a juror's duties. In few quarters of the South, however, is the negro unable to get full and exact justice in the courts, whether the jury be white or black. Immediately after the war, when there was general alarm and irritation, there may have been undue severity in sentences and extreme rigor of prosecution. But the charge that the people of the South have, in their deliberate and later moments, prostituted justice to the oppression of this dependent people, is as false as it is infamous. There is abundant belief that the very helplessness of the negro in court has touched the heart and conscience of many a jury, when the facts should have held them impervious. In the city in which this is written a negro, at midnight, on an unfrequented street, murdered a popular young fellow, over whose grave a monument was placed by popular subscription. The only witnesses of the killing were the friends of the murdered boy. Had the murderer been a white man, it is believed he would have been convicted. He was acquitted by the white jury, and has since been convicted of a murderous assault on a person of his own color. Similarly, a young white man, belonging to one of the leading families of the State, was hanged for the murder of a negro. Insanity was pleaded in his defense, and so plausibly that it is believed he would have escaped had his victim been a white man.

I quote on this point Mr. Benjamin H. Hill, who has been prosecuting attorney of the Atlanta, Ga., circuit for twelve years. He says: "In cities and towns the negro gets equal and exact justice before the courts. It is possible that, in remote counties, where the question is one of a fight between a white man and a negro, there may be a lingering prejudice that causes occasional injustice. The judge, however, may be relied on to correct this. As to negro jurors, I have never known a negro to allow his lawyer to accept a negro juror. For the State I have accepted a black juror fifty times, to have him rejected by the opposing lawyer by order of his negro client. This has occurred so invariably that I have accepted it as a rule. Irrespective of that, the negro gets justice in the courts, and the last remaining prejudice against him in the jury-box has passed away. I convicted a white man for voluntary manslaughter under peculiar circumstances. A negro met him on the street and cursed him. The white man ordered him off and started home. The negro followed him to his house and cursed him until he entered the door. When he came out, the negro was still waiting. He renewed the abuse, followed him to his store, and there struck him with his fist. In the struggle that followed, the negro was shot and killed. The jury promptly convicted the slayer."

So much for the relation between the races in the South, in churches, schools, social organizations, on the railroad, and in theaters. Everything is placed on the basis of equal accommodations, but separate. In the courts the blacks are admitted to the jury-box as they lift themselves into the limit of qualification. Mistakes have been made and injustice has been worked here and there. This was to have been expected, and it has been less than might have been expected. But there can be no mistake about the progress the South is making in the equitable adjustment of the relations between the races. Ten years ago nothing was settled. There were frequent collisions and constant apprehensions. The whites were suspicious and the blacks were restless. So simple a thing as a negro taking an hour's ride on the cars, or going to see a play, was fraught with possible danger. The larger affairs—school, church, and court—were held in abeyance. Now all this is changed. The era of doubt and mistrust is succeeded by the era of confidence and good-will. The races meet in the exchange of labor in perfect amity and understanding. Together they carry on the concerns of the day, knowing little or nothing of the fierce hostility that divides labor and capital in other sections. When they turn to social life they separate. Each race obeys its instinct and congregates about its own centers. At the theater they sit in opposite sections of the same gallery. On the trains they ride each in his own car. Each worships in his own church, and educates his children in his schools. Each has his place and fills it, and is satisfied. Each gets the same accommodation for the same money. There is no collision. There is no irritation or suspicion. Nowhere on earth is there kindlier feeling, closer sympathy, or less friction between two classes of society than between the whites and blacks of the South to-day. This is due to the fact that in the adjustment of their relations they have been practical and sensible. They have wisely recognized what was essential, and have not sought to change what was unchangeable. They have yielded neither to the fanatic nor the demagogue, refusing to be misled by the one or misused by the other. While the world has been clamoring over their differences they have been quietly taking counsel with each other, in the field, the shop, the street and cabin, and settling things for themselves. That the result has not astonished the world in the speediness and the facility with which it has been reached, and the beneficence that has come with it, is due to the fact that the result has not been freely proclaimed. It has been a deplorable condition of our politics that the North has been misinformed as to the true condition of things in the South. Political greed and passion conjured pestilential mists to becloud what the lifting smoke of battle left clear. It has exaggerated where there was a grain of fact, and invented where there was none. It has sought to establish the most casual occurrences as the settled habit of the section, and has sprung endless jeremiads from one single disorder, as Jenkins filled the courts of Christendom with lamentations over his dissevered ear. These misrepresentations will pass away with the occasion that provoked them, and when the truth is known it will come with the force of a revelation to vindicate those who have bespoken for the South a fair trial, and to confound those who have borne false witness against her.

One thing further need be said, in perfect frankness. The South must be allowed to settle the social relations of the races according to her own views of what is right and best. There has never been a moment when she could have submitted to have the social status of her citizens fixed by an outside power. She accepted the emancipation and the enfranchisement of her slaves as the legitimate results of war that had been fought to a conclusion. These once accomplished, nothing more was possible. "Thus far and no farther," she said to her neighbors, in no spirit of defiance, but with quiet determination. In her weakest moments, when her helpless people were hedged about by the unthinking bayonets of her conquerors, she gathered them for resistance at this point. Here she defended everything that a people should hold dear. There was little proclamation of her purpose. Barely did the whispered word that bespoke her resolution catch the listening ears of her sons; but for all this, the victorious armies of the North, had they been rallied again from their homes, could not have enforced and maintained among this disarmed people the policy indicated in the Civil Rights bill. Had she found herself unable to defend her social integrity against the arms that were invincible on the fields where she staked the sovereignty of her States, her people would have abandoned their homes and betaken themselves into exile. Now, as then, the South is determined that, come what may, she must control the social relations of the two races whose lots are cast within her limits. It is right that she should have this control. The problem is hers, whether or not of her seeking, and her very existence depends on its proper solution. Her responsibility is greater, her knowledge of the case more thorough than that of others can be. The question touches her at every point; it presses on her from every side; it commands her constant attention. Every consideration of policy, of honor, of pride, of common sense impels her to the exactest justice and the fullest equity. She lacks the ignorance or misapprehension that might lead others into mistakes; all others lack the appalling alternative that, all else failing, would force her to use her knowledge wisely. For these reasons she has reserved to herself the right to settle the still unsettled element of the race problem, and this right she can never yield.

As a matter of course, this implies the clear and unmistakable domination of the white race in the South. The assertion of that is simply the assertion of the right of character, intelligence, and property to rule. It is simply saying that the responsible and steadfast element in the community shall control, rather than the irresponsible and the migratory. It is the reassertion of the moral power that overthrew the scandalous reconstruction governments, even though, to the shame of the republic be it said, they were supported by the bayonets of the General Government. Even the race issue is lost at this point. If the blacks of the South wore white skins, and were leagued together in the same ignorance and irresponsibility under any other distinctive mark than their color, they would progress not one step farther toward the control of affairs. Or if they were transported as they are to Ohio, and there placed in numerical majority of two to one, they would find the white minority there asserting and maintaining control, with less patience, perhaps, than many a Southern State has shown. Everywhere, with such temporary exceptions as afford demonstration of the rule, intelligence, character, and property will dominate in spite of numerical differences. These qualities are lodged with the white race in the South, and will assuredly remain there for many generations at least; so that the white race will continue to dominate the colored, even if the percentages of race increase deduced from the comparison of a lame census with a perfect one, and the omission of other considerations, should hold good and the present race majority be reversed.

Let no one imagine, from what is here said, that the South is careless of the opinion or regardless of the counsel of the outside world. On the contrary, while maintaining firmly a position she believes to be essential, she appreciates heartily the value of general sympathy and confidence. With an earnestness that is little less than pathetic she bespeaks the patience and the impartial judgment of all concerned. Surely her situation should command this, rather than indifference or antagonism. In poverty and defeat,—with her cities destroyed, her fields desolated, her labor disorganized, her homes in ruins, her families scattered, and the ranks of her sons decimated,—in the face of universal prejudice, fanned by the storm of war into hostility and hatred,—under the shadow of this sorrow and this disadvantage, she turned bravely to confront a problem that would have taxed to the utmost every resource of a rich and powerful and victorious people. Every inch of her progress has been beset with sore difficulties; and if the way is now clearing, it only reveals more clearly the tremendous import of the work to which her hands are given. It must be understood that she desires to silence no criticism, evade no issue, and lessen no responsibility. She recognizes that the negro is here to stay. She knows that her honor, her dear name, and her fame, no less than her prosperity, will be measured by the fullness of the justice she gives and guarantees to this kindly and dependent race. She knows that every mistake made and every error fallen into, no matter how innocently, endanger her peace and her reputation. In this full knowledge she accepts the issue without fear or evasion. She says, not boldly, but conscious of the honesty and the wisdom of her convictions: "Leave this problem to my working out. I will solve it in calmness and deliberation, without passion or prejudice, and with full regard for the unspeakable equities it holds. Judge me rigidly, but judge me by my works." And with the South the matter may be left—must be left. There it can be left with the fullest confidence that the honor of the republic will be maintained, the rights of humanity guarded, and the problem worked out in such exact justice as the finite mind can measure or finite agencies administer.

29 The Relationship of the Whites to the Negroes

In 1901 there was an almost unbridgeable chasm beween Negro and white in the South. W. E. Burghart Du Bois was regarded as a radical left-wing Negro who viewed members of his race as capable of full participation as citizens. George T. Winston, President of the North Carolina College of Agriculture and Mechanic Arts, held a diametrically opposite view. President Winston looked upon the Negro as an appealing but undependable child who until some unspecified future period would have to be led along the path of improvement by white men. He expressed his views when most southern states had revised their constitutions along the Mississippi Plan of disfranchising Negroes. In President Winston's mind "Sambo" was at last out of the statehouse and would remain in the cotton fields forever if he had anything to do with it.

There are few better articles stating the southern white man's restrictive attitude toward the Negro. Professor Winston expressed here the belief the Negro was a brutal child, irresponsible, and constitutionally lazy. He was untrustworthy and was incapable of self-improvement. Nevertheless Professor Winston did propose a Hampton Institute or a Tuskegee for every congressional district. And, curiously, he all but advocated miscegenation as one way to strengthen the character of the Negro race in the South, while lamenting the breakdown in communications between the races. The effect of what he advocated, however, was the erection of a barrier between free men.

Since the abolition of slavery a great change has taken place in the relations of the whites to the Negroes in the Southern states. This change has been one not merely of ownership and legal authority, but of personal interest, of moral influence, of social and industrial relations.

To-day there is practically no social intercourse between the two races, excepting such as exists between the Negroes and the most degraded whites. It was far different in slavery. Then the two races mingled freely together, not on terms of social equality, but in very extended and constant social intercourse. In almost every household the children of the two races played and frolicked together, or hunted, fished or swam together in the fields, streams and forests. During my childhood and boyhood the greater portion of my play-time was spent in games and sports with Negroes. Scarcely any pleasure was so great to a southern child as playing with Negroes. In the long summer evenings we would play and romp until bed-time in the spacious yard surrounding the house, or in the garden or neighboring fields. I remember well how the evenings would fly by, and how my mother would grant repeated extensions of time, "just to play one more game of fox-and-geese, or hide-the-switch." Some of the songs that we sang and some of the games that we played, part singing, part acting, part dancing, still linger in my memory and carry me back to the happiness of childhood. Always in my childhood memories, especially in happy memories, I find associated together my mother, my home, and the Negro slaves.

During the winter evenings, when it was disagreeable out of doors, I would get permission for four or five Negro boys and girls to play with me in the library, or in the nursery. Here we would play indoor games; jack-straws, blind-man's buff, checks, checkers, pantomime, geography puzzles, conundrum matches and spelling bees. Frequently I would read the Negroes fairy stories, or show them pictures in the magazines and books of art.

George T. Winston, "The Relationship of the Whites to the Negroes," *Annals of the American Academy of Political and Social Science* 18 (July 1901), 105–118.

I remember how we used to linger over a beautiful picture of Lord William Russell bidding adieu to his family before going to execution; and how in boyish way I would tell the Negroes the story of his unhappy fate and his wife's devotion. Another favorite picture was the coronation of Queen Victoria. How we delighted in "Audubon's Birds" and in the beautifully colored plates and animals in the government publications on natural history. The pleasure was by no means one-sided. To our hotchpot of amusement and instruction the Negroes contributed marvelous tales of birds and animals, which more than offset my familiar reminiscences of Queen Victoria and Lord Russell.

It was a great privilege during slavery for the white children to visit Negro cabins at night and listen to their folk lore. Those delightful stories immortalized by Joel Chandler Harris, in the character of Uncle Remus, I heard many times in my youth, and many others besides equally delightful. There is a marvelous attraction between a white child and a Negro; even between a little child and a grown Negro. I always found it a pleasure to sit in the cabins and watch them at work. It was a pleasure just to be with them. I have eaten many a meal with my father's slaves in their cabins, always treated with consideration, respect and affection, but not greater than I myself felt for the master and mistress of the humble cabin. My mother would have punished severely any disrespect or rudeness on my part toward the older Negroes. I would not have dared to call them by their names. It was always "Uncle Tom" or "Aunt Susan," when I addressed them. This form of appellation was common in the South between whites and blacks. Even a strange Negro, whose name was not known, however humble he might be, was saluted on the high road, when passed by a respectable white person, with the friendly greeting of "Howdye, Uncle," or "Howdye, Auntie."

Social intercourse between white and black during slavery was not confined to children. Not infrequently the Negro women would come to the "White House" to see the mistress, often in the evenings, sitting and chatting in the nursery or the ladies' sitting room. Visits to the slave cabins were made regularly, oftentimes daily, by the white women of the household, who went not merely to visit the sick and inspect the children, to advise and direct about work and household matters, but to show their personal interest in and regard for the Negroes themselves, not as slaves, nor workers, but as individuals, as human beings, and sometimes as dear friends. In short, a social visit was made; not upon terms of social equality, but still a social visit, during which the news of the plantation or neighborhood, and occasionally of the larger world, was exchanged and discussed. This custom existed to some extent even on large plantations, where the slaves were more isolated and herded together in larger numbers. On small farms, where the races were about equal numerically, and in all households there was constant and very familiar contact between white and black. The white women in the Southern households usually aided and directed the work of the Negroes. The mistress sewed or cut garments in the same room with the slave seamstresses. The lady's maid slept upon a couch or pallet in her lady's chamber, or the one adjoining. The cooks, dining-room servants, nurses, laundresses, coachmen, house-boys, gardeners, shoemakers, carpenters, blacksmiths and mechanics generally were in daily enjoyment of a very considerable degree of social intercourse with the white race. They entered into the traditions and spirit of the family to which they belonged, defended its name and its honor, accepted in a rude way its ideas of courtesy, morality and religion, and thus became to a considerable degree inheritors of the civilization of the white race. It was this semi-social intercourse between the two races, without any approach to social equality, this daily and hourly contact producing personal interest, friendship and affection, added to the industrial training of slavery that transformed the Negro so quickly from a savage to a civilized man.

The one great evil connected with race familiarity, the evil of licentiousness and miscegenation, while degrading to the white race was not entirely harmful to the Negro. Nearly all the leaders of the Negro race, both during slavery and since, have been Mulattoes; and the two really great men credited to the Negro race in the United States have been the sons of white fathers, and strongly marked by the mental and moral qualities of the white race. The Mulatto is quicker, brighter, and more easily refined than the Negro. There is a general opinion among Southern people that he is inferior morally; but I believe that his only inferiority is physical and vital. It cannot be denied that the Negro race has been very greatly elevated by its Mulatto members. Indeed, if you strike from its records all that Mulattoes have said and done, little would be left. Wherever work requiring refinement, extra intelligence and executive ability is performed, you will find it usually directed by Mulattoes.

But the social intercourse between the races in the South, which was so helpful to the blacks, has now practically ceased. The children of this generation no longer play and frolic together. White ladies no longer visit Negro cabins. The familiar salutation of "Uncle" or "Auntie" is no longer heard. The lady's maid sleeps no more by the bedside of her mistress. The Southern woman with her helpless little children in solitary farm house no longer sleeps secure in the absence of her husband with doors unlocked but safely guarded by black men whose lives would be freely given in her defence. But now, when a knock is heard at the door, she shudders with nameless horror. The black brute is lurking in the dark, a monstrous beast, crazed with lust. His ferocity is almost demoniacal. A mad bull or a tiger could scarcely be more brutal. A whole community is now frenzied with horror, with blind and furious rage for vengeance. A stake is driven; the wretched brute, covered with oil, bruised and gashed, beaten and hacked and maimed, amid the jeers and shouts and curses, the tears of anger and of joy, the prayers and the maledictions of thousands of civilized people, in the sight of school-houses, court-houses and churches is burned to death. Since the abolition of slavery and the growing up of a new generation of Negroes, crimes that are too hideous to describe have been committed every month, every week, frequently every day, against the helpless women and children of the white race, crimes that were unknown in slavery. And, in turn, cruelties have been inflicted upon Negroes by whole communities of whites, which, if attempted during slavery, would have been prevented at any sacrifice. I do not hesitate to say that more horrible crimes have been committed by the generation of Negroes that have grown up in the South since slavery than by the six preceding generations in slavery. And also that the worst cruelties of slavery all combined for two centuries were not equal to the savage barbarities inflicted in retaliation upon the Negroes by the whites during the last twenty years. This condition of things is too horrible to last. It must grow better; or else grow worse, and by its own fury destroy both black and white.

Between the older generations in the South there is still warm affection. Whenever I visit my old home, all the Negroes that are able, come to see me, many traveling considerable distances. The last time I was there my nurse and playmate, a woman of fifty years, about six years my elder, threw her arms around me and wept like a child, completely overcome with emotion. She was honest, virtuous, industrious, intelligent, affectionate and faithful. She had been raised from childhood by my mother and had slept every night in my mother's bed room. I am sure that every member of my father's family would have risked his life to protect her. And she would have greatly preferred death to seeing misfortune or disaster visit our family. My youngest brother's nurse, dying about ten years after emancipation, made her will and left her little store of goods and property, worth perhaps a hundred dollars, to her white nursling, "little Master Robert." A few days ago a Negro man was pardoned from the State penitentiary in North Carolina, by the Governor. The following letter secured his pardon. It was written by his former master and playmate, a captain in the Confederate army, an ex-member of Congress, a Democratic member of the recent State Legislature:

To His Excellency Honorable CHARLES B. AYCOCK, *Governor of North Carolina.*

Dear Sir: I respectfully and earnestly petition you to pardon William Alexander, a Negro convicted of burglary in the year 1889, in Mecklenburg County. William was born on my father's plantation, and is about fifty-eight or fifty-nine years old, one or two years my junior. I need only state that his father was our coachman and his mother our cook, to show you my opportunity was good for knowing him. He was my slave, and his father and mother died on my plantation. William was not smart, or, to use a plantation term, was less bright than any of the young Negroes on the plantation. Knowing both of the Negroes connected with him in the burglary, I feel no hesitation in assuring you that I believe that they persuaded him to join them. William has now served about twelve years. This is an excessive punishment for a Negro of a low order of intelligence. If he came of a bad family, I would not ask his pardon. His family is as good as any Negro family in this state. He is the only one that has ever been indicted for crime. I could get others to sign a petition, but it would be a favor for me, not him, for an ordinary Negro confined in the penitentiary for twelve years is a forgotten man. Governor, I pray you to pardon William Alexander; and, if he will, he can return to my plantation where the friend of his boyhood will give him a home.

Very respectfully,

S. B. ALEXANDER.

Raleigh, N. C., *March 26, 1901.*

The industrial relations of the races have also undergone great changes in the South, though not so marked as the changes in social and personal relations. Under slavery almost all the labor of the South was performed by Negroes, or by Negroes and whites working side by side. The South was lacking in manufactures, and used little machinery. Its demand for skilled labor was not large, but what demand existed was supplied mainly by Negroes. Negro carpenters, plasterers, bricklayers, blacksmiths, wheelwrights, painters, harnessmakers, tanners, millers, weavers, barrelmakers, basketmakers, shoemakers, chairmakers, coachmen, spinners, seamstresses, housekeepers, gardeners, cooks, laundresses, embroiderers, maids of all work, could be found in every community, and frequently on a single plantation. Skilled labor was more profitable than unskilled, and therefore every slave was made as skilful as was possible under a slave system. The young Negroes were brought up to labor, from an early age. The smartest girls were trained to domestic service in its various branches, and became practically members of the family, so far as careful training was concerned. Many of them

could sew, knit, crochet, embroider, cut, fit and make garments,
clean up house, wash and iron, spin and weave, even more skil-
fully than the mistress who had taught them. All the garments
that I wore in childhood were made by Negroes or by my
mother, with the single exception of the hat. Negro lads who
showed aptitudes for trades, were hired out under a sort of
apprentice system, and taught to be skilful as carpenters,
masons, smiths, and the like. The Negro artisans were very
jealous of their rights, and stood upon their professional skill
and knowledge. I remember, one day, my father, who was a
lawyer, offered some suggestions to one of his slaves, a fairly-
good carpenter, who was building us a barn. The old Negro
heard him with ill-concealed disgust, and replied: "Look here,
Master, you'se a first-rate lawyer, no doubt; but you don't
know nothing 'tall 'bout carpentering. You better go back to
your law books." The most accomplished housemaid, maid-of-
all-work, laundress, nurse, dining-room servant, in our household was a woman named Emily, and the most accomplished
man-of-all-work, carpenter, coachman, 'possum-hunter, fisher-
man, story-teller, boy amuser, was Emily's brother, Andrew.
They had been given to my father in his youth by my grandfather, and had attended him to college, working in the dining-
room, to pay for his education. They were present at my father's
wedding, and for twenty years remained members of the household, exceedingly useful and skilful; and, I may add, exceedingly privileged characters. They far surpassed in efficiency and
versatility any white laborers in the county. I remember, one
Sunday, the family came home earlier than usual from church,
there being no services on account of the illness of the minister.
On entering his bed room my father beheld a strange and yet
familiar looking Negro arrayed in dress-suit standing in front
of the mirror, with arms akimbo, and swallow-tails of the coat
switching from side to side in token of pride and satisfaction. It
was Emily, arrayed in her master's best suit, enjoying a new
sensation. No punishment was inflicted on her. Nor do I remember that any of my father's slaves were ever punished, except
such switching as was given the children, on which occasions I

was usually present, a most unwilling participant and fellow-victim.

When emancipation came at the close of the Civil War, it was understood by the average Negro to mean freedom from labor. Freedom, leisure, idleness was now his greatest pleasure. How delightful it was to tell old master now that he had business in town and couldn't work to-day; to leave the plow and hoe idle; to meet other Negroes on the streets, to spend the day loafing, chatting, shouting, oftentimes drinking and dancing or quarreling and fighting. Sambo was now a gentleman of leisure, and he enjoyed it to the full. It was easy to live in the South. The mild climate and fertile soil, the abundance of game in forest and stream, the bountiful supply of wild fruits, the accessibility of forests with firewood free to all, the openhanded generosity and universal carelessness of living made it possible for the average Negro to idle away at least half his time and yet live in tolerable comfort.

The national government, to guard against distress among the Negroes and to prevent oppression by the whites, neither of which was at all possible, now established throughout the South, for the distribution of food and clothing and the administration of justice between the races, the Freedman's Bureau. This institution was in every respect most unfortunate. The Negro ran away from his old master's cornfield and his appeals to work in order to enjoy the free bounty of the federal government. I knew a Negro to walk one hundred miles in order to obtain half a bushel of corn meal from the bureau. In the time required he might have earned by labor four and a half bushels, or nine times what he got by begging. But the evils of idleness, although great, would soon have passed away, if the two races had been left alone. The Southern whites were familiar with and very tolerant of the Negro's weaknesses and petty vices. They looked upon him with sympathy and sorrow, with friendship and affection, rather than with anger, resentment, and hostility. They were anxious to see him go to work even more diligently than in slavery, acquire property, and improve his moral and physical condition. The races still remained very close together, in their daily lives, interests and affections. They might have worked out a future along lines far different from those they are now following. It was decreed otherwise by fate.

The bestowal of political rights upon the Negro, the dis-franchisement of almost every prominent white man in the South, the migration from the North of political carpetbaggers and their manipulation of the Negro vote, the Civil Rights Bill, the Force Bill, the zeal of educational and religious mission-aries, most of whom preached and practiced the social and civil equality of the races; in short, the dark, dismal and awful night of Reconstruction, following swift upon the storm of Civil War with its unparalleled destruction of life and property, now threatened the very foundations of civilizations in all the South-ern states. The bonds between the races were broken at last. The Negro did not endorse all the demands that were made in his behalf. He knew they were impossible. Still he was pro-foundly influenced by them. In slavery he was like an animal in harness; well trained, gentle and affectionate; in early freedom the harness was off, but still the habit of obedience and the force of affection endured and prevented a run-away. In Re-construction came a consciousness of being unharnessed, un-hitched, unbridled and unrestrained. The wildest excesses followed. The machinery of government was seized in every Southern state by men recently slaves, now guided by political adventures. Southern halls of legislation, once glorified by the eloquence of Patrick Henry, the wisdom of Marshall, or the patriotism of Washington, now resounded with the drunken snorings or the unmeaning gibberish of Cuffee and Sambo. Negro strumpets in silks and satins led wild orgies at inaugural balls in marble halls that blushed and closed their eyes. "Uncle Tom" and "Aunt Susan" were now entirely vanished. The fam-ily cook now demanded to be known as Mrs. Jackson, and the chambermaid as Miss Marguerite. I know an unmarried Negress, about twenty-five years of age, the mother of three illegitimate children, who requires her own children to call her on all occasions, "Miss Mary." It was not a time for the learning of new trades by the emancipated race. It was not a time for new industries, or increased efficiency of labor. The Negro was intoxicated with the license of freedom; the North was blinded by sentimentality and the passions of war; the South was fighting for civilization and existence. It is all over now. I forbear to characterize it further. Some day the historian, the poet, the painter, the dramatist will picture Reconstruction, and will make the saddest picture in the annals of the English-speaking race.

But Reconstruction is ended at last. For the first time since 1870 the National House of Representatives contains not a single Negro.

For the first time in our history the American Negro is almost friendless. The North, tired of Negro politicians and Negro beggars, is beginning to say: "We have helped the Negro enough; let him now help himself and work out his own salvation." The South, worn out with strife over the Negro and supporting with difficulty its awful burden of Negro ignorance, inefficiency and criminality, is beginning to ask whether the race is really capable of development, or is a curse and a hindrance in the way of Southern progress and civilization.

The two races are drifting apart. They were closer together in slavery than they have been since. Old time sympathies, friendships and affections created by two centuries of slavery, are rapidly passing away. A single generation of freedom has almost destroyed them. Unless a change is made, coming generations will be separated by active hatred and hostility. The condition of the Negro is indeed pitiful; and his prospects for the future are dark and gloomy. There is no solution of the problem, unless it is dealt with from the standpoint of reason and experience, without prejudice or fanaticism.

The Negro is a child race. If isolated from the world and left to himself, he might slowly grow into manhood along separate lines and develop a Negro civilization; but in the United States such isolation and such development are quite impossible. The Negro here is bound to be under the tutelage and control of the whites. No legal enactment, no political agitation, no scheme of education can alter this fact. It is better for the Negro that it should be so; better that he should be dispersed among the white people, living with them and learning their ways, than to be deported to Africa, or segregated somewhere in America, to work out slowly a separate and distinct Negro civilization.

The tutelage of the Negro is not yet complete. It lasted through six generations of slavery, directed by Southern whites. It has continued through one generation of freedom, directed by Northern whites, acting through Federal legislation, through Federal courts, through political, educational and religious missionaries working among the Negroes in the Southern states. The folly and the futility of Northern tutelage is now fully demonstrated; and the Negro is again under the tutelage of the South, to remain there until the race problem is finally settled.

The real question is not one of tutelage *versus* self-development, but whether the necessary tutelage of the Negro under the white race shall be one of friendship and sympathy or one of prejudice and hostility. To such a question only one answer is possible. It would be a cruelty greater than slavery to leave this helpless race, this child race, to work out its own salvation in fierce and hostile competition with the strongest and best developed race on the globe. The Negro can expect no peculiar development. He must aim at white civilization; and must reach it through the support, guidance and control of the white people among whom he lives. He must regain the active friendship and affection of the Southern whites. He will do so if let alone by the North. The South once liked him and loved him, and will do so again if he will permit and deserve it. The North, through force of arms and legal enactment, has given him physical freedom; but moral and intellectual freedom must come through the help of the descendants of his former masters. If this help be not given, there is no hope for the race. Against the prejudice and passion, the neglect and oppression, the competition and hostility which will inevitably result from a continuance of the relations now existing between the two races in the South the Negro will be ground to powder. His progress depends absolutely upon the restoration of friendly relations to the whites. Nor is this a matter of easy accomplishment. Two things are requisite;

1. The withdrawal of the Negro from politics.
2. His increased efficiency as a laborer.

The withdrawal of the Negro from politics is now being accomplished by legislation in the various Southern States. If this is interrupted by the North, and the old battle of Reconstruction fought again, the result will be the complete and final estrangement of the two races, with prejudice and hostility too intense to permit their living peaceably together.

Greater industrial efficiency would prove an everlasting bond between the races in the South. It is the real key to the problem. Let the Negro make himself indispensable as a workman, and he may rely upon the friendship and affection of the whites. But the best energies of the race since emancipation have been diverted from industrial fields into politics, preaching and education. Until recently its leaders have not regarded industrial effort as a means of progress. But public sentiment in the South still welcomes the Negro to every field of labor that he is capable of performing. The whole field of industry is open to him. The Southern whites are not troubled by his efficiency but by his inefficiency. For a full generation the Negro has had opportunity to control every industry in the South. Had he devoted himself, upon emancipation, to manual labor and the purchase of land instead of politics, religion and education, he would own to-day at least one-half the soil of the Southern states.

There is abundant room for Northern philanthropy in helping to uplift the Southern Negro. A Hampton Institute, or a Tuskegee, should be established in every congressional district. But this alone will not suffice. The Negro laborer, like the white laborer, needs the industrial training of his daily employer. He needs, daily and hourly, the sympathy, encouragement, instruction, admonition and restraint of his white employer. These are given to the white boy or girl; and are received usually with willingness and profit. But such help is not given to the Negro; nor is it desired. Negro children are less courteous to white people now than white children were to Negroes during slavery.

The Negro race is a child race and must remain in tutelage for years to come; in tutelage not of colleges and universities, but of industrial schools, of skilled and efficient labor, of character building by honest work and honest dealing, of good habits and good manners, of respect for elders and superiors, of daily employment on the farm, in the household, the shop, the forest, the factory and the mine. Slavery gave the Negro a better industrial training than he has to-day. Freedom has increased his zeal and his opportunity, but diminished his skill. The door of his opportunity will not always be open. He must enter now. If he do not, he will remain for a while among the races of the earth a dull and stupid draught animal; and finally will pass away, incompetent. But, with the help of the white race he may obtain opportunity to develop his powers, he may subdue his animal passions and cultivate his gentler emotions, may train his physical strength into skill and power, may grow from childhood into mature manhood; and in the providence of God may yet add strength to the civilization of a people, who, through the tutelage of slavery, with sorrow and tears, with labor and anguish, with hope and charity brought him from barbarism to civilization, from heathenism to Christianity.

30 Relations of the Negroes with the Whites

At the turn of the century W. E. Burghart Du Bois read a paper to a section of the American Political Science Association that spelled out, perhaps more clearly than had ever been done before, the areas in southern life where friction occurred unnecessarily between whites and blacks. Packed in the short essay was a review of the whole gamut of failures from economic discriminations to the denial of political rights. Du Bois reviewed for his white audience many of the innermost attitudes and reactions of Negroes to the basic discriminations they suffered.

In his discussion of white supremacists' efforts to drive the Negro from the polls, Du Bois made an eloquent plea for a reconsideration of the issue. No one speaking for the Negro at this early period in the twentieth century, not even the Civil Rights Commission, has stated so clearly that the only way the Negro could hope to improve his status on all fronts was full and responsible exercise of the ballot. Too, the Negro had a right to trial by jury and judge free of the biases of the color line. Despite the fact the white Southerner has long boasted that he almost alone has understood the Negro, Du Bois pointed out the fact he could not differentiate between Negroes of character and those lacking it. He cited the dignified accomplishments of Paul Lawrence Dunbar and the ghastly end of Sam Hose, who was lynched in Georgia.

Du Bois spoke realistically to his white listeners where Booker T. Washington had been cautious, eloquent, and pleading in his famous Atlanta Exposition speech (see Document 54).

IN THE DISCUSSION OF GREAT SOCIAL PROBLEMS IT IS EXTREMELY difficult for those who are themselves actors in the drama to avoid the attitude of partisans and advocates. And yet I take it that the examination of the most serious of the race problems of America is not in the nature of a debate but rather a joint endeavor to seek the truth beneath a mass of assertion and opinion, of passion and distress. And I trust that whatever disagreement may arise between those who view the situation from opposite sides of the color line will be rather in the nature of additional information than of contradiction.

The world-old phenomenon of the contact of diverse races of men is to have new exemplification during the new century. Indeed the characteristic of the age is the contact of European civilization with the world's undeveloped peoples. Whatever we may say of the results of such contact in the past, it certainly forms a chapter in human action not pleasant to look back upon. War, murder, slavery, extermination and debauchery—this has again and again been the result of carrying civilization and the blessed gospel to the isles of the sea and the heathen without the law. Nor does it altogether satisfy the conscience of the modern world to be told complacently that all this has been right and proper, the fated triumph of strength over weakness, of righteousness over evil, of superiors over inferiors. It would certainly be soothing if one could readily believe all this, and yet there are too many ugly facts, for everything to be thus easily explained away. We feel and know that there are many delicate differences in race psychology, numberless changes which our crude social measurements are not yet able to follow minutely, which explain much of history and social development. At the same time, too, we know that these considerations have never adequately explained or excused the triumph of brute force and cunning over weakness and innocence.

    W. E. Burghart Du Bois, "Relations of the Negroes with the Whites," *Annals of the American Academy of Political and Social Science* 18 (July 1901), 121–140.

It is then the strife of all honorable men of the twentieth century to see that in the future competition of races, the survival
of the fittest shall mean the triumph of the good, the beautiful
and the true; that we may be able to preserve for future civilization all that is really fine and noble and strong, and not continue
to put a premium on greed and impudence and cruelty. To
bring this hope to fruition we are compelled daily to turn more
and more to a conscientious study of the phenomena of race
contact—to a study frank and fair, and not falsified and colored
by our wishes or our fears. And we have here in the South as
fine a field for such a study as the world affords: a field to be
sure which the average American scientist deems somewhat
beneath his dignity, and which the average man who is not a
scientist knows all about, but nevertheless a line of study which
by reason of the enormous race complications, with which God
seems about to punish this nation, must increasingly claim our
sober attention, study and thought. We must ask: What are the
actual relations of whites and blacks in the South, and we must
be answered not by apology or fault-finding, but by a plain,
unvarnished tale.

In the civilized life of to-day the contact of men and their relations to each other fall in a few main lines of action and communication: there is first the physical proximity of homes and dwelling places, the way in which neighborhoods group themselves,
and the contiguity of neighborhoods. Secondly, and in our age
chiefest, there are the economic relations—the methods by
which individuals co-operate for earning a living, for the mutual
satisfaction of wants, for the production of wealth. Next there
are the political relations, the co-operation in social control, in
group government, in laying and paying the burden of taxation.
In the fourth place there are the less tangible but highly important forms of intellectual contact and commerce, the interchange
of ideas through conversation and conference, through periodicals and libraries, and above all the gradual formation for
each community of that curious *tertium quid* which we call public opinion. Closely allied with this come the various forms of
social contact in every-day life, in travel, in theatres, in house

gatherings, in marrying and giving in marriage. Finally, there are the varying forms of religious enterprise, of moral teaching and benevolent endeavor.

These are the principal ways in which men living in the same communities are brought into contact with each other. It is my task this afternoon, therefore, to point out from my point of view how the black race in the South meets and mingles with the whites, in these matters of every-day life.

First as to physical dwelling, it is usually possible, as most of you know, to draw in nearly every Southern community a physical color line on the map, to the one side of which whites dwell and the other Negroes. The winding and intricacy of the geographical color line varies of course in different communities. I know some towns where a straight line drawn through the middle of the main street separates nine-tenths of the whites from nine-tenths of the blacks. In other towns the older settlement of whites has been encircled by a broad band of blacks; in still other cases little settlements of nuclei of blacks have sprung up amid surrounding whites. Usually in cities each street has its distinctive color, and only now and then do the colors meet in close proximity. Even in the country something of this segregation is manifest in the smaller areas, and of course in the larger phenomena of the black belt.

All this segregation by color is largely independent of that natural clustering by social grades common to all communities. A Negro slum may be in dangerous proximity to a white residence quarter, while it is quite common to find a white slum planted in the heart of a respectable Negro district. One thing, however, seldom occurs: the best of the whites and the best of the Negroes almost never live in anything like close proximity. It thus happens that in nearly every Southern town and city, both whites and blacks see commonly the worst of each other. This is a vast change from the situation in the past when through the close contact of master and house-servant in the patriarchal big house, one found the best of both races in close contact and sympathy, while at the same time the squalor and dull round of toil among the field hands was removed from the sight and hearing of the family. One can easily see how a person who saw slavery thus from his father's parlors and sees freedom on the streets of a great city fails to grasp or comprehend the whole of the new picture. On the other hand the settled belief of the mass of the Negroes that the Southern white people do not have the black man's best interests at heart has been intensified in later years by this continual daily contact of the better class of blacks with the worst representatives of the white race.

Coming now to the economic relations of the races we are on ground made familiar by study, much discussion and no little philanthropic effort. And yet with all this there are many essential elements in the co-operation of Negroes and whites for work and wealth, that are too readily overlooked or not thoroughly understood. The average American can easily conceive of a rich land awaiting development and filled with black laborers. To him the Southern problem is simply that of making efficient workingmen out of this material by giving them the requisite technical skill and the help of invested capital. The problem, however, is by no means as simple as this, from the obvious fact that these workingmen have been trained for centuries as slaves. They exhibit, therefore, all the advantages and defects of such training; they are willing and good-natured, but not self reliant, provident or careful. If now the economic development of the South is to be pushed to the verge of exploitation, as seems probable, then you have a mass of workingmen thrown into relentless competition with the workingmen of the world but handicapped by a training the very opposite to that of the modern self-reliant democratic laborer. What the black laborer needs is careful personal guidance, group leadership of men with hearts in their bosoms, to train them to foresight, carefulness and honesty. Nor does it require any fine-spun theories of racial differences to prove the necessity of such group training after the brains of the race have been knocked out by two hundred and fifty years of assiduous education in submission, carelessness and stealing. After emancipation it was the plain duty of some one to assume this group leadership and training of the Negro laborer. I will not stop here to inquire *whose* duty it was

—whether that of the white ex-master who had profited by
unpaid toil, or the Northern philanthropist whose persistence
brought the crisis, or of the National Government whose edict
freed the bondsmen—I will not stop to ask *whose* duty it was,
but I insist it was the duty of *some one* to see that these workingmen were not left alone and unguided without capital, landless,
without skill, without economic organization, without even the
bald protection of law, order and decency; left in a great land
not to settle down to slow and careful internal development, but
destined to be thrown almost immediately into relentless, sharp
competition with the best of modern workingmen under an economic system where every participant is fighting for himself,
and too often utterly regardless of the rights or welfare of his
neighbor.

For we must never forget that the economic system of the
South to-day which has succeeded the old régime is not the
same system as that of the old industrial North, of England
or of France with their trades unions, their restrictive laws,
their written and unwritten commercial customs and their long
experience. It is rather a copy of that England of the early
nineteenth century, before the factory acts, the England that
wrung pity from thinkers and fired the wrath of Carlyle. The rod
of empire that passed from the hands of Southern gentlemen
in 1865, partly by force, partly by their own petulance, has never
returned to them. Rather it has passed to those men who have
come to take charge of the industrial exploitation of the New
South—the sons of poor whites fired with a new thirst for wealth
and power, thrifty and avaricious Yankees, shrewd and unscrupulous Jews. Into the hands of these men the Southern
laborers, white and black, have fallen, and this to their sorrow.
For the laborers as such there is in these new captains of industry neither love nor hate, neither sympathy nor romance—it
is a cold question of dollars and dividends. Under such a system
all labor is bound to suffer. Even the white laborers are not yet
intelligent, thrifty and well trained enough to maintain themselves against the powerful inroads of organized capital. The
result among them even, is long hours of toil, low wages, child

labor, and lack of protection against usury and cheating. But among the black laborers all this is aggravated, first, by a race prejudice which varies from a doubt and distrust among the best element of whites to a frenzied hatred among the worst; and, secondly, it is aggravated, as I have said before, by the wretched economic heritage of the freedmen from slavery. With this training it is difficult for the freedman to learn to grasp the opportunities already opened to him, and the new opportunities are seldom given him but go by favor to the whites.

Left by the best elements of the South with little protection or oversight, he has been made in law and custom the victim of the worst and most unscrupulous men in each community. The crop-lien system which is depopulating the fields of the South is not simply the result of shiftlessness on the part of Negroes but is also the result of cunningly devised laws as to mortgages, liens, and misdemeanors which can be made by conscienceless men to entrap and snare the unwary until escape is impossible, further toil a farce, and protest a crime. I have seen in the black belt of Georgia an ignorant, honest Negro buy and pay for a farm in installments three separate times, and then in the face of law and decency the enterprising Russian Jew who sold it to him pocketed money and deed and left the black man landless, to labor on his own land at thirty cents a day. I have seen a black farmer fall in debt to a white storekeeper and that storekeeper go to his farm and strip it of every single marketable article—mules, plows, stored crops, tools, furniture, bedding, clocks, looking-glass, and all this without a warrant, without process of law, without a sheriff or officer, in the face of the law for homestead exemptions, and without rendering to a single responsible person any account or reckoning. And such proceedings can happen and will happen in any community where a class of ignorant toilers are placed by custom and race prejudice beyond the pale of sympathy and race brotherhood. So long as the best elements of a community do not feel in duty bound to protect and train and care for the weaker members of their group they leave them to be preyed upon by these swindlers and rascals.

This unfortunate economic situation does not mean the hindrance of all advance in the black South, or the absence of a class of black landlords and mechanics who, in spite of disadvantages, are accumulating property and making good citizens. But it does mean that this class is not nearly so large as a fairer economic system might easily make it, that those who survive in the competition are handicapped so as to accomplish much less than they deserve to, and that above all, the personnel of the successful class is left to chance and accident, and not to any intelligent culling or reasonable methods of selection. As a remedy for this, there is but one possible procedure. We must accept some of the race prejudice in the South as a fact—deplorable in its intensity, unfortunate in results, and dangerous for the future, but nevertheless a hard fact which only time can efface. We cannot hope then in this generation, or for several generations, that the mass of the whites can be brought to assume that close sympathetic and self-sacrificing leadership of the blacks which their present situation so eloquently demands. Such leadership, such social teaching and example, must come from the blacks themselves. For sometime men doubted as to whether the Negro could develop such leaders, but to-day no one seriously disputes the capability of individual Negroes to assimilate the culture and common sense of modern civilization, and to pass it on to some extent, at least, to their fellows. If this be true, then here is the path out of the economic situation, and here is the imperative demand for trained Negro leaders of character and intelligence, men of skill, men of light and leading, college-bred men, black captains of industry and missionaries of culture. Men who thoroughly comprehend and know modern civilization and can take hold of Negro communities and raise and train them by force of precept and example, deep sympathy and the inspiration of common blood and ideals. But if such men are to be effective they must have some power—they must be backed by the best public opinion of these communities, and able to wield for their objects and aims such weapons as the experience of the world has taught are indispensable to human progress.

Of such weapons the greatest, perhaps, in the modern world is the power of the ballot, and this brings me to a consideration of the third form of contact between whites and blacks in the South—political activity.

In the attitude of the American mind toward Negro suffrage, can be traced with singular accuracy the prevalent conceptions of government. In the sixties we were near enough the echoes of the French Revolution to believe pretty thoroughly in universal suffrage. We argued, as we thought then rather logically, that no social class was so good, so true and so disinterested as to be trusted wholly with the political destiny of their neighbors; that in every state the best arbiters of their own welfare are the persons directly affected, consequently it is only by arming every hand with a ballot—with the right to have a voice in the policy of the state—that the greatest good to the greatest number could be attained. To be sure there were objections to these arguments, but we thought we had answered them tersely and convincingly; if some one complained of the ignorance of voters, we answered: "Educate them." If another complained of their venality we replied: "Disfranchise them or put them in jail." And finally to the men who feared demagogues and the natural perversity of some human beings, we insisted that time and bitter experience would teach the most hardheaded. It was at this time that the question of Negro suffrage in the South was raised. Here was a defenseless people suddenly made free. How were they to be protected from those who did not believe in their freedom and were determined to thwart it? Not by force, said the North; not by government guardianship, said the South; then by the ballot, the sole and legitimate defense of a free people, said the Common Sense of the nation. No one thought at the time that the ex-slaves could use the ballot intelligently or very effectively, but they did think that the possession of so great power, by a great class in the nation would compel their fellows to educate this class to its intelligent use.

Meantime new thoughts came to the nation: the inevitable period of moral retrogression and political trickery that ever follows in the wake of war overtook us. So flagrant became the political scandals that reputable men began to leave politics alone, and politics consequently became disreputable. Men began to pride themselves on having nothing to do with their own government and to agree tacitly with those who regarded public office as a private perquisite. In this state of mind it became easy to wink at the suppression of the Negro vote in the South, and to advise self-respecting Negroes to leave politics entirely alone. The decent and reputable citizens of the North who neglected their own civic duties grew hilarious over the exaggerated importance with which the Negro regarded the franchise. Thus it easily happened that more and more the better class of Negroes followed the advice from abroad and the pressure from home and took no further interest in politics, leaving to the careless and the venal of their race the exercise of their rights as voters. This black vote which still remained was not trained and educated but further debauched by open and unblushing bribery, or force and fraud, until the Negro voter was thoroughly innoculated with the idea that politics was a method of private gain by disreputable means.

And finally, now, to-day, when we are awakening to the fact that the perpetuity of republican institutions on this continent depends on the purification of the ballot, the civic training of voters, and the raising of voting to the plane of a solemn duty which a patriotic citizen neglects to his peril and to the peril of his children's children—in this day when we are striving for a renaissance of civic virtue, what are we going to say to the black voter of the South? Are we going to tell him still that politics is a disreputable and useless form of human activity? Are we going to induce the best class of Negroes to take less and less interest in government and give up their right to take such an interest without a protest? I am not saying a word against all legitimate efforts to purge the ballot of ignorance, pauperism and crime. But few have pretended that the present movement for disfranchisement in the South is for such a purpose; it has been plainly and frankly declared in nearly every case that the object of the disfranchising laws is the elimination of the black man from politics.

Now is this a minor matter which has no influence on the main question of the industrial and intellectual development of the Negro? Can we establish a mass of black laborers, artisans and landholders in the South who by law and public opinion have absolutely no voice in shaping the laws under which they live and work. Can the modern organization of industry, assuming as it does free democratic government and the power and ability of the laboring classes to compel respect for their welfare—can this system be carried out in the South when half its laboring force is voiceless in the public councils and powerless in its own defense? To-day the black man of the South has almost nothing to say as to how much he shall be taxed, or how those taxes shall be expended; as to who shall execute the laws and how they shall do it; as to who shall make the laws and how they shall be made. It is pitiable that frantic efforts must be made at critical times to get lawmakers in some states even to listen to the respectful presentation of the black side of a current controversy. Daily the Negro is coming more and more to look upon law and justice not as protecting safeguards but as sources of humiliation and oppression. The laws are made by men who as yet have little interest in him; they are executed by men who have absolutely no motive for treating the black people with courtesy or consideration, and finally the accused lawbreaker is tried not by his peers but too often by men who would rather punish ten innocent Negroes than let one guilty one escape.

I should be the last one to deny the patent weaknesses and shortcomings of the Negro people; I should be the last to withhold sympathy from the white South in its efforts to solve its intricate social problems. I freely acknowledge that it is possible and sometimes best that a partially undeveloped people should be ruled by the rest of their stronger and better neighbors for their own good, until such time as they can start and fight the world's battles alone. I have already pointed out how sorely in need of such economic and spiritual guidance the emancipated Negro was, and I am quite willing to admit that if the representatives of the best white southern public opinion were the ruling and guiding powers in the South to-day that the con-

ditions indicated would be fairly well fulfilled. But the point I
have insisted upon and now emphasize again is that the best
opinion of the South to-day is not the ruling opinion. That to
leave the Negro helpless and without a ballot to-day is to leave
him not to the guidance of the best but rather to the exploitation
and debauchment of the worst; that this is no truer of the South
than of the North—of the North than of Europe—in any land, in
any country under modern free competition, to lay any class of
weak and despised people, be they white, black or blue, at the
political mercy of their stronger, richer and more resourceful
fellows is a temptation which human nature seldom has and
seldom will withstand.

Moreover the political status of the Negro in the South is
closely connected with the question of Negro crime. There can
be no doubt that crime among Negroes has greatly increased
in the last twenty years and that there has appeared in the slums
of great cities a distinct criminal class among the blacks. In
explaining this unfortunate development we must note two
things, (1) that the inevitable result of emancipation was to
increase crime and criminals, and (2) that the police system
of the South was primarily designed to control slaves. As to the
first point we must not forget that under a strict slave régime
there can scarcely be such a thing as crime. But when these
variously constituted human particles are suddenly thrown
broadcast on the sea of life, some swim, some sink, and some
hang suspended, to be forced up or down by the chance currents
of a busy hurrying world. So great an economic and social revolution as swept the South in '63 meant a weeding out among
the Negroes of the incompetents and vicious—the beginning of
a differentiation of social grades. Now a rising group of people
are not lifted bodily from the ground like an inert solid mass,
but rather stretch upward like a living plant with its roots still
clinging in the mold. The appearance, therefore, of the Negro
criminal was a phenomenon to be awaited, and while it causes
anxiety it should not occasion surprise.

Here again the hope for the future depended peculiarly on
careful and delicate dealing with these criminals. Their offenses

at first were those of laziness, carelessness and impulse rather than of malignity or ungoverned viciousness. Such misdemeanors needed discriminating treatment, firm but reformatory, with no hint of injustice and full proof of guilt. For such dealing with criminals, white or black, the South had no machinery, no adequate jails or reformatories and a police system arranged to deal with blacks alone, and which tacitly assumed that every white man was *ipso facto* a member of that police. Thus grew up a double system of justice which erred on the white side by undue leniency and the practical immunity of red-handed criminals, and erred on the black side by undue severity, injustice and lack of discrimination. For, as I have said, the police system of the South was originally designed to keep track of all Negroes, not simply of criminals, and when the Negroes were freed and the whole South was convinced of the impossibility of free Negro labor, the first and almost universal device was to use the courts as a means of re-enslaving the blacks. It was not then a question of crime but rather of color that settled a man's conviction on almost any charge. Thus Negroes come to look upon courts as instruments of injustice and oppression, and upon those convicted in them as martyrs and victims.

When now the real Negro criminal appeared and, instead of petty stealing and vagrancy, we began to have highway robbery, burglary, murder and rape, it had a curious effect on both sides of the color line; the Negroes refused to believe the evidence of white witnesses or the fairness of white juries, so that the greatest deterrent to crime, the public opinion of one's own social caste was lost and the criminal still looked upon as crucified rather than hanged. On the other hand the whites, used to being careless as to the guilt or innocence of accused Negroes, were swept in moments of passion beyond law, reason and decency. Such a situation is bound to increase crime and has increased it. To natural viciousness and vagrancy is being daily added motives of revolt and revenge which stir up all the latent savagery of both races and make peaceful attention to economic development often impossible.

But the chief problem in any community cursed with crime

is not the punishment of the criminals but the preventing of the young from being trained to crime. And here again the peculiar conditions of the South have prevented proper precautions. I have seen twelve-year-old boys working in chains on the public streets of Atlanta, directly in front of the schools, in company with old and hardened criminals; and this indiscriminate mingling of men, women and children makes the chain-gangs perfect schools of crime and debauchery. The struggle for reformatories which has gone on in Virginia, Georgia and other states is the one encouraging sign of the awakening of some communities to the suicidal results of this policy.

It is the public schools, however, which can be made outside the homes the greatest means of training decent self-respecting citizens. We have been so hotly engaged recently in discussing trade schools and the higher education that the pitiable plight of the public school system in the South has almost dropped from view. Of every five dollars spent for public education in the State of Georgia the white schools get four dollars and the Negro one dollar, and even then the white public school system, save in the cities, is bad and cries for reform. If this be true of the whites, what of the blacks? I am becoming more and more convinced as I look upon the system of common school training in the South that the national government must soon step in and aid popular education in some way. To-day it has been only by the most strenuous efforts on the part of the thinking men of the South that the Negro's share of the school fund has not been cut down to a pittance in some half dozen states, and that movement not only is not dead but in many communities is gaining strength. What in the name of reason does this nation expect of a people poorly trained and hard pressed in severe economic competition, without political rights and with ludicrously inadequate common school facilities? What can it expect but crime and listlessness, offset here and there by the dogged struggles of the fortunate and more determined who are themselves buoyed by the hope that in due time the country will come to its senses?

I have thus far sought to make clear the physical economic
and political relations of the Negroes and whites in the South as
I have conceived them, including for the reasons set forth, crime
and education. But after all that has been said on these more
tangible matters of human contact there still remains a part
essential to a proper description of the South which it is difficult
to describe or fix in terms easily understood by strangers. It is,
in fine, the atmosphere of the land, the thought and feeling, the
thousand and one little actions which go to make up life. In
any community or nation it is these little things which are most
elusive to the grasp and yet most essential to any clear conception of the group life, taken as a whole. What is thus true of all
communities is peculiarly true of the South where, outside of
written history and outside of printed law, there has been going
on for a generation, as deep a storm and stress of human souls,
as intense a ferment of feeling, as intricate a writhing of spirit
as ever a people experienced. Within and without the sombre
veil of color, vast social forces have been at work, efforts for
human betterment, movements toward disintegration and despair, tragedies and comedies in social and economic life, and
a swaying and lifting and sinking of human hearts which have
made this land a land of mingled sorrow and joy, of change and
excitement.

The centre of this spiritual turmoil has ever been the millions
of black freedmen and their sons, whose destiny is so fatefully
bound up with that of the nation. And yet the casual observer
visiting the South sees at first little of this. He notes the growing
frequency of dark faces as he rides on, but otherwise the days
slip lazily on, the sun shines and this little world seems as happy
and contented as other worlds he has visited. Indeed, on the
question of questions, the Negro problem, he hears so little that
there almost seems to be a conspiracy of silence; the morning
papers seldom mention it, and then usually in a far-fetched
academic way, and indeed almost every one seems to forget
and ignore the darker half of the land, until the astonished
visitor is inclined to ask if after all there *is* any problem here.
But if he lingers long enough there comes the awakening: per-

haps in a sudden whirl of passion which leaves him gasping
at its bitter intensity; more likely in a gradually dawning sense
of things he had not at first noticed. Slowly but surely his eyes
begin to catch the shadows of the color line; here he meets
crowds of Negroes and whites; then he is suddenly aware that he
cannot discover a single dark face; or again at the close of a
day's wandering he may find himself in some strange assembly,
where all faces are tinged brown or black, and where he has
the vague uncomfortable feeling of the stranger. He realizes at
last that silently, resistlessly, the world about flows by him in
two great streams. They ripple on in the same sunshine, they
approach here and mingle their waters in seeming carelessness,
they divide then and flow wide apart. It is done quietly, no
mistakes are made, or if one occurs the swift arm of the law and
public opinion swings down for a moment, as when the other
day a black man and a white woman were arrested for talking
together on Whitehall street, in Atlanta.

Now if one notices carefully one will see that between these
two worlds, despite much physical contact and daily intermingling, there is almost no community of intellectual life or
points of transferrence where the thoughts and feelings of one
race can come with direct contact and sympathy with the
thoughts and feelings of the other. Before and directly after the
war when all the best of the Negroes were domestic servants
in the best of the white families, there were bonds of intimacy,
affection, and sometimes blood relationship between the races.
They lived in the same home, shared in the family life, attended
the same church often and talked and conversed with each
other. But the increasing civilization of the Negro since has
naturally meant the development of higher classes: there are
increasing numbers of ministers, teachers, physicians, merchants, mechanics and independent farmers, who by nature and
training are the aristocracy and leaders of the blacks. Between
them, however, and the best element of the whites, there is
little or no intellectual commerce. They go to separate churches,
they live in separate sections, they are strictly separated in all
public gatherings, they travel separately, and they are begin-

illig to read different papers and books. To most libraries, lectures, concerts and museums Negroes are either not admitted at all or on terms peculiarly galling to the pride of the very classes who might otherwise be attracted. The daily paper chronicles the doings of the black world from afar with no great regard for accuracy; and so on throughout the category of means for intellectual communication; schools, conferences, efforts for social betterment and the like, it is usually true that the very representatives of the two races who for mutual benefit and the welfare of the land ought to be in complete understanding and sympathy are so far strangers that one side thinks all whites are narrow and prejudiced and the other thinks educated Negroes dangerous and insolent. Moreover, in a land where the tyranny of public opinion and the intolerance of criticism is for obvious historical reasons so strong as in the South, such a situation is extremely difficult to correct. The white man as well as the Negro is bound and tied by the color line and many a scheme of friendliness and philanthropy, of broad-minded sympathy, and generous fellowship between the two has dropped still-born because some busy-body has forced the color question to the front and brought the tremendous force of unwritten law against the innovators.

It is hardly necessary for me to add to this very much in regard to the social contact between the races. Nothing has come to replace that finer sympathy and love between some masters and house servants, which the radical and more uncompromising drawing of the color line in recent years has caused almost completely to disappear. In a world where it means so much to take a man by the hand and sit beside him; to look frankly into his eyes and feel his heart beating with red blood—in a world where a social cigar or a cup of tea together means more than legislative halls and magazine articles and speeches, one can imagine the consequences of the almost utter absence of such social amenities between estranged races, whose separation extends even to parks and street cars.

Here there can be none of that social going down to the people; the opening of heart and hand of the best to the worst, in generous acknowledgment of a common humanity and a common destiny. On the other hand, in matters of simple alms-giving, where there be no question of social contact, and in the succor of the aged and sick, the South, as if stirred by a feeling of its unfortunate limitations, is generous to a fault. The black beggar is never turned away without a good deal more than a crust, and a call for help for the unfortunate meets quick response. I remember, one cold winter, in Atlanta, when I refrained from contributing to a public relief fund lest Negroes should be discriminated against; I afterward inquired of a friend: "Were any black people receiving aid?" "Why," said he, "they were *all* black."

And yet this does not touch the kernel of the problem. Human advancement is not a mere question of almsgiving, but rather of sympathy and co-operation among classes who would scorn charity. And here is a land where, in the higher walks of life, in all the higher striving for the good and noble and true, the color line comes to separate natural friends and co-workers, while at the bottom of the social group in the saloon, the gambling hall and the bawdy-house that same line wavers and disappears.

I have sought to paint an average picture of real relations between the races in the South. I have not glossed over matters for policy's sake, for I fear we have already gone too far in that sort of thing. On the other hand I have sincerely sought to let no unfair exaggerations creep in. I do not doubt but that in some Southern communities conditions are far better than those I have indicated. On the other hand, I am certain that in other communities they are far worse.

Nor does the paradox and danger of this situation fail to interest and perplex the best conscience of the South. Deeply religious and intensely democratic as are the mass of the whites, they feel acutely the false position in which the Negro problems place them. Such an essentially honest-hearted and generous people cannot cite the caste-leveling precepts of Christianity, or believe in equality of opportunity for all men, without coming to feel more and more with each generation that the present draw-

ing of the color line is a flat contradiction to their beliefs and
professions. But just as often as they come to this point the
present social condition of the Negro stands as a menace and a
portent before even the most open-minded: if there were nothing to charge against the Negro but his blackness or other
physical peculiarities, they argue, the problem would be comparatively simple; but what can we say to his ignorance, shiftlessness, poverty and crime: can a self-respecting group hold
anything but the least possible fellowship with such persons and
survive? and shall we let a mawkish sentiment sweep away the
culture of our fathers or the hope of our children? The argument
so put is of great strength but it is not a whit stronger than the
argument of thinking Negroes; granted, they reply, that the condition of our masses is bad, there is certainly on the one hand
adequate historical cause for this, and unmistakable evidence
that no small number have, in spite of tremendous disadvantages, risen to the level of American civilization. And when by
proscription and prejudice, these same Negroes are classed with,
and treated like the lowest of their people simply *because* they
are Negroes, such a policy not only discourages thrift and intelligence among black men, but puts a direct premium on the
very things you complain of—inefficiency and crime. Draw lines
of crime, of incompetency, of vice as tightly and uncompromis-
ingly as you will, for these things must be proscribed, but a color
line not only does not accomplish this purpose, but thwarts it.

In the face of two such arguments, the future of the South
depends on the ability of the representatives of these opposing
views to see and appreciate, and sympathize with each other's
position; for the Negro to realize more deeply than he does at
present the need of uplifting the masses of his people, for the
white people to realize more vividly than they have yet done
the deadening and disastrous effect of a color prejudice that
classes Paul Lawrence Dunbar and Sam Hose in the same despised class.

It is not enough for the Negroes to declare that color prejudice
is the sole cause of their social condition, nor for the white South
to reply that their social condition is the main cause of prejudice.

They both act as reciprocal cause and effect and a change in neither *alone* will bring the desired effect. Both must change or neither can improve to any great extent. The Negro cannot stand the present reactionary tendencies and unreasoning drawing of the color line much longer without discouragement and retrogression. And the condition of the Negro is ever the excuse for further discrimination. Only by a union of intelligence and sympathy across the color line in this critical period of the Republic shall justice and right triumph.

31 A Racial Credo

One of the most thoughtful Southerners of the 1920s to 1940s was Howard W. Odum of the University of North Carolina. Odum's thinking was often well in advance of his fellow Southerners, and no subject intrigued him more than troubled racial relations. Without employing the methodology or phraseology of modern sociologists and social scientists he had the knack of cutting straight through to the heart of the race issue. In 1943 he published his book *Race and Rumors of Race*. This was the era of rumors of "Eleanor Clubs" and stories of "shoving societies." More specifically it was an age of highly perceptible changes in racial relations. It was not difficult at all to start almost any sort of a rumor of Negro rebellion among the southern Whites.

The phenomena of the persistent rumors was itself a revealing fact in southern life. Howard W. Odum undertook to examine the essential elements of prejudice against the Negro by devising a credo which would list all of the prevailing beliefs, current and traditional. In this list he mentioned every racial cliché that had ever been uttered by the Southerner and white Americans generally about the Negro.

NOW THE BARE STATEMENT OF AN ORGANIC CREDO, WHICH WOULD startle even most southerners appeared crude and harsh. So, here

Howard W. Odum, *Race and Rumors of Race: Challenge to American Crisis* (Chapel Hill: The University of North Carolina Press, 1943), 18–21.

again, it was important to repeat and repeat the question: Was it true that the South believed these things about the Negro? Or, if not, now that it was put down in black and white as the composite feeling and folkways of the South, what part of it was *not* true? Of course, no southerner ever wrote such a credo for himself and no one ever heard a southerner parading his credo as such. Yet, tested and checked in private life, in religious attitudes, in politics and law, and in the defense mechanisms of the region, in the great body of common folk, was this the South's credo and was it the heart of the whole drama?

Without an understanding of the South's organic feelings and beliefs it was not possible to explain such violent reactions to episodes and experiences which appeared to outsiders as mere commonplace behavior. Keeping in mind the variations of a composite credo and ratio of different groups of southerners who might dissent, and also the possible comparison with what people in the other regions held, it seemed important to ask again and again whether the white South would face the issue of its beliefs. Here, again, as always, there were paradox and contrast. While one group of leaders would protest the unfairness to the South of the presentation of such a credo, another large group would seem to say, "Sure, of course, that's what we believe. Why mention it? Everybody knows the Negro is just a Negro." Yet it was in many ways a startling credo that seemed to be the heart of the crisis. It seemed possible to count a score of units in the total and to ask again, Was it true that the South believed:

1. That the Negro was a Negro and always would be that and nothing more.

2. That, being a Negro, and different from the white man he therefore could not be expected ever to measure up to the white man's standards of character and achievement.

3. That, not being capable of full achievement and being of an inferior race, it was logical that he should be kept in an inferior place, which is "his place."

4. It followed that this was a white man's country, and that therefore the white man would dominate in about whatever way he chose. Laws and resolutions only made matters worse.

5. Political equality and equal educational opportunities, if given to the Negro, would lead to social equality and the mixture of races, which was contrary to all the major premises of the southern way of life.

6. Furthermore, political and social equality would lead to the domination of the white South by the Negroes and their northern supporters.

7. Discrimination and segregation, therefore, were necessary to keep the Negro in his place and protect the interests and integrity of the whites.

8. It was assumed, from this point on, by the best of the South, that the Negro, when kept within his rightful sphere, should not be treated unkindly or unjustly.

9. That he should be given fair trials and protected by law.

10. That he should be paid a living wage. Since, however, his standards of living were lower, he could live on less than a white man could.

11. That if given too much pay, he would waste the money and get out of bounds to his own harm as well as to the detriment of the South.

12. That the Negro was by nature inclined to criminal behavior, partly because of his animal nature and partly because of his irresponsibility and immorality.

13. Moreover, the Negro was better off in the South where he was "understood" and where his best friends were.

14. That, while as a race the Negro was inferior and generally untrustworthy, as an individual he was often honest, loyal, lovable, capable, and even talented and distinguished. Yet this was the exception.

15. That his music, his carefree, patient disposition, his homely philosophy added interest and color and richness to the culture of the South.

16. That recognition should be given to the Negro for having made outstanding progress in many fields since being freed from slavery.

17. Yet the Negro in general was not capable of taking great responsibility or of assuming leadership.

18. That no self-respecting southerner would work under Negro supervision.

19. That if the New Dealers, northerners, and reformers would let the South and the Negro alone, peaceful adjustments of the race problem could be made.

20. That those who were inviting the Negro to discontent and trying to force his participation in industry and politics on an equal basis were fomenting race riots which would hurt both whites and Negroes and the total Nation in the long run.

21. And that, finally, this was not a debatable issue.

There were, of course, various self-evident facts with reference to such a credo. In the first place, there were some variations from the norm as indicated in this credo. Yet, for all practical purposes this made little difference, since it was the mode of southern attitude and folkways which gave rise to points of tension, conflict, and the like. This credo was presented, not because there was anything new in it, but rather in order to highlight and make more vivid the folkways of the South concerning the Negro. Such a bold and bald statement of a credo was so vivid that it was perhaps surprising to southerners and, therefore, might go a long way toward explaining why the other regions of the Nation have rediscovered a level of their own national life with which they were either not acquainted or which they had forgot. The credo was in such complete contradistinction to the urgings and demands that were being made on the South in the name of war and freedom and Americanism that the resulting tension and conflict were easily explainable. It had to be repeated often that the understanding of the realistic folkways of the South was necessary also to explain the reaction of so many people from other regions to what seemed to them arbitrary, unreasonable, and entirely unfair attitudes and procedures in the South with reference to the simplest, most common, everyday, reasonable expectations of the Negro for life, liberty, and the pursuit of happiness.

That is, unless the full meaning of the southern folkways concerning the Negro was clearly understood, most of the incidents, stories, and happenings that had been basic to recent race tension and conflict would themselves be unreasonable and unexplainable. On the contrary, to the South, sensing its concept of the biracial society, what had happened seemed so simple and logical as to need no other explanation than that it had happened.

32 The Durham Manifesto

Negro leaders met in Durham, North Carolina, in 1942 and drafted a statement of views on what the Negro "wants and is expecting of the post-war South and Nation." This statement was reminiscent of questions that had arisen during World War I. In that case it was white leadership that had expressed apprehensiveness of what the Negro veteran returning from war for the first time as a fully participating soldier would demand of the region. This question in 1918 gripped some thoughtful Southerners with fear. The Durham statement was clear and comprehensive, and—as responsible southern whites admitted—was eminently fair. It touched on the key points at which the Negro had suffered his more serious discriminations, and offered possible procedures by which the anguish of the race problem could be lessened. Negroes sought relief from political discriminations and agricultural oppressions, and they requested an improved type of education for their people. Otherwise they predicted serious social difficulties. Wisely they saw that in the war, and in the period following it, the American Negro would become a symbol of discrimination against minority groups throughout the world.

In Atlanta at a southern regional meeting, in 1942, and a year later in Richmond, Virginia, Negroes and whites together considered the Manifesto. White leadership, however, later displayed timidity when charged with socialism, race-mixing, and communism by such southern demagogic politicians as Governor Eugene Talmadge of Georgia, and the Durham Manifesto went largely unheeded. No doubt failure to heed this statement of racial needs was one of the

348

South's major blunders. It allowed the position of leadership to slip away from the more conservative Negro, and in time a militant extra-regional Negro crusade was to assault every rampart of southern racial discrimination, going far beyond the modest Durham requests in its demands for changes.

THE WAR HAS SHARPENED THE ISSUE OF NEGRO-WHITE RELATIONS in the United States, and particularly in the South. A result has been increased racial tensions, fears, and aggressions, and an opening up of the basic questions of racial segregation and discrimination, Negro minority rights, and democratic freedom, as they apply practically in Negro-white relations in the South. These issues are acute and threaten to become even more serious as they increasingly block, through the deeper fears aroused, common sense consideration for even elementary improvements in Negro status, and the welfare of the country as a whole. . . .

POLITICAL AND CIVIL RIGHTS

We regard the ballot as a safeguard of democracy. Any discrimination against citizens in the exercise of the voting privilege, on account of race or poverty, is detrimental to the freedom of these citizens and to the integrity of the State. We therefore record ourselves as urging now:

a. The abolition of the poll tax as a prerequisite to voting.

b. The abolition of the white primary.

c. The abolition of all forms of discriminatory practices, evasions of the law, and intimidations of citizens seeking to exercise their right of franchise.

Exclusion of Negroes from jury service because of race has been repeatedly declared unconstitutional. This practice, we believe, can and should be discontinued now.

Civil rights include personal security against abuses of police power by white officers of the law. These abuses, which include wanton killings, and almost routine beatings of Negroes,

New South 7 (December 1952), 6–8.

whether they be guilty or innocent of an offense, should be stopped now, not only out of regard for the safety of Negroes, but out of common respect for the dignity and fundamental purpose of the law. It is the opinion of this group that the employment of Negro police will enlist the full support of Negro citizens in control of lawless elements of their own group.

In the public carriers and terminals, where segregation of the races is currently made mandatory by law as well as by established custom, it is the duty of Negro and white citizens to insist that these provisions be equal in kind and quality and in character of maintenance.

Although there has been, over the years, a decline in lynchings, the practice is still current in some areas of the South, and substantially, even if indirectly, defended by resistance to Federal legislation designed to discourage the practice. We ask that the States discourage this fascistic expression by effective enforcement of present or of new laws against this crime by apprehending and punishing parties participating in this lawlessness. If the States are unable, or unwilling to do this, we urge the support of all American citizens who believe in law and order in securing Federal legislation against lynching.

The interests and securities of Negroes are involved directly in many programs of social planning and administration. . . . We urge the use of qualified Negroes on these boards, both as a means of intelligent representation and a realistic aid to the functioning of these bodies.

INDUSTRY AND LABOR

Continuing opposition to the employment of Negroes in certain industries appears to proceed from (1) the outdated notions of an economy of scarcity, inherited from an industrial age when participation in the productive enterprises was a highly competitive privilege; (2) the effects of enemy propaganda designed to immobilize a large number of potentially productive workers in the American war effort; (3) the age-old prejudices from an era when the economic system required a labor surplus which competed bitterly within its own ranks for the privilege of work; (4) the established custom of reserving technical processes to certain racial groups; and (5) craft monopolies which have restricted many technical skills to a few workers.

Our collective judgment regarding industrial opportunities for Negroes may be summarized as follows:

The only tenable basis of economic survival and development for Negroes is inclusion in unskilled, semi-skilled, and skilled branches of work in the industries or occupations of the region to the extent that they are equally capable. . . .

There should be the same pay for the same work.

Negro workers should seek opportunities for collective bargaining and security through membership in labor organizations. . . . We deplore the practice of those labor unions which bar Negroes from membership, or otherwise discriminate against them, since such unions are working against the best interest of the labor movement. . . .

EDUCATION

As equal opportunity for all citizens is the very foundation of the democratic faith, and of the Christian ethic which gave birth to the ideal of democratic living, it is imperative that every measure possible be taken to insure an equality of education to Negroes and, indeed, to all underprivileged peoples.

Basic to improvement in Negro education is better schools, which involves expenditures by States of considerably more funds for the Negro schools. This group believes that a minimum requirement now is (a) equalization of salaries of white and Negro teachers on the basis of equal preparation and experience; (b) an expanded school building program for Negro schools designed to overcome the present racial disparity in physical facilities; this program to begin as soon as building materials are available; (c) revision of the school program in terms of the social setting, vocational needs, and marginal cultural characteristics of the Negro children; and (d) the same length of school term for all children in local communities. . . .

The education of Negroes in the South has reached the point at which there is increased demand for graduate and professional training. This group believes that this training should be made available equally for white and Negro eligible students in terms defined by the United States Supreme Court in the decision on the case of *Gaines* versus *The University of Missouri.*

Where it is established that States cannot sustain the added cost of equalization, Federal funds should be made available to overcome the differentials between white and Negro facilities and between Southern and national standards.

It is the belief of this group that the special problems of Negro education make demands for intelligent and sympathetic representation of these problems on school boards by qualified persons of the Negro race. The education of Negro youth can be measurably aided by the use of Negro enforcement officers of truancy and compulsory education laws.

AGRICULTURE

The South is the most rural section of the Nation, and Negroes, who constitute 33 percent of its population, are responsible for an important share of the agricultural production on Southern farms. . . . We suggest the following measures as means of increasing the production of the area, raising the status and spirits of Negro farmers, and of improving the region's contribution to the total war effort:

1. Establishment of sufficient safeguards in the system of tenancy to promote the development of land and home ownership and more security on the land, by: (a) written contracts; (b) longer lease terms; (c) higher farm wages for day laborers; (d) balanced farm programs, including food and feed crops for present tenants and day laborers.

2. Adequate Federal assistance to Negro farmers should be provided on an equitable basis.

3. The equitable distribution of funds for teaching agri-

culture in the Negro land grant colleges to provide agricultural research and experimentation for Negro farmers.

4. The appointment of qualified Negroes to governmental planning and policy making bodies concerned with the common farmer, and the membership of Negro farmers in general farmers' organizations and economic cooperatives, to provide appropriate representation and to secure maximum benefits to our common wealth.

MILITARY SERVICE

We recognize and welcome the obligation of every citizen to share in the military defense of the nation and we seek, along with the privilege of offering our lives, the opportunity of other citizens of full participation in all branches of the military service, and of advancement in responsibility and rank according to ability.

Negro soldiers, in line of military duty and in training in the South, encounter particularly acute racial problems in transportation and in recreation and leave areas. They are frequently mistreated by the police. We regard these problems as unnecessary and destructive to morale. . . .

SOCIAL WELFARE AND HEALTH

This group believes that minimum health measures for Negroes would include the following:

a. Mandatory provisions that a proportion of the facilities in all public hospitals be available for Negro patients;

b. That Negro doctors be either included on the staff for services to Negro patients, according to their special qualifications, or permitted as practitioners the same privilege and courtesy as other practitioners in the public hospitals;

c. That Negro public health nurses and social workers be more extensively used in both public and private organizations.

We advocate the extension of slum clearance and erection of low-cost housing as a general as well as special group advantage.

The Federal government has set an excellent precedent here with results that offer much promise for the future. . . .

The effect of the war has been to make the Negro, in a sense, the symbol and protagonist of every other minority in America and in the world at large. Local issues in the South, while admittedly holding many practical difficulties, must be met wisely and courageously if this Nation is to become a significant political entity in a new international world.

33 The Negro Wants Full Equality

Following the drafting of the *Durham Manifesto,* W. T. Couch, Director of The University of North Carolina Press, commissioned an extensive examination of the Negro's wants in an open American society. He, however, was not quite prepared for the results. In an introduction to the composite book, *What the Negro Wants,* Couch observed that the more conservative Negro authors began their discussion at about the point where the publisher had thought the more radical ones would conclude their essays. Couch's introductory essay was in a sense a lecture to his authors on the ancient associations of the races in the South, and he restated the fundamental belief that much more time would have to elapse before racial equality could be achieved.

One of the most judicious yet forceful statements was the following essay by Roy Wilkins. In an even temper but in forthright terms, this young Negro leader discussed the frustrations and disappointments of his race in American society, and he reviewed the failures of Negroes to achieve freedom and equality even through laws and court decisions. There was a long gap between a legal expression and the actual accomplishment of equal treatment of the races. In a clear analysis the author outlined the inconsistencies that were so apparent in America during World War II when the fascists' racial attitudes were so heavily under fire. He viewed the Negro soldier returning at the end of the war to a no more free or equal life than at the end of World War I. He did, however, place confidence in the organized Negro to bring about change, and he assured his readers that Negro soldiers were not fighting and dying in battles around the globe just to maintain the status quo.

355

The book *What the Negro Wants* went largely unread in the South. Had Southerners read the essays by the more articulate Negroes of the period they would not have been taken so by surprise a decade later.

In the time since Pearl Harbor there has been, perhaps, more heated and constant discussion of the so-called Negro problem in this country than in any similar period.

The war stimulated the discussion. The war stimulated the Negroes. The war alarmed many whites and threw practically the entire white South, including persons hitherto regarded as "liberals" on the race question, into hysterics.

For this war *was* not like other wars. As the second act to 1914–1918, it was on a broader stage and the actors spoke plain lines from behind little make-up. The villians talked of "master races," of force, of the significance of the individual, of the might and power of the state, of the necessity of conquest and slavery.

These were things that 13,000,000 American Negroes, even though "educated" in Mississippi, could understand easily. If they had any difficulty with the words "fascism" and "totalitarianism" Hitler resolved their fogginess by speaking plainly of Negroes as half-apes. They knew where they stood.

Well, Hitler had made himself plain—what about those who opposed Der Fuehrer? What were they going to say? Britain's rule of her colonies is not exactly a secret to the dark people of the world. How would the perpetrators of the smelly Caribbean colonial policy (even then under fire and furious cover-up) answer the man with the mustache? What would the rulers of India, the overlords of Kenya, the collaborators with Smuts of South Africa, the guardians of White Australia, say to Berchtesgaden? And America, bursting, as always, with indignation, what would she, with her Dixie, say to the Wilhelmstrasse, the Krupps, and the Wehrmacht?

Rayford W. Logan, ed., *What the Negro Wants* (Chapel Hill: The University of North Carolina Press, 1944), 113–132.

From a ship off Newfoundland came the Atlantic Charter, but before American Negroes, always cynical, could reason out its weaknesses, Winston Churchill settled all speculation by replying to a question bluntly and unequivocally that the Charter applied only to the nations of Europe conquered by Hitler. The question had been cabled by natives in West Africa, who, like their brothers behind the Jim Crow walls in America, just could not believe the fine words of the Charter.

America, meanwhile, so accustomed to setting the Negro outside any moral and ethical considerations, had been going about its business as though no conflict existed between its high pronouncements and its practices.

When, in 1939 and 1940, it began building up its army and navy by voluntary enlistment, it took no Negro volunteers. Negro lads stormed enlistment offices from coast to coast and were turned down in batches of as high as 100. In Charlotte, N.C., a Negro high school teacher who accompanied four of his students to a recruiting office was set upon and beaten by a sergeant.

The excuse was that there were only four regiments of Negroes in the regular army, that they were not too far under strength since many men in them had re-enlisted as a career, and that an act of Congress would be required to authorize the formation of any more "Negro" units.

An official of the Army Air Forces wrote NAACP a one-sentence letter in the summer of 1940 saying it was "not contemplated" that Negroes would be admitted to the aristocratic air forces.

All the while our leading statesmen, our radio stations, our newspapers, were denouncing the dictators, racial and religious bigotry, force and brutality. They were extolling democracy, humanitarianism, equality of peoples. They were wringing their hands and tearing their hair over the Austrians, the Czechs, the Danes, Norwegians and the rest.

Black America listened to the radio, read the newspapers. Here was language it could understand. If it was cause for international weeping that Jews were beaten in Berlin and scourged into a loathesome ghetto in Warsaw, what about a tear for black ghettos in America? If the aggressors in Central Europe and Asia should be quarantined, what about the aggressors on the racial front here?

So there was discussion among the Negroes. Many of the whites, caught up between their words and their deeds, saw the point but resolved stubbornly to give no ground. An old world was being shattered around them, their own words were promising the destruction of Hitlerism, but they insisted that "their own Negroes" should remain *in status quo*.

Hitler jammed our white people into their logically untenable position. Forced to oppose him for the sake of the life of the nation, they were jockeyed into declaring against his racial theories—publicly. Europe was overrun. Britain had its back to the wall. It was a hop, skip and a jump from Ostend to the Thames estuary, and from there to the Hudson and the towers of Lower Manhattan. Latin America looked to Franco and Hitler. Australia was trembling. India and the whole Far East were watching and weighing.

America had to rally, to stave off disaster, to talk for time, to prepare to fight for its very life. It had to say: "Down with Hitlerism! Down with the Master Race theory! Away with racial bigotry!" If these words would rally men and gain precious support, perhaps our crumbling world could be saved.

But the irritation at having to say these things in their extremity, and the anger at the literal interpretation of them by the belabored Negro made our white people angrier and angrier in their insistence upon the status quo.

In the scholarly *Virginia Quarterly* for the Autumn of 1942, John Temple Graves, Southern editor and columnist, spoke his mind on "The Southern Negro and the War Crisis," bemoaning the stirring of the Southern Negroes in time of war by "Northern agitators," by the Roosevelt administration and Mrs. Roosevelt.

> Negro leaders outside the South . . . made the war an occasion for the most intensive campaign ever launched against any and every differential, minor or major, between white man and black. They have chosen to go crazy with their championings, scouring the land for trouble . . . making plain beyond ques-

tion an intent to use the war for settling overnight the whole, long, complicated, infinitely delicate racial problem.

Hard on the heels of Editor Graves came Editor Virginius Dabney of the Richmond, Va., *Times Dispatch,* with an ominous article in the January, 1943, *Atlantic Monthly,* entitled "Nearer and Nearer the Precipice." Like Graves, Dabney decried agitators, shuddered at the thought of Negroes aspiring to political and social equality, reiterated the utter impossibility of abolishing segregation. He predicted that pressure of Negroes toward these goals would bring about "an interracial explosion which may make the race riots of the first World War and its aftermath seem mild by comparison. . . . There may also be far-reaching and heavily adverse effects upon the colored peoples of China, India, and the Middle East—peoples whose attitude can be of crucial importance to the Allies in the war."

Latest expression, at this writing, has come again in the *Atlantic* for January, 1944, in an article, "How the South Feels," by David L. Cohn. No editor, but a business man of means, Mr. Cohn echoes Messrs. Graves and Dabney: segregation is here to stay, the agitators must beware, In fact, the whole problem is *insoluble.*

Now, it may be asked, what demands and what procedures aroused these furious pronouncements? What does the Negro want? Well, Negroes are demanding nothing new or startling. They are asking nothing they had not asked before Hitler came to power, before war had brought German armies within sight of the white cliffs of Dover. They are asking nothing inconsistent with the declared war aims of the United Nations. They are asking nothing inconsistent with the Constitution and the Bill of Rights.

They asked then, and they ask now simply complete equality in the body politic. They could not in self-respect ask less. If it has seemed in the past that certain segments of the Negro population and certain leaders have demanded less, closer study will show that the goal has always been complete equality. There is considerable evidence that the master politician on the race question, Booker T. Washington, carelessly nominated as the "half-loaf" leader, envisioned complete equality as the goal for his people. A shrewd man, thoroughly in tune with his time and its people, Washington *appeared* to be an appeaser and did his great work under that protective cloak.

It was inevitable that there should emerge, as the Negro made progress, a group which felt that the time had come for bolder words and more direct steps toward the goal. The Negro was here to stay. The terror of the Reconstruction had not wiped him out or submerged him completely. The years of lynching had not intimidated him. He was to be a citizen, with a citizen's rights, and the battle was pitched accordingly. The Niagara Movement, an all-Negro organization, came into being and later merged with the National Association for the Advancement of Colored People, formally organized in 1909.

From the very beginning the NAACP was for complete equality. It is not generally known that William English Walling, a white Kentuckian, wrote the words which stimulated the organization of the NAACP. In the *Independent,* of September 3, 1908, Walling had an article on the race riots in Springfield, Illinois, in the course of which he declared:

> Either the spirit of the abolitionists, of Lincoln and Lovejoy must be revived and we must come to treat the Negro on a plane of *absolute political and social equality,* [italics mine] or Vardaman and Tillman will soon have transferred the race war to the North. . . . Yet who realizes the seriousness of the situation, and what large and powerful body of citizens is ready to come to their aid?

A little band of white and colored citizens responded to the Walling piece and issued a formal Lincoln's Birthday Call in 1909. Drafted by Oswald Garrison Villard, then owner and editor of the New York *Evening Post,* this call demanded equality of opportunity, equality before the law, an end to disfranchisement, abolition of segregation of the races, equality in education, and an end to mob violence. It voiced what was to be the recurring theme of the NAACP down the years: attacks upon citizenship rights of Negroes are attacks upon democracy and upon white Americans as well.

Oo, thirty-five years ago equality—political and social equality —was the stated goal of an organized body of white and Negro Americans. This, then, is no new World War II doctrine of the NAACP, trotted out to solve the race problem overnight. Yet Dabney could write in January, 1943: "The NAACP *now* [italics mine] is not only for 'absolute political and social equality,' but it has declared war to the death on all forms of racial segregation." The NAACP declared for this objective in 1909 and has been working assiduously toward its attainment ever since.

It is significant that this crusade has been conducted in the American tradition. There have been no cells of terrorists, no extra-legal activities. The pattern has been petition and protest, legal redress, lobbying, legislative activity, education, and persuasion. And, implicit and explicit in all activities, has been the theme of equality.

The earliest sustained work of the NAACP had to do with the crime of lynching. Security of the person from violence was a paramount problem, with lynchings in the early fifth of the century averaging more than 100 a year. In tackling lynching the Association had first to grapple with the cloak of sex which the defenders of lynching used to justify the crime. It determined by painstaking study that in less than 20 percent of lynchings was *any sort* of sex crime charged, and that in only 16 percent of the cases was rape charged. Thus, 80 out of every 100 victims of mobs were done to death for something other than crimes against white women.

Fifteen thousand persons took part in a silent protest parade against lynching down New York's Fifth Avenue in 1917. Charles Evans Hughes addressed a mass meeting in Carnegie Hall in 1919. The Dyer federal anti-lynching bill, forerunner of numerous others, passed the House in 1922 and was filibustered to death in the Senate shortly thereafter. Full and half-page display advertisements were inserted in daily newspapers in 1922, telling such a compelling story of the lynching evil that one Pacific Coast daily offered to carry the display without cost.

Pickets paraded before Albert Hall in London, decrying American lynchings. Feature articles appeared in dailies in faraway Sydney, Australia. Books, magazine articles, pamphlets, petitions, meetings and conferences spread the story. Filibusters merely helped scatter the education farther afield.

The story was getting across to America and the world that the Negro was a human being, was an American citizen presumably possessing inalienable rights which were being grievously and bestially violated, so that proud and free America could hardly hold its head high enough to escape the stench. Did we have courts? And to what end? Did we have a Constitution? For whom? What of our vaunted slogan, "Equal Justice Under Law"?

As the years went by, the skill and the pressure increased. Succeeding anti-lynching bills in the national capitol suffered the same fate as the Dyer bill: passage in the House, death by filibuster in the Senate, under both Democratic and Republican majorities. But the education went on, sped by the forces of opposition. Whereas in 1919 hardly any man of prominence, or any man of promising career would speak out against lynching, in 1938 when the last bill was killed in a 21-day filibuster, no man, or newspaper, or institution of any importance could be found to defend lynching. Public opinion had been completely reversed in twenty years, even to the extent that a number of Southern newspapers not only deplored lynching, but endorsed federal legislation against it.

The goal in this fight was equality: equality before the law, equality in security of the person, equality in human dignity. The campaign is not ended, but the point has been made, more than a toehold has been won. There will be, undoubtedly, more lynchings and more riotous outbreaks, but instead of being in the stream of public opinion, they will be counter to it; they will be against an established principle. As such they can be handled, just as any other crime is handled.

Hand in hand with the continuous struggle against lynching and mob violence went the legal battles in the courts of the land. In its thirty-five years of existence, the NAACP has carried twenty-one cases to the United States Supreme Court. It has won nineteen cases, lost one, and one is pending as this is written In addition, it has handled thousands of cases in the lower courts.

The Supreme Court cases decided Constitutional rights of Negroes as citizens: equality in the body politic. Although the record is full of brilliant examples of legal procedure involving many questions, the outstanding example would seem to be the famous Elaine, Arkansas (Phillips County), riot cases which began in 1919 and ended in 1923. In this one action, covering 79 defendants, were the items of mob violence, mob domination of court procedure, service of Negroes on juries, and the enforcement of contracts.

Negro farmers of Phillips County had received no accounting from plantation owners on their cotton from June, 1918, to July, 1919. Feeling that they had been more than patient, they organized themselves into the Progressive and Household Union of America, engaged a law firm in Little Rock either to get a settlement or to sue the landlords. At a meeting in a small Negro church at Hoop Spur in October, 1919, a shot was fired into the church from the outside. The farmers stopped planning and returned the fire. A white man was killed and rioting ensued. Troops were ordered into the county. All available local and state police, as well as hundreds of deputized citizens joined the soldiers in a county-wide man-killing spree. Newspapers blazoned the affair as an "insurrection," thus justifying the wanton and indiscriminate killing of Negroes.

Eight hundred Negroes were arrested. A "Committee of Seven" held a kangaroo court and directed that 12 prisoners should die and 67 others be imprisoned. The courts faithfully followed directions. Five of the men were tried at one time and given death in a matter of six minutes. Counsel was provided by the court the day before trial, but did not consult with defendants, put no witnesses on the stand, made no address to the jury.

The Arkansas Supreme Court heard the appeals of the twelve men sentenced to death, granted new trials to six, affirmed the conviction of the others. On retrial the six were again convicted and again had their convictions reversed on the ground Negroes had been excluded from the jury panel.

From then on, the story is a complicated one of appeals, suits for various writs, changes of venue, transfers to federal courts, two unsuccessful attempts to get before the United States Supreme Court, one hairbreadth snatching of six doomed men from the death house, and finally, in 1922, a review by the highest court in the land.

In its opinion in this case, *Moore* v. *Dempsey*, 261 U.S. 86, handed down in February, 1923, the court reversed itself in *Frank* v. *Mangum*, 237 U.S. 309, and held that a trial in a court dominated by mob sentiment was not due process of law within the meaning of the Fourteenth Amendment. In the Frank case, arising in Georgia, the Jewish defendant, now known to be innocent, was convicted of attacking and killing a little girl, and then lynched. The court had held that since the forms of the law had been observed, it could not examine into the atmosphere of the trial. The Arkansas lawyers, out of the long, bitter legal tangle in the Elaine cases, bristling as they were with injustices crying aloud for attention, managed to get the story into their brief. A Negro and a white lawyer brought this battle to a victorious close by putting all 79 defendants "on the street."

But here again the objective was equality. Had it not been so, the Negro farmers would have accepted the status quo, would have agreed that *as Negroes* they had no right to demand, after the fashion of white men, an accounting for their crops. They would not have dared order suits to recover. They would not have dared shoot back. After the riot their lawyers and their friends and the NAACP would not have dared muster every skill in the tenacious fight, in a mob atmosphere, for their freedom.

Equality was the prize—equality of opportunity as farmers, equality in the courts of the land, the right to serve on juries, to avail themselves of writs, to have their motives, their provocations, their actions judged as free men among free men.

And this struggle for equality carried over into the quest for the purple badge of a democratic nation, the right to exercise the franchise. The very first case carried to the United States Supreme Court by the NAACP was a challenge of a then popular device for disfranchising Negroes, the Grandfather Clause.

Inserted in many state constitutions in the South, this clause set forth, in varying language, that no person might vote whose grandfather was not eligible to vote in 1860. In 1915 the highest court held this clause to be unconstitutional, but, needless to say, the opinion did not enfranchise the Negroes.

Mindful that there can be no equality in a democracy where citizens are barred from the ballot box, the NAACP has kept up the campaign in the courts and in the public conscience to strike down the barriers. Two cases were taken up from Texas challenging the so-called White Democratic Primary, and the Supreme Court opinion went against the state. A third case was carried up by an independent group of Texas Negro citizens and the decision this time was in favor of Texas. A new case is pending, having been argued first in November, 1943, and re-argued in January, 1944.

Along with these legal assaults on disfranchisement has gone a crusade against the poll tax requirement for voters which prevents an estimated 10,000,000 citizens (6,000,000 white and 4,000,000 Negro) from voting. If the poll tax can be eliminated and the Democratic primaries opened to Negro citizens, two stalwart props of inequality will have been struck down. Others will remain, not the least of which will be force and intimidation, but eventually these will have to go, also.

In the original Call to form the NAACP in 1909 there was this phrase: "recent history in the South shows that in forging chains for the Negroes, the white voters are forging chains for themselves." In no phase of this ever-continuing fight for equality for the Negro is this truism demonstrated more clearly than in the campaign for political equality. Here it becomes plain that the free ballot for the Negroes means a greater and stronger democracy for *all* Americans. Tenaciously the NAACP has clung throughout the years to its thesis that inequality for the Negro opens the way to inequality for other Americans and thus weakens the nation.

In the field of education the effort to achieve equality has gone steadily forward. Here, from the outset, America was receptive and responsive. Education is a fetish of our country; we have believed it somehow to be a magic cure-all. The chief inequality in education for Negroes lay (and still lies) in the system of separate, or segregated schools for the two races.

These inequalities in per capita expenditure, equipment, buildings, school term, teachers' salaries, and curricula, are too well known to be set forth in detail here. Most spectacular and easily-grasped illustration is the per capita expenditure for Mississippi, where the money expended for white children is roughly nine times as great as that expended for Negroes, although Negroes form 49 percent of the population.

A vulnerable point in the system of segregation seemed to be the salary differential between white and colored teachers in the same local system, who have the same training and experience and perform essentially the same duties. These differentials have been attacked in courts by attorneys for the NAACP, acting at the request of individual teacher-plaintiffs, or organized groups of Negro teachers. The results have been reasonably successful, having forced equalization of salaries in localities in 13 states. The greatest single victory was that in Norfolk, Virginia, where an opinion was secured from the United States Circuit Court of Appeals which has tended to influence some local boards of education to equalize salaries on presentation of a petition, without actual court procedure.

Another vulnerable sector from the standpoint of the Constitution, was the denial of graduate and professional training to Negroes in tax-supported state institutions. In the famous Gaines case, where the University of Missouri was the defendant, the United States Supreme Court in December, 1935, held that a state either must supply equal separate facilities to Negroes for graduate and professional study or admit them to existing graduate institutions. Missouri chose to set up a separate law school for Negroes, and later a separate school of journalism, but the law school has been closed for lack of funds and students, and the journalism school is being staffed, beginning February 1, 1944, with faculty members from the University of Missouri.

The Gaines decision did not get a single Negro into a Southern graduate school, but it riveted the Negro's claim to equality under the Constitution; it set under way numerous plans for providing graduate instruction. One border state proceeded to admit a few Negro graduate students to its university without publicity. Missouri seems to have demonstrated that a separate graduate institution is not the way out. A case is still pending in the courts against the University of Kentucky. The Negroes, members of state legislatures, heads of state universities, and white laymen are busy debating not whether the Negro is entitled to this training, but how it shall be made available. The right to it has been established as the law of the land: equality of opportunity.

The stubborn resistance to these latest moves in the field of education lies in the adherence to segregation as a pattern of life for the two races. The NAACP has maintained from the beginning that discrimination and inequality are inherent in the segregated pattern. There can be no equality *with* segregation. A hundred examples could be cited, but the Jim Crow public school system would seem to be all the proof needed. Complete equality, therefore, envisons the abolition of the segregated school.

On the economic front powerful obstacles to the attainment of equality have been encountered, but progress has been made. Equal pay for the same work has been the underlying theme. The sharecropping system of Southern agriculture has held millions of Negroes—and poor whites—in virtual economic slavery, impoverishing the entire region as it has impoverished its victims. Employers and trade unions, in and out of the South, have blocked industrial employment of the Negro. The "lock-out" of the Negro worker by many of the craft unions has been matched by the policy of many employers. Lately, by their pronouncements and practices of no discrimination the industrial unions have eased the Negro's position and driven the crafts to the defensive.

But underneath, especially in the South, is the bugaboo of segregation. Workers at a war plant in Baltimore struck in the fall of 1943 to force the management to install separate toilets for Negroes. The Atlanta city council expressed opposition to the establishment of a regional office of the Fair Employment Practices Committee in that fair city because it was proposed to have Negro and white *clerks* working in the same office. A Negro messenger, elevator operator, or cleaning man would have caused no trouble. The bitter opposition to the CIO in the South stems not alone from that region's aversion to organized labor, but from the equality within the CIO and the non-segregation of its members. The fight on various organizations of tenant farmers and sharecroppers had as one of its targets the non-segregation policy.

Like most other phases of the so-called Negro problem, this denial of opportunity to Negro workers is not confined to the South. Anti-Negro feeling has broken out in industrial plants in many Northern centers, notably Detroit, where in June 1943, 25,000 white workers quit the Packard plant because *three* Negroes had been upgraded, according to seniority rules, to work on machines.

The NAACP has been hammering away for equality of opportunity in employment, attacking policies of discrimination and exclusion, and instituting legal action in individual cases deemed to advance the general cause. The first round in what may be a notable achievement was won in January, 1944, when a Providence, R.I., judge held that auxiliary unions, created especially for Negroes by the Boilermakers' union, were not legal in the state, and that Negro boilermakers must be considered members of regular locals. There is some indication that the Boilermakers' international union may agree to alter its policy and accept Negroes as full members. At any rate, there is an important element within the union working toward this goal.

Most significant activity of the NAACP, in cooperation with other groups, was the mobilization of pressure which resulted in the issuance of an Executive Order by President Roosevelt in June, 1941, forbidding discrimination in employment in any war industry or government agency because of race, creed, color, or national origin. The order also created the Fair Employment Practices Committee, which has become a by-word as the FEPC, during its short, stormy career.

Fierce opposition to FEPC has come from the segregationists. Its work has been branded as an attempt to "tear down the social fabric of the South," and in its one big case against sixteen Southern railroads, its findings that flagrant discrimination exists as a policy against Negroes as railroad firemen have been openly defied by both carriers and unions. Of course, FEPC activity is an attack upon the social fabric of the South, in the broadest sense of "social." It aims at equality of opportunity and reward, and any system or practice of any union or employer, in the North or South, which operates to deny that opportunity may be considered under attack. The immediate cause for the creation of the FEPC was the shameless exclusion of Negroes from employment at a time when manpower was desperately needed to speed the war effort. The personnel managers who slammed doors in the faces of Negro applicants, and the union members who refused to work beside them were failing the nation in time of war. Something had to be done as a war measure. But the sure justification for the FEPC thesis lies not alone in the war of the present, but in the basic conception of the American democratic ideal.

It should be said that in normal peace times the Negro feels most strongly about economic proscription. He is insulted and humiliated in other phases of life and resentment will flare white hot at the moment. But on the limitation in employment his feeling is no spasmodic thing. He sees immigrants come to his America and get jobs he cannot get. He works as a "helper" all his life in a trade and teaches white apprentices who, in a few years, earn twice his wage and become his superiors. Each night he goes to his ghetto home. Each payday his working wife adds her bit to his bit to make a total barely sufficient to keep the household together, to keep the children in school, to pay the small insurance premiums. Or, he gets a high school or college education, but must content himself with jobs far below his talents.

He wants the bars down so that men may find their level, the dice players, business men, mechanics, professors, thieves, clerks, playboys, laborers, and the rest. He wants equality of opportunity to work at any job for which he is fitted, and to earn the pay and promotions that go with that job.

And then there is the whole area of relations encompassing what may be called the movement of citizens, their enjoyment of public accommodations. The Jim Crow railroad car symbolizes to the Negro his proscription in public. Until this war arrived it was thought that resentment of the Jim Crow car was confined to Northern Negroes who had occasional business in the South. But it has been discovered that great masses of Negroes who have lived all their lives in the South and are familiar with its mores are bitter against the Jim Crow car, the separated seats in buses and trolleys, the filthy waiting rooms, the insolent ticket sellers and equally insolent sandwich counter attendants, both white and colored, and the arrogant, ignorant and brutal bus and trolley drivers. Contrary to some assertions, the flare-ups over these facilities have not been confined to Northern Negro soldiers in training in the South; if the truth be told, *all* Negroes except the minority of hat-in-hand variety deeply resent this separation. They took spontaneous advantage of the court decision in the case brought by former Congressman Arthur W. Mitchell of Illinois against the Chicago Rock Island and Pacific Railroad for denying him Pullman accommodations from Memphis to Hot Springs, Arkansas, a case which brought the opinion from the Supreme Court that Negroes may not be denied first class tickets or all accommodations which go with such tickets, including dining and lounge car facilities. Countless instances have been reported of Negroes in the Southern hinterland boarding trains and quoting this decision to conductors and others.

The Negro wants to be able to go to parks, playgrounds, beaches, pools, theatres, restaurants, hotels, taverns, tourist camps, and other places of public amusement and accommodation without proscription and insult. The question comes immediately: does this mean *with whites?* The answer must be in the affirmative. If the Negro's goal is complete equality, complete acceptance as a member of the American public, then he wants access to these accommodations on an equality with other Americans. The popular and instantaneous question of whether he wants to "thrust" himself "where he is not wanted" is supposed to flabbergast him. Who is "wanted" where, and by whom? During the Dewey racket-busting crusade in New York several years ago it was revealed that the king man in the huge organized prostitution ring lived in a tower apartment in one of the world's famous hotels on Manhattan's Park Avenue, the same tower apartments which housed a former President of the United States, which gave shelter to the First Lady of China, and to the former King of England! Yet a respectable Negro business man, tendering the correct tariff to the room clerk, would have been hustled out by house detectives like a criminal!

Is a hotel a membership club, or a theatre a drawing room? If a public bathing beach or pool or tennis court is restricted to "wanted" persons, why do we have the Racquet Club, Newport, Southampton, and their prototypes over the land?

In this general category comes the all-important matter of housing. The Negro wants to be free to rent or buy a house according to his standards and his means. If he can afford a $10,000 home, he does not want to be forced to build it in a $2,500 neighborhood. If he can pay $50 a month rent, he wants $50 in value, in a $50 locality; he does not want to be forced to pay $50 for a $40 home in a $30 neighborhood.

He wants all the municipal services—water, gas, light, sewerage, garbage collection, sidewalks and paving—on the same basis they are furnished to other citizens. Here again the pattern of enforced segregation is an obstacle and must be removed. Doubtless there will always be some voluntary segregation, as there is with other racial groups, but the ghetto must go. It does not seem to be known generally that in several communities in the South, Negro and white families live side by side in some streets without friction. Muskogee, Okla., among others, has such a section.

In this connection, as with other phases of the problem, the

Negro is weary of the fallacious and oft-repeated argument that he is not a taxpayer, that white people bear the burden of such improvements as he receives. That this contention could be advanced seriously in this day of rudimentary economic intelligence among the masses of people only demonstrates the flimsy construction of the façade behind which the opposition parades.

These goals represent, then, what the Negro wants. The record of struggle toward the objectives is too long, too persistent, too studded with recurring efforts following failure to admit of doubt as to the ends sought. Here has been set forth only the latter phases of the fight—that covering the thirty-five years of the NAACP and the few prior years of the Niagara Movement. But the demands were voiced long before the Emancipation Proclamation. The great Frederick Douglass, chief spiritual father of the "no-compromise" school, was clamoring for full and complete equality even as a slave. Later he was to thunder his insistent message from platforms in the North and in England.

The leaders of the complete equality school have as their ancestors, besides Douglass, Sojourner Truth, Harriet Tubman, the insurrectionists Nat Turner, Denmark Vesey, and the rest. Behind these are the nameless hundreds whose indomitable spirits and will to freedom drove them from slave cabins through strange lands and unknown dangers to liberty in far Canada.

Not to be forgotten, too, are the mothers and fathers, newly-freed, who worked, sacrificed, and saved that their children might become what Mr. Lincoln's proclamation and the Thirteenth, Fourteenth and Fifteenth amendments said they should be. These people did not sacrifice for half-measures. They had had to take crumbs, but crumbs were not for their children and grandchildren. Their eyes were on complete equality.

All this explains the repeated challenges to the status quo, the long fight against lynching, the recourse to the courts again and again on the same issue. This explains the migrations to the North and West.

If these be the true yearnings of Negro Americans, how shall the, be satisfied? That, now, is the problem of the American whites. In truth, the so-called Negro problem is really a white problem. In recent years the Southern whites have been trying to spread the responsibility for a solution to the nation as a whole; but any unbiased student must see that, regardless of the outbreaks here and there outside the South, the responsibility for initiating remedial action is upon the South. Indeed, nothing makes the Southerner froth more than attempts from without the South to do something about the situation. Governmental remedies for general situations which include the Negro have drawn heavy fire, even from so-called white "liberals."

What are the Southern whites going to do about it, aside from repeating over and over that they intend to do nothing, that the Negro must be satisfied with the status quo?

The Negro is here. He is thoroughly American. He thinks and lives in the American tradition. He learns from American text books about the Revolutionary war, about independence, the spirit of America—and equality. He reads the newspapers and magazines. He goes to the movies and he listens to the radio. Once every four years he has that wondrous educational experience, a Presidential election.

It ought to be apparent, therefore, that the Negro, even in peace times, cannot be insulated from the stream that is America. This is doubly true in a war where race, color, democracy, fascism, equality, freedom, and slavery are shouted from every microphone, screamed from every headline.

No "agitators" were needed to point out to him the discrepancies between what we said we were fighting for, and what we did to him. He did not need the NAACP to show him that it sounds pretty foolish to be *against* park benches marked "Jude" in Berlin, but to be *for* park benches marked "Colored" in Tallahassee, Florida.

It is pretty grim—not foolish—to have a black boy in uniform get an orientation lecture in the morning on wiping out Nazi bigotry, and that same evening be told he can buy a soft drink only in the "Colored" post exchange!

Yes, it's a problem for the white people. They have got to
make up their minds. Pearl Buck puts it this way:

> But be that as it may, the real point is that our democracy
> does not allow for the present division between a white ruler race
> and a subject colored race, and we ought to make up our minds
> as to what we want and then move to accomplish it. If the
> United States is to include subject and ruler peoples, then let
> us be honest about it and change the Constitution and make it
> plain that Negroes cannot share the privileges of the white peo-
> ple. True, we would then be totalitarian rather than democratic;
> but if that is what we want, let us say so and let us tell the Negro
> so. Then the white Americans will be relieved of the necessity of
> hypocrisy and the colored people will know where they are. They
> may even settle down into a docile subject race, so long as we
> are able to keep the weapons of rebellion from them—and these
> include education.

Our country *could* eliminate the Negro as a citizen, but the
dangers to other groups, and the precedent that would be set
argue against it.

The Negro intends, from all present appearances, to "sit
tight" on his demands. He cannot do otherwise, unless he means
to retreat at a time when America and the world are moving
forward. There is no indication that he intends this retreat.
These goals, as has been shown, are no hastily manufactured
items, incident to the beginning of World War II. They are the
very warp and woof of Negro life. He stands ready to cooperate with anyone on their realization who recognizes them as the
ends to be achieved.

It has been said that not all the armored divisions of both
the Axis and Allied armies can force the South to revise its system of social segregation. It has been said again that if such a
demand is made seriously, every white male below the Potomac
will spring to arms and another civil war will rend the nation.

These are ominous pronouncements, calculated, through the
threat of bloodshed, to give the Negro and his friends pause.
But there is no sign of fright in the ranks of the darker Ameri-

cans. They seem confident that the tides of social upheaval abroad in the world today cannot be channeled by the men and women north and south of the Ohio River who wish to keep them in "their place." The armored divisions will not have to be brought into play. The tremendous surges of the peoples of Russia and Asia and Africa may prove more powerful than tanks or guns. The urgent necessity for the building of a peace between the Western Powers and the rest of the world, founded upon respect for the peoples outside the Anglo-American fold, will be a spur not to be lightly evaluated. Such a peace, in a shrunken world, could not avoid affecting the status of the Negro minority in our country.

And then there is the wholly unknown quantity of the attitude of our returning soldiers, white and black. There is no guaranty, as has been asserted by former Governor Sam Jones of Louisiana in a magazine article, that all the white soldiers of the South are fighting to maintain white supremacy. No doubt many of them are fighting for America as they have known it, and that would include white supremacy, but certainly many of them have had their eyes opened by their travels and by the blood and death which have respected no man because of his color.

Certain it is that the Negro soldiers are not fighting and dying to maintain the status quo for their race. The young Negro fighter pilots from Punta Gorda, Fla., and Emory, Miss., who were among those shooting down Nazi planes in the fierce fighting over the Anzio beachhead are not risking their lives to intrench further the way of life obtaining in their home towns. The Negro Marines in the South Pacific, the black engineers, the colored quartermaster units getting the supplies through the mud and heat and cold of the battle-fronts, are not working for the status quo. The lads who drove bulldozers in fifty below zero to build the Alaskan highway, who hacked their way through Burmese jungles to build the Ledo road, are not returning to run a bulldozer on the Mississippi levees for 20 cents an hour. Nor will they take kindly, to put it in its mildest form, to surly suggestions as to their "place." Their place now is in front of the bullets of the enemy, and below the bombs in enemy planes. Bullets, or threats of bullets, are not likely to cause them to bow and scrape once they are home.

No, the threats of civil war will not turn the trick. The American demands of the Negro are there, made in the American manner, rooted in the American ideal. They are not to be brushed aside, and something more than fulmination and bluster is indicated from the opposition. The next move is up to white Americans, and particularly white Southern Americans.

34 The Governor's Appeal

The United States Supreme Court confirmed the *Brown* v. *Board of Education* decision in its second hearing (1955) of the arguments on how to implement the mandate that the public schools of the United States be desegregated. Southerners had hoped that the attorney generals of the southern states could persuade the Court to take a traditional or moderate course in this matter. Instead, the Court ordered immediate preparations for desegregation. By this time, extremist forces had organized to resist as far as they could the Court's mandate. The more conservative forces of state government still believed there was an orderly way to avoid compliance. In some cases it was proposed that the state interpose its power between the schools and the United States government. The successful industrialist Luther H. Hodges was Governor of North Carolina, and he clearly favored the course of action which his state had followed since 1890. After considerable discussion of the immediate problem at several levels of the government, Governor Hodges spoke to white and colored citizens alike from the studios of WUNC-TV on August 8, 1955. This statement shows what a large number of responsible Southerners believed at this time. Yet Governor Hodges' speech was to raise considerable criticism from both whites and Negroes—from the more liberal whites like Paul Green because it seemed not to face the real problem, and from Negroes because they believed it a repetition of ancient segregationist views.

TONIGHT I WANT TO DISCUSS WITH YOU—THE PEOPLE OF NORTH Carolina—that subject which is uppermost in the minds of all of us—our public schools and segregation. North Carolina now stands at the crossroads! Our choice of which road we shall follow will involve all that has been accomplished in the past through the determined efforts of our forefathers to provide us with a good system of public schools; it will also involve the future of our children—and our children's children. Make no mistake here! Let there be no misunderstanding! We hold in our minds and hearts the past, the present, and the future of our beloved state. I urge, therefore, that you consider what I say to you tonight with full realization of the consequences of your decisions.

In order that we can approach our subject in a proper context —that is, with an understanding of what has happened in the past—I would like to take time to review for you briefly some of the background of education in North Carolina.

Like all the Southern states, North Carolina was dealt a crushing blow by the War Between the States. In the words of a distinguished historian: "North Carolina entered upon the [post war] period with her public assets dissipated, her industries destroyed, her railroads wrecked, her educational institutions closed, her public debt piled up in crushing proportions, and with a political problem that for two generations absorbed those energies that should have been left free to develop economic, social, and intellectual resources of the state." In 1866, the General Assembly closed the doors of the common schools, which had survived the stresses and strains of the war. It succumbed to the fear of poverty, the fear of taxes, and, above all, to the fear of mixed schools for white and Negro children.

The constitution of 1868 required the General Assembly to provide for a system of public schools with a minimum term of

James W. Patton, ed., *Messages, Addresses, and Public Papers of Luther Hartwell Hodges, Governor of North Carolina 1954–1961* (Raleigh: Council of State, State of North Carolina, 1963), vol. I, 199–214.

four months each year and compulsory attendance for each child between the ages of six and eighteen years up to a total of sixteen months or four years. Schools and their problems became involved in the bitter political struggles of the Reconstruction period and even when home rule was returned to the state in 1877, our people were so poor that they could not adequately support a strong system of public schools. In fact it was with difficulty that our public schools were even kept in operation during this time of unbelievable poverty and hardship.

For example, in 1880 the superintendent of public instruction reported that the average value of a schoolhouse in the state was exactly $47.67. The average monthly pay of white teachers was just $24.11 per month, and for Negro teachers $19.93 per month. With an average term of less than three months, the total annual pay of a white teacher was under $75 and of a Negro teacher, less than $60. I mention these facts to show you our beginnings in the long and bitter battle to have and to hold adequate public education for the children of the state.

As the years passed, some improvement was shown, but the financial panic of 1893 hit our state very hard. Cotton dropped to five cents per pound, and other products of our farms sold at equally low prices. At the turn of the century our people were still very poor, and we did not have sufficient resources to maintain an adequate system of public schools. Along with our sister Southern states, we ranked at the bottom of the nation.

Then came our great educational governor, Charles B. Aycock. Under his able and dynamic leadership, our state literally lifted itself by its own bootstraps. With Aycock we began a march of progress that has never since been halted.

In his campaign of 1900, Aycock repeatedly championed the cause of universal education. In his message to the General Assembly in 1903, Governor Aycock, who had been the leading figure in the white supremacy campaign in 1900, threw his weight against the division of school taxes by races. In speaking against the proposed division of taxes by races, he said: "The amendment proposed is unjust, unwise and unconstitutional. It would wrong both races, would bring our state into condemnation of a just opinion elsewhere, and would mark us as a people who have turned backward."

Aycock won his battle for universal education—an equal but *separate* education for white and Negro children was on the road to becoming a reality.

Since the time of Aycock, we have never ceased to go forward in public education and today our school system represents an investment of over $400,000,000, and it touches the lives of approximately 30,000 teachers and around 1,000,000 school children.

It is extremely difficult for the average citizen to visualize what our school system means to the state. Our schools are the very backbone of our culture and our economic progress. They have produced a well-balanced and prosperous community.

In 1900, 20 percent of our white population over ten years of age, and a higher ratio for Negroes, could not read and write. There were only 75,000 North Carolinians employed in industry out of a total population of 2,000,000, and they were earning only $216 annually. There were only thirty public high schools and a total enrollment therein of approximately 2,000 students. Only 200 pupils were graduated from high schools in 1900. In 1950, 73 percent of our school age population was attending school. In 1947, *only* 2.7 percent of the total population—white and Negro—fourteen years of age or older was unable to read and write.

I have reviewed the history, growth, and importance of our public school system because these facts are needed for a full understanding of what is involved in the matters we must now consider.

As you know, the public policies of North Carolina with respect to the operation of the schools or any other governmental activity are determined by the General Assembly. During the past session of this body, the laws governing the schools of the state were rewritten and new legislation was enacted which placed the pupil enrollment powers in the hands of local school boards. In order to guard against creating any impression that this rewriting of the school laws and placing the enrollment powers in the local boards was designed to encourage mixing of races, I joined in supporting the introduction of a resolution through which the General Assembly could express the public policy of this state with respect to the question of mixing races in the schools. That resolution was passed unanimously, and I would like now to read it for you:

A JOINT RESOLUTION STATING THE POLICY OF THE STATE OF NORTH CAROLINA WITH REFERENCE TO THE MIXING OF THE CHILDREN OF DIFFERENT RACES IN THE PUBLIC SCHOOLS OF THE STATE, AND CREATING AN ADVISORY COMMITTEE ON EDUCATION

Whereas, Governor William B. Umstead, shortly before his death, appointed a Special Advisory Committee on Education, composed of outstanding citizens of our state of both races, to study the difficult and far-reaching problems presented by the May 17, 1954, decision of the Supreme Court of the United States on the question of segregation in the public schools, and our present Governor, Honorable Luther H. Hodges, recommissioned that committee soon after assuming the duties of Governor of North Carolina, and said committee filed its report with the Governor on December 30, 1954, which report stated, among other things, the following:

"The mixing of the races forthwith in the public schools throughout the state cannot be accomplished and should not be attempted. The schools of our state are so intimately related to the customs and feelings of the people of each community that their effective operation is impossible except in conformity and with community attitudes. The committee feels that the compulsory mixing of the races in our schools, on a state-wide basis and without regard to local conditions and assignment factors other than race, would alienate public support of the schools to such an extent that they could not be operated successfully.";

And whereas, His Excellency, the Governor of North Carolina, has transmitted the report of this special committee to this General Assembly recommending it as the policy for this state to follow;

And whereas, The Attorney General of the State of North Carolina has filed a brief with the Supreme Court of the United States in the pending segregation cases before said Court, which brief states, among other things, the following:

"The people of North Carolina know the value of the public school. They also know the value of a special structure in which two distinct races can live together as separate groups, each proud of its own contribution to that society and recognizing its dependence upon the other group. They are determined, if possible, to educate all of the children of the state. They are also determined to maintain their society as it now exists with separate and distinct racial groups in the North Carolina community.

"The people of North Carolina firmly believe that the record of North Carolina in the field of education demonstrates the practicability of education of separate races in separate schools. They also believe that the achievements of the Negro people of North Carolina demonstrates that such an educational system has not instilled in them any sense of inferiority which handicaps them in their efforts to make lasting and substantial contributions to their state."

Now, therefore, be it resolved by the House of Representatives, the Senate concurring:

Section 1. That the report of the Governor's Special Advisory Committee on Education and the brief of the Attorney General of North Carolina, filed in the Supreme Court of the United States in the pending segregation cases, are hereby approved as a declaration of the policy of the State of North Carolina with respect to the serious problems in public education created by the opinion of the Supreme Court of the United States handed down on May 17, 1954.

Section 2. That the mixing of the races in the public schools within the state cannot be accomplished and if attempted would alienate public support of the schools to such an extent that they could not be operated successfully.

This resolution also created the Advisory Committee on Education for the express purpose of making a continuing study of school problems growing out of the Supreme Court decision and providing advice and counsel to the General Assembly, the governor, the State Board of Education, and county and local school boards throughout the state. This committee was appointed some weeks ago and is headed by the Honorable Thomas J. Pearsall of Rocky Mount. Its other members are:

Senator Lunsford Crew of Halifax County
Senator William Medford of Haywood County
Representative Cloyd Philpott of Davidson County
Representative Edward Yarborough of Franklin County
Colonel William T. Joyner of Wake County, and
Mr. R. O. Huffman of Burke County

Now we come to the May, 1955, decision of the Supreme Court of the United States in which the Court reaffirmed its May, 1954, decision announcing that henceforth the Constitution of the United States will not permit racial discrimination with respect to the enrollment of pupils in the public school system and added that a prompt and reasonable start must be made toward compliance with the decision.

We did not agree with the decision, and our state made every effort possible to persuade the Court to reach a different conclusion. Under our form of federal government, the Supreme Court by a new interpretation of the United States Constitution, no matter how much we may disagree with this new interpretation, can nullify any conflicting state constitutional provision, state law, or state policy. This is true even though the new interpretation overrules the well-established "separate but equal" doctrine which had previously been declared by this same Court to be the law of the land with respect to public education and upon which our state had relied during its desperate struggle to establish adequate schools for both races. Therefore, the decision of the Supreme Court and the policy of the state as set out by the General Assembly had to be examined to determine if there was any way in which both could remain in effect at the same time. We knew that if they could not, then the General Assembly would have to take action with respect to the continued operation of the public schools.

Probably because there was no definite time limit in the decision and because of the general and unspecific language of the Supreme Court, leaders of our General Assembly publicly expressed the conviction that no special session was necessary.

With the advice of the then attorney general, the late Honorable Harry McMullan, and his staff, I agreed with this conclusion, but at the same time the attorney general's office and I viewed the possible long-range effects of the decision with grave concern. Thereafter, on the night of June 6, I made a report over television and radio in which I discussed some of the serious problems created by the decision, but I also pointed out to the people that the decision did not forbid a dual system of schools in which the children of each race voluntarily attend separate schools and that the Court had never said that any state must set up a single school system, mixing the children of both races.

At the beginning of the hearings held in South Carolina recently, Federal Judge John J. Parker, chief judge of the United States Court of Appeals for the Fourth Circuit and a native of North Carolina, made a statement in which he pointed out what the United States Supreme Court had decided and what it has not decided in its latest decision. I would like to quote this statement in part:

> It [the Court] has not decided that the federal courts are to take over or regulate the public schools of the states. It has not decided that the states must mix persons of different races in the schools or must require them to attend schools or must deprive them of the right of choosing the schools they attend.
>
> What it has decided and all that it has decided is that a state may not deny to any person on account of race the right to attend any school that it maintains. This, under the decision of the Supreme Court, the state may not do directly or indirectly; but, if the schools which it maintains are open to children of all races, no violation of the Constitution is involved even though the children of the different races voluntarily attend different schools, as they attend different churches.
>
> Nothing in the Constitution or in the decision of the Supreme Court takes away from the people freedom to choose the schools they attend. The Constitution, in other words, does not require integration. It merely forbids discrimination.

When I made my television and radio report, I also said that many responsible people had freely predicted that considerable time must pass and a number of test cases must be decided before the full effects of the Court's opinion could be known. Some time has now passed and the Virginia and South Carolina test cases, which were already before the Supreme Court, have been decided. Honorable William B. Rodman, our new attorney general, has stated publicly that if all local boards set up study committees to make thorough studies of the problems created by the Court's decision, he believes that for the current year school operations as in the past will not be interfered with by the courts. Our Advisory Committee on Education has within the last few weeks recommended that all local school boards set up committees to study the problem and that during the 1955–56 school year, the schools continue to operate on the same basis of enrollment as has been used in the past. I joined in these recommendations.

The ultimate effects of the Supreme Court's decision on North Carolina can now be fairly well determined. This decision indirectly informs us that within the next few years our efforts expended with so much sacrifice to provide separate but equal educational opportunities for the races in order that we might maintain the older culture of the white race and encourage the growth of the new and rapidly developing culture of the Negro race are to be undone unless—and this is important—*unless we can, through good will and pride in the integrity of our respective racial cultures and way of life, continue our separate schools voluntarily.*

It is my sincere and abiding hope that we can do this.

Let us look at the situation squarely and directly. Let us realize with full knowledge that if we are not able to succeed in a program of voluntary separate school attendance, the state within the next year or so will be face to face with deciding the issue of whether it shall have some form of integrated public schools or shall abandon its public schools. And let me express something here with all the seriousness of which I am capable: Citizens or organizations that attempt to force us into deciding this issue will, in my opinion, have done North Carolina the greatest disservice ever done it in the 180 years of its existence as a state.

Most of us in North Carolina are proud of our way of life

and when I say "most of us" I speak as governor of all the people of the state—Negroes and whites. We are not ashamed of the opportunities that we have labored so hard to provide for both races. The Negro citizens of this state need not, and it is my belief, do not consider themselves second-rate citizens because they go to their own schools, any more than they consider themselves second-rate Christians because they go to their own churches.

I would like, for the next few minutes, to address a few remarks directly to the citizens of North Carolina who are members of the Negro race.

You Negro citizens have every right to be proud of your progress in North Carolina. You and your fathers and mothers before you, in accordance with your economic ability, have taken an admirable part in the struggle for the public schools of the state. Your race has made great contributions to North Carolina, including many, many outstanding leaders in various fields of endeavor. The success of these leaders was accomplished, not over any protests of the white race, but in most cases grew out of the devoted friendship and assistance of white citizens. I doubt that there is one among you who is not personally familiar with numerous instances in which white citizens of your community have extended a helping hand to Negro citizens in furtherance of something the Negro citizens sought to accomplish. Nor has this sort of thing been limited to whites helping Negroes. The Negroes in our state have also made their contributions to members of the white race in things they have tried to do. In other words, in North Carolina the races have lived together in a friendly relationship of mutual helpfulness which has been a source of great pride to all of us and the object of praise from throughout the nation. Our state has thereby moved forward and the Negro race has made the most astounding progress of any race in all history.

In spite of this outstanding record of good race relationships here in North Carolina, we are being made the object of a campaign by an organization which seems determined to destroy our interracial friendship and divide us into camps of racial antagonism. This organization is known as the National Association for the Advancement of Colored People and, apparently is the declared enemy of the principle that the Negro race can take care of its own children as well as can any other race. Although this group avows that the end it seeks is equality, its leaders have obviously convinced themselves that you are not capable of assuming equality. A race which can achieve equality has no need to lose itself in another race. Yet, that is what the NAACP would have you do.

This selfish and militant organization, seeking to promote its own ideas of social conduct, has used every means at its command to convince you that you cannot develop your own culture within your own race and thereafter that you must be ashamed of your color and your history by burying it in the development of the white race. In short, this organization would destroy your identity as a race.

Have any of you ever heard of any real leaders of any race who set out to raise the standards and pride of their race by encouraging its members to lose their identity in complete merger with other races? I do not believe you have. Furthermore, I am convinced that any organization which honestly sought the welfare of your race as a race would not encourage such a course of action. I believe that by virtue of your actions, not only in the past but in the future, you have and will continue to offer convincing proof that you do believe yourselves capable of developing your children within the framework of your own racial culture.

Did you know that here in our state we employ as many Negro teachers as do the seven states of New York, Pennsylvania, Illinois, Ohio, Michigan, California, and Indiana all put together? New York State has approximately the same Negro population as North Carolina, namely, about one million Negro residents. Yet North Carolina employs five times as many Negro teachers as does New York. It would seem to me that if the out-of-state leaders of the NAACP really want to promote fair treatment for the Negro race, they might better spend their time correcting discriminations against Negro teachers by some of their own states instead of trying to create ill will and distrust between the races in North Carolina.

Any stigma you may have felt because of laws requiring segregation in our public schools has now been removed by the courts. No right thinking man resents your desire for equality under the law. At the same time, no right thinking man would advise you to destroy the hopes of your race and the white race by superficial and "show-off" actions to demonstrate this equality. Only the person who feels he is inferior must resort to demonstrations to prove that he is not. A person convinced of his own equality, of his own self-respect, of his own race respect, needs no demonstration to bolster his own convictions. Nevertheless, the leaders of the NAACP would urge you to make such demonstrations by refusing to attend schools in which the teaching personnel are members of your own race. Already this group is urging lawsuits and petitions for integration in the face of the decrees recently handed down by the federal courts in South Carolina and Virginia which make it clear that integration is not required by law and that more time will be needed to deal with the problem.

The policies formulated by leaders of this organization tend to create the only kind of situation in which an organization such as it is can survive—that is, one of distrust, antagonism, resentment and confusion. If the leaders of the NAACP ever allow you to make it clear that you have faith and confidence in the ability and competence of your own schools and your own teachers by refusing to demand admission to schools attended by white children, the principal reason for the existence of their organization in North Carolina would end. Of course, their leaders realize this and so in the interest of preserving their NAACP organization, if for no other, they will, so they have declared, try to push you into lawsuits over school admissions. They will thereby, if they are successful, force you into repudiating your own schools, your own teachers, your own race.

Now let me put the issue to you substantially as it was put in a recent editorial appearing in one of the state's newspapers—

that is, purely on the basis of your own self-interest in your own children. Put on this basis, your problem and the problem of your true leaders is this: How can you get the best education for your children? Can you do it by mixing them in the public schools through force of law and risking the abandonment of the public schools? Or through having them attend separate schools by choice?

If the choice is for voluntary separate school attendance, you can count on at least as good an education for your children as they are getting now. If our past experience is any teacher, your schools will become progressively better as facilities are increased and teaching improves.

On the other hand, if your answer is integration by force of law with the attendant risks, nobody knows how much education the children of either race will get. How good the schools will be or whether there will be any schools are matters dependent upon human reactions which no one can foretell with certainty. Certain it is, however, that the white citizens of this state will *resist integration strenuously, resourcefully, and probably with growing bitterness.* Resistance will take the form of delay of every kind so long as possible. And how long will that be? That depends on many factors including the judges and the determination and resourcefulness of both sides. Our history shows how difficult, if not impossible, it is to change by court rulings long established customs. When the law runs up against human nature and the popular will, something has to give, and not infrequently it is the law which is changed or modified, as in the "noble experiment" of prohibition.

Abolition of the public schools and their replacement to a most uncertain extent by private ones is a last-ditch and double-edged weapon. If that weapon is ever used in North Carolina, its result will be appalling in ignorance, poverty, and bitterness. Generations of both races will suffer by it immeasurably, and it is *likely that the Negro citizens will suffer most.*

North Carolina's public education system is the pride and prop of the state, and it must be preserved if we want to continue to make progress. It is founded on the faith and sacrifice and

will of the people. But if that foundation is weakened or shattered by changing the system into something radically different
from what it is now, nobody knows what will happen to the
schools.

And so my earnest request of you Negro citizens of North
Carolina is this: Do not allow any militant and selfish organization to stampede you into refusal to go along with this program I am proposing in the interest of our public schools; take
pride in your race by attending your own schools; and make it
clear that any among you who refuse to cooperate in this effort
to save our public school system are not to be applauded but are
to be considered as endangering the education of your children and as denying the integrity of the Negro race by refusing
to remain in association with it.

Let there be no mistake or misunderstanding about this
thing! Those who would force this state to choose between
integrated schools and abandonment of the public school system will be responsible if in the choice we lose the public school
system for which North Carolinians of both races have fought
so hard and find to our eternal sorrow the personal racial bitterness which North Carolinians of both races have avoided so
successfully. We must as whites and Negroes work together
to solve this problem. Men of both races of good will and faith
will be needed and must be had!

I would not be fair or candid with you—the people of North
Carolina—if I were not to confess that in this crucial hour I am
greatly concerned for the future of our public school system
and for the welfare and happiness of approximately a million
school children. To be aware of danger, to be conscious of impending tragedy, does not mean that we quail before it or that
we give vent to panic. On the other hand, it would be foolish not
to look the truth in the face. That I am trying to do tonight. The
wise man, and for that matter, the brave man, does not blind
himself to fearful consequences, nor does he ignore the tragic
possibilities of life. When I raise the possibility that all other
remedies having failed, North Carolina might withhold support
of the public schools, I do not thereby seek to frighten anyone.

I simply state that facts and circumstances logically lead to that possibility. Therefore, what I say to you tonight is in no sense an appeal to fear, but rather in truth an appeal to reason. As our superintendent of public instruction, the Honorable Charles F. Carroll, has already said: "Over one million of our school children in whose hearts, minds and hands rests much of the destiny of this state, are innocent parties to this segregation matter and they must not become its *victims*." I repeat that I earnestly hope we can continue to preserve our public schools! I pray that you will have faith as I have—faith that we will so do.

In addressing some of my remarks directly to the Negro citizens of the state, I do not mean that we white citizens of North Carolina do not have an equally substantial responsibility in determining the success or failure of this voluntary program to save our public schools. On the contrary, we perhaps have the greatest responsibility of all; and the manner in which we should, in my opinion, discharge this responsibility is what I would like to discuss with you for the next few minutes.

Many of us, including myself, have at one time or another expressed the conviction that the overwhelming majority of the Negro citizens of North Carolina would, if left free from agitation and outside influence, prefer to have their own schools. If there were no agitation it is my continued belief that our problem would be solved. However, we may well recognize at the outset that there is and will be agitation. This means then that our job, yours and mine and the Negro citizens', will be to overcome the effects of this agitation. The way we can do this is by using every proper means to convince our Negro friends that we are sincere when we say that our way of life, as compared with that in states mixing races in the schools, is to the advantage of the Negro race as well as it is to the white race. We must achieve this program in a friendly and cooperative spirit. Never let it be charged that there is any coercion in our efforts since, of course, if there is coercion then there can be no voluntary program. We should set out to accomplish this program in good faith and with every intention of carrying out a truly voluntary separate school attendance. If we can do this, we can have high hopes for its success. This is evidenced by a recent statement made by an elected Negro city councilman of Durham: "If Negro children of the Walltown section of the city were given their own choice in the matter, they would walk past Durham High School [which is the school white students attend] to attend Hillside High School [which is the school Negro students attend]. They have stronger ties at Hillside."

I shall suggest to the members of our Advisory Committee on Education that they promote in every school district and community in North Carolina a program of encouraging voluntary choice of separate schools; that members of both races be invited to take part in organizations to encourage such voluntary actions and to improve race relations; and that each organization compile and make available factual material which will show that voluntary separate school attendance is both feasible and desirable. This is not a problem which can be left solely to officials in Raleigh or to officials anywhere else. It must be carried on by each of you and by all of you, and will require the best that is in you—both as to ideas and willingness to work. I hope all of you will cooperate.

Our Advisory Committee on Education with headquarters and staff in Raleigh, Agriculture Building, Rooms 556–558, is available for contact by your organizations as well as by local school boards. They will make every effort to furnish you with the kind of material you need and with suggested programs as to how you can carry out this campaign. They have engaged a staff and it stands ready to help you.

I know that many of you, even as you dedicate yourselves to helping carry out the program I have recommended, are concerned as to how we should meet any situations that might arise during the school year immediately ahead. Fortunately, the last General Assembly enacted legislation which sets up a procedure whereby local school boards may pass on applications of persons dissatisfied with their enrollment assignment. Local boards can do this in accordance with conditions in their own locality and will be in the best position to know how to deal with each particular situation. The decisions of the local boards are made subject to appeal to the Superior Court where a jury will determine the facts involved. From the Superior Court, an appeal is available to the Supreme Court of North Carolina.

This law provides tests or standards which can be used to govern the admission of pupils. These standards which are to guide local school boards are: orderly and efficient administration of public schools; the effective instruction of the pupils enrolled therein; and the health, safety, and general welfare of such pupils. I believe that this law furnishes an adequate system of determining in a lawful way whether or not a particular child shall attend a particular school. Meanwhile, let's take this thing step by step, learning as we go, watching the cases from states already in the court, studying decisions and actions of judges who handle these cases. Let's see how successful will be our efforts with the program I am suggesting; let's find out if lawsuits are brought where and why. Let each local school group have its study committee to analyze its own conditions and problems; and also, in the meanwhile, we should continue our schools as they have been. It would be foolish to do otherwise. I repeat—no court has told us or will tell us that we must mix races in schools. Neither can the courts operate our schools. That's up to us. Let's do it in fairness and good spirit but with firmness and courage.

I would like, at this time, to thank all of you for the many hundreds of letters and telegrams which you have sent me from every section of North Carolina supporting my position in this segregation matter. I need your constant help, your prayers, and best wishes. I do not have the wisdom to tell you what will happen in the years ahead. I don't think anyone is that smart and I feel that as your governor I don't help our state or our public schools by inflammatory or prejudical remarks. I think like most of you, and I believe in the same things you believe in. I am convinced that a system of separate schools for the races is the best interest of us all and I pledge to you that I will exert every effort to maintain such a system. We all want to preserve our

public schools. They have been the backbone of our progress—
social and economic. It would be a tragedy if anyone forced us
to abandon them.

In conclusion, let me say as I have said before: We in North
Carolina have remained comparatively calm and restrained during this difficult period, but that hasn't meant we don't feel
strongly on the subject. We have approached our problems not
as two races, antagonistic to each other, but as one citizenry
determined to do what is best for both races and for our children. If we can keep this attitude we will without changing our
beliefs come through this situation with our public school system intact and with our basic traditions intact. It is my intention to do everything I can to see that this happens.

Thank you, fellow citizens, for your patience in listening and
for your great help in facing this serious problem.

35 North Carolina and the Negro

In the summer of 1963 the piedmont area of North Carolina was disturbed by a series of mass demonstrations, in some cases nearly resulting in violence. Both Negroes and diehard whites became involved, and for a time it seemed the trouble would spread over a wide area. After the demonstrations in the town of Lexington, Governor Terry Sanford took active steps to deal with the issues raised by the protestors. His aide, General Capus Waynick, assembled 150 Negro leaders in Raleigh on June 25, 1963, when Governor Sanford made a statement to them about the state's position in the face of the demonstration.

Internal evidence in the Governor's statement indicates that he was genuinely disturbed by future prospects of an open race war. He was positive in his declaration that North Carolina would maintain order. He told his hearers that the demonstrations had served their purposes, and he appealed for a dignified discussion of the issues involved. He used the illustration of a North Carolina soldier who said he was to blame for violent demonstrations because he had stood by without expressing his own feelings to white people earlier. This Negro soldier's sense of being discriminated against no doubt reflected his race's unhappiness in North Carolina.

You are here at our invitation to find a better way to express your hopes, desires, and aspirations. You must find a way

Memory F. Mitchell, ed., *Messages, Addresses, and Public Papers of Terry Sanford, Governor of North Carolina, 1961–1965* (Raleigh: North Carolina History Commission, 1966), 597–599.

not only which expresses the depth and breadth of your dissatisfaction, but which also encourages people to assist in opening up jobs and other opportunities.

The device of the mass demonstration has largely served its purpose in North Carolina. It got across your message and the urgency that had not been fully understood prior to then.

A penetrating insight came from a soldier, who happens to be a North Carolina Negro, who wrote: "I am as much to blame for the riots on the streets of Lexington as those who were there. For it was I who stood aside, saying and doing nothing for many years, and all the while some white people thought I was happy and content when I knew it wasn't so."

The demonstrations have shown just how unhappy and discontented you are, how anxious you are to remove, and remove right now, the indignities and injustices which have been visited upon your parents and their parents.

These demonstrations have been followed by progress for you, but you would be making a mistake to assume that the demonstrations alone, as such, brought your progress. The demonstrations brought the message, and the message, in its truth and fullness, stirred the action which brought your progress. This may be a subtle distinction, but it is an important distinction, and it has great meaning for your future.

The mass demonstration awoke and jolted many people, but this method had reached the point of diminishing returns in its latter days destroying good will, creating resentment, losing friends, and not influencing people.

There are thousands of North Carolinians with both the desire and the ability to start removing indignities and injustices, so the long-range response of good will, fairness, and full job opportunity depends on mutual respect, not intimidation.

These mass demonstrations also had reached the point where I, as head of the executive branch of government, responsible for law enforcement, peace and order, was required to establish a firm policy for North Carolina. My responsibility for public safety required that I take action before danger erupted into violence.

I do not intend to let mass demonstrations destroy us. It would be unfortunate if I were called on to prove this. As head of the executive branch, I am entitled to the support of all good citizens, and I call on you to join with others in holding down strife.

I hope you will not declare war on those who urge courses of reason at this time.

There indeed are people in the land today who say that the white man is your enemy and war is necessary.

Not so!

Emphatically not so in North Carolina!

Your enemy and mine is a system bequeathed us by a cotton economy, kindled by stubbornness, intolerance, hotheadedness, north and south, exploding into war and leaving to our generations the ashes of vengeance, retribution, and poverty.

The way to fight this common enemy is education, up and down the line and across the board.

The way to fight this enemy is to open up job opportunities for everybody, everywhere, on the basis of ability and training, without regard to race. As a state we cannot afford to use only part of our human resources.

The way for you to fight this enemy is through dignity, clearly and forcefully stating your honest feelings, seeking understanding and accomplishment, through good will which is at hand in so many places. This kind of leadership and responsible example by you would be applauded and widely accepted across the nation.

That is why you are here. The story this morning is not the story of mass demonstrations. The real story is not beclouded by the story of possible violence, of the force, the danger, with failure to establish clearer understanding.

The story this morning is the reasonable story of what you think and why. I believe that is important.

General Capus Waynick is the representative of the Governor's Office. If this forum is of advantage, then we can hold others in other cities, as an alternative to potentially dangerous and generally misunderstood mass demonstrations. I am sure that North Carolina mayors and other leaders will co-operate fully. I am sure that they are willing to discuss all things with you and assist you in many ways.

Now is the time for men and women of good faith to put North Carolina above the distressing clamor of racial conflict.

Now is the time for reason to prevail.

36 The Golden Out-of-Order Plan

Above the screams of the rabble-rousers could be heard the voice of Harry Golden of Charlotte, North Carolina. The editor of the *Carolina Israelite* enjoyed baiting the extremists with his pungent observations on their comic antics. Using the effective device of humor he held them up to public ridicule. First Golden proposed that the main source of race difficulties in the schools was the principle that Negroes and whites should not sit down together; this was one of the great dangers of race-mixing. Therefore he suggested that all the seats be removed from schoolrooms and other public places so that everybody would remain vertical. Golden next suggested his "out-of-order" plan to solve the water fountain problem. By such proposals he pointed out that hostile attitudes toward desegregating many public facilities were no more than a gossamer of prejudice anyway.

WHILE I STILL HAVE FAITH IN THE GOLDEN VERTICAL NEGRO Plan, which I announced last summer, I have found it difficult to get a School Board to try it—(take the seats out of the classrooms, and let the kids stand, since no one pays the slightest attention to a vertical Negro).

Now, however, I am on much firmer ground. This time I sub-

Harry Golden, "The Golden Out-of-Order Plan," *New South* 12 (April 1957), 13.

mitted my plan to a successful test, and I am ready to formally announce—THE GOLDEN "OUT-OF-ORDER" PLAN.

I tried my Plan in a city of North Carolina where the Negroes represent thirty-nine percent of the population.

I prevailed upon the manager of a department store to shut the water off in his "white" water fountain and put up a sign, "Out-of-order." For the first day or two the "whites were hesitant, but little by little they began to drink out of the water fountain belonging to the "coloreds"—and by the end of the third week everybody was drinking the "segregated" water; with not a single, solitary complaint to date.

I believe the test is of such sociological significance that the Governor should appoint a special committee of two members of the House and two Senators to investigate the GOLDEN "OUT-OF-ORDER" PLAN. We kept daily reports on the use of the unsegregated water fountain which should be of great value to this committee. This may be the answer to the necessary uplifting of the "white" morale. It is possible that the "whites" may accept desegregation if they were assured that the segregated facilities still exist, albeit, "Out-of-order."

As I see it now the key to my plan is to keep the "Out-of-order" sign up for at least two years. We must do this thing gradually.

PART 5 The South in Social Chaos

During the latter quarter of the nineteenth-century the South was caught in a web of social problems from which its leaders lacked the will and resources to break free. One immense problem was Reconstruction's legacy of violence. Contemporary newspapers were filled with reports of crimes of all sorts committed by whites and blacks alike. Most counties were poorly equipped to care properly for criminals. Jails were insecure, filthy, and ill-managed, and in no southern state was there a penitentiary adequate to handle the great flow of convicts. Public expense involved in caring for prisoners increased with each succeeding decade, and governors and legislators were unwilling to levy taxes and appropriate sufficient funds to provide sufficient prisoner care.[1]

Even though the states' treatment of criminals had been a matter of national concern prior to 1860, Southerners for the most part looked upon the convict as a ward of the state for purposes of punishment rather than rehabilitation. His body

[1] C. Van Woodward, *Origins of the New South*, 212–215, 232–234, 424–425; Francis Simkins, *A History of the South*, 2nd ed. rev. enl. (New York: Knopf, 1953), 508–512; E. Franklin Frazier, *The Negro in the United States*, 646–647; Francis W. Coker, "Lynchings," *Encyclopedia of the Social Sciences*, IX, 639–643; *Report, Southern Commission on the Study of Lynchings and What They Mean.*

belonged to the state to be used or sold at will. In practice the abuse of convicts by leasing them to private companies was an act of criminality; many times it was more brutal than was the act for which the man was convicted. Convict leasing provoked serious criticism, and states were forced to discontinue the practice. Prisoner abuses, however, were continued in some places by use of chain gangs.[2]

Even more offensive than ill treatment of convicts was the practice of lynching. From 1865–1960 the reputation of the South was besmirched by the frequent occurrence of lynchings. These were provoked by almost as many causes as there were lynchings. Manslaughter was actually the chief excuse, though in the public mind the crime most often avenged was rape.[3] The Congress made numerous attempts to enact anti-lynching legislation, but these were thwarted either by filibusters or by maneuvers on the part of the powerful southern bloc in Congress.

[2] Louis N. Robinson, "Prison Labor," *Encyclopedia of the Social Sciences*, XII, 415–419.

[3] Gunar Myrdal et al., *An American Dilemma*, 558–566; Walter White, *Rope and Faggott: A Biography of Judge Lynch* (New York: A. A. Knopf, 1929); Arthur F. Raper, *The Tragedy of Lynching* (Montclair, N.J.: Patterson Smith, 1969); Thomas D. Clark, *The Southern Country Editor*, 226–244.

37 Rural Public Health

No greater problem beset the South at the turn of the twentieth century than that of poor health. Deficient diet, heavy parasitic infection, and constant exposure to malaria all took their toll. Lack of medical knowledge was partly responsible for this condition, but ignorance, poverty, and indifference were even more to blame. No one was better qualified to comment on rural conditions of health and poverty than the famous medical researcher Dr. Charles Wardell Stiles. In 1909 he was with the Public Health and Marine Hospital Service in Washington, D.C. Within the next decade, 1910–1920, Dr. Stiles was to have an important impact on the South through the crusade for eradication of hookworm.

RELIABLE VITAL STATISTICS FOR THE SOUTHERN RURAL DISTRICTS are lacking, so that in comparing present medical conditions with those prior to 1865 one must rely upon three chief sources of information, namely, (1) scattered articles in medical journals, (2) the memory of older physicians, and (3) theoretical deductions as to what will occur under certain conditions. In

Charles Wardell Stiles, "The Industrial Conditions of the Tenant Class (White and Black) as Influenced by the Medical Conditions," in *Economic History, 1865–1910*, ed. James Curtis Ballagh, *The South in the Building of the Nation*, vol. VI (Richmond: The Southern Historical Publications Society, 1909), 594–601.

view of these premises, no article written on this subject can claim to be free from criticism.

Again, the average person who lives or travels in the South does not visit the rural tenant classes nor does he look for disease. Statements, therefore, from one who has become interested in these tenants and their diseases will not be in harmony with the experience of the average traveler or resident.

That prior to 1860 the sanitary surroundings and the health conditions of the tenant white class were, at least in some districts, as wretched as they are to-day can be safely deduced both from the medical literature and from testimony of various physicians. That the tenant negroes are living under decidedly poorer sanitary surroundings and are in poorer average health than were the slaves is the testimony of every physician interviewed, and this testimony is supported by the self-evident fact that slaves were property too valuable to be permitted to live generally under the insanitary surroundings now noticed as the rule among the average country negroes. An unusually intelligent negro physician recently said: "Before the war the white man took care of us and he knew how to do it; since the war we negroes have had charge of ourselves and we have been going from bad to worse."

In any area in which different races live, complicated medical conditions may be expected to exist. In our South, with the white man and the black races, we find both European (or temperate) and African (or tropical) diseases, of which each class has spread to the other race: tuberculosis to the negroes, and malaria, hookworm disease, Cochin-China diarrhea, amebic dysentery, and filariasis to the whites. The well-to-do classes are able to surround themselves with good sanitary conditions, especially in cities, whereby they escape, to a greater or less extent, the effects of the diseases not only of the opposite, but also of their own race, but the poorer, namely, the tenant classes of both races living under poor sanitary surroundings have to bear the brunt of the burden of the diseases, not only of their own race, but in addition of those contracted from the other race. Under these circumstances, we must be prepared to find that the Southern tenants, living under anything less than ideal sanitary conditions, are not in such good state of health as are the tenants in other parts of the country where these medical complications do not exist.

That the sanitation surrounding the rural tenants in the South is ideal, probably no one will claim. That in numerous instances it is little better than medieval Europe and frequently no better than that described for the present savage tribes of Africa must be admitted by persons conversant with the facts. For instance, in examining a plantation on which there were sixty white hands, the only privy found on the estate was one reserved for the owner's family; on another plantation there was a settlement of eight negro houses, not one of which had a privy. That these cases are not exceptional is shown by the fact that records of 4,645 farm houses scattered over six of the Southern states show that 55.2 per cent. of these had no privy of any kind. A very high percentage, at least 30 per cent., according to conservative estimates, of the rural schools, and a very much higher percentage of the rural churches, are absolutely devoid of the most elementary toilet facilities.

With the insanitary conditions so prevalent in the South, it need not be surprising that the tenant labor is inefficient and the death rate high. As the sanitary conditions under which the negroes are living are in general much worse than those for the whites, and as the nourishment of the blacks is so irregular and poor, the present much higher death rate and the low degree of efficiency among the negroes need cause no surprise.

Admitting that the vital statistics of the Twelfth Census (1900) are very far from perfect, the following comparison is worthy of serious consideration: (1) The average negro population for the entire country is 11.6 per cent., the average typhoid death-rate 46.5 deaths per 100,000 inhabitants. (2) Fifteen states have an average negro population of 34.34 per cent., and an average typhoid death rate of 72.7. (3) Seventeen other states have an average negro population of 2.48 per cent., and an average typhoid death rate of 39.25. (4) The eighteen non-negro states have an average negro population of 0.42 per cent., and an average typhoid death rate of 25.51. (5) The typhoid death rates for the registration area are: white males,

37.4; negro males, 75.3; white females, 27.4; negro females, 56.3.

The popular belief that tuberculosis is rare in the rural districts can not be accepted as applying generally to the South, either for the whites or the blacks.

It is impossible to make even a rough estimate of the number of deaths due to the tropical or the African diseases in the rural South, but from present indications an estimate that 30 per cent. of the rural tenants harbor hookworm infection is not excessive.

The general testimony is that the immoral diseases are relatively uncommon among the rural whites (except in certain districts), but excessively common among the rural blacks. In fact, unless some change in this respect develops in the not too distant future, the more generally common of these will soon solve the negro problem.

The habitations of the rural tenants are, as a class (with exceptions, of course) very inferior. Light is valued so little that it is common to find the homes without windows. Were it not for the cracks and chimneys, the ventilation would be even worse than it is now. The people seem to fear night air, and this evil is intensified among the negroes by a more or less wide spread habit of covering the head at night with the bed clothes.

The food varies considerably. I have been with families in a comparatively poor financial condition where the table was fairly good, but in the majority of instances the diet is monotonous, and the food poorly cooked and it is served in a manner which decreases rather than increases the appetite. This point can not be considered as at all peculiar to the South, for the same general conditions are found elsewhere. Still, when we compare a very poor Southern tenant family, white or black, with a very poor family in the West, or in Germany, the fact can not be escaped that with the poor style or even lack of privy on the Southern farms, the fecal pollution of food through flies is excessive in comparison. This point, however, may be made equally well against some of the smaller hotels.

Having painted the foregoing rather black picture of conditions, let us turn to the outlook for their betterment.

The first point to be made is that we are discussing the *tenants*, namely, persons who live in houses and under sanitary conditions *provided by landlords*. The absence of a privy at 52.2 per cent. of the farm houses tabulated was not due to the ignorance of tenants, but to the thoughtlessness and ignorance of the better educated white landlord. The latter, one of the finest men in the world to meet, would not think of eating at a table with a negro, but it does not seem to occur to him that he and his family daily run the risk of eating negro fecal material carried to their food by flies which have bred and fed in the nearby woods used by his tenants or servants in lieu of a privy. There is a popular idea, more or less widespread among the tenant classes, that a privy is not conducive to health, and the landlord, intelligent as to most matters, fails to see the importance of preventing soil pollution in order to insure better health for his own and his tenants' children. This intelligent man takes it as established that he can not run stock on the same small pasture year after year without having an outbreak of disease (due of course to intense soil pollution), but he forgets to apply the same principle to his tenants. The privy is man's invention which enables him to keep his family year after year on the same restricted premises; a failure to have a sanitary privy means soil pollution and resulting disease. As it is the landlord, rather than the tenant, who provides the house and its annexes, it is on the landlord rather than the tenant that the responsibility must be placed for the present conditions under which so many tenants live.

Given now the privy, would it be used? If a sanitary toilet is built, there will be more or less difficulty in inducing the whites, especially the men, to use it; there will be much greater difficulty in inducing the negroes to use it.

Still the outlook is much brighter than at first appears. In case of the tenant whites it should be recalled that the mother is by far the most important member of the family. Once gain her for sanitation (and this is not difficult) and the reform is half completed.

Of the negroes one can not speak so confidently. Admitting

that there are many exceptions, still the average negro (especially of the younger generation) whom one meets is so superficial, thoughtless, and undependable, that I am pessimistic as to the outlook. Possibly my fears are ungrounded, but I do fear, nevertheless, that the chaingang will eventually have to be requisitioned as a school in which to teach the rural negro the ordinary decencies of civilized sanitation.

Next to the sanitary privy, I would urge that greater housekeeping conveniences be placed in the tenant homes so that the women may have a less harsh life. The burden on the tenant wife is a severe one—and one unnecessarily intensified by poor health due to insanitary surroundings.

More fresh air, more sunlight, and more cleanliness in the home, combined with a sanitary toilet and better housekeeping facilities would soon so increase the efficiency and reduce the death rate among the tenant class that the labor problem would be solved to a greater extent and child-labor, instead of being justified as it is at present as the less of two evils, would to a great extent disappear.

38 Convict Labor in Georgia

When Woodrow Wilson formed a law partnership with Edward Ireland Renick in 1883, he found he had a tremendous amount of leisure time waiting for clients to appear. He looked about him to discover social conditions in Georgia, and busied himself writing essays on the state and the New South. One of the most offensive practices of the "redeemer" administrations in the South was that of saving money at the expense of human welfare. Practically no provisions were made in Georgia's budget for care of criminals sentenced to the penitentiaries. The cheapest way to handle this problem was to lease convicts to private lessors for a negligible annual sum.

The convict system shocked Wilson as a conscientious Calvinist; he saw in it a sin against humanity as well as a prostitution of the powers of the state. Accordingly Wilson prepared the following essay, which he submitted to his old friend Robert Bridges for use in the *New York Evening Post*. Although there were scores of articles criticizing the convict leasing system, none was more incisive than Wilson's.

IT MAY BE SAID WITH TRUTH THAT, ALTHOUGH SHE HAS KNOWN nothing since the war of the old system of penitentiary confine-

Woodrow Wilson, "Convict Labor in Georgia," *New York Evening Post* (March 7, 1883); in Arthur Link, ed., *The Papers of Woodrow Wilson*, vol. II (Princeton: Princeton University Press, copyright © 1967), 306–311.

ment, Georgia is still experimenting in systems of convict labor. Her policy toward her criminals has vacillated as much as have the purposes and whims of her legislators in regard to all other matters of government. Something like her present plan of convict labor was adopted as early as 1866, but many and differing laws relating to the subject have since been enacted, and even now nobody can be certain that the system will long remain unchanged. An influential minority of Georgians, firm in their convictions, and perhaps growing in numbers, are much dissatisfied with it; every legislature tinkers with it, and nobody seems to regard it as a settled thing.

The history of the system in this State is much like the history of similar systems in neighboring States. It took its rise in that impatience of taxation which is still its main support and strength—an impatience which was like to have emptied the old penitentiary sooner than it did. The last report of Mr. J. W. Nelson, the present Principal Keeper of convicts in Georgia, shows that fifty years ago, under the old penitentiary régime, when the prison roll contained but two hundred names, the expense of maintaining the prisoners after the old fashion was considered by the taxpayers so heavy a burden that by the Act of 24th of December, 1831, the penitentiary was actually abolished. By that act an attempt was made to return to the laws of the imperfect code which had been in force previous to 1816, and, as a supplement to that code, the whipping-post was erected to serve as a terror to those who were prone to commit certain minor crimes. But the laws of 1816 speedily proved inadequate to the needs of 1832. The Legislature of that year was constrained to open again the doors of the State prison, and, in spite of the fact that the taxes collected for the support of the convicts were still always paid with a very bad grace by the people, and that more than one serious attack was made upon the administration of the penitentiary, no further legislative step was taken in the matter until 1866. By an act of that year the General Assembly authorized Governor Jenkins to farm out the convicts to private persons on the best terms possible. But the times were then too troublous for the regular and legal birth of such a system, or indeed of any new policy of peaceful administration, for all law was in suspense; the hand of the Federal Government was on the South, and Governor Jenkins was soon displaced by military rule. General Ruger assumed command of the State, and undertook the executive direction of its affairs in the name of the Federal authorities: and he it was who acted upon the suggestion of the Assembly in the matter of the disposition of the convicts by instituting the present system. He found the prisons of the State crowded and without proper management, and, in May, 1868, thought it convenient and expedient to lease out a number of the convicts. In July of the same year he made a second lease; and in the following November his successor, Rufus B. Bullock, reconstruction Governor of Georgia, contracted with Messrs. Grant and Alexander to lease the entire convict force of the State on easy terms.

Such was the beginning of the present policy of convict leasing. Since 1868 very few legislatures have refrained from meddling with the system. After making trial from 1871 to 1874 of short leases for terms of from one to two years, and after extending the maximum term to five years in 1874, the law now provides for leases for at least twenty years in ordinary cases. The number of lessees is made to depend upon considerations of convenience. The law of 1876 authorized an experiment of which nothing has come. The Governor was instructed to require the principal leasing company, which was constituted a corporation for the purposes of the act, to procure at its own expense a suitable site, either an island off the coast of Georgia or some other place within the limits of the State, of which the Governor should approve, and on that site to erect, at its own expense, under the Governor's direction, "suitable, convenient, safe, healthy, and commodious prisons, barracks, hospitals, guard-houses, and all other dwellings necessary for the safe keeping and comfort of the convicts." This establishment, entirely under private management, save for the presence of one or two officers, such as a physician and a chaplain, appointed by the Governor, was to have been known as the State Penitentiary, and was to have been convict headquarters rather than the common criminals' prison, the act contemplating that certain convicts should be kept within the walls while all the rest worked without in mines and quarries, or on roads and canals. But the scheme broke down, and this novel experiment of a private penitentiary under governmental supervision gave place to the existing arrangements, which may be very briefly described.

There are at present about 1,200 convicts in the hands of the several lessees. They are scattered throughout the State in guarded camps where they can best serve the purposes of the contractors, some mining coal for Senator Brown, some mining iron ore, some quarrying granite, others making brick, others constructing tramways, and still others building railroads. A large force has for several years been assigned by the State, without charge, to the proprietors of the Marietta and North Georgia Railroad, by a special act which contemplated similar contributions of labor on the part of the State to other railroad companies. For each convict the regular lessees pay the paltry sum of $20 per annum, enabling the State to realize yearly for the lease of the whole force about $25,000. The conditions of lease are that the treatment of the convicts shall be "in accordance with existing regulations"; in short, that they are to be well cared for and humanely dealt with; that they are never to be worked upon Sunday, nor for more than ten hours on any other day; and that they are never to be corporeally punished except by some one person in each camp regularly appointed to administer punishment, and by him only when punishment is absolutely necessary for the preservation of discipline. The lessees further undertake to clothe and lodge the convicts comfortably, to be answerable in damages for all escapes, and to release promptly such as may be pardoned or may have served out their terms, dismissing them with a good suit of citizen's clothes and money enough to take them to their homes. For the fulfilment of these conditions the lessees give such bond, with security, as is deemed sufficient by the Governor; and their diligence and good faith in the performance of their obligations are sought to be assured by the supervision of the Assistant

Keeper, who makes monthly visits to each of the camps in the name of the State, and files in the Governor's office frequent reports of the results of his inspection. Besides the Principal and Assistant Keepers, the State also employs a physician, to make frequent professional visits to the camps, with a view to securing proper sanitary regulations, as well as for the purpose of rendering his services to the sick.

Such, in brief, is the convict system of Georgia. It is, at least, a consistent one. The State gets altogether rid of the care of all of its criminals[.] It extends its policy of leasing even to cases of misdemeanor, for one section of the law of 1874 provides that persons sentenced to fine, or fine and costs, with alternative imprisonment, may bind themselves, in a sort of penal apprenticeship, for the alternative period of imprisonment, to such persons, approved of by the judge who passed sentence, as shall consent in writing to pay the fine. In such cases the hirer is considered the bailee of the convict and may surrender him to the officers of the court if at any time he grossly misbehaves or attempts to escape.

The criticisms and objections to which this system is open are obvious. In the first place, if intended to operate for the pecuniary advantage of the State, the revenues derived from it are miserably small as compared with the income which might be secured from the system. Both Alabama and South Carolina lease their convicts to private persons, but they get much higher rates than Georgia lessees have ever paid. In Alabama the convicts are divided into three classes, according to their capacity for labor. For those who are capable of the most efficient work the government obtains prices falling very little below the highest market price of labor; for those less efficient good wages are paid, and those least efficient are let out for their maintenance. In South Carolina a somewhat similar plan is adopted, the prices obtained by the State being there proportioned to the kind of labor for which the convicts are engaged. But South Carolina does not lease out all her convicts; she is more thrifty; she retains a number in her well-ordered penitentiary, and there trains them in the handicrafts. The shoes made at the South Carolina

Penitentiary are purchased all over that State as the best shoes made for ordinary wear. To a careful and provident system, such as her neighbors have established, Georgia, however, makes no pretence. In her eyes one convict is worth no more than another; and the $25,000 which the leases yearly bring into her coffers fully compensates her as an addition to the pleasure of getting rid of the care of all her criminals.

But the economic objection to the system is the least serious of all. It is not desirable that the chief end of the State in this matter should be to make as much money as possible out of the lease of her criminals. Manifestly, it is a system which is open to gross abuses. The entire care and discipline of the convicts is intrusted to private individuals whose interest it is to get as much gain as possible out of their purchased punitive authority. The friends of the present system insist, that the convicts are treated for the most part without harshness and with a due regard for their health and comfort. But it is known that very disgraceful things have happened in consequence of the fact that the sexes have not always been kept carefully separate in the camps, and it is reasonable to conclude that, in their eagerness to get as much work as possible out of the laborers who are thus put absolutely at their disposal, the lessees do not hesitate to make every hour an hour of toil and drudgery, to the neglect of all those reformatory methods and influences for which government is nowadays always expected to provide.

Indeed, it is evident that the system is quite incompatible with modern ideas of the duty which society owes to the criminal classes. No effort ought to be spared to educate and elevate the inmates of our prisons. No outlay, however great, is wasted which is devoted to the training of convicts in the handicrafts or to their moral and intellectual elevation. No such betterment of the condition of this unhappy class can, however, be accomplished in Georgia convict camps under present circumstances, for the men who people these camps are hired not for their own benefit, but for the gain of their hirers. True, these lessees are bound by the law to observe such plans of reform as may be prescribed by the State; but they are visited only once a month by the public inspector, and they do not pretend to have employed the convict forces for any other purpose than that of profit to themselves. They are restrained from gross abuses of their power by penal statutes and by that salutary authority which has been given to the Governor, to summarily forfeit their lease upon any breach of the law or of their contracts; but they can use their employees without bettering them, and still keep safely within the letter of both contract and law.

If the object of conviction be punishment, it is obviously open to question whether the Georgia system of convict labor at all answers even that end. The majority of the convicts are of the lower class of negroes, who are accustomed to the severest and meanest kinds of manual work, and who are neither punished nor humiliated by being compelled to drudge in chains. The prevailing sentiment of the negroes upon this subject was well illustrated by a conversation between two colored men which I accidentally overheard the other day. The burden of their talk was that if one of their fellows were to rob them of their small savings or of their scanty stores of household wealth, it would neither afford them any satisfaction nor restrain him from committing similar crimes in future if he were sent to work for Mr. Brown in the mines; and they declared their conviction that the whipping-post would be better for all concerned.

But the gravest objections that can be urged against this system rest upon higher grounds even than these. For who can defend a system which makes the punishment of criminals, that high prerogative of government, a source of private gain? Who can justify a policy which delegates sovereign capacities to private individuals? How high an estimate will criminals put upon the dignity and power of government when they see that their own punishment for disobedience of the regulations of that government is made a source of private emolument?

39 The Suppression of Lawlessness in the South

Lawlessness was one of the heaviest burdens the post-war South had to bear. There seems actually to have been little distinction between problems experienced by states with predominantly Negro populations and those with overwhelming numbers of white people. Kentucky, for instance, after 1870 was beset by crime that disrupted law enforcement efforts in several counties and revealed serious weaknesses in the state government. In the following essay, however, J. M. Stone views the crime situation in Mississippi as arising from the predominance of Negroes in the state's population. In most of the writings of this period Southerners were quick to blame the illiterate Negro for increased crime, but almost never did they plead for major improvement in public education. When they did speak of education it was a fourth grade education of exceedingly indifferent quality, which white Southerners considered sufficient to remedy many conditions which troubled the region. In this essay Stone also views the problem of lynching, but stresses the hopeful fact that not all criminals charged with raping white women were lynched.

THE TITLE OF THIS ARTICLE IMPLIES THAT THE SOUTHERN STATES present conditions differing from those of other sections of the

J. M. Stone, "The Suppression of Lawlessness in the South," *North American Review* 158 (April 1894), 500–506.

United States, and requiring remedial treatment of a special or extraordinary character. There is an element of truth in this idea, but a correct and comprehensive understanding of the subject requires careful and exact discrimination. It is true that the presence of the negro race in large numbers in the Southern States is a fact that distinguishes, in many ways, the conditions of society in those States from those of Northern communities. It is very far from true, however, that extraordinary or peculiar remedies are required or would prove useful or efficacious. On the contrary the elements of ignorance and immorality that tend to lawlessness in the South are not different in quality from those existing elsewhere, though they are more extensive and prevalent, in a relative point of view, when compared with communities with exclusively white populations.

The white race of the South has the same general and fundamental moral and intellectual qualities, and the same racial instincts and characteristics, that distinguish the race elsewhere. The subject of organized society, public morality and good government, as well as the principles that regulate private obligations and duties, are unquestionably regarded by the best classes of white people in the South as they are accepted and regarded by the people in the other States. And moreover, the better class of negroes in the South share with their white fellow-citizens the desire for the moral as well as the material improvement and advancement of our commonwealths.

The elements of ignorance and illiteracy, with an accompanying low standard of morality, prevailing widely among the negro population in the South, constitute in the broadest sense the only peculiar and abnormal features that characterize the existing situation in the Southern States. While these circumstances, complicated by the friction of race prejudice, *prima facie* seem to call for special methods of treatment, and new or novel remedies, yet after careful examination and reflection, and upon an exact and thoughtful analysis, the evident impracticability, in our form of government, of heroic or empirical legal measures for the suppression of individual crimes resolves the problem at last into one that must be dealt with by ordinary legal remedies and moral forces necessarily involving a slow and tedious process.

In view of the former condition of slavery, the negroes of the South, since their emancipation, have done well, and all that could have been expected, in the direction of moral and mental advancement; but a vast deal remains to be done. The important and practical question that now presents itself is, What measures and remedies are best adapted to the solution of the problem of bringing the races into more harmonious relations, and for continuing the improvement that is now slowly going on?

The negro question, the race question, or the Southern question, as it has been indifferently termed, has been voluminously discussed from every point of view. The best thought of the country has been directed to its solution or adjustment, but the inquiry has always proceeded upon the fallacious assumption that a satisfactory result could only be accomplished by artificial, legal, or force methods; whereas it is continually becoming clearer that the problem is too complicated and the environment by far too ramified and intricate for drastic or rapid treatment, and that we must be content to wait patiently and hopefully the slow but certain operation of those great moral forces and principles that underlie our social structure, and that uniformly direct human actions in the greatest concerns of races and peoples. It seems now to be the consensus of public thought and opinion on this subject that external interference cannot possibly promote the solution of this Southern problem or lessen its tension, and that at last it must be left in the hands of the communities immediately and directly concerned in its settlement and adjustment. It is not, however, within the purpose of this paper to discuss the political phases of this question, but only to consider the fact of political and race antagonisms in their relations to the commission and suppression of crime.

The white race of the South, charged as it is with the responsibility of government in the Southern States, has accepted the responsibility, which was unavoidable, of dealing with this race issue with all that is involved in it. The measure of this trust is correctly appreciated, and its difficulties are not underestimated, nor can either of these considerations be disregarded when it is remembered that the white men of the South, above all others, are vitally concerned in the just and proper accomplishment of this task. This consideration stands as a guaranty of our earnest purpose to secure the prosperity and welfare of these Southern communities; a consummation which involves necessarily the greatest good to the greatest number of individuals of both races, resting firmly upon a broad and just basis.

. . . Racial antagonisms between the whites and blacks have been a serious disturbing element, and have impaired, in a measure, the proper administration of the criminal laws in this State [Mississippi]. The inharmonious relations between the races are due very largely to political causes which happily, are diminishing under the operation of the suffrage clause of the State constitution of 1890, which places an educational qualification upon the elective franchise. Instead of the enormous negro majorities that formerly existed, there is now in the State a large majority of white electors, and the apprehensions and uneasiness in respect to the former ignorant and incompetent mass of voters have disappeared, and public disorders and disturbances, and the various forms of lawlessness having their origin in political causes, have ceased to occur, and there is no reasonable apprehension of their reappearance.

Notwithstanding the great modification or removal of the political tension, there remains a great mass of ignorance and illiteracy accompanied by a low standard of morality among the negro population, and there also remain the prejudices of race and caste which operate as an irritant, and which obstruct and impair, in a measure, the perfectly just and impartial administration of the criminal jurisprudence of the State. The criminal laws of the State are perfectly just, and entirely equal and impartial in all their terms, in respect to the two races; and the judges, without exception, in their rulings and decisions, act with impartiality, though the verdicts of the juries in criminal cases are not always responsive to the justice of the case. Offences against property are not more numerous in Mississippi than in other States, and the civil laws in respect to private property rights are generally administered by the courts and juries with justice and impartiality between the races. It may be fairly asserted that property and property rights of every kind are generally protected as effectually as in other States, and a healthy public opinion prevails in the State in respect to this subject, and public sentiment is steadily advancing to a higher appreciation of the value of human life.

Conflicts between the races have happily ceased to occur. A far better feeling prevails between the whites and the blacks, and a just recognition of personal rights is gradually but steadily suppressing a former spirit of lawlessness. I can perceive no reason why, under the continued and steady pressure of this improving public sentiment, the race question should not gradually and finally cease to operate upon or affect the administration of the criminal laws of the State. When the magnitude of the upheaval of the social and political elements of the South that followed the emancipation and political enfranchisement of the slave population is considered, and the turbulence, public disorders, and bloodshed that unhappily marked the period of reconstruction is remembered, the present condition of public affairs in Mississippi is far from unsatisfactory. As the result of these periods of disorder, there naturally followed a marked increase of crimes of a homicidal nature, as is shown by the statistics of the State Penitentiary. Thus in the year 1879, in a prison population of 997, there were 247 convicts under sentence for murder, manslaughter, and homicidal assaults. In 1881 the total number of convicts was 876, and the number of this class of crimes was 237. Again in 1883, in a total of 763, there were 205 cases of this class. The following later statistics indicate the persistent continuance of this form of crime. Thus in the year 1890, in a prison population of 485, there were in the aggregate 219 convicts under sentence of imprisonment for murder, manslaughter, and homicidal assault. In the year 1891, in a total of 543 convicts, 268 were under sentence for these crimes. In the year 1892, in a total of 601, there were 272 convicts sentenced for these crimes; while in 1893 the total prison population was

767, with 334 convicts under sentence for these homicidal offences. The white and black convicts are shown in the following proportions: In the year 1890, whites 50 and negroes 435; in 1891, whites 54, negroes 489; in 1892, whites 47, and negroes 533; in 1893, whites 120, while there were 647 negro convicts.

During the year 1893, as shown by the records of the Supreme Court of the State, there were appeals from convictions in twenty-six murder cases, ten of manslaughter and nine of homicidal assaults, making a total of forty-five convictions by juries for homicidal offences which were reviewed by the Supreme Court. Of the murder cases nine were convictions of white men, and in the manslaughter cases one-half were white offenders. The proportion or percentage of crime is very much larger with the negroes than the whites, as will appear from the relative population of the two races. The whole population of the State, as shown by the Census of 1890, is 1,289,600, of which 544,851 are whites, and 747,749 are negroes. The relative proportions of crime show one negro convict for every 1,155 of negro population, and one white convict to every 4,540 of white population.

The period embracing the years 1875 and 1876, and perhaps 1877, exhibited a high percentage of crime. The State-prison register of the year 1877 showed a total of 1,012 convicts in the state prison, and in the year 1878 the number had increased to 1,056, the blacks largely predominating. In October, 1893, the date of the last prison report, the total number of convicts was 767. This decrease in the prison population indicates a decrease in crime, and the increase in the number of white convicts from 50 in the year 1890, to 120 in the year 1893, in my judgment, is an evidence that the law is being more effectually enforced against white offenders. Both of these indications are unquestionably in the right direction.

. . . There are occasional instances of lynching of negroes charged with the offence of criminal assault upon white women. But the instinct that prompts this form of lawlessness is not peculiar to the white race of the South, though for obvious reasons it is more frequent than in the Northern States. It is a mistake, however, to suppose that lynching is not the exception, for the prison reports show that for the year 1890 there were thirty-one convicts under sentence for this crime; in 1891 there were twenty-eight under like sentence; in 1892 there were twenty-five of such convicts; and in 1893 there were twenty-seven convicts under sentence for this crime. These statistics show clearly that ordinarily the law takes its proper course in the punishment of this most infamous of crimes, and that the lynching of the offenders is the exception, and not the rule.

The complete eradication of what is commonly termed lynch law, especially in this class of offences, has been found in all the States of the American Union a difficult, if not an impossible, task. It is obviously more difficult of treatment in the large negro populations of the South than in white communities. The death penalty has been imposed by the statutes of the State for this offence, and under the influence of this penalty I think there has been a decrease in the commission of this crime, and as the effect of an improving public sentiment there is a more general disposition to leave the trial and punishment of this class of offenders to the courts of the State. The remedies to be applied and the agencies to be employed in effecting a still further improvement in the enforcement of the law and the suppression of crime must flow naturally from the great moral forces that underlie our civilization. As the negro advances in intelligence his conceptions of the duties of citizenship will improve, and he will more distinctly and clearly perceive the duty of all members of society to obey the laws of the state. It is not above his comprehension to understand that his welfare and immunity from punishment, not to speak of his prosperity and advancement, depend upon his observance of the rights of others. He is steadily learning this lesson. On the other hand it is becoming clearer to the white race, that the highest condition of prosperity and improvement must finally rest upon a condition or basis involving the prosperity and contentment of the negroes, who form the great body of peasantry in the Southern States, for no country can be great or prosperous with an oppressed and discontented peasantry.

Mississippi, out of its slender resources, is spending over a million and a half dollars annually in public education, and educational facilities are provided for all the children of the State. Negro illiteracy is decreasing, and if the common-school system of public education is a potent agency in the suppression of crime, satisfactory results from this source may be confidently anticipated. Education of public thought finds its way quickly into the jury box, and improves the quality of verdicts in the just and impartial enforcement of the criminal laws. In a limited way, and as incidental to the main purpose, the technicalities of criminal law by which the guilty sometimes escape, and the delays of criminal procedure so favorable to the law-breakers, might be remedied, and a better jury system might be provided.

The white men of the South have dealt with those formidable conditions substantially as any other white men would have done. It may be fairly claimed for them that they have accomplished as much as any others in their place would have accomplished, and it may be conceded that they have probably committed as many errors. As it is, they have done their best, and the present condition of improvement is not unsatisfactory, in view of the magnitude of the undertaking. The most gratifying feature in the situation is that the trend of public thought and action is steadily in the direction of justice and fair dealing, while there is nothing in view to indicate retrogression. On the contrary, everything promises a continuance of the improvement in the relations between the races and the continued moral and material advancement of the people.

40 Lynch Law and the Emmett Till Case

Between 1874 and 1930 southern rural editors presented varying points of view in their weekly journals with almost monthly regularity. The following brief comments reflect most of the thoughts on this subject.

Terrible was his crime and terribly did he expiate it. But who will say his fate was not a just one? While the laws of Tennessee make highway robbery a capital and rape only a penitentiary offense, such scenes as that Friday night will be enacted. Public opinion, which is stronger than all law, sustains such proceedings and under the circumstances public opinion is not wrong.[1]

We are not in favor of lynch law as a general thing, but think that every case of rape should be met with instant death from the people. It will learn the blacks a lesson that naught else will—particularly where the case is of such an aggravating character as the one to which allusion is made above [a Negro had been charged with raping a young white girl]. Never in our lives have we seen so many accounts of rape by Negroes upon white ladies as in the past few weeks. Every paper is filled with accounts of them. Let our people make a determination to hang or *burn on the spot*, everyone caught in the act, and we guarantee it will put a quietus on it when nothing else will.[2]

[1] *Jackson* (Tennessee) *Whig and Tribune*, June 27, 1774.
[2] *Oglethorpe* (Georgia) *Echo*, September 3, 1875.

We do not think that white men will quit hanging black men until black men quit outraging white women. The law ought to be sustained, but public sentiment is to a law what the ground under a house is to the superstructure. The public sentiment is not part of the law, the ground is not part of the house, but neither law nor house can stand on nothing.[3]

Lee Walle, a Negro, assaulted a white woman in Memphis one day this week, and the dusky Lee has since climbed the golden stairs by the rope route. It is an unwritten law in Mississippi and the South that rape means rope and this law will continue as unchangeable as the laws of the Medes and the Persians. As long as black brutes continue to lay hands on the fair women of the South, just so long will mob law obtain.[4]

We prefer that the law be allowed to deal with such cases, but so long as disgraceful, heathenish scenes enacted at the burning of Sam Hose are not re-enacted, we shall not go out of our way to censure the mob.[5]

The practice of lynching, with two possible exceptions, last took place on August 28, 1955, in Tallahatchie County, Mississippi. Emmett Till, a fourteen-year-old Chicago Negro boy was said to have been kidnapped and murdered by Ray Bryant and J. W. Milan, white men. Till was accused of having "wolf whistled" at the wife of one of the men. A mutilated body was recovered from the Tallahatchie River, but there was a question about positive identification of the corpse, although Till's mother said it was her son's body.

The two white men were brought to trial in September 1955, and on the 23rd of that month were acquitted by an all white male jury, even though Bryant and Milan admitted to kidnapping the boy. This kidnapping and murder, and the miscarriage of justice at the hands of the jury received world-wide newspaper coverage. Quickly the name Till became synonymous with brutality and murder. These editorials, drawn from four southern newspapers, reflect the public anger aroused by the incident.

[3] *Whig and Tribune,* September 12, 1875.
[4] *Ackerman* (Mississippi) *Choctaw Plaindealer,* July 28, 1893.
[5] *Greensboro* (Georgia) *Herald,* July 29, 1899.

ATLANTA CONSTITUTION

In Sumner, Miss., a 14-year-old Negro boy afflicted physically (and some suggested mentally) by polio, was killed.

Reportedly his lynching, or murder (a matter of semantics), resulted from his "wolf whistle" or "insulting remarks" directed at the wife of a community storekeeper.

Apparently there was no immediate action. Some three days afterwards he was taken from the home of his uncle and killed.

The two men charged with this killing now have been acquitted. The sheriff testified they had admitted abducting the boy. But there were no witnesses to the death.

The prosecution conducted a vigorous case. It was obvious Mississippi was stirred. The lynching, or murder, was brutal. A boy had been killed for an act for which a boy of another color would have been whipped or reprimanded. The state's prosecutors valiantly and honestly sought a conviction.

The jury, summoned by due process, declared the defendants not guilty. That's that. But some person, or persons, are guilty.

The burden remains with Mississippi and with the conscience of the people of the county or counties involved.

Someone killed a 14-year-old boy. He would not have been killed had it not been for his color.

What will Mississippi and Sumner do about it so that the Communists of Russia and of China may not say that in our country the law means one thing for one person and another thing for another?

This crime, unhappily, is known the world around. Unfortunately, the verdict will not conclude the case.

Someone, or some persons, are guilty. That's an uncomfortable fact.

The burden still rests on Mississippi.

WINSTON-SALEM JOURNAL

The acquittal of the two white men in Sumner, Mississippi, in the slaying of a young Negro boy last month was not unexpected, Nor were the cries of "shameful and "shocking" that followed the verdict.

The jury trial is the essence of justice in the English-speaking world. It has been devised through centuries of trial and error, and today it stands as one of the finest achievements of civilized man. But it is not perfect, for man is not perfect, nor are his accomplishments. There are times when the jury trial leads to the wrong verdict. The Sumner jury may be guilty of miscarriage of justice. The best judge of that will be someone who was present throughout the trial, not someone who read about the trial hundreds or thousands of miles away.

If there has been a miscarriage of justice in Mississippi, as some believe, then that is a terrible thing. But more terrible, and something that emotions raised by the outcome of the trial should not obscure, is the existence in this country of a state of mind that makes it possible, even easy, for a teen-aged boy to be kidnapped and murdered, whatever his alleged offense may have been. There were indications that this attitude was a thing of the past. The murder of young Emmett Till is evidence to the contrary, and that is frightening. In the days ahead, as the South tries to work out some difficult problems, we will all do well to remember they can best be solved in an atmosphere of co-operation and good will. Violence, such as flared in Mississippi last month, solves nothing. It only makes things worse. It can wipe out the slow gains of years. It must not be permitted to happen.

CHATTANOOGA TIMES

. . . No one could justly condemn the State of Mississippi for the crime. But once the crime was committed, it became Mississippi's duty to carry the case to a final conclusion. The case was not ended with the acquital of Bryant and Milan of murder. What happened to Emmett Till is the unanswered question which will plague Mississippi and the South until it is answered.

The preceding editorials were reprinted in the *New South* 10 (October 1955), 10–11.

The judge and prosecuting staff have even been commended by the NAACP for their conduct during the trial. The Negro press correspondents at the trial signed a memorandum warmly praising the judge. The community is also to be commended. Although all who had anything to do with the trial were said to have received floods of letters reeking of racial antagonism, none of this was in evidence around the courthouse. . . .

Many questions remain unanswered, however, and this uncertainty suits the purposes of Communists and the type of agitators who foment hatred for the South. Propaganda feeds on such grim mysteries.

No one expects Till to show up alive. The jury, with its "reasonable doubt" might have been shocked into unconsciousness if the Negro boy had suddenly appeared alive in the courtroom as the verdict was being delivered. Evidently the Chicago boy has been murdered and Mississippi should not rest until the mystery is cleared. The kidnapping was a crime, the murder would have been monstrous.

"What happened to 14-year-old Emmett Till?" will be asked time and time again. And until it is answered, we of the South can only admit that Emmett Till is a damaging symbol—another skeleton in the South's closet.

RICHMOND TIMES-DISPATCH

With 14-year-old Emmett Till admittedly kidnapped by two white men, and with no trace of him found thereafter—according to the defense version which was accepted by the jury—the case is having wide repercussions.

It is bound to raise in many minds the question whether there is one law in the South for Negroes and another for whites.

The only basis on which the South can hope to support arguments in behalf of the "separate but equal" doctrine is on a basis of absolute fair treatment for the Negro.

This case would look a lot better at the bar of public opinion if somebody would give a plausible identification of the body found in the Tallahatchie if, in fact, it is not that of Emmett Till.

PART 6

The Segregation Rationale

In the beginning of the uneasy decade that opened this century James Kimball Vardaman of Mississippi put into angry phrases the sentiments of white supremacists all across the South. A master of trans-illiteration, but thoroughly incapable of using subtleties, Vardaman was blunt and bruising in stating his racial views. To him the Negro was intellectually and physically inferior to the white man. Throughout the history of man the Negro had remained a dawdler in the morasses of savagery and ignorance.[1] Rivaling his contemporary Benjamin Tillman of South Carolina, the Mississippian spread intense hatred of the Negro all across his state.

Succeeding to Vardaman's mantle in later years, Theodore G. Bilbo continued to utter the bitterest sorts of tirades against the Negro. Proclaiming him inferior when measured by any standard, both Vardaman and Bilbo found in the defenseless black an excellent instrument for fanning sentiments in their political campaigns. Bilbo put himself on semi-permanent record in his book, *Take Your Choice*. In a chapter entitled "The Dangers of Amalgamation" he "scientifically" substantiated his views by generously quoting self-styled anthropologists and social scien-

---

[1] Harris Dickson, "The Vardaman Idea," *The Saturday Evening Post*, April 27, 1907, CLXXIX, 3–5.

tists who supplied him with ideas. There was no doubt in his
mind that Negroes were incapable of building a culture for
themselves, or that Negroes had behind them no meaningful
history.[2]

Where Vardaman and Bilbo revealed their hatred of the Negro in plain language, other, and more pious critics sought biblical support for their views. The Reverend G. T. Gillespie of
Jackson, Mississippi, for instance, revived the whole scriptural
arguments advanced by pro-slavery ministers in the decades
immediately before the Civil War.[3] The White Citizens
Councils gave wide publicity to these timeworn arguments.
Private pamphleteers also promulgated similar concepts.

Obviously there was little relationship between the views of
the racial extremists and the social and economic realities in the
South. Southerners less interested in prejudicial abstractions
than in the advancement of their region answered their neighbors in various ways. Practical-minded state officials and businessmen spoke in economic terms. Writers like William Faulkner refuted the Vardamans and Bilbos by citing more serious
threats to civilization by racial discrimination. Nevertheless
southern congressmen served the past as though the ghostly
hands of Vardaman and Bilbo directed their actions, when they
attempted to frustrate passage of civil rights legislation in the
1960s, and as late as 1968 George Corley Wallace of Alabama
threatened to make a national issue of racial and sectional
difficulties.[4]

[2] Theodore G. Bilbo, *Take Your Choice,* 198–241.
[3] Clement Eaton, *A History of the Old South* (New York: Macmillan,
1949), 384–388.
[4] *Congressional Record,* July 13, 1956, 12760–12761.

41 The Vardaman Idea

No Southerner, not even Pitchfork Ben Tillman of South Carolina, stirred so much bitter hatred of the Negro as did James Kimball Vardaman of Mississippi. In his campaign speeches in small rural Mississippi towns he often influenced his listeners to commit outrageous acts against Negro citizens. But like all the racists and demagogues, Vardaman had his apologists. In the following document, first published in *The Saturday Evening Post*, Harris Dickson, the novelist and short story writer, presented the "Vardaman Idea" to the American public. He discussed about all of the excuses for racial discrimination that the segregationists have ever advanced. Beyond this Dickson related the "Vardaman Idea" to the wisdom of ancient peoples as well as to the philosophy of Abraham Lincoln, Louis Agassiz, the Koran, and Freud. In his tirades against the Negro, Governor Vardaman insisted he was only saying what Thomas Jefferson, Lincoln, and the others would have said had they lived in Mississippi in 1907.

"VARDAMANISM!" "DEMAGOGIC APPEALS!" "NEGROPHOBIA!" By these and like expressions the Governor of Mississippi is frequently pointed out as the Apostle of the Rabid Idea. College professors, highly educated and unco-wise, accord to him the unique distinction of originating a new creed.

Harris Dickson, "The Vardaman Idea," *The Saturday Evening Post* 179 (April 27, 1907), 3–5.

James K. Vardaman must smile guiltily at all of this, must wonder how long the deception can last, how long it will be before his rank plagiarism will be discovered and himself unmasked as a mere believer in the repetitions of history.

Here is the Vardaman Idea—a very simple matter, after all. It does not take two men and a boy to comprehend it:

> The negro should never have been trusted with the ballot. He is different from the white man. He is congenitally unqualified to exercise the most responsible duty of citizenship. He is physically, mentally, morally, racially and eternally the white man's inferior. There is nothing in the history of his race, nothing in his individual character, nothing in his achievements of the past nor his promise for the future which entitles him to stand side by side with the white man at the ballot-box.
>
> This inestimable privilege was thrust upon the negro snatching him out of his twenty thousand barbaric years and placing him shoulder to shoulder with the heir of all the ages. This was a stupendous blunder, worse than any crime, and the sober second thought of the nation should correct it.
>
> We must repeal the Fifteenth and modify the Fourteenth Amendment to the Constitution of the United States. Then we shall be able in our legislation to recognize the negro's peculiarities, and make laws to fit them. This would leave the matter precisely as was intended by the fathers of the Republic.

This is what Vardaman says, and a vast number of patriotic citizens who are standing face to face with the sordid problem think practically the same thing. . . .

Under present conditions the negro rarely comes in direct competition with the white man, either North or South. At the North this is because there are so few negroes in proportion to the total population—even these few being in most cases barred from trades unions and like organizations.

In the South the negro was formerly well under control; he is now drifting rapidly from all control; yet he cannot be reckoned the white man's rival. The white mechanic and farmer work side by side with him in peace.

Should the negro be forced upon his own resources into competition with whites, he must stand or fall by the natural law of survivorship. If he cannot survive he must die. Such is nature's law. It is a matter of common knowledge that no like race has ever been able to survive in competition with the whites.

The negro's greatest safety and greatest happiness require that he should be spared a battle which gives no quarter. Should that competition come into the trades, it means that the white man, because of superior competency and intelligence, will demand the best places and the best wages; in commerce the white man will outwit him, in politics control him, in war annihilate him. . . .

His sole place in history is the one accorded him by his enterprising neighbor—a driven slave sculptured upon the resting-place of kings.

Left alone, contented in his jungle, he had progressed backward and become a feeder upon human flesh, a polygamist, without religion, family ties or morals. He was the inventor and promulgator of slavery, the patentee and proprietor of cannibalism—these being the twin institutions which he had contributed to human progress.

The Egyptians observed these traits of the negro which had kept him at a standstill, and promptly assigned the reason. Oddly enough, it is the same reason given by Lincoln, Stanley, Livingstone, Vardaman et al. ad infinitum—"the skull of the negro is different. They had the elongated skull, the low, prominent forehead, hollow temples, thick lips, broad shoulders, salient breast, undeveloped lower part of the body"—all minutely described by careful hands which now repose as mummies in royal mausoleums beside the Nile.

Modern science teaches that the sutures in the skulls of the Caucasian races remain open and loosely jointed until the late maturity of manhood, thus giving the white man's brain an opportunity to expand into highest possible development of mental power. With the African these sutures close at a comparatively early period in youth; the skull becomes permanently ossified, of extraordinary thickness—well-nigh impermeable. There is little difference between children of the two races. It is no uncommon thing to see a negro child that is exceedingly bright, learning with ease. But nature seems to have said: "Thus far shalt thou learn, and no further." Development beyond a certain point seems to be absolutely forbidden by the physical, the purely mechanical, structure of his skull. Possibly the Egyptians knew all these details, possibly not; but they did say "his skull is different."

Curiously enough, we find these early Egyptians deploring the evil effect upon their race caused by an admixture of negro blood. It seems uncanny in this twentieth century of grace to hear this faraway protest against miscegenation, and to reflect how little human-kind has changed. . . .

The black man reappeared in history again and again, but only as an article of unholy commerce. Virginia enacted the first recorded laws in restraint of the slave trade, which were promptly vetoed by successive Kings of England.

The American Colonies won their independence. A second war was fought, and the white man freed the black.

Throughout these sixty turbulent centuries the negro knew nothing of history. He had contributed nothing to the onward march, and gained nothing from it. All the peoples of the world had blazoned their names upon the great book of the world's events—all save one.

Humankind passed through sixty centuries of bloodshed, convulsion and tutelage—the leaven to make it wise and free. But all these centuries of change left no impress upon the stolid and changeless negro. Immutable as the graven sphinx he stood stock-still, wondering at these restless nations who dreamed their glittering dreams, beyond his comprehension. Of all created things he alone escaped the universal uplifting, the world-wide betterment. As he was in the beginning, so is he now. For six thousand years he had bred and multiplied in his jungle. That was all.

Upon many obelisks of ancient Egypt the pen and inkstand are oft-repeated hieroglyphics. Six thousand years later the negro is disfranchised in Mississippi because he cannot read or write. Descriptions of him to-day by such explorers as Stan-

Icy, Livingstone, DuChaillu are but repetitions of what the Egyptians wrote upon their papyrus scrolls. Mr. Charles Francis Adams, in the *Century Magazine*, after a visit to Africa, abandons all previous theories which he had so ably advanced. He tells the same story of hopeless barbarism, and urges that a difference be made in our fundamental law to fit the negro's limitations. This is Vardaman's position to a T.

When the strong hand which controls the negro relaxes its grasp, like the released plummet, he drops by sheer force of gravity into his natural level. The wild horse of Texas must be kept under saddle and constantly reminded of the compulsory civilization to which he is subject. Slip his halter for a moment only and he is again the bucking bronco, "a branded hide full o' hell," as madly resentful of harness as if leather had never touched his back. Let him taste an hour of freedom, and he must be captured, broken and civilized again.

When French restraint in Hayti and San Domingo was removed the negro returned to barbarism at once. His rapid reversion in Liberia is "as natural as the return of the sow that is washed to her wallowing in the mire," to quote Professor Barringer.

The Congo native has not advanced an inch in civilization from contact with the Portuguese; in Senegal he has gained nothing of the French; Cecil Rhodes built an Empire at the Cape—and the naked negro is still the servant of them all. There must be a reason for this. In no place upon the broad globe has he met a more kindly protection, better teaching and a more tolerant charity for his invincible limitations than in the Southern States of America. These people have taught him all he knows.

It is very clear that by himself and of himself the negro has no aspirations. Where all of his neighbors live in mud huts and feed upon human flesh, huts and fat friends are good enough for him. He is imitative, but his imitation does not reach the basic virtues of his model.

In isolated instances this imitation may succeed to all external appearance. But beneath the skin remains the changeless savage, without real foundation upon which to build cultured and moral gentlemen as judged by Anglo-Saxon standards. . . .

The present negro population of Africa is estimated at double the entire population of the United States—without semblance of civilization, not a schoolhouse, not a newspaper, not a law. The door of hope has rusted on its hinges for lack of a hand to open it.

Such is the phylogeny, the life-history, of the negro race, unbroken generations of barbarism which have fixed their characteristics indelibly upon him. Our American negroes for the most part came from the West Coast; they are Guinea blacks, the easy prey and hereditary bondmen of other slave nations. All historians and explorers agree in assigning to them the lowest position in the scale of Equatorial Africa—except that of the Bushman. Travelers and missionaries to-day describe in most revolting terms these negroes at home. They are naked cannibals, selling their own flesh and blood when they do not eat it, precisely what the Afro-American voter would be had he been left to his own devices. And this is the type to which, from all historical evidence, these same Afro-American voters would speedily revert if the enforced civilization of the white man were suddenly removed. Instances of this reversion might be indefinitely quoted upon the highest authority. Why should the negro revert? Because he has not been long enough out of his natural state to create for himself a second nature strong enough to overcome the first. Twenty thousand years of jungle habit cannot be eradicated in a day.

With him there has been no voluntary transition. Left to himself he has never done anything for himself—has never shown the slightest inclination to better his condition. Redpath says: "The black peoples of Nigritian stock do not choose to exert themselves beyond the range of purely natural wants."

To this the writer must add his personal testimony as to present conditions, based upon intimate knowledge of the negro, and twenty years' experience in criminal courts. If the plain truth were told it would shock a sensitive world more deeply than all the harrowing stories of the slave ships. The negro is not immoral, he is simply unmoral. As Froude says of him, "He never felt the guilt of sin."

None of these delinquencies draws upon the negroes the disapproval of their own people. There is no punishment of any kind, no loss of social prestige, no frown, no inconvenience. Serving a term in the penitentiary is often regarded as a badge of aristocracy. One negro will say of another: "Better let dat nigger alone; dat's a bad nigger; he's been in the pentenshiarry seven times." He who wins the homage wears it.

All of this being true, unquestionably, undeniably true, is, or is not, the negro different from the white man? The Egyptian thought so; Lincoln said so; Vardaman maintains it.

Their social condition is accepted as a matter of course throughout the South; it causes no comment, and the laws in that regard are not pretended to be enforced. To enforce these laws would fill the prisons and empty the fields. It is a common thing to see a family of brothers and sisters in three or four different shades. No lady ever inquires into the personal character of her servant—she dare not.

When our Anglo-Saxon ancestors ran wild in the northern forests they were men of clean lives—one husband, one wife. The family was the unit out of which they built their government. Upon the purity of their hearthstones and the sanctity of their homes they cemented the foundations of a granite empire.

No white man ever falls so low or becomes so lost to decency that he forgets the first few years of his life. His teachings at a gentle mother's knee and the guidance of a respected father abide with him forever.

It is a melancholy fact that the negro, as a race, has none of these. When the young negro goes forth into the world—God pity him!—he has no such anchorage to hold him steady in the storm. Herein lies the vital essence of the negro problem.

For instance, take a negro boy from Mississippi, send him to the public schools and the high schools; then some philanthropist, perhaps, pays his tuition at Harvard, gives him an education, a bulldog, a silk hat and patent-leather shoes. What can that make of him with such a home behind him and such an instinct within himself? It is quite impossible to make gentlemen by veneer.

The negro cannot be remodeled by beginning at the ballot, the highest duty of citizenship, and then working downward. The cleansing process must begin in his home, in his private character, at the elemental duties, and work upward. Schooling may sharpen his intellect, but it does not make character.

White men have earned preeminence by centuries of struggle. They possess rights and duties to-day which it would have been impossible for them to comprehend a thousand years ago. Nations and individuals are alike; they must grow by their own efforts, or the growth is flabby. The body must be strengthened by physical exercise, each man for himself. No man can take exercises for another. The white man cannot, by law, confer his own instincts, his genius for government, his capacity and power of comprehension upon the negro.

Unable as he is to control himself, the negro is singularly tractable and amenable to control by his well recognized superiors. For this reason the Egyptians, Romans and Turks paid higher prices for them than for other slaves. They never fretted in captivity; it was their natural state.

The negro throve and attained his highest development in slavery. Transplanted to a new country, where the climate suited him, where he was not raided, massacred and eaten, he multiplied like imported rabbits in Australia. During slavery their children were well cared for, and there was a wonderful increase. But since freedom came, this has been checked by the frightful mortality among their infants. Men and women alike lead such irregular lives that new diseases, utterly unknown before the war, sweep them off like sheep. Since the war the percentage of black insane in Mississippi, as compared with whites, has increased four hundred per cent. Tuberculosis, formerly unknown, is now extremely common.

The fathers of the present generation were better men than their sons—healthier, more reliable, more industrious. There were better artisans and mechanics among the slaves than among free men to-day. Young negroes are idler, more vicious, and have been educated into six hundred per cent, more criminality.

Left to his own devices, the negro produces only twenty-seven per cent of the cotton crop, despite the popular idea that he makes it all. The English president of a Southern railway system once told the writer that for twenty years they had been gradually eliminating negroes from all positions of responsibility where negligence would cause loss of life or property. These are facts, open, notorious facts, which no man can gainsay.

The South has had its bitter dose of negro voters. We took it not in a sugar-coated pill, nor in a capsule, but straight. Negroes governed the country for eight years after the war, and increased the war debts fivefold. Four years of unparalleled war left the Southern States with an average debt of seven millions; negro rule in eight years of profound peace and abject poverty multiplied these debts to an average of thirty-four millions. War is less expensive than peace under negro domination.

Vardaman knows these things; we all know them. The Vardaman Idea is growing. It is an accepted fact in the South—although there are differences of opinion as to its present expediency. It is being whispered by politicians of both parties in the Border States, under their breath, for the negro wields the balance of power. Lifelong Republicans in Maryland have been driven temporarily into Democratic ranks upon this issue—the ligament which binds the solid South. [. . . .]

Vardaman is six feet, black-haired, erect as an Indian, wide-hatted, white-cravated, stalwart and picturesque. A man of intensive personality, he says what he thinks, and says it in unmistakable English. Then he backs it up with all the might that in him lies.

His propensity for speaking out in meeting without regard for diplomacy has kept him on the fighting-line all his life. But Vardaman would be happy nowhere else.

Before the Spanish War he was editing a newspaper at Greenwood, Mississippi. He preached intervention. Then he deemed it his duty to help fight the war he had advocated. Leaving wife and family, he enlisted as a private in the First Mississippi Volunteers. A neighboring company elected him captain, but the Governor of Mississippi refused to commission him. His indignant company wanted to disband, but Vardaman held them together and forced the election of another leader. He immediately reënlisted in the Fifth U.S. Volunteers of yellow fever immunes, although himself not immune. The situation at fever-stricken Santiago was so desperate that Colonel Roosevelt and other officers, in the famous round-robin, said if they were not taken out of there they would die. Vardaman, with the Fifth Immunes, was sent to relieve them. A few months after his arrival in Cuba he was appointed Major. [. . . .]

After ten months in Cuba, Vardaman returned to Mississippi, ran for Governor, and was defeated. Four years later he was elected.

There has never been a Governor in the South who has striven more earnestly to protect negroes. He has pardoned more negroes than white men. He broke up the White Cap organization, and sent many of them to the penitentiary for outrages upon negroes.

On one occasion a lynching was threatened in a distant county. Vardaman rushed to the scene on a special train, and personally brought the negro back to Jackson, where he would be safe until the day of trial. This is only one instance. There are many others. His administration of State affairs has been scrupulously honest and successful; even his enemies concede that much.

The necessity for the repeal of the Fifteenth Amendment is not so much for the protection of the white man against the encroachment of the black man as it is to protect the black man against inevitable destruction by the white man. If we undertake to adjust the white man's civilization to the negro it lifts him to a condition and atmosphere in which he cannot live, any more than a fish can live out of the water. Neither can we draw the white man down to his level. Therefore, we have got to make laws for the utterly distinct moral and intellectual requirements of the respective races. Thomas Jefferson saw that more than a hundred years ago. Abraham Lincoln realized it fifty years ago. Every observant man in the South knows and feels it to-day.

42 The Vardaman Idea Brought up to Date

Theodore G. Bilbo was a lineal philosophical descendant of James K. Vardaman. In his book, *Take Your Choice,* he cleverly selected sources that gave his writing the color of authority for the undiscriminating reader. In this particular chapter he turned anthropologist and proved to his own satisfaction that the Negro was inferior as measured by any conceivable standard of physical nature or accomplishments. His arguments were old ones, but his message came at the moment when the South was being aroused by post-World War II racial demands. Thus Bilbo's ideas were widely circulated by speeches and publicity. There is, however, no way of knowing how many people read his book, or how many segregationists now know of its existence.

At this point, it should be pointed out that no attempt will be made here to reconcile the different theories as to the origin of the races of mankind. We leave the reader to his own conclusions concerning the plan which was used by the Creator of the Heavens and the Earth in creating and separating the different races. The fact that God did ordain the division of the people of the earth into separate races as a part of the Divine plan is sufficient for our purpose. We do not know that for thou-

Theodore G. Bilbo, *Take Your Choice* (Poplarville, Mississippi: Dream House Pub. Co., 1947), 82–93.

sands of years, the races have been constituted practically as they are today and grouped into three great divisions: the white, the yellow, and the black. We also know that from the dawn of history the different races have left a record of their accomplishments and achievements upon the pages of time, and from the chronicle we can compare their qualities, abilities, and their contributions to the progress of mankind.

. . . we found that all the great civilizations of the world have been produced by the white race. Could this have been accidental? Over thousands of years, north, south, east, and west, everywhere, under all conditions, Caucasian man has manifested his conquering, victorious qualities. Throughout the years, history records no achievements of the Negro race which challenge in any manner whatsoever the superiority of the culture and civilization of the white man.

. . . The history of civilization and culture, is the history of the Caucasian race. Great and glorious cities, monuments, and Coliseums, amphitheatres and cathedrals, empires and nations have testified to the ability of the white man. He has bridged the rivers, spanned the oceans, conquered continents, and built mighty civilizations out of the wildernesses. Great men, world leaders, brilliant minds that have mastered things material and spiritual, all the endless creations of art, science, literature, law, religion, and of every activity known to man blaze across the pages of history to give evidence of the superior ability of the white race. It was by the white man's brain that the atoms of creation were split and the atomic bomb became the greatest power on earth.

The negro has had just as long as the white man to develop a civilization of his own. Thousands and tens of thousands of years have passed, and the black man has not lifted his people from the darkness of Africa. If the white and black races are equal in ability, then why have they not produced equal civilizations? Or why has not the African exhibited his ability to reproduce civilization and culture after the way has been blazed for him? It is a matter of historical truth that no Negro race has ever initiated a civilization and "only when it is mixed with some other can it even be initiated into one." This may well be said to be the real reason why the American Negro is feverishly and unrelentingly demanding the integration of his kind into every phase of the white man's civilization—in the churches and schools, in politics and government, in the army and navy, and in the air. The only known request that he has not made is for the permission to help handle the atomic bomb! He is afraid of that "bug"!

There were some American Negroes who were repatriated by the American Colonization Society to West Africa and established the Republic of Liberia in 1847. However, they have provided us with no startling revelations of the black man's ability because even in the creation of the Liberian Republic the Negroes adopted almost in toto the Constitution of the United States. The only noted changes which they made in adopting the American Constitution for their form and scheme of government were two amendments: (1) an amendment to provide specifically that no white man should ever vote in the Republic of Liberia, (2) an amendment to provide that no white man should ever own a foot of land in Liberia. This second provision, however, does not prevent the leasing of the lands of Liberia to traders, merchants, and manufacturers.

The accomplishments of the white and black races in world history prove without a shadow of a doubt the inequality of the two races. "Wherefore by their fruit ye shall know them." The white man has shown his superior ability by the great civilizations and cultures which he has created.

White Americans who have built the civilization of the new world are the descendants of the white men who created the civilization of Europe. Whether a descendant of the Nordic or Mediterranean or Alpine branch of the white race, the white man in America can look back with pride at the accomplishments of his racial family. "Every human being unites in himself the blood of thousands of ancestors, stretching back through thousands of years," and the white man has a right to be proud of his world-conquering Caucasian blood.

. . . Historically and scientifically, the inferiority of the Negro race when compared to the white race is both a proved and obvious fact. It is wholly unnecessary to compile statistics and opinions of distinguished physicians and ethnologists who classify the Negro as inferior to the Caucasian. The following quotations from the works of Dr. Robert B. Bean are typical of the conclusions of scholars who have studied the Negro race:

> The frontal region of the Negro skull has been repeatedly shown to be much smaller than that of the Caucasian. Considering this fact, the conclusion is reached that the Negro has a smaller proportion of the faculties pertaining to the frontal lobe than the Caucasian. The Negro, then, lacks reason, judgment, apperception, affection, self-control, will power, orientation, ethical and esthetic attributes, and the relation of the ego (of personality or self) to environment.
>
> The conclusion is that the brain of the Negro is smaller than the brain of the white, the stature is also lower, and the body weight is less, and any crossing of the two races results in a brain weight relative to the proportion of white blood in the individual.
>
> The skull capacity of the Negro has been repeatedly demonstrated to be less than that of the Caucasian.*

From the beginning of time down to the present day, the Negro race has been weighed in the scales and found wanting. Although those who are advocating complete equality for the whites and blacks in the United States claim that "a modern science" supports their demands, neither this argument nor their shouts against what they call "racial prejudice" can refute facts and logic. The chief points which are characteristic of the Negro race may be listed as follows:

1. The abnormal length of the arm, which on the average exceeds that of the Caucasian by about two inches.

2. The projection of the jaws and the facial angle which is about 70 as compared with 82 for the Caucasian.

3. Weight of the brain, which indicates cranial capacity of 35 ounces, as compared with 20 for the highest gorilla and 45 for the Caucasian.

* William P. Pickett, *The Negro Problem; Abraham Lincoln's Solution* (New York: Putnam's Sons, 1909), 10–11.

4. Full black eye, with black iris and yellowish sclerotic coat.

5. Short flat snub nose with dilated nostrils and concave ridge.

6. Thick protruding lips, plainly showing the inner red surface.

7. High and prominent cheek bones.

8. Exceedingly thick cranium, enabling the Negro to butt with the head and resist blows which would break any ordinary European skull.

9. Correspondingly weak lower limbs with a broad flat foot with low instep and heel projecting backwards.

10. Deep brown or blackish complexion which is in some cases distinctly black.

11. Short, black hair, elliptical or almost flat in section and distinctly woolly.

12. Thick skin, mostly hairless, and emitting a peculiar rancid odor.

13. Frame of medium height, thrown somewhat out of the perpendicular by the shape of the pelvis, the spine, and the backward projection of the head.

14. Cranial sutures, which close much earlier than in the other races and thus seem to arrest the growth of the brain at an earlier age.

The Negroes in the United States have been citizens for some eighty years. During this time, they have advanced and made notable progress, but they have accomplished nothing which will refute the age-old proof of the inferiority of the Negro race in comparison to the Caucasian.

. . . We are fully aware that there are different theories being currently publicized as to the reason for the inferiority of the Negro race. However, whether this status is the result of a natural and inherent inferiority never to be overcome or whether it is caused, as sometimes contended, by the fact that the Negro is a backward race, thousands of years behind the white man in civilization and culture, the practical result is the same. If inequality and inferiority exist, then the doctrine of the equality of the races is absolutely false. And if this theory is unfounded and untrue, then the proponents of racial equality have no basis upon which to argue that the blacks should be given full equality with the whites in this country, including the right of intermarriage.

We hear much about the so-called equality of the races from certain Negroes who seek to defy the laws of God and man in order to mix and mingle and intermarry with white people, but we seldom hear them express any gratitude to white Americans and particularly to Southern white Americans for what has been done for the Negro in America. The slave traffic may have been evil and horrible and the institution of slavery may have been wrong; nevertheless, slavery in America definitely left the Negro in a better condition than it found him. The savage, cannibalistic, barbarian Negro slaves were fed, clothed, civilized, and taught Christianity.

. . . Environment has placed the American Negro in the midst of a great civilization produced by the white man, but neither environment nor education can change the basic traits and characteristics of the race to which the Negro in the United States belongs.

. . . There are certain mental, physical, and moral characteristics which belong to the Negro race. And these characteristics are thus attributed to the race which has never produced a great civilization in world history, and one which has produced very little indeed during the years of its existence in America. The most outstanding leaders which have come from the Negro race would have passed unnoticed if their skin had been white. They have been prominent in this country because they were Negroes.

WERE IT NOT FOR THE SUPER-SENSITIVE MONGRELS OF NORTH AMERICA, THERE WOULD BE NO CLAMOR FOR "EQUALITY" OF RACES; NOR WOULD THERE BE ANY EMINENT "NEGROES." BOOKER WASHINGTON WAS A MULATTO, FREDERICK DOUGLASS WAS A MULATTO. BRUCE, TURNER, DU BOIS, MILLER—THESE ARE NOT NEGROES! WERE THEY WHITE MEN THEY WOULD BE OBSCURE, BUT BY SOCIAL CUSTOM AND LAW THEY ARE RECOGNIZED TO BE NEGROES, AND AS SUCH THEY STAND AT THE HEAD OF THEIR RACE.

History and science refute the doctrine of the equality of the white and Negro races which is proclaimed by the proponents of racial equality in the United States today. There are inequalities and differences between the white and black races, and all the history of civilization affirms that the superior position belongs to the Caucasian. The Negroid writers and the negrophilists will continue to deny the facts of history and the findings of science for they are color-blind, but white America must realize these truths and accept them as a basis from which we must work to bring about an adequate and permanent solution to the Negro problem.

If any Negro reads this chapter and has just reason to think that he does not possess the inferior qualities of mind, body, and spirit which the greatest and most reliable scientists—students of the comparative qualities of the races—have pointed out, then let him thank God for that portion of white blood which flows through his veins because of the sin of miscegenation on the part of one or more of his ancestors.

43 A Christian View of Segregation

In the nineteenth century when the anti-slavery crusade was reaching a crescendo, Southerners turned to the Scriptures to find justification for owning slaves. This quest was repeated after 1954 when segregation was threatened by court decision. The compiler of the following scriptural references is unknown. This document was a propaganda sheet published and distributed by the Mississippi Citizens' Councils in 1955. However, some of the entries are the same ones that involved the Reverend G. T. Gillespie and Dr. Ernest Trist Thompson in a vigorous exchange of views over scriptural interpretations.[1] In this case implications are that God cursed Ham for his unseemly conduct in the presence of his father Noah. This was not so. God did not curse anyone. Rather it was Noah who did the cursing, and there is sound reason for questioning his sobriety at the time. The Citizens' Councils propagandist did not represent scriptural fact in once again offering the hoary old Biblical arguments that God meant the Negro to be inferior.[2]

THE OLD TESTAMENT

Genesis 1:25.   And God made the beast of the earth after his kind, and cattle after their kind, and

[1] The Thompson attack on Dr. Gillespie's views occurred in a Southern Presbyterian Assembly in 1955.
[2] "Is Segregation Unchristian?" Citizens' Council Collection, University of Kentucky Library.

	everything that creepeth upon the earth after his kind: and God saw that it was good.
Genesis 6.2.	That the sons of God saw the daughters of men that they were fair, and they took them wives of all which they chose.
Genesis 6:10.	And Noah begat three sons, Shem, Ham, and Japheth.
Genesis 9:22.	And Ham, the father of Canaan, saw the nakedness of his father, and told his two brethren without.
Genesis 9:24.	And Noah awoke from his wine, and knew what his younger son had done unto him.
Genesis 9:25.	And he said, cursed be Canaan a servant of servants shall he be unto his brethren.
Genesis 9:26.	And he said, blessed be the Lord God of Shem; and Canaan shall be his servant.
Genesis 9:27.	God shall enlarge Japheth, and he shall dwell in the tents of Shem; and Canaan shall be his servant.
Genesis 10:6.	And the sons of Ham; Cush, and Mizraim, and Canaan.
Genesis 10:20.	These are the sons of Ham, after their families, after their tongues, in their countries, and in their nations.
Genesis 11:6.	And the Lord said, Behold, the people is one, and they have all one language, and this they begin to do, and now nothing will be restrained from them, which they have imagined to do.
Genesis 11:7.	Go to, let us go down, and there confound their language, that they may not understand one another's speech.
Genesis 11:8.	So the Lord scattered them abroad from

G. T. Gillespie, *A Christian View of Segregation* (Winona, Mississippi, 1954).

thence upon the face of the earth; and they left off to build the city.

Genesis 11:9.
Therefore is the name of it called Babel; because the Lord did there confound the language of all the earth: and from thence did the Lord scatter them abroad upon the face of all the earth.

Genesis 15:1.
And he said unto Abram, know of a surety that thy seed shall be a stranger in the land that is not theirs; . . .

Genesis 24:3.
And I will make thee swear by the Lord, the God of heaven and the God of the earth, that thou shalt not take a wife unto my son of the daughters of the Canaanites, among whom I dwell.

Genesis 24:4.
But thou shalt go unto my country, and to my kindred, and take a wife unto my son Isaac.

Genesis 28:6
When Esau saw that Isaac had blessed Jacob, and sent him away to Padanaram, to take him a wife from thence; and that as he blessed him he gave him a charge, saying, Thou shalt not take a wife of the daughters of Canaan;

Genesis 28:7.
And that Jacob obeyed his father and his mother, and was gone to Padanaram.

Leviticus 19:19.
Ye shall keep my statutes. Thou shalt not let thy cattle gender with a diverse kind; thou shalt not sow thy field with mingled seed; neither shall a garment mingled of linen and woolen come upon thee.

Leviticus 20:24.
. . . ; I am the Lord your God, which have separated you from other people.

Numbers 36:5.
And Moses commanded the children of Israel according to the word of the Lord, say-

	ing, the tribe of the sons of Joseph hath said well.
Numbers 36:6.	This is the thing which the Lord doth command concerning the daughters of Zelophehad, saying, Let them marry to whom they think best, only to the family of the tribe of their father shall they marry.
Deuteron. 7:3.	Neither shalt thou make marriage with them; thy daughter thou shalt not give unto his son, nor his daughter shalt thou take unto thy son.
Deuteron. 7:6.	For thou art an holy people unto the Lord thy God; the Lord thy God hath chosen thee to be a special people unto himself, above all people that are upon the face of the earth.
Deuteron. 28:32.	Thy sons and thy daughters shall be given unto another people, and thine eyes shall look, and fail with longing for them all the day long; and there shall be no might in thine hand.
Deuteron. 32:31.	For their rock is not as our Rock, even our enemies themselves being judges.
Joshua 23:12.	Else if ye do in any wise go back, and cleave unto the remnant of these nations, even these that remain among you, and shall make marriages with them, and go in unto them, and they to you;
Joshua 23:13	Know for a certainty that the Lord your God will no more drive out any of these nations from before you; but they shall be snares and traps unto you, and scourges in your sides, and thorns in your eyes, until ye perish from off this good land which the Lord your God hath given you.

Jeremiah 13:23.   Can the Ethiopian change his skin, or the leopard his spots. . . .

Malachi 3:6.   For I am the Lord, I change not; . . .

THE NEW TESTAMENT

Matthew 5:17.   Think not that I am come to destroy the law, or the prophets; I am not come to destroy, but to fulfill.

Matthew 15:13.   Every plant, which my heavenly Father hath not planted, shall be rooted up.

Matthew 15:14.   Let them alone: they be blind leaders of the blind. And if the blind lead the blind, both shall fall into the ditch.

Acts 17:26.   And hath made of one blood all nations of men for to dwell on all the face of the earth, and hath determined the times before appointed, and the bounds of their habitation;

Hebrews 13:8.   Jesus Christ the same yesterday, and today, and forever.

44 North Carolina at the Crossroads

It is doubtful that any other southern state had so much to lose by an outbreak of racial terror and extremism after 1940 as North Carolina. The state was well on its way to becoming highly industrialized, and since 1945 it had made a tremendous and imaginative effort to attract new industries. Already having a satisfactory industrial foundation, it was in a better position than most of the other southern states to increase industrialization. In 1954 it was caught in a dilemma. Basically its people were opposed to desegregation, and for a time its Governor fumbled around trying to establish a course of action. Governor Luther H. Hodges in his first utterances gave reason to believe that North Carolina might try to follow the course of the lower southern states.

In 1958 Malcolm Seawell, the Attorney General of North Carolina, spelled out clearly the course his state would have to pursue to avoid disaster. Speaking to the North Carolina Bankers Association, Trust Section, he reviewed what had happened and pleaded with his listeners that North Carolina not be swayed by extremists on either side of the integration-segregation issue.

NORTH CAROLINA IS NOW AT THE CROSSROAD. IT HAS COME TO THE place and to the time when it must make a decision not alone for today but for all of the days that lie ahead of it as a sovereign

New South 14 (January 1959), 3–5.

state. Since the case of *Brown* vs. *Board of Education,* which was handed down on May 17, 1954, by the Supreme Court of the United States, there have been many spokesmen, including attorneys, judges, governors and laymen, who have declared that the decision in the Brown case is not the law of the land and that it need not be obeyed.

Many people have taken the position that the Supreme Court had no right to "legislate" or to hand down the decision in the Brown case, and that, since the Supreme Court had no right to hand down such a decision, there is no obligation on the part of people to obey or to accept the Brown decision as the law.

In Arkansas, we have had presented to us a view (a long range one) of what may happen to people who seek to evade the law of the land. The school board in Little Rock submitted a plan for gradual integration, starting with the senior high school and working down through the various grades, with desegregation to be accomplished in the 1960s. This plan was acceptable to the federal courts and never reached the Supreme Court, although tacit approval of the original Little Rock plan was given by the Supreme Court in its decision of Sept. 29, involving the Little Rock School Board.

The governor of Arkansas, Orval Faubus, won a sweeping victory for reelection as governor of that state upon a platform defiant to the law of the land. When the Supreme Court of the United States, in affirming the Circuit Court of Appeals, denied Little Rock a two-and-a-half year stay, the governor of Arkansas immediately called a session of the state legislature to pass laws conforming to a constitutional amendment giving him power to lease public schools to private individuals or corporations for the operation by the private individuals or corporations of segregated schools.

This action the Supreme Court of the United States has now declared is unconstitutional. The people of this state and elsewhere recall with revulsion the action of the President of the United States in sending troops to Little Rock, Ark. Soldiers with bayoneted rifles around the high school of Little Rock will long remain in the memory of the people of this nation.

But, whatever our thoughts about the Supreme Court of the United States, its interpretation of the Constitution of the United States becomes the law of the land, and whatever our personal feelings about that law may be, the signs at the crossroad where we now stand as a people clearly spell out to us that there can be neither defiance nor evasion of the law of the land.

To remedy that condition, our state is making an all-out effort to attract industry to North Carolina, to improve farming conditions, and to make this more and more a state of greater opportunities to the people who are here and to those who will be attracted here.

No large businesses will desire to locate in a state where its employees will not have available for their children the opportunity to be educated. When school doors are closed, progress must of necessity, and for many reasons, come to an end.

Not only is it my oath-bound duty to support and maintain the Constitution of the United States and its laws, and the Constitution of the State of North Carolina and its laws not inconsistent with the Constitution of the United States, but it is my duty as a citizen, just as it is your duty, to promote the welfare of all of the people of North Carolina.

While I have said over and over again that I do not like what the Supreme Court of the United States has done and what it continues to do in the field of public education, it is my duty as a public official and as a citizen to urge the people of North Carolina to consider what havoc defiance will bring to us.

It is not a pleasant thing to speak out for obedience to the law and then to receive letters such as the following, which was, of course, unsigned: "When the peoples of North Carolina want your advice on education, they will ask for it. When did you join the NAACP, you nigger lover."

However distasteful may be the job which is assigned by law to me, I intend to take my stand on the side of law—and neither through public utterance nor in any other manner will I seek to advise a people to take any other stand than that which I know under law is the only stand we may take. If this is politically inexpedient, dangerous or fatal, I'll just have to be content with what the future holds for me.

The most damaging blows yet given to the attempts on the part of people who, in good faith, seek to keep alive public education in the South have been given by Orval Faubus of Arkansas.

We here in North Carolina are not in the same boat as are the people of Arkansas, and, while there has been some small demonstration by that putrid outfit which calls itself the Ku Klux Klan, any resentment on the part of the people as a whole has been kept in check by them—and that's the way it should be.

Recently, in two successive issues of the *U.S. News and World Report*, which is a highly regarded weekly news magazine, the statement was made that it was the general consensus that North Carolina had the best program dealing with integration of any of the states involved. We have been called a "middle of the road state," because of the fact that we, under our own North Carolina laws, do not seek to nullify the law of the land, nor avoid it, nor to defy it. We simply seek to work out what is best for all of our people, and, under law, to preserve free public education.

We must not be swayed by extremists on either side. We must, in good faith, take that middle-course, which will, under law, save us.

Those states which seek to evade have been and will continue to be unsuccessful, and, to those states, there are but two avenues which remain open—an obedience to the law or avoidance of the law. To avoid the law, the state merely goes out of the business of public education. That day should never come to North Carolina.

Let me give you some idea of the investment which we as a people have in public education in North Carolina, when that investment (if such is ever possible) is expressed in dollars and cents. The state budget for public education in North Carolina in the year 1958–59 is $162,060,000. The total cost of our schools in this state for the year 1956–57 was $169,000,000. Of this cost, the state paid $132,000,000, local governments participated in the amount of $29,500,000 and the federal government partici- pated to the tune of $7,554,000. Throughout this state the total value of public school buildings is approximately $600,000,000. This figure of $600,000,000 is the present value of school build- ings and equipment and does not reflect a replacement value. Replacement value would be considerably in excess of $1,000,- 000,000.

Over the years since the state first entered the field of public education under a program sponsored by our great governors, the major portion of our tax dollar has gone into our public schools. We have worked out a system which has as its aim the equalization of public education for all of our children, regard- less of their place of residence. This has been done so that a child in a rural or small town community may receive an educa- tion here in North Carolina comparable to that received in this state by children in the larger and wealthier communities.

But public education can never have a dollar valuation placed upon it. Our schools are there for a purpose, and that is that our children may be educated and may grow up to be a blessing to their communities, to their state and to mankind. This year in our public schools, we have approximately 1,086,000 children. That is the figure which should be more compelling to us than the dollar mark. The school population is increasing year by year, and our obligations to the children are increasing with every new school year.

It is unthinkable to me that any people possessed of their senses would say, in effect: "We will close our schools and let our children grow up in ignorance." In small part, we are seeing that happen in other states, particularly to the immediate north of us.

Based upon the figures which I have already given you, if the schools in North Carolina should be closed for one day, it would result in a loss of 6,028 child years of education. In other words, it would take one child 6,028 years of perfect attendance to make up this total loss. And, of course, on the basis of the number of children in school, to close the schools for a year would result in the loss of 1,085,000 child years.

I need not tell you that there is a relationship, not given to accurate mathematical calculations, between education and income. As a rule, the better educated the child, the more income he will have. Our state, despite its great strides in all fields of endeavor, remains too near the bottom in per capita income.

45 American Segregation and the World Crisis

On November 10, 1955, in Memphis, Tennessee, members of the Southern Historical Association heard William Faulkner give his views on segregation. He made a strong plea for freedom of all Americans and cited the position the United States occupied in the free world. Unfortunately Faulkner could never quite make himself clear on the race issue. The following statement is direct and clear, and so was a subsequent letter, published December 1, in the Commercial *Appeal*. However, other statements by this famous southern author suggest that he may have had ambivalent attitudes toward the racial disturbance that went on about him.

For the moment and for the sake of the argument, let's say that, a white Southerner and maybe even any white American, I too curse the day when the first Negro was brought against his will to this country and sold into slavery. Because that doesn't matter now. To live anywhere in the world of A.D. 1955 and be against equality because of race or color, is like living in Alaska and being against snow.

Inside the last two years I have seen (a little of some, a good deal of others) Japan, the Philippines, Siam, India, Egypt, Italy,

William Faulkner, "American Segregation and the World Crisis," from *Three Views of the Segregation Decisions*, Foreword by Bell I. Wiley (Atlanta: Southern Historical Association, 1956), 9–12.

West Germany, England and Iceland. Of these countries, the only one I would say definitely will not be communist ten years from now, is England. And if these other countries do not remain free, then England will no longer endure as a free nation. And if all the rest of the world becomes communist, it will be the end of America too as we know it; we will be strangled into extinction by simple economic blockade since there will be no one anywhere anymore to sell our products to; we are already seeing that now in the problem of our cotton.

And the only reason all these countries are not communist already, is America, not just because of our material power, but because of the idea of individual human freedom and liberty and equality on which our nation was founded, and which our founding fathers postulated the name of America to mean. These countries are still free of communism simply because of that—that belief in individual liberty and equality and freedom —that one belief powerful enough to stalemate the idea of communism. We have no other weapon to fight communism with but this, since in diplomacy we are children to communist diplomats, and in production we will always lag behind them since under monolithic government all production can go to the aggrandizement of the State. But then, we don't need anything else, since that idea—that simple belief of man that he can be free—is the strongest force on earth; all we need to do is, use it.

Because it is glib and simple, we like to think of the world situation today as a precarious and explosive balance of two irreconcilable ideologies confronting each other; which precarious balance, once it totters, will drag the whole world into the abyss along with it. That's not so. Only one of the forces is an ideology, an idea. Because the second force is the simple fact of Man: the simple belief of individual man that he can and should be free. And if we who so far are still free, want to continue to be free, all of us who are still free had better confederate, and confederate fast, with all others who still have a choice to be free—confederate not as black people nor white people nor pink nor blue nor green people, but as people who still are free with all other people who still are free; confederate together and stick together too, if we want a world or even a part of a world in which individual man can be free, to continue to endure.

And we had better take in with us as many as we can get of the nonwhite peoples of the earth who are not completely free yet but who want to be and intend to be, before that other force which is opposed to individual freedom, befools and gets them. Time was when the nonwhite was content to—anyway, did— accept his instinct for freedom as an unrealizable dream. But not any more; the white man himself taught him different with that phase of his—the white man's—own culture which took the form of colonial expansion and exploitation based and morally condoned on the premise of inequality not because of individual incompetence, but of mass race or color. As a result of which, in only ten years, we have watched the nonwhite peoples expel, by bloody violence when necessary, the white man from all of the middle east and Asia which he once dominated. And into that vacuum has already begun to move that other and inimical power which people who believe in freedom are at war with— that power which says to the nonwhite man: "We don't offer you freedom because there is no such thing as freedom; your white overlords whom you just threw out have already proved that to you. But we offer you equality: at least equality in slavedom; if you are to be slaves, at least you can be slaves to your own color and race and religion."

We, the western white man who does believe that there exists an individual freedom above and beyond this mere equality of slavedom, must teach the nonwhite peoples this while there is yet a little time left. We, America, who are the strongest force opposing communism and monolithicism, must teach all other peoples, white and nonwhite, slave or (for a little while yet) still free. We, America, have the best chance to do this because we can do it here, at home, without needing to send costly freedom expeditions into alien and inimical places already convinced that there is no such thing as freedom and liberty and equality and peace for all people, or we would practice it at home.

The best chance and the easiest job, because our nonwhite

minority is already on our side; we don't need to sell them on America and freedom because they are already sold; even when ignorant from inferior or no education, even despite the record and history of inequality, they still believe in our concepts of freedom and democracy.

That is what America has done for them in only three hundred years. Not *to* them: *for* them, because to our shame we have made little effort so far to teach them to be Americans, let alone to use their capacities to make of ourselves a stronger and more unified America:—the people who only three hundred years ago were eating rotten elephant and hippo meat in African rain-forests, who lived beside one of the biggest bodies of inland water on earth and never thought of a sail, who yearly had to move by whole villages and tribes from famine and pestilence and human enemies without once thinking of a wheel, yet in only three hundred years in America produced Ralph Bunche and George Washington Carver and Booker T. Washington, who have yet to produce a Fuchs or Rosenberg or Gold or Greenglass or Burgess or McLean or Hiss, and for every prominent communist or fellow-traveler like Robeson, there are a thousand white ones.

I am not convinced that the Negro wants integration in the sense that some of us claim to fear he does. I believe he is American enough to repudiate and deny by simple American instinct any stricture or regulation forbidding us to do something which in our opinion would be harmless if we did it, and which we probably would not want to do anyway. I think that what he wants is equality, and I believe that he too knows there is no such thing as equality *per se*, but only equality *to:* equal right and opportunity to make the best one can of one's life within one's capacity and capability, without fear of injustice or oppression or threat of violence. If we had given him this equal right to opportunity ninety or fifty or even ten years ago, there would have been no Supreme Court decision about how we run our schools.

It is our white man's shame that in our present southern economy, the Negro must not have economic equality; our double shame that we fear that giving him more social equality will jeopardize his present economic status; our triple shame that even then, to justify ourselves, we must becloud the issue with the purity of white blood; what a commentary that the one remaining place on earth where the white man can flee and have his blood protected and defended by law, is Africa—Africa: the source and origin of the people whose presence in America will have driven the white man to flee from defilement.

Soon now all of us—not just Southerners nor even just Americans, but all people who are still free and want to remain so—are going to have to make a choice. We will have to choose not between color nor race nor religion nor between East and West either, but simply between being slaves and being free. And we will have to choose completely and for good; the time is already past now when we can choose a little of each, a little of both. We can choose a state of slavedom, and if we are powerful enough to be among the top two or three or ten, we can have a certain amount of license—until someone more powerful rises and has us machine-gunned against a cellar wall. But we cannot choose freedom established on a hierarchy of degrees of freedom, on a caste system of equality like military rank. We must be free not because we claim freedom, but because we practice it; our freedom must be buttressed by a homogeny equally and unchallengeably free, no matter what color they are, so that all the other inimical forces everywhere—systems political or religious or racial or national—will not just respect us because we practice freedom, they will fear us because we do.

[*Editor's note*—On December 1, Mr. Faulkner extended views expressed in his Memphis paper with the following statement]:

The question is no longer of white against black. It is no longer whether or not white blood shall remain pure, it is whether or not white people shall remain free.

We accept insult and contumely and the risk of violence because we will not sit quietly by and see our native land, the

South, not just Mississippi but all the South, wreck and ruin itself twice in less than a hundred years, over the Negro question.

We speak now against the day when our Southern people who will resist to the last these inevitable changes in social relations, will, when they have been forced to accept what they at one time might have accepted with dignity and goodwill, will say, "Why didn't someone tell us this before? Tell us this in time?"

46 The Moral Aspects of Segregation

Speaking from the same platform with William Faulkner (see Document 45), Benjamin E. Mays, President of Morehouse College, Atlanta, told members of the Southern Historical Association in most eloquent terms that segregation was immoral. But even more impressively he told white Southerners that if the battle for freedom for 15,000,000 Negroes was lost, then it would also be lost for 145,-000,000 whites. Mays, an eloquent and wise southern Negro, outlined clearly the problems of the new age in the South in which race problems would have to be considered on the basis of morality. There is sharp contrast between Dr. Mays's sense of religious morality in racial matters and the views expressed by the Reverend G. T. Gillespie that were distributed as two Citizens' Council propaganda sheets.

WHENEVER A STRONG DOMINANT GROUP POSSESSES ALL THE POWER, political, educational, economic, and wields all the power; makes all the laws, municipal, state and federal, and administers all the laws; writes all constitutions, municipal, state and federal, and interprets these constitutions; collects and holds all the money, municipal, state, and federal and distributes all the

Benjamin E. Mays, "The Moral Aspects of Segregation," *Three Views of the Segregation Decisions,* foreword by Bell I. Wiley (Atlanta: Southern Historical Association, 1956), 13–18.

money; determines all policies—governmental, business, political and educational; when that group plans and places heavy burdens, grievous to be borne, upon the backs of the weak, that act is immoral. If the strong group is a Christian group or a follower of Judaism both of which contend that God is creator, judge, impartial, just, universal, love and that man was created in God's image, the act is against God and man—thus immoral. If the strong group is atheistic, the act is against humanity— still immoral.

No group is wise enough, good enough, strong enough, to assume an omnipotent and omniscient role; no group is good enough, wise enough to restrict the mind, circumscribe the soul, and to limit the physical movements of another group. To do that is blasphemy. It is a usurpation of the role of God.

If the strong handicaps the weak on the grounds of race or color, it is all the more immoral because we penalize the group for conditions over which it has no control, for being what nature or nature's God made it. And that is tantamount to saying to God, "You made a mistake, God, when you didn't make all races white." If there were a law which said that an illiterate group had to be segregated, the segregated group could go to school and become literate. If there were a law which said that all peoples with incomes below $5,000 a year had to be segregated, the people under $5,000 a year could strive to rise above the $5,000 bracket. If there were a law which said that men and women who did not bathe had to be segregated, they could develop the habit of daily baths and remove the stigma. If there were a law which said that all groups had to be Catholics, the Jews and Protestants could do something about it by joining the Catholic Church. But to segregate a man because his skin is brown or black, red or yellow, is to segregate a man for circumstances over which he has no control. And of all immoral acts, this is the most immoral.

So the May 17, 1954, Decision of the Supreme Court and all the decisions against segregation are attempts on the part of the judges involved to abolish a great wrong which the strong has deliberately placed upon the backs of the weak. It is an attempt on the part of federal and state judges to remove this stigma, this wrong through constitutional means, which is the democratic, American way.

I said a moment ago that if the strong deliberately picks out a weak racial group and places upon it heavy burdens that act is immoral. Let me try to analyze this burden, segregation, which has been imposed upon millions of Americans of color. There are at least three main reasons for legal segregation in the United States.

1. The first objective of segregation is to place a legal badge of inferiority upon the segregated, to brand him as unfit to move freely among other human beings. This badge says the segregated is mentally, morally, and socially unfit to move around as a free man.

2. The second objective of segregation is to set the segregated apart so that he can be treated as an inferior: in the courts, in recreation, in transportation, in politics, in government, in employment, in religion, in education, in hotels, in motels, restaurants and in every other area of American life. And all of this has been done without the consent of the segregated.

3. The third objective of legalized segregation follows from the first two. It is designed to make the segregated believe that he is inferior, that he is nobody and to make him accept willingly his inferior status in society. It is these conditions which the May 17, 1954, Decision of the Supreme Court and other federal decisions against segregation are designed to correct—to remove this immoral stigma that has been placed upon 16 million Negro Americans, and these are the reasons every thinking Negro wants the legal badge of segregation removed so that he might be able to walk the earth with dignity, as a man, and not cringe and kow-tow as a slave. He believes that this is his God-given right on the earth.

Segregation is immoral because it has inflicted a wound upon the soul of the segregated and so restricted his mind that millions of Negroes now alive will never be cured of the disease of inferiority. Many of them have come to feel and believe that they are inferior or that the cards are so stacked against them that it is useless for them to strive for the highest and the best. Segregate a race for ninety years, tell that race in books, in law, in courts, in education, in church and school, in employment, in transportation, in hotels and motels, in the government that it is inferior—it is bound to leave its damaging mark upon the souls and minds of the segregated. It is these conditions that the federal courts seek to change.

Any country that restricts the full development of any segment of society retards its own growth and development. The segregated produces less, and even the minds of the strong group are circumscribed because they are often afraid to pursue the whole truth and they spend too much time seeking ways and means of how to keep the segregated group in "its place." Segregation is immoral because it leads to injustice, brutality, and lynching on the part of the group that segregates. The segregated is somebody that can be pushed around as desired by the segregator. As a rule equal justice in the courts is almost impossible for a member of the segregated group if it involves a member of the group imposing segregation. The segregated has no rights that the segregator is bound to respect.

The chief sin of segregation is the distortion of human personality. It damages the soul of both the segregator and the segregated. It gives the segregated a feeling of inherent inferiority which is not based on facts, and it gives the segregator a feeling of superiority which is not based on facts. It is difficult to know who is damaged more—the segregated or the segregator.

It is false accusation to say that Negroes hail the May 17, 1954, Decision of the Supreme Court because they want to mingle socially with white people. Negroes want segregation abolished because they want the legal stigma of inferiority removed and because they do not believe that equality of educational opportunities can be completely achieved in a society where the law brands a group inferior. When a Negro rides in a Pullman unsegregated he does it not because he wants to ride with white people. He may or may not engage in conversations with a white person. He wants good accommodations. When he eats in an unsegregated diner on the train, he goes in because he is hungry and not because he wants to eat with white people. He goes to the diner not even to mingle with Negroes but to get something to eat. But as he eats and rides he wants no badge of inferiority pinned on his back. He wants to eat and ride with dignity. No Negro clothed in his right mind believes that his social status will be enhanced just because he associates with white people.

It is also a false accusation to say that Negroes are insisting that segregated schools must be abolished today or tomorrow, simultaneously all over the place. As far as I know, no Negro leader has ever advocated that, and they have not even said when desegregation is to be a finished job. They do say that the Supreme Court is the highest law of the land and we should respect that law. Negro leaders do say that each local community should bring together the racial groups in that community, calmly sit down and plan ways and means not how they can circumvent the decision but how they can implement it and plan together when and where they will start. They will be able to start sooner in some places than in others and move faster in some places than in others but begin the process in good faith and with good intent. To deliberately scheme, to deliberately plan through nefarious methods, through violence, boycott and threats to nullify the Decision of the highest law in the land is not only immoral but it encourages a disregard for all laws which we do not like.

We meet the moral issue again. To write into our constitutions things that we do not intend to carry out is an immoral act. I think I am right when I say that most of our states, certainly some of them, say in their constitutions "separate but equal." But you know as well as I do that on the whole the gulf of inequality in education widened with the years. There was no serious attempt nor desire in this country to provide Negroes with educational opportunities equal to those for whites. The great surge to equalize educational opportunities for Negroes did not begin until after 1935 when Murray won his suit to enter the law school of the University of Maryland. It is also clear that the millions poured into Negro education in the last 20 years were appropriated not so much because it was right but in an endeavor to maintain segregation.

We brought this situation upon ourselves. We here in the South have said all along that we believe in segregation but equal segregation. In 1896 in the Louisiana case, *Plessy* versus *Ferguson,* the United States Supreme Court confirmed the doctrine "separate but equal." But from 1896 to 1935 there was practically nothing done to make the separate equal. When Murray won his case in 1935, we knew we had to move toward equalization. Since 1935 many suits have been won.

It would have been a mighty fine thing if we had obeyed the Supreme Court in 1896 and equalized educational opportunities for Negroes. If we had done that the problem would have been solved because gradually the separate school system would have been abolished and we would have been saved from the agony and fear of this hour. We didn't obey the Supreme Court in 1896 and we do not want to obey it now.

Let me say again that the May 17, 1954, Decision of the Supreme Court is an effort to abolish a great evil through orderly processes. And we are morally obligated to implement the Decision or modify the federal constitution and say plainly that this constitution was meant for white people and not for Negroes and that the Declaration of Independence created mostly by the mind of the great southerner, Thomas Jefferson, was meant for white people and not for Negroes. Tell the world honestly that we do not believe that part of the Declaration of Independence which says in essence that all men are created equal, that they are endowed by their creator with certain inalienable rights, that among these are life, liberty and the pursuit of happiness.

We are morally obligated to abolish legalized segregation in America or reinterpret the Christian Gospel, the Old and New Testaments, and make the Gospel say that the noble principles of Judaism and Christianity are not applicable to colored peoples and Negroes. Tell the world honestly and plainly that the Fatherhood of God and the Brotherhood of Man cannot work where the colored races are involved. We are morally obligated to move toward implementing the Decision in the deep south or lose our moral leadership in the world. If we do not do it, we must play the role of hypocrisy, preaching one thing and doing another. This is the dilemma which faces our democracy.

The eyes of the world are upon us. One billion or more colored people in Asia and Africa are judging our democracy solely on the basis of how we treat Negroes. White Europe is watching us too. I shall never forget the day in Lucknow, India, when nine reporters from all over India questioned me for 90 minutes about how Negroes are treated in the United States. I shall remember to my dying day the event in 1937 when the principal of an untouchable school introduced me to his boys as an untouchable from the United States. At first it angered me. But on second thought I knew that he was right. Though great progress has been made, for which I am grateful, I and my kind are still untouchables in many sections of the country. There are places where wealth, decency, culture, education, religion, and position will do no good if a Negro [seeks service]. None of these things can take away the mark of untouchability. And the world knows this.

Recently a group of colored students from Asia, Africa, the Middle East and South America were visiting an outstanding Southern town. All the colored people except those from Africa and Haiti could live in the downtown hotels. The Africans and the Haitians had to seek refuge on the campus of a Negro College. That incident was known to all the other colored students and it will be told many times in Europe, Asia, Africa—and it will not help us in our efforts to democratize the world.

Not long ago a Jew from South Africa and a man from India were guests of a Negro professor. He drove them for several days through the urban and rural sections of his state. The Negro, the host, a citizen of the United States, could not get food from the hotels and restaurants. His guests, one a Jew and the other an Indian, had to go in and buy food for him. The man who introduced me in India as an untouchable was right. The Negro is America's untouchable.

Two or three years ago a friend of mine was traveling in

Germany. He met a German who had traveled widely in the United States. He told my friend that he hangs his head in shame every time he thinks of what his country did to the Jews— killing six millions of them. But he told my friend that after seeing what segregation has done to the soul of the Negro in the South, he has come to the conclusion that it is worse than what Hitler and his colleagues did to the Jews in Germany. He may be wrong but this is what he is telling the people in Germany.

Make no mistake—as this country could not exist half slave and half free, it cannot exist half segregated and half desegregated. The Supreme Court has given America an opportunity to achieve greatness in the area of moral and spiritual things just as it has already achieved greatness in military and industrial might and in material possessions. It is my belief that the South will accept the challenge of the Supreme Court and thus make America and the South safe for democracy.

If we lose this battle for freedom for 15 million Negroes we will lose it for 145 million whites and eventually we will lose it for the world. This is indeed a time for greatness.

47 The Congressional Manifesto

Southern representatives in the summer of 1956 believed that they could influence the Congress's consideration of new civil rights legislation. Eighty-three members signed a manifesto stating that the impending legislation would in essence create a police state. According to them, the Civil Rights Act not only involved discriminations against the Negro but would result in a serious invasion of the rights of all Americans. They believed court trials would occur without juries, and that the United States Attorney General would be able to bypass states in the trial of civil rights cases. The manifesto was presented by Congressman William Tuck of Virginia, and was signed by members of the House from twelve southern states. No Kentucky representatives signed the manifesto.

WHEREAS UNDER THE GUISE OF PIOUS LANGUAGE THE CIVIL-RIGHTS bill, H. R. 627, proposes to establish a Commission on Civil Rights, and to provide for an additional Assistant Attorney General, and further purports to strengthen the civil-rights statutes and protect the right to vote; and

Whereas the truth is that these combined proposals if enacted into law would constitute a flagrant violation of States' rights; would result in further concentration of power in the Federal

U.S. *Congressional Record*, July 13, 1956, 12760–12761.

Government and vest unprecedented powers in the hands of the Attorney General, and would intrude the authority of the Federal Government into matters which, under our Constitution, are expressly reserved to the States and to the people: Now, therefore, be it

Resolved, That we, the undersigned Members of the United States House of Representatives, conscious of the grave and far-reaching consequences involved in it, hereby pledge our unqualified opposition to this iniquitous legislation and, confident of the soundness of our position, express the following cogent reasons that impel us to take this united stand.

The bill authorizes the Commission, with the aid of paid investigators and "voluntary" pressure groups and professional informers, to launch a sweeping "investigation of allegations" which might lead them to believe that "unwarranted economic pressure" is supposedly being exerted by private individuals over others, because of their religion as well as their race. In addition, and wholly unrelated to race or religion, the Commission is directed to "study and collect information concerning economic, social and legal developments" and "to appraise the laws and policies of the Federal Government" in the entire field of so-called civil rights. The term "civil rights" itself is not defined; and what would constitute unwarranted pressure, economic, social and legal developments, and the scope of the appraisal and investigation, are left to the whim of the Commission. And through the power of subpena the Commission could compel any person to testify and open his books to public inspection.

The proposed additional Assistant Attorney General would be in charge of a special Civil Rights Division to be created and which would be manned by a vast horde of lawyers and investigators. A politically minded Attorney General could subject the governments of States, counties, towns and localities and the officials and citizens of the same to insults, intimidation and terror, against which there would be no redress.

Armed with the power which this legislation would expressly confer, the Attorney General, even without the consent of the plaintiffs, could file purely private law suits by and for private citizens against their neighbors. In no case would it be necessary to prove the commission of any overt act, and under the bill the Attorney General could obtain an injunction on a simple allegation that the defendant "is about to engage in an attempt" to do something that the lawyers in the Civil Rights Division conceive to be objectionable. All actions would be filed in the Federal Courts and tried without a jury, and Congress, for the first time in history, would specifically permit the Attorney General to by-pass State law and ignore available local remedy. This device to concentrate more power in the Federal Government and to flout States' rights is an insult to all liberty loving American citizens.

Under the Constitution the States are the sole judges of the qualifications of voters and throughout the long history of the United States the manner in which our elections are held has been a time-honored function of the States. The broad language of the bill would open practically the entire field of elections, including State primaries, to Federal intervention. The intrusion of the Federal Government into this field has not heretofore been permitted or even considered, except in precise instances clearly defined by the Fourteenth and Fifteenth Amendments. If additional powers in matters of elections are deemed to be necessary to be vested in the Federal Government, then Congress should attack the problem squarely by proposing an amendment to the Constitution.

No one has the wildest idea of the purpose for which the extraordinary powers created by this legislation will be employed and to grant them by such vague language as is contained in the bill approaches recklessness.

The people in the United States who entertain notions that the so-called racial issue is paramount in the sum total coverage of these proposals are due for a rude awakening when their own real civil rights will be invaded if this legislation should be adopted. Our real civil rights spring from the Bill of Rights which, among other things, provides that all matters not prohibited to the States nor delegated to the Federal Government are reserved to the States or the people.

It is an unfortunate fact, however, that this bill will add further fuel and flame to discord engendered by certain agitators and if adopted could only result in deterioration of the goodwill and harmonious relations existing between the races and grievous injury to the steady progress and advancement of the very people whom the proponents profess to assist; be it, therefore, further

Resolved, That we invite and urge every Member of like mind in the House of Representatives and in the Senate, where the rules of procedure are more flexible, to join with us in the employment of every available legal and parliamentary weapon to defeat this sinister and iniquitous proposal.

PART 7 The Hood and the Cross

SOUTHERNERS YET UNBORN WILL COME TO RUE THE DAY IN THE troubled era of Reconstruction when the hooded order of the Ku Klux Klan was formed. It is doubtful that this order has ever in its history achieved a single thing of constructive social significance. Its stated objectives could have been achieved much more permanently and constructively by the normal approaches of a democratic society. Certainly the two twentieth-century revivals of the Klan have been highly detrimental to law and order, and to human dignity in the South.[1] Historically, the Klan in the 1920s exposed the cause of white protestant Americans in terms of rigid religious fundamentalism.[2] Its tentacles reached deep into the fibre of southern social and political life. The Klan's leaders were shabby men seeking power and wealth far beyond their capacity to manage or understand. Fortunately they never achieved their objectives.

In the late 1930s the latent spirit of bigotry and Klanism once

[1] Arnold S. Rice, *The Ku Klux Klan in American Politics* (Washington, D.C.: Public Affairs Press, 1962); *passim*, Charles C. Alexander, *The Ku Klux Klan in the Southwest* (Lexington: University of Kentucky Press, 1965).

[2] H. W. Evans, *The Modern Menace of Immigration*, and *The Public School Problem in America.* Anonymous, *A Fundamental Klan Doctrine, and Constitution and Laws of the Knights of the Ku Klux Klan* (Atlanta: n.p., 1924).

479

again came to the surface. This time the anti-Negro and anti-social progress philosophy of the order was even more pronounced. Its white trash leadership undertook to re-order southern society with bludgeon, threats, and all other forms of intimidation.[3] The United States Congress has found it almost impossible to devise and get enacted an anti-Klan law which would not jeopardize the whole structure of American fraternal organization. The success or failure of the Ku Klux Klan in the South has rested with the governors and the attorney generals, and with a tolerant or enraged public opinion.[4]

[3] Rice, *op cit.*, and Alexander, *op. cit. Southern Politics in State and Nation*, 52–53, 434–435, 263–264.

[4] James W. Patton, ed., *Papers and Messages of Luther H. Hodges*, and Memory F. Mitchell, ed., *Papers and Messages of Terry Sanford*.

48 Hollow Appeal to Reason

In 1924 the voluble Hiram Wesley Evans of Dallas and Atlanta looked on all mankind, except Negroes, Jews, and Catholics, as brothers under the skin. He believed that men could sit down together and reason matters out to a logical conclusion. From the following discussion, though, one can imagine how easily the Imperial Wizard or his minions of the Ku Klux Klan could be persuaded to listen to reason on any subject. In a fine bit of ambivalence he sets forth the philosophy of the revived Ku Klux Klan in such a way that it sounds like a new patriotic society.

Evans was captivated by the sight of printer's ink and he fed a constant flow of pamphlets to the klaverns all over the country. None of these, however, stated so clearly the misty philosophy of the Klan as the following slender pamphlet. Not even the constitution and bylaws or the laughable ritual outlining so many antics gave so clear an insight. This philosophy of 100 percent Americanism under a bed sheet and the cover of secrecy and darkness was fraught with the bitterest sort of intolerance. To use the word "reason" in connection with Klan procedure was absurd.

ONE SEES MUCH THESE DAYS ABOUT THE KLAN BEING RACIALLY and religiously intolerant. Any organization (the Klan not ex-

Hiram W. Evans, *Come Now, Let Us Reason Together* (Atlanta: n.p., 1924), 3–14.

481

cepted) should be willing to prove itself worthy by showing a ready inclination, not only to have its methods examined but to freely assist. That must be a poor line of goods which a salesman, in his effort to place on the market, is unwilling to allow his prospective customer to examine. If the Klan deserves even a tithe of the things uttered against it, it has no right to exist in free America, or anywhere else. It is to be admitted that many of the critics of the Klan are sincere. As Klansmen, we also hope those who are not agreeable to us will admit that we, too, are sincere. Nothing can be accomplished by wrangling. Exchanging condemnations only tends to stir up anger. The Klan devoutly hopes the day will come, and believes that day is dawning, when the public will cease its indulgence in moral lynch law, (and one type of lynch law is as bad as the other), and, instead of condemning this American organization without a trial, will grant to it the rights vouchsafed under the Constitution—that of a fair and impartial trial by jury. The Klan is perfectly willing, in fact it prays for such a trial. All it asks is the right to state its case before a fair and impartial jury. But, remember, the jury must be fair and impartial. Indeed, it cannot be fair, unless it is impartial. It is to be wondered if our fellow-Americans, being as zealous as we for our beloved country, realize the extremely difficult situation into which they have forced the Klan by condemning it without a hearing, and further, by compelling it to appeal for its life before a jury of biased minds?

Cases are too numerous where a judge, who has sworn to be fair and impartial, has charged a jury of investigation to condemn and declare as outlaws the members of the Ku Klux Klan, even before the organization had been brought to trial to determine the correctness or the falsity of the judge's charge. Candidates have announced for high office, having as a plank in their platform, a statement in behalf of religious toleration, and another plank in their same platform declaring against the members of the Ku Klux Klan. The inconsistency of such conditions speaks for itself. The Klan solemnly asserts it has not had fair and impartial treatment at the hands of the people. But it has been investigated by the highest law-making body of our nation, and has been exonerated and given a clean bill of health. It has been incorporated by the law of the land. It has been accepted by thousands and tens of thousands of ministers of the Gospel, public school teachers, and others of equally high repute. It lays no claim to authority or power. It makes no effort against organized society. It seeks no one's life, nor property, nor name. It seeks no favor but the good will of Jesus Christ. It possesses no tenet that is inimical or contrary to the Constitution of the United States. It has no creed but such as is harmonious with the Protestant expression of New Testament Christianity. Why, therefore, the constant, the unrelenting, the unfraternal, the persistent effort on the part of some people, or some publications, to express glaring untruths against this movement? Have we come to the point as a nation when we have ceased to be fair-minded? Do we vehemently protest against the lynching of a man for some hideous crime, and at the same time morally lynch hundreds of thousands of the best men ever born to America? As surely as he is burnt who plays with fire, or as surely as he is befouled, who slings mud, so surely will the persistent indulgence in the groundless infliction of injury result unfortunately to those employing this method. At this juncture, one is strikingly reminded of Saul of Tarsus, who, when he became the amiable Christ-like Paul, admitted he had been guilty of many forms of crime in opposing the policies of Jesus, and said that he thought, during the days of his persecuting, he was doing God service. No doubt those in America, both individuals and publications, think they are performing a patriotic duty when they call the Klan all kinds of unseemly names, and accuse it of racial and religious intolerance, to say nothing of the many other accusations.

We as Klansmen, are as willing to grant sincerity to our critics, as we are desirous of having them grant the same to us. In fairness of mind, let us approach the question. The Klan is either guilty or innocent. There can be no middle ground. The Klan does not seek for any middle ground. In fact, the Klan admits it deserves every kind of punishment its critics have wished it, if it should be proved guilty.

Let us consider the charge of racial and religious intolerance.

To a Klansman that charge is ridiculously absurd, but to say it is such, does not prove anything to our critics. We have to go further than that. Suppose we imagine ourselves to be seated around a conference table. Nations of divergent beliefs and dissimilar blood have done as much. Why cannot we of the same blood do likewise? Place the Klan on trial. Allow it to state its case. The public is well acquainted with the definition of intolerance. The Klan submits this point to the consideration of the jury: It is possible there can exist two kinds of Klans—one in the imagination of the reading public, and formed by the fabrications of non-Klan, (we shall not say anti-Klan) publications,—the other Klan is the one that exists in reality. Between the two, there is an unmeasured distance, indeed, between the two, there is a great gulf fixed. Klansmen are too honorable, too patriotic, too intelligent, too respectable, to belong to or to tolerate that kind of organization which the average non-Klan newspaper persists in picturing to the public mind. Right there Klansmen and the rest of us fellow-Americans have a common starting point. Like the great American Secretary of State, we can practice Hughes' diplomacy by beginning with our agreements, rather than with our differences. Let it be reiterated, Klansmen must heartily agree with non-Klansmen in their unequivocal condemnation of the Ku Klux Klan as expressed or as interpreted in the average non-Klan publication. Klansmen are not surprised at the vehement protest on the part of their fellow-Americans against such a monstrosity as is this newspaper Klan.

Klansmen would have been greatly surprised, in fact would have been disappointed, if their true fellow-Americans had withheld protests when this newspaper monstrosity began to be introduced to the uninformed minds of the public. The reason why Klansmen did not also join in the protests is because they know the average non-Klan newspaper production is a travesty on the good looks of pure Americanism. Sometimes, by actual mistake, the wrong cut will be inserted in a newspaper over a name that does not belong to it.

The purpose of the Ku Klux Klan is not yet understood by the people in general. It is (sad to relate) an American tendency to muddy the waters when an issue is pending. Shrewd lawyers, suborned witnesses, and other agents at times are relied on to divert the attention of the jury from the real issue of a case to some inconsequential matter. This custom is too well known to all Americans to demand proof. The same method has been indulged in with reference to the Ku Klux Klan. Those who are fair-minded are, in the course of time, going to demand a fair and impartial trial of the Klan. Also, those of discriminating mind are going to look behind this effort of muddying the waters in order to see why such was resorted to. Right there will be found the real cause of the greater amount of opposition to the Klan. As in the case of Daniel, when his critics were bent upon his defeat, they could find nothing against him but his religion, so it is with the Klan. "Let them hear who have ears to hear."

In the course of time, things will be better for the Klan. At present the movement is young. Those who are in it admit mistakes, just as any new machinery works awkwardly at first, but as everybody makes mistakes, we shall have to let that matter give way to a fact of deeper import. How has the Klan treated its mistakes? There is the crux of another matter. Be it said, the Klan has profited by its mistakes, and is working far better than it ever has before, and, no doubt, better than it was dreamed of. Soon the people will become acquainted with the Klan's real self. They will cease looking at the picture printed in the non-Klan publications over the name of the Klan, and, after being introduced to the Klan itself, and having beheld it with their own eyes, will at once discover the mistake of the non-Klan press of imposing on the credulity of the people by printing this false photographic Klan. To change the figure, the public is now too near the mountain. When the public will have traveled far enough to look back upon the mountain, they will then see it in its true perspective. There exists an exact parallel between the present situation and that of the early Christian church. The generation in which the church originated condemned the movement, and killed the Christ. It took other generations to arise and call Him blessed. In the meantime, Klansmen need to be, and will be, patient, for they have the inward consciousness that their cause is just.

Now let us look at the charge accusing the Klan of being

racially and religiously intolerant. The very reverse is true, and here is the Klan's answer. In the qualifications for membership into the Klan, the words, "Catholic," "Jew," or "Negro" are not one time mentioned. As to race, the Klan does believe in the supremacy of the White race, and for that belief has no apology to make. But in believing in the supremacy of the White race, it does not advocate that those of another race shall forfeit any of the rights granted them by the Constitution of the United States. In the qualifications for membership into the Klan, the word "white" is used. By inference, it could be said the Negro would, therefore, not be eligible for membership into the Klan. But why single out the Negro? The same disqualification for membership into the Klan would apply to the Chinaman, who is yellow, or to the Malay, who is brown, etc.

Moreover, many of the critics of the Klan seem to take the position that membership in the Klan is equivalent to citizenship in the United States, at least they seem to charge Klansmen with believing that. But such is far from the truth. *Klansmen hold that all citizens of the United States are entitled to all privileges granted every other citizen under the Constitution.* When it comes to religion, the qualifications for membership into the Klan, state "one must be a believer in the tenets of the Christian religion," but not one word is said about the Jew, nor against the Jew. He has howled before he was hit. If the Klan is to be condemned for believing in the tenets of the Christian religion, then all it says is—Let it be condemned. It has no apologies to make for believing in Jesus Christ. But the Klan's critics at this point seem to jump to another inference, which is a gratuitous assumption, namely: they seem to charge the Klan with believing that only those who are Christians are citizens of the United States. The Klan does not believe this. The Klan never has said this. The Klan is simply stating its own religious belief, but as readily grants the other man to believe as he would wish, even as does the Klan demand the right to its own belief. But why single out the Jew on this point? Why say, because the Klan believes in Jesus Christ, that the Klan is against the Jew? The Klan itself does not say so. It is only the critics of the Klan, or those who are the self-appointed interpreters of the Klan who make such a ridiculous charge. Instead of the Klan stirring up trouble among religionists, or among the races, it has been these self-appointed interpreters of the Klan upon whom such condemnation should fall. When it comes to the point of personal belief the Klan respectfully requests that all non-Klansmen remain silent, while the Klan speaks for itself.

Then there comes the charge of anti-Catholicism, which like the others, is also a groundless supposition. It is but a part of this grotesque photograph labeled, "The Klan;" but, in reality, it is the drawing of a diseased imagination on the part of some overzealous critics whose zeal has exceeded their knowledge. As has been stated, the requirements for membership into the Klan do not contain the word "Catholic" at all. The requirements for membership do say that those who seek admittance into the Klan must be native-born citizens of this country, who owe no allegiance of any nature to any foreign government, or institution, or sect, or ruler, or person, etc. This is not aimed at the Roman Catholic any more than it could be aimed at the Buddhist, or the Confucianist, or the Mohammedan, or anybody else who owes any allegiance to any foreign person, either civil or religious. Why, then, all this hue and cry on the part of Roman Catholics about the Klan being religiously intolerant? The only thing the Klan is seeking to do in its effort to organize native-born Americans, is to unite those whose interests, of any nature whatsoever, are wholly and solely concentrated in the United States of America and here alone. That is what the Klan means by its expression "100% American." It does not mean that the members of the Klan are any more "American" than any one else, but it does mean that those who are members of the Klan are, beyond dispute, "American, 100%." It means that we owe no allegiance of any nature whatsoever to any man on earth outside the United States, and, when it comes to spiritual affairs, it means we owe no allegiance to any man on earth, but to the Man, Christ Jesus, Who is in Heaven. When our critics began to realize this, they will see the inoffensiveness of the movement, and will cease caricaturing it, as has heretofore been so persistently done.

To end this article here would be incomplete, because there

has not been given a reason for the Klan. In union there is strength. It seems every race, and every religion, and every color in the United States has been organized except those people who are native-born, white, Gentile, Protestants. The foreigners, and their descendants in this country are organized along their racial and national lines. They have their schools; they speak their foreign languages; they have their publications printed in their foreign tongue and they have their churches, where other than the English language is employed. This organizes them and tends to keep them aloof. The Negro has his processes of organization and seeks to conserve and unite his characteristic abilities. The Roman Catholics have their processes of organizations, their rituals and customs, their ecclesiastical tongue, which is not the English language. These things, and others, tend to keep them united. The Jews have their organizations and keep alive the customs of their fathers, religiously, socially and economically. This tends to unite them.

To recapitulate the foreigner, being organized, leaves the native-born. The Negro being organized, leaves the White native-born. The Roman Catholic being organized, leaves the White, native-born Protestant. The Jews being organized, leaves the White, native-born, Protestant, Gentile. It is this last named individual whom the Klan seeks to organize. Up to the present he (the White, native-born, Protestant, Gentile), has not been organized. Being in a disorganized state, he has been the victim of exploitation on the part of any organized element that has sought his possessions. He has lived in his own country, but has been victimized in one way or another by strangers. They voted him when they wished, they exploited him in their greed, they used him in other ways, as their avarice dictated. And now, they seek to disfranchise him in his own country and deny him the rights of the Constitution written by his own fathers! But such a day is passing. The White, native-born, Protestant, Gentile is organizing! He is not seeking to injure others, but is seeking to defend himself, and if his organizing be charged as criminal, let the answer be made, he is doing only what his critics have already done before him!

Nor can this article end here. It would be selfish if it did. The Klan is far more than a self-defense organization. At heart the Klan wishes well to every one of those other organized divisions of American citizenship, but the Klan sees, that is to say, these White, native-born, Protestant, Gentiles see that the best interests of all these other organized forces would be jeopardized, as well as our own interests, if the policies of government are not directed by those who not only have the interests of the government at heart, but who, by their birth and inheritances, possess a sympathetic understanding for America. People who have just come to this country, or who within a ridiculously short period of time become full-fledged citizens, are not capacitated to run this government like that man, or that woman, who has inherited the spirit of Bunker Hill and Valley Forge. People who have a religion inimical, or contradictory, to the religion possessed by those men who penned the Declaration of Independence, cannot as intelligently interpret that immortal document as can he or she who has inherited the religion of the American forefathers.

Foreigners, non-Protestants, non-Gentiles, non-Whites, as well as the native-born, White, Protestant, Gentiles, are likened unto various passengers or families on the same ship. That ship is the government of the United States, and if, through false steering, the ship goes on the rocks, every one on board will suffer loss. Too long have we relegated the affairs of our government into the hands of others, ourselves failing to give it the attention it has deserved. The recent World War woke us up to our dereliction. We saw our mistake, and solemnly agreed, then and there, to hereafter give more attention to our government. Klansmen believe firmly that the class of men and women whom they represent are better capacitated to run this government than are those who are foreign, in tongue, in spirit, or in anything else.

We do not say they are not citizens—we do not say they have no rights that we do not have—we only speak of capacity, and *American capacity,* at that. Should this government be run on the rocks by the mismanagement of some semi-foreign navigator, (and one can be foreign in religion, as well as in blood), all would suffer equally. The contention of the Klan is: if White, native-born, Protestant, Gentiles be organized, such will result as a blessing to every one else in this country, because it will be to the salvation of this country. If America be saved, the foreigner who is here, and the non-Protestant, and the non-Christian, and the non-White will all be equal participants in the salvation. This is the aim of the Klan and this is what the Klan is trying to have the people to comprehend. Our prayer is: "God open their eyes, that they may see." Surely our critics have indulged in enough groundless vituperation. It is now time to get over one's splenetic disorder, and calmly sit at the conference table that we might be fair one to another.

49 Human Relations Ku Klux Klan Style

The Ku Klux Klan was shocked in North Carolina by the Lumbee Indians who resented the hoodlums from South Carolina and North Carolina burning a cross in protest of the Indians' racial differences. The Indians dealt with this problem directly by a vigorous physical retaliation which Klansmen could understand, and on January 30, 1958, Governor Luther H. Hodges sharply condemned the Klan for its inexcusable action by its assault upon an Indian public meeting. He did not, however, censor the Indians for striking back with force. For a time the Klan was in a state of disorder and high disfavor with the people of North Carolina. The fact Klansmen had been routed by the Indians caused them to be ridiculed for their cowardice and high-handedness in disrupting a perfectly orderly public assembly.

THE RECENT INCIDENT IN MAXTON INVOLVING CITIZENS OF ROBEson County and a small group of outsiders claiming to be members of the Ku Klux Klan is of serious concern to the thoughtful citizens of North Carolina who are determined as I am that we shall maintain law and order.

It is of concern because we know that several people could easily have been killed or seriously injured on that occasion.

James W. Patton, ed., *Messages, Addresses, and Public Papers of Luther H. Hodges, Governor of North Carolina 1954–1961* (Raleigh: Council of State, State of North Carolina, 1963), vol. II, 586–588.

It is of concern because such an incident is an assault on peace and good order, and a slur on the name of our state.

It is of concern because of the possible stimulus to other and more serious future incidents.

In the last few days there have been intimations and threats to the effect that the Klan will at some future date assemble an armed gathering in Robeson County or at other places and put on a big show of force to further intimidate the people of this state. There have been threats that bands of armed men from out of the state will come into North Carolina.

I want my position to be clearly understood.

The responsibility for the Maxton incident rests squarely on the irresponsible and misguided men who call themselves leaders of the Ku Klux Klan.

The Ku Klux Klan and its leaders who rant against Communism actually give aid and comfort to Communist Russia. The Klan is responsible for provoking incidents that are exploited in propaganda by Russia and other Communist nations.

I believe that all people have the right to express their views and try to persuade others, in a peaceful manner, to agree with them. However, no one and no group has the right to impose his views on others by intimidation, by night-riding excursions, cross-burnings and other overt acts designed to intimidate individual citizens.

The Ku Klux Klan has shown itself to be an organization of violence and intimidation. The consequences of its usual activities are the unlawful oppression of individual citizens, or else the arousement, incitement, and provocation of groups of citizens which lead to public disorder.

Let me say:

(1) To the alleged leaders of the Ku Klux Klan—Your message of hate and violence is a mockery to the religion you often profess. Not many years ago, there were other misguided men who were in your position of alleged Klan leadership. They violated the laws of North Carolina. They were tried and convicted in our courts of law by juries composed of citizens of this state. They were sent to prison. I hope that such events will not have to be repeated.

(2) To those few citizens who may be beguiled and misled into joining or giving aid or comfort to the Klan—Our basic freedoms and liberties that all citizens cherish can only be maintained and protected under a system of law and order. No group can be permitted, on whatever pretext or cause, to gather in armed bands, ride about in the night time for the purpose of threatening other citizens with violence, and on occasion committing acts of violence. No group can be allowed, under our system of law and order, to act in such a way as to incite other citizens to riot or disorder. I ask that you beware of false and fraudulent leadership. Some of the so-called leaders in the Klan who have assumed imposing titles have turned out to be religious imposters with criminal records. Many of these individuals, we are convinced, are interested only in what money they can extort from gullible citizens or the publicity they can gain for themselves for a time. When you associate yourselves with such men, you not only associate yourselves against law and order, but against the overwhelming numbers of your neighbors and fellow citizens who are law abiding, who do not want or need an organization whose creed spawns hate and violence.

(3) To those citizens who have no sympathy for the Klan or deplore what it is and what it does—Do not help the Klan by crowding to their meetings out of curiosity to see what might happen. Do not allow them to provoke you to attempt group action against the Klansmen. To do these things is to do exactly what the Klan leaders desire.

I recognize the great obligation that newspapers, radio and television stations, and other news media have to report the news whether it is good or bad. However, we all know that an over-zealousness in "finding" news can sometimes result in the unfortunate "making" of news. There is some evidence in the Maxton incident that the Klan leaders had decided not to go ahead with that meeting, but changed their minds when they were encouraged by the publicity they were getting before the meeting and saw the potential notoriety they would gain if the meeting was held. It is significant that, according to estimates, scores of news representatives were on the scene the night of the Maxton incident.

I am confident that our news media will continue to be aware of the danger of unwittingly contributing to incidents by providing what amounts to promotional publicity of Klan meetings. Of course, we need to throw the full light of public disclosure on all those individuals who take an active part in Klan matters. Identification of names, addresses, and past records of such individuals is a salutary thing and in the public interest.

Our sheriffs, chiefs of police, and all local law-enforcement officers have the immediate and primary responsibility for maintaining law and order in their respective communities. They do a good job. I want each of them to know that I, with all other state officials and agencies, stand ready to assist them at any time such assistance is needed.

We will maintain law and order in North Carolina.

50 The Ku Klux Klan Has to Go

By 1953 the North Carolina legislature was fed up enough with the nefarious activities of the Ku Klux Klan to pass a strong anti-Klan law. There has long been an incipient cluster of Klanism in that state, and not infrequently members got themselves involved in all sorts of long-nosed meddling with the lives of people, even to involving the law enforcement authorities in North and South Carolina in an issue of interstate Klan raiding. Too, members of the order became involved in a commotion with the Lumbee Indians, in which the Indians fought back successfully. Despite the new law, after 1954 the Klan activities became intensified, especially after Congress began debates on the civil rights laws. Governor Terry Sanford made his petition quite clear on June 22, 1964, when he reiterated the contents of the General Statutes relating to Klan activities. No southern governor has ever been so positive and clear on this subject. Had the other governors taken so firm a stand the Klan never would have gotten beyond the stage of holding a few poorly attended meetings at some clearing in the pine woods.

BECAUSE THERE IS A GROWING CONCERN ACROSS THE STATE, I THINK it is necessary to remind the people involved that the Ku Klux Klan is not going to take over North Carolina.

Memory F. Mitchell, ed., *Messages, Addresses, and Public Papers of Terry Sanford, Governor of North Carolina 1961–1965* (Raleigh: North Carolina History Commission, 1966), 623–624.

Taking the law into their hands, running people away, burning crosses, making threats, wearing hoods, are all illegal practices and are not going to be permitted.

In 1953, the General Assembly, following the conviction of a number of members of the Ku Klux Klan, passed a law with teeth in it.

It was designed primarily by Clifton L. Moore, then the solicitor who prosecuted the Klan members, who now is Associate Justice of the North Carolina Supreme Court.

Here are the teeth, here is what is provided, here is what is against the law:

1. It is against the law to belong to certain kinds of organizations: "It shall be unlawful for any person to join . . . solicit members for . . . or assist in any way any secret political society. . . ." G.S. 14–12.3.

A secret society "shall mean any two or more persons . . . combined or united for any common purpose whatsoever, who shall use among themselves any certain grips, signs or password, or who shall use for the advancement of any of their purposes or as a part of their ritual any disguise of the person, face or voice or any disguise whatsoever. . . ." G.S. 14–12.1.

"The term 'secret political society' shall mean any secret society, as hereinbefore defined, which shall at any time have for a purpose the hindering or aiding the success of any candidate for public office, or the hindering or aiding the success of any political party or organization, or violating any lawfully declared policy of the government of the State or any of the laws and constitutional provisions of the State." G.S. 14–12.1.

"The term 'secret military society' shall mean any secret society . . . when members are illegally armed, or . . . have for a purpose the engaging in any venture by members thereof which shall require the illegal armed force. . . ." G.S. 14–12.1.

2. It is against the law to use "any signs, grips, passwords, disguise of the face, person or voice, or any disguise whatsoever in the furtherance of any illegal secret political purpose. . . ." G.S. 14–12.4.

3. It is against the law to permit such a secret society to meet. G.S. 14–12.5.

4. It is required that the regular meeting places be marked. It is against the law to meet elsewhere unless newspaper notice is given two days in advance. It is required that the membership lists be available. G.S. 14–12.6.

5. It is against the law for a person over sixteen years old to wear a mask, hood, or device whereby the person, face, or voice is disguised, to be in a public place, or demand entrance or go into some one else's residence. G.S. 14–12.8, 12.9.

6. It is against the law to burn a cross on the property of another without first getting written permission. G.S. 14–12.12.

The FBI has been asked to keep a running investigation.

The State Highway Patrol is being instructed to watch for violations.

Local law enforcement officers should also watch for violations.

Superior Court solicitors have the responsibility for bringing the indictments, and I am sure they will do so where they uncover violations.

Let the KKK get this clear. I am not going to tolerate their illegal actions, and the people of North Carolina are not going to put up with it.

I repeat, the KKK is not going to take over North Carolina.

51 The Ku Klux Klan and the Industrial South

The detrimental influence of the Ku Klux Klan on the movement of new industry into the South has been mentioned in many sources. Not infrequently the *Wall Street Journal* and *New York Times* either made surveys or carried local reports of the disastrous economic results of Klan outbreaks. No testimony, however, was so eloquent as this brief letter from Lewis Lawrence of Alexander City, Alabama.

WOULDN'T YOU KNOW THAT THE KKK WOULD GET OUT ITS LITERA-ture at the most inopportune time. This morning, not long after coming into the Chamber office, an industrial prospect walked in, and we began talking about the excellent opportunities and facilities which Alexander City offers his firm. After talking for some lengths, he stated that all these things seemed to be true, but that the KKK literature which he found on his windshield wiper this morning left a bad taste in his mouth, and a bad impression about the community. He states that attitudes of a community were important to his firm, and that when they heard about the incident, he was not too sure about their reaction as to their wishing to continue to consider Alexander City as a possible location.

I tried to explain that such material must have come from outside Alexander City. Unfortunately, I am afraid the damage has been done, and that we can forget this particular person's firm as a potential industrial prospect.

Lewis Lawrence, Mgr.
Chamber of Commerce, Inc.

52 The Modern
Ku Klux Klan

Southern editors have a rather good record in publicizing their attitudes toward the Ku Klux Klan. Grover Hall of the *Montgomery* (Alabama) *Advertiser,* Julian and Cora Harris of the *Columbus* (Georgia) *Sun,* and other editors have been forthright in condemning the Klan. Hall and the Harrises won Pulitzer Prizes for their editorials on the subject. The editor of the *Columbus* (Georgia) *Ledger* was equally courageous in branding the Klan a cowardly organization in the following document. In plain words he spelled out the sordid objectives of the various organizations that functioned under an assortment of names, but were Ku Kluxers all the same. This editorial condemnation is comparable to the official scoldings by Governors Luther H. Hodges and Terry Sanford of North Carolina.

THERE MUST BE NO MISUNDERSTANDING—AND THERE SHOULD NOT be, on the record—about the nature of Kluxism, under whatever name. When several KKK organizations were placed on the attorney general's list of subversive organizations and also after several states passed anti-masking and anti-cross burning laws, Kluxism faded away for a while. In the last year or so—trading on resentment of the Supreme Court's school desegregation

New South, 12 (April 1957), 14.

decision—several groups have tried to revive Kluxism under different but similar KKK names. But if the names are changed, the motives evidently are not.

The Kluxers are not interested only in expressing dissent with the Supreme Court decision. This is the appeal they have for some who do not understand the movement. They have shown over and over that they are hate groups and that the hatred is not limited to the school decision or Negroes. A bunch of Kluxists drew a crowd of about 300, including children and curious spectators, in Warner Robins a week ago Saturday night (although they boasted 15,000 would attend). Here is how *The Macon Telegraph* described it:

"At the maximum the spectacle drew 300 curious observers and as the rantings and ravings against Catholics, Jews and Negroes proceeded in typical KKK style, the meager audience dwindled more and more."

Heading up the U. S. Klans, Knights of the Ku Klux Klans, which is one of the new names, is a man in Atlanta with a police record. He told an audience in Conway, S. C., last fall that he was building a "strong and vicious organization." He said progress was being made in Texas and shortly thereafter Atty. Gen. John Shepperd sent a notice to all Texas prosecutors to notify his office if any of the Atlanta group showed up in their areas.

He quoted Texas laws against masked or hooded groups, and attached a Fulton County police "mug" shot of the alleged "Imperial Wizard."

This same character told a cross-burning gathering at Stone Mountain (near Atlanta) that the Klan would, in effect, observe only "laws that are just."

Klansmen appeared at a meeting addressed by the notorious hate-peddler John Kasper in Birmingham . . . and Kasper said he was "deeply honored" and "We need all the rabble rousers we can get. . . . We want trouble and we want it everywhere we can get it." Kasper has a long record of peddling hate booklets, directed mostly against Jews, in New York and Washington. He is a darling of the Kluxists and evidently from what he said in Birmingham returns the affection.

That is Kluxism—a proposition dedicated to hate of all but white protestants; of observing laws with which it agrees and otherwise being the law. Kluxism remains subversive under any name.

53 Hard Times for the Klan

For the most part the modern Ku Klux Klan of the South is composed of white trash—but violent white trash, as shown by a series of incidents that occurred on the North Carolina-South Carolina border in February 1952. Public officials dealt the Klan a blow, but in trying to formulate legislation the North Carolina Legislature warned of the possible dangers to innocent and constructive organizations which unintentionally would be brought under laws that would destroy the Klan. Meanwhile, the Solicitor of Robeson County, North Carolina, outlined clearly to the Klan hoodlums that freedom and the right to protection existed for all people.

THE PRESENT-DAY KU KLUX KLAN IS A FAR CRY FROM THE POWER-ful "Invisible Empire" which terrorized the South and parts of the North in the Twenties. It now consists of a few third-rate satrapies ruled by power-hungry little men who spend much of their time quarreling among themselves. Yet in limited areas these terrorist splinter groups are still a serious threat to safety of the person.

The Association of Carolina Klans, headed by a self-styled "Grand Dragon" named Thomas L. Hamilton, is one such group. It achieved notoriety in 1950 when some of its members raided

"Hard Times for the Klan," New South, 7 (March-April 1952), 6–7.

a Negro nightclub in Horry County, S. C. A gun-fight ensued, and when the shooting was over one Klansman, a Conway policeman, lay dead and abandoned by his companions. Since that time, Horry's Sheriff C. E. Sasser has waged a running campaign against the organization.

MASKED FLOGGERS

Members of the same group have been active across the state line in North Carolina. During the past thirteen months, more than a dozen persons have been flogged by masked nightriders in Columbus County. Many of the victims were white persons whose morals did not suit the floggers' fancy. Among the few local persons who dared speak out against this lawlessness were two newspaper editors, who rightly termed it "a reign of terror."

Some of these high-riding Klansmen recently had a nasty fall. On February 16, some forty agents of the FBI staged a surprise roundup of members of the now defunct Fair Bluffs Klavern. All ten of those arrested were indicted by a special federal grand jury on charges of abduction and conspiracy.

A few weeks later, the Columbus County sheriff, aided by state agents, dealt the Klan another blow. This time eleven men were arrested and charged with kidnapping and assault.

At about the same time, the sheriff of nearby Robeson County apprehended fifteen alleged Klansmen, charged with violation of an old statute which forbids membership in secret political organizations. Three renounced their membership and were released; the rest denied the charge and were placed under bond.

DEMAND STATE LAWS

Too often, arrest in such cases is not followed by conviction. It remains to be seen whether North Carolina will change the pattern. But one thing is unmistakable: the public revulsion against the Klan and its principles is angry and widespread. One index is the demand in North Carolina for state laws that will permanently end such terrorism. The Attorney General of the state is considering a measure that would outlaw the Klan and other organizations which conspire to take the law into their own hands.

Such sweeping legislation has its dangers, as Alexander F. Miller, the Southern director of the Anti-Defamation League, recently pointed out. Alternatively, the ADL suggests the following as effective ways to curb the Klan's illegal actions without endangering the constitutional right of association:

1. Klan members associate secretly to conspire against the public order and safety. The secrecy can be stripped from the Klan by a Secret Society Registration Act which requires the membership list, the officials and finances of certain secret societies, such as the Klan, to be registered with the Secretary of State and open to public inspection.

2. Klan violence is usually committed under cover of masks, hoods, or robes. Obviously an anti-mask law such as has been passed recently by four Southern States will remedy this evil.

3. The Klan intimidates its intended victims by terroristic signs and symbols, especially cross burnings. The use of these symbols can be limited and prohibited by appropriate law such as is now on the books in Georgia.

4. The Klan has sometimes infiltrated the law enforcement machinery. This problem can be solved by legislation providing that each law enforcement officer take periodic oaths that he is not a member of the Ku Klux Klan or any like organization.

Such laws, vigorously enforced would be another way of saying what the Solicitor of Robeson County recently told a group of arrested Klansmen:

> You understand physical force, but there is another force which we wish to impress upon you. The same law which has protected you all your lives is not your individual or collective possession. It belongs to the rich and to the poor, to the Negro, to the white, to the Indian, to the native born, to the foreign born, to the protestant, to the Catholic, and to the Jew. It is going to stay that way.

PART 8 Spokesmen of the South

SPOKESMEN OF THE SOUTH MULTIPLIED RAPIDLY AFTER 1880. Some of them cried out against the excesses of Reconstruction while others publicized the region's great social and economic promise.[1] Historically, the South had racial, educational, and cultural problems. To claim its share of the great American heritage it had to depart radically from many old ways of life.[2] To try to accomplish this both newspapers and national periodicals opened their columns freely to spokesmen for the New South.[3] Among the new crop of writers were Henry W. Grady, George Washington Cable, Booker T. Washington, Josephus Daniels, and John Spencer Bassett.[4] In time, educational crusades were publicized by all sorts of writers, and articles that appeared with regularity in the journals.

No statement prior to the rendering of the decision in *Plessy* v. *Ferguson* was more reassuring to Southerners than Booker T. Washington's widely publicized Atlanta speech. In 1895 he

---

[1] Thomas D. Clark and Albert D. Kirwan, *The South Since Appomattox, a Century of Regional Change*, 202–228.

[2] C. Vann Woodward, *Origins of the New South, 1877–1913*, pp. 142–174.

[3] This was especially true of the *Century* and *Scribner's* magazines. The South received wide notices in the national newspaper press.

[4] Clark and Kirwan, 208–227.

enunciated, in an extremely eloquent oration before the Southern States Cotton Exposition audience, the doctrine of economic equality but social separateness. He captivated his audience with his words, even if he failed to impress upon it the seriousness of his theme of the Negro's struggle to gain certain equalities.[5]

In the field of education there was a veritable multitude of spokesmen and crusaders for improved schooling.[6] Edwin A. Alderman was one of the ablest of southern educators, and like Charles McIver and Charles Brantley Aycock of North Carolina he understood intimately the central problems of prodding Southerners into action.[7] If Alderman, McIver, Aycock, and J. L. M. Curry spoke of education in institutional terms, the ubiquitous Walter Hines Page spoke as a layman viewing his fellow Southerners as inadequately functioning human beings. His "Forgotten Man" speech was a ringing indictment of lack of southern cultural accomplishment.[8] In the 1920s H. L. Mencken added further reason for the South's cultural self-consciousness when he published his "Sahara of the Bozart" in the *American Mercury*.[9] In response, Gerald W. Johnson, a fellow writer and Baltimore neighbor, made his own analysis, and in a somewhat wrathful reply in the *Mercury* revealed the failures of the regional critics to take into consideration the more

[5] Booker T. Washington, *Up from Slavery* (New York: Garden City, 1901), 221–226, and *The Future of the American Negro* (Boston: Small, Maynard & Company, 1899) develops much more fully this famous Negro's views on his race's place in American society.

[6] Dabney, *Universal Education in the South;* J.A.C. Chandler et al., "History of the Social Life of the Southern States," *The South in the Building of the Nation*, vol. X, 237–427.

[7] Three solid biographies of the North Carolina educational leaders are: Dumas Malone, *Edwin A. Alderman: A Biography* (New York: Doubleday, Doran & Company, Inc. 1940); Oliver H. Orr, Jr., *Charles Brantley Aycock;* and Rose Howell Holder, *McIver of North Carolina* (Chapel Hill: The University of North Carolina Press, 1957).

[8] Walter Hines Page, *The Rebuilding of Old Commonwealths*, 1–45.

[9] Henry L. Mencken, "The Sahara of the Bozart," *Prejudices: Second Series* (New York: Alfred A. Knopf, 1920), 136–154.

pertinent facts about the South. His reply, in fact, was an answer to several decades of criticism.[10]

Decades later two progressive governors of North Carolina voiced a new spirit for their state. Luther H. Hodges and Terry Sanford viewed not only North Carolina but the South through broader perspectives of educational and social needs. In many respects they seemed to answer the biting strictures of Walter Hines Page and H. L. Mencken in terms of the unfolding twentieth century.[11]

[10] Gerald W. Johnson, "The South Takes the Offensive," *The American Mercury* (May 1924), 70–78.

[11] James W. Patton, ed., *Messages, Addresses, and Public Papers of Luther Hartwell Hodges, Governor of North Carolina 1954–1961*, 2 vols.; Memory F. Mitchell, ed., *Messages, Addresses, and Public Papers of Terry Sanford, Governor of North Carolina 1961–1965*.

54 Cast Down Your Buckets

After a tremendous amount of publicity and promotion, southern businessmen, especially those of Atlanta, opened the Cotton States' Exposition in September 1895. True to the custom of the times there was almost a continuous stream of oratory from the moment the Exposition opened until it closed. For the first time a large public gathering in the South heard a superb orator; Booker T. Washington of the Tuskegee Institute was invited to speak for his race which was so obviously a major factor in the production of cotton. This was Professor Washington's opportunity to decry failures to treat the Negro as a productive force, and to assure the great audience that the two races could live side by side separately but perhaps equally. A year later the United States Supreme Court enunciated such a doctrine in *Plessy* v. *Ferguson.*

Booker T. Washington's speech was extremely short as nineteenth-century southern orations went, but it was indeed forceful in its dramatic allusions. His critics said he confirmed the white man's prejudices, but the press all across the nation had extravagant praise for the speech.

Mr. President and Gentlemen of the Board of Directors and Citizens:

Booker T. Washington, *Up from Slavery, an Autobiography* (New York: Garden City, 1901), 221–222.

One third of the population of the South is of the Negro race. No enterprise seeking the material, civil, or moral welfare of this section can disregard this element of our population and reach the highest success. I but convey to you, Mr. President and Directors, the sentiment of the masses of my race when I say that in no way have the value and manhood of the American Negro been more fittingly and generously recognized than by the managers of this magnificent exposition at every stage of its progress. It is a recognition that will do more to cement the friendship of the two races than any occurrence since the dawn of our freedom.

Not only this, but the opportunity here afforded will awaken among us a new era of industrial progress. Ignorant and inexperienced, it is not strange that in the first years of our new life we began at the top instead of at the bottom; that a seat in Congress or the State Legislature was more sought than real estate or industrial skill; that the political convention or stump-speaking had more attraction than starting a dairy farm or truck garden.

A ship lost at sea for many days suddenly sighted a friendly vessel. From the mast of the unfortunate vessel was seen a signal: "Water, water; we die of thirst!" The answer from the friendly vessel at once came back: "Cast down your bucket where you are." A second time the signal, "Water, water; send us water!" ran up from the distressed vessel, and was answered: "Cast down your bucket where you are." And a third and fourth signal for water was answered, "Cast down your bucket where you are." The captain of the distressed vessel, at last heeding the injunction, cast down his bucket, and it came up full of fresh, sparkling water from the mouth of the Amazon River. To those of my race who depend upon bettering their condition in a foreign land, or who underestimate the importance of cultivating friendly relations with the Southern white man who is their next-door neighbor, I would say: "Cast down your bucket where you are"—cast it down in making friends, in every manly way, of the people of all races by whom we are surrounded.

Cast it down in agriculture, mechanics, in commerce, in domestic service, and in the professions. And in this connection it is well to bear in mind that whatever other sins the South may be called to bear, when it comes to business, pure and simple, it is in the South that the Negro is given a man's chance in the commercial world, and in nothing is this Exposition more eloquent than in emphasizing this chance. Our greatest danger is that in the great leap from slavery to freedom we may overlook the fact that the masses of us are to live by the productions of our hands, and fail to keep in mind that we shall prosper in proportion as we learn to dignify and glorify common labor, and put brains and skill into the common occupations of life; shall prosper in proportion as we learn to draw the line between the superficial and the substantial, the ornamental gew-gaws of life and the useful. No race can prosper till it learns that there is as much dignity in tilling a field as in writing a poem. It is at the bottom of life we must begin, and not at the top. Nor should we permit our grievances to overshadow our opportunities.

To those of the white race who look to the incoming of those of foreign birth and strange tongue and habits for the prosperity of the South, were I permitted, I would repeat what I say to my own race, "Cast down your bucket where you are." Cast it down among the eight million Negroes whose habits you know, whose fidelity and love you have tested in days when to have proved treacherous meant the ruin of your firesides. Cast down your bucket among these people who have without strikes and labor wars tilled your fields, cleared your forests, builded your railroads and cities, brought forth treasures from the bowels of the earth, and helped make possible this magnificent representation of the progress of the South. Casting down your bucket among my people, helping and encouraging them as you are doing on these grounds, and, with education of head, hand, and heart, you will find that they will buy your surplus land, make blossom the waste places in your fields, and run your factories. While doing this, you can be sure in the future, as in the past, that you and your families will be surrounded by the most patient, faithful, law-abiding, and unresentful people that the world has seen. As we have proved our loyalty to you in the past, in nursing your children, watching by the sick bed of your mothers and fathers, and often following them with tear-dimmed eyes to their graves, so in the future, in our humble way, we shall stand by you with a devotion that no foreigner can approach, ready to lay down our lives, if need be, in defense of yours, interlacing our industrial, commercial, civil, and religious life with yours in a way that shall make the interests of both races one. In all things that are purely social we can be as separate as the fingers, yet one as the hand in all things essential to mutual progress.

There is no defense or security for any of us except in the highest intelligence and development of all. If anywhere there are efforts tending to curtail the fullest growth of the Negro, let these efforts be turned into stimulating, encouraging, and making him the most useful and intelligent citizen. Effort or means so invested will pay a thousand per cent interest. These efforts will be twice blessed—"Blessing him that gives and him that takes."

There is no escape through law of man or God from the inevitable:

> *The laws of changeless justice bind*
> *Oppressor with oppressed;*
> *And close as sin and suffering joined*
> *We march to fare abreast.*

Nearly sixteen millions of hands will aid you in pulling the load upward, or they will pull, against you, the load downward. We shall constitute one third and more of the ignorance and crime of the South, or one third its intelligence and progress; we shall contribute one third to the business and industrial prosperity of the South, or we shall prove a veritable body of death, stagnating, depressing, retarding every effort to advance the body politic.

Gentlemen of the Exposition, as we present to you our humble effort at an exhibition of our progress, you must not expect overmuch. Starting thirty years ago with ownership here and there in a few quilts and pumpkins and chickens (gathered from miscellaneous sources), remember, the path that has led from these to the inventions and production of agricultural implements, buggies, steam engines, newspapers, books, statuary carving, paintings, the management of drugstores and banks, has not been trodden without contact with thorns and thistles. While we take pride in what we exhibit as a result of our independent efforts, we do not for a moment forget that our part in this exhibition would fall far short of your expectations but for the constant help that has come to our educational life, not only from the Southern states, but especially from Northern philanthropists, who have made their gifts a constant stream of blessing and encouragement.

The wisest among my race understand that the agitation of questions of social equality is the extremist folly, and that progress in the enjoyment of all the privileges that will come to us must be the result of severe and constant struggle rather than of artificial forcing. No race that has anything to contribute to the markets of the world is long, in any degree, ostracized. It is important and right that all privileges of the law be ours, but it is vastly more important that we be prepared for the exercise of those privileges. The opportunity to earn a dollar in a factory just now is worth infinitely more than the opportunity to spend a dollar in an opera house.

In conclusion, may I repeat that nothing in thirty years has given us more hope and encouragement, and drawn us so near to you of the white race, as this opportunity offered by the Exposition; and here bending, as it were, over the altar that represents the results of the struggles of your race and mine, both starting practically empty-handed three decades ago, I pledge that, in your effort to work out the great and intricate problem which God has laid at the doors of the South, you shall have at all times the patient, sympathetic help of my race; only let this be constantly in mind, that while, from representations in these buildings of the product of field, of forest, of mine, of factory, letters, and art, much good will come, yet far above and beyond material benefits will be that higher good, that, let us pray God, will come in a blotting out of sectional differences and racial animosities and suspicions, in a determination to administer absolute justice, in a willing obedience among all classes to the mandates of law. This, coupled with our material prosperity, will bring into our beloved South a new heaven and a new earth.

55 Education in the South

One of the most important crusaders for educational advancement in the South at the turn of the nineteenth century was Edwin A. Alderman. He took an active part in the campaign in North Carolina to build a public school system. Later he became President of Tulane University, and then President of the University of Virginia. President Alderman's observations on the background of the drive to develop universal education have marked historical significance. He also revealed a kind of racial liberalism which should have been heeded more respectfully in the South at the beginning of the twentieth century.

You have asked me to write on Education in the South. All the years of adult life spent in educational service in the South give me some right, perhaps, to speak. I have a desire to set forth, briefly, what has been done, and what needs to be done, in order to build up, in the southern portion of our Union, an educational system adequate to the needs of an industrial democracy fretted by a stupendous racial question.

Some things ought, by this time, to be tolerably fixed in the consciousness of every thoughtful American citizen, and need

Edwin Anderson Alderman, "Education in the South," *The Outlook,* 68 (August 3, 1901), 775–780.

not call, therefore, for lengthy exposition or argument. Education in democracies is not a question of philanthropy or expediency, but of life and death. As democracy has not yet proven its right to exist as the ultimate form of government, neither has statesmanship evolved even a tolerably wise system of universal education. Many of the problems of the South are also problems of the North and the East. Educational systems, it should be understood, are forced upon peoples by the pressure of real or apparent social needs, and are not superimposed by mere individual intelligence or will.

The period of time between 1810 and 1860 was for the South a period of isolation, during which, holding itself proudly aloof from the ferments of the modern world, it went its own way and created its own individual, dramatic, militant social forms, with their blending of splendid virtues and fatal weaknesses. There was need for political leadership and for the willful, masterful man. Private academies, seminaries, colleges, and universities arose to supply this need, and it is doubtful if there were anywhere in the world, outside of Scotland, better schools for the training of the few than existed in the South prior to the Civil War, and there issued from them the smallest but the strongest and most alert political force that Christendom has ever seen. The value and dignity of the common man—the single individual—to society was not realized, unhappily, and, therefore, the common school with rural conditions to struggle against, could not take root in the South. The value of all the public-school property of the Southern States prior to 1870 did not equal the cost of one great, modern high-school building to-day. Of course slaves could not be educated systematically and remain slaves.

The quality of no people in history has ever been more grimly tested than the quality of the Southern people from 1860 to 1880, which period might be described as the period of war and submersion. I shall not dwell upon it here. Its heroisms stir my blood, its sufferings touch my heart, its achievements arouse my pride. The first vivid recollection of my life was a glimpse of the regnant face of General Lee in 1869, and hence the shadows of this time of anarchy, of poverty, and prejudice of the world darkened the days of my childhood. The burden upon the men of the time was to maintain racial integrity, to establish new institutions for strange new needs, to find a clue to modern economic systems, to earn bread for their children and the children of their slaves, and, hardest of all, to conquer pride and to keep their spirits sweet and unspoiled. Defeat and disaster could not destroy their English consciousness and their inflexible purpose to rule their own local affairs. Let us forgive them any lack of philosophical insight or academic viewpoints, as we must forgive our brethren of the North some tragic blundering and some tactless philanthropy. It is sufficient praise of these men, molding in unquiet times a new life, to say that fifteen years after the war had ceased we found ourselves living in a new world of friendly feeling, of waning intolerance, of educational desire, and of marvelous material prosperity.

From 1880 until now has been the period of awakening and achievement, and the South has entered at last upon its probation as a member of the modern world. Southern people have taken deeply to heart the conviction that no civilization can grow great in poverty. The Southern boy now reaching up into life has many other ambitions besides statesmanship. He wants to know how to build bridges, to manufacture raw material, to set up machinery, to organize industry, to exploit material resources, and in general to get money together. This is the most deeply rooted idea in the Southern mind to-day. It existed as a controlling impulse in the early days of the century, but slavery paralyzed it, and the present movement is in the nature of a renaissance. There need be no fears that the South will fail to look after the industrial education of its sons and daughters in the new century. Indeed, there are signs that it may overdo it, after the zigzag fashion of educational and social movement. Already the dollarless man has some difficulty in explaining himself away, and it is almost amusing to behold sleepy little towns, that once dozed under the sun, black and dirty and busy and happy, sending salable products all around the earth. I rejoice in this industrial impulse. The test of character will come in the using of the wealth so obtained, but it is altogether wise to obtain the wealth and to possess the mechanical skill.

The South has also taken to heart the conviction that the chief problem of every society is to realize its highest self in life and in law, not by personal courage or raw individualism, but by scholarly activity and community effort. An examination of statistics will reveal many noble and impressive beginnings in the direction of this self-realization. State universities destroyed by war have been revived and new ones established on broader foundations in every Southern State. It is difficult to speak too warmly of the work done by these institutions. They are directed and taught by able and unselfish scholars, holding high ideals, and they do what they attempt to do honestly and well. They are crippled by poverty and by the mania for the multiplication of small colleges, but I believe it is true to say that they accomplish more on small means than any institutions except the Scottish universities. The sum of all their endowments does not equal the endowments of any one of a half dozen Northern and Western institutions. What strength they have is internal—the strength of moral energy, of faith in the belief that they are the symbols of the benign force that shall work out the good life of their land. What strength they need is the strength of endowment, of apparatus, of ample and even magnificent surroundings, that they may arise so sharply and clearly out of low levels that they may set new standards and establish new conceptions of college life. The material they have to work upon is of the best—simple, healthy minded, earnest young Americans of unmixed blood, who are reaching up into life through sacrifice and toil, and who have the Scottish faith in and enthusiasm for the dignity and power of knowledge.

The colleges of the churches have been the objects of great sacrifice and heroism. Some of them, it must be frankly confessed, have no reason to exist save that of denominational pride, but a goodly number of them are great forces for good, manned by scholars, and are sending out yearly well-trained men into Southern life. Private philanthropy, almost unknown in antebellum days, and still timid, has endowed a few institutions, like

Vanderbilt University, Tulane University, Newcomb College, a department of Tulane; Converse College, and Trinity College in North Carolina. Only three of these were endowed by people of Southern birth, and their endowments are so small that they still need most of the equipment necessary to great universities. The aristocratic and theological systems neglected industrial training entirely, and made provision only for the fortunately born and well-to-do classes among women. The land-grant colleges born out of the wisdom of the National Government have arisen to supply the first neglect, and a juster and broader view of life has tardily remedied the neglect of a century by the creation of colleges for women modern in spirit and of approved power and promise. Successful efforts have been made to train teachers both in normal schools to which they were bidden to come, and by a widespread system of institutes which went to their doors.

Lastly, and greatest of all, a system of public schools for whites and blacks supported by public taxation, and this means largely taxation of the whites, has been established in every Southern community, and is being slowly strengthened under stupendous difficulties. The movement received its first impulse in the cities and towns, and from them has spread like a blessed contagion, as each community perceived its value. The city schools of the Southern States are as good as any in the land, for the reason that they command the services of the very finest and highest types of young Southern womanhood and manhood. The principle of local taxation for schools as well as for jails and poorhouses has been written in the statute books, and the commitment of the leaders of public thought, however faintly, to this principle of local taxation for schools is the surpassing achievement of this period of awakening. That the child has a right to be educated, that it is the State's duty to guard and maintain that right, is now in the South an axiom in public policy. Fifteen years ago this was a proposition to be debated, but to-day it is a truism, and measures the growth of the public conscience and intelligence during that period of time. Sophisms and doctrinaire theories have fallen away, and the

people of the South are asking this question, How shall we build
a worthy system of education for all the people? Their earnestness is made manifest in the fact that they tax themselves in
proportion to their wealth more heavily than the rich urban
communities of the country. One must go back to the days of
Horace Mann for the spirit of this movement. It has been more
than a movement. It has been a crusade against hampering tradition, false individualism, and racial entanglement. The leader
of it has been J. L. M. Curry—a rare blending of the grace and
charm of the old time with the vigor and freedom of the new.
Around him have gathered a group of young Southern scholars
and a few older heads of wisdom and civic virtue. These men,
whose names I dare not mention, lest I omit some, deserve well
of their time, for, though disheartened, they have never been
daunted, and they are now able to see as a result of their pleading a new kind of leadership and a new type of statesman appearing in Southern politics—the educational statesman—the
man who bases his campaign upon popular education, who
stands or falls on the principle of taxation of property for the
creation of intelligence, citizenship, and ampler institutional
life. Charles B. Aycock, the new Governor of North Carolina,
is, perhaps, the most conspicuous example of the Southern ideal-
ist lifted beyond partisanship, and carrying into politics the
heart of a reformer and the training of a scholar, but the type
may be found in other gubernatorial chairs and places of power.

The South then has traveled far in educational growth, and
deserves high praise, but after all it has not traveled very far
and its journey has just begun. The South is a rural community.
Four-fifths of its people live in the country. This is a tremendous
obstacle to educational progress. The first great need of this
rural community is more money with which to provide a nine
months' school for its children in every school district, with
better-paid and better-equipped teachers. The average length
of the rural-school term in the South does not much exceed
twelve weeks out of the year. A nine months' school term would
give birth to secondary schools, and they in turn would
strengthen universities and colleges. The money needed for this

great end must come from home, from the people who see its
influence upon the lives of their children, and it is my belief
that these people will gladly spend this money when they are
aroused and enlightened and made to feel in their marrow and
bones its vital importance. It is difficult to arouse democracies,
and especially rural democracies. They must be talked to and
pleaded with and written at in effective ways, and the people
of the South are still old-fashioned enough to submit to this.
The greatest opportunity ever offered to constructive philanthropy lies just here, in my judgment. If there existed in each
Southern State a group of able men, of power and proven experience, guided in a systematic way, whose business it was to
cover the territory of that State in an untiring campaign of education for a number of years, the close of the first decade of this
century would see the wise adjustment of most of the educational difficulties of the South. There would be opportunities
for these men to teach the teachers and the people, to convert
clever politicians and journalists into educational statesmen, to
transform State Legislatures into educational associations, to
suggest wiser educational organization, and to stimulate to
helpfulness and benevolence the growing wealth of the South.
It was not the fashion in the South of the past, nor is it much
the fashion of the present, save among women, to give money
to education, partly because Southern people are in the accumu-
lative stage of money-getting, after an experience of direst poverty, and partly because, as a stunting inheritance from that
poverty, they have grown accustomed to the use of small means
for great objects. The law of philanthropy, however, is local.
If Southern institutions are to grow great, Southern wealth must
lead in that movement. The temper of the Southern States is
just ready for this campaign of education. It is in the mood to
be helped to self-help.

The interest on a few million dollars would put this movement on an enduring basis. If the Peabody Fund has stimulated
its thousands to encouraging beginnings, this would influence
its tens of thousands to splendid finalities. Is it too much to hope
that there will arise some genius of social co-operation who will

undertake to make possible this great agency—some Pierpont
Morgan of the educational world, with his eyes upon the common people who work in the shadows of the world, and upon
a land somewhat overborne with difficult and vexed problems?

The next great need of the South in education is a scientific
co-relation of the various branches of its so-called educational
system. Education is one whole process. Primary, secondary,
higher are mere convenient terms, like day and night, month and
year. There is a deadly reality in these unrealities in our educational system. That system is unconnected, uncoordinated, and
self-sufficient. The public schools, the high schools, the colleges
and universities are not articulated in sympathetic ways, but
stand off and war against each other as if they were rivals. Feeble
colleges multiply. There are more mono-hippic colleges and universities in Tennessee and Texas than there are universities on
the continent of Europe. New ones are established yearly, and
begin a career of ineffectual achievement and heroic poverty.
Much of this, of course, is due to mistaken educational enthusiasm, local and denominational pride, and commercial interpretations of culture. Great harm results in the setting up of false
ideas of liberal training, in the cheapening of historic degrees,
in preventing lofty, genuine leadership, high above clamor or
poverty of politics. It is my belief that each Southern State ought
to appoint an educational commission of five or more able students of education to investigate the subject of educational organization and taxation, and report for discussion some large
unwasteful plan in the room of the atomistic agencies now
going at great, delicate concerns, as freebooters go to battle.

The third great need of the South is a few amply, even mag-
nificently, equipped institutions set at logical and strategic
points in its area, where a sound, modern, various learning
might be taught to the young men and women who must direct
our life. These institutions should be especially effective in the
subjects of technology, economics, sociology, and philosophy,
for these are our issues for the next twenty years. The cities
should take care of their own schools, and they will do so. The
churches should take care of their own, where they exist pri-

marily for church purposes. The State universities and the land-grant colleges, simply as such, are proper charges upon the State itself, and civic self-respect demands that they be so maintained, and maintained generously. Colleges for the training of teachers will grow naturally out of enlarged facilities for popular education. A union of all forces—ecclesiastical, civic, and philanthropical—are needed, however, to create inspiring institutions, and, in addition, there must be some certainty that the institutions so aided have proven their right to exist and occupy such a geographical position as will insure their indefinite growth. There are only six or eight such institutions in the Southern States between Johns Hopkins on the North and Tulane University on the South, including these two institutions. Hampton Institute and Tuskegee Institute ought to be continually strengthened as the great training-grounds and experiment-stations for the education of the negro race. To establish new colleges while the potentially great institutions struggle on in poverty, turning away precious young scholars because they have no loan funds or fellowships or scholarships, is a piece of pure folly. If it is desired to furnish the highest kind of technical instruction, strengthen that department in the strongest of these institutions. It is my belief that departments of philosophy and sociology, amply endowed for the scholarly study of social conditions and for the inculcation of right theories of life in three or four of these colleges, would accomplish more results in ending the reign of the empiric and the politician, and ushering in the trained thinker, the sympathetic, orderly minded man, than two-thirds of the money spent on negro education since 1870. Booker Washington, with his great gifts of heart and brain, will live in history merely as a racial phenomenon, without lasting effect upon his time, if there does not come to him the intelligent sympathy of the white men of the South, trained to justice and power in the handling of social questions.

The fourth and acutest need of the South—perhaps I might say of our whole country—is an ever-widening circle of scholars whose minds are set upon the building of their institutions in righteousness and wisdom rather than upon obtaining the reward of their own smartness. We have suffered much from men who settled things first and learned about them afterwards. We need men who know about things before settling them, and who are dowered with social sympathy and faith in the common man. The "brave, free scholar," as pictured by Emerson in his memorable address, is the man who sees things as they are and hates violence; who has no fear of oppression, because he is strong; who cannot be deceived, because he has been trained and knows truth from mania and the fates of nations and the experiences of cities of men; who cannot be terrorized, because he is not afraid; who cannot be starved, because his hands have skill and his brain has cunning. This real sort of scholar is needed to aid in the transformation of unthinking, careless men, without tastes or wants, into men with ideals; men who can see the relation of law to society and what it means to defy law even to protect innocence; men who can see the beauty and the interest of life; men who love their towns, their villages, their front yards, back yards, highways, parks, schools, and libraries, and thus, proceeding upward, grow into a finer notion of the perils and privileges of republican citizenship. His coming, too, would make an end to the time when it would be possible to estimate Southern thought in the gross, and to predict, in advance, Southern action in bulk.

The education of the negro demands another article, and my limit of space is reached. This much must be said, however. The South has never been in so generous and thoughtful a mood toward the negro race as it is to-day, while his disfranchisement is going on apace in every Southern State. This is a movement to get rid of the negro as a menacing political factor, disturbing the judgment of men and arousing their passions in order to get a breathing-spell in which to think on him righteously and justly as a human being, as a racial problem, as a black man, who cannot be sent away and who cannot be permitted to dominate intelligence. It is the first moment since the colossal folly of his enfranchisement that Southern men could *think* about the question at all, and their deepest conviction now is that, having established forever their dominance and integrity as a race, they must justify themselves to posterity by acting toward the negro in a spirit of justice and wisdom. Indeed, this movement of disfranchisement goes deeper than that, and is altogether beneficent in its purposes. It means at bottom that the right to vote is a right to be won by intelligence and character, and to be won by the ignorant white man as well as by the ignorant black man. If the Filipino or the Porto Rican ever shares in our Government, he will do so after generations of preparation for the sacred right. Ignorance, whether in whites or blacks, in North or South, in cities or in countries, ought to be subjected to the same test. There are many millions of negroes in the South. It might as well be confessed that much of the $25,000,000 spent on them by Northern philanthropy has been literally wasted, and much of the $100,000,000 spent on them by Southern taxation has been likewise wasted, but this waste is almost as much the fault of those who spent it as it is of the negroes who received it. The attempt to put the negro in possession of the traditional culture of the Anglo-Saxon race was an absurd piece of American haste. Putting behind us, then, the era of wrong ideals of education, of sentimentalism, and of much solemn nonsense, let us go forward another step. The negro must be educated. Ignorance is no remedy for anything. Any other theory is monstrous. I indulge in no fantasies, or prophecies, or forecasts, optimistic or pessimistic. I cannot foresee the future any more than John C. Calhoun could foresee Booker Washington delighting and instructing a Charleston audience. Our duty is with the present, to use such knowledge and sympathy as we have, and let the future do likewise. It is wise and just to help the black man to character and usefulness; but I cannot reiterate too strongly my belief that the white man is and ought to be and will be the controling force, and that he will act toward the negro in the light of his training. The education, therefore, of one untaught white man to the point that knowledge and not prejudice will guide his conduct, and that he must deal with these people in justice and kindness, is worth more to the black man himself than the education of ten negroes. The Southern people need help for the noble discharge of this mighty task, not bald, smug alms-giving; not the altruism of the remote nor the cocksure theories of the unaffected, but substantial, brotherly confidence and help from their fellow-countrymen of every section. One of the encouraging notes of the times is the growth of this large confidence and sympathy with the Southern man in his dealings with the negro.

56 The Educational Needs of the South

The year 1904 was a crucial one in many ways for the southern educational crusade. In this period some directions had already been set; the General and Southern Educational boards were now having a genuine impact. For the first time the region as a whole was to get a rather clear statistical view of its educational situation.[*] Much had been published in periodicals and newspapers, but by the turn of the century more attention was given precise statistics. This fact was made immediately evident in the new statements by educational leaders. S. C. Mitchell delivered the following address in New York at a dinner given by Richard C. Ogden. Subsequently he repeated it in Richmond, and it was then published in the *Outlook*. Mitchell's terms are general, but the paper summarizes the historical background of the crusade for universal education in the South and outlines several of the central problems.

THE ADVENT OF THE GENERAL AND SOUTHERN EDUCATION BOARDS marked a distinct epoch in the development of the South. Even before the present renaissance, here and there an aggressive man or woman was striking for a higher educational ideal. Such workers the Southern Education Board heartened and made

[*] Charles L. Coon, *Facts About Southern Educational Progress, A Present Day Study in Public School Maintenance for Those Who Look Forward* (Raleigh: North Carolina Dept. of Education, 1905).

528

more effective by drawing them together in bold and concerted action. The patriotic motives which animated the leaders of the movement, and the wisdom and tact which characterized its advance, soon silenced criticism. Fresh and widespread enthusiasm was given to the educational cause through the press, secular and religious, and through the admirable addresses of the agents of the Boards. I have heard Dr. Fraser speaking upon practical phases of education to vast crowds upon the banks of the Rappahannock, and Mr. St. George Tucker addressing throngs of country people gathered under an arbor at the foot of the Blue Ridge. Such meetings have been held in all parts of Virginia, with most encouraging results. By way of indicating how vital is the work undertaken, and the necessity therefor, a brief retrospect of the conditions in the South may not be out of place.

In the Atlantic Ocean there is only one gulf current, but in the nineteenth century there were three gulf currents. These three streams of tendency are as traceable, as measurable, and as potent in their influence as that resistless river in the sea. What, now, were these three tendencies in the nineteenth century?

I. *Liberal.* The liberal tendency of that age was both the strongest and the most easily discernible. The French Revolution, which ushered in the nineteenth century, was a frenzy for freedom. Before the rush of its emancipating spirit there went down in irretrievable ruin the absolutist governments which had held in bondage the continent of Europe. Stein's memorable edict of the 9th of October, 1807, abolishing serfdom in Prussia, is not so much an achievement of individual genius as the most vivid expression of the differences between the old and new Europe. Other countries followed perforce, even Russia freeing her serfs in 1861. The odious distinctions of feudalism, with the obsolete privileges of the aristocrat, were one after another swept away; equality for all before the law was established; liberal constitutions were wrested from despots; the press was unmuzzled;

S. C. Mitchell, "The Educational Needs of the South," *The Outlook* 76 (February 13, 1904), 415–419.

labor was unshackled; in a word, every man was given a chance. It is pleasing to recall that it was our fathers of 1776 who intoned the dominant note of that great century. Jefferson's Declaration of Independence is the prelude to the French Revolution and its far-reaching liberal influences.

II. *National.* The national tendency in the nineteenth century was hardly less strong than the liberal. The two tendencies, the liberal and the national, though separable, were found usually working in unison. Nationality is to a race what personality is to a man. The desire of each race to set up housekeeping for itself, to live under its own vine and fig tree, to feel the full force of the spirit of kinship in its unifying effect, to attain to complete racial individuality—this intense and spontaneous yearning for nationality was to transform the map of Europe in the nineteenth century. We can note only the results. Heroic Greece led off in 1829; Belgium succeeded in 1830, Holland being individualized at the same time; Italy and Germany made good their nationality in 1870; and eight years thereafter Rumania, Servia, and Montenegro reached the same goal. Poland, Ireland, and Hungary, despite heroic struggles to form nations, have failed, while yesterday the Macedonians in the Balkan peninsula were in arms against the Turk in order to win the prize of nationality for themselves. Who can doubt that they will attain it, the Berlin Treaty of Beaconsfield to the contrary notwithstanding? The stars in their courses fight for progress. Nationality has shown itself an electric and resistless force.

III. *Industrial.* The industrial tendency of the nineteenth century was also marked. Invention kept pace with liberty and nationality. On the 5th of January, 1769, James Watt announced his patent "for a method of lessening the consumption of steam and fuel in fire engines." That is regarded as the birthday of England's manufacturing supremacy, as well as marking the transition in all progressive States from the exclusively agricultural to the industrial status. In 1787 a clergyman of Kent, Cartwright, produced the power-loom. Six years later a Connecticut school-teacher, living in Georgia, invented the cotton-gin. What changes followed may be faintly suggested by recalling the fact that in 1784 an American ship landed eight bales of cotton at Liverpool, and the custom-house officers seized them, on the ground that cotton was not a product of the United States. Coal, steam, steel, electricity—these made a new earth, giving magic wealth and power to nations in the van, such as England, Germany, and France. Society became dominantly industrial.

Circumstances—cruel circumstances that bring tears at the thought—had shut the South out of a share in these three mighty influences of that century. Destiny seemed to have arrayed her against them, in spite of the fact that in the closing quarter of the eighteenth century Virginia's own sons were pioneers in the advocacy of national and liberal measures. Such is the pathos and irony of the civil tragedy. Madison, as the father of the Constitution; Washington, putting his strong stamp upon the Federal executive; Marshall, giving force to the Federal judiciary; and Jefferson, drafting the preliminary ordinance of 1787, excluding slavery from the Northwest Territory—these men and measures appeared prophetic of a destiny for the South the reverse of what ensued. The shift in the scene was made by Eli Whitney in his invention, in 1793, of the cotton-gin, which rendered slavery profitable in the raising of cotton, a product so well suited to the climate and soil of the South.

As a result, the South found itself at variance with the rapid changes which had swept over the world during the first half of the nineteenth century. The South was led by this train of circumstances—

(1) To hold on to slavery in opposition to the liberal tendency of the age.

(2) To insist upon States' rights in opposition to nationality.

(3) To content herself with agriculture alone, instead of embracing the rising industrialism.

It was an instance of arrested development. The facts do not permit us to escape this conclusion, notwithstanding that there was so much of nobility, chivalry, and beautiful life in the old South to love and admire. It was these historic forces—the liberal, national, and industrial—that won at Appomattox over the South, in spite of the genius of Lee, the heroism of her sons, and the sacrifices of her daughters.

If this be the interpretation of the confused forces in that time that tried men's souls, then certain duties become clear as to the South of our day. These are—

(1) To liberalize it in thought.

(2) To nationalize it in politics.

(3) To industrialize it in production.

Gratifyingly are these new forces at work—forces which are to re-create the commonwealths of the South in all that makes for progress and power. Education is a present ferment; industrialism, especially in cotton and iron mills, is making vast strides; the Panama Canal will put us on the pathway of the world. We are beginning to see that "if cotton is ever king, its scepter will be a spindle." By such alignments with this wondrous mother-age, we shall enable the South to take her rightful part in determining the National destiny.

The task, therefore, of the present educational movement is to help on these progressive tendencies. How can that best be done? What are the greatest educational needs of the South at this time? They are, in my opinion, two: teachers and publicists. The first will leaven the masses, while the second will flank the demagogue. It would be hard to say which of these two needs is the more pressing, the uplifting of the masses or the proper leading of the public mind.

As concerns the negro, his primary need is likewise for teachers and leaders, moral, well trained, and deeply sensible of race responsibility. Such a man will say, with the Apostle, "Who is weak, and I am not weak? Who is made to stumble, and I burn not?" Needless to say that some such leaders the negroes now have. No other race has made such progress, if you consider the depths from which it has risen and the difficulties which it has encountered. It took a thousand years to train the Teuton, from the fifth to the fifteenth centuries. He who condemns the negro because of his lack of will power either in work or morals would do well to remember that slavery weakens that special faculty in man.

The negro can neither be deported nor repressed, but, by means of the slow and sure forces of education and religion,

he is becoming capable in industry and moral in society. About
such a process there is nothing dramatic, not to say tragic; but
it is just, humane, and feasible—in a word, statesmanlike. It is
of course understood that by education and religion for the
negro I mean very practical things. His education must be
both mental and manual, and his religion must be wholly moral.
Fitness for life is the thing desired. Before the negro there
stand four doors through which he may perhaps force an entrance: (1) thrift, (2) education, (3) religion, and (4) politics.
The pity is that he bolted first for the last door—politics. But
this mistake is correcting itself, as he sees that suffrage is a
privilege to be gained only by the worthy, reckoned according
to property and intelligence. This burrowing notion is inciting
him more and more to press into the gateways of thrift, education, and religion. An anti-negro plank in the next Democratic
platform would be the worst political blunder as regards the
South since the passage of the Fugitive Slave Law.

Such being the conditions in the South, we must have more
normal schools, especially for women, better pay for our teachers in the common schools, longer sessions than at present, expert
school superintendents, and, to secure these, National aid for
education given through the agency of the State according
to illiteracy, and available only after a minimum rate of taxation
has been levied.

The other need of the South to which I alluded is that of
publicists in larger numbers. And by this term I mean, not office-
seekers—they, alas! are legion—but men who can bring scientific intelligence to bear upon the economic, social, and political
conditions confronting us. Such men may influence the public
mind through the press, or as legislators, or as teachers, or as
financiers, or in any other of the numerous callings open to
forceful leaders. The two things requisite in such a class of
publicists are the spirit of social service and specialized intelligence. The advent to power in several Southern States of
men thus endowed is one of the most hopeful signs of the times.
The conditions in the South resulting from the war have given

the demagogue his day, his hey-day. Excluded largely from wholesome contact with National politics, and hence not knowing the steadying responsibilities of vast public trusts, the average politician has found in the appeal to the prejudices of the people an exhaustless mine of sordid profit. Naturally, his own powers have become contracted to the limits of the prejudices which he has tried to congeal. The stock in trade of the politician has been to dangle the bones of the skeleton in the Southern closet. At the faintest sound of that gruesome noise, all the children were straightway hushed, independence of thought and action vanished, and the stage was left bare for the wiles of the demagogue. Democracy, which is often neither economical nor efficient, ceased to become educative—losing thereby its essential virtue. There was no opposition party to fulfill the healthful function of criticism. Am I mistaken in believing that there is a general tendency upon the part of the thoughtful people of the South to escape from these leading-strings? This in part is the explanation of the new constitutions which largely remove the negro from politics. The ex-slave had enslaved the South. Democracy is government by discussion; but where only one party exists the discussion becomes a monologue. The zest of political life and the interplay of social forces disappeared. As a result, the public mind of the South became, not so much stagnant, as a fertile field for all sorts of political vagaries. The solidarity of the South came to mean the inertness of a mass. From such sterile conditions aggressive and discriminating leadership was hardly to be expected. Happily, all of this is now changing. In my opinion, no public speaker in the South to-day can intone a more responsive note than that of nationality. This was to me the remarkable fact disclosed at the Southern Education Conference in Richmond last spring. It became evident, as the discussions progressed, that each of the Southern speakers had, in the secrecy of his own study, reached this conclusion as to nationality, believing, forsooth, his own opinion in that regard to be novel and individual. When all came together upon this candid platform, it was with surprise that each found his own view to be the reigning opinion.

57 The Forgotten Man

In June 1897, Walter Hines Page, the expatriate North Carolinian, was invited to deliver an address at the State Normal and Industrial School for Women. Page had earlier edited a newspaper in Raleigh, and was one of the organizers of the famous Watauga Club. He was very much concerned with the failure of his fellow Southerners to recognize that they really held the key to their region's progress. Whatever damages they had suffered from the Civil War or the indignities of Reconstruction, the fate of the New South rested in the hands of the people. According to Page the first and most necessary reform was the establishing of a system of universal education. He told his audience that the turn of the century was an age that demanded new approaches to southern problems, and that the old educational procedures were no longer suitable. Graphically Page portrayed for his audience the man of the masses who could be made productive, but at present acted as a brake on southern civilization because he had been passed by. It was time to lift up forgotten men, women, and children, said this expatriate southern writer and lecturer. The South could yet begin to catch up if only it would establish a system of public schools that would permit those capable of acquiring an education to advance from kindergarten all the way to graduation from a state university.

WE HAVE OFTEN REMINDED OURSELVES AND INFORMED OTHER people that we have incalculable undeveloped resources in

North Carolina, in our streams, our forests, our mines, our quarries, our soil—that Nature has been most bountiful; so that our undeveloped resources invite men under the pleasantest conditions to productive industry. And so they do. But there is one undeveloped resource more valuable than all these, and that is the people themselves. It is about the development of men that I shall speak, more particularly about the development of forgotten and neglected men.

. . . The doctrine of equality of opportunity is at the bottom of social progress, for you can never judge a man's capacity except as he has opportunity to develop it. When we make a social study, we must come face to face with all the men who make up the social body, seeing them as they are, and not through the medium of our traditions nor by their estimates of themselves.

From this point of view let me make a very rapid and general survey of the culture of men in North Carolina—of the social structure and the social forces that have shaped our civilization.

In the days of our fathers the social structure was to a slight extent aristocratic, but it was much less aristocratic than the social structure was, for example, in Virginia or in South Carolina. The mass of the people were common people; they lived directly out of the soil and they had the manners and the virtues and the limitations of a simple agricultural population, which was much the same in the early part of the century in all countries where a livelihood was easily obtained. They were nearly all of English and Scotch, and Scotch-Irish stock. Most of them were sprung from peasants of sturdy qualities; a very few from gentlemen; and some were descended from forced and hired immigrants. Taken all together they were a common people, capable of as sound development as the population of any other State. But they were ignorant, as the common people in all lands were a hundred years ago.

. . . These things I mention not in blame of our ancestors. It is out of just such stock that the men came who to-day rule the

Walter Hines Page, *The Rebuilding of Old Commonwealths* (New York: Doubleday, Page & Company, 1902), 1–47.

world. But I mention these things because we ourselves have written and spoken much nonsense about ourselves and about our ancestors and have made ourselves believe that we were in some way different from other sturdy folk and that we were in some way better than other common people. Thus we have come to put a false value on our social structure, and we have never looked ourselves in the face and seen ourselves as others see us. This false view has done incalculable hurt. All social progress must begin with a clear understanding of men as they are.

. . . We are all common folk, then, who were once dominated by a little aristocracy, which, in its social and economic character, made a failure and left a stubborn crop of wrong social notions behind it—especially about education.

There lingers one very striking relic of the aristocratic structure of opinion in North Carolina—a certain timidity on the part of our leaders in dealing with the public, a timidity on the part of the leaders, which we have falsely called conservatism on the part of the people, a hesitation to trust the people's judgment. It cropped out humorously on this platform yesterday. Mr. Scarborough declared that our people were conservative—very conservative! You must consider what they are ready for and what they are not ready for, for they are very conservative. A half hour later, while narrating the career of Dorothea Dix, Mr. Carr showed how one woman of enthusiasm came here from Massachusetts and induced the State to spend for a single institution at one time (and that an asylum for the insane) a larger sum than the whole annual resources of the State government; and no man has from that day to this made objection to the expenditure. Our whole history is full of such incidents. Almost every noteworthy thing that we have done has been done in obedience to an impulse. Conservative? We are the most impulsive people imaginable. But if "conservatism" so overcome any one who hears me in the very conservative things that I have to say, it must be understood that I speak only for myself. I speak out of my own ignorance only, and I speak, I regret to say, only as a spectator of your noble work.

. . . The politician has been the greater popular hero, but the preacher has had much the greater influence. For a century he was by far our greatest man—the man of the largest original power and of the strongest character. He inherited the heroic qualities of the pioneers, and he led a life at once serene and active. He was a primitive sort of character, genuine and fearless. If our traditions overrate the political leaders that we have produced, they as greatly underrate the early preachers.

Now let us see what these two powers that ruled our fathers did for the education of the masses. The first conception of education was the aristocratic conception, and the first system of teaching was controlled by those who held political power; it was the old system of class education. It did not touch the masses. They had no part in it. They grew up with the idea that education was a special privilege: they did not aspire to it, did not believe that it was attainable, and at last they came to believe that it was not desirable, certainly that it was not necessary. They remained illiterate, neglected, forgotten. There was no substantial progress in broadening educational opportunities in North Carolina from the time of the colony till the beginning of the civil war, except the noteworthy and noble work that was done just before the war to develop a public school system. This notable and noteworthy effort gives us good reason to hold those who made it, chief among whom was Calvin H. Wiley, in grateful remembrance.

I commend to you most earnestly as of the first importance a thorough study of our social beginnings and development— not always as it has been described by our historians, but from original sources. You will clear your minds of the hazy exaggerations that we get from tradition. Many traditional heroes will disappear, and many whose names have been forgotten or are seldom heard will re-appear as real heroes. Among these will be the group of men who strove forty years ago or more to establish a public school system. But their scheme, like Jefferson's own great scheme, was doomed to await a later time for its development.

Later than the aristocratic system of education and overlapping it, came the ecclesiastical system. In establishing and developing this, the preachers did valiant service. They were colporteurs and they carried religious books to the people. The churches established, besides preparatory schools for boys and girls, three schools for men which grew into colleges. At first they were established for the education of preachers, but they broadened their field of labour and became schools of general culture, and most admirable service they have done. The denominational educational movement was broader in its benefits than the old aristocratic educational movement had been, for these colleges were open to the common people and they proclaimed the desirability of general education. Still they were class institutions; each was a school of a sect. Universal education, universal free education, was not on their programme. Some men whom the State had neglected were now remembered by the churches, especially if they were of an emotional temperament and felt "called" to preach. The way towards general education was broadening, but the very conception of education was yet a class conception. It was provided less for the sake of the people than for the sake of the church.

The forgotten man remained forgotten. The aristocratic scheme of education had passed him by. To a less extent, but still to the extent of hundreds of thousands, the ecclesiastical scheme also passed him by. The general level of education was almost as low as it had ever been. Both the aristocratic and the ecclesiastical plans held undisputed sway till a time within the memory of us all. But in the meantime education had been making more rapid conquests—developing in method and extending its benefits in other States and in other lands—than in any preceding time in the history of the world.

Tried by the tests of this progress, what have the aristocratic system and the ecclesiastical system of education to show for themselves?

First, what did they do for their own favoured classes? North Carolina is one of the old thirteen States. The aristocratic system had free play here for nearly a hundred years, and the ecclesiastical system has had free play for at least half as long.

They established our university and our denominational colleges. Excellent as these are, they do not rank with the best institutions of most of the other original thirteen States—of Virginia, nor of New Jersey, nor of New York, nor of Connecticut, nor of Massachusetts. Nor have they trained even a select body of scholars that have been or are in any way famous. Make another test: there are no great libraries in the State, nor do the people yet read, nor have the publishing houses yet reckoned them as their patrons, except the publishers of school books. By any test that may be made, both these systems of education failed even with the classes that they appealed to. One such test is the test of emigration from the State. In 1890 there were living in other States 293,000 persons who were born in North Carolina. One in eight of every native of the State then living had gone away. When we remember that almost every one of these emigrants went to States where taxes are higher and schools are more numerous and better and where competition is more fierce, and when we remember that they went away from a State that is yet sparsely settled and richer in natural opportunities than most of the States to which they went, the failure of these systems becomes painfully obvious.

If a slave brought $1,000 in old times, it ought to be safe to assume that every emigrant from the State has an economic value of $1,000. This emigration therefore had up to 1890 cost us $293,000,000—a fact that goes far to explain why we are poor. To take the places of these 293,000 emigrants, after twenty years of organized effort to induce immigration 52,000 immigrants born in other States had come here, a large proportion of whom had come for their health. But counting the sick and the dying at $1,000 each, we had still lost $241,000,000 by the transaction. This calculation gives a slight hint of the cost of ignorance and of the extravagance of keeping taxes too low.

Next, what did these systems of education do for the masses? In 1890, twenty-six per cent. of the white persons of the State were unable even to read and write. One in every four was wholly forgotten. But illiteracy was not the worst of it; the worst of it was that the stationary social condition indicated by gen-

erations of illiteracy had long been the general condition. The
forgotten man was content to be forgotten. He became not only
a dead weight, but a definite opponent of social progress. He
faithfully heard the politicians on the stump praise him for
virtues that he did not have. The politician told him that he
lived in the best State in the Union, told him that the other
politician had some hare-brained plan to increase his taxes, told
him as a consolation for his ignorance how many of his kinsmen
had been killed in the war, told him to distrust anybody who
wished to change anything. What was good enough for his
fathers was good enough for him. Thus the forgotten man became a dupe, became thankful for being neglected. And the
preacher told him that the ills and misfortunes of this life were
blessings in disguise, that God meant his poverty as a means
of grace, and that if he accepted the right creed all would be
well with him. These influences encouraged inertia. There could
not have been a better means to prevent the development of the
people.

I have thus far spoken only of the forgotten man. I have done
so to show the social and educational structure in proper perspective. But what I have come to speak about is the forgotten
woman. Both the aristocratic and the ecclesiastical systems made
provision for the women of special classes—the fortunately born
and the religious well-to-do. But all the other women were forgotten. Let any man whose mind is not hardened by some worn-
out theory of politics or of ecclesiasticism go to the country in
almost any part of the State and make a study of life there,
especially of the life of the women. He will see them thin and
wrinkled in youth from ill prepared food, clad without warmth
or grace, living in untidy houses, working from daylight till
bed-time at the dull round of weary duties, the slaves of men
of equal slovenliness, the mothers of joyless children—all un-
educated if not illiterate. Yet even their condition were endurable if there were any hope, but this type of woman is
encrusted in a shell of dull content with her lot; she knows no
better and can never learn better, nor point her children to a
higher life. If she be intensely religious, her religion is only

an additional misfortune, for it teaches her, as she understands
it, to be content with her lot and all its burdens, since they prepare her for the life to come. Some *men* who are born under
these conditions escape from them; a *man* may go away, go
where life offers opportunities, but the women are forever helpless.

And this sight every one of you has seen, not in the countries
whither we send missionaries, but in the borders of the State of
North Carolina, in this year of grace. Nor is it an infrequent
sight. There are thousands and thousands of such women in our
population.

Now one of the two things is true—either these forgotten
men and women are incapable of development, and belong to
a lower order of intelligence than any other people of Anglo-
Saxon stock; or our civilization, so far as they are concerned, has
been a failure. Of course there is no doubt which of these sup-
positions is true; for these people are capable of development,
capable of unlimited growth and elevation. But, if they be
capable of development, then both the aristocratic and the ecclesiastical systems of society have failed to develop them.

Since both the politician and the preacher have failed to lift
this life after a century of unobstructed opportunities, it is time
for a wiser statesmanship and a more certain means of grace.

. . . In my judgment there has been no other event in North
Carolina since the formation of the American Union that is
comparable in importance to this new educational progress.
The movement now has such momentum that nothing can
hinder the complete development of the public school system till
every child is reached. When every inhabited township votes a
local tax to supplement the State tax, the taxes you now levy will
seem small and will be increased. According to the last published reports of the Commissioner of Education, the total sum
spent per year per pupil in the public schools was still lower
in North Carolina than in any State except South Carolina. It
was only $3.40. In Georgia it was nearly $6.50, in Virginia it
was nearly $9, in Indiana it was $20, in Michigan nearly $20, in
Wisconsin $21, in Minnesota nearly $30, in the new State of
North Dakota it was nearly $33.50—nearly ten times the ex-

penditure per pupil that was made in North Carolina. None of these States is richer than your own in possibilities. The ability to maintain schools is in proportion rather to the appreciation of education than to the amount of wealth. We pay for schools not so much out of our purses as out of our state of mind. For example, there is a man in Moore County who had two children at school at the expense of somebody else. Although he did not pay their bills, he took them from school the other day because, he said, the charge for tuition was too high. He is the frankest and most faithful believer of our old-time economic creed that I have ever known.

. . . *A public school system generously supported by public sentiment, and generously maintained by both State and local taxation, is the only effective means to develop the forgotten man, and even more surely the only means to develop the forgotten woman.*

Even ten years ago, many men in North Carolina did not stand on this platform. Now I hear that few oppose such a programme, and those few you will soon educate for sheer pity.

. . . The most sacred thing in the Commonwealth and to the Commonwealth is the child, whether it be your child or the child of the dull-faced mother of the hovel. The child of the dull-faced mother may, for all you know, be the most capable child in the State. At its worst, it is capable of good citizenship and a useful life, if its intelligence be quickened and trained. Several of the strongest personalities that were ever born in North Carolina were men whose very fathers were unknown. We have all known two such, who held high places in church and state. President Eliot said a little while ago that the ablest man that he had known in his many years' connection with Harvard University was the son of a brick mason. The child, whether it have poor parents or rich parents, is the most valuable undeveloped resource of the State.

But the day is past when worn-out theories hold us in captivity, and we owe its passing chiefly to the idea that this institution stands for. Our whole life will soon be delivered from the bondage of ignorance by our hitherto forgotten women.

. . . May I go forward a step further in the development of

public education that must in due time follow this delivery from the bondage of the old systems? The extension of free preparatory schools in every part of the State is leading to the establishment of free high schools, such as already exist in some towns, as in Greensboro and in Durham, and in other larger towns. These will draw to themselves the intellectual interests of the whole community and make the public school system the pride of our people. I know towns where every enlightening interest centres in the high school. Lectures are given there on literature and on music and on practical subjects as well, by the most learned men and women. Parents pursue courses of study with their children. The whole life of such towns is lifted to a high intellectual level. In some such towns private schools exist only to train those boys and girls who are too dull or backward to keep pace with the rest—a sort of asylums for the stupid.

. . . The opportunity exists in North Carolina to establish a similar system by a single effort and without any considerable increase of expenditure. We have our State University, most useful and vigorous under its recent President, and its present one, and we have our three larger and older denominational colleges—Davidson College with its solidity and old-time dignity, Wake Forest College, a striking demonstration of what people of moderate means may at any time do when they work with united purpose, and Trinity College with its new life made possible by its generous benefactors. We have all these and the other State schools and denominational schools for boys and for girls. If they could all be united into one great school, it would at once become by far the most efficient and noteworthy institution in the South. And there is no reason why it should not become one of the greatest seats of learning in the Union. If the doors of such an institution were thrown open free to every boy and girl in the State, and there were free schools to train them for it, we should no longer talk of forgotten men and women; and people from other States would seek homes here. These counties would be peopled at last by as useful and as cultivated a population as any in the United States.

Nor need the religious influence of any of the denominational colleges suffer by such a move when the time for it comes. Every one might have its own dormitory and religious supervision over pupils of its own sect. A definite movement of this sort has already been made where the denominational schools have shown a wish to become a part of the system of public education.

But I have wandered too far from the problems of the immediate present. Such things as I have spoken of, we may look for in the future. What may we not look for in the future? Whatever I might say in prophecy would be as inadequate as all that I might say in congratulation. Great changes come as silently as the seasons. I am no more sure of this spring time than I am of the rejuvenation of our society and the lifting up of our life. A revolution is in progress, and this institution is one of the first and best fruits of it. I declare in truth and soberness, that this is the most inspiring sight that I have ever seen in North Carolina, for before the moral earnestness of well-trained women social illusions vanish and worn-out traditions fall away.

O earnest young Womanhood of the Commonwealth, we that had forgotten you now thankfully do you honour. Many a man with the patriotic spirit that is our inheritance has striven to lift dead men's hands from our stagnant life and has been baffled by a century's inertia. I speak the gladdest speech of my life when I say that *you* have lifted them. This institution and your presence is proof that the State has remembered the forgotten woman. You in turn will remember the forgotten child; and in this remembrance is laid the foundation of a new social order. The neglected people will rise and with them will rise all the people.

58 Sahara of the Bozart

In that period of radical change in the South, the 1920s, Henry L. Mencken, a rising literary figure living on the periphery of the South, surveyed the region and proclaimed it a barren land indeed so far as literary, cultural, and intellectual accomplishments were concerned. He found not one thing to commend in the South's cultural history since 1865. It had produced in his opinión no single literary figure worthy of mention, no painters, sculptors, musicians, scientists, theologians, or historians who could claim distinction. Indisputably Mencken overlooked some Southerners who had made contributions such as Thomas Nelson Page, Mary Noailles Murphree, James Lane Allen, George Washington Cable, Henry Watterson, and others. He treated Joel Chandler Harris as no more than the Negro's amanuensis. It was true, however, that most of these had not produced immortal literature. They were nostalgic and sentimental, if not vapid, at times. In Mencken's mind the South was dominated by men and women who took more pride in the day-to-day little gains of the region than in the larger and more enduring social and artistic values.

Mencken's essay made the South highly self-conscious. Even non-literary people were aroused by the piece, and some of them responded defensively and naively. Ironically Mencken made his Jove-like observation at the moment when young Southerners such as Faulkner, Glasgow, Cabbell, Roberts, and others were coming of age and soon would produce some of the best books and poems in American literature. There remained, it is true, the unwashed and

546

illiterate, but these too became important as characters in future books.

> Alas, for the South! Her books have grown fewer—
> She never was much given to literature.

In the lamented J. Gordon Coogler, author of these elegiac lines, there was the insight of a true poet. He was the last bard of Dixie, at least in the legitimate line. Down there a poet is now almost as rare as an oboe-player, a dry-point etcher or a metaphysician. It is, indeed, amazing to contemplate so vast a vacuity. One thinks of the interstellar spaces, of the colossal reaches of the now mythical ether. Nearly the whole of Europe could be lost in that stupendous region of fat farms, shoddy cities and paralyzed cerebrums: one could throw in France, Germany and Italy, and still have room for the British Isles. And yet, for all its size and all its wealth and all the "progress" it babbles of, it is almost as sterile, artistically, intellectually, culturally, as the Sahara Desert. There are single acres in Europe that house more first-rate men than all the states south of the Potomac; there are probably single square miles in America. If the whole of the late Confederacy were to be engulfed by a tidal wave tomorrow, the effect upon the civilized minority of men in the world would be but little greater than that of a flood on the Yang-tse-kiang. It would be impossible in all history to match so complete a drying-up of a civilization.

I say a civilization because that is what, in the old days, the South had, despite the Baptist and Methodist barbarism that reigns down there now. More, it was a civilization of manifold excellences—perhaps the best that the Western Hemisphere has ever seen—undoubtedly the best that These States have ever seen. Down to the middle of the last century, and even beyond, the main hatchery of ideas on this side of the water was across the Potomac bridges. The New England shopkeepers

and theologians never really developed a civilization; all they
ever developed was a government. They were, at their best,
tawdry and tacky fellows, oafish in manner and devoid of imagination; one searches the books in vain for mention of a salient
Yankee gentleman; as well look for a Welsh gentleman. But in
the south there were men of delicate fancy, urbane instinct
and aristocratic manner—in brief, superior men—in brief, gentry. To politics, their chief diversion, they brought active and
original minds. It was there that nearly all the political theories
we still cherish and suffer under came to birth. It was there that
the crude dogmatism of New England was refined and human-
ized. It was there, above all, that some attention was given to
the art of living—that life got beyond and above the state of a
mere infliction and became an exhilarating experience. A certain noble spaciousness was in the ancient southern scheme of
things. The *Ur*-Confederate had leisure. He liked to toy with
ideas. He was hospitable and tolerant. He had the vague thing
that we call culture.

But consider the condition of his late empire today. The picture gives one the creeps. It is as if the Civil War stamped out
every last bearer of the torch, and left only a mob of peasants
on the field. One thinks of Asia Minor, resigned to Armenians,
Greeks and wild swine; of Poland abandoned to the Poles. In all
that gargantuan paradise of the fourth-rate there is not a single
picture gallery worth going into, or a single orchestra capable of
playing the nine symphonies of Beethoven, or a single opera-
house, or a single theater devoted to decent plays, or a single
public monument (built since the war) that is worth looking at,
or a single workshop devoted to the making of beautiful things.
Once you have counted Robert Loveman (an Ohioan by birth)
and John McClure (an Oklahoman) you will not find a single
southern poet above the rank of a neighborhood rhymester.
Once you have counted James Branch Cabell (a lingering sur-
vivor of the *ancien régime:* a scarlet dragonfly imbedded in
opaque amber) you will not find a single southern prose writer
who can actually write. And once you have—but when you
come to critics, musical composers, painters, sculptors, archi-

tects and the like, you will have to give it up, for there is not even a bad one between the Potomac mud-flats and the Gulf. Nor an historian. Nor a sociologist. Nor a philosopher. Nor a theologian. Nor a scientist. In all these fields the south is an awe-inspiring blank—a brother to Portugal, Serbia and Esthonia.

Consider, for example, the present estate and dignity of Virginia—in the great days indubitably the premier American state, the mother of Presidents and statesmen, the home of the first American university worthy of the name, the *arbiter elegantiarum* of the western world. Well, observe Virginia to-day. It is years since a first-rate man, save only Cabell, has come out of it; it is years since an idea has come out of it. The old aristocracy went down the red gullet of war; the poor white trash are now in the saddle. Politics in Virginia are cheap, ignorant, parochial, idiotic; there is scarcely a man in office above the rank of a professional job-seeker; the political doctrine that prevails is made up of hand-me-downs from the bumpkinry of the Middle West —Bryanism, Prohibition, vice crusading, all that sort of filthy claptrap; the administration of the law is turned over to professors of Puritanism and espionage; a Washington or a Jefferson, dumped there by some act of God, would be denounced as a scoundrel and jailed overnight. Elegance, *esprit*, culture? Virginia has no art, no literature, no philosophy, no mind or aspiration of her own. Her education has sunk to the Baptist seminary level; not a single contribution to human knowledge has come out of her colleges in twenty-five years; she spends less than half upon her common schools, *per capita*, than any northern state spends. In brief, an intellectual Gobi or Lapland. Urbanity, *politesse*, chivalry? Go to! It was in Virginia that they invented the device of searching for contraband whisky in women's underwear. . . . There remains, at the top, a ghost of the old aristocracy, a bit wistful and infinitely charming. But it has lost all its old leadership to fabulous monsters from the lower depths; it is submerged in an industrial plutocracy that is ignorant and ignominious. The mind of the state, as it is revealed to the nation, is pathetically naïve and inconsequential. It no longer reacts with energy and elasticity to great problems. It has fallen to the bombastic trivialities of the camp-meeting and the chautauqua. Its foremost exponent—if so flabby a thing may be said to have an exponent—is a statesman whose name is synonymous with empty words, broken pledges and false pretenses. One could no more imagine a Lee or a Washington in the Virginia of to-day than one could imagine a Huxley in Nicaragua.

I choose the Old Dominion, not because I disdain it, but precisely because I esteem it. It is, by long odds, the most civilized of the southern states, now as always. It has sent a host of creditable sons northward; the stream kept running into our own time. Virginians, even the worst of them, show the effects of a great tradition. They hold themselves above other southerners, and with sound pretension. If one turns to such a commonwealth as Georgia the picture becomes far darker. There the liberated lower orders of whites have borrowed the worst commercial bounderism of the Yankee and superimposed it upon a culture that, at bottom, is but little removed from savagery. Georgia is at once the home of the cotton-mill sweater and of the most noisy and vapid sort of chamber of commerce, of the Methodist parson turned Savonarola and of the lynching bee. A self-respecting European, going there to live, would not only find intellectual stimulation utterly lacking; he would actually feel a certain insecurity, as if the scene were the Balkans or the China Coast. The Leo Frank affair was no isolated phenomenon. It fitted into its frame very snugly. It was a natural expression of Georgian notions of truth and justice. There is a state with more than half the area of Italy and more population than either Denmark or Norway, and yet in thirty years it has not produced a single idea. Once upon a time a Georgian printed a couple of books that attracted notice, but immediately it turned out that he was little more than an amanuensis for the local blacks—that his works were really the products, not of white Georgia, but of black Georgia. Writing afterward *as* a white man, he swiftly subsided into the fifth rank. And he is not only the glory of the literature of Georgia; he is, almost literally, the whole of the literature of Georgia—nay, of the entire art of Georgia.

Virginia is the best of the south to-day, and Georgia is perhaps the worst. The one is simply senile; the other is crass, gross, vulgar and obnoxious. Between lies a vast plain of mediocrity, stupidity, lethargy, almost of dead silence. In the north, of course, there is also grossness, crassness, vulgarity. The north, in its way, is also stupid and obnoxious. But nowhere in the north is there such complete sterility, so depressing a lack of all civilized gesture and aspiration. One would find it difficult to unearth a second-rate city between the Ohio and the Pacific that isn't struggling to establish an orchestra, or setting up a little theater, or going in for an art gallery, or making some other effort to get into touch with civilization. These efforts often fail, and sometimes they succeed rather absurdly, but under them there is at least an impulse that deserves respect, and that is the impulse to seek beauty and to experiment with ideas, and so to give the life of every day a certain dignity and purpose. You will find no such impulse in the south. There are no committees down there cadging subscriptions for orchestras; if a string quartet is ever heard there, the news of it has never come out; an opera troupe, when it roves the land, is a nine days' wonder. The little theater movement has swept the whole country, enormously augmenting the public interest in sound plays, giving new dramatists their chance, forcing reforms upon the commercial theater. Everywhere else the wave rolls high—but along the line of the Potomac it breaks upon a rock-bound shore. There is no little theater beyond. There is no gallery of pictures. No artist ever gives exhibitions. No one talks of such things. No one seems to be interested in such things.

As for the cause of this unanimous torpor and doltishness, this curious and almost pathological estrangement from everything that makes for a civilized culture, I have hinted at it already, and now state it again. The south has simply been drained of all its best blood. The vast blood-letting of the Civil War half exterminated and wholly paralyzed the old aristocracy, and so left the land to the harsh mercies of the poor white trash, now its masters. The war, of course, was not a complete massacre. It spared a decent number of first-rate southerners—perhaps even some of the very best. Moreover, other countries, notably

France and Germany, have survived far more staggering butcheries, and even showed marked progress thereafter. But the war not only cost a great many valuable lives; it also brought bankruptcy, demoralization and despair in its train—and so the majority of the first-rate southerners that were left, broken in spirit and unable to live under the new dispensation, cleared out. A few went to South America, to Egypt, to the Far East. Most came north. They were fecund; their progeny is widely dispersed, to the great benefit of the north. A southerner of good blood almost always does well in the north. He finds, even in the big cities, surroundings fit for a man of condition. His peculiar qualities have a high social value, and are esteemed. He is welcomed by the codfish aristocracy as one palpably superior. But in the south he throws up his hands. It is impossible for him to stoop to the common level. He cannot brawl in politics with the grandsons of his grandfather's tenants. He is unable to share their fierce jealousy of the emerging black—the cornerstone of all their public thinking. He is anaesthetic to their theological and political enthusiasm. He finds himself an alien at their feasts of soul. And so he withdraws into his tower, and is heard of no more. Cabell is almost a perfect example. His eyes, for years, were turned toward the past; he became a professor of the grotesque genealogizing that decaying aristocracies affect; it was only by a sort of accident that he discovered himself to be an artist. The south is unaware of the fact to this day; it regards Woodrow Wilson and Col. John Temple Graves as much finer stylists, and Frank L. Stanton as an infinitely greater poet. If it has heard, which I doubt, that Cabell has been hoofed by the Comstocks, it unquestionably views that assault as a deserved rebuke to a fellow who indulges a lewd passion for fancy writing, and is a covert enemy to the Only True Christianity.

What is needed down there, before the vexatious public problems of the region may be intelligently approached, is a survey of the population by competent ethnologists and anthropologists. The immigrants of the north have been studied at great length, and any one who is interested may now apply to the Bureau of Ethnology for elaborate data as to their racial strains, their stature and cranial indices, their relative capacity for education, and the changes that they undergo under American *Kultur*. But the older stocks of the south, and particularly the emancipated and dominant poor white trash, have never been investigated scientifically, and most of the current generalizations about them are probably wrong. For example, the generalization that they are purely Anglo-Saxon in blood. This I doubt very seriously. The chief strain down there, I believe, is Celtic rather than Saxon, particularly in the hill country. French blood, too, shows itself here and there, and so does Spanish, and so does German. The last-named entered from the northward, by way of the limestone belt just east of the Alleghenies. Again, it is very likely that in some parts of the south a good many of the plebeian whites have more than a trace of negro blood. Interbreeding under concubinage produced some very light half-breeds at an early day, and no doubt appreciable numbers of them went over into the white race by the simple process of changing their abode. Not long ago I read a curious article by an intelligent negro, in which he stated that it is easy for a very light negro to pass as white in the south on account of the fact that large numbers of southerners accepted as white have distinctly negroid features. Thus it becomes a delicate and dangerous matter for a train conductor or a hotel-keeper to challenge a suspect. But the Celtic strain is far more obvious than any of these others. It not only makes itself visible in physical stigmata —*e. g.*, leanness and dark coloring—but also in mental traits. For example, the religious thought of the south is almost precisely identical with the religious thought of Wales. There is the same naïve belief in an anthropomorphic Creator but little removed, in manner and desire, from an evangelical bishop; there is the same submission to an ignorant and impudent sacerdotal tyranny, and there is the same sharp contrast between doctrinal orthodoxy and private ethics. Read Caradoc Evans' ironical picture of the Welsh Wesleyans in his preface to "My Neighbors," and you will be instantly reminded of the Georgia and Carolina Methodists. The most booming sort of piety, in the south, is not incompatible with the theory that lynching is a

benign institution. Two generations ago it was not incompatible
with an ardent belief in slavery.

It is highly probable that some of the worst blood of western
Europe flows in the veins of the southern poor whites, now poor
no longer. The original strains, according to every honest historian, were extremely corrupt. Philip Alexander Bruce (a Vir-
ginian of the old gentry) says in his "Industrial History of Virginia in the Seventeenth Century" that the first native-born
generation was largely illegitimate. "One of the most common
offenses against morality committed in the lower ranks of life in
Virginia during the seventeenth century," he says, "was bas-
tardy." The mothers of these bastards, he continues, were chiefly
indentured servants, and "had belonged to the lowest class in
their native country." Fanny Kemble Butler, writing of the
Georgia poor whites of a century later, described them as "the
most degraded race of human beings claiming an Anglo-Saxon
origin that can be found on the face of the earth—filthy, lazy,
ignorant, brutal, proud, penniless savages." The Sunday-school
and the chautauqua, of course, have appreciably mellowed the
descendants of these "savages," and their economic progress and
rise to political power have done perhaps even more, but the
marks of their origin are still unpleasantly plentiful. Every now
and then they produce a political leader who puts their secret
notions of the true, the good and the beautiful into plain words,
to the amazement and scandal of the rest of the country. That
amazement is turned into downright incredulity when news
comes that his platform has got him high office, and that he is
trying to execute it.

In the great days of the south the line between the gentry and
the poor whites was very sharply drawn. There was absolutely
no intermarriage. So far as I know there is not a single instance
in history of a southerner of the upper class marrying one of the
bondwomen described by Mr. Bruce. In other societies characterized by class distinctions of that sort it is common for the
lower class to be improved by extra-legal crosses. That is to say,
the men of the upper class take women of the lower class as
mistresses, and out of such unions spring the extraordinary

plebeians who rise sharply from the common level, and so propagate the delusion that all other plebeians would do the same thing if they had the chance—in brief, the delusion that class distinctions are merely economic and conventional, and not congenital and genuine. But in the south the men of the upper classes sought their mistresses among the blacks, and after a few generations there was so much white blood in the black women that they were considerably more attractive than the unhealthy and bedraggled women of the poor whites. This preference continued into our own time. A southerner of good family once told me in all seriousness that he had reached his majority before it ever occurred to him that a white woman might make quite as agreeable a mistress as the octaroons of his jejune fancy. If the thing has changed of late, it is not the fault of the southern white man, but of the southern mulatto women. The more sightly yellow girls of the region, with improving economic opportunities, have gained self-respect, and so they are no longer as willing to enter into concubinage as their grand-dams were.

As a result of this preference of the southern gentry for mulatto mistresses there was created a series of mixed strains containing the best white blood of the south, and perhaps of the whole country. As another result the poor whites went unfertilized from above, and so missed the improvement that so constantly shows itself in the peasant stocks of other countries. It is a commonplace that nearly all negroes who rise above the general are of mixed blood, usually with the white predominating. I know a great many negroes, and it would be hard for me to think of an exception. What is too often forgotten is that this white blood is not the blood of the poor whites but that of the old gentry. The mulatto girls of the early days despised the poor whites as creatures distinctly inferior to negroes, and it was thus almost unheard of for such a girl to enter into relations with a man of that submerged class. This aversion was based upon a sound instinct. The southern mulatto of to-day is a proof of it. Like all other half-breeds he is an unhappy man, with disquieting tendencies toward anti-social habits of thought, but he is intrinsically a better animal than the pure-blooded descendant of the old poor whites, and he not infrequently demonstrates it. It is not by accident that the negroes of the south are making faster progress, economically and culturally, than the masses of the whites. It is not by accident that the only visible aesthetic activity in the south is wholly in their hands. No southern composer has ever written music so good as that of half a dozen white-black composers who might be named. Even in politics, the negro reveals a curious superiority. Despite the fact that the race question has been the main political concern of the southern whites for two generations, to the practical exclusion of everything else, they have contributed nothing to its discussion that has impressed the rest of the world so deeply and so favorably as three or four books by southern negroes.

Entering upon such themes, of course, one must resign one's self to a vast misunderstanding and abuse. The south has not only lost its old capacity for producing ideas; it has also taken on the worst intolerance of ignorance and stupidity. Its prevailing mental attitude for several decades past has been that of its own hedge ecclesiastics. All who dissent from its orthodox doctrines are scoundrels. All who presume to discuss its ways realistically are damned. I have had, in my day, several experiences in point. Once, after I had published an article on some phase of the eternal race question, a leading southern newspaper replied by printing a column of denunciation of my father, then dead nearly twenty years—a philippic placarding him as an ignorant foreigner of dubious origin, inhabiting "the Baltimore ghetto" and speaking a dialect recalling that of Weber & Fields—two thousand words of incandescent nonsense, utterly false and beside the point, but exactly meeting the latter-day southern notion of effective controversy. Another time, I published a short discourse on lynching, arguing that the sport was popular in the south because the backward culture of the region denied the populace more seemly recreations. Among such recreations I mentioned those afforded by brass bands, symphony orchestras, boxing matches, amateur athletic contests, shoot-the-chutes, roof gardens, horse races, and so on. In reply another great southern journal denounced me as a man "of wineshop temperament, brass-jewelry tastes and pornographic predilections." In other words, brass bands, in the south, are classed with brass jewelry, and both are snares of the devil! To advocate setting up symphony orchestras is pornography! . . . Alas, when the touchy southerner attempts a greater urbanity, the result is often even worse. Some time ago a colleague of mine printed an article deploring the arrested cultural development of Georgia. In reply he received a number of protests from patriotic Georgians, and all of them solemnly listed the glories of the state. I indulge in a few specimens:

> Who has not heard of Asa G. Candler, whose name is synonymous with Coca-Cola, a Georgia product?
> The first Sunday-School in the world was opened in Savannah.
> Who does not recall with pleasure the writings of . . . Frank L. Stanton, Georgia's brilliant poet?
> Georgia was the first state to organize a Boys' Corn Club in the South—Newton county, 1904.
> The first to suggest a common United Daughters of the Confederacy badge was Mrs. Raynes, of Georgia.
> The first to suggest a state historian of the United Daughters of the Confederacy was Mrs. C. Helen Plane (Macon convention, 1896).
> The first to suggest putting to music Heber's "From Greenland's Icy Mountains" was Mrs. F. R. Goulding, of Savannah.

And so on, and so on. These proud boasts came, remember, not from obscure private persons, but from "Leading Georgians" —in one case, the state historian. Curious sidelights upon the ex-Confederate mind! Another comes from a stray copy of a negro paper. It describes an ordinance lately passed by the city council of Douglas, Ga., forbidding any trousers presser, on penalty of forfeiting a $500 bond, to engage in "pressing for both white and colored." This in a town, says the negro paper, where practically all of the white inhabitants have "their food prepared by colored hands," "their babies cared for by colored hands," and "the clothes which they wear right next to their

skins washed in houses where negroes live"—houses in which
the said clothes "remain for as long as a week at a time." But
if you marvel at the absurdity, keep it dark! A casual word, and
the united press of the south will be upon your trail, denouncing
you bitterly as a scoundrelly Yankee, a Bolshevik Jew, an agent
of the Wilhelmstrasse. . . .

Obviously, it is impossible for intelligence to flourish in such
an atmosphere. Free inquiry is blocked by the idiotic certainties
of ignorant men. The arts, save in the lower reaches of the gospel
hymn, the phonograph and the chautauqua harangue, are all
held in suspicion. The tone of public opinion is set by an upstart
class but lately emerged from industrial slavery into commercial
enterprise—the class of "hustling" business men, of "live wires,"
of commercial club luminaries, of "drive" managers, of forward-
lookers and right-thinkers—in brief, of third-rate southerners
inoculated with all the worst traits of the Yankee sharper. One
observes the curious effects of an old tradition of truculence
upon a population now merely pushful and impudent, of an old
tradition of chivalry upon a population now quite without imagination. The old repose is gone. The old romanticism is gone.
The philistinism of the new type of town-boomer southerner is
not only indifferent to the ideals of the old south; it is positively
antagonistic to them. That philistinism regards human life, not
as an agreeable adventure, but as a mere trial of rectitude and
efficiency. It is overwhelmingly utilitarian and moral. It is in-
conceivably hollow and obnoxious. What remains of the ancient
tradition is simply a certain charming civility in private intercourse—often broken down, alas, by the hot rages of Puritanism,
but still generally visible. The southerner, at his worst, is never
quite the surly cad that the Yankee is. His sensitiveness may
betray him into occasional bad manners, but in the main he is a
pleasant fellow—hospitable, polite, good-humored, even jovial.
. . . But a bit absurd. . . . A bit pathetic.

59 Separate and Unequal

By the mid-twentieth century the South was forced to re-examine the principle of "separate but equal" set forth in *Plessy* v. *Ferguson.* Those Southerners familiar with the imbalances between education of Negro and white students asked whether the present system was not actually widening the chasm between the two groups. Southern legislators generally acknowledged that unequal educational conditions existed, when all of the assemblies enacted sales tax levies to help eliminate the physical inequalities between the races. But there was more involved than mere buildings, buses, and classroom equipment. Other inequalities occurred in the vital areas of teacher qualification, educational traditions, and lack of basic preparation of great masses of students to take advantage of better educational opportunities.

The following excellent analysis illustrates statistically the failure of the South to educate both races. It appeared in 1947 when *Brown* v. *Board of Education* was but a remotely disturbing threat for the future.

As WE SAID BEFORE, PEOPLE WHO FIND IT CONVENIENT TO BLAME all the South's problems on the Negro usually try to explain away the South's lack of education in the same way. But this is

From "In-the-Red Schoolhouse," *Report* of the Southern Regional Council (1947), 14–18.

only half the truth. It is true, of course, that the low educational status of the South's large Negro population is a big factor in the region's poor showing in comparison with the rest of the nation. For instance, going back to the draftees who couldn't write their own names: nine out of the ten were Southerners, and six of the nine (66.7 per cent) were Negroes. But, as we also said before, that only means that the South has failed to provide proper education for the Negro.

Let's see how badly we have failed. We have already found that six out of 100 Southern adults in 1940 had never been to school. If we break this down by race, we see that the proportion of white adults with no schooling whatever was 3.2 per cent, which compares favorably with the national average of 3.1 per cent. On the other hand, more than twelve out of every 100 Negro adults (12.3 per cent) in the South had never been to school. The same disadvantage to the Negro carries through in all other measurements of education and educational opportunity. For example, 12 out of 100 white adults (12.2 per cent) had dropped out of school before they reached the fifth grade—but more than one-third of Negro adults (37.6 per cent) had left school before the fifth grade. Worst of all is the record for high school: one in ten white adults had finished high school, but only about two in every one hundred Negro adults (2.3 per cent) had completed four years of high school study. The Southern Negro has even greater disadvantages when it comes to a college education. About five out of every 100 white adults (4.6 per cent) in the South in 1940 had been to college four years or more: only one in every 100 Negro adults (0.9 per cent) had gone that far.

These facts, of course, show only how badly the South has educated the Negro in the past. What about the educational opportunities for Negro boys and girls today? There is no doubt that in recent years the South has made progress in Negro education, but it still has a long way to go. Let's analyze the facts in the 1940 census when 86.5 per cent of the school-age children in the non-Southern states were enrolled in school. In the South that year 75.1 per cent of white children of school age were enrolled; 72.6 per cent of Negro children were enrolled. This isn't a great difference, but if we break it down into grammar and high school groups we find Negro youth at a great disadvantage in terms of the follow-through of education. In the elementary grades (ages five through 13) 79.8 per cent of white children and 76.8 per cent of Negro children were enrolled in the South. But in the junior high and high school group there is a wide difference: 71.6 per cent of Southern white children of secondary school age (14 to 17) were enrolled; only 63.8 per cent of Negro children of the same age were in junior high and high schools.

There are many reasons for the Southern Negro's lack of education and educational opportunity. One of them is the poor quality of training offered in Negro public schools. We have already seen that the qualifications of white teachers in the South are inferior to that of teachers in other parts of the Nation. The training of the average Negro teacher in the South is even lower. Oklahoma was the only one of 12 Southern states where the proportion of Negro teachers with four or more years of college education almost equalled that of white teachers. In fact, the percentage of Negro teachers with four or more years of college training for the twelve states ranged from a low of 9.1 per cent in Mississippi to 65.8 per cent in Oklahoma. In nine of these Southern states the proportion of Negro teachers with this much training was less than 40 per cent. More than two-thirds of the Negro teachers in Alabama, Arkansas, Florida, Georgia, Louisiana, Mississippi and South Carolina had not received four years of college education. In other words, the training of Negro teachers in the South is not enough to enable them to do the best kind of teaching job: the greater part of them have only two years or even less of college education.

Again we come to the money problem—teacher pay. The salaries of Negro teachers in the South are much lower than those of white teachers. Oklahoma, which had the highest percentage of well-trained teachers, naturally turns out to have paid the highest average salaries received by Negro teachers in the South—$971 a year. In the next highest ranks for average

AVERAGE SALARIES OF NEGRO AND WHITE TEACHERS
(1939–40)

State	*Average Salary* *Negro*	*Average Salary* *White*
Oklahoma	$971	$ 998
Kentucky	959	873°
Texas	667	1,153
North Carolina	645	910
Virginia	608	908
Florida	583	1,147
Louisiana	504	1,193
Alabama	408	874
Georgia	403	901
South Carolina	391	953
Arkansas	375	638
Mississippi	235 [285]	821

(Tennessee—not available.)

° The unusual fact that average salaries in Kentucky are higher for Negro teachers than for white teachers must be explained by pointing out that the Negro population of Kentucky is comparatively small and that the poor quality of schools for white children in some rural areas, the mountains and the mining communities brings down the average for white teachers.

teacher pay were Texas, $667 a year; North Carolina, $645 a year; and Virginia, $608 a year. In seven of the 12 Southern states average yearly salaries for Negro teachers ranged from $583 in Florida to $285 in Mississippi. The widest difference between salaries of white and Negro teachers was also in Mississippi: $821 a year for white teachers, compared with $285 for Negro teachers.

These figures are for 1939–40, and in recent years there has been organized action throughout the South by Negro citizens, with the cooperation of forward-looking white citizens, to assure Negro teachers equal pay (on the basis of qualifications) with white teachers. Here and there some improvements have been made or are being made. And the war years have undoubtedly brought changes to the over-all condition of Negro teacher-training in the South. More recent scattered records show that in some Southern areas during World War II and after Negro teachers had better training than white teachers. This was because the best-trained white teachers were drawn off into better-paying war-and-boom jobs, but educated Negroes, with fewer opportunities in business and industry, still took up teaching. On the whole, however, white teachers are still ahead of Negro teachers in both training and salaries in the South. It was estimated, on the basis of 1939–40 salaries, that it would take nearly 25 million dollars to bring Negro teachers' pay up to the equal of white teachers in 11 Southern states.

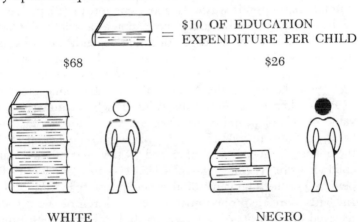

= $10 OF EDUCATION EXPENDITURE PER CHILD

$68 $26

WHITE NEGRO

THERE'S A REASON: If the Negro in the South is poorly educated there are reasons for it. One reason is that so much less is spent for Negro education. The average expenditure—per child—for Negro education in the South is little more than one-third of the average for Southern white pupils.

Negro schools in the South are handicapped with a heavy "teacher load," heavy even in comparison with Southern white schools, which we have seen do not have enough teachers. Earlier we noted that the U. S. Office of Education said that in 1941–42 the ratio in 17 Southern and border states was 28.6

white pupils per teacher and 36.1 Negro pupils per teacher. The Negro teacher-load was heavier than the white in every Southern state except Kentucky and Oklahoma, and in three states—Arkansas, Louisiana and Mississippi—the ratio in Negro schools was more than 40 pupils per teacher.

All of this boils down to the question of how much money is spent for Negro education in the South. From what we have just seen we can guess that it is pitifully small. It is. Here is the comparison of education dollars spent per pupil, Negro and white, in 12 states, all but one in the Southern Region. In 1941–42 the average yearly expenditure was $68.04 for one white pupil and only $26.59 for one Negro pupil. The expenditure for Negro pupils was only about one-fourth (27 per cent) of the average expenditure for the Nation as a whole. We have already seen that the average education expenditure per classroom for Negroes in 17 Southern and border states was only $477, compared with $1,166 for whites in the same region and $2,199 for the rest of the Nation. We find the same great inequality when we examine the value of school property. The value of school property for Negroes was reported for nine Southern states in 1942. The value of Negro school property in these states, where between 25 and 30 per cent of the school children were Negroes, was $84,348,411—only one-tenth (9.5 per cent) of the total value of all school property in those states. In short, more than one-fourth of the children of those states received the benefits of only one-tenth of the education funds.

We have seen that rural education is generally inferior to urban education throughout the South. The disadvantage to Negro school children in the rural South is even greater than it is to white children. Since about two-thirds of our Negro population lives on farms and in small towns, the problem of rural education is especially severe for Southern Negroes—in terms of dollars spent for education, school facilities, teacher-training, and enrollment and attendance. In other words, although the Negro all over the South is handicapped in education opportunities, the odds are even greater against rural Negro boys and girls.

60 The South on the Rise

Torn by the storm following the rendering of the *Brown v. Board of Education* decision, Southerners realized that they had to expend all of their energies to bring their schools up to the national average. At the same time, southern political leaders undertook to find some means of circumventing the Supreme Court's decision. Governor Terry Sanford of North Carolina, in a vein somewhat reminiscent of the pleas of the great educational governor of that state, Charles Brantley Aycock, addressed the South Carolina Educational Week Conference in Columbia in July 1961. There is no really discernible trace of resistance to the court decision in his plea that Southerners look about them at their place in the nation, and understand that they have to hustle just to keep in sight of other sections' educational progress. He pleaded not for universal education—that had been accomplished—but he asked that the South achieve quality education. This latter challenge was bigger than one state or even the whole region could meet alone; it demanded a national consideration. The South could rise again but this time its weapons would be textbooks, classrooms, and adequate educational effort at all levels.

THE SOUTH IS RISING AGAIN! IT IS NOT RISING AGAIN THROUGH secession from the union, nor through insurrection, nor through

Memory F. Mitchell, ed., *Messages, Addresses, and Public Papers of Terry Sanford, Governor of North Carolina 1961–1965* (Raleigh: North Carolina History Commission, 1966), 150–158.

nullification. It is rising again through education, through industry, through commerce, and through agriculture.

It is rising through the excercise of its long-neglected literary talents, through its research in the scholarly fields and in the applied sciences. It is rising to heights that will make the great accomplishments of the "Old South" pale by comparison.

The South is moving again into the mainstream of American life.

Now that it is moving, the South deserves a chance to work out its future without free advice from people who neglect their own problems in order to give ill-informed attention to ours. It is doubtful that we will have it. The issues are too alive, too complex, too pressing, and too emotional.

The South has been on the defensive too long. The defensive position is not conducive to positive thought and action. But positive thought and action are what we must have today in the South and in the nation. We must and we intend to move out of the defensive. If there is to be a New South, it must have a new policy—a policy consistent with the national conscience, to be sure, but a policy which also will preserve that which is best of the South's distinctive culture and enable it to realize its highest potential for good. We can move from the defensive to national leadership, and this we must do because the very future of the nation depends on what we are able to accomplish.

What should the new southern policy be? To the extent that education is basic to the achievement of our national goals, and nothing is more basic to it, education must be the foundation of progress in the South. The issue must not be whether there will be education. The issue must be whether the education that is available is appropriate, of excellent quality, and adequately supported.

North Carolina has settled the question. It does not intend to turn back. We have faced the bleak alternatives to better schools, and we have chosen to expand and improve our schools.

The clarion call for better schools has replaced the rebel yell as the voice of the South, and it deserves the attention of a national audience which usually is only too willing to hear the opposite. Education across the nation is crying for direction and leadership. Well, let's lead.

North Carolina is on the move as is South Carolina and, indeed, the entire South. It is backing up its promises with money in unprecedented amounts.

The General Assembly of North Carolina recently appropriated over $100 million in enrichment funds for public education.

The General Assembly of North Carolina has met the challenge of the times by that action. The South Carolina legislature, I am told, also has moved to meet that challenge. We cannot do the job that needs doing in education without money provided by those legislatures.

But money, whether it is provided by the city council, the legislature, or the Congress, cannot do the job alone.

As James Bryant Conant put it: "The road to better schools will be paved by the collective action of the local citizenry. The responsibility for the sorely needed upgrading of our schools cannot be passed to the state legislatures or to Congress. The responsibility rests on every citizen in the land."

But though the support must come from the people and their elected representatives, the educating must come from the teachers. You educators must not fail, for all else depends on you as we seek our regional and national goals.

I would hope that those in education, self-assured in their own competency, would leave their minds wide open for all criticism and new ideas. Those who are motivated to sharp criticism of existing institutions from their own sincere concern make a valuable contribution to the advancement of our society.

Now is the time for fresh approaches, bold action, tearing away from any tinge of self-satisfaction, an appreciative willingness to give all thoughts and suggestions a fair audience.

I have noted in some of my friends and associates in the field of education, a group in which I count myself to be a member, a tendency to be oversensitive. Criticism of the school system too often evokes criticism of the person making the criticism.

I welcome all ideas, thoughts, suggestions, criticism—even

harsh and blunt criticism. I do not pretend to take all advice, but I do try to listen and weigh and profit by all advice which comes my way.

A case in point is Admiral Hyman C. Rickover. Here a distinguished scientist, a patriot of the highest order, a man moved by an overriding concern for the future of democracy is suspected of being against the school system because he is harsh in his criticism. I will admit that I suspect he occasionally deliberately overstates his case, takes an unusually blunt stance, slaps harder than is needed, in order to shock us to attention. This is his method, but not his purpose, and we might in candor concede that his method is justified by our laxness in many areas.

I say those of us charged with the future of education, in a democracy can take criticism and that we will expect and welcome it. In this way we will profit, and democracy will profit and survive.

I would not follow all the suggestions of Admiral Rickover, and perhaps not any of them exactly, but I use him as an example because the reaction to his prodding has been extreme.

For example, consider these statements of Rickover:

> We are now confronted with clear-cut evidence that in the all-important field of education our true competitive position against other certain advanced nations is unsatisfactory. The wall behind which we have been nursing the illusion that "our schools are the best in the world" is being rudely pulled down and we must face up to the truth, remedy our educational errors and do a great deal better by our children.

There is no answer in this statement, but there is much truth, and we will do well to look back over our shoulders to see indeed that our adversaries are gaining on us.

Continuing to quote:

> The enormous wealth [of America has been] a mighty prop to self-esteem. . . . Thus protected against the harsh facts of life, it is easy to imagine oneself superior, not just in wealth but in other things as well. This is a pleasant illusion, but it may have consequences not even the richest can afford.

Here, perhaps, is a key to the reason the youth is in a better position to move into national leadership. We have had less reason to become haughty and vain, and we know we have a job to do in building our opportunities.

And again:

> . . . not even so rich a people as we can *afford* underpaid and undereducated teachers, absence of academic standards, and a philosophy of fun and games at school. . . .

Now don't jump at conclusions by saying to yourself we can't have inflexible national standards. Maybe we can't, but put your mind to working on how we can have academic standards which afford goals and measure achievement. That is the way to put blunt criticism to work running in your favor.

And don't get miffed when I quote "fun and games" by thinking, "well, we certainly don't have that in our schools." Maybe you don't, but too many do, and we are all too lax in too many ways.

I am saying to educators let's be our own harshest critics. Let's seek out our shortcomings, look for ways of improvement, and get on with the job.

Take the four things I have just mentioned: underpaid teachers, undereducated teachers, absence of academic standards, "fun and games."

Teachers are underpaid. I am responsible for that, and all citizens are responsible. I said across my state that this was problem number one. The people agreed, the General Assembly agreed, and we are moving to higher pay.

Many people have asked: "How will paying a teacher more convert her into a better teacher than she was last year?" The answer is twofold. We have to start paying more before we start attracting an adequate number of qualified people. This is no chicken or egg dilemma. Higher pay must come first.

The other answer is immediate. Higher pay demonstrates that we have confidence in our teachers, that we understand the priority of education, and that we believe in upgrading its importance. This leads to improved morale and a terrific challenge, and every teacher worth his salt immediately starts trying to do a better job.

When I speak of undereducated teachers, I am not restricting myself to the teachers in the classrooms who hold something less than "A" certificates. I am speaking also of those teachers who have taken an overdose of courses of *how* to teach and who have had far too few courses of *what* to teach.

It is time that our schools of education bring the courses on subject matter into balance with the courses on teaching methods.

I think there would be no argument from this audience if I observe that in the field of academic standards an "A" on arithmetic in one school, or in one county, does not equal an "A" on the same subject in another school or in another county. The results of entrance examinations for college freshmen prove the inequality of academic standards of various schools and various counties and various states.

We might sum up the problem of the overemphasis on "fun and games" this way: It is true that all work and no play makes Johnnie a dull boy. But all play and no work at school will make Johnnie an ignorant boy. And it will make him a poor boy when he goes out into the world to compete for a job.

Carolinians have always understood that education is the means by which our states must reach their full potential growth in both economic and human values. At the turn of the century, Walter Hines Page made the following statement of faith:

> I believe in the free public training of both the hands and the mind of every child born of woman.
>
> I believe that by the right training of men we add to the wealth of the world. All wealth is the creation of man, and he creates it only in proportion to the trained uses of the community; and, the more men we train, the more wealth everyone may create.
>
> I believe in the perpetual regeneration of society, in the immortality of democracy, and in growth everlasting.

We have had our successes and we have made progress and we have a remarkable record considering that we suffered many years of struggle against the oppressive tactics of vindictive victors as an aftermath of the Civil War. But whatever our successes, it is not enough for the rapidly advancing scientific, changing world we now enter.

The job is not finished. What we have really done is to create new and unlimited opportunities.

The late Dr. Howard Odum of the University of North Carolina, and a native of Georgia, showed clearly that the South need not continue to be known as the "nation's economic problem number one." While we do not have everything, he pointed out, we do have in abundance those resources that really matter—soil, water, climate, rainfall, and people—most of all we have a stock of sturdy and able people. We only need to develop fully this human resource. That again justifies our reliance on education as the path to all other objectives.

Quality education is no mean goal! For all other goals we seek for the South can be measured by the quality, the scope, the reach of our educational efforts.

Education is the foundation of economic improvement. We in the South are concerned, vitally, with industrial development, farm income, the economic growth, the chance of all to make a better living; and because of this we must give top priority to education.

Education is the foundation of democracy. We are concerned with defending the principles of freedom, of individual liberties, of free enterprise, of equality and dignity of man; and therefore, we seek the fulfillment of these principles through quality education we offer our boys and girls.

Education is the foundation of the needs and hopes of the nation. We are concerned with our part in the world, and we are concerned with the peace of the world, and therefore, we must adequately educate the scientists, the statesmen, and the citizenry who will fully understand and are equipped to defend and promote the ideals of our dynamic democracy of the twentieth century.

Education, put in the bleakest terms, is survival. Here in our own small part of the free world, we can do no less than seek the best as we prepare to do our part to defend America and the free world.

And education, put in its brightest terms, is life and growth, and happiness. We are not here merely to make a living. We are talking about the fundamental when we are talking about education, and our goal is worthy of the best we have in mind, and heart, and spirit.

The training the teachers are giving in the classrooms is ultimately going to be more important than the training being given on the parade fields of Fort Jackson and Fort Bragg—and I am not minimizing the importance of the army posts.

How well the students perform is going to have a greater effect on history than how well a missile performs at Cape Canaveral.

The South must improve its schools if it expects to improve its economy.

Yet despite this, we have for too long in the South expected our teachers to work for apples and yearbook dedications.

North and South Carolina are properly concerned when anyone attempts to cut our tobacco parity below 90 per cent. Yet we have been giving our sons and daughters something less than 66 per cent of the national educational parity.

The South, like the rest of the nation, needs to take a long, hard look at itself to see where it stands now, and to see where it hopes to stand and where it will stand twenty years from now.

Our public school system is southern, and we have no desire to make it northern or anything other than southern. But that does not require us to be provincial in our efforts to prepare our children to take part in life. We have been forced, by the sheer impact of the change taking place in this modern day America, to place our children in competition with children from every section of the country.

The present day businessman cannot rely on competition solely from his own county or even his own state. Products from all over America, and indeed all over the world, flow in daily to compete against the products he is selling here in this state. If he is a manufacturer, he can rest assured that a new industry from outside the South will soon come in, and he will have to meet the new demands for labor and other resources.

If the child is setting out to become a lawyer, he can no longer plan to make a living on criminal cases and a few civil actions in the JP courts. He may be practicing in what we think of as a one-horse town, but he still must match wits with bonding attorneys from Wall Street, tax attorneys trained by the federal government, and corporation lawyers sent out by General Motors and Standard Oil. The attorney today competes with these experts, and beats them from time to time, or he must give up any hope of a successful career.

Even to get into a medical school today, a student must match his wits against those who come from all over the country to get the relatively few openings in our crowded medical schools. In practice, the doctor must make use of the most complex medicines and methods of modern science.

In all of these areas, the child from the South can no longer think in terms of how good he is in his own community; he must be competent to equal those all across the nation. We may still revel in the stories of the Old South, but when it comes down to the hard, everyday problem of making a living, there just aren't many of us picking cotton anymore. And the public school system which is geared to those times will do our children the greatest disservice in preparing them for a race they can never win, a life they can never live to its fullest.

The South, like the rest of the nation, needs to ask itself again the questions which Edwin Markham angrily asked:

> Is this the thing the Lord God made and gave
> To have dominion over sea and land. . . ?
> How will you ever straighten up this shape;
> Touch it again with immortality:
> Give back the upward looking and the light;
> Rebuild in it the music and the dream?

Through education! That is how. Education will straighten up this shape, touch it again with immortality, give it back the upward looking and the light. But education that is designed for the few, the rich and the privileged will not do it. Education that does not take him into account, or rejects him if it notices him at all, will never straighten up this shape or heal his immedicable woes.

Great southerners have long recognized this truth. Thomas Jefferson knew that an educated citizenry is a necessary prerequisite to free government. Woodrow Wilson, another southerner, knew that universal education is a necessary prerequisite to making the world safe for democracy.

But this is not the only area of educational need. The South, like the rest of the nation, needs also to look at the other end of the educational system—the colleges and the universities.

Only three of the thirteen southern states rank above the national average in the percentage of their adult population with four or more years of college education. North Carolina is not among them. It is thirty-ninth among the fifty states. South Carolina ranks higher, but not high enough to boast. Your state is thirty-second among the fifty states.

I do not minimize the need for more money in higher education, either public or private. More money must be provided—substantially more money. But the South will not keep faith with the future if we do not take into account the tremendous backlog of educational demand that exists on the part of honest, hardworking people who simply do not have the price. It is a reality we must face. It is a reality the South must take into account as it shapes a new college policy for the future.

Universal quality education will provide the cornerstone for a prosperous New South—a South that can again lead the nation.

The place to begin is with the beginning: in the public schools. Here we must reappraise our curriculum. North Carolina is seeking a new curriculum, a curriculum with power—"power in itself to challenge the latent germ of genius, great or small, classical or modern, academic or technical, that every educable human being has within him in some degree." It is only in the light of this curriculum study that we are investing another $100 million toward the achievement of this goal. We await results with hope and with confidence, but meanwhile we work.

This, however, is not enough for the foundation. The key to

quality education is quality teaching. And one of the keys to quality teaching is quality teacher education, both pre-service and in-service teacher education. It must be said to the credit of professional education in North Carolina and South Carolina that it, too, is taking a positive stand for progress. There can be no doubt that the leadership now being exerted by the profession will bring new quality, of rich meaning, to the instruction in tens of thousands of classrooms in the state.

The junior colleges and the church-supported colleges must play important roles in the higher education of our states. How else shall we face the doubling of college enrollments certainly within the next decade? How else will we be able to reach the young men and women who simply do not have the price of a residential college education?

The need for industrial, or the so-called terminal-technical education is increasing. At the present time a survey of every job opportunity in North Carolina is being made, and the survey will lead to complete, accurate descriptions of the requirements of each of these thousands of jobs. On the basis of this survey, curricular standards will be set up and state wide courses of instruction leading to certification of technicians will be established. These will form the curriculum of North Carolina's new system of industrial education centers, which, although begun only in 1958, are now reaching over 15,000 adults.

I am informed that South Carolina is moving quickly in this field of industrial education.

At the head of our educational system, and carrying the heaviest responsibility for its leadership are our senior colleges and universities with their graduate schools and various professional programs. These institutions serve as the brain centers, as sources of ideas and plans for much of our life. The specialized leaders who come from these institutions become the trusted leaders in many fields, and the standard they set is determined in a large part by the standard to which they have been challenged by those institutions. As we support these institutions to the best possible performance, we insure that our leadership will have the opportunity to develop to its fullest.

Quality education which we seek cannot be delivered by a city

council, or a legislature, or the Congress, although their help is
essential in starting the march. Quality education is complex,
difficult, constant in required attention, and it will demand the
best in effort by school boards, the state agencies, the superintendents, the principals, the teachers, the parents, the students,
and indeed all the citizens of this university, this city, this state,
and this nation.

The hour is at hand when South Carolina, North Carolina,
and all the South can rise again and march again. We will make
this march not with bayonets but with textbooks. We will not be
firing on Fort Sumter. We will be firing on the dungeons of
ignorance.

We will make this march by reaching out and grasping the
hands of our most priceless possession, our children and our
grandchildren.

61 The South in a Rapidly Changing World

No Southerner was in a better position to view his region against a background of national and international changes than was Secretary of Commerce Luther H. Hodges in April 1964. A highly intelligent man, he had served a long apprenticeship as businessman and then as Governor of North Carolina. Portions of this address at the University of Alabama reflect a change of viewpoints from those expressed earlier, in the author's public address to the citizens of North Carolina in 1955 (see Document 34). He was optimistic in his belief that the South would at last close many of the gaps that had hindered the region in the past, but he was also positive that southern people had to change many of their approaches to both southern and national problems. The South was going nowhere if it proposed to go alone. Hodges was certain, moreover, that both human and material resources had to be processed intelligently. People would have to be trained to the fullest possible extent of their abilities in order to help the South realize its economic potential.

THE POLITICAL, SOCIAL, AND ECONOMIC ASPECTS OF THIS [RACIAL and technological] change in the world are all crucial for the future of the Deep South. But I have not sought to limit my-

Luther H. Hodges, "What Kind of America," from *The Deep South in Transition*, ed. Robert B. Highsaw (University, Alabama: University of Alabama Press, 1964), 30–44.

self to any one of these categories. In the first place, I find it very difficult to separate these aspects of how people live and move forward together. And, secondly, I would suggest humbly and sincerely that the Deep South is not going anywhere, if it proposes to go alone. And the same can be said of any other region of this great country, or of any other country on this troubled earth of ours.

There is not much that can be said about the political future of a region or a nation these days without taking into consideration its economic and social developments. No area or society can realize its full economic potential without undergoing some significant changes in its political attitudes and its social patterns. And the failure to deal constructively with explosive social forces can wreck the best laid plans of politicians, economists, businessmen, and laboring men.

These changes and potential changes are interdependent. We can try to separate them, try to triangulate human existence in an effort to understand ourselves and our society better, but we cannot escape the fact that life is not lived, or work done, or history made in tight little compartments. Nor can we compartmentalize our lives or our thoughts of our southern society. If we try to make progress in one area and try to cling to that part of the past that is outmoded, we will inevitably fail in both. And if we try to talk and think about the South as if it had some mystical and independent destiny, our talk and thought will be irrelevant to the future.

Not many people today seriously are chanting "save your Confederate money, boys, the South will rise again." But there is a more sophisticated appeal to southern pride and sentiment which suggests that the South, in coming into its own economically, is going to forge ahead of the rest of the nation, and thus will avenge the wrongs done to it in the past by inheriting the nation, if not the earth, economically. Today, we rejoice in the progress the whole South has made in the last two or three decades. There has been a virtual revolution in southern agriculture since the end of World War II, as well as a rapid growth of its industry. Along the Gulf Coast there has grown up a magnificent petrochemical complex. On the Savannah River there is a $2 billion nuclear production facility, as well as nuclear research facilities on southern university campuses. The South is a leader in the utilization of educational television. And here in Alabama, at Huntsville, as well as Cape Kennedy in Florida, and at other southern locations, the South stands on the threshold of the space age.

But, as a governor of a southern state, I was constantly aware of the larger context in which I had to work—a context ranging far beyond the South and even the United States. For example, I was concerned long before it became a headline matter with the United States' balance of payments deficit and the drain on our nation's gold reserves. This was having a very indirect, but nevertheless very powerful impact upon our efforts to create more jobs in North Carolina.

What was happening? Our country—our businessmen, our tourists, and our government—was spending more in other countries than foreign countries were spending with us. Dollars were accumulating in the hands of these foreign holders at an alarming rate, and there was a growing tendency for them to convert their dollars into gold from our reserves. They were afraid we would be forced to devalue the dollar—reduce its value in terms of gold—to prevent the exhaustion of our reserves, and also to reduce the prices of American exports, so we could sell more abroad and thereby earn more to offset our overseas expenditures. But the dollar is the keystone of the international monetary system and of our whole system of international trade. It is accepted by buyers and sellers the world over because it is "as good as gold." So devaluation of the dollar, and the destruction of this trading system built up again after World War II, was unthinkable. And it probably would have been ineffective because other countries would have devalued too, to maintain the same rates of exchange.

All of this meant that the United States had to keep its interest rates high to prevent even more money from flowing abroad —attracted by the prospects of earning more in foreign banks that pay even higher rates of interest. But higher interest rates at home tend to discourage businessmen from borrowing money to invest in new plants which would create more jobs. It also encouraged corporations with surplus cash to put it into savings accounts rather than use it to expand or modernize their facilities. And when fewer new plants are being built and fewer older plants expanded, North Carolina and Alabama and every other state has a much harder time of attracting or creating new industrial jobs for its workers, who have been leaving our farms at a rapid pace and looking for jobs in the towns and cities. Fortunately, the run on our gold reserves has been reduced to a trickle. This Administration convinced foreign dollar holders that we would not devalue our currency. We have also worked out some special arrangements with foreign governments and their central banks to safeguard the dollar from future speculation. But we still have a serious deficit problem, and it concerns the Deep South as much as it does the New York bankers who handle the bulk of our international gold and currency transactions.

It is important to you that our national export expansion program, sponsored by the United States Department of Commerce, should succeed. Your prospects for future economic growth will be affected by the vigor with which businessmen in other parts of the country enter and succeed in the foreign market, just as their growth will be affected by how Deep South businessmen accept the challenge to sell more abroad.

It is important to your future that we modernize our industrial plants throughout the United States. Much of our equipment is older than the machines put in place, with much United States' aid, since World War II in Western Europe and Japan. This lack of modernization impairs our productivity. We are not producing goods as cheaply as we could to win more sales in other countries and to meet the competition of foreign goods in American markets. It is also important to your future that we do a better job of applying scientific research to our civilian production, to creating new growth products and new industrial processes, and that we develop more of our potential scientific and technical brainpower, so we will have enough of these trained people for our civilian economy, as well as for our space and defense efforts. Right now the Japanese are applying as much scientific and engineering brainpower to civilian products as we are, on a per capita basis, and the West Germans are applying more.

It is important to your future that we have an expanding national economy, and that this growth take place with relative price stability. Business, labor and government must work together to stimulate our growth rate, so we will create the additional jobs we need, without the kind of inflation that could impair our domestic living standards and price American goods out of world markets.

Most important to your future is the realization that most of our problems are not North Carolina problems, or Alabama problems, or southern problems, or even in many cases American problems. Our big concerns are the problems of free men everywhere, the problems of how to achieve greater prosperity, more individual dignity and freedom, and a securer peace for all men, whatever their race, their creed, their nationality, or their present situation in life. There can be no future for the Deep South, or for the South as a whole, as a separate entity, as something apart from, fearful of, or indifferent to, the powerful forces shaping the future of our nation and the world. The world's problems are the South's problems, and the problems that face the people of the southern states are very properly the concern of people everywhere. Many people outside the South are finding that what they thought were problems peculiar to the South are explosive problems in their own communities. I regret that any community has these problems. Nevertheless, the realization of these problems represents progress in understanding the scope of the racial problem in America and in the world. Indeed, this understanding is necessary to the achievement of meaningful equality of opportunity for all people.

The rest of the nation is far less different from the South than it has imagined, and this has come as something of a shock to them. And the South has not yet fully realized how like the rest of the country it has become. Both sides need to adjust their thinking. The recent past makes it very clear that the future of the South lies in becoming more and more like the rest of the nation, and the really meaningful question is: What is our nation to become?

Despite the growth of southern cities and our industry, we still tend to think of the South as being much more agricultural than the rest of the nation. But there has been a real revolution in southern agriculture since 1940. In that year, 34 per cent of all employment in the South was in farm jobs. In the nation as a whole, farm jobs accounted for only 19 per cent of total employment. But in 1960, farm employment in the South had plunged to only 9 per cent of total employment—while dropping to 7 per cent in the United States as a whole. The South is now only a percentage point or two away from being just like the rest of the nation in the farm/nonfarm divisions of its labor force. Farm mechanization and the creation of many new jobs in industry and the service occupations have been transforming southern life. Far from being a land of sharecroppers, the South is now essentially a land of farming by machines and chemicals. The index of mechanization in the South is now equal to that for the nation as a whole.

There are wide variations among the states and within them. North Carolina has more small farms than any other southern state, despite the fact that it also has a great deal of industry— adding more value by manufacturing than Connecticut and ranking eleventh among the 50 states in manufacturing. But the fact remains that 90 per cent of all southern families are non-farm families. Here in Alabama, 88 per cent of your families are off the farm, for all practical economic purposes, even though many of them still may be living on the land.

The South also closely resembles the rest of the nation in its nonfarm occupational mix. In 1960, the percentage distribution of employed persons in various occupations in the South was about what it was in the rest of the nation ten years earlier. In 1964 the South is probably even closer to the national employment pattern. The big growth in job opportunities in the

United States in the decade of the 1950's was not in factory jobs. It was in service and professional and technical jobs. And the South has been following that national trend. While the South had an increase of 23 per cent in craftsmen, foremen, and kindred workers, and a 19 per cent increase in factory operatives in the decade, its service workers increased 36 per cent, clerical workers 50 per cent, and professional and technical workers 52 per cent. White-collar occupations have absorbed more of our work force since 1956 than blue-collar jobs. And the number of workers in our country's service industries has exceeded the number in goods-producing industries since 1949. The shift has been toward jobs that require more and better education, and education is the key to raising the productivity and per capita income of the South.

In 1932, southern per capita income was only 53 per cent of the national figure. Twenty years later, after World War II and the growth of the early postwar period, it was 73 per cent of the national figure. The most recent figure, for 1962, is 76 per cent, or more than three-fourths of the national level. But whether the gap closes further or even slips backwards in the next decade depends largely upon the kind of educational effort the South makes. The rest of the country is also moving ahead, and as the Red Queen explained to Alice in *Through the Looking Glass:* "It takes all the running you can do to keep in the same place. If you want to get somewhere else, you must run at least twice as fast as that."

It was estimated some time back that, if the South continued to support its educational system at the level of the 1950's— which because of increased enrollments would require a doubling of school expenditures—the region would find in 1975 that it had been slipping, not gaining on the national standard of living. It would drop from 76 per cent of the national per capita income to only 67 per cent. If, on the other hand, the South raised its level of educational support to the national average, it was projected that southern per capita income would rise to 84 per cent of the national figure in 1975, and would be almost double what it was in 1960. Southern personal income would be almost tripled, and the southern market in 1975 would be, by itself, more than half as large as the entire United States market in 1960.

As the South meets its challenges, it will become more and more like the rest of the United States and can make a great contribution to the nation. It will still be different from the United States as New England is different from the United States as a whole, or as the Midwest and the Pacific Northwest have a flavor all their own. But essentially the destiny of the South is to become what America becomes, and hopefully our contribution from the South will make for a better America. The South, in the larger sense, will be what America will be, and southerners can really only affect the destiny of their region by acting as Americans to help shape the character and destiny of their country in a rapidly changing world.

What kind of America is this going to be?

Is this going to be an America in which all of our fellow citizens, without regard to race, color, or creed, have a decent standard of living?

Is this going to be an America which has found ways of living in relative peace and harmony with other countries, including those that have radically different cultures and social systems? Will we be humble and generous in our attitudes and actions?

Is this going to be an America that is at peace within itself.

Is this going to be an America that believes in brotherhood and the American dream of freedom and equality of opportunity for all?

Is this going to be an America that refuses to be torn apart by hatred and violence, because it is capable of recognizing legitimate grievances and of moving to rectify those things which are wrong and long overdue for righting?

These are some of the really challenging questions that have to be answered in Alabama, in North Carolina, in New York and Wisconsin, and Maryland and California, if we are to have a destiny worthy of American traditions. These are the kinds of problems that knock insistently at our door—at all of our doors, whether you are students, or professors, or businessmen, or housewives, or public officials—knocking and demanding the best that is in us, demanding that we accept the call to leadership, that we make the nation's crucial human problems our individual, personal concerns.

This America of ours is the richest society ever known to man. Last year our gross national product topped $600 billion, and the take-home-pay of Americans totaled more than $400 billion, after taxes. Yet there are about 35 million Americans—one-fifth of our total population—who shared, not one-fifth or even one-tenth of that vast sum. Their share was less than one-twentieth of the disposable personal income of the United States. Only $11 billion a year would raise all of these families, including more than 11 million children, out of the poverty category as it is currently defined in the United States. If a dole would solve the basic problems of these people, we could wipe out poverty in America almost overnight. But a dole is not what these people need. They need something much more difficult to mobilize. They need an aroused America, a country determined to attack the root causes of poverty, a people willing to give of their ingenuity, their concern, and their means, in their own communities, to help us make a successful final assault on poverty in America. It means that you and I, all over the nation, should not just ride from a lovely home in a modern car to a modern office, but should look around our towns and cities to see how our fellow citizens are living.

In our city slums, in our rural shacks, in the camps of migrant workers, on our Indian reservations, around long-closed mine shafts, there is real privation, frustration, and degradation. There is disease and delinquency and crime. There is poverty that is real, painful, and seemingly hopeless and self-perpetuating—and intensely personal! We need to find ways in our local communities, in our states, and through our national government, to break this tragic chain of ignorance, apathy, and want. We need to discover ways of making better use of our existing welfare and economic development programs, including the community development programs of the Commerce Department's vital Area Redevelopment Administration. We need to develop new and bolder approaches to some of these ancient problems—such as the regional approach of the Appalachia Commission, which seeks to revitalize an area of some 16 million people extending from northern Alabama to the Pennsylvania coal fields.

We can stop wringing our hands over the large number of our young men who fail the pre-induction examinations given by the armed services under the Selective Service program. We can, instead, try to equip these young men for productive work, through the Job Corps program recommended to the Congress by President Johnson. We can give them better educations, and we must. An astonishing one-third of all our southern young men examined under the Selective Service program from 1950 through 1962 failed to pass the mental qualification test. In North Carolina it was 34.5 per cent. In Alabama it was more than 40 per cent, in Mississippi it was 45 per cent—or four times the 11.5 per cent figure for the rest of the nation. Should we not in the South ask ourselves the question—why such a difference?

These figures reflect, not upon the inherent ability of our people, but upon the lack of education or the quality of the education we have been giving our youth. We must realize that, in addition to trying to correct the deficiencies of the past, we are challenged to raise the level of support for our schools at every level. And we must challenge our schools at all levels to do a better job of training. Our citizens must demand better leadership and support this leadership to the limit. We must make even greater sacrifices for the future, if we are not to saddle our country and our region with large numbers of men and women who, because of inadequate educations today, will be of little value to our economy, or themselves, in tomorrow's even more complex, highly technical society.

Our ability to make some of the greater expenditures needed to realize the full potential of the South in a growing America will depend upon what happens in our relations with other countries, and especially with the Soviet bloc countries. There has been a marked turn for the better in our relations with the

Soviet Union, an improvement stemming from a mutual understanding that each side has the power and the determination
to defend its vital national interests, but that neither country
wants to unleash a nuclear holocaust. No one knows what the
future may hold for our relations with the Soviet Union or with
its various allies and satellite states. But whether we can develop
slowly more normal relations with these countries, through
limited agreements or through expanding trade in non-strategic
goods, it is as important to the future of the South as anything
that might happen in Dixie itself.

We can safely and logically expand our non-strategic trade
with the Soviet bloc countries in Europe. Most of these goods
are already available to these countries from other Western
industrial nations. In 1962, all of the countries of the free world
sold nearly $4.5 billion worth of goods to the Soviet bloc in
Europe. And of these sales, about half—$2.2 billion—were
shipments from Japan and our North Atlantic Treaty Organization allies. United States sales totaled only $125 million, and
these were largely agricultural commondities. With so many
sources of supply for modern industrial goods, one country such
as the United States cannot prevent the Soviet Union from
obtaining the things it needs to develop its economy. We have
to be realistic in the application of our export controls, and our
people must be sophisticated enough to recognize opportunities to serve our national interest by expanding trade as well
as by restricting it.

There is, of course, no challenge facing America which demands greater realism than the explosive problem of equal opportunity for all our citizens, regardless of race, creed, or color.
This is a problem which could tear America apart. It could destroy all hopes for developing the potential of the South, all efforts to maintain the United States as a bulwark of freedom and
democratic self-government, and all dreams of building a world
in which no man's hand is raised in anger against his brother. It
could plunge this great country of ours into an orgy of hatred
and violence in which today's militants on both sides would
be devoured by more extreme leadership tomorrow, and to-

morrow's extremists by even more radical leaders the day after. We are witnessing a social revolution centering on the demands of Negro rights, and given the whole history of this nation and of the world itself, the ultimate outcome cannot be in doubt. The Negro in America cannot be forever denied equal opportunity and the full measure of human dignity without the abandonment of everything America has stood for in the history of Western civilization. The Negro deserves better treatment, and he must surely get it.

Our good sense will not permit us to continue to sanction the waste of the talents of our Negro citizens. We are educating all of our citizens at great expense, and then allowing a large number of these trained people to be used in jobs far below their potential. Far too many trained Negro engineers are still sweeping floors, sorting mail, and digging ditches. Trained stenographers are working as maids. Trained electricians are raking leaves, and men trained as draftsmen can find jobs only as construction laborers. Significantly, one of the reasons for our low per capita income in the South is the widespread underemployment of Negroes in our labor force. Less than half of our Negro families are headed by persons with full-time, year-round jobs. Too many Negro men and women are confined to jobs that produce little for them or for those who employ them —to jobs which in other parts of the country have been partially eliminated by machines, with a resulting rise in the average productivity and average incomes of the people in those areas.

The South can never realize its full potential as long as a substantial portion of its population is functioning far below its capacity. We cannot maintain the employment traditions of a plantation economy and expect to be a leader or even a full participant in a highly technical national and international economy. But even if the South or the nation could afford this waste, it would not be possible to maintain in an open, democratic society practices and traditions which an overwhelming majority of the people know in their hearts to be unfair, intolerable, and morally wrong. This is the reality we must face, if we are to make the difficult adjustments and accommodations that are necessary to prevent a rending of our social fabric by extremists on both sides.

There are those, white and Negro, who would rather see America pulled apart than have it wear a cloth that is not cut according to their own measurements. But these extremists cannot prevail in a nation, in a state, or in a community, whose citizens are willing to speak for what is right and to work for what is good. They cannot prevail if enough Americans are willing to accept a full share of the responsibility for determining what America is to become.

Let it be said clearly again and again. We must all respect the law and obey the law. Change it if we will, but obey it until and unless it is changed. And this message is to white and Negro alike, of whatever shades of color and whatever shades of opinion. It is also to bad politicians (most politicians are good, honest leaders)—to those politicians who incite and encourage trouble to garner votes for themselves. This sort of politician should be rebuked and refused support. Most of us throughout this great nation –the South, the West, the East, and North—are moderate in our thinking and in our actions. Let's be unafraid as we face today's problems. Let's be courageous and firm in our support of what is right. It is up to each of us to help decide what America is to become.

We can help history decide whether America had the power to bring out the best in her citizens, whether it could inspire them with compassion for the unfortunate, whether it could sustain their faith in the future in a revolutionary world, whether it could give them a permanent passion for justice and truth and the achievement of the brotherhood of man. America's challenges are our challenges, and America's hope for the future lies in our response to them.

62 Full Circle of Failure

Fourteen years have elapsed since the United States Supreme Court rendered its momentous decision in *Brown* v. *Board of Topeka Education*. During this period the South has undergone at least three phases of responses to what the Court proclaimed to be the "law of the land." In the following document, Glenda Bartley has summarized the results of this decision and the tremendous amount of other court decisions and legislation which have followed. The results, so far as carrying out the Court's mandate, have been negative. There has been a serious disregard for the law, and a psychological maiming of thousands of children who have been subjected to the traumatic experience of a discrimination worse than the traditional types.

IN THE LONG DECADE BETWEEN THE SUPREME COURT'S FIRST DECISION in *Brown* v. *Topeka Board of Education* and passage of the Civil Rights Act of 1964, faith in the ability of federal courts to affect substantial integration in the public schools of the South had sharply diminished. At the time Congress gave legislative sanction to the nation's fundamental law, there were only 34,105 (1.17) percent of Negro enrollment, Negro children attending school with whites in the eleven southern states. Hope now hinged on Title VI of the act, which contained the

Glenda Bartley, "The Full Circle of Failure," *Lawlessness and Disorder, Report* of the the Southern Regional Council (Atlanta, 1968), 1–15.

590

ingredients for a small revolution. Then, for three, bitter, frustrating, defeated years, attention was focused on the enforcement agency for Title VI—the Department of Health, Education and Welfare. It seemed that HEW's Office of Education with its power to cut off federal funds now had the weapon to wring compliance from the previously unbudgeable South, that school desegregation would cease to be a phenomenon of urban tokenism.

Essentially, the shift away from the courts to the executive branch made school desegregation wholly an administrative matter.

In the first year of this administrative era (1965) the Office of Education issued guidelines for compliance with the act. The freedom-of-choice clause (theoretically allowing parents to send their children to any school in a given system) in these guidelines, and in those issued subsequently, still placed the burden of desegregation on Negro school children and their parents, but the weight of resistance was shifted from southern legislatures to individual school administrators. Neither the novices at HEW nor experienced observers outside the South calculated the nature and ability of their new adversaries. School administrators in a region yet uncommitted to education are a lonely and beleaguered lot. (Support for education as a regional panacea is more dogma than dollars.) Early outraged protest over federal intervention and federal control soon settled into the sure manipulation by one parallel bureaucracy of the other.

It was also during the brief period before schools opened under the first guidelines that the real violence set in. The previous ten years had been relatively free of it in the matter of school desegregation. There was Mansfield, and Clinton, and Little Rock, and New Orleans, where screaming mother-mobs appeared on television as the first wave of mass media theater of the absurd. But the violence was done mostly to psyches of the few Negro children. During the first judicial era (1954–64), the mode of southern private resistance was as often economic as physical terrorism. And the targets of the bombs, beatings, burnings, bullets, firings, credit cut-offs, and foreclosures were most often not parents who tried to send their children to "white" schools, but people who tried to gain access to public accommodations, register to vote, and the like. This was largely because there were virtually no Negro parents making the attempt in the rural areas and small towns where the varieties of terrorism have been most virulent. In the cities, where most of the (token) school desegregation occurred during the first judicial era, the terrorism was mainly within the schools, a low-grade, day-by-day torture of the Negro children by their schoolmates, teachers, and administrators.

Out in the rural areas of the South, where law enforcement was repressive before it became fashionable to be so, the advent of the guidelines, the threat that black children might actually go to school with white children, brought a wave of terror unmatched since post-Reconstruction whites rode around in bedsheets. And economic retaliation against the few Negroes who chose the "white" school did not abate.

In September, 1965, 184,308 (6.1 percent) Negro children enrolled in "white" schools.

In spite of the increased violence and the pitifully small number of Negroes in desegregated situations, there was a national misunderstanding of what was happening in the South. There were several reasons for this. The administrative experiment was taking place in rural areas of the South—crossroads towns and hamlets as ill-geared for news coverage as Ulverstone, Tasmania. And, since there had been virtually no desegregation at all before, any small gain was often hailed as a triumph. Another reason for the national misunderstanding was perhaps caused by national news media's probably unconscious wish to have done with the violence attendant on any significant social change in the South. This passion for tranquility, for order, has led many a responsible reporter, magazine, newspaper, and television network to announce the advent of another school year as an occasion of "increased desegregation," or even "massive desegregation . . . without violence." (An example of such was the story which ran under a headline proclaiming that school desegregation swept peacefully across Dixie: the story itself recounted instances of desegregators' homes fired into—as many as 32 times—in three towns in one state alone.)

March, 1966, brought new guidelines aimed at plugging some of the loopholes that observers felt accounted for the debacle during the first year of the administrative era. Freedom-of-choice, the most commonly used southern compliance method, remained. The choice forms were mailed that spring; federal negotiations with individual districts continued; a few school systems, notably in Alabama and Mississippi (with their unpopular national image), had their funds terminated; private agencies, already cognizant they were doing the federal government's job, sent field workers to persuade Negro parents to choose the "white" school.

In 1966 there were 2,598,842 (or 88 per cent of the Negro enrollment) in all-Negro schools, more, due to population increases and the amount of desegregation, than had attended segregated schools in the year of the first *Brown* decision.

New guidelines were issued in December, 1966, but it was about over—the administrative era. Negro parents, target of every trick known to a national minority accustomed to working its will on the nation in matters of race, were getting tired. Negro children, in all too many instances in desegregated schools abused, excluded from activities, were disillusioned. Private agencies' field workers, who had often been Negroes' only assurance that all of white America was not hostile, that they and their children were not totally alone, were reluctantly pulling out.

When school opened in September, 1967, 86 per cent of southern Negro students remained in segregated schools. Figures for the Deep South were more depressing: Alabama, 94.6; Mississippi, 96.1; South Carolina, 93.6; Georgia, 90.1; and Louisiana, 93.3.

Defeat for the administrative experiment in education in the only large nation without a national school system came for a number of reasons. Freedom-of-choice was a fatal blunder. It allowed the violence to work its will, permitted white terrorists a victory denied their "respectable" counterparts of the 1950's. Negro parents, who had from the first simply been interested in getting their children the best education available, failed to see the educational value of losing a job, being shot at, in order that the children might attend a school only a little less bad than the "Negro" one. Even without white resistance, the free choice concept in its pure form is an administrative impossibility. Realizing this early on, authors of guidelines and court orders as well were forced to attach exemption clauses (read as loopholes by southern schoolmen) taking into account such physical realities as "proximity," "overcrowding" and the like.

The confounding of Title VI was perhaps present all along within the same act. Title IV, little noticed in 1964, has haunted all the efforts launched under Title VI. There are many districts in the South which are like Washington, D. C., where the school population is mostly Negro and defies conventional zoning or other plans to make it desegregated. Such districts in the South are still overwhelmingly rural, but Atlanta, Memphis, Richmond, and other cities are already, or soon will be, in this category. Title IV prohibits "bussing" to achieve racial balance. How then desegregate minority Negro districts, or large school systems in which *de facto* housing segregation perpetuates school segregation? Pairing (making one elementary school serve grades 1–2, another grades 3–4, etc., drawing children from wider geographic areas in the process), said some experts. Combination pairing-zoning, said others. And still others suggested educational parks, federally financed in fringe areas to accommodate suburban whites and ghetto blacks. This would be achieved with urging from (the same) Title IV's technical assistance teams and pressure of fund termination from Title VI (carrot and stick, repeated *ad nauseum*—the carrot magically to overcome heretofore sacrosanct district boundaries, to say nothing of county lines and jurisdictions hallowed in the South, but the other part of the formula, the basic question, ignored—

WHAT STICK?). The restriction on bussing eliminated the possibility of drawing up zone plans which would ultimately destroy the dual school structure—erase the designations "Negro" and "white."

It is therefore useless (and even cruel) to criticize too strongly the failure of the Office of Education to map a strategy other than freedom-of-choice.

The weapon—termination of federal funds—did not prove effective. Most often the sufferers were the pitiful black schools. Many southern superintendents seem to hold to the philosophy that "Negro" and "federal" are synonymous terms. These schoolmen use federal school funds, like those allotted under Title I of the Elementary and Secondary Education Act for upgrading education in "deprived" areas, to bring Negro schools' per pupil expenditures up to the level afforded "white" schools by local finances.

Perhaps the best summary of the failure of the administrative experiment is contained in an example of massive school desegregation as it swept non-violently across Unadilla, Georgia.

Roy Hunter was beaten by schoolmates more than once at Unadilla High School and received threats on his life up until the moment of his singular dark presence in the graduation exercises from that seat of learning. Three years before, in 1965, his mother, fired from her job, had found a dead bear on her front porch—local whites' reminder that her eight children had chosen the wrong school. Finally, in 1968, Unadilla lost its federal money—200,000 badly needed dollars. All but $25,000 of that money had gone to the Negro school—much of it spent for lunches (upgrading education in the South is all too often a matter of feeding children who get little food at home). The community raised tax millage to replace the $25,000, and the superintendent announced that since the system no longer received federal funds, the "white" school would no longer accept black children. The Hunter children had been the only desegregators all along. Displaying the kind of courage that seems required of those who still believe in this country's fundamental law, they again attended the "white" school in the fall of 1968.

March 29, 1967, marked the advent of the second judicial era
in school desegregation. The Fifth Circuit Court of Appeals,
sitting *en banc* (full court), directed each state within the
circuit to take all necessary affirmative action to bring about a
"unitary school system in which there are no Negro schools and
no white schools—just schools."

In October, 1967, the Supreme Court refused to review the
order, and the National Association for the Advancement of
Colored People declared the Fifth Circuit ruling to be "the most
influential school desegregation opinion" since *Brown* vs. *Topeka.* Indeed it was. In effect it gave legal sanction to the guidelines, while insisting that freedom-of-choice plans would be
thoroughly examined by the courts to determine whether the
method was working.

On May 27, 1968, the Supreme Court issued a similar ruling,
stating that,

> In desegregating a dual system of public education, a plan uti-
> lizing student "freedom-of-choice" is not an end in itself but is only
> a means to the constitutionally required end, the abolition of the
> system of segregation and its effects, and, if it proves effective, it
> is acceptable, but, if it fails to undo segregation, other means must
> be used to achieve that end.

Clearly freedom-of-choice had failed in almost every instance
to abolish "the system of segregation and its effects."

The decisions renewed hope, all but bludgeoned to death
by more than a decade of too many Unadillas, an Ezekiel's
Wheel kind of hope that freedom-of-choice itself would be
abolished. At the same time civil rights and legal agencies were
renewing their efforts to desegregate southern schools, Education Commissioner Harold Howe, II, was expressing federal
relief at the re-entrance of the courts in a manner which should
have been ominous to those who were anticipating a new concerted effort by executive and judicial branches. Howe said:
"Our policies are clearly supported by the courts. . . . It's not as

necessary now as it formerly was for those of us in Education
to have a role in civil rights compliance."

A federal district court in Alabama had issued an order (also
in March, 1967) which would, in fact, result in a collision of the
two branches of the federal government in the matter of school
desegregation. *Lee* v. *Macon County* placed 99 of Alabama's 118
school districts under court order. These were districts that
had formerly been operating under HEW guidelines. During the
summer of 1967, HEW declared that the Lanett, Alabama,
school system was not in compliance with the guidelines and
was therefore ineligible for federal aid; Lanett school officials
protested that they were now under a court-approved plan, and
in July the court held that it was the court's responsibility to
determine whether school systems were in compliance with its
order. Urging HEW to continue investigations and to report any
failures to comply, the court warned, however, that HEW
could only take action with its specific approval.

But meanwhile, all across the South during 1967 and the
spring and summer of 1968 old school cases were reopened and
new ones filed. Results were familiar to those old enough to
remember *Brown I* and *Brown II*. District courts in numerous
cases overthrew freedom-of-choice plans and ordered school
boards to submit geographic zoning plans drawn so as to afford
substantial desegregation.

In many respects the new judicial era was exactly like the old.
It introduced an entirely new concept in equal education to
southern whites. No less revolutionary than the Supreme Court's
announcing in 1954 that separate educational facilities were
inherently unequal was the idea that desegregation meant white
children attending formerly "Negro" schools. Freedom-of-choice
had been the interim separate but equal, not a transitional concept, but educational dogma. HEW's acceptance of gradualism
was not nearly so damning as its acceptance of the southern
solution. Freedom-of-choice meant Negroes, as many as could
stand it, in white schools. New, court ordered, the zone concept
literally meant mixing the schools. Administrators (the South,
they said, the *people*, simply weren't ready for it, no sir) re-

luctantly drew up the new plans.* Through the late spring and early summer resistance grew. Just as in the first judicial era, it was mainly the cities of the South that were affected. And the resistance had a citified, sophisticated new look, not seen since the administrative experiment moved the issue to the rural South. Committees, organizations (Stand Together and Never Divide, etc.) of white parents formed (reformed, in many instances—a new generation of resisters) to fight for freedom-of-choice. Almost without exception they were victorious.

The new judicial era fell victim to many of the traps that had plagued the old one. Federal judges, admittedly not educators, were often forced to believe elaborate arguments by schoolmen that what the courts requested was simply not (immediately) possible. Redraw all school boundaries . . . 75,000 children involved . . . teachers already assigned . . . overcrowding . . . undercrowding . . . BUSSING . . . You see, your honor, we would very much like to comply with the court order, and we will . . . but not now. (A federal district judge in Mississippi recently ruled that, since whites would pull out of a zone-desegregated school system, freedom-of-choice was constitutional. This bit of tortured judicial reasoning was engendered by a poll, conducted by whites, of whites in the district. The poll revealed that white parents would refuse to send their children to public schools; therefore, no desegregation would exist. So, freedom-of-choice would, at least in theory, allow more desegregation.)

Also, pressure by white parents in many locales had almost the same effect as threats by southern legislatures a decade before. These parents, through their organizations, said they would, and in some instances did, close the schools down rather than desegregate them. (In Chesterfield County, South Carolina, schools were closed for a week due to protests by white parents. They were reopened September 15, 1968, after the board reinstituted the freedom-of-choice plan.)

---

* The Supreme Court stated in *Brown II* (1955): "It should go without saying that the vitality of these constitutional principles cannot be allowed to yield simply because of disagreement with them." *Brown v. Board of Education of Topeka*, 1955, 349 U.S. 294, 75 S.Ct. 753, 99 L.Ed. 1083.

Mobile, Alabama, seemed to sum up the first year of the new judicial era: The Mobile case had been in court for many years. The system was operating under freedom-of-choice. In 1967 two per cent of Negro school children attended "white" schools. The Fifth Circuit Court of Appeals in March, 1968, instructed the school board to adopt a rigid (no provisions for transfers within the system to avoid attending a desegregated school) zone plan, which would have placed about 1,400 white children in formerly all-Negro schools. White parents organized (Stand Together, etc., and Whites Organized for Rights Keeping); the area's state senator filed a motion in federal court seeking to overturn the new ruling on grounds it would be unsafe for white children to attend all-Negro schools. After a summer of legal battling the federal district judge who had issued the initial order came up with a plan allowing senior high schools to operate under freedom-of-choice, requiring specified attendance zones for elementary and junior high schools, and permitting more liberal transfers within the attendance zones. When school opened in September, an estimated 3,500 Negroes were in formerly all-white schools; but very few whites were in formerly all-Negro ones.

Mississippi, as usual, was the epitome of frustration, confusion, and a certain hope. School cases in 50 of Mississippi's 148 districts are to be reopened in the fall. A spokesman for the NAACP Legal Defense and Educational Fund, Inc., the most active agency in the legal battle for school desegregation, was confident that in most of those districts freedom-of-choice would be discarded and zone or pairing plans required. The spokesman also stated that such action would result in whites pulling out of the public schools in several districts. "It depends on the district," he said. "Where whites are proud of the schools, where the schools are good, whites will stay. In the Delta, where schools are bad, whites will probably pull out." He cited Corinth, a relatively prosperous community in northern Mississippi, as an example of a good school system's holding whites in spite of a comprehensive zone plan that would result in substantial desegregation. Though Mississippi still has a tuition grant statute, which theoretically could support private schools, there is little chance of indefinite survival. The Legal Defense Fund spokesman, wise in the ways of Mississippi, and still hopeful, said, "Whites will probably go through the full cycle of resistance and come back to reconciliation again—just as they did before." He felt that the South might yet solve the problem of desegregation before the North began, really, to grapple with it.

THE PATTERN OF FAILURE

There was the chance, a slim one, that the courts might succeed, might assure justice at last to school children in the South. But all the foregoing history indicates failure, and the results of the first year of the second judicial era bear out this gloomy prophecy. Though no official figures were available in late September, 1968, the old pattern seemed to hold. A few more Negroes in school with whites in the cities; in some instances rural "Negro" schools closed and the entire student body absorbed by the "white" ones; a minuscule number of whites in formerly all-Negro schools. The second judicial era would, it seemed, encounter the same dilemma that doomed the first one: Governor Lurleen Wallace, paraphrasing another Southerner who flouted the law when it suited him to do so, said of the Fifth Circuit ruling, "They have made their decision, now let them enforce it."

Why those who had lived through the first era, had watched the few children life-scarred for the privilege of entering a *building*, fanned the old hope again is probably irrelevant. But the results of fourteen long years of methodizing, legalizing, computerizing, analyzing, and finally, mortifying what is, after all, the basic right of every American child—the right to a good education, the right to enter any building to get that education —will long be felt in this nation.

We teach children, all children, that the United States of America is dedicated to law and order. We lie. We have shown a generation of American children, in the public institution closest to their lives, the schools, that this nation's fundamental law need not be obeyed; we have clearly demonstrated to them that what we expect is their conformity to lip service to the shibboleth. What will be the awful effects of this lie upon children, black and white alike? What depths of disillusionment when they hear us say "law" and observe only "order?"

After a generation has beheld successful evasion, rationalized vacillation, outright flaunting of the law, only a country absolutely wedded to the totalitarian concept of order without law could turn on the victims of lawlessness and accuse them of destroying the fabric of society.

Index

THE AMERICAN HERITAGE SERIES

THE COLONIAL PERIOD

THE REVOLUTIONARY ERA TO 1789

THE YOUNG NATION

Hamilton, Alexander *Papers on Public Credit, Commerce, and Finance* AHS 18 Samuel McKee, Jr., J. Harvie Williams

Jefferson, Thomas *The Political Writings of Thomas Jefferson: Representative Selections* AHS 9 Edward Dumbauld

Madison, James *The Political Thought of James Madison* AHS 39 Marvin Meyers

Gallatin, Albert *Selected Writings of Albert Gallatin* AHS 40 E. James Ferguson

The Government and the Economy, 1783–1861 AHS 65 Carter Goodrich

Marshall, John *John Marshall: Major Opinions and Other Writings* AHS 42 John P. Roche

Democracy, Liberty, and Property: The State Constitutional Conventions of the 1820's AHS 43 Merrill D. Peterson

THE MIDDLE PERIOD

Social Theories of Jacksonian Democracy: Representative Writings of the Period 1825–1850 AHS 1 Joseph L. Blau

Jacksonian Civilization: A Documentary History AHS 85 Edward Pessen

Channing, William Ellery *Unitarian Christianity and Other Essays* AHS 21 Irving H. Bartlett

The Writings of Justice Joseph Story AHS 45 Henry Steele Commager

Manifest Destiny AHS 48 Norman A. Graebner

Slavery in America AHS 66 Willie Lee Rose

The Antislavery Argument AHS 44 Jane and William Pease

Calhoun, John C. *A Disquisition on Government and Selections from the Discourse* AHS 10 C. Gordon Post

Lincoln, Abraham *The Political Thought of Abraham Lincoln* AHS 46 Richard Current

The Radical Republicans and Reconstruction, 1861–1870 AHS 47 Harold Hyman

THE LATE NINETEENTH CENTURY

Late Nineteenth Century American Liberalism AHS 26 Louis Filler

The Forging of American Socialism: Origins of the Modern Movement AHS 24 Howard H. Quint